Mathematics for
Business Applications

Mathematics for Business Applications

HAROLD D. SHANE

Baruch College
City University of New York

CHARLES E. MERRILL PUBLISHING COMPANY
A Bell & Howell Company
Columbus, Ohio

Published by
CHARLES E. MERRILL PUBLISHING COMPANY
A Bell & Howell Company
Columbus, Ohio 43216

This book was set in Times Roman
The production editor was Frances Margolin.
The cover was designed by Will Chenoweth.

Library of Congress Catalog Card Number 75-16595
International Standard Book Number 0-675-08668-X

2 3 4 5 6 7 8—81 80 79 78 77 76

Printed in the United States of America

PREFACE

This book is designed for a full-year course in mathematics. The text is divided into four parts arranged in order of increasing reliance upon algebraic competence and mathematical sophistication. In addition, there is an Introduction which contains a brief review of arithmetic and algebra for those who feel the need of it. Parts I and II require only elementary algebra. Part III requires a somewhat greater degree of mathematical sophistication, and Part IV depends upon a knowledge of intermediate algebra. I have tried to motivate the mathematical concepts by applications. When it seemed necessary to develop the mathematical machinery first, I have tried to include applications as soon as reasonable.

Parts I and III are relatively more mathematical and less applied, while Parts II and IV are mostly applications. In fact, at Baruch College we teach Parts I and III in the first semester and Parts II and IV in the second. By doing so, semester one becomes a general course in mathematics equally valuable to students of business, social sciences, psychology or the liberal arts. Since calculus is treated largely as the mathematics of economic theory, the second term then becomes a course in mathematics of finance and economics, particularly useful to students of accountancy and administration.

I have taught all the material in this book to many, many classes of students almost exactly as it is written here. Most of them enjoy it this way and understand the material. They find some of the nonbusiness applications particularly fascinating. In fact, when I tell them that the Markov chain analysis of the basic math sequence in 8.7 is a simple version of what we are using for future planning here, they usually ask to see the complete study.

As you can probably tell, my first acknowledgement goes to my students, who have really taught me about mathematics, education, and myself. Second, to my colleagues, who are my severest critics. Particularly helpful suggestions have been made by Warren Gordon, Sheldon Koenig, Al Friedland, and Frank Saidel. Third, to my wife,

Mita, who solved most of the exercises and to my daughters, Lisa and Erica, who helped in the best way they knew. I also wish to thank Selma Lippman, my secretary, who typed the manuscript and without whose invaluable aid I would never have had the time to write any book. Special notes of acknowledgement go to David C. Trunnell, whose many sound recommendations were incorporated into the text, and to Pete Hutton, my editor, advisor and friend. And thanks to Frances Margolin and all those other people at Charles E. Merrill, who made the entire project possible.

H. D. S.

TO THE INSTRUCTOR

Some may not wish to cover all the material in the text. However, the topics are arranged within each part so that you may break off at the end of a chapter without having lost out on the applications. For example, if you stop Part I after chapter 1, you will still have seen linear programming. If you make it through chapter 2, you will revisit linear programming, including the simplex method. Chapter 3 culminates in input-output analysis, but if you leave it out, the only other topics you will lose are game theory and Markov chains. Similarly, if you stop Part II after chapter 4, you will have seen the most common business application used by nonbusinessmen. On the other hand, chapter 6 on advanced topics in finance is fairly specialized.

In Part III, probability has been developed without combinations and permutations. My experience has been that when done in the traditional order, students get so wound up in the counting problems that they lose sight of probability. In addition, in real applications, probabilities are not determined by combinatorics but by statistical studies of the occurrence or nonoccurrence of events of interest. If you stop after chapter 7, you will have covered all the basic ideas of probability, mathematical expectation, and game theory. It is also possible to omit chapter 8 completely, but Markov chains offer a beautiful amalgam of matrix algebra and probability. Finally, just enough combinatorics is done in chapter 9 to introduce the most important applied probability distributions: the hypergeometric, the binomial, and the normal.

Part IV is very carefully designed because it is usually at the end that people start running out of time. By the middle of chapter 10, economic optimization problems are discussed by doing applications immediately after the first derivative formulas are stated. By the end of chapter 10, the calculus of algebraic functions is completed. If you wish, you can skip chapter 11, although you would miss continuous compounding of interest, elasticity of demand, and exponential growth and decay. However, you would be able to get on to antidifferentiation.

In chapter 12, the integral is handled as an antiderivative with the Riemann sum given only at the end.

A good one-semester course in mathematics for business and social science students would be all of chapter 1; chapter 2, sections 2.1–2.5; all of chapter 3; chapter 7, sections 7.1–7.10; chapter 8, sections 8.1–8.3; chapter 10, sections 10.1–10.7. For a good one-semester finite mathematics course, follow the preceding syllabus but substitute the balance of chapter 8 and sections 9.1, 2, 4, and 5 for chapter 10.

One warning on chained problems: In two chapters of the book, certain exercises are continued from section to section. These occur in sections 7.6, 7.7, 7.8, numbers 4 through 14, and in sections 8.5, 8.6, numbers 7 through 10. In almost every case, the same number has been reserved in each section for corresponding exercises.

If you do not like flipping back and forth, there are sufficient other exercises that these can be avoided. However, some are interesting problems, and you might wish to save them until the completion of the last section involved.

CONTENTS

*This book is dedicated to the memory of my father,
Jack Shane.*

Introduction

Review of
Arithmetic and Algebra

The material in the main body of this text assumes a certain familiarity with arithmetic and algebra. This introduction is for those of you who feel a need to review this prerequisite material. Each major topic (letters A through K) is briefly reviewed; and each includes a selection of exercises. The subtopics are numbered consecutively 1 through 33.

Before starting any portion of the text, you should review Topics A and B. In addition, the guide below is provided for those topics you might wish to study before beginning particular chapters of the text.

GUIDE

Chapter	Topics	Chapter	Topics
1	G, I, J, K	7	C, D, G, J
2	C, G, I	8	C, D, G
3	C, D	9	C, D, E
4	C, E, G	10	C, D, E, F, G, H, J
5	C, G	11	C, D, E, F, G, H, J
6	C, G	12	C, D, E, F, G, H, J

A. Addition and Subtraction of Signed Numbers

Let us begin by reviewing some of the basic laws of addition that hold for all numbers.

1. *The commutative law.* In symbols

$$a + b = b + a$$

In words, when adding two numbers, the order in which they are written is immaterial. For example,

$$36 + 112 = 112 + 36 = 148$$

2. *The associative law.* In symbols

$$(a + b) + c = a + (b + c)$$

In words, when adding three numbers, it does not matter which two are added first. Notice the algebraic convention that an expression in parentheses is to be calculated first. Thus

$$(7 + 11) + 19 = 18 + 19 = 37$$
$$7 + (11 + 19) = 7 + 30 = 37$$

The combined and repeated usage of these two laws allows you to rearrange a sum of numbers into any convenient order for purposes of addition.

3. *The role of zero.* In symbols

$$a + 0 = 0 + a = a$$

In words, zero added to any number does not change the number.

4. *The definition of* $-b$. The negative of a number b is defined as that number which when added to b sums to zero. In symbols

$$b + (-b) = 0$$

There is a distinction here that is sometimes confusing. For example, the negative of 5 is -5. The negative of -8 is $+8$. Thus, the symbol $-a$ may actually denote a positive number. We repeat, if a is negative, then $-a$ is positive.

Moreover, it is a simple consequence of the definition to show that

$$a + (-b) = a - b$$

and

$$a - (-b) = a + b$$

5. *The absolute value of a number.* The symbol $|b|$ is called the absolute value of b. The absolute value of a positive number or zero is the number itself. The absolute value of a negative number is the number with the sign changed from $-$ to $+$. Thus, $|12| = 12$, $|-10| = 10$ and $|0| = 0$. From property (4), the definition can be written as $|b| = b$ if b is positive and $-b$ if b is negative.

6. *The addition and subtraction of signed numbers.* When two negative numbers are added, the sum is found by adding the absolute values of the two numbers and assigning a negative sign to the result. When adding a positive number and a negative number, find the difference between the absolute values of the numbers. Assign the result the sign of the number with the larger absolute value. For example,

$$-7 + (-11) = -18$$
$$-7 + 15 = \quad 8$$
$$-16 + 12 = \quad -4$$

In a business context, these rules are easy to remember. Think of positive numbers as gains and negative numbers as losses. Now, adding two losses produces a loss equal to their sum. Adding a gain and a loss will produce a net gain if the gain is larger and a net loss if the loss is larger.

When subtracting signed numbers, simply recall that $-(-a) = a$, $-a = -(+a)$, and $-a = +(-a)$. For example,

$$15 - (-28) = 15 + 28 = 43$$
or
$$-6 - 15 = -6 + (-15) = -21$$
or
$$-16 - (-63) = -16 + 63 = 47$$

7. *Removal of parentheses.* Due to the associative law, we may write

$$a + (b + c) = a + b + c$$
or
$$a + (b - c) = a + b - c$$

without changing the value.

If a minus sign precedes a parentheses, we may remove the parentheses by changing the sign of each term in the interior. For example,

$$-(7 - 4) = -(3) = -3$$

could be written

$$-(7 - 4) = -7 + 4 = -3$$

Using these rules, we may rearrange sums of positive and negative numbers at will. For example,

$$(56 - 35) + (73 - 18) - (61 + 10) - (35 - 43)$$

may be evaluated in many ways. You may first perform the operations in the parentheses:

$$(56 - 35) + (73 - 18) - (61 + 10) - (35 - 43)$$
$$= 21 + 55 - 71 - (-8) = 21 + 55 - 71 + 8$$
$$= 21 + 55 + 8 - 71 = 84 - 71 = 13$$

Alternatively, you can remove all parentheses first.

$$(56 - 35) + (73 - 18) - (61 + 10) - (35 - 43)$$
$$= 56 - 35 + 73 - 18 - 61 - 10 - 35 + 43$$

Now group all the positive and negative numbers together.

$$56 + 73 + 43 - 35 - 18 - 61 - 10 - 35$$
$$= 56 + 73 + 43 - (35 + 18 + 61 + 10 + 35)$$
$$= 172 - 159 = 13$$

Notice in the next to last line we inserted a parenthesis preceded by a minus sign and therefore changed all the signs inside. For example,

$$-11 - 12 + 3 = -(11 + 12 - 3) = -20$$

EXERCISES

Reduce the following expressions to a single number:

1. $3 + 5 =$

2. $3 - 7 =$
3. $-19 + 76 =$
4. $(3 - 5) + 11 =$
5. $119 - (61 - 78) =$
6. $6 - (-8) =$
7. $-4 - (-17) =$
8. $(183 - 61) - (63 + 41 - 11) =$
9. $-62 - (31 - 85) =$
10. $-(17 - 11 + 61) - (35 + 7 - 66) =$

Remove parentheses, then evaluate:

11. $(56 - 35) + (-13 + 6) - (14 + 2) =$
12. $-(17 - 11) + (13 - 6) + (-6 - 5) =$
13. $(6 + 15 - 63 - 21) + (-3 - 6 + 91) =$
14. $-(-3 - 66 + 11) - (36 + 95) =$

When you have "nested parentheses," you must either compute the value within the innermost set first or remove parenthesis, remembering to use the rules on every term within. For example, $-[16 + (-3 + 5)]$ may be calculated in several different ways.

$$-[16 + (-3 + 5)] = -[16 + 2] = -18$$
$$-[16 + (-3 + 5)] = -[16 - 3 + 5] = -[21 - 3] = -18$$
$$-[16 + (-3 + 5)] = -16 - (-3 + 5) = -16 + 3 - 5 = -18$$

Now try:

15. $-[66 - (11 - 28) - 4] =$
16. $[17 - (28 - 6) + 13] - 180 =$
17. $-\{28 - [16 + (-35 + 11) - (12 - 9)] - 1\} + 61 =$

B. Multiplication of Signed Numbers

When two expressions are combined by addition, they are called *terms*. When they are multiplied, they are called *factors*. The result is called the *product*. In arithmetic, the product is usually indicated with a × sign. Thus,

$$3 \times 15 = 45$$

When using symbols, the times sign may be mistaken for the letter x, so instead we write

$$a \cdot b \qquad \text{or} \qquad (a)(b) \qquad \text{or} \qquad a(b) \qquad \text{or just} \qquad ab$$

to represent a times b. Hence we may write

$$3 \times 5 = 3 \cdot 5 = (3)(5) = 3(5) = 15$$

Of course, we may not write 35 because it would be read thirty-five. Multiplication also satisfies certain basic rules.

8. *The commutative law.*

$$ab = ba$$

9. *The associative law.*

$$a(bc) = (ab)c$$

Just as for addition, these two rules allow the factors to be rearranged in any way within a product.

10. *The role of 1.* Any number multiplied by 1 is unchanged. In symbols,

$$(1)(a) = a$$

11. *The distributive law.*

$$a(b + c) = ab + ac$$

For example,

$$7(3 + 11) = 7(14) = 98$$
$$7(3 + 11) = (7)(3) + 7(11) = 21 + 77 = 98$$

12. *The role of -1.*

$$(-1)a = -a \text{ for any } a$$

13. *The role of 0.*

$$(0)(a) = 0 \text{ for any } a$$
$$\text{If } ab = 0, \text{ then either } a = 0 \text{ or } b = 0 \text{ or both}$$

14. *Multiplication using negative numbers.*

If a or b is negative, then $ab = -|a||b|$

If both a and b are negative, then $ab = |a||b|$

That is, the product of two numbers with the same sign is positive; the product of numbers of opposite sign is negative. For example,

$$(-3)(7) = -21 \qquad (4)(-8) = -32 \qquad (-5)(-11) = 55$$

Also remember this rule when applying the distributive law. For example,

$$(-3)(7 - 5) = (-3)(7) - (-3)(5) = -21 - (-15) = -21 + 15 = -6$$

EXERCISES

Reduce to a single number:

1. $(-4)(5) =$
2. $(-7)(-12) =$
3. $-6(15 - 11) =$
4. $(14 - 18)(13 - 17) =$
5. $(15 - 18)(26 - 13 - 10 - 3) =$
6. $(-3)(-11)(-6) =$
7. $(-2)(4)(-4)(3) =$
8. $(-2)(-3)(6 - 7) =$
9. $[(2)(-3) + 6](12) =$
10. $[-3(6 - 5) + (-11)](6 - 9) =$

C. Fractions, Decimals, and Percent

Given any number b except zero, it is possible to define a number $1/b$, called the *reciprocal of* b, such that $b(1/b) = 1$. The expression $1/0$ is undefined, since no number will satisfy the requirement that $(b)(0) = 1$. The product of any whole number a times the reciprocal of another whole number b is written $a(1/b) = a/b$ and is called a *fraction*. The product $a(1/b)$ is the same as dividing a by b. Thus,

a/b, $a(1/b)$, and $a \div b$ are different notations for the same operation. Because of this, the rules for division of signed numbers are the same as for multiplication of signed numbers. That is, a/b is positive if a and b have like signs and is negative if they have unlike signs. For example, $(-10)/(-5) = 2$ and $(-16)/4 = -4$. In the fraction a/b, a is called the *numerator* and b is called the *denominator*. Complicated fractions are usually written $\dfrac{a}{b}$ for clarity. If not, parentheses must be used. For example,

$$14/2 + 5$$

would be interpreted as $7 + 5 = 12$. If you mean

$$\frac{14}{2 + 5} = 2$$

you must write

$$14/(2 + 5)$$

In general, multiplication and division operations are to be done first. Thus,

$$(5)(2) + 3 = 10 + 3$$

If you need to add first, put parentheses around the terms to be added.

$$5(2 + 3) = (5)(5) = 25$$

Multiplication takes precedence over division. Thus,

$$1/2a = \frac{1}{2a}$$

If you want 1/2 times a, write

$$(1/2)(a) \qquad \text{or} \qquad a(1/2) = a/2$$

There are many properties of fractions which are required in order to satisfy the commutative, associative, and distributive laws. These are discussed in the next section.

15.   *The cancellation rule.*   If a/b is any fraction and both numerator and denominator are multiplied or divided by any nonzero number, the fraction does not change. Thus,

$$\frac{a}{b} = \frac{ac}{bc} = \frac{a \div c}{b \div c} \text{ for any } c \neq 0$$

This allows us to reduce fractions to "lowest terms." For example,

$$\frac{14}{35} = \frac{14 \div 7}{35 \div 7} = \frac{2}{5}$$

Fractions may also be expressed as decimals and percents. A fraction is converted into decimal form by long division. The result will be a decimal that terminates, such as $1/4 = 0.25$, or a decimal that repeats (immediately or eventually), such as $5/6 = 0.833 \ldots$. A fraction in which the numerator is larger than the denominator will turn out as a whole number plus a fractional part. Thus, $16/5 = 3\frac{1}{5}$ or 3.2. The term *percent* means per 100. Thus $0.17 = 17/100$ or 17 parts per hundred $= 17\%$. To convert a decimal to percent, simply multiply by 100. To convert a percent to a decimal, divide by 100. For example, $0.193 = 19.3\%$ and $116\% = 1.16$. When multiplying, dividing, adding, or subtracting decimals or percents, use the same techniques as for whole numbers. For example, 6% of $150 is (150) $(6\%) = (150)(0.06) = \$9.00$.

EXERCISES

Convert the following fractions to (a) a decimal and (b) percent:

1. 1/5
2. 2/9
3. 3/8
4. −7/16
5. 11/7
6. 155/80
7. −6/4
8. 17/12
9. −12/17
10. 8/(−3)
11. A store marks up merchandise 50%. What does an item purchased for $70 sell for?
12. An item is marked down from $80 to $75. What is the percentage markdown?

13. A store gives a 12% discount for cash customers. What is the discount on a $165 item?

14. A bank pays 7.9% interest. What is the interest on $430?

15. A store marks prices up 20%. What is the purchase price as a percentage of sales price?

D. Addition, Subtraction, Multiplication, and Division of Fractions

16. *The product of two fractions.*

$$\frac{a}{b} \cdot \frac{c}{d} = \frac{ac}{bd}$$

For example,

$$\frac{-3}{4} \cdot \frac{5}{7} = \frac{-15}{28}$$

Remember that a whole number b may be thought of as $b/1$. Thus

$$7(6/5) = \frac{7}{1} \cdot \frac{6}{5} = \frac{42}{5}$$

17. *The quotient of two fractions.*

$$\frac{a}{b} \div \frac{c}{d} = \frac{a}{b} \cdot \frac{d}{c}$$

That is, to divide by a fraction, invert the divisor and multiply. For example,

$$\frac{-2}{3} \div \frac{-8}{7} = \frac{-2}{3} \cdot \frac{7}{-8} = \frac{-14}{-24} = \frac{14}{24} = \frac{7}{12}$$

18. *The sum or difference of two fractions.* If two fractions have the same denominator, add them (or subtract them) by combining the numerators. Thus,

$$\frac{7}{8} + \frac{3}{8} = \frac{10}{8} = \frac{5}{4}$$

or
$$\frac{9}{11} - \frac{2}{11} = \frac{7}{11}$$

If the fractions have different denominators, first use the cancellation rule to write them as fractions with the same denominator. For example, to compute

$$\frac{5}{6} + \frac{3}{10}$$

proceed as follows: Each fraction may be written with denominator 30. Thus

$$\frac{5}{6} = \frac{25}{30} \quad \text{and} \quad \frac{3}{10} = \frac{9}{30}$$

Hence,

$$\frac{5}{6} + \frac{3}{10} = \frac{25}{30} + \frac{9}{30} = \frac{34}{30} = \frac{17}{15}$$

19. *Least common denominators.* In the last example, we used 30 as the "common denominator" of the two fractions. We could just as easily have used 60. Thus,

$$\frac{5}{6} + \frac{3}{10} = \frac{50}{60} + \frac{18}{60} = \frac{68}{60} = \frac{17}{15}$$

We used 30 because it was smaller. In fact, 30 is called the *least common denominator*, because it is the smallest number that is a multiple of both 6 and 10. It is also called the *least common multiple of 6 and 10.* Using the least common denominator will save work in combining fractions; here is another application of least common multiple.

A supermarket sells apple juice in a 32-ounce bottle for 53¢ and in a 40-ounce bottle for 65¢. Which is a better buy? The usual suggestion is to figure the price per ounce. Thus, in the 32-ounce bottle, we have $53/32 = 1.65625$¢ per ounce. In the 40-ounce bottle, we have $65/40 = 1.625$¢ per ounce. Thus the 40-ounce bottle is really cheaper. However, there is a way to figure this out without using long division. The least common multiple of 32 and 40 is 160. Actually five 32-ounce bottles contain 160 ounces, and four 40-ounce bottles contain 160 ounces. Hence, in 32-ounce bottles, 160 ounces cost $5(53¢) = \$2.65$. In 40-ounce bottles, 160 ounces cost $4(65¢) = \$2.60$. Now you not only know that the 40-ounce bottle is cheaper, but you also know how much you can save over several purchases.

EXERCISES

Reduce the following expressions to a simple fraction:

1. $5/6 + 1/4 =$
2. $7/8 - 5/11 =$
3. $-2/3 + 11/12 =$
4. $(-1/6)(-3/5) =$
5. $(7/8) \div (7/3) =$
6. $(2/9)(5/3 + 4/3) =$
7. $(1/5)(9/13 - 4/13) =$
8. $(-11/12 + 9/16) \div (5/8) =$
9. $(6/7) \div (5/12 - 3/5) =$
10. $(2/3)(7/6)(9/11) =$
11. $(-3/4)(26/11) + (-3/8) =$
12. $(2/3 - 3/4) \div (3/4 - 9/16) =$

Give the answer to the following as a percentage:

13. $(2/3)(1/5) =$
14. $1/4 + 0.42 =$
15. $(2/3)(6\%) =$
16. $-0.61 + 5.3\% + 2/21 =$
17. $(12\%)(0.15)(-2/3) =$
18. $(0.16)(3/5 - 3/7) =$
19. $(-2.15) \div (2.2 - 1/5) =$
20. $(-2.15) \div (-3/8) =$
21. Which is a better buy, a three-quart container of milk for $1.15 or a four-quart container for $1.56?
22. Which is a better buy, a 5 lb 4 oz box of detergent at $2.59 or a 2 lb 4 oz box at $1.09?
23. Which is a better buy, a 12 oz box of cereal at 63¢ or a 1 lb 4 oz box at 91¢?
24. Which is a better buy, 6½ oz of tuna fish at 67¢ or 3 oz of tuna fish at 29¢?

E. Exponential Notation

For short, we denote the product $(b)(b)$ as b^2 or $(b)(b)(b)$ as b^3. In general,

20.   If n is a natural number, then b^n is the product of n b's. That is,

$$\underbrace{b \cdot b \ldots b}_{n \text{ times}} = b^n$$

In this notation, n is called the *exponent* and b, the *base*. For example,

$$2^4 = 2 \cdot 2 \cdot 2 \cdot 2 = 16$$
$$(-3)^5 = (-3)(-3)(-3)(-3)(-3) = -243$$

From this definition, certain properties must follow.

21.   (a) $b^n b^m = b^{n+m}$
      (b) $b^n \div b^m = b^{n-m}$
      (c) $(ab)^n = a^n b^n$
      (d) $(a^n)^m = a^{nm}$

For example,

$$x^5 \cdot x^2 = x^{5+2} = x^7$$
$$x^8 \div x^6 = x^{8-6} = x^2$$
$$(2y)^3 = 2^3 y^3 = 8y^3$$
$$(z^4)^3 = z^{(4)(3)} = z^{12}$$

These same rules apply to exponents which may be negative or zero. However, in order that they be consistent, we must have

22.   (e) $b^{-n} = 1/b^n$
      (f) $b^0 = 1$

For example,

$$x^5 y^3 \div x^7 y^3 = x^{5-7} y^{3-3} = x^{-2} = 1/x^2$$

Furthermore, it is possible to define a meaning for fractional exponents as follows: For any b, we define $b^{1/q}$ to be the number having the property that

$$(b^{1/q})^q = b$$

For example, $8^{1/3}$ is the number satisfying the relationship $(8^{1/3})^3 = 8$. Since we know that $2^3 = 8$, it must be that $8^{1/3} = 2$. This is also called the *cube root* of 8 and is written $\sqrt[3]{8}$. In general,

$$b^{1/q} = \sqrt[q]{b}$$

When $q = 2$, we write

$$b^{1/2} = \sqrt{b}$$

called the *square root of b*. The symbol $\sqrt[q]{}$ is called a *radical*. If there is no *index* number q shown, we understand that $q = 2$. If we want $b^{p/q}$, we use property (d) and write it as $(b^{1/q})^p$ or $(b^p)^{(1/q)}$, whichever is more convenient. For example,

$$(16)^{3/4} = (16^{1/4})^3 = (2)^3 = 8$$
$$(27x^3)^{2/3} = (27)^{2/3}(x^3)^{2/3} = (27^{1/3})^2 x^{3(2/3)}$$
$$= 3^2 x^2 = 9x^2$$
$$\left(\frac{x^6}{8}\right)^{-2/3} = \frac{x^{-4}}{8^{-2/3}} = 8^{2/3}x^{-4} = 4x^{-4}$$

Notice that the square of any real number must be positive. That is, $b^2 = b \cdot b$. If b is positive, $b \cdot b$ is positive. If b is negative, the product of two negative numbers is still positive; hence, $b \cdot b$ is positive. Therefore, the square root of a negative number is not real. In general, $b^{p/q}$ is not a real number if q is even and b is negative. For example, $(-8)^{3/4}$ is not real but $(-8)^{-2/3}$ is real and equals $1/4$.

EXERCISES

Simplify as much as possible:

1. $4^3 3^2 =$

2. $4^{-2}8 =$

3. $[(2)(-3)]^3 =$

4. $(3a)^2 =$

5. $(-2a)^{-1} =$

6. $x^5 x^{-3} =$

7. $x^{1/2} \div x^{3/2} =$

8. $(x^{2/3})^{-3} =$

9. $(x^{2/3})^{(3/4)} =$

10. $y^{-6}b^{-3}y^4b^8 =$

11. $(xy)^4(x^2y)^{-3} \div (xy^{1/4})^4 =$

12. $(27x^3y^{-6})^{(-2/3)} =$

F. Factoring Algebraic Expressions

Frequently it is important to be able to find the factors that make up a product. The simplest case is a direct application of the distributive law.

23. *Removing a common factor.* Given an expression of the form $ab + ac$, it may be rewritten by the distributive law as

$$ab + ac = a(b + c)$$

This may be very useful in simplifying fractions. Thus,

$$\frac{2a + 2b}{7a + 7b} = \frac{2(a + b)}{7(a + b)}$$

Now, numerator and denominator may be divided by the quantity $a + b$ to yield

$$\frac{2a + 2b}{7a + 7b} = \frac{2(a + b)}{7(a + b)} = \frac{2}{7}$$

Notice that we may divide out (or cancel) a common factor in numerator and denominator of a fraction. We may not cancel a factor from only one term. Thus,

$$\frac{2x + 1}{2x + 3} \neq \frac{x + 1}{x + 3}$$

That is, you cannot divide out the 2 which is a factor of the first term in both numerator and denominator.

Sometimes the common factor is tricky. For example,

$$3a + ab + 3c + bc = a(3 + b) + c(3 + b)$$

We have factored a from each of the first two terms and c from each of the last two. However, now we see that $(3 + b)$ is a common factor of each of the two terms; hence,

$$a(3 + b) + c(3 + b) = (3 + b)(a + c)$$

One fringe benefit of common factors is the possibility of combining like terms. Thus,

$$7a + 6a = a(7 + 6) = 13a$$

or

$$-15x + 7x = x(-15 + 7) = -8x$$

or

$$-6abc - 11abc = (-6 - 11)abc = -17abc$$

That is, if the "letter" parts of the two terms are the same, they may be combined by combining the numerical coefficients properly. In the case $(3ab - 9ac)$, the letter parts are not identical. However, there is a common factor $3a$, so we have

$$3ab - 9ac = 3a(b - 3c)$$

Sometimes we may apply the laws of exponents to factoring. Thus,

$$3x^5 + 12x^3$$

has a common factor $3x^3$,

$$3x^5 + 12x^3 = 3x^3(x^2 + 4)$$

24.   *Binomials.*   If we multiply $(a + b)(c + d)$, the result is

$$(a + b)(c + d) = (a + b)c + (a + b)d = ac + bc + ad + bd$$

You could factor this by successive applications of removing a common factor. However, if we took a product such as

$$(x + 2)(x + 3) = x^2 + 5x + 6$$

the individual numerical terms have been combined. Nevertheless, by good guessing you could find the factors. In general,

$$(x + u)(x + v) = x^2 + (u + v)x + uv$$

Clearly then, if $x^2 + bx + c$ is to have factors $(x + u)(x + v)$, then $uv = c$ and $u + v = b$.

For example, consider

$$x^2 - 5x + 4$$

Since $c = 4$ is positive, the factors u and v must have the same sign. Since $b = -5$ is negative, the sum of u and v must be negative. Hence, u and v must both be negative and their product must be 4. The only whole numbers possible are $-4, -1$ and $-2, -2$. Trial will show that $-4, -1$ is correct and

$$x^2 - 5x + 4 = (x - 1)(x - 4)$$

It is a little more difficult to handle

$$ax^2 + bx + c$$

but trial and error will work if there are simple factors.

25. *Difference of two squares.* One special factorization that comes up frequently is

$$a^2 - b^2 = (a - b)(a + b)$$

For example,

$$4x^2 - 9y^2 = (2x)^2 - (3y)^2 = (2x - 3y)(2x + 3y)$$

26. *The perfect square.* Another special form is

$$(a + b)^2 = a^2 + 2ab + b^2$$

For example,

$$(x - 4y)^2 = x^2 + 2(x)(-4y) + (-4y)^2 = x^2 - 8xy + 16y^2$$

It is also common to combine two types of factoring. For example, $x^3 - 16x$ may be factored in two stages. First, remove a common factor.

$$x^3 - 16x = x(x^2 - 16)$$

Now, the second factor is the difference of two squares. Hence,

$$x^3 - 16x = x(x^2 - 16) = x(x - 4)(x + 4)$$

EXERCISES

Factor the following:

1. $3ax + 6ay$
2. $3a^2x - 9ax^2$
3. $3ax^2 - 3ay^2$
4. $x^2 - 5x - 6$
5. $x^2 + 12x - 13$
6. $x^2 - xy + 3y - 3x$
7. $x^4 - 16y^4$
8. $a^2 + 2ab + b^2$
9. $4x^2 + 4xy + y^2$
10. $x^3 + 6x^2y + 9xy^2$
11. $2x^2 - 5x$
12. $2x^2 - 5x - 7$
13. $x^3 - x^2 - 2x$
14. $x^3y - xy$
15. $x^3 + 3x^3 - x^2 - 4x^2$
16. $ab^2 + a^2b + 3ab$
17. $x^2z^2 - 4x^2t^2z + 4t^4x^2$
18. $4x^3y^2 - 8x^3z^2$
19. $x^2 - y^2 + x^2 + 2xy + y^2$
20. $x^3 + 12x^2y + 20xy^2$

G. Solutions of Linear Equations

An expression in which two quantities are related by an equal sign is called an *equation*. If an equation involves a symbol such as x, it may be true for all values of x or for only some values of x. An equation such as

$$3x^2 + 5x^2 = 8x^2$$

is true for all x and is called an *identity*. An equation such as

$$4x = 8$$

is true only for $x = 2$. It is called an *open sentence* or *conditional equality*. To "solve an equation" means to find all values of x for which the equation is true. In order to solve the equation, you may add (or subtract) any quantity to both sides of the equation, or you may multiply (or divide) both sides of the equation by any number other than zero. The object is to rearrange the equation so that the unknown is isolated. For example,

$$3x + 7 = 13$$

is a linear equation. That is, it involves x only to the first power. To isolate x, first subtract 7 from both sides, yielding

$$3x + 7 - 7 = 13 - 7$$
$$3x = 6$$

Now divide both sides by 3, yielding

$$\frac{3x}{3} = \frac{6}{3} \qquad x = 2$$

This is the solution. It should be checked by substituting $x = 2$ in the original equation. See if you can follow these steps:

$$3x - 12 = 4x + 6$$
$$3x - 12 - 4x = 4x + 6 - 4x$$
$$-x - 12 = 6$$
$$-x - 12 + 12 = 6 + 12$$
$$-x = 18$$
$$x = -18$$

Of course, with practice you can do many steps at one time.

Many simple verbal descriptions lead to linear equations. For instance, a salesman is paid $100 per week plus a commission of 5% of the total sales he makes. Last week he earned $620. What was his sales total? To solve, let x = amount of total sales. Now, the commission is 5% of x or $(0.05)x$. Hence, his earnings for the week are given by

$$100 + (0.05)x = 620$$

Subtracting 100 from both sides,

$$(0.05)x = 520$$

Multiplying by 20, we have

$$x = \$10,400$$

EXERCISES

Solve for x:

1. $2x = 6$
2. $x + 5 = 12$
3. $15 - x = -6$
4. $12 + 3x = 2$
5. $16.2 = x - 3.5$
6. $1.4x + 3 = 6.6$
7. $2x - 3 = 6x + 9$
8. $2x - (4x - 9) = 3x + 6$
9. $x + [3 - (5 + 4x)] = 6 - (3 - 2x)$
10. $(0.5)(x - 4) = 1.3x + 2.2$
11. $\frac{1}{2}x + \frac{2}{3} = 2x - 4$
12. $(1/3)(x + 6) = x + 2$
13. $(x + 5)/12 = 7$
14. $(x - 5)/14 = 0$
15. $(2x + 3)/6 = (x - 1)/5$
16. $(0.4)(x - 6) = (0.25)(x + 0.2)$
17. If eggs cost 75¢ per dozen, how many eggs can you buy for $23.25?
18. In New York City, sales tax is 8%. If the tax on an item is $1.60, what was the sales price? If the total cost including tax was $32.40, what was the price?
19. Books ordered by mail sell for $7.00 a piece plus a fixed $1.00 for handling. How many books were ordered if the bill was $57.00?

20. A man has seven more dimes than he has nickels. If he has $2.50 in dimes and nickels, how many of each does he have?

21. A man is twice as old as his son. Ten years ago, he was three times as old as his son was then. How old is the man?

22. Two men are waiting for trains. Mr. Abel waits ten minutes and then takes the local, which averages 30 miles per hour. Mr. Baker waits thirty minutes and then takes the express, which averages 50 miles per hour. They arrive at their destination at the same time. How long did the express take for the trip?

H. Quadratic Equations

An equation of the form $ax^2 + bx + c = 0$ with a, b, and c constants is called a *quadratic equation*. If the quadratic expression on the left-hand side can be factored easily, we may reason as follows:

$$x^2 - 3x - 4 = 0$$

Factoring yields

$$(x - 4)(x + 1) = 0$$

We have now the product of two numbers equaling zero. Therefore, one or the other must be zero to satisfy the equation. Hence, either $x - 4 = 0$ or $x + 1 = 0$. The two possible solutions are

$$x = 4 \qquad \text{or} \qquad x = -1$$

27. If we cannot find the factors easily, we apply the *quadratic formula*, which states that the roots of

$$ax^2 + bx + c = 0$$

are given by

$$x = \frac{-b \pm \sqrt{b^2 - 4ac}}{2a}$$

For example, the roots of

$$2x^2 + 3x - 9 = 0$$

are

$$x = \frac{-3 \pm \sqrt{(3)^2 - (4)(2)(-9)}}{2(2)} = \frac{-3 \pm \sqrt{81}}{4}$$

That is, $x = \dfrac{-3 + 9}{4} = 3/2$ and $x = \dfrac{-3 - 9}{4} = -3$. Of course, this equation could have been factored, as we now see.

$$2x^2 + 3x - 9 = (2x - 3)(x + 3)$$

Consider another example.

$$x^2 + 2x - 2 = 0$$

$$x = \frac{-2 \pm \sqrt{(2)^2 - 4(1)(-2)}}{2} = \frac{-2 \pm \sqrt{12}}{2}$$

Now, $\sqrt{12} = \sqrt{4}\,\sqrt{3} = 2\sqrt{3}$

Therefore,

$$x = -1 \pm \sqrt{3}$$

and the two roots are

$$x = -1 + \sqrt{3} \qquad \text{and} \qquad x = -1 - \sqrt{3}$$

which cannot be further simplified.

28. If, for some equation, the expression $b^2 - 4ac$, called the *discriminant*, is equal to zero, then there is only a single root to the quadratic. If the discriminant is negative, the roots involve the square root of a negative number, which is imaginary; and the equation does not have real numbers as solutions. In this text, there are no applications that involve imaginary or complex numbers.

EXERCISES

Solve by factoring:

1. $x^2 - 8x - 9 = 0$
2. $x^2 + 4x - 21 = 0$
3. $x^2 + 9x + 20 = 0$
4. $x^2 - 9x + 18 = 0$

5. $x^2 + 4 = 5x$

6. $x^2 - x = 6$

7. $2x^2 - 11x + 5 = 0$

8. $2 - x = 3x^2$

9. $3x^2 - 4 = x$

10. $x^2 = 11x + 26$

Solve by quadratic formula, finding only real roots:

11. $x^2 - 2x - 5 = 0$

12. $x^2 - x - 1 = 0$

13. $4x^2 = 1 - 4x$

14. $2x^2 - x - 1 = 0$

15. $3x^2 - 6 = x$

16. $x - x^2 = 7$

Solve, finding only real roots:

17. $x^2 - x - 12 = 0$

18. $6x^2 - 11x - 10 = 0$

19. $x^2 - 4x - 7 = 0$

20. $3x^2 + x - 4 = 0$

21. $2x^2 - 3x + 6 = 0$

22. $5x^2 - 7x - 2 = 0$

I. Two Equations in Two Unknowns

Consider the following problem: Erica and Lisa have $18.00 between them. Erica has $8.00 more than Lisa. How much does each have?
   If we let

$$x = \text{Erica's money}$$

and

$$y = \text{Lisa's money}$$

then

$$x + y = 18$$

$$x - y = \ \ 8$$

We have two equations in two unknowns, x and y. We want the values for which both equations are true. There are two methods of solving.

29. *Substitution.* Solve one equation for y in terms of x (or x in terms of y), and substitute into the other equation. Thus, solving the first equation for y yields

$$y = 18 - x$$

Substituting into the second equation,

$$x - (18 - x) = 8$$
$$x - 18 + x = 8$$
$$2x = 26$$
$$x = 13$$

Knowing x, we have $y = 18 - 13 = 5$. You may now check by direct substitution in the original equations.

$$13 + 5 = 18$$
$$13 - 5 = 8$$

30. *Elimination of one variable.* Add a multiple of one equation to the other so as to arrive at a new equation with only one variable. In the last example,

$$x + y = 18$$
$$x - y = 8$$

Adding the two equations,

$$2x + 0 = 26$$
$$x = 13$$

Now substitute into either equation to yield $y = 5$. Again, you should check by substitution. As another example, consider

$$2x - 3y = 1$$
$$3x + 4y = 10$$

In order to eliminate y, we could multiply the second equation by 3/4 and then add. It is easier to multiply the first equation by 4 and the second by 3 and then add.

$$8x - 12y = 4$$
$$9x + 12y = 30$$
$$\overline{17x = 34}$$
$$x = 2$$

Substituting into either equation, we get $y = 1$. Again, you should check your answer.

EXERCISES

Solve:

1. $x - y = -2$
    $x + y = 4$

2. $2x + y = 12$
    $x - 3y = 4$

3. $2s - 3t = 1$
    $3s + 5t = 68$

4. $x = 6 - t$
    $t = 7 - 2x$

5. $6x + t = 0$
    $3x + 15 = 2t$

6. $-9 - t = 3y$
    $9 + 2y = t$

7. A bottle and a cork cost $1.10; the bottle costs $1.00 more than the cork. How much does each cost?

8. A man has 16 nickels and dimes totalling $1.30. How many of each type of coin does he have?

9. A book company charges the same amount for each book and a fixed delivery charge for any shipment. The bill for seven books is $23.00. The bill for 13 books is $41.00. What is the shipping charge and the charge per book?

10. A family with two adults and five children paid $20.00 for circus tickets. A family with four adults and two children paid $24.00 for circus tickets. How much does an adult's ticket cost and how much does a child's ticket cost?

J. Inequalities

The symbol $<$ is read "less than." The statement $a < b$ is read "a is less than b." It means that $b - a$ is positive. Thus,

$$3 < 5 \qquad -3 < 0 \qquad -7 < -4$$

When reversed, $>$ is read "greater than." Thus,

$$-2 > -11 \qquad \tfrac{1}{2} > -2 \qquad 16.2 > 12.9$$

The symbols $\leq$ and $\geq$ are read "less than or equal to" and "greater than or equal to" respectively. If we write $x < 4$, we mean that x is any number less than 4. If we write $x \leq 4$, we mean x is any number up to and including 4.

Sometimes we have inequalities like

$$2x + 6 \leq 26$$

To solve the inequality means to isolate x just as in solving an equation. In handling inequalities, the following rules must be observed:

31.   (a)   The same number may be added to both sides of an inequality without changing it; that is, if $a > b$, then $a + c > b + c$.

(b)   If both sides of an inequality are multiplied by a positive number, the inequality is unchanged; that is, if $a > b$ and $c > 0$, $ac > bc$.

(c)   If both sides of an inequality are multiplied by a negative number, the inequality is reversed; that is, if $a > b$ and $c < 0$, $ac < bc$. These rules will hold whether we work with $<$, $>$, $\leq$, or $\geq$. Thus, to solve

$$2x + 6 \leq 26$$

first subtract 6 from both sides (that is, add -6). This does not change the inequality and yields

$$2x \leq 20$$

Now divide both sides by 2 (that is, multiply by 1/2). Since 1/2 is positive, the inequality is maintained and reduces to $x \leq 10$.

Take a business example. A case of soda costs $3.00. The cost of delivery is $5.00 regardless of the number of cases ordered. What is the largest number of cases that can be purchased for $73.00? Let

x = number of cases. The cost of x cases is $3x + 5$. We must have $3x + 5 \leq 73$ or $3x \leq 68$ or $x \leq 22\frac{2}{3}$. Therefore, if only whole cases can be ordered, we may order at most 22 cases.

EXERCISES

Solve the following inequalities:

1. $x + 3 \leq 5$

2. $2x - 3 \geq 5$

3. $2x - 3 < 3x - 11$

4. $7x - 6 \leq 4(x - 2)$

5. $6x > 5x$

6. $2x - 11 \leq 3x + 4(x - 6)$

7. Erica is three years older than Lisa. The sum of their ages is less than 27. What is the oldest Lisa can be?

8. A store sells records for $4.50. It buys the records for $2.50. In addition, it has overhead costs of $200 per week. What is the smallest number of records it must sell each week in order to have a weekly profit of at least $300?

K. Some Geometry

32. Given any angle A, it is possible to define certain trigonometric quantities associated with A. The three fundamental trigonometric quantities are: sine of A, abbreviated sin A; cosine of A, abbreviated cos A; and tangent of A, abbreviated tan A. If A is less than 90° it may be located in a right triangle, and the trigonometric values may be expressed in terms of the lengths of the sides of the triangle, as shown in Figure 1.

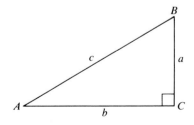

Figure 1

$$\sin A = a/c \qquad \cos A = b/c \qquad \tan A = a/b$$

In addition, for any right triangle, the sides must satisfy

33. *The Pythagorean theorem.* If a and b are the legs of a right triangle and c is the hypotenuse (side opposite the right angle), then $a^2 + b^2 = c^2$.

Analytic geometry, with which chapter 1 begins, assumes that it is possible to identify all the real numbers with points along a number line. Usually such a line is drawn with the numbers increasing from left to right as shown in Figure 2. Numbers other than whole numbers fit in between them in their appropriate locations.

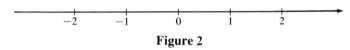

Figure 2

Number inequalities may be represented as portions of the number line. For example, $x \leq 2.5$ is shaded in Figure 3. A double inequality such as $-1.5 \leq x \leq 1$ is graphed as in Figure 4.

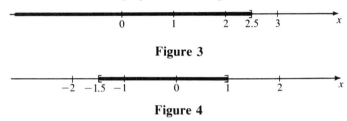

Figure 3

Figure 4

EXERCISES

1. Given a right triangle with legs of length 3 and 4. Find the length of the hypotenuse. Let A be the angle opposite the shortest side. Find $\sin A$, $\cos A$, and $\tan A$.

2. Repeat Exercise 1 for the triangle with one leg 5 inches long and hypotenuse 13 inches long.

3. The sum of the angles of any triangle is $180°$. A right angle is $90°$. The sine of $30°$ is $1/2$. Draw a right triangle with a $30°$ angle in it. Let the shortest side of the triangle be 5 units long. Find the lengths of the other sides. Find $\cos 30°$ and $\tan 30°$.

4. If one angle of a right triangle is $45°$, then the legs are of equal length. This is called an *isosceles* right triangle. If the legs of an

isosceles right triangle are each 3 units long, find the length of the hypotenuse. Find sin 45°, cos 45°, tan 45°.

5. Find the lengths of the legs of an isosceles right triangle with hypotenuse of length 2.

6. Graph the inequalities:
   (a) $-2 \leq x \leq -1$
   (b) $0 \leq x \leq 6$
   (c) $-1/2 \leq x \leq 1/2$
   (d) $12 \leq x \leq 15.9$

7. Solve the following inequalities and graph the solutions:
   (a) $-2x + 3 \leq 11$
   (b) $x - 6 \geq 5 - 3x$
   (c) $3 \leq 3x \leq 6$
   (d) $12 \leq -3x \leq 15$

PART I

Linear Methods

1

Lines and Linear Programming

1.1 Linear Equations

Coordinate geometry is one of the most useful tools in the analysis of business and economic problems. With coordinate geometry, algebraic formulas may be translated into *graphs*. In many cases, having the graph is the end of the problem. As you know from everyday experience, a picture may be far more informative than a collection of data or a formula. In other cases, you can draw conclusions from the picture and thus find a solution to a problem that would otherwise appear to be quite difficult.

The study of coordinate geometry begins with a universe consisting of all ordered pairs of real numbers. Examples of points in this universe are $(1, 4)$, $(-1/2, 5)$, $(3.6, -2.1)$, $(0, \pi)$ and $(0.3, \sqrt{2})$. Because the pairs are *ordered*, $(1, 2)$ and $(2, 1)$ are two different points. When coordinate axes are introduced in a plane, every ordered pair is associated with a point in the plane; and, conversely, every point in the plane has attached to it a unique ordered pair of coordinates. In case you have forgotten, let us briefly review how this is done. First, as in figure 1, a pair of number lines are drawn at right angles to one another, intersecting at the point zero on each line. The horizontal line is called the *x*-axis and the vertical line is called the *y*-axis. Now, construct a vertical line through any point in the plane. At the point where this line crosses the *x*-axis is a number called the *x-coordinate* (or *abscissa*) of the point. Now construct a horizontal line through the point. At the point where this line crosses the *y*-axis is a number called the *y-coordinate* (or *ordinate*) of the point. If the point is called *P*, and its coordinates are (x, y), then we can refer to it as $P(x, y)$. In figure 1, the points $P(1, 2)$, $Q(-1, 1/2)$ and $R(-2, -2\frac{1}{4})$ are shown. Notice that every point on the *x*-axis has ordinate 0 and every point on the *y*-axis has abscissa 0. The point where the axes intersect, called the *origin*, has coordinates $(0, 0)$.

If we have a formula or some other rule expressing the relationship between two quantities *x* and *y*, then we may plot all the points whose coordinates satisfy the rule. The resulting picture is the graph of the relationship. Similarly, you could give a verbal description of a desired graph and find the relationship between the coordinates which would

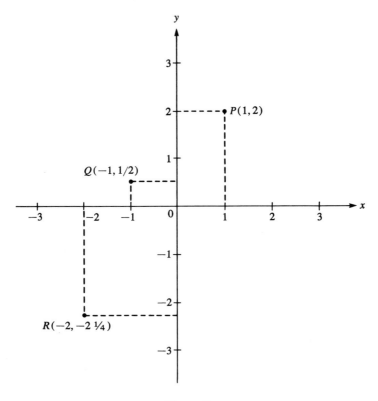

Figure 1

produce such a graph. For example, the vertical line crossing the x-axis at 3 would be described by the rule $x = 3$ and $y =$ anything. Since the last restriction is no restriction at all, we shall simply refer to this graph as "the line $x = 3$." In general, any vertical line will be represented by the equation $x = a$, where a is some constant. If a is positive, then the line lies to the right of the y-axis. If a is negative, the line lies to the left of the y-axis. The equation $x = 0$ is the y-axis. A horizontal line has equation $y = b$, where the line crosses the y-axis at $(0, b)$. If b is positive, then the line lies above the x-axis; if b is negative, the line lies below the x-axis. Of course, the equation $y = 0$ is the x-axis.

Let us now consider some lines not parallel to either axis. To begin, we take a line L_1 passing through the origin and making an angle α with the positive x-axis (see figure 2). If $P(x, y)$ is any point on the line, other than the origin, then $\tan \alpha = y/x$. Using the symbol $m = \tan \alpha$, we obtain $m = y/x$ or $y = mx$ as the equation of the line. If we consider another line L_2, parallel to L_1 and cutting the y-axis at $(0, b)$, then for each x-value the y-value on L_2 will be simply b more than the value on L_1 (see figure 3). That is, the equation of this line will be $y = mx + b$. In this equation, m is called the slope of the line and b is called the y-intercept. It should be obvious that if two nonvertical lines are parallel, then they have the same slope. Figure 4 shows some typical graphs of lines of the form $y = mx + b$. How does one draw the graph of such a line?

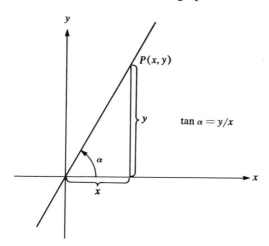

Figure 2

Example 1 Graph the straight line whose equation is $y = -2x + 4$.

According to Euclid, two points determine a straight line. Hence, we need only substitute two values of x, find the corresponding values of y, plot

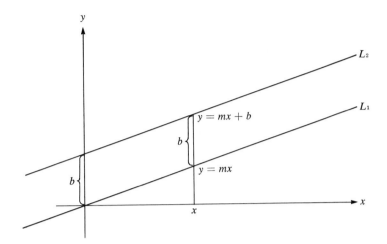

Figure 3

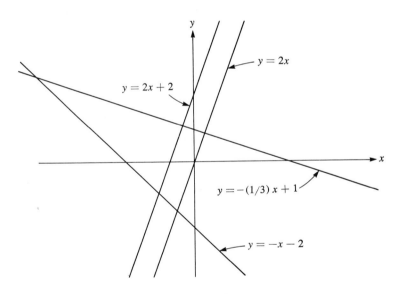

Figure 4

these two points and draw the line. So when $x = 0$, $y = 4$; and when $x = 1$, $y = 2$. Thus, $(0, 4)$ and $(1, 2)$ lie on the line and the graph is shown in figure 5.

Example 2 Find the equation of a line of slope 3, which passes through the point $(-1, 4)$.

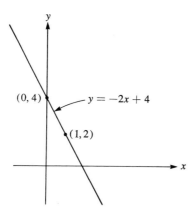

Figure 5

The equation of the line must be $y = 3x + b$, since it has slope 3. In addition, the equation must be true for $x = -1$ and $y = 4$. That is,

$$4 = 3(-1) + b$$
$$4 = -3 + b \qquad b = 7$$

Hence, the required equation is $y = 3x + 7$.

Example 3 Find the equation of the line which passes through $(2, 9)$ and $(-5, -6)$.

The equation is $y = mx + b$, which must be true at both points. Therefore,

$$9 = 2m + b$$
$$-6 = -5m + b$$

Here we have two equations in two unknowns, m and b. To solve, we subtract the lower equation from the upper, which yields

$$15 = 2m - (-5m)$$
$$15 = 7m$$
$$m = 15/7$$

Substituting into the first equation, we get

$$9 = 2(15/7) + b$$
$$9 = 30/7 + b$$
$$b = 9 - 30/7 = 63/7 - 30/7 = 33/7$$

Hence, the required equation is

$$y = (15/7)x + 33/7$$

which looks nicer if both sides are multiplied by 7 to yield

$$7y = 15x + 33$$

In Example 3, we see that given two points on a line, we are able to determine the slope of the line. Now, let us try to do this in general. Suppose we know that a line passes through two points $P(x_1, y_1)$ and $Q(x_2, y_2)$. Following the pattern in the example,

$$y_2 = mx_2 + b$$
$$\underline{y_1 = mx_1 + b}$$
$$y_2 - y_1 = mx_2 - mx_1$$
$$y_2 - y_1 = m(x_2 - x_1)$$
$$m = \frac{y_2 - y_1}{x_2 - x_1} \quad \text{if } x_2 \neq x_1$$

This is called the *slope formula*. Of course, if P and Q are different points and $x_2 = x_1$, the line is vertical and the slope is undefined.

Example 4   Use the slope formula to solve the problem in Example 3.

In this case $x_1 = 2$, $y_1 = 9$, $x_2 = -5$ and $y_2 = -6$, so

$$m = \frac{-6 - 9}{-5 - 2} = \frac{15}{7}$$

Therefore,

$$y = (15/7)x + b$$

and using the point $(2, 9)$,

$$9 = (15/7)2 + b$$
$$b = 33/7$$

and $y = (15/7)x + 33/7$, as before.

In Examples 2 and 4, we were faced with the problem of knowing the slope of a line and one point on the line and needing to know its equation. Using the slope formula, you will find that it is easy to find a general solution to this problem. Let L be a line with slope m, passing through the point $P(x_1, y_1)$. Let (x, y) be any other point on the line. Now, using the slope formula with (x, y) playing the role of Q, we have

$$m = \frac{y - y_1}{x - x_1}$$

that is,

$$y - y_1 = m(x - x_1)$$

This is called the point-slope formula for a straight line.

Example 5 Using the point-slope formula, rework Example 4. We have $m = 15/7$ and $(x_1, y_1) = (2, 9)$. Hence the equation is

$$y - 9 = (15/7)(x - 2)$$

Multiplying both sides by 7, we have

$$7y - 63 = 15(x - 2)$$
$$7y - 63 = 15x - 30$$
$$7y = 15x + 33$$

which is the same equation obtained previously.

The slope formula also gives us a good indication of what the slope really represents. If we always think of Q as lying to the right of P, then the denominator, $x_2 - x_1$, is always positive. If Q is higher than P, the numerator is also positive; hence, m is positive. So if the line is rising as you go from left to right, the slope is positive; otherwise it is negative. A zero slope indicates that the numerator is zero, which means that $y_2 = y_1$ and the line is horizontal. A line which makes a 45° angle with the x-axis has slope $+1$ (-1 means 45° below the positive x-axis). Large slopes indicate steepness and small slopes indicate a gentle rise or fall.

We have seen that the equation of a line may take one of three forms:

1. $x = a$, a vertical straight line,
2. $y = b$, a horizontal straight line,
3. $y = mx + b$, any other line.

Of course, Form 2 is only a special case of Form 3 with $m = 0$. All this can be summarized in the following.

THEOREM 1 Every equation of the form $Ax + By = C$, A and B not both zero, is the equation of a straight line. A, B and C are constants. (Accordingly, every such equation is called a *linear equation*.)

Proof If $A = 0$, $B \neq 0$, $By = C$, $y = C/B$, which is a horizontal line. If $B = 0$, $A \neq 0$, $Ax = C$, $x = C/A$, which is a vertical line. If neither A nor B is zero,

$$Ax + By = C$$
$$By = -Ax + C$$
$$y = (-A/B)x + C/B$$

which is of the form $y = mx + b$.

Example 6 Find the slope and y-intercept of the line, with the equation $3x + 4y = 8$. Find the x-intercept, too. (The x-intercept is the point where the line crosses the x-axis.)

The equation is $3x + 4y = 8$, which we solve for y:

$$4y = -3x + 8$$
$$y = (-3/4)x + 2$$

Therefore, the slope is $-3/4$ and the y-intercept is $(0, 2)$. To find the x-intercept, we must find the value of x for which $y = 0$. In other words, substitute $y = 0$ in the equation and solve for x.

$$3x + 4(0) = 8$$
$$3x = 8 \qquad x = 8/3$$

So the x-intercept is $(8/3, 0)$.

In general, unless a line passes through the origin, the easiest way to draw the graph of a line is to plot its x- and y-intercepts.

Example 7 Plot the line $3x + 5y = 10$.

Let $x = 0$. We have $5y = 10$, $y = 2$, that is, the y-intercept is 2. Let $y = 0$. We have $3x = 10$, $x = 10/3$; the x-intercept is $10/3$. The graph is shown in figure 6.

In business, the description of production costs is frequently a straight line. Suppose, for example, that a manufacturer has fixed overhead costs of D dollars. Suppose further that the cost of manufacturing a particular item is m dollars. If the assembly line produces x items, then the total cost C of producing these items is

$$\text{Cost} = \text{Overhead} + (\text{Cost per item}) \times (\text{Number of items})$$

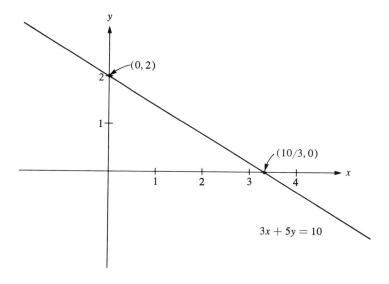

Figure 6

or in symbols, $C = D + mx$

Thus, plotting C versus x, we obtain a straight line. The slope of the line is the cost of producing each individual item and the C-intercept is the overhead.

Suppose that the manufacturer sells his goods for P dollars per item. Then his total revenue R is

Revenue = (Price per item) × (Number of items)

or in symbols $R = Px$

Thus, plotting R versus x, we have a straight line through the origin with slope P. If we plot the graph of cost and revenue on the same set of axes, the point at which they intersect is called the *breakeven point*. It is the number of sales at which revenue equals cost. Alternatively, you could simply take profit S as revenue minus cost.

$$S = R - C = Px - (D + mx) = (P - m)x - D$$

The profit graph is again linear. This time the slope is $P - m$ and the y-intercept is $-D$. The x-intercept of this line gives the number of sales at which S changes from negative (i.e. a loss) to positive (i.e.

a profit.) Of course, this must be the same x as that attained by finding the intersection of the cost line and revenue line.

Example 8   A businessman has fixed overhead of $2,000 and manufacturing costs of $20 per item. If the sales price of each item is $30, analyze his profit and loss picture. His cost equation is

$$C = 2,000 + 20x$$

His revenue equation is

$$R = 30x$$

To find the point of intersection of these lines, set $R = C$, yielding

$$30x = 2,000 + 20x$$
$$10x = 2,000$$
$$x = 200$$

Thus, when sales reach 200 items, the breakeven point is reached. When sales exceed 200, the manufacturer begins to show a profit.
    Alternatively, we may write

$$S = 30x - (2,000 + 20x)$$
$$S = 10x - 2,000$$

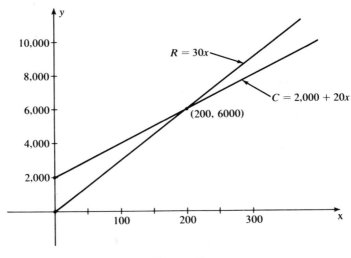

Figure 7

Figure 7 shows R and C lines on the same set of axes. Figure 8 shows the profit line. Notice that the x-intercept of profit is the same as the x-value at which $C = R$.

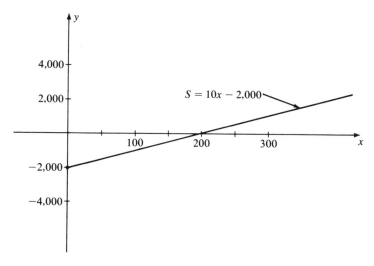

Figure 8

EXERCISES

1. Find the equations of the lines whose slopes and y-intercepts are
   (a) 2, 4
   (b) $-3, 0$
   (c) $0, -2$
   (d) $1/2, -1/2$
   (e) $-1/4, 3$

2. Find the equations of the lines with the given slopes and passing through the given points:
   (a) $-3, (2, 5)$
   (b) $1/2, (-2, 0)$
   (c) $1/6, (0, 0)$
   (d) $-1/4, (2, -2)$

3. Find the slope, x- and y-intercepts of $2x - 5y = 6$. Plot the line.

4. Find the equation of the line parallel to the line in Exercise 3 passing through $(-1, 7)$. Plot the line.

5. Plot the line $2x + 6y + 11 = 0$. Find the area of the triangle formed by the line, the x-axis and the y-axis.

6. Find the equation of the vertical line passing through the x-intercept of the line in Exercise 5.

7. Find the equations of the two lines parallel to $y = -3$, and 4 units away from it.

8. Find the equations of the line passing through the given pair of points:
   (a) $(1/2, -2)$ and $(1/4, -1/4)$
   (b) $(0, -9)$ and $(-1/2, 3)$
   (c) $(-1/3, 2/3)$ and $(0, 0)$
   (d) $(1, -5)$ and $(2, -5)$
   (e) $(1/2, 16)$ and $(1/2, -73)$
   (f) $(0, 4)$ and $(-7, 0)$

9. Plot the lines in Exercise 8.

10. Find the equation of the line whose y-intercept is 3 and whose x-intercept is -5.

11. Find the equation of a line whose y-intercept is 4 and such that the area of a triangle formed by the line and the two axes is 20 square units.

12. The area of a triangle formed by the line and the two axes is 40 and the slope of the line is -5. Find the equation of the line.

13. Find the length of the portion of the line $7x + 12y = 84$ that is cut off by the two axes.

14. Plot the points $(-1, -7)$, $(4, 2)$ and $(8, 4)$. Do they lie on the same line?

15. Repeat the analysis of Example 8, p. 42, for fixed overhead of $2,500, cost per item $30, and sales price of $45 per item.

16. Suppose the manufacturer in Exercise 15 can manage to reduce his overhead to $1,200. How does this affect his breakeven point?

17. Suppose that the manufacturer in Exercise 15 is forced to cut his sales price to $35 in order to move his goods. How does this affect his breakeven point? Assume that his overhead remains $2,500, and his cost per item remains $30.

18. If a manufacturer has fixed costs of $700, a cost per item for production of $20, and expects to sell at least 100 items, what should he set as his sales price to guarantee breaking even?

19. If the manufacturer in Exercise 18 wishes to guarantee profits of at least $600, how should he set his sales price?

20. A businessman discovers that when he makes 1,000 items, his costs are $800. When he makes 1,500 items, his costs are $1,200.

Assuming that his costs are linear, find his overhead and cost per item. Plot the cost graph.

21. A businessman discovers that he breaks even when his total sales is \$3,000 and his sales price is \$50. If his fixed overhead is \$1,200, find his production cost per item and find his profit when he produces 130 items.

1.2 Linear Inequalities

In this section we would like to discuss the graphs of relationships of the forms $Ax + By \leq C$, or $Ax + By \geq C$. For simplicity, let us simply discuss inequalities of the first type; everything we say will carry over to the other. To begin, we may add (or subtract) equal quantities to both sides of an inequality without changing it. If we multiply both sides of an inequality by a positive number, the inequality will be unchanged; if multiplied by a negative number, it will be reversed. In either case, we can reduce the inequality to one of three types:

1. $x \leq a$ or $x \geq a$,
2. $y \leq b$ or $y \geq b$,
3. $y \leq mx + b$ or $y \geq mx + b$.

In the first case, $x = a$ is a vertical line. For all points to its left, $x < a$; for all points to its right, $x > a$. In the second case, $y = b$ is a horizontal line. For all points below the line, $y < b$; for all points above the line, $y > b$. In the third case, we have similar behavior. That is, if $P(x_1, y_1)$ is below the line $y = mx + b$, then P lies on some line parallel to the original line, which will have equation $y = mx + b_1$, and b_1 is less than b. Thus at $x = x_1$, $y = mx_1 + b$, on the original line, and $y_1 = mx_1 + b_1$. Since $b_1 < b$, $y_1 < mx_1 + b$. Thus, every straight line acts as a boundary dividing the plane into two regions. In one, $Ax + By < C$, and in the other, $Ax + By > C$. The graph of $Ax + By \leq C$ then consists of the line $Ax + By = C$ and all the points on one side of the line. The only problem is, How does one determine which is the proper side? Very simply, since all the points on one side of the line satisfy the inequality and all the points on the other side do not, we test any particular point and see whether or not it works. If it does, then all the points on that side of the line do! Usually the origin is a good point to try.

Example 9 Plot the graph of the inequality $3x + 4y \leq 12$.

First we plot the line $3x + 4y = 12$. The x-intercept is 4, the y-intercept is 3 (see figure 9). Now we test to see if the origin satisfies the inequality. Substituting $x = 0$, $y = 0$, we obtain

$$3(0) + 4(0) \leq 12$$
$$0 \leq 12$$

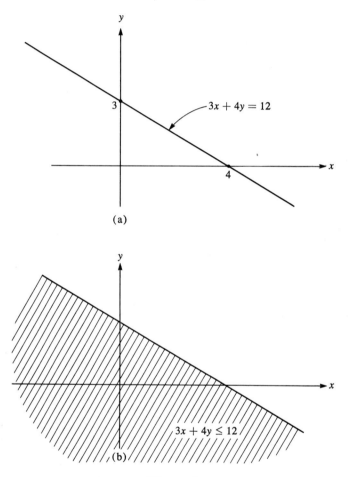

(a)

(b)

Figure 9

which is true. Hence the origin and all other points below or on the line constitute the graph shown in figure 9b. If the origin is not usable, try any other point. An example follows.

Example 10 Plot the graph of $y \leq 3x$.

The line $y = 3x$ passes through the origin. Therefore, we must try a different point. Take (0, 1), which lies above the line. Substituting, we see that $1 \leq 0$ is not a true statement, so the inequality is satisfied by all points below or on the line. See figure 10.

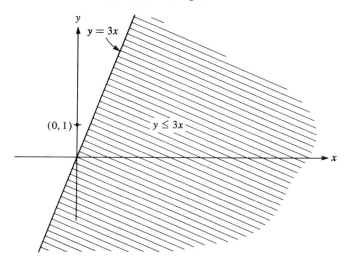

Figure 10

EXERCISES

1. Plot the graph of $2x - 5y \leq 10$.

2. Plot the graph of $3x + 11y + 8 \leq 0$.

3. Find the inequality which has the following region as its graph:
   (a) The boundary is a straight line of slope -3 passing through (2, 5) and the region includes the point (4, 6).
   (b) The boundary is a straight line passing through (1/2, 1/2) and $(-1, 3)$; and $(-5, 12)$ is included in the region.
   (c) All the points below or on the line $y = 7$ and to the right of or on $x = -3$.
   (d) All the points whose abscissa is between $-1/4$ and 3, inclusive, and whose ordinate is no greater than 6.

4. Plot the region consisting of all points satisfying the following inequalities simultaneously:

$$x \geq 2 \quad \text{and} \quad x \leq 5$$

5. Plot the regions satisfying all the given inequalities:
   (a) $x \geq 1, x \leq 5, y \leq x$

(b) $x \geq 1, y \geq 0, y \leq 5 - x$.

6. What inequalities describe the strip between $y = 3x - 2$ and $y = 3x + 7$?

7. What region is described by the inequalities $y \leq x$ and $y \geq x + 1$?

1.3 Linear Programming

One of the newest and most applicable branches of mathematics deals with the solution of problems which involve only linear equations and linear inequalities. This area is called *linear programming*. Most real problems in this discipline deal with many unknowns and involve many inequalities. We shall investigate some more or less artificial problems which can be handled without the help of computers or calculating machines but which expose the fundamental ideas which are involved.

Let us begin with the following: A company sells boxes of mixed nuts under two different brand labels. Under the regular label, a box of nuts contains 4 ounces of pecans, 8 ounces of cashews and the remainder peanuts. Under the special quality label, a box contains 1 ounce of pecans, 9 ounces of cashews and the remainder peanuts. The company can afford to use 40 ounces of pecans and 108 ounces of cashews at a time. The supply of peanuts is unlimited. Let us try to describe this situation mathematically.

$$x = \text{the number of boxes of regular to be sold}$$
$$y = \text{the number of boxes of special to be sold}$$

Now,

$$4x + y = \text{total number of ounces of pecans used}$$
$$8x + 9y = \text{total number of ounces of cashews used}$$

Not knowing the size of the box, we do not know how many ounces of peanuts will be used, but the supply of peanuts is unlimited anyway. According to the description, the number of ounces of pecans may not exceed 40 and the number of ounces of cashews may not exceed 108. Thus, we have the following set of "constraints":

$$4x + y \leq 40$$
$$8x + 9y \leq 108$$
$$x \geq 0$$
$$y \geq 0$$

where the last two inequalities indicate that one cannot make a negative number of boxes. Graphically, this collection of constraints restricts our attention to a region of feasible solutions, which has been labelled F in figure 11. Geometrically, F consists of all points in the first quadrant (i.e. above the x-axis and to the right of the y-axis), which are simultaneously below the line $4x + y = 40$ and the line $8x + 9y = 108$, plus all the points on the boundaries. The region is bounded by the quadrilateral $OPQR$, where O is the origin, P is the y-intercept of $8x + 9y = 108$, R is the x-intercept of $4x + y = 40$, and Q is the point of intersection of the two lines.

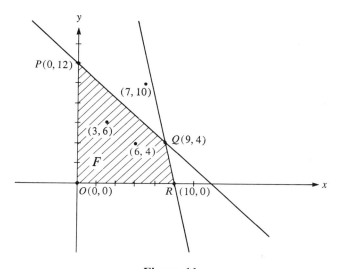

Figure 11

We can now see that the points $(6, 4)$ and $(3, 6)$ are feasible solutions but $(7, 10)$ is not. It is difficult to tell from the graph whether $(6, 7)$ is feasible or not. Checking the first inequality we have $4(6) + 7 \le 40$, which is true, but checking the second inequality, we see $8(6) + 9(7) \le 108$, which is not true. Hence, $(6, 7)$ is not feasible and there is no way to make 6 boxes of regular and 7 boxes of special without running out of nuts first!

Of course, Q was obtained by solving the equations of the two lines simultaneously. That is,

$$4x + y = 40 \qquad (1)$$
$$8x + 9y = 108 \qquad (2)$$

Doubling the first equation and subtracting it from the second, we have

$$8x + 9y = 108$$
$$\underline{-(8x + 2y = 80)}$$
$$7y = 28$$
$$y = 4$$

Substituting into Eq. (1) yields

$$4x + 4 = 40$$
$$4x = 36$$
$$x = 9$$

To be on the safe side, check the answer by substituting into Eq. (2):

$$8(9) + 9(4) = 108$$

which is correct.

Suppose now that the company makes a profit of 40¢ on each box of regular and 30¢ on each box of special. How many of each should be made in order to maximize the profit? Calling the profit in cents M, we have

$$M = 40x + 30y$$

For example,

$$M = 40(6) + 30(4) = 360¢ = \$3.60 \quad \text{at } (6, 4)$$
$$M = 40(3) + 30(6) = 300¢ = \$3.00 \quad \text{at } (3, 6)$$

and

$$M = 40(0) + 30(12) = 360¢ = \$3.60 \quad \text{at } (0, 12)$$

Is there any way to determine the point at which M is the greatest without actually checking every point in F? Let us see if we can find a geometric interpretation of the expression for profit (known as the objective function).

If we rewrite the objective in the form

$$30y = -40x + M$$
$$y = (-4/3)x + M/30$$

we see that we have a line of slope $-4/3$ and y-intercept $M/30$. To find the maximum possible value of M, we must find the line parallel to $y = (-4/3)x$ which intersects F and has the largest possible y-intercept. In figure 12, several members of the family of lines are shown. For $M = 150$ and for $M = 360$, the line crosses F, so lots of feasible points give these values of M. For $M = 540$, the line completely misses F, so there are no feasible points for which this value can be obtained. Notice that as M increases, the line moves upward. From the geometry, it appears that the maximum possible value of M will occur at the value for which we pass from F. That is, in this case, the line which goes through $Q(9, 4)$ will have the greatest feasible value of M. In fact, at $(9, 4)$, $M = 40(9) + 30(4) = 480\rlap{/}{c} = \$4.80$. Thus, the optimal production scheme is to make 9 boxes of regular, 4 boxes of special and show a profit of \$4.80.

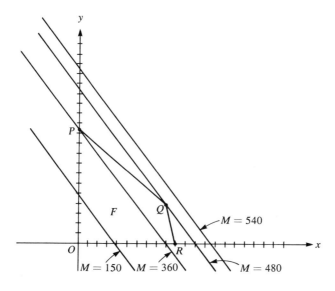

Figure 12

Let us do some further analysis of the problem. Consider table 1.

Table 1

Point	Pecans Used	Cashews Used	Pecans Left	Cashews Left	Profit
(0, 0)	0 oz	0 oz	40 oz	108 oz	0
(3, 6)	18 "	78 "	22 "	30 "	$3.00
(6, 4)	28 "	84 "	12 "	24 "	3.60
(0, 12)	12 "	108 "	28 "	0 "	3.60
(10, 0)	40 "	80 "	0 "	28 "	4.00
(9, 4)	40 "	108 "	0 "	0 "	4.80

From the table it appears that the point of optimum profit is attained when the supply of both kinds of nuts is exhausted. However, this is *not* always the case. In fact, let us reconsider the problem assuming three different possible profit structures: Case I, the one we have already considered; Case II, the profit on regular is 5¢/box and the profit on special is 50¢/box; Case III, the profit on regular is 50¢/box and the profit on special is 5¢/box. We now have three different profit functions:

$$M_1 = 40x + 30y$$
$$M_2 = 5x + 50y$$
$$M_3 = 50x + 5y \quad \text{(Consider table 2.)}$$

Table 2

Point	Profit			
	Case I	Case II	Case III	
(0, 0)	0	0	0	
(3, 6)	$3.00	$3.15	$1.80	
(6, 4)	3.60	2.30	3.20	
(0, 12)	3.60	6.00	.60	Cashews Used Up
(10, 0)	4.00	.50	5.00	Pecans Used Up
(9, 4)	4.80	2.45	4.70	Both Used Up

Although tables 1 and 2 are in no sense exhaustive of all possibilities, they seem to indicate that the maximum in every case is attained at a point at which at least one item is used up. This, of course, is sensible since if some of each were left over, we could pack a little more and increase the profit. Of course, we are assuming that we could pack up a fractional number of boxes. If we were to restrict attention to solutions in whole numbers only, we would enter the realm of a closely related subject called *integer programming*. At any rate, the result also makes sense geometrically, since the points at which maxima are attained correspond to vertices of the region *F*. Clearly, a line moving upward must last touch *F* at one of the corners. What then decides which vertex is the right one? The answer is simply the slope of the objective. Figure 13 shows the three objectives we have considered and illustrates the reason that each is optimized at a different vertex.

One of the first problems dealt with by the technique of linear programming was called the diet problem. A simplified version of the diet problem is the following. A diet supplement is made from a mixture of wheat germ and soy flour. The composition of one ounce of each, in terms

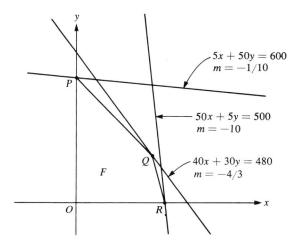

Figure 13

of Vitamin A, Vitamin B and Vitamin C, is shown in table 3. (The figures are purely imaginary.)

Table 3

	Vitamin A	Vitamin B	Vitamin C	Cost
Wheat Germ	2 units	5 units	3 units	11¢/oz
Soy Flour	1 "	3 "	2 "	6¢/oz

Find the mixture of the two ingredients satisfying the following conditions. First, the mixture must contain at least 20 units of A, 58 units of B and 36 units of C. Second, the cost should be as low as possible. To solve the problem, we shall proceed as in the previous example.

x = number of ounces of wheat germ in the mixture
y = number of ounces of soy flour in the mixture

Then we have the following constraints:

$$2x + y \geq 20 \quad \text{(units of Vitamin A)}$$
$$5x + 3y \geq 58 \quad \text{(units of Vitamin B)}$$
$$3x + 2y \geq 36 \quad \text{(units of Vitamin C)}$$
$$x \geq 0$$
$$y \geq 0$$

where the last two constraints again express the condition that one cannot mix up a negative number of ounces of a substance. The objective is to minimize the cost, $C = 11x + 6y$. Graphing the region F of feasible solutions (see figure 14), we see that the region has four vertices, (0, 20), (2, 16), (8, 6) and (12, 0). Again the optimal solution would occur at one of the vertices. Checking these four points, we obtain the following: at (0, 20), $C = 120¢ = \$1.20$; at (2, 16), $C = 118¢ = \$1.18$; at (8, 6), $C = 124¢ = \$1.24$; and at (12, 0), $C = 132¢ = \$1.32$. Thus, we claim that the most economical mixture is 2 ounces of wheat germ to every 16 ounces of soy flour with a resulting cost of \$1.18.

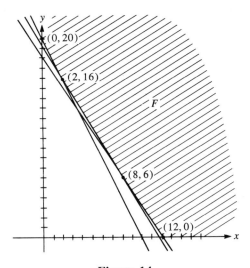

Figure 14

It is interesting to note that if the price of wheat germ were to drop to 10¢/ounce, we would be faced with an odd situation. In that case, $C = 10x + 6y$. Checking the vertices we find the following: at (0, 20), $C = \$1.20$; at (2, 16), $C = \$1.16$: at (8, 6), $C = \$1.16$; and at (12, 0), $C = \$1.20$. The optimal point then occurs at two adjacent vertices. Therefore, either point is a suitable choice. Moreover, any point on the line segment joining them is also an optimal point! This happens because the objective is parallel to the segment and hence every point on the segment gives the same y-intercept and hence the same value to C. The equation of the line in question is $10x + 6y = 116$, which passes through (2, 16) and (8, 6). In addition, the point halfway between is (5, 11) and this also gives the value \$1.16 to the objective as will any other point on the segment.

EXERCISES

1. Plot the regions described by the following sets of inequalities:
   (a) $x \geq 1$
      $x \leq 5$
      $y \geq 2$
      $y \leq 2x + 6$
   (b) $x \leq 5$
      $y \geq -2$
      $y \leq x + 6$
   (c) $x + 3y \geq 4$
      $4x + y \geq 10$
      $x \geq 0$
      $y \geq 0$
   (d) $2x + y \leq 10$
      $2x + y \geq 5$
      $y \leq 3x$
      $y \geq (1/2)x$
   (e) $x + 4y \leq 40$
      $x + 2y \leq 30$
      $x \leq 23$
      $x \geq 0$
      $y \geq 0$

2. Find a set of inequalities which describes a quadrilateral with vertices $(1, 6)$, $(3, 7)$, $(1/2, 2)$ and $(5, 0)$.

3. Find a set of inequalities which describes a pentagon with vertices $(0, 0)$, $(0, 10)$, $(5, 9)$, $(6, 6)$ and $(7, 0)$.

4. For Exercise 1, (a)–(e), find the maximum and minimum values of $P = 3x + 5y$ and $C = 2x - 7y$ on each of the regions.

5. Solve the mixed-nut example in the text if each box must weigh one pound (16 ounces) and if there are only 66 ounces of peanuts available.

6. A candy manufacturer makes two basic types of merchandise. The pertinent information is displayed in the following table:

Type	Coconut Used/Box	Chocolate Used/Box	Profit/Box
Coconut-covered Chocolate	1 ounce	14 ounces	$2.00
Chocolate-covered Coconut	10 "	1 "	3.00

He has available 150 ounces of coconut and 154 ounces of chocolate. How many boxes of each should he make in order to maximize his profit?

7. After Christmas, a toy store has a collection of leftover ornaments to get rid of. The store owner decides to make up two types of "bargain packs" and run a sale. The first type of pack contains 2 strings of lights and 5 angels and sells for $1. The second type of pack contains 3 strings of lights and 3 angels and sells for $2. He has 42 strings of lights and 78 angels available. How many of each type should he make up in order to maximize his receipts? If he wishes to maximize his receipts at a time when he has used up all the ornaments, what possible prices could he charge for the second type of pack? (The price of the first is fixed at $1.)

1.4 Enumeration of Vertices

From the examples in the preceding section the form of a general linear programming problem in two variables seems clear. The problem always consists of a statement of the form "maximize (or minimize) some objective, subject to certain constraints." To be more precise, the statement is usually presented in the following format:

Maximize (or minimize): $Q = Dx + Ey$

$$\text{Subject to: } A_1x + B_1y \leq C_1 \tag{1}$$
$$A_2x + B_2y \leq C_2 \tag{2}$$
$$\vdots$$
$$A_kx + B_ky \leq C_k \tag{k}$$

although some of the inequalities may appear to be reversed.

The method of attack also seems to be clear. That is, take all possible pairs of constraint inequalities, replace them by equations and solve simultaneously, thereby obtaining all points of intersection. By the geometry of the situation, some of these intersection points will be the vertices of F and the others will lie outside the region of feasible solutions. So one must then check each point of intersection and ascertain whether or not it lies in F. This is accomplished by simply substituting the coordinates in each of the k constraint inequalities. Those which satisfy them all are of interest, the others are not. For the points of interest, we evaluate Q. The largest number obtained is the maximum possible value of Q and the smallest is the minimum possible value of Q (subject to the constraints, of course). This method of "enumeration of vertices" is perhaps best illustrated by a simple example. Consider the following problem:

$$\text{Maximize: } Q = 3x - 4y$$

Subject to: $x + 4y \leq 10$	(1)
$4x + y \leq 10$	(2)
$x \geq 0$	(3)
$y \geq 0$	(4)

We see that we shall have to solve six systems of two equations in two unknowns. In particular they are Eqs. (1) and (2), Eqs. (1) and (3), Eqs. (1) and (4), Eqs. (2) and (3), Eqs. (2) and (4) and Eqs. (3) and (4). Solving Eqs. (1) and (2) simultaneously yields

$$x + 4y = 10$$
$$4x + y = 10$$

The reader may check that the point of intersection is $(2, 2)$ Solving Eqs. (1) and (3) yields

$$x + 4y = 10$$
$$x = 0$$

It is easy to see that the point of intersection is $(0, 2\frac{1}{2})$. Continuing in this manner, we may summarize our results in tabular form (see table 4).

Table 4

Equation Pair	Point	Is the Point in F?	Value of Q	Remarks
(1) and (2)	(2, 2)	Yes	-2	—
(1) and (3)	(0, 2½)	Yes	-10	Minimum value
(1) and (4)	(10, 0)	No	—	Does not satisfy Eq. (2)
(2) and (3)	(0, 10)	No	—	" " " " (1)
(2) and (4)	(2½, 0)	Yes	7½	Maximum value
(3) and (4)	(0, 0)	Yes	0	—

We have additionally noted in the last section that when the maximum of the objective function occurs at two different vertices, it is the same at every point on the line segment joining them.

EXERCISES

1. Maximize $w = 3x - y$, subject to

$$x + 2y \geq 4$$
$$x + y \leq 12$$
$$2x + 4y \leq 30$$
$$x \geq 0$$
$$y \geq 0$$

2. Maximize $P = 3x + 2y$, subject to

$$x + y \leq 5$$
$$x + 2y \leq 6$$
$$x \geq 0$$
$$y \geq 0$$

3. Maximize $P = 10x + y$, subject to

$$x + y \geq 1$$
$$5x + y \leq 10$$
$$x + 2y \leq 11$$
$$x \geq 0$$
$$y \geq 0$$

4. Minimize $C = 50x + 40y$, subject to

$$2x + 3y \geq 240$$
$$2x + y \geq 120$$
$$x \geq 0$$
$$y \geq 0$$

5. For which value(s) of M will the minimum of $C = Mx + 40y$ occur at (30, 60) in the region described by the constraints in Exercise 4?

6. A quart of A costs \$2.00 and contains 2 oz of "Zing." A quart of B costs \$3.00 and contains 6 oz of "Zing." A mixture of A and B consisting of at least 10 quarts and having at least 30 oz of "Zing" is needed. What is the minimum cost of the mixture?

7. A tailor has 80 square yards of cotton material and 120 square yards of wool material. A suit requires 1 sq yd of cotton and 3 sq yd of wool. A dress requires 2 sq yd of each. How many of each garment should the tailor make in order to maximize his income, if a suit sells for $80 and a dress for $50?

8. In an ecology drive, the town of Cleanup sets a goal of processing at least 40 tons of paper, 30 tons of aluminum cans and 50 tons of glass bottles each month. Roundups of garbage made in residential and commercial districts show the following distribution of material:

Type of District	Paper	Aluminum	Glass	Cost/Pickup
Commercial	3 tons	1 ton	1 ton	$50
Residential	1 ton	1 "	5 "	25

How many pickups of each kind should be made in order to minimize the cost of the project?

9. A hospital patient is being fed intravenously. His diet is a mixture of two fluids, A and B. One unit of A contains 5 grams of protein and 100 calories, and one unit of B contains 10 grams of protein and 50 calories. His total protein intake must be at least 50 grams and may not exceed 100 grams. In addition, for proper metabolism, more of fluid B than fluid A must be administered. Find the mixture of the two fluids that maximizes his caloric intake.

10. The candy manufacturer in Exercise 6, Section 1.3, decides to add 6 ounces of peanuts to each type of candy. Resolve the problem assuming he wishes to use only 180 ounces of peanuts.

2

Systems of Equations

2.1 Simple Systems

Consider the following problem: Jackson's Pharmacy fell victim to a fire the day after receiving a small shipment from the warehouse. The shipment consisted of 15 cases of cold tablets, vitamins, and aspirins having a total value of $92. The cold tablets were valued at $7.00 per case, the vitamins at $10.00 per case, and the aspirins at $3.00 per case. Mr. Jackson recalled that there was one fewer case of aspirins than of the other two combined. How many cases of each type were in the shipment?

This problem involves three unknown quantities. Let

x = number of cases of cold tablets

y = number of cases of vitamins

z = number of cases of aspirins

In equation form, the given information is

$$x + y + z = 15$$
$$7x + 10y + 3z = 92$$
$$x + y - z = 1$$

Here we have three equations in three unknowns, a situation we have not yet encountered. In this chapter, we shall develop an efficient way to handle such problems. In fact, the methods developed enable you to find all solutions to a general system of n linear equations in m unknowns where m and n are not necessarily the same. Please notice that we deal only with systems of "linear" equations, that is, equations in which the unknowns appear only to the first power. If the equations involve only two unknowns, then we know that graphically they represent straight lines, and we are looking for the point of intersection of the lines. In this case, three things can happen. First, the lines could have one point of intersection (even if there are several lines). Algebraically, this would mean that the system of equations has a unique solution. In other words, there exists exactly one ordered pair which satisfies all the equations simultaneously. A second possibility is that the lines have no point in common. When you have three lines, for example, it is usual to have them form a triangle. That is, each intersects the other but there is no point common to all three. In this case, we say the equations are "incompatible" and there is no solution. Even two equations in two unknowns can be incompatible if they represent parallel lines, since parallel lines never intersect. The third possibility is that all the equations are different representations of the same line. In that case any point on the line is a solution of the system, and hence we have an infinite number of solutions. Such a system is called "redundant." When more than two unknowns are present, many variations on this theme are possible; however, all reduce to one of these three situations: The system has a unique solution; the system is incompatible; or the system is redundant.

Let us then look at the problem of solving the equations. The underlying idea is to replace the system of equations with an equivalent system in which the roots can be identified. By equivalent systems we mean two systems having identical roots. For example, solve

$$x + y = 3$$
$$x - y = 4$$

Adding the two equations, we have $2x = 7$, $x = 3\frac{1}{2}$, which we substitute into the first equation, yielding $3\frac{1}{2} + y = 3$, $y = -1/2$. Now, what have we really done? We have added the two equations, producing a new equation, $2x = 7$. We have combined this with the first equation to form a new system:

$$x + y = 3$$
$$2x \quad\ = 7$$

This new system is equivalent to the original one and we can obtain its roots by inspection (almost).

The important question is, What operations can you perform on a system of linear equations that will produce a new system having the same roots? There are three allowable operations:

1. Any two equations may be interchanged.
2. Any equation may be multiplied (or divided) by any number other than zero.
3. Any equation may be replaced by the equation obtained by adding to it any multiple of any other equation.

A few parenthetical remarks are appropriate here. First, in (1), it seems obvious that the order in which you write the equations should be immaterial. Second, in (2), you cannot multiply by zero, since this would eliminate the equation. Third, in (3), adding any multiple also allows subtracting any multiple, since this amounts to simply adding a negative multiple. This operation is the most important one as you will see in the first example.

In the following, we have labeled the equations for easy identification:

$$x + y + z = 2 \qquad (1)$$
$$x + 2y - z = 6 \qquad (2)$$
$$x - y + 2z = -3 \qquad (3)$$

First, we replace Eq. (2) by Eq. (2) − Eq. (1) and we replace Eq. (3) by Eq. (3) − Eq. (1). By performing these operations, we eliminate x from all but the first equation.

$$x + y + z = 2 \qquad (1)$$
$$y - 2z = 4 \qquad (2)$$
$$-2y + z = -5 \qquad (3)$$

Next, we replace Eq. (3) by Eq. (3) + 2 times Eq. (2). This has the effect of giving us a "triangular configuration" with the last equation having only one unknown; the next to last, two unknowns; and the first, all three.

$$x + y + z = 2 \qquad (1)$$
$$y - 2z = 4 \qquad (2)$$
$$-3z = 3 \qquad (3)$$

We may now read off the solutions by "back substitution." Solving Eq. (3) yields $z = -1$. Substituting this into Eq. (2), we have $y + 2 = 4$,

$y = 2$. Substituting these two values into Eq. (1) yields $x + 2 - 1 = 2$, $x = 1$. Thus, $x = 1$, $y = 2$ and $z = -1$.

Let us recapitulate what has been done, for this is the method to be used. First, we added suitable multiples of the first equation to each of the others in order to eliminate the first unknown from all but the first equation. Next, we added suitable multiples of the second equation to all those below it, in order to eliminate the second unknown from all of them. In this case, of course there is only one equation below the second. If there were more unknowns, we would continue in this manner, aiming for the triangular form. For example,

$$x - y + z + 2w = 0 \tag{1}$$
$$x + y + 2z - 3w = 13 \tag{2}$$
$$x \quad - z + w = -4 \tag{3}$$
$$x - y + 2z \quad = 7 \tag{4}$$

Clearing x from Eqs. (2), (3) and (4), we have

$$x - y + z + 2w = 0 \tag{1}$$
$$2y + z - 5w = 13 \quad \text{[Obtained from Eq. (2)} - \text{Eq. (1)]} \tag{2}$$
$$y - 2z - w = -4 \quad \text{[Obtained from Eq. (3)} - \text{Eq. (1)]} \tag{3}$$
$$z - 2w = 7 \quad \text{[Obtained from Eq. (4)} - \text{Eq. (1)]} \tag{4}$$

Clearing y from Eqs. (3) and (4) yields

$$x - y + z + 2w = 0$$
$$2y + z - 5w = 13$$
$$-\frac{5}{2}z + \frac{3}{2}w = \frac{-21}{2} \quad \text{[Obtained from Eq. (3)} - 1/2 \text{ Eq. (2)]}$$
$$z - 2w = 7$$

Multiplying Eq. (3) by -2 (in order to eliminate fractions), we obtain

$$x - y + z + 2w = 0 \tag{1}$$
$$2y + z - 5w = 13 \tag{2}$$
$$5z - 3w = 21 \tag{3}$$
$$z - 2w = 7 \tag{4}$$

Clearing z from Eq. (4) yields

$$x - y + z + 2w = 0 \qquad \text{(1)}$$
$$2y + z - 5w = 13 \qquad \text{(2)}$$
$$5z - 3w = 21 \qquad \text{(3)}$$
$$-\frac{7}{5}w = \frac{14}{5} \quad \text{[Obtained from Eq. (4)} - 1/5 \text{ Eq. (3)]} \qquad \text{(4)}$$

We now have the triangular pattern and upon back substitution,

$$w = -2 \qquad 5z + 6 = 21 \qquad z = 3 \qquad 2y + 3 + 10 = 13$$
$$y = 0 \qquad x - 0 + 3 - 4 = 0 \qquad x = 1$$

It is left to the reader to substitute these numbers into the original system and see that we do indeed have the roots of the system.

EXERCISES

Solve the systems of equations in Exercises 1 – 12.

1. $x + 3y = 6$
   $x - 3y = 12$

2. $x - 2y + 2z = -3$
   $x + y - z = 0$
   $x - 3y - 3z = -16$

3. $x + 2y - 2z = 4$
   $2x - y + 3z = 1$
   $3x + z = -2$

4. $3x - 4y + 3z = -6$
   $x - 2y + 6z = -4$
   $2y + 9z = -2$

5. $2x + 6y - z + 2w = 4$
   $x - y + z - 2w = -5$
   $2x + y - 3z + 6w = 3$
   $x - y + 4z = 9$

6. $x - z = 2$
   $y + w = 9$
   $x + w = 8$
   $x - y = -1$

7. $\begin{aligned} 3x + 7y - z &= -6 \\ x + 2y + 3z &= 5 \\ 2x - 4y + 5z &= 16 \end{aligned}$

8. $\begin{aligned} 2x - 3y + z &= 7 \\ x + y - 4z &= -8 \\ -2x + 3y + 2z &= -1 \end{aligned}$

9. $\begin{aligned} x + 2y - z &= 3 \\ 2x + 5y + 2z &= -5 \\ -3x + 4y - 4z &= 22 \end{aligned}$

10. $\begin{aligned} -x + y + z &= -2 \\ 6x - 7y + 3z &= 21 \\ 5x + y + 3z &= -13 \end{aligned}$

11. $\begin{aligned} x + y + z - w + t &= 1 \\ x + 2y - 3z \qquad\quad + 2t &= -26 \\ x \qquad + 2z + 2w - t &= 23 \\ -x - y - z + 3w + 4t &= -15 \\ 2x + y \qquad\quad + w + t &= -1 \end{aligned}$

12. $\begin{aligned} x - y &= 2z - x + t \\ 2x - y &= 3z - w - 2 \\ y &= 3x - 3z \\ 2t + 2w &= z - y \\ x + z &= 2w - 2y - t \end{aligned}$

13. Solve the Jackson Pharmacy problem in the text.

14. The Board of Trustees of a small hospital assumes that the daily operating expenses E can be expressed by the formula $E = a + bx + cy$ where a = overhead, b = cost per patient, x = number of patients, c = cost per resident physician, and y = number of resident physicians. When there are 50 patients and 5 physicians in the hospital, the expense is found to be \$6,050. When there are 40 patients and 2 physicians, the expense is \$4,840. When there are 30 patients and one physician, the expense is \$3,770. Find a, b, and c.

15. A stationery supplier wishes to clear his inventory of 124 boxes of pencils, 72 boxes of ball pens, and 32 boxes of erasers. He finds that his major customers order supplies as follows: A package A order is 5 boxes of pencils, 2 of ball points, and 1 of erasers. A package B order is 4 boxes of pencils, 4 of ball points, and 2 of erasers. A package C order is 2 boxes of pencils, 3 of ball points, and 1 of erasers. How many packages of each type should be made up?

2.2 Systems with Nonunique Solutions

Suppose one is faced with the problem of solving a system in which the number of unknowns and the number of equations are not the same. We will still apply the same technique. For example,

$$x - y + z + w = 6 \tag{1}$$
$$2x - 3y + 3z + w = 7 \tag{2}$$
$$x + y - z - 3w = 4 \tag{3}$$

In this system of three equations in four unknowns, we begin by eliminating x from the last two equations:

$$x - y + z + w = 6$$
$$- y + z - w = -5 \quad [\text{Eq. (2)} - 2 \text{ times Eq. (1)}]$$
$$2y - 2z - 4w = -2 \quad [\text{Eq. (3)} - \text{Eq. (1)}]$$

Now using Eq. (2) to eliminate y, we have

$$x - y + z + w = 6$$
$$- y + z - w = -5$$
$$-6w = -12 \quad [\text{Eq. (3)} + 2 \text{ times Eq. (2)}]$$

From Eq. (3), we have $w = 2$. Substituting into Eq. (1) and Eq. (2), we have

$$x - y + z + 2 = 6$$
$$- y + z - 2 = -5$$

yielding

$$x - y + z = 4$$
$$- y + z = -3$$

Here we see that we can choose any value for z and still find correct values for x and y. That is, let $z = k$ and substitute into Eq. (2):

$$-y + k = -3$$
$$-y = -3 - k$$
$$y = 3 + k$$

Now, substitute into Eq. (1):

$$x - (3 + k) + k = 4$$

$$x - 3 - k + k = 4$$
$$x - 3 = 4$$

Thus, the general solution to this system is $x = 7$, $y = 3 + k$, $z = k$ and $w = 2$, where k is any number whatsoever! Thus, we have a redundant system. Some possible solutions are $x = 7$, $y = 3$, $z = 0$, $w = 2$ (the case $k = 0$); $x = 7$, $y = 113$, $z = 110$, $w = 2$ (the case $k = 110$); $x = 7$, $y = 0$, $z = -3$, $w = 2$ (the case $k = -3$); and $x = 7$, $y = 3\frac{1}{4}$, $z = 1/4$, $w = 2$ (the case $k = 1/4$). The reader should check that all the above, including the general formula, are solutions by seeing that they do satisfy the equations. A remark is in order here about redundant systems. Usually the solution involves an arbitrary number (called a *parameter*), k, and all the values change as k changes. This system is only partly redundant in that x and w are completely determined and only y and z depend upon the parameter.

As a second example, let us consider the following:

$$x - y + z = 6 \tag{1}$$
$$x + 3y - 2z = 8 \tag{2}$$
$$4y + 4z = 11 \tag{3}$$
$$x - 7y + 9z = 16 \tag{4}$$

We begin as usual:

$$x - y + z = 6$$
$$4y - 3z = 2 \qquad [\text{Eq. (2)} - \text{Eq. (1)}]$$
$$4y + 4z = 11$$
$$-6y + 8z = 10 \qquad [\text{Eq. (4)} - \text{Eq. (1)}]$$

Eliminating y yields

$$x - y + z = 6$$
$$4y - 3z = 2$$
$$7z = 9 \qquad [\text{Eq. (3)} - \text{Eq. (2)}]$$
$$\frac{7}{2}z = 13 \qquad [\text{Eq. (4)} + 3/2 \text{ times Eq. (2)}]$$

We now use the third equation to eliminate z from all the equations below it:

$$x - y + z = 6$$
$$4y - 3z = 2$$
$$7z = 9$$
$$0 = 17/2 \qquad [\text{Eq. (4)} - 1/2 \text{ times Eq. (3)}]$$

The last equation is now clearly an impossible or absurd statement. No matter what values of x, y and z are chosen, $0 \neq 17/2$. But this system is equivalent to the original one. Hence, the original system is incompatible. This is *not* the inevitable result of having more equations than unknowns. In fact, if Eq. (4) of the original system had been

$$x - 7y + 9z = 15/2$$

when the triangularization had been completed the final system would have turned out:

$$x - y + z = 6$$
$$4y - 3z = 2$$
$$7z = 9$$
$$0 = 0$$

The last line is perfectly valid and we would be able to solve by back substitution in the usual manner, obtaining $x = 173/28$, $y = 41/28$ and $z = 9/7$.

EXERCISES

Solve the systems in Exercises 1 through 10 wherever possible.

1. $x - y + z = 3$
      $2x + 2y - 3z = 7$
      $x - 2y + z = 8$
      $x + 2y + 3z = 11$

2. $x - y + z = 3$
      $2x + 2y - 3z = 7$
      $x - 2y + z = 8$
      $x + 2y + 11z = 49$

3. $x - y = -1$
      $3x + y = 3$
      $2x + 2y = 4$
      $6x - 4y = -3$

4. $\begin{aligned} x + y &= 2 \\ 3x + 5y &= 9 \\ 2x - 4y &= -5 \\ x + 4y &= 8 \end{aligned}$

5. $\begin{aligned} x - y + z &= 3 \\ 2x + 2y - 3z &= 7 \\ x - 5y + 6z &= 2 \\ 11x - 7y + 6z &= 34 \end{aligned}$

6. $\begin{aligned} x - y + z &= 3 \\ 2x + 2y - 3z &= 7 \\ x - 2y + z &= 8 \\ 2x + y - z &= 2 \end{aligned}$

7. $\begin{aligned} x + 3y &= 6 \\ 3x - y &= 5 \\ -x + 7y &= 7 \\ 2x - 4y &= -1 \end{aligned}$

8. $\begin{aligned} x + 2y + 3z - 6w &= 12 \\ -x + y - 2z + 6w &= 9 \\ x + 5y + 4z - 6w &= 30 \end{aligned}$

9. $\begin{aligned} x - y + z + w &= 4 \\ x + 2y - 3z + w &= 3 \\ x - y + z &= 6 \end{aligned}$

10. $\begin{aligned} x + 2y + 3z - 6w &= 12 \\ -x + y - 2z + 6w &= 9 \\ x + 5y + 4z - 6w &= 33 \end{aligned}$

2.3 Solutions of Systems Using Tableaus

To save writing and to make solution of systems possible on a computer (which cannot do algebra), an ingenious technique has been developed. This method involves suppressing the symbols for the unknowns and recording only their coefficients while performing the allowable operations on the equations. In short, a tableau or "matrix" of the coefficients in the system is constructed. For example, corresponding to the system

$$x - 3y + z = 6$$
$$2x + 3y = 9$$
$$x + 15y - z = 4$$

the tableau is:

$$\begin{pmatrix} 1 & -3 & 1 & \vdots & 6 \\ 2 & 3 & 0 & \vdots & 9 \\ 1 & 15 & -1 & \vdots & 4 \end{pmatrix} \begin{array}{l} \text{Row 1} \\ \text{Row 2} \\ \text{Row 3} \end{array}$$

The "rows" are the coefficients of x, y and z and the righthand member of each equation in turn. Note that the numbers are carefully lined up in columns so that one can always tell to which unknown the coefficient is attached. For this reason, it is necessary to enter a 0 whenever an unknown is not present. Rows are numbered from top to bottom and the columns are numbered from left to right. Thus, one may refer to the entry in Row 2, Column 3, which in this case is 0. Thus in the second equation, the coefficient of the third unknown is zero.

To solve the system, one may perform all the allowable operations on equations on the rows of the matrix. That is,

1. any row may be multiplied by any nonzero number. Multiplying a row by a number thus means multiplying every entry by that number.
2. any two rows may be interchanged.
3. any multiple of one row may be added to any other row. Adding two rows means, of course, adding the elements in like columns.

A new matrix obtained by any of these operations or any combination of them is said to be "row equivalent" to the original. That is, row equivalent matrices represent equivalent systems. Let us attack the system given at the beginning of this section by this method. In solving equations, one first uses the first equation to eliminate the first unknown from all succeeding ones. In matrix form, this means use the first row to make all entries below it in the first column zero. That is, replace Row 2 by Row 2 minus twice Row 1 and replace Row 3 by Row 3 minus Row 1:

$$\begin{pmatrix} 1 & -3 & 1 & \vdots & 6 \\ 0 & 9 & -2 & \vdots & -3 \\ 0 & 18 & -2 & \vdots & -2 \end{pmatrix}$$

Next, we clear the second unknown from all equations beyond the second, i.e., we clear everything below Row 2 in the second column. To do this, we double Row 2 and subtract it from Row 3, which yields

$$\begin{pmatrix} 1 & -3 & 1 & \vdots & 6 \\ 0 & 9 & -2 & \vdots & -3 \\ 0 & 0 & 2 & \vdots & 4 \end{pmatrix}$$

We have now completed the triangularization. The third row reads

$$2z = 4$$

so $z = 2$. The second row reads

$$9y - 2z = -3$$

since $z = 2$, $9y - 4 = -3$, $9y = 1$, $y = 1/9$. The first row reads

$$x - 3y + z = 6$$

Substituting, we have

$$x - 1/3 + 2 = 6 \qquad x = 13/3$$

We shall use the symbol $\sim$ to indicate equivalence. Let us attempt to solve the following:

$$\begin{array}{rcrcrcr} x & + & y & + & z & = & 2 \\ x & & & + & z & = & 4 \\ & & y & - & z & = & -5 \\ x & - & 2y & - & z & = & 5 \end{array}$$

which in matrix form is

$$\begin{pmatrix} 1 & 1 & 1 & \vdots & 2 \\ 1 & 0 & 1 & \vdots & 4 \\ 0 & 1 & -1 & \vdots & -5 \\ 1 & -2 & -1 & \vdots & 5 \end{pmatrix} \sim \begin{pmatrix} 1 & 1 & 1 & \vdots & 2 \\ 0 & -1 & 0 & \vdots & 2 \\ 0 & 1 & -1 & \vdots & -5 \\ 0 & -3 & -2 & \vdots & 3 \end{pmatrix}$$

$$\sim \begin{pmatrix} 1 & 1 & 1 & \vdots & 2 \\ 0 & -1 & 0 & \vdots & 2 \\ 0 & 0 & -1 & \vdots & -3 \\ 0 & 0 & -2 & \vdots & -3 \end{pmatrix} \sim \begin{pmatrix} 1 & 1 & 1 & \vdots & 2 \\ 0 & -1 & 0 & \vdots & 2 \\ 0 & 0 & -1 & \vdots & -3 \\ 0 & 0 & 0 & \vdots & 3 \end{pmatrix}$$

The triangularization is complete and the last row reads $0 = 3$. Again, we have an incompatible system. Were you able to fill in the operations as we went from matrix to matrix? Let us try it again, only change the last equation to

$$x - 2y - z = 2$$

This will change the matrix only in that the entry in Row 4, Column 4, will be 2 instead of 5. Now

$$\begin{pmatrix} 1 & 1 & 1 & \vdots & 2 \\ 1 & 0 & 1 & \vdots & 4 \\ 0 & 1 & -1 & \vdots & -5 \\ 1 & -2 & -1 & \vdots & 2 \end{pmatrix}$$

and we begin by clearing the first column,

$$\begin{pmatrix} 1 & 1 & 1 & \vdots & 2 \\ 0 & -1 & 0 & \vdots & 2 \\ 0 & 1 & -1 & \vdots & -5 \\ 0 & -3 & -2 & \vdots & 0 \end{pmatrix}$$
Row 2 — Row 1
Unchanged
Row 4 — Row 1

Next we clear Column 2,

$$\begin{pmatrix} 1 & 1 & 1 & \vdots & 2 \\ 0 & -1 & 0 & \vdots & 2 \\ 0 & 0 & -1 & \vdots & -3 \\ 0 & 0 & -2 & \vdots & -6 \end{pmatrix}$$
Row 3 + Row 2
Row 4 — 3 times Row 2

Finally we clear Column 3,

$$\begin{pmatrix} 1 & 1 & 1 & \vdots & 2 \\ 0 & -1 & 0 & \vdots & 2 \\ 0 & 0 & -1 & \vdots & -3 \\ 0 & 0 & 0 & \vdots & 0 \end{pmatrix}$$
Row 4 — 2 times Row 3

The equations now read

$$\begin{aligned} x + y + z &= 2 \\ -y &= 2 \\ -z &= -3 \\ 0 &= 0 \end{aligned}$$

The equations are compatible and solving by back substitution yields

$$z = 3 \qquad y = -2 \qquad x = 1$$

EXERCISES

1-12. Redo problems 1-12 in Section 2.1 in tableau form.

13-22. Redo problems 1-10 in Section 2.2 in tableau form.

23. Solve:
$$x - y + z = 6$$
$$x + 2y + z = 11$$
$$3x \qquad + 3z = 23$$
$$2x + 13y + 2z = 37$$
$$-x + 13y - z = 14$$

24. Solve:
$$x - 3y + z = -2$$
$$2x - 5y + 2z = -3$$
$$-x + 7y + 3z = 2$$
$$2x - y + 6z = -3$$

25. Solve:
$$x - y + 7z = 16$$
$$3x - 2y - 4z = 12$$
$$5x - 4y + 10z = 46$$

26. A three-digit number may be expressed as $100h + 10t + u$, where h is the hundreds digit, t is the tens digit, and u is the units digit [for example, $345 = 100(3) + 10(4) + 5.$] For a certain three-digit number, the sum of the digits is 18; the tens digit is equal to the sum of the other two; and if the digits are reversed, the new number is 99 less than the original number. Find the number.

27. For a certain three-digit number, the sum of the digits is 16, the middle digit is the sum of the end digits, and interchanging the units and tens digit will make the number 27 less than the original number. Find the number.

28. A man had $4.46 in pennies, nickels, and dimes. There were 94 coins in all and ten more nickels than dimes. How many coins of each type did he have?

29. Ties Unlimited stocks $1 ties, $2 ties, and $4 ties. If it has a total inventory of 7,000 ties valued at $12,000, how many ties of each kind may it possibly have? If there are exactly 2,000 $2 ties, how many $1 and $4 ties are there?

30. The price of a quart of milk, two dozen eggs, and two loaves

of bread is \$3.05. The price of two quarts of milk and a dozen eggs is \$1.60. The price of three quarts of milk, three dozen eggs, and a loaf of bread is \$4.20. What are the prices of the three commodities?

2.4 Method of Complete Elimination

The method of triangularization and back substitution is the single most efficient way to solve systems of equations. It combines a largely arithmetic technique with some very simple algebra. However, there is an extension of this method which involves only arithmetic. We shall refer to this technique as *complete elimination*. Complete elimination begins in exactly the same way as triangularization. However, instead of clearing all rows below the one with which you are operating, you clear all rows above and below. To be more precise, the steps are as follows.

1. Subtract suitable multiples of the first equation from all others in order to eliminate the first unknown from all but the first equation.
2. Subtract suitable multiples of the second equation from all above and below it in order to eliminate the second unknown from all but the second equation.
3. Continue in this manner, leaving only the third unknown in the third equation, the fourth unknown in the fourth equation, and so on.

When the elimination is completed, you will be able to read off the answers by inspection.

Naturally, as in the method of triangularization, it is most efficient to use this technique in tableau form. As an example, let us solve

$$x + 2y - 2z = -5$$
$$2x + 5y + z = 12$$
$$-5x - 10y + 9z = 21$$

Writing the system in tableau form, we have

$$\begin{pmatrix} 1 & 2 & -2 & -5 \\ 2 & 5 & 1 & 12 \\ -5 & -10 & 9 & 21 \end{pmatrix}$$

We begin by clearing the first column,

$$\begin{pmatrix} 1 & 2 & -2 & \vdots & -5 \\ 0 & 1 & 5 & \vdots & 22 \\ 0 & 0 & -1 & \vdots & -4 \end{pmatrix} \quad \begin{array}{l} \text{Unchanged} \\ \text{Row } 2 - 2 \text{ times Row } 1 \\ \text{Row } 3 + 5 \text{ times Row } 1 \end{array}$$

Since the entry in Row 3, Column 2 has turned out to be zero, we would now be finished if we only wanted to triangularize. However, for purposes of complete elimination we must still clear the second and third columns. So we continue, clearing Column 2,

$$\begin{pmatrix} 1 & 0 & -12 & \vdots & -49 \\ 0 & 1 & 5 & \vdots & 22 \\ 0 & 0 & -1 & \vdots & -4 \end{pmatrix} \quad \begin{array}{l} \text{Row } 1 - 2 \text{ times Row } 2 \\ \text{Unchanged} \\ \text{Unchanged} \end{array}$$

We now work on Column 3,

$$\begin{pmatrix} 1 & 0 & 0 & \vdots & -1 \\ 0 & 1 & 0 & \vdots & 2 \\ 0 & 0 & -1 & \vdots & -4 \end{pmatrix} \quad \begin{array}{l} \text{Row } 1 - 12 \text{ times Row } 3 \\ \text{Row } 2 + 5 \text{ times Row } 3 \\ \text{Unchanged} \end{array}$$

Thus, the three equations now read $x = -1$, $y = 2$, and $-z = -4$, that is, $z = 4$.

Let us take an example with more unknowns than equations.

$$\begin{aligned} x + y - z + 2w &= 5 \\ 2x - 2y + 3z + 7w &= -5 \\ x + 2y \quad\quad - w &= 2 \end{aligned}$$

In tableau form,

$$\begin{pmatrix} 1 & 1 & -1 & 2 & \vdots & 5 \\ 2 & -2 & 3 & 7 & \vdots & -5 \\ 1 & 2 & 0 & -1 & \vdots & 2 \end{pmatrix}$$

$$\sim \begin{pmatrix} 1 & 1 & -1 & 2 & \vdots & 5 \\ 0 & -4 & 5 & 3 & \vdots & -15 \\ 0 & 1 & 1 & -3 & \vdots & -3 \end{pmatrix} \quad \begin{array}{l} \text{Unchanged} \\ \text{Row } 2 - 2 \text{ times Row } 1 \\ \text{Row } 3 - \text{Row } 1 \end{array}$$

In order to avoid fractions, let us interchange Rows 2 and 3.

$$\begin{pmatrix} 1 & 1 & -1 & 2 & \vdots & 5 \\ 0 & 1 & 1 & -3 & \vdots & -3 \\ 0 & -4 & 5 & 3 & \vdots & -15 \end{pmatrix}$$

$$\sim \begin{pmatrix} 1 & 0 & -2 & 5 & \vdots & 8 \\ 0 & 1 & 1 & -3 & \vdots & -3 \\ 0 & 0 & 9 & -9 & \vdots & -27 \end{pmatrix} \quad \begin{array}{l} \text{Row } 1 - \text{Row } 2 \\ \text{Unchanged} \\ \text{Row } 3 + 4 \text{ times Row } 2 \end{array}$$

$$\sim \begin{pmatrix} 1 & 0 & -2 & 5 & \vdots & 8 \\ 0 & 1 & 1 & -3 & \vdots & -3 \\ 0 & 0 & 1 & -1 & \vdots & -3 \end{pmatrix} \quad \begin{array}{l} \text{Unchanged} \\ \text{Unchanged} \\ \text{Row } 3 \text{ divided by } 9 \end{array}$$

$$\sim \begin{pmatrix} 1 & 0 & 0 & 3 & \vdots & 2 \\ 0 & 1 & 0 & -2 & \vdots & 0 \\ 0 & 0 & 1 & -1 & \vdots & -3 \end{pmatrix} \quad \begin{array}{l} \text{Row } 1 + 2 \text{ times Row } 3 \\ \text{Row } 2 - \text{Row } 3 \\ \text{Unchanged} \end{array}$$

There is no fourth row; hence we may not clear the fourth column, and we stop. The last equation reads $z - w = -3$. Letting $w = k$, $z = -3 + k$. The second equation reads $y - 2w = 0$, $y = 2k$. The first equation reads $x + 3w = 2$, $x = 2 - 3k$. Notice that this considerably simplifies the back substitution.

One final example:

$$\begin{aligned} x - y + z + 2w &= 3 \\ -x + y - z + w &= 3 \\ x - 2y + z + 3w &= 4 \end{aligned}$$

In tableau form,

$$\begin{pmatrix} 1 & -1 & 1 & 2 & \vdots & 3 \\ -1 & 1 & -1 & 1 & \vdots & 3 \\ 1 & -2 & 1 & 3 & \vdots & 4 \end{pmatrix}$$

$$\sim \begin{pmatrix} 1 & -1 & 1 & 2 & \vdots & 3 \\ 0 & 0 & 0 & 3 & \vdots & 6 \\ 0 & -1 & 0 & 1 & \vdots & 1 \end{pmatrix} \quad \begin{array}{l} \text{Unchanged} \\ \text{Row } 2 + \text{Row } 1 \\ \text{Row } 3 - \text{Row } 1 \end{array}$$

We would like to operate with Row 2 to clear Column 2. However, this is not possible since the entry in Row 2, Column 2 is 0. Therefore, we shall interchange Rows 2 and 3:

$$\begin{pmatrix} 1 & -1 & 1 & 2 & \vdots & 3 \\ 0 & -1 & 0 & 1 & \vdots & 1 \\ 0 & 0 & 0 & 3 & \vdots & 6 \end{pmatrix}$$

$$\begin{pmatrix} 1 & 0 & 1 & 1 & \vdots & 2 \\ 0 & -1 & 0 & 1 & \vdots & 1 \\ 0 & 0 & 0 & 3 & \vdots & 6 \end{pmatrix} \quad \begin{matrix} \text{Row 1 } - \text{ Row 2} \\ \text{Unchanged} \\ \text{Unchanged} \end{matrix}$$

We would now like to clear Column 3, but it is already cleared except for the first row. With only zeroes below it, there is no way to do any more. However, we may use Row 3 to clear Column 4. Dividing Row 3 by 3 and then subtracting it from each of the other rows yields

$$\begin{pmatrix} 1 & 0 & 1 & 0 & \vdots & 0 \\ 0 & -1 & 0 & 0 & \vdots & -1 \\ 0 & 0 & 0 & 1 & \vdots & 2 \end{pmatrix}$$

and we read off the solution: $w = 2$, $y = 1$, and $x = -z$, where z may be anything. This type of situation comes up infrequently, but you should realize that it can be handled. As we have seen, when everything in the column you wish to work with has been cleared below the row you are up to, simply skip that column and go on to the next one. In the last example, we skipped over Column 3 to Column 4.

EXERCISES

1-30.   Redo the problems of Section 2.3 using complete elimination.
Solve the following systems by complete elimination.

31. $x - 3y + z = -2$
       $2x - 5y + 2z = -3$
       $-x + 7y + 3z = 2$

32. $x - 3y + z = -2$
       $3x - 8y + 3z = -5$
       $x + 2y + 5z = -1$
       $4y + 4z = 0$

33. $\quad x + 2y - 3z = 6$
$\quad\quad 2x + 3y + 4z = 1$
$\quad\quad 3x + 2y + 5z = 0$

34. $\quad x + 2y - 3z = 6$
$\quad\quad 2x + 3y + 4z = 1$
$\quad\quad 3x + 2y + 5z = 0$
$\quad\quad 6x + 7y + 6z = 7$

35. $\quad x + 2y - z + w = 1$
$\quad\quad 3x - y + 2z - w = -1$
$\quad\quad 2x - 2y + 3z = 5$
$\quad\quad 2x + 3y - 2z + w = -3$

36. $\quad\quad 2y - z = 3$
$\quad\quad 2x + 3y - z = 8$
$\quad\quad x + y + z = 7$

37. $\quad x + y + z + w = 16$
$\quad\quad 2x + 2y - 3z + w = 9$
$\quad\quad 3x + 3y + 4z - 2w = 6$

38. $\quad x + 2y - 3z + w = 6$
$\quad\quad 2x + 3y + 4z + w = 1$
$\quad\quad 3x + 2y + 5z + w = 0$

39. $\quad x + 2y - 3z = 5$
$\quad\quad -x + 3y + 4z = 3$
$\quad\quad 2x - z = 4$
$\quad\quad 3x + 4y = 11$

40. $\quad\quad z + 6w = 1$
$\quad\quad y - z = 2$
$\quad\quad x + y = 3$
$\quad\quad y + 3w = 2$

2.5 Linear Programming Revisited

As an application of the method of complete elimination, we shall consider a purely algebraic method of solving linear programming problems. The student should recall that by the enumeration of vertices one may solve a linear programming problem without resorting to the geometric construction. However, in a fairly large problem, the number of vertices soon becomes so enormous that a more efficient technique is required. The technique which we shall discuss is called the *simplex procedure*. The beauty of the simplex procedure is that one needs only to detect vertices that fall in the region of feasible solutions. Additionally, starting from one feasible vertex, the procedure will lead you to another feasible solution for which the objective function is larger, and it will tell you to stop when the optimal solution is reached. Finally, the steps are so routine and repetitious that the whole method is readily programmed for use by computers, thus making it applicable to large-scale problems.

To fix the ideas, let us take a specific example in standard form.

$$\text{Maximize:} \quad P = x + 2y$$
$$\text{Subject to:} \; 3x + y \leq 15$$
$$3x + 4y \leq 24$$
$$x \geq 0$$
$$y \geq 0$$

Notice that the standard form involves three basic requirements:

1. The objective is to be maximized.
2. The unknowns must be nonnegative.
3. The other constraints must be of the form

$$ax + by + \cdots + ew \leq k$$

for unknowns $x, y, \ldots, w$.

To start, figure 1 shows the geometric solution. We see that the objective P is maximized at $(0, 6)$ where $P = 12$. However, let us see how to solve the problem algebraically.

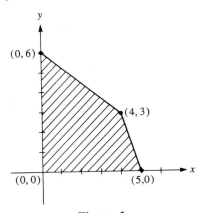

Figure 1

First, we convert the inequalities into equalities by introducing non-negative slack variables r, s and we convert the objective into the equation $-x - 2y + P = 0$. Thus,

$$
\begin{aligned}
3x + y + r &= 15 \\
3x + 4y + s &= 24 \\
-x - 2y + P &= 0
\end{aligned}
$$

We rewrite this system in a special matrix form called the *simplex tableau*.

x	y	r	s	P	
3	1	1	0	0	15
3	4	0	1	0	24
−1	−2	0	0	1	0

This represents three equations in five unknowns, which has many solutions. We shall read only the simplest solution detectable by inspection, namely,

$$
\begin{aligned}
r &= 15 \\
s &= 24 \\
P &= 0 \\
x &= 0 \\
y &= 0
\end{aligned}
$$

That is, if in a column we have several nonzero entries, then that unknown is assigned the value zero. Now, clearly the solution we have corresponds to the vertex $(0, 0)$ and $P = 0$ which is surely not the optimal solution. Since the last row says $-x - 2y + P = 0$, if we increase either x or y we also increase P since the sum must remain zero. Which should we increase? Every unit increase in y causes two units increase in P. But every unit increase in x causes one unit increase in P. Hence, it seems reasonable to increase y. By how much should we increase y? The first equation says $3x + y + r = 15$. The largest possible value of y is attained at $x = r = 0$. Hence $y = 15$. However, if $y = 15$, the second equation becomes

$$
\begin{aligned}
3x + 4(15) + s &= 24 \\
3x + s &= -36
\end{aligned}
$$

This means either x or s must be negative, which is not allowed. Hence, the maximum allowable value of y is attained when $x = s = 0$ in the second equation. That is,

$$4y = 24 \qquad y = 6$$

Now, in order to read $y = 6$ as part of the solution of the problem, we must perform a complete elimination clearing all of Column 2 except in Row 2. We shall call the element in Row 2, Column 2, the "pivotal element," which we circle thus:

x	y	r	s	P	
3	1	1	0	0	15
3	④	0	1	0	24
−1	−2	0	0	1	0

x	y	r	s	P		
11/4	0	1	−3/4	0	9	Row 1 − 1/4 × Row 2
3/4	1	0	1/4	0	6	Row 2 ÷ 4
1/2	0	0	1/2	1	12	Row 3 + 1/2 × Row 2

The solution reads $x = 0$, $y = 6$, $r = 9$, $s = 0$, $P = 12$. This corresponds to the vertex $(0, 6)$, which is the optimal point. How do we know? The last equation reads

$$(1/2)x + (1/2)s + P = 12$$

Since the coefficients of x and s are positive, any increase in either causes P to become smaller. Hence, we must stop.

Let us review the method used. First, to find the pivotal element we identified the proper column by taking the one with the most negative entry at the bottom. Having picked the proper column, the proper row was found as follows: Take the ratio of the last element in each row to the element in the selected column. The row for which this ratio is the least is the proper one. In the last example, we chose the second column because its last entry was −2. The pertinent ratios were then 15/1 for the first row and 24/4 for the second row. Hence, the second row was chosen.

How do we know when to stop? When there are no more negative entries in the last row! For example, take the same problem, only make the objective function $P = 2x + y$. That is,

$$\text{Maximize: } P = 2x + y$$
$$\text{Subject to: } 3x + y \leq 15$$
$$3x + 4y \leq 24$$
$$x \geq 0$$
$$y \geq 0$$

The tableau is

x	y	r	s	P	
③	1	1	0	0	15
3	4	0	1	0	24
−2	−1	0	0	1	0

The most negative entry, -2, is in the x-column. The corresponding ratios are 15/3 and 24/3. Hence, the 3 in the upper left-hand corner has been circled as the pivotal element. Carry out the total elimination process on the x-column:

x	y	r	s	P	
1	1/3	1/3	0	0	5
0	③	−1	1	0	9
0	−1/3	2/3	0	1	10

We still have a negative element in the y-column; hence P may be increased further by introducing y into the solution. We compute the pertinent ratios, which are $5 \div (1/3) = 15$ and $9/3 = 3$. The pivotal element is then the 3 circled above. Perform the total elimination on the y-column:

x	y	r	s	P	
1	0	4/9	−1/9	0	4
0	1	−1/3	1/3	0	3
0	0	5/9	1/9	1	11

We now have no negative entries in the last column. We stop the process and read the solution:

$$x = 4$$
$$y = 3$$
$$r = 0$$
$$s = 0$$
$$P = 11$$

It is easy to see geometrically that this is the optimal solution. Notice that in the first example, the final answer showed one of the slack variables r to equal 9. That is, there is some slack in the solution. In other words, if 15 and 24 represent the total quantities of certain resources, then in this solution something is left over at the optimal point. In the second example, both slack variables are zero, indicating that the best solution utilizes the total resources available.

It should be noted that the simplex procedure offers one other advantage. Since it is totally arithmetic, the technique will work with any number of variables. Let us try one somewhat larger problem.

The New York Nut Co. packages 8-ounce jars of nuts under three different labels, Econo-nut, All-nutz and Lux-O-nut. Each is a mixture of peanuts, cashews and almonds. In the following table, we have the breakdown and profit per jar for each of the three:

	Peanuts	Cashews	Almonds	Profit
Econo-nut	6 oz	1 oz	1 oz	10¢
All-nutz	4 "	3 "	1 "	20¢
Lux-O-nuts	2 "	2 "	4 "	30¢

Suppose the total number of ounces available of peanuts, cashews and almonds are 800, 600 and 300 ounces respectively. How many of each jar should be prepared in order to maximize the profit?

Let

$$x = \text{number of jars of Econo-nut}$$
$$y = \text{number of jars of All-nutz}$$
$$z = \text{number of jars of Lux-O-nuts}$$

Then the problem becomes

$$\text{Maximize: } P = 10x + 20y + 30z$$
$$\text{Subject to: } \quad 6x + 4y + 2z \leq 800$$
$$x + 3y + 2z \leq 600$$
$$x + y + 4z \leq 300$$
$$x \geq 0$$
$$y \geq 0$$
$$z \geq 0$$

We introduce three slack variables r, s, t and arrive at the simplex tableau:

x	y	z	r	s	t	P	
6	4	2	1	0	0	0	800
1	3	2	0	1	0	0	600
1	1	④	0	0	1	0	300
-10	-20	-30	0	0	0	1	0

We have circled the pivotal element in the above. After total elimination the tableau is

x	y	z	r	s	t	P	
5.5	3.5	0	1	0	$-.5$	0	650
.5	②.⑤	0	0	1	$-.5$	0	450
.25	.25	1	0	0	.25	0	75
-2.5	-12.5	0	0	0	7.5	1	2250

Again, we have circled the pivotal element. After total elimination, the tableau is

x	y	z	r	s	t	P	
4.8	0	0	1	-1.4	.9	0	20
.2	1	0	0	.4	$-.2$	0	180
.2	0	1	0	$-.1$	.3	0	30
0	0	0	0	4	5	1	4500

There are now no negative entries in the last row. Hence we read the solution: $x = 0$, $y = 180$, $z = 30$, $r = 20$, $s = 0$, $t = 0$, $P = 4500$. Thus, the company should sell 180 jars of All-nutz, 30 jars of Lux-O-nuts and no Econo-nut. The number $r = 20$ indicates that 20 ounces of peanuts will be left over. The optimal profit is $P = 4500¢ = \$45$ if this procedure is followed.

A few closing remarks are in order. Suppose when choosing the pivotal element two columns tie for having the most negative bottom entry. We may then choose either column first. Having chosen a column, we are supposed to select the pivotal element as the one for which a certain ratio is smallest. This is not quite accurate. If the smallest ratio is negative, this corresponds to a negative value for the unknown, which is not allowed in the set of feasible solutions. Hence, we should say, Choose the element for which one obtains the smallest nonnegative ratio. Again, if there is a tie for lowest in this case, choose the one you wish.

EXERCISES

1. Maximize: $x + 2y + 3z$
    Subject to: $2x + y + z \leq 2$
    $4x + 2y + z \leq 2$
    $x, y, z \geq 0$

2. Maximize: $2w - x + 3y + z$
    Subject to: $3w - x - y + z \leq 4$
    $w - x + y + z \leq 1$
    $2w + x + 2y \leq 7$
    $w, x, y, z \geq 0$

3. Maximize: $P = x + 3y$
    Subject to: $y \leq 5$
    $3x + 5y \leq 34$
    $2x + y \leq 18$
    $x \geq 0$
    $y \geq 0$

4. A coffee manufacturer makes 50¢ profit on each can of instant coffee, and 35¢ profit on each can of regular coffee. The manufacturer must include for use in each can beans from both Brazil and Colombia. In his storeroom he has available 1,200 ounces of Brazilian beans and 1,500 ounces of Colombian beans. If each can of instant coffee requires 4 oz of Brazilian beans, and 3 oz of Colombian beans, while each can of regular coffee requires 2 oz of Brazilian beans and 3 oz of Colombian beans, how many cans of each type should the manufacturer produce to maximize his profit?

5. Maximize: $4x - 6y + 2z$

   Subject to: $2x + 2y + 2z \leq 8$

   $\qquad\quad x \quad\ \ - z \leq 2$

   $\qquad\quad x, y, z \geq 0$

6. Maximize: $4x + 3y + 7z$

   Subject to: $\ x + 2y + 3z \leq 100$

   $\qquad\quad 3x + \ y + 3z \leq 100$

   $\qquad\qquad x, y, z \geq \quad 0$

7. Suppose that in the New York Nut Co. example in the text, the company changes the contents of the Econo-nut jar by substituting an extra ounce of peanuts for the almonds. Suppose that by doing so the company increases the profit to 15¢/jar. How many of each type jar should they now market?

8. A television assembly plant divides its operation among three shops, electronic assembly, cabinet assembly, and packing and shipping. The plant assembles cheap floor models, portables and luxury floor models. The table below shows the man hours needed for each model, the number of hours available in each shop and the price on each type of model. Find the number of each type to be manufactured to maximize total sales.

	Electronic Assembly	Cabinet Assembly	Packing and Shipping	Price
Cheap Model	3	2	2	$350
Portable Model	2	1	2	$300
Deluxe Model	3	4	2	$600
Hours Available	105	120	70	

2.6 Artificial Variables and the Dual Problem

In the last section we dealt with linear programming problems in standard form. However, in chapter 1, we solved many linear programming problems in which some or all of the inequalities were in nonstandard form or in which the objective was to be minimized rather than maximized. Could we apply this simplex method to a problem in other than standard form? The answer is yes. In fact, there are many ways to adapt the technique. We shall consider one way. Take the following example:

$$\text{Minimize: } C = x + 2y$$
$$\text{Subject to: } x - y \leq 4$$
$$2x + y \geq 4$$
$$4x - y \leq 8$$
$$x, y \geq 0$$

We would naturally first introduce nonnegative slack variables to make the constraints into equalities. In the first and third inequalities, we must add something, but in the second, we must subtract a suitable slack variable, yielding

$$x - y + r \qquad\quad = 4$$
$$2x + y \qquad - s \quad\; = 4$$
$$4x - y \qquad\qquad + t = 8$$
$$x, y, r, s, t \geq 0$$

Furthermore, we must adjust the objective so that the problem becomes a maximization problem. This is accomplished by letting $P = -C = -x - 2y$. Now maximizing P is the same as minimizing C. The objective rewritten in equation form is $x + 2y + P = 0$ and the simplex tableau is

x	y	r	s	t	P	
1	-1	1	0	0	0	4
2	1	0	-1	0	0	4
4	-1	0	0	1	0	8
1	2	0	0	0	1	0

This tableau has two drawbacks. First, the only solution which can be read off directly is $x = 0$, $y = 0$, $r = 4$, $s = -4$, $t = 8$ and $P = 0$, which is not a feasible solution since one variable has a negative value. Second, even if there were a feasible solution, we have no negative elements in the last row and hence no way to find a pivotal element and get started.

The first problem is avoided by introducing an "artificial" variable u into the second equation, making it

$$2x + y - s + u = 4$$

Of course, if two variables in the basic solution were negative, we would need two artificial variables and so on. In this case, the basic solution is now

$$x = y = s = P = 0 \qquad u = 4, r = 4, t = 8$$

We have seen that the objective function is not modified when slack variables are introduced. However, you would not want the solution to a linear programming problem to yield a nonzero value for an artificial variable. Therefore, a new objective $Q = P - nu$, where n is a large number, is introduced when an artificial variable is brought in. This new objective will be at its maximum only when P is maximized and $u = 0$. The resulting problem which may be attacked by the simplex procedure is

Maximize: $Q = -x - 2y - nu$

Subject to: $x - y + r \qquad\qquad = 4$

$\qquad\qquad 2x + y \qquad - s + u \quad = 4$

$\qquad\qquad 4x - y \qquad\qquad + t = 8$

$\qquad\qquad x, y, r, s, t, u \geq 0$

and in tableau form we have

x	y	r	s	u	t	Q	
1	-1	1	0	0	0	0	4
2	1	0	-1	1	0	0	4
4	-1	0	0	0	1	0	8
1	2	0	0	n	0	1	0

What is lacking is a negative element in the last row and its associated pivotal element. In order to have an equivalent system of equations with negative elements in the last row, we will eliminate u from the fourth equation by subtracting n times Row 2 from Row 4. The new tableau is

x	y	r	s	u	t	Q	
1	-1	1	0	0	0	0	4
2	1	0	-1	1	0	0	4
4	-1	0	0	0	1	0	8
$1-2n$	$2-n$	0	n	0	0	1	$-4n$

We may now begin the simplex procedure. Our choice is to leave n as it is and use some algebra or substitute some large number for n and just use arithmetic. We shall do the latter. In this problem, $n = 20$ is considerably larger than any other number so let us make this substitution. The largest negative entry is in the x-column. The possible ratios are 4/1, 4/2, 8/4. Since the last two are equal we may pick either the 2 or the 4 as the pivot. Let us take the 2, which simplifies fractions. We have

x	y	r	s	u	t	Q		
1	-1	1	0	0	0	0	4	
①	1/2	0	$-1/2$	1/2	0	0	2	Row 2 $\div$ 2
4	-1	0	0	0	1	0	8	
-39	-18	0	20	0	0	1	-80	

x	y	r	s	u	t	Q		
0	$-3/2$	1	1/2	$-1/2$	0	0	2	Row 1 $-$ Row 2
1	1/2	0	$-1/2$	1/2	0	0	2	Row 2
0	-3	0	2	-2	1	0	0	Row 3 $-$ 4 $\times$ Row 2
0	3/2	0	1/2	39/2	0	1	-2	Row 4 $+$ 39 $\times$ Row 2

For each unknown, the last entry is now positive; the process stops and we read $x = 2$, $r = 2$, $t = 0$, $y = 0$, $s = 0$, $u = 0$, $Q = -2$. Since r, s, t are slack variables, the pertinent information is $x = 2$, $y = 0$ and $Q = P = -C = -2$, that is, $C = 2$.

Let us summarize this technique. The steps are as follows:

1. Convert all the inequalities to equalities by adding or subtracting suitable slack variables.
2. In any equation where a slack variable has been subtracted, add an artificial variable in order to guarantee a feasible point from which to begin the simplex procedure.

3. Adjust the objective function in two stages. First, if the objective is to minimize, replace the objective function by its negative (if the object is to maximize, do nothing). Second, subtract from the objective function n times each artificial variable, where n is an arbitrarily large number.

4. Form the simplex tableau. As a first step, use suitable row operations to clear the last row in each artificial variable column.

5. Begin the regular simplex procedure and carry it through to completion.

For set-ups which are exactly the reverse of standard form, there are better procedures. In particular, there is a technique based on the so-called "dual problem," which is more efficient than the one given here. The advantage of artificial variables is that they enable you to handle all kinds of linear programming problems.

Let us consider the case where a real linear programming problem develops into a form which is exactly the opposite of the standard form. That is, the objective is to be minimized rather than maximized, and all the inequalities are of the form $ax + by + \cdots + ew \geq k$ rather than $ax + by + \cdots + ew \leq k$. In such a case we apply the method of duality. For every minimization problem, there is a corresponding maximization problem called the dual (and vice versa). For example, in business your objective is usually to maximize profit. This may be posed in two ways: Maximize revenue, subject to the limitation that the various costs may not exceed preset limits, or minimize costs, subject to the limitation that revenues may not fall below certain preset limits. These two are dual problems. The mathematical dual of a linear programming problem is easy to attain by the following method.

Suppose that we have analyzed a problem to yield the format

$$\text{Minimize: } C = 2x + 5y$$
$$\text{Subject to: } x + 2y \geq 30$$
$$3x + y \geq 20$$
$$2x + y \geq 10$$
$$x, y \geq 0$$

The dual problem is formed by first introducing as many new variables as there are inequalities in the original problem. In this case, there are three inequalities (we ignore the $x, y \geq 0$, which are part of every problem suitable for simplex procedure). Call these variables u, v, w. We now read *down* the inequalities in the original problem to find the inequalities in the dual. Reading down, the x-coefficients are 1, 3, 2 in the inequalities and 2 in the objective. Our first inequality in the dual will have 1, 3, 2 as the coefficients of u, v, w and 2 as the constant, yielding

$$u + 3v + 2w \leq 2$$

Notice that since in the original problem the inequalities are $\geq$, in the dual they are $\leq$. Reading down the y-coefficients similarly, we obtain

$$2u + v + w \leq 5$$

Finally, the objective function is found by reading down the constant side of the inequalities; that is,

$$P = 30u + 20v + 10w$$

and the dual problem is

Maximize: $P = 30u + 20v + 10w$

Subject to: $u + 3v + 2w \leq 2$

$2u + v + w \leq 5$

$u, v, w \geq 0$

The value of P attained as the maximum in the dual is identical to the value of C which is minimum in the original problem.

There are several advantages to being able to convert problems to their duals. The first and most obvious is that it is far simpler than using artificial variables, which are then necessary only when a problem involves mixed inequalities. Second, most computers have library programs that handle either maximization or minimization problems; one program might be more convenient to use than the other. A third, less obvious advantage is demonstrated in the preceding example. The dual is in proper format for the simplex procedure but it involves three variables. If that had been the given problem, its dual would have been the original problem, which involves only two variables and hence could be solved geometrically. Since the geometric solution is generally easier to find, you might wish to solve the dual problem to avoid the simplex procedure. Doing so would yield the optimal value of the objective, but would not give the values of the variables for which it is attained. However, let us look again at our example.

If the reader solves the original problem geometrically, he should find that C is minimized at $x = 30$, $y = 0$, and $C = 60$. Solving the dual problem by the simplex, we have the tableau

u	v	w	r	s	P	
①	3	2	1	0	0	2
2	1	1	0	1	0	5
-30	-20	-10	0	0	1	0

We have circled the pivotal element as usual. After one complete elimination, we have

u	v	w	r	s	P	
1	3	2	1	0	0	2
0	-5	-3	-2	1	0	1
0	70	50	30	0	1	60

There are no negative entries in the last row, and so the procedure is completed. We read off the solution $u = 2$, $s = 1$, $P = 60$, $v = w = r = 0$. Notice that $P = 60$ is the same as the value of C which solves the original problem. Also notice that the bottom entries in the slack variable columns give the values of x and y, namely 30 and 0, that solve the original problem. This seemingly magical result is not an accident. However, the mathematical explanation of why it works is beyond the scope of this book. To repeat, after solving the dual problem, the final simplex tableau will display the solution to the original problem as the last entries in the slack variable columns.

EXERCISES

1. Redo the first example in the text assuming that 4 were chosen as the pivot.

2. Use the simplex procedure to

$$\text{Minimize:} \quad x + 4y$$
$$\text{Subject to:} \quad 4x + y \geq 5$$
$$5x - y \leq 4$$
$$-x + 2y \leq 10$$
$$x, y \geq 0$$

3. Use the artificial variables to

$$\text{Minimize: } x + 7y$$
$$\text{Subject to: } 2x + y \geq 10$$
$$x + y \geq 9$$
$$2x + 5y \geq 24$$
$$x, y \geq 0$$

4. Use the simplex procedure to

$$\text{Minimize: } 2x - 3y$$
$$\text{Subject to: } 2x - y - z \geq 3$$
$$x - y + z \geq 2$$
$$x, y, z \geq 0$$

5. Use the simplex procedure to

$$\text{Minimize: } -x + 2y$$
$$\text{Subject to: } 5x - 2y \leq 3$$
$$x + y \geq 1$$
$$-3x + y \leq 3$$
$$-3x - 3y \leq 2$$
$$x, y \geq 0$$

6. A processing plant can handle at most twelve tons of material in any one day. From a ton of high grade ore, it can extract three pounds of A and one pound of B. From a ton of low grade ore, it can extract one pound of A and two pounds of B. It has standing orders to meet or exceed fifteen pounds of A and twenty pounds of B each day. If it costs \$40 to process a ton of high grade ore and \$10 to process a ton of low grade ore, find the production pattern that will minimize daily costs.

7. For the same conditions as in Exercise 6, suppose that the sole customer is the government, which pays a price based on a fixed percent profit based on cost, so that the object is to maximize cost. Now find the optimal procedure.

8. A dietician must prepare a mixture of two foods A and B. Each unit of A contains 20 grams of protein, 25 grams of carbohydrate, and costs 40 cents. Each unit of B contains 15 grams of protein,

18 grams of carbohydrate, and costs 25 cents. What is the cheapest mixture of A and B that must contain at least 400 grams protein and 600 grams carbohydrate?

9. A dietician is planning weekly food purchases for a school. He can buy foods I, II, and III costing $56, $37, and $12 per package, respectively. The unit concentrations of nutrients per package are tabulated as follows:

	I	II	III
Protein units	100	75	15
Fat units	80	30	5
Carbohydrate units	5	30	100

Dietary requirements are at least 1,000 units of protein, at least 1,500 units of carbohydrates, and at most 500 units of fat. How much of each food should be bought to satisfy the requirements at minimum cost?

10. Redo Exercise 3 by setting up the dual problem and applying the simplex procedure to it. Check your answer by the geometric method.

11. Solve the following problem by the simplex method and check your answer by solving its dual geometrically.

$$\text{Maximize: } P = 11x + 36y + 40z$$
$$\text{Subject to: } x + 4y + 2z \le 2$$
$$x + 3y + 5z \le 3$$
$$x, y, z \ge 0$$

12. Check the solution to Exercise 1, Section 2.5 by solving its dual geometrically.

13. Check the solution to Exercise 6, Section 2.5 by solving its dual geometrically.

14. Solve by any method:

$$\text{Minimize: } C = 90x + 25y + 36z$$
$$\text{Subject to: } 5x + 2y + 3z \ge 17$$
$$4x + 3y + 9z \ge 24$$
$$x, y, z \ge 0$$

3

Matrices

3.1 Matrices and Matrix Addition

A matrix is a rectangular array of numbers. In chapter 2 we encountered matrices used to represent systems of linear equations, and we studied those operations upon and with the rows of a matrix used to solve the equations. However, matrices occur in many other contexts and have many applications. We shall use boldface print for the symbol representing a matrix. For example, we may write

$$\mathbf{A} = \begin{pmatrix} 1 & -3 & 3 \\ 4 & 5 & 0 \end{pmatrix}$$

The horizontal lines of numbers are called the *rows* of the matrix, and the vertical lines of numbers are called the *columns* of the matrix. The rows are numbered from top to bottom and the columns from left to right. Thus, the first row of $\mathbf{A}$ is

$$(1 \quad -3 \quad 3)$$

and the third column of $\mathbf{A}$ is

$$\begin{pmatrix} 3 \\ 0 \end{pmatrix}$$

If a matrix has m rows and n columns, it is called an m by n matrix ($m \times n$). Thus, $\mathbf{A}$ is 2×3.

Each number in a matrix is called an *entry* and is identified by giving its row and column designation. The entry in Row i and Column j of $\mathbf{A}$ is denoted a_{ij}. If two matrices $\mathbf{A}$ and $\mathbf{B}$ have the same numbers of rows and columns, they are said to have the same *shape*. We say that $\mathbf{A} = \mathbf{B}$ if they are the same shape and have the same entries in like locations. That is, $\mathbf{A} = \mathbf{B}$ if $a_{ij} = b_{ij}$ for all possible values of i and j. Let us look at some examples. Let

$$\mathbf{A} = \begin{pmatrix} 1 & 2 \\ 3 & 4 \end{pmatrix} \qquad \mathbf{B} = \begin{pmatrix} 1 & 3 \\ 2 & 4 \end{pmatrix} \qquad \mathbf{C} = \begin{pmatrix} 1 & 2 \\ 2 & 4 \end{pmatrix}$$

All of these matrices have the same shape, 2×2. However, are any two equal? Consider $\mathbf{A}$ and $\mathbf{B}$. They have the same entries but not in the same locations. Therefore, $\mathbf{A} \neq \mathbf{B}$. The matrices $\mathbf{A}$ and $\mathbf{C}$ differ in one entry, for $a_{21} = 3$ but $c_{21} = 2$. Therefore, they are not equal. Similarly, $\mathbf{B} \neq \mathbf{C}$, and hence no two are equal.

Let us consider the following: A real estate company has three brokers, Mr. Josephs, Mr. Sheldon, and Mr. Warren. Each sells houses and vacant lots. The sales by each man for the first two months of the year are:

January Sales

	Houses	Lots
Mr. Josephs	$70,000	$10,000
Mr. Sheldon	40,000	3,000
Mr. Warren	0	15,000

February Sales

	Houses	Lots
Mr. Josephs	$35,000	$7,000
Mr. Sheldon	30,000	0
Mr. Warren	90,000	1,000

If we represent the January sales in thousands of dollars by a matrix $\mathbf{J}$ and the February sales by a matrix $\mathbf{F}$, then

$$\mathbf{J} = \begin{pmatrix} 70 & 10 \\ 40 & 3 \\ 0 & 15 \end{pmatrix} \qquad \mathbf{F} = \begin{pmatrix} 35 & 7 \\ 30 & 0 \\ 90 & 1 \end{pmatrix}$$

The matrix of total sales **T** would be

$$\mathbf{T} = \begin{pmatrix} 105 & 17 \\ 70 & 3 \\ 90 & 16 \end{pmatrix}$$

In other words, each entry in **T** is simply the sum of the corresponding entries in **J** and **F**. In fact, we shall take this to be the definition of the sum of two matrices. That is, if **A** and **B** are two matrices of the same shape, then the matrix $\mathbf{C} = \mathbf{A} + \mathbf{B}$ is the matrix of the same shape and such that $c_{ij} = a_{ij} + b_{ij}$ for all possible choices of i and j.

Example Find a, b, and c if

$$\begin{pmatrix} a & 0 & -1 \\ 3 & b & 5 \end{pmatrix} + \begin{pmatrix} -2 & 6 & c \\ 3 & 1 & -3 \end{pmatrix} = \begin{pmatrix} 4 & 6 & -2 \\ 6 & 4 & 2 \end{pmatrix}$$

Adding the two matrices on the lefthand side of the equation yields

$$\begin{pmatrix} a-2 & 6 & c-1 \\ 6 & b+1 & 2 \end{pmatrix} = \begin{pmatrix} 4 & 6 & -2 \\ 6 & 4 & 2 \end{pmatrix}$$

Since equal matrices must have the same entries in corresponding locations, we must have

$$a - 2 = 4, \; a = 6; \; b + 1 = 4, \; b = 3; \; c - 1 = -2, \; c = -1$$

Now, if one were to take $\mathbf{A} + \mathbf{A}$, the results would be a matrix, each of whose entries is twice the corresponding entry in **A**. It would be nice to write $\mathbf{A} + \mathbf{A} = 2\mathbf{A}$. In order to do so, one must define the product of a number k and a matrix **A** as follows: Let the entry in Row i, Column j of **A** be a_{ij}. The corresponding entry in $k\mathbf{A}$ would be ka_{ij}. In particular, if one forms the matrix $(-1)\mathbf{A}$, then $\mathbf{A} + (-1)\mathbf{A}$ will be a matrix with all zero entries. We shall call this a zero matrix and designate it **Z**. If any $m \times n$ matrix **A** is added to an $m \times n$ zero matrix, we have $\mathbf{A} + \mathbf{Z} = \mathbf{A}$.

If, as with numbers, we define $-\mathbf{A}$ to be the matrix which when added to **A** gives **Z** (that is, $-\mathbf{A} + \mathbf{A} = \mathbf{Z}$), then it is easy to see that $-\mathbf{A} = (-1)\mathbf{A}$ and we can add and subtract matrices just like numbers. For example, solve for x, y, z and w:

$$\begin{pmatrix} 1 & -x \\ 0 & 2 \end{pmatrix} + 2\begin{pmatrix} 1 & -1 \\ 2 & 1 \end{pmatrix} - 3\begin{pmatrix} 1 & -1 \\ y & 6 \end{pmatrix} = \begin{pmatrix} z & 0 \\ 11 & w \end{pmatrix}$$

Performing the indicated operations on the lefthand side yields

$$\begin{pmatrix} 0 & -x+1 \\ 4-3y & -14 \end{pmatrix} = \begin{pmatrix} z & 0 \\ 11 & w \end{pmatrix}$$

Now equating like elements, we have

$$
\begin{aligned}
z &= 0 \\
-x+1 &= 0 \qquad x = 1 \\
4-3y &= 11 \qquad y = -7/3 \\
w &= -14
\end{aligned}
$$

EXERCISES

In exercises 1 and 2, you are given the following matrices.

$$\mathbf{A} = \begin{pmatrix} -1 & 2 & 3 \\ 1 & -1 & 4 \end{pmatrix}, \ \mathbf{B} = \begin{pmatrix} 1 & -2 & -3 \\ 2 & 2 & 0 \end{pmatrix}, \ \mathbf{C} = \begin{pmatrix} 1 & 0 & 1 \\ -2 & -1 & 3 \end{pmatrix},$$

$$\mathbf{U} = (1 \quad -1 \quad 2 \quad 3)$$
$$\mathbf{V} = (0 \quad 2 \quad -1 \quad 4) \quad \mathbf{W} = \begin{pmatrix} 3 \\ 2 \\ -5 \end{pmatrix}$$

1. Find if possible:
    (a) $\mathbf{A} + \mathbf{B}$
    (b) $\mathbf{A} + \mathbf{U}$
    (c) $2\mathbf{V} - 4\mathbf{U}$
    (d) $\mathbf{C} - (\mathbf{A} + \mathbf{B})$
    (e) $3\mathbf{W}$
    (f) $5\mathbf{B}$
    (g) $3\mathbf{A} + 4\mathbf{B} - 5\mathbf{C}$
    (h) $\mathbf{W} - \mathbf{U}$
    (i) $(-1/2)\mathbf{W}$

2. Solve for $\mathbf{X}$:
    (a) $\mathbf{A} + \mathbf{B} + \mathbf{X} = \mathbf{Z}$
    (b) $\mathbf{U} - \mathbf{X} = \mathbf{V}$
    (c) $2\mathbf{A} - 3\mathbf{X} = 4\mathbf{C}$
    (d) $2\mathbf{U} - 3\mathbf{X} = 4\mathbf{V}$

3. Solve for a, b, and c, if possible:

$$a\begin{pmatrix} 1 & 0 \\ 3 & 5 \end{pmatrix} + b\begin{pmatrix} 2 & 0 \\ 1 & 4 \end{pmatrix} = c\begin{pmatrix} 1 & 0 \\ 3 & 2 \end{pmatrix}$$

4. Let **R** be a 4×2 matrix with $r_{ij} = i - j$. Find **R**.

5. Let **S** be a 3×3 matrix with s_{ij} being 1 if i is greater than j and being zero otherwise. Find **S**.

6. Find all possible 2×2 matrices **Y** having the following properties: $y_{11} = y_{21} - 3$, $y_{12} = 2y_{21}$, and the sum of all the entries is 1.

7. The price of a box of cigars is $7.00 and carries a $2.00 tax. The price of a carton of cigarettes is $4.00 and carries a $1.00 tax. Let **A** be a 2×2 matrix with first row (7 2) and second row (0 0). Let **B** be a 2×2 matrix with first row (0 0) and second row (4 1). A store orders 200 boxes of cigars and 500 cartons of cigarettes. What does the matrix $200\mathbf{A} + 500\mathbf{B}$ represent?

8. Consider the matrices **A** and **B** in Exercise 7. Suppose a store ordered a supply of cigars and cigarettes at a total cost of $375.00 of which $80.00 was tax. How many of each were ordered?

3.2 Matrix Algebra

Having defined the sum of two matrices, it is natural to wish to define the product. Addition and subtraction of matrices are carried out in a very natural manner. The same shall not be true for multiplication. You may well wonder about the choice of definition. However, as the applications develop, the reasons for this choice should become clear.

To begin, let us introduce a little further terminology. A matrix with only one row will be called a *row vector* and its entries will be called *components*. Thus,

$$\mathbf{u} = (-1 \quad 2 \quad 3 \quad 5)$$

is a four-component row vector. Similarly, a matrix with only one column will be called a *column vector*. Thus,

$$\mathbf{v} = \begin{pmatrix} 1 \\ 0 \\ 12 \end{pmatrix}$$

is a three-component column vector. Since vectors are just matrices of a special shape, there is nothing new to say about addition and subtraction of vectors. However, we shall now define the product of a row and a column vector.

Definition   If $\mathbf{u}$ is an n-component row vector, $\mathbf{u} = (u_1, u_2, \ldots, u_n)$, and v is an n-component column vector,

$$\mathbf{v} = \begin{pmatrix} v_1 \\ v_2 \\ \vdots \\ v_n \end{pmatrix}$$

then the product of $\mathbf{u}$ and $\mathbf{v}$ is

$$\mathbf{uv} = u_1 v_1 + u_2 v_2 + \cdots + u_n v_n$$

Notice that the product is just a number. For example,

$$(1 \quad -2 \quad 4)\begin{pmatrix} 2 \\ 3 \\ 7 \end{pmatrix} = (1)(2) + (-2)(3) + (4)(7) = 24$$

A simple bookkeeping procedure may now be expressed in compact form by using vector notation. Suppose that a stationery order reads "3 rolls of tape @ 27¢, 4 pads of paper @ 29¢, and 12 ball point pens @ 19¢." If we write the amounts ordered as a vector $\mathbf{A} = (3 \quad 4 \quad 12)$ and the prices for each item as a vector

$$\mathbf{P} = \begin{pmatrix} .27 \\ .29 \\ .19 \end{pmatrix}$$

then we see that $\mathbf{AP} = 3(.27) + 4(.29) + 12(.19) = \$4.25$ is the total bill.

Having defined the product of two vectors, we shall use it to define the product of two matrices.

Definition   If $\mathbf{A}$ is an $m \times n$ matrix and $\mathbf{B}$ is an $n \times q$ matrix, then the product $\mathbf{C} = \mathbf{AB}$ is an $m \times q$ matrix with entries c_{ij} defined by the rule: c_{ij} is the product of Row i of $\mathbf{A}$ and Column j of $\mathbf{B}$.

In order for this definition to hold, the rows of $\mathbf{A}$ must have as many components as the columns of $\mathbf{B}$. If $\mathbf{A}$ is $m \times n$, then the number of components in each row of $\mathbf{A}$ is n. Similarly, if $\mathbf{B}$ is $p \times q$, then the number of components in each column of $\mathbf{B}$ is p. Thus, in order to form the product $\mathbf{AB}$, we must have $n = p$. For example, let

$$A = \begin{pmatrix} 2 & 1 & 3 & 4 \\ -1 & 3 & 0 & 2 \\ 1 & -1 & 2 & -2 \end{pmatrix} \quad \text{and} \quad B = \begin{pmatrix} 1 & -1 \\ 2 & 0 \\ 1 & 1 \\ 3 & 5 \end{pmatrix}$$

Here, A is 3 × 4 and B is 4 × 2. Hence, we can form the product AB but *not* the product BA! The resulting matrix AB will have three rows and two columns. In fact

$$AB = \begin{pmatrix} 2 & 1 & 3 & 4 \\ -1 & 3 & 0 & 2 \\ 1 & -1 & 2 & -2 \end{pmatrix}\begin{pmatrix} 1 & -1 \\ 2 & 0 \\ 1 & 1 \\ 3 & 5 \end{pmatrix} = \begin{pmatrix} 19 & 21 \\ 11 & 11 \\ -5 & -9 \end{pmatrix}$$

By the way, the simplest way to perform this multiplication is to start by multiplying Row 1 of A by each column of B until you run out of columns. The resulting products form the first row of AB. Now do it again, using the second row of A to form the second row of AB. Keep going until you run out of rows. You are now finished, and the number of rows and columns will come out straight automatically. However, just as a check, remember if A is $m \times n$ and B is $n \times q$, then AB will be $m \times q$.

Let us see how the product was obtained in this case. We multiplied the first row of A by the second column of B

$$(2 \quad 1 \quad 3 \quad 4)\begin{pmatrix} 1 \\ 2 \\ 1 \\ 3 \end{pmatrix} = 2 \cdot 1 + 1 \cdot 2 + 3 \cdot 1 + 4 \cdot 3 = 19$$

which is then entered as the first row, first column of the product matrix. We next took the first row of A times the second column of B, $2 \cdot (-1) + 1 \cdot 0 + 3 \cdot 1 + 4 \cdot 5 = 21$ which became the second entry in the first row of the product. We are now out of columns in B. Hence, we begin forming products using the second row of A. Row 2 of A times Column 1 of B is $(-1) \cdot 1 + 3 \cdot 2 + 0 \cdot 1 + 2 \cdot 3 = 11$, entered in Row 2, Column 1 of the product. We continue in this manner, exhausting all columns of B for each row of A until all three rows of A have been used. The last product formed is Row 3 times Column 2, $1 \cdot (-1) + (-1) \cdot 0 + 2 \cdot 1 + (-2) \cdot 5 = -9$.

Let us try an application. Referring to the three real estate brokers on page 98, we had a matrix J describing their January sales and a matrix **F** describing their February sales. Suppose that each salesman receives a 10% commission on sales of houses and a 5% commission on sales of lots. If we express the commission rates as a vector

$$\mathbf{P} = \begin{pmatrix} .10 \\ .05 \end{pmatrix}$$

then the product

$$\mathbf{JP} = \begin{pmatrix} 70 & 10 \\ 40 & 3 \\ 0 & 15 \end{pmatrix}\begin{pmatrix} .10 \\ .05 \end{pmatrix} = \begin{pmatrix} 7 + 0.5 \\ 4 + 0.15 \\ 0 + 0.75 \end{pmatrix} = \begin{pmatrix} 7.5 \\ 4.15 \\ 0.75 \end{pmatrix}$$

gives the January commissions for the three salesmen in thousands of dollars. Thus, Mr. Josephs (first row) earned $7,500 in January. Mr. Sheldon (second row) earned $4,150, and Mr. Warren (third row) earned $750. The product **FP** must give the February commissions of the three men. Moreover, it must be true that the sum of the commissions for the two months combined must equal the commission received on the total sales for the two months. That is, $\mathbf{JP} + \mathbf{FP} = (\mathbf{J} + \mathbf{F})\mathbf{P}$. In other words, the example seems to indicate that multiplication of matrices will satisfy the distributive law with respect to matrix addition.

Let us take another example. We are given three tables. Table 1 gives the price per gross for stationery supplies. Table 2 gives the number of gross of each item shipped to each store in certain chains. Table 3 gives the number of chain stores in each of several cities.

Table 1

	Pencils	Pads	Erasers
Price	3.00	4.00	2.00
Shipping	.50	1.00	.50

Table 2

	Barbix Stores	Milban Stores	Newhill Stores	Coldel Stores
Pencils	2	4	1	6
Pads	2	0	1	3
Erasers	2	6	1	0

Table 3

	New York	Chicago	Boston
Barbix	1	2	1
Milban	0	3	2
Newhill	6	1	0
Coldel	2	2	2

Calling the cost matrix **A**, the number shipped per store matrix **B**, and the stores per city matrix **C**, we have **A** is 2×3, **B** is 3×4 and **C** is 4×3. We may form

$$\mathbf{AB} = \begin{pmatrix} 3 & 4 & 2 \\ .5 & 1 & .5 \end{pmatrix} \begin{pmatrix} 2 & 4 & 1 & 6 \\ 2 & 0 & 1 & 3 \\ 2 & 6 & 1 & 0 \end{pmatrix} = \begin{pmatrix} 18 & 24 & 9 & 30 \\ 4 & 5 & 2 & 6 \end{pmatrix}$$

Here we have multiplied cost per item by number of items per store, yielding cost to each store. Thus, for example, each Milban store (Column 2) is billed \$24 for stationery and \$5 for shipping. If we then multiply this by **C**, forming **(AB)C**, we get the total cost billed in each city. That is,

$$\mathbf{(AB)C} = \begin{pmatrix} 18 & 24 & 9 & 30 \\ 4 & 5 & 2 & 6 \end{pmatrix} \begin{pmatrix} 1 & 2 & 1 \\ 0 & 3 & 2 \\ 6 & 1 & 0 \\ 2 & 2 & 2 \end{pmatrix}$$

$$= \begin{pmatrix} 132 & 177 & 124 \\ 28 & 37 & 26 \end{pmatrix}$$

If, on the other hand, we had first formed **BC**, getting the amount shipped to each city, and then formed **A(BC)**, we should also end up with the total cost billed in each city. That is, **(AB)C = A(BC)**. In general, this associative law will hold. That is, **(AB)C = A(BC)** if all the products are defined. Hence, we can drop the parentheses and simply write **ABC**.

Please notice that we are very careful to maintain the order of multiplication. Thus, **(AB)C = A(BC)**, but we cannot write **AB = BA**! There are several reasons for this. First, it is entirely possible that **AB** is defined but **BA** is not. In fact, this is the case in the last example. But consider **B** and **C** in the last example. We could form **BC** and, having a 3×4 multiplying a 4×3, end up with a 3×3 matrix. The product **CB** could also be formed but the result would be 4×4. Thus **CB ≠ BC**. However, suppose we have square matrices. What then? Well, the product of two $(m \times m)$'s will be $m \times m$ no matter which is put first. Let us try

$$E = \begin{pmatrix} 1 & 1 \\ 2 & 1 \end{pmatrix} \quad \text{and} \quad F = \begin{pmatrix} -1 & 2 \\ 0 & 3 \end{pmatrix}$$

Now

$$EF = \begin{pmatrix} -1 & 5 \\ -2 & 7 \end{pmatrix} \quad \text{and} \quad FE = \begin{pmatrix} 3 & 1 \\ 6 & 3 \end{pmatrix}$$

Again, $EF \neq FE$.

You may wonder if it is ever possible that $AB = BA$. In fact, it is possible in certain special cases. Let us look at one. If A is a square matrix, then certainly we may define $A^2 = AA$. Similarly, we may define $A^3 = AAA$, which, thanks to the associative law, is the same as $A(AA) = A(A^2) = (AA)A = A^2A$. In general, if C and B are powers of some matrix A, then $CB = BC$. In other words, $(A^k)(A^m) = (A^m)(A^k)$.

We see that multiplication of a vector and a matrix is simply a special case of matrix multiplication. A variety of bookkeeping operations can be handled this way. For example, if we multiply a matrix A by a vector $U = (1, 1, \ldots, 1)$ with a suitable number of components, the resulting vector UA has as components the column sums of A. Thus, using A from the preceeding example,

$$(1, 1)\begin{pmatrix} 3 & 4 & 2 \\ .5 & 1 & .5 \end{pmatrix} = (3.5, 5, 2.5)$$

we have a vector of total cost including shipping for each item. Multiplying a matrix D by V, a column vector of all ones, will yield for DV a vector of row sums. Thus, in the preceding example, BC is the matrix giving the numbers of pencils, pads and erasers shipped to New York, Chicago and Boston. The vector $(BC)V$ gives the grand total of pencils shipped, pads shipped and erasers shipped.

$$\begin{pmatrix} 2 & 4 & 1 & 6 \\ 2 & 0 & 1 & 3 \\ 2 & 6 & 1 & 0 \end{pmatrix}\begin{pmatrix} 1 & 2 & 1 \\ 0 & 3 & 2 \\ 6 & 1 & 0 \\ 2 & 2 & 2 \end{pmatrix}\begin{pmatrix} 1 \\ 1 \\ 1 \end{pmatrix} = (71, 33, 47)$$

We see that 71 gross of pencils, 33 gross of pads and 47 gross of erasers have been shipped.

Summarizing, we see that matrix addition is commutative and associative; that is

$$A + B = B + A \qquad (1)$$

$$(A + B) + C = A + (B + C) \qquad (2)$$

Matrix multiplication is associative but not commutative

$$(AB)C = A(BC) \qquad (3)$$

$$AB \neq BA \qquad (4)$$

and multiplication is distributive over addition

$$(A + B)C = AC + BC \qquad D(A + B) = DA + DB \qquad (5)$$

Interestingly, a zero matrix used in multiplication works like the number zero. Any matrix multiplied by **Z** gives **Z**(**AZ** = **Z**; **ZA** = **Z**). Of course, in such a statement it may be necessary to have two different meanings for **Z**. Thus, if **A** is 2×3 and **Z** is a 3×4 zero matrix, then **AZ** is a 2×4 zero matrix.

Unlike numbers, if a matrix product **AB** is zero, it is possible that neither **A** nor **B** is zero. For example, suppose

$$A = \begin{pmatrix} 1 & -1 \\ -1 & 1 \end{pmatrix} \quad \text{and} \quad B = \begin{pmatrix} 1 & 1 \\ 1 & 1 \end{pmatrix}$$

Now $AB = \begin{pmatrix} 0 & 0 \\ 0 & 0 \end{pmatrix} = BA$. Here both the products **AB** and **BA** are zero but neither is a zero matrix!

EXERCISES

1. Given $A = \begin{pmatrix} -1 & 0 \\ 1 & 2 \\ 3 & 1 \\ -4 & -1 \end{pmatrix}$, $B = \begin{pmatrix} 2 & 1 \\ -1 & 3 \\ -3 & 0 \\ 5 & 8 \end{pmatrix}$ and $C = \begin{pmatrix} 1 & 2 \\ -3 & 5 \end{pmatrix}$,

   compute whichever of the following are well defined:
   (a) **AB** + **C**
   (b) (**A** + **B**)**C**
   (c) **A** + **BC**
   (d) **AC** + **B**
   (e) (2**A** − 3**B**)**C**
   (f) **C**(**B** − **A**)

2. Given $D = \begin{pmatrix} 0 & 1 \\ -2 & 3 \end{pmatrix}$, $E = \begin{pmatrix} 2 & -1 \\ 1 & -2 \end{pmatrix}$ and $F = \begin{pmatrix} -3 & 2 \\ 1 & 4 \end{pmatrix}$,

(a) verify $(DE)F = D(EF)$;

(b) verify $D(E + F) = DE + DF$;

(c) show that $(D + E)(D + E) \neq D^2 + 2DE + E^2$. What does $(D + E)(D + E)$ equal?

3. Given $A = \begin{pmatrix} 1 & 2 \\ -1 & -2 \end{pmatrix}$ and $B = \begin{pmatrix} 2 & 4 \\ -1 & -2 \end{pmatrix}$, show that $AB = Z$ but $BA \neq Z$.

4. Given $A = \begin{pmatrix} 2 & -3 \\ -2 & 3 \end{pmatrix}$, find a matrix B for which $AB = Z$.

5. Solve for x:

$$(x, 2)\left[\begin{pmatrix} 2 & 3 \\ -5 & 4 \end{pmatrix} - 2\begin{pmatrix} 1 & 2 \\ -3 & -1 \end{pmatrix} \right]\begin{pmatrix} 3 \\ x \end{pmatrix} = 33$$

6. For A, B, C, D, E, F defined in Exercises 1 and 2, compute

(a) $A(D + 3E - 2F)$;

(b) $(A + B)(F + 2C)$.

7. Compute GH and HG where $G = (-1, 2, 4)$ and $H = \begin{pmatrix} 1 \\ 3 \\ 5 \end{pmatrix}$.

8. Let $K = \begin{pmatrix} 1 & 1 \\ 1 & 1 \end{pmatrix}$. Show that $K^2 - 2K = Z$.

9. Table 1 shows the vitamin contents per gram in three diet supplements R, S and T. Table 2 shows the number of grams of the diet supplements in two different mixtures, M_1, M_2, of these supplements. Compute the table which shows the units of the four vitamins in the two mixtures.

Table 1

	R	S	T
Vitamin A	1	0	2
B	11	2	1
C	8	2	3
D	0	5	0

Table 2

	M_1	M_2
R	3	2
S	1	3
T	2	1

10. A new mixture is made up using the ingredients described in Exercise 9 by taking 1/3 of mixture 1 and 2/3 of mixture 2. Letting

$$\mathbf{w} = \begin{pmatrix} 1/3 \\ 2/3 \end{pmatrix}$$

describe the contents of the new mixture as a matrix product involving $\mathbf{w}$.

11. For the store order example in the text, verify that $(\mathbf{AB})\mathbf{C} = \mathbf{A}(\mathbf{BC})$. For the real estate sales example in the text, verify that $\mathbf{JP} + \mathbf{FP} = (\mathbf{J} + \mathbf{F})\mathbf{P}$.

3.3 Identities and Inverses

For matrix addition, we have encountered a zero matrix $\mathbf{Z}$, which plays the role of zero in addition. There also exists a class of matrices $\mathbf{I}$, which play the role of one in multiplication, that is, $\mathbf{AI} = \mathbf{IA} = \mathbf{A}$. Again, we remark that if $\mathbf{A}$ is $m \times n$, then $\mathbf{I}$ will have to be $n \times n$ in the expression $\mathbf{AI}$, and $\mathbf{I}$ will have to be $m \times m$ in the expression $\mathbf{IA}$. The form of $\mathbf{I}$ is particularly simple. It is a square matrix with all zero entries, except along the diagonal that runs from top left to bottom right (called the principal diagonal). Along this diagonal the entries are all one. Thus,

$$\mathbf{I}^{(2 \times 2)} = \begin{pmatrix} 1 & 0 \\ 0 & 1 \end{pmatrix} \qquad \mathbf{I}^{(3 \times 3)} = \begin{pmatrix} 1 & 0 & 0 \\ 0 & 1 & 0 \\ 0 & 0 & 1 \end{pmatrix}$$

and so on.

The question is then, Does there exist an inverse matrix for any matrix $\mathbf{A}$? That is, does there exist a matrix $\mathbf{B}$ such that $\mathbf{BA} = \mathbf{I}$? For example, for

$$\mathbf{A} = \begin{pmatrix} 0 & 0 \\ 1 & 2 \\ 1 & 1 \end{pmatrix} \qquad \mathbf{B} = \begin{pmatrix} 1 & -1 & 2 \\ 0 & 1 & -1 \end{pmatrix}$$

we have

$$\mathbf{BA} = \begin{pmatrix} 1 & -1 & 2 \\ 0 & 1 & -1 \end{pmatrix} \begin{pmatrix} 0 & 0 \\ 1 & 2 \\ 1 & 1 \end{pmatrix} = \begin{pmatrix} 1 & 0 \\ 0 & 1 \end{pmatrix} = \mathbf{I}$$

Thus, we would say $\mathbf{B}$ is a "left inverse" for $\mathbf{A}$. Unfortunately,

$$\mathbf{AB} = \begin{pmatrix} 0 & 0 \\ 1 & 2 \\ 1 & 1 \end{pmatrix} \begin{pmatrix} 1 & -1 & 2 \\ 0 & 1 & -1 \end{pmatrix} = \begin{pmatrix} 0 & 0 & 0 \\ 1 & 1 & 0 \\ 1 & 0 & 1 \end{pmatrix} \neq \mathbf{I}$$

Hence, **B** is not a "right inverse" for **A**.

For $m \times n$ matrices, $m \neq n$, there is no way in which one can construct a single matrix **B**, so that $\mathbf{AB} = \mathbf{I}$ and $\mathbf{BA} = \mathbf{I}$. However, for square matrices the opposite is true. That is, if $\mathbf{AB} = \mathbf{I}$, then $\mathbf{BA} = \mathbf{I}$ and we can refer to **B** as the multiplicative inverse of **A**. We shall designate this matrix $\mathbf{A}^{-1}$ and call it "**A** inverse."

To find $\mathbf{A}^{-1}$, one could proceed directly from the definition. For example, let

$$\mathbf{A} = \begin{pmatrix} 2 & 1 \\ 1 & 1 \end{pmatrix}$$

We seek

$$\mathbf{A}^{-1} = \begin{pmatrix} a & b \\ c & d \end{pmatrix}$$

So that $\mathbf{AA}^{-1} = \mathbf{I}$. Thus,

$$\begin{pmatrix} 2 & 1 \\ 1 & 1 \end{pmatrix} \begin{pmatrix} a & b \\ c & d \end{pmatrix} = \begin{pmatrix} 1 & 0 \\ 0 & 1 \end{pmatrix}$$

This yields

$$2a + c = 1 \qquad 2b + d = 0$$
$$a + c = 0 \qquad b + d = 1$$
$$a = 1, c = -1 \qquad b = -1, d = 2$$

The result is

$$\mathbf{A}^{-1} = \begin{pmatrix} 1 & -1 \\ -1 & 2 \end{pmatrix}$$

It is wise to check this by showing that $\mathbf{A}^{-1}\mathbf{A} = \mathbf{I}$, thus verifying that although we solved for $\mathbf{A}^{-1}$ by seeking a right inverse, the resulting matrix is also the left inverse.

Unfortunately, not all matrices are invertible. For example, if one attempts to solve

$$\begin{pmatrix} 1 & 1 \\ 2 & 2 \end{pmatrix} \begin{pmatrix} a & b \\ c & d \end{pmatrix} = \begin{pmatrix} 1 & 0 \\ 0 & 1 \end{pmatrix}$$

the result is

$$a + c = 1 \qquad b + d = 0$$
$$2a + 2c = 0 \qquad 2b + 2d = 1$$

Both sets of equations are incompatible and hence $\begin{pmatrix} 1 & 1 \\ 2 & 2 \end{pmatrix}^{-1}$ does not exist.

Let us try a 3×3 matrix.

$$\mathbf{A} = \begin{pmatrix} 1 & -1 & 2 \\ 1 & -2 & 3 \\ 3 & -1 & 2 \end{pmatrix} \qquad \mathbf{A}^{-1} = \begin{pmatrix} a & d & g \\ b & e & h \\ c & f & i \end{pmatrix}$$

$$\mathbf{AA}^{-1} = \begin{pmatrix} 1 & -1 & 2 \\ 1 & -2 & 3 \\ 3 & -1 & 2 \end{pmatrix} \begin{pmatrix} a & d & g \\ b & e & h \\ c & f & i \end{pmatrix} = \begin{pmatrix} 1 & 0 & 0 \\ 0 & 1 & 0 \\ 0 & 0 & 1 \end{pmatrix}$$

$a - b + 2c = 1$	$d - e + 2f = 0$	$g - h + 2i = 0$
$a - 2b + 3c = 0$	$d - 2e + 3f = 1$	$g - 2h + 3i = 0$
$3a - b + 2c = 0$	$3d - e + 2f = 0$	$3g - h + 2i = 1$

An inspection of the three sets of equations shows that if we write them in matrix form, the lefthand side is in every case the same. We wish to solve

$$\begin{pmatrix} 1 & -1 & 2 & \vdots & 1 \\ 1 & -2 & 3 & \vdots & 0 \\ 3 & -1 & 2 & \vdots & 0 \end{pmatrix} \quad \begin{pmatrix} 1 & -1 & 2 & \vdots & 0 \\ 1 & -2 & 3 & \vdots & 1 \\ 3 & -1 & 2 & \vdots & 0 \end{pmatrix} \quad \begin{pmatrix} 1 & -1 & 2 & \vdots & 0 \\ 1 & -2 & 3 & \vdots & 0 \\ 3 & -1 & 2 & \vdots & 1 \end{pmatrix}$$

Since the required row operations would be the same in each case, we may as well solve them all at once! Thus we write

$$\begin{pmatrix} 1 & -1 & 2 & \vdots & 1 & 0 & 0 \\ 1 & -2 & 3 & \vdots & 0 & 1 & 0 \\ 3 & -1 & 2 & \vdots & 0 & 0 & 1 \end{pmatrix}$$

Now, the first three columns are $\mathbf{A}$ and the last three columns are $\mathbf{I}$. Let us start solving by complete elimination:

$$(\mathbf{A} \vdots \mathbf{I}) = \begin{pmatrix} 1 & -1 & 2 & \vdots & 1 & 0 & 0 \\ 1 & -2 & 3 & \vdots & 0 & 1 & 0 \\ 3 & -1 & 2 & \vdots & 0 & 0 & 1 \end{pmatrix}$$

$$\sim \begin{pmatrix} 1 & -1 & 2 & \vdots & 1 & 0 & 0 \\ 0 & -1 & 1 & \vdots & -1 & 1 & 0 \\ 0 & 2 & -4 & \vdots & -3 & 0 & 1 \end{pmatrix} \qquad \begin{array}{l} \text{Row 1} \\ \text{Row 2} - \text{Row 1} \\ \text{Row 3} - 3 \times \text{Row 1} \end{array}$$

$$\sim \begin{pmatrix} 1 & 0 & 1 & \vdots & 2 & -1 & 0 \\ 0 & 1 & -1 & \vdots & 1 & -1 & 0 \\ 0 & 0 & -2 & \vdots & -5 & 2 & 1 \end{pmatrix} \qquad \begin{array}{l} \text{Row 1} - \text{Row 2} \\ (-1) \text{ Row 2} \\ \text{Row 3} + 2 \times \text{Row 2} \end{array}$$

$$\sim \begin{pmatrix} 1 & 0 & 0 & \vdots & -1/2 & 0 & 1/2 \\ 0 & 1 & 0 & \vdots & 7/2 & -2 & -1/2 \\ 0 & 0 & 1 & \vdots & 5/2 & -1 & -1/2 \end{pmatrix} \qquad \begin{array}{l} \text{Row 1} + 1/2 \times \text{Row 3} \\ \text{Row 2} - 1/2 \times \text{Row 3} \\ -1/2 \times \text{Row 3} \end{array}$$

Let us interpret. Remember that the last three columns represent the righthand sides of each of the three systems in turn. So we have $a = -1/2$, $b = 7/2$, $c = 5/2$; $d = 0$, $e = -2$, $f = -1$; $g = 1/2$, $h = -1/2$, $i = -1/2$. That is, the row operations that have reduced **A** to **I** have simultaneously reduced **I** to $\mathbf{A}^{-1}$. In other words, our final matrix is $(\mathbf{I}\!:\!\mathbf{A}^{-1})$, so

$$\mathbf{A}^{-1} = \begin{pmatrix} -1/2 & 0 & 1/2 \\ 7/2 & -2 & -1/2 \\ 5/2 & -1 & -1/2 \end{pmatrix} = (1/2)\begin{pmatrix} -1 & 0 & 1 \\ 7 & -4 & -1 \\ 5 & -2 & -1 \end{pmatrix}$$

Again, the student should check this result. Naturally, this same technique would be used for 2×2, 4×4 or any other square matrix.

Suppose one wished to solve the system

$$x - y + 2z = 3$$
$$x - 2y + 3z = 4$$
$$3x - y + 2z = 5$$

Let the matrix of coefficients be

$$\mathbf{A} = \begin{pmatrix} 1 & -1 & 2 \\ 1 & -2 & 3 \\ 3 & -1 & 2 \end{pmatrix}$$

Let

$$\mathbf{X} = \begin{pmatrix} x \\ y \\ z \end{pmatrix}$$

and let

$$\mathbf{B} = \begin{pmatrix} 3 \\ 4 \\ 5 \end{pmatrix}$$

We have the system written as

$$\mathbf{AX} = \mathbf{B}$$

Multiplying both sides of this equation by $\mathbf{A}^{-1}$, we have

$$\mathbf{A}^{-1}\mathbf{AX} = \mathbf{A}^{-1}\mathbf{B}$$
$$\mathbf{IX} = \mathbf{A}^{-1}\mathbf{B}$$
$$\mathbf{X} = \mathbf{A}^{-1}\mathbf{B}$$

Since we just computed $\mathbf{A}^{-1}$, we have, in other words,

$$\begin{pmatrix} x \\ y \\ z \end{pmatrix} = (1/2)\begin{pmatrix} -1 & 0 & 1 \\ 7 & -4 & -1 \\ 5 & -2 & -1 \end{pmatrix}\begin{pmatrix} 3 \\ 4 \\ 5 \end{pmatrix} = (1/2)\begin{pmatrix} 2 \\ 0 \\ 2 \end{pmatrix} = \begin{pmatrix} 1 \\ 0 \\ 1 \end{pmatrix}$$

Thus, $x = 1$, $y = 0$, $z = 1$ solves the system.

Does it pay to solve a system this way? Surely not, since the row operations needed to invert the matrix are more extensive than those needed to solve the system. Of course, if one had reason to need the solution to $AX = B$ for several different B's, then it might pay to do the operations once and compute A^{-1}.

EXERCISES

1. Given $A = \begin{pmatrix} -1 & 2 \\ 1 & 3 \end{pmatrix}$, $B = \begin{pmatrix} -1 & 3 \\ 2 & -4 \end{pmatrix}$, find AB, $(AB)^{-1}$, A^{-1} and B^{-1}. Show that $B^{-1}A^{-1} = (AB)^{-1}$.

2. Show that if A and B are any two invertible matrices, $(AB)^{-1} = B^{-1}A^{-1}$.

3. Use A and B in Exercise 1 to show that $(A + B)^{-1} \neq A^{-1} + B^{-1}$.

4. Given $A = \begin{pmatrix} 1 & -1 \\ 2 & -3 \end{pmatrix}$, $B = \begin{pmatrix} 4 & -1 & 2 \\ 2 & 1 & 3 \end{pmatrix}$ and $C = \begin{pmatrix} 2 & 0 & 1 \\ -1 & 2 & 1 \end{pmatrix}$, find $A^{-1}B + 3C$.

5. (a) Find A^{-1} if

$$A = \begin{pmatrix} 1 & 2 & -3 \\ 2 & 3 & 4 \\ 3 & 2 & 5 \end{pmatrix}$$

   (b) Solve the following system of equations:

$$x + 2y - 3z = 6$$
$$2x + 3y + 4z = 1$$
$$3x + 2y + 5z = 0$$

6. (a) Find A^{-1} if

$$A = \begin{pmatrix} 1 & 2 & -2 \\ 2 & 5 & 1 \\ -5 & -10 & 9 \end{pmatrix}$$

   (b) Solve the following system of equations:

$$x + 2y - 2z = -5$$
$$2x + 5y + z = 12$$
$$-5x - 10y + 9z = 21$$

7. Simplify:

$$\begin{pmatrix} 1 & 3 \\ 0 & -2 \\ 2 & 4 \end{pmatrix} \begin{pmatrix} 13 & 3 \\ 2 & -2 \end{pmatrix}^{-1} - 3 \begin{pmatrix} 2 & -1 \\ 2 & 3 \\ 3 & 0 \end{pmatrix}$$

8. Find a matrix **B** such that **AB** = **I**, where $\mathbf{A} = \begin{pmatrix} 1 & 2 & 1 \\ -1 & 4 & 3 \end{pmatrix}$.

9. (a) Find $\mathbf{A}^{-1}$ if

$$\mathbf{A} = \begin{pmatrix} 1 & -1 & 3 & 2 \\ 2 & -2 & 2 & -1 \\ 3 & 0 & 0 & -2 \\ 4 & 3 & 1 & 1 \end{pmatrix}$$

(b) Find $\mathbf{A}^{-1}$ if

$$\mathbf{A} = \begin{pmatrix} 1 & 2 & -1 & 1 \\ -1 & -3 & 4 & 2 \\ 2 & 2 & 3 & -2 \\ 3 & 2 & 1 & 1 \end{pmatrix}$$

10. Given

$$\mathbf{AB} = \begin{pmatrix} 2 & 1 & -1 & 3 \\ 0 & 2 & 1 & 4 \\ -1 & 2 & 0 & 1 \end{pmatrix}$$

find **B**, if

(a) $\mathbf{A} = \begin{pmatrix} 1 & -1 & 2 \\ 2 & 1 & 0 \\ 0 & 3 & 1 \end{pmatrix}$

(b) $\mathbf{A} = \begin{pmatrix} 1 & -1 & 2 \\ 2 & 2 & 0 \\ 1 & -2 & 4 \end{pmatrix}$

3.4 Input–Output Analysis

One of the simplest economic applications of matrix algebra is input–output analysis. Consider the relationships between two departments in a large company. In particular, take the Tool Shop and the Repair Shop. Now in order for the Tool Shop to turn out work, it requires input from the Repair Shop (to repair imperfect equipment) and also from itself (to make its own tools.) Similarly, the Repair Shop requires some of its own resources and also the output from the Tool Shop in order to function. Let us suppose that for the Repair Shop to generate one man-hour of work it requires an input of 0.1 man-hours of Repair Shop time and 0.3 man-hours of Tool Shop time. Further suppose that for the Tool Department to generate one man-hour of work requires inputs of 0.5 man-hours from Repair and 0.2 man-hours from Tool Shop.

We display this as a matrix

$$\begin{array}{cc} & \text{Repair shop} \quad \text{Tool shop} \\ \begin{array}{c} \text{Repair} \\ \text{shop} \\ \text{Tool} \\ \text{shop} \end{array} & \begin{pmatrix} 0.1 & 0.5 \\ 0.3 & 0.2 \end{pmatrix} \end{array}$$

The first column of this input-output matrix gives the inputs needed for one man-hour of production in the Repair Shop, and the second column gives the inputs needed for a unit of production in the Tool Shop. Finally, let us assume that the size of the staff is such that the weekly output capacities of the Repair and Tool Shops are 800 and 600 man-hours respectively.

In order to generate these outputs, input of $(0.1)(800) + (0.5)(600)$ from the Repair Shop and $(0.3)(800) + (0.2)(600)$ man-hours from the Tool Shop are required. That is, if we call the input-output matrix

$$\mathbf{A} = \begin{pmatrix} 0.1 & 0.5 \\ 0.3 & 0.2 \end{pmatrix}$$

and the output vector

$$\mathbf{X} = \begin{pmatrix} 800 \\ 600 \end{pmatrix}$$

the input requirements are given by the vector

$$\mathbf{Y} = \mathbf{AX}$$

In other words,

$$\mathbf{Y} = \begin{pmatrix} 0.1 & 0.5 \\ 0.3 & 0.2 \end{pmatrix} \begin{pmatrix} 800 \\ 600 \end{pmatrix} = \begin{pmatrix} 380 \\ 360 \end{pmatrix}$$

We see that the Repair Shop has an 800 man-hour capacity, of which 380 are needed just to keep these two shops operating. The remaining 420 are surplus available to other departments which draw upon the Repair Shop. Similarly, the Tool Shop has a 240 man-hour excess capacity. Naturally, a complete input-output analysis of a large company would involve all departments and would require the use of an $n \times n$ matrix, where n would be the number of departments and would be of considerable size. Nevertheless, the analysis would be the same. Whenever a $\mathbf{Y}$ component is less than the corresponding component of the $\mathbf{X}$ vector there would be a surplus which could then be sold to an outside user. Hopefully this is the case for the production line. If a $\mathbf{Y}$ component is greater than the $\mathbf{X}$ component, an outside producer must provide some of the commodity. This situation would be expected in many areas, as very few companies are totally self-sufficient. Finally, where the $\mathbf{X}$ and $\mathbf{Y}$ components are equal, we have a department which produces just enough output for internal consumption. We note in passing that this type of analysis may be applied to entire national economies where the various industries play the roles of the departments. Clearly, this analysis could also be applied to noneconomic systems such as closed ecological environments to determine self-sufficiency.

In all cases, we have $\mathbf{Y} = \mathbf{AX}$, where $\mathbf{A}$ is the input-output matrix, $\mathbf{X}$ is the output capacity, and $\mathbf{Y}$ is the required input. If it turns out that $\mathbf{Y} = \mathbf{X}$, the system is in perfect equilibrium, satisfying its own needs and only its own needs. If not, we may write $\mathbf{X} - \mathbf{Y} = \mathbf{D}$. Since $\mathbf{D}$ is the amount by which the output capacity exceeds the input needs, $\mathbf{D}$ represents the amounts of the various outputs which are available to an outside user. Writing the last equation in the form $\mathbf{Y} = \mathbf{X} - \mathbf{D}$ and substituting into $\mathbf{Y} = \mathbf{AX}$ yields

$$\mathbf{X} - \mathbf{D} = \mathbf{AX}$$

$$\mathbf{X} - \mathbf{AX} = \mathbf{D}$$

$$\mathbf{IX} - \mathbf{AX} = \mathbf{D}$$

$$(\mathbf{I} - \mathbf{A})\mathbf{X} = \mathbf{D}$$

In this last form, we may look at another version of the problem. Suppose that we know the outside consumer demand for each of our products or services. We represent this information as a vector $\mathbf{D}$

and ask how much production capacity we must have in order to meet the demand. That is, we know **D** and wish to find **X**. We solve $(I - A)X = D$ by multiplying both sides of the equation by $(I - A)^{-1}$, giving

$$(I - A)^{-1}(I - A)X = (I - A)^{-1}D$$
$$IX = (I - A)^{-1}D$$
$$X = (I - A)^{-1}D$$

For example, suppose that in the original example, the other departments in the company require an increase to 400 man-hours of Repair Shop time and 500 man-hours of Tool Shop time. Now

$$D = \begin{pmatrix} 400 \\ 500 \end{pmatrix} \qquad A = \begin{pmatrix} 0.1 & 0.5 \\ 0.3 & 0.2 \end{pmatrix}$$

and

$$I - A = \begin{pmatrix} 1 & 0 \\ 0 & 1 \end{pmatrix} - \begin{pmatrix} 0.1 & 0.5 \\ 0.3 & 0.2 \end{pmatrix}$$
$$= \begin{pmatrix} 0.9 & -0.5 \\ -0.3 & 0.8 \end{pmatrix} = (1/10) \begin{pmatrix} 9 & -5 \\ -3 & 8 \end{pmatrix}$$

Computing $(I - A)^{-1}$ yields

$$(I - A)^{-1} = (10/171) \begin{pmatrix} 24 & 15 \\ 9 & 27 \end{pmatrix}$$

and

$$X = (I - A)^{-1}D = (10/171) \begin{pmatrix} 24 & 15 \\ 9 & 27 \end{pmatrix} \begin{pmatrix} 400 \\ 500 \end{pmatrix} = (10/171) \begin{pmatrix} 17100 \\ 17100 \end{pmatrix}$$
$$= \begin{pmatrix} 1000 \\ 1000 \end{pmatrix}$$

Thus, the capacity of both shops must be increased to 1,000 man-hours to meet the corporate demands. Notice that the internal structure is such that an increase in capacity of 200 man-hours in the first shop (from 800 to 1,000) was needed to increase the output surplus by 20 man-hours (from 380 to 400). Such analyses may well determine policy decisions. For example, in this case it might be wiser to purchase the additional repair service from an outside source rather than invest in such a large increase in capacity.

EXERCISES

1. Given the input-output matrix

$$A = \begin{pmatrix} 1/4 & 1/3 \\ 1/2 & 1/4 \end{pmatrix}$$

   (a) If the output capacity is $\begin{pmatrix} 100 \\ 300 \end{pmatrix}$ find the input vector.

   (b) For which components is there an output surplus and how much is it?

   (c) Find the output capacity needed to generate a surplus vector $\begin{pmatrix} 75 \\ 150 \end{pmatrix}$.

2. Follow the directions of Exercise 1 for

$$A = \begin{pmatrix} 0.3 & 0.2 & 0.2 \\ 0.1 & 0.4 & 0.4 \\ 0.1 & 0.1 & 0.6 \end{pmatrix}$$

   if in (a) the output capacity is

$$\begin{pmatrix} 10 \\ 20 \\ 40 \end{pmatrix}$$

   and in (c) the required surplus is

$$\begin{pmatrix} 20 \\ 10 \\ 50 \end{pmatrix}$$

3. Find all vectors **X** for which the system described by

$$A = \begin{pmatrix} 0.2 & 0.8 \\ 0.4 & 0.6 \end{pmatrix}$$

   is in equilibrium. That is, input equals output.

4. Repeat Exercise 3 for

$$A = \begin{pmatrix} 0.1 & 0.3 & 0.6 \\ 0.2 & 0.3 & 0.5 \\ 0.4 & 0.6 & 0 \end{pmatrix}$$

5. For the input-output matrix of Exercise 1, if the inputs generated are given by

$$Y = \begin{pmatrix} 20 \\ 50 \end{pmatrix}$$

find the output capacity.

6. Repeat Exercise 5 for the matrix of Exercise 2 and

$$Y = \begin{pmatrix} 130 \\ 210 \\ 160 \end{pmatrix}$$

7. A study of the Payroll and Accounting offices of a large firm shows that in order for the Payroll office to generate one man-hour of work it requires an input of 0.3 man-hours of time from the Accounting office and 0.2 man-hours from the Payroll office. The Accounting Department requires 0.1 hours of Payroll office time and 0.4 hours of Accounting office time as inputs for one-hour output.
    (a) Display the input-output matrix.
    (b) If the output capacity is 250 man-hours in Accounting and 120 hours in Payroll, find the required inputs. Find the surplus available to other departments.
    (c) Suppose that other departments require a 15-hour increase in time available from these two offices. By how much must the capacity of each office be increased?

8. Reconsider the firm in Exercise 7. Suppose that a secretarial pool is started that requires 0.1 man-hours input from each of the other two departments for each man-hour generated and whose services are required by the Accounting Department only for 0.1 man-hours for each hour generated.
    (a) If the pool has a total output capacity of 80 man-hours, what are now the surplus capacities of the three departments?
    (b) What must the capacity of the secretarial pool be in order that the output surplus from Accounting and Payroll is maintained at previous levels?

PART II

Mathematics of Finance

4

Progressions and Depreciation

4.1 Arithmetic Progressions

What property is shared by the following sequences?

$$1, 3, 5, 7, 9, 11, \ldots$$

$$-1, 2, 5, 8, 11, 14, \ldots$$

$$1, 1\frac{1}{2}, 2, 2\frac{1}{2}, 3, 3\frac{1}{2}, \ldots$$

$$100, 75, 50, 25, 0, -25, \ldots$$

In each case, the difference between successive terms is a constant. If we denote the first term in the sequence by u_1, the second term u_2, and so on, the nth term u_n, then the rule for formation of the terms may be written $u_{n+1} - u_n = d$ where d is called the *common difference*. In the first case, $d = 2$; in the second, $d = 3$; in the third, $d = 1/2$; and in the fourth, $d = -25$. This type of sequence is called an *arithmetic progression*. It is easy to work out the general properties of such a progression. The fundamental formula may be rewritten,

$$u_{n+1} = u_n + d$$

123

If we call the first term a, then

$$u_1 = a$$
$$u_2 = a + d$$
$$u_3 = a + d + d = a + 2d$$
$$u_4 = a + 2d + d = a + 3d$$
$$\vdots$$
$$u_n = a + (n - 1)d$$

In the sequence $-1, 2, 5, 8, \ldots$, we have $a = -1$, $d = 3$, and the nth term is $u_n = -1 + 3(n - 1)$.

To find the sum of an arithmetic progression, write

$$S_n = a + (a + d) + (a + 2d) + \cdots + [a + (n - 1)d]$$
$$S_n = na + d + 2d + 3d + \cdots + (n - 1)d$$
$$S_n = na + [1 + 2 + 3 + \cdots + (n - 1)]d$$

We now must sum $X_n = 1 + 2 + 3 + \cdots + (n - 2) + (n - 1)$. To do so, we shall write X_n twice, first with the terms in increasing order and second with the terms in decreasing order. Thus

$$X_n = \quad 1 \quad + \quad 2 \quad + \quad 3 \quad + \cdots + (n - 2) + (n - 1)$$
$$X_n = (n - 1) + (n - 2) + (n - 3) + \cdots + \quad 2 \quad + \quad 1$$

Add the two equations:

$$2X_n = \underbrace{n + n + \cdots + n}_{(n-1) \text{ times}} = n(n - 1)$$

Thus,

$$X_n = \frac{n(n - 1)}{2}$$

$$S_n = na + \frac{n(n - 1)d}{2}$$

$$= n\left[a + \frac{(n - 1)d}{2}\right]$$

$$= n\left[\frac{2a + (n - 1)d}{2}\right] = n\left[\frac{a + u_n}{2}\right]$$

That is, the sum of the first n terms is the average of the first and last terms multiplied by the number of terms.

Suppose we take the progression 100, 75, 50, 25, . . . ; the tenth term is $u_{10} = 100 + 9(-25) = -125$ and the sum of first ten terms,

$$S_{10} = \frac{10(100 - 125)}{2} = -125$$

EXERCISES

1. Find the fifteenth term of sequence 2, 5, 8, 11, 14, ... Find the sum of the first 45 terms.

2. The third term of an arithmetic progression is 3 and the fifth term is -2. Find the fourth term.

3. The nth term of an arithmetic progression is a and the $(n + 2)$nd term is b. Find the $(n + 1)$st term.

4. The nth term of a progression is $u_n = 2 + 5(n - 1)$. Find the sum of the first ten terms.

5. The fourth term of an arithmetic progression is -1 and the ninth term is 14. Find the first term and the sum of the first thirty terms.

6. The fourth term of an arithmetic progression is 13 and the seventh term is 22. Find the first term, the common difference, and the sum of the first sixty terms.

7. Find the sum of all the even numbers from 22 to 200, both inclusive.

8. The first term of an arithmetic progression is 6 and the sum of the first twelve terms is 20. Find the common difference.

9. The sum of the first seven terms of an arithmetic progression is 15, and the sum of the first eleven terms is 10. Find the first four terms of the progression.

4.2 Straight-Line and Sum-of-Integers Depreciation

The most common business application of the arithmetic progression is in the depreciation of assets. Suppose that a company or individual invests in a piece of equipment, building, or other tangible asset that does not have an unlimited life expectancy. Let the value of that item when new be V. Now it is not reasonable to carry that item on your books at value V year after year, only to have it drop to value zero in the year in which it finally wears out. Instead, you normally write off the value of the item by some systematic plan over the item's expected lifetime. There are several ways in which this can be done. The simplest is to assume that the item depreciates by a fixed amount each year. That is, assume that the value of the item plotted versus time will have a constant downward slope. In other words, it is a straight line with y-intercept V. The slope must be chosen so that the value of the item will be 0 at the time at which the item is expected to wear out. In this straight-line depreciation scheme, the slope is very simple to calculate.

Suppose we wish to depreciate the item over a period of n years. Then we know that it must lose V/n in each year. Accordingly, letting A_n be the value after the nth year, we have

$$A_0 = V,\ A_1 = V - V/n,\ A_2 = V - 2V/n,\ \ldots,\ A_n = V - nV/n = 0$$

In general, the value after the kth year will be $A_k = V - kV/n$. Now this is clearly an arithmetic progression with $a = V$ and $d = -V/n$, the only difference being that we have started numbering with zero instead of 1, so that the formula gives the proper value after the kth year.

For example, suppose that a taxi driver values his cab at \$5,000 when new. Suppose also that he anticipates a usable life of 4 years, at which time he will junk the car. If he decides to take a straight-line depreciation of the value of the cab, then he will write off \$5,000/4 = \$1,250 in each year. Thus the value of the cab after each of the successive years will be \$3,750, \$2,500, \$1,250, \$0.

Of course, it is not necessary that an asset be depreciated down to zero. It is perfectly reasonable for the cab driver to assume that there will be some salvage value to his car at the time that he disposes of it. Similarly, a company may buy a building which is valued with the land it sits on at \$200,000. If the company assumes that the land is worth \$20,000 and that the building has a usable life of 30 years, then it will depreciate only \$180,000 (=\$200,000 − 20,000) over the 30-year period. Thus, the write-off will be \$180,000/30 = \$6,000 per year. In this case, after k years the value of the asset will be \$200,000 − $3,000k = A_k$.

In general, suppose that the value of the asset when new is A and the amount to be depreciated is V. Then the value of the asset after k years is

$$A_k = A - kV/n$$

Although straight-line depreciation is a perfectly acceptable accounting procedure, it does fail to reflect reality in many cases. For example, it is widely recognized that some things depreciate far more when they are new than in later years. The best-known example is a new car. For such assets it is usual to assume a different depreciation scheme. The most common ones are "fixed percent," "double declining balance," and "sum-of-integers." In this section we shall discuss the sum-of-integers method. The other two shall be considered in Section 4.4.

For the sum-of-integers technique, we assume that the usable life of the asset is n years. Now let the sum of the integers from one to n be denoted by N. That is, $N = 1 + 2 + 3 + \cdots + n$. We know from the last section that $1 + 2 + 3 + \cdots + (n - 1) = n(n - 1)/2$. Adding n to both sides of this equation yields $1 + 2 + 3 + \cdots + n = n(n + 1)/2$. Thus $N = n(n + 1)/2$. The depreciation in the first year is taken to be n/N times the amount to be depreciated, V. In the second year, the depreciation is taken to be $(n - 1)/N$ times V, and so on. In the last year the depreciation is just $1/N$ times V. It is easy to see that the sum of these values will be exactly V and that each year the amount of depreciation is less than the preceding year.

As an example, consider the taxi cab worth $5,000 with a usable life of 4 years. Here, $n = 4$, $N = 4(4 + 1)/2 = 10$. The fractional depreciation in successive years is 4/10, 3/10, 2/10, and 1/10. That is, in the first year the cab depreciates $2,000 [$=(4/10)($5,000)]$. In the second year the depreciation is $1,500, in the third year $1,000, and in the last year $500. In tabular form, we have Table 1.

Table 1

End of Year Numbered	Amount Depreciated	Value of Asset
0	0	$5,000
1	$2,000	3,000
2	1,500	1,500
3	1,000	500
4	500	0

Notice that the total of the Amount Depreciated column is equal to the initial value of the asset. A logical question to ask at this time is: Is it possible to have a simple formula for the value of the asset after k years? In other words, can we find the value of the asset at any time without the entire table? Notice that in the example, the amounts depreciated in each year form an arithmetic progression with $a = $2,000$ and $d = -500$. In general, the amounts depreciated in any year form an arithmetic progression with $a = nV/N$ and $d = -V/N$.

Therefore, the total depreciated by the end of the kth year may be easily computed as the sum of the first k terms of an arithmetic progression. The value of the asset at that time is simply the initial value minus the total depreciation.

For example, let us reconsider the building and land worth $200,000 together. To make the numbers come out easily, let us suppose that the land is worth $14,000, so that we wish to depreciate $186,000 over 30 years. In the sum-of-integers technique, $n = 30$, $N = (30)(31)/2 = 465$, and $V = \$186,000$. We now reduce the initial value of the asset, $A = \$200,000$, by appropriate fractions of V in successive years. To be precise, the annual depreciations will be $(30)(186,000)/465$, $(29)(186,000)/465$, . . . , $(1)(186,000)/465$. Of course, the values are most easily found by noticing that $186,000/465 = 400$. Then, in the first year, the depreciation is $(30)(400) = 12,000$; in each succeeding year, this amount will drop by 400. Thus, the first few rows of the depreciation table would be as shown in Table 2.

End of Year Numbered	Amount Depreciated	Value of Asset
0	0	$200,000
1	$12,000	188,000
2	11,600	176,400
3	11,200	165,200
4	10,800	154,400

Suppose that we wished to know the value of the asset after 20 years. We notice that the amounts depreciated form an arithmetic progression with $a = 12,000$ and $d = -400$. In general, these would be $a = nV/N$ and $d = -V/N$. Now the twentieth term of this progression is $u_{20} = a + 19d = 12,000 + 19(-400) = 4,400$. Thus, the depreciation in the twentieth year is $4,400, and the total depreciation up to and including the twentieth year is the sum of the first twenty terms of the progression, which as we know is simply $20(12,000 + 4,400)/2 = 164,000$. Therefore, the value of the asset remaining at that time is $200,000 - 164,000 = \$36,000$.

It is interesting to note the rate at which the sum-of-integers method shows depreciation. In the last example, twenty years represented 2/3 of the life of the building. The write-off in that time would be $164,000/186,000 = 82/93$ or about 8/9 of the total value. Similarly, in the taxi cab example, after three years (3/4 of the life of the cab), the write-off amounts to $4,500/5,000 = 9/10$ of the value.

EXERCISES

1. A machine worth $10,000 new and having a scrap value of $500 is to be depreciated over a ten-year life. Write depreciation tables for this write-off by both the straight-line and sum-of-integers methods.

2. A house and land together are worth $45,000, of which the land is worth $3,000. If the house has an expected remaining life of 20 years, what will be value of the asset after eight years under straight-line depreciation? How much under sum-of-integers depreciation? Compare the two methods after ten years and twelve years.

3. Suppose that the machine in Exercise 1 could just as well be assumed to have a twelve-year life and no scrap value. Which valuation would give the greater depreciation for the first five years under straight-line depreciation? Under sum-of-integers depreciation?

4. A company invests in a machine worth $20,000 new which has a scrap value of $2,000 and a usable life of twelve years. Two years later it purchases another machine having a value of $16,000 and no scrap value after eight years. Find the total value of the two machines on the books five years later if straight-line depreciation is used.

5. Repeat Exercise 4 with sum-of-integer depreciation.

6. A $50,000 house and land is depreciated over 25 years by the straight-line method. If after ten years the asset is valued at $24,000, find the value of the land. (Only the value of the house is depreciated; the value of the land is assumed to remain constant.)

7. Repeat Exercise 6 for sum-of-integers depreciation if the value after ten years is $29,500.

4.3 The Geometric Progression

In this section, we shall consider another kind of progression formed by adherence to a simple rule. Consider, for example, the sequence of numbers

$$3, 3/2, 3/4, 3/8, 3/16, \ldots,$$

where each number is 1/2 of the preceding one. Another possibility might be

$$1, -3, 9, -27, 91, -243, \ldots,$$

where each number is −3 times the preceding number. Both these sequences are said to be *geometric progressions*.

The characterization of a geometric progression, $u_1, u_2, u_3, \ldots$, is that

$$u_{k+1} = ru_k$$

Here r is called the *common ratio* since $u_2/u_1 = r$; $u_3/u_2 = r$; $u_4/u_3 = r$; . . . . If $u_0 = a$, then $u_1 = ar$; $u_2 = ar^2$; $u_3 = ar^3$, ... In the first sequence given above, $a = 3$ and $r = 1/2$. The general term $u_k = 3(\frac{1}{2})^k$. Notice that the numbering starts with zero so that the third term is $u_2 = 3(\frac{1}{2})^2 = 3/4$; the sixth term is $u_5 = 3(\frac{1}{2})^5$; and so forth. In the second sequence we have $a = 1$ and $r = -3$. The term $u_k = (-3)^k$.

Suppose you wished to sum the first k terms of a geometric progression. We shall designate this by S_k. For the first example given, we have

$$S_1 = 3$$
$$S_2 = 3 + 3/2 = 9/2$$
$$S_3 = 3 + 3/2 + 3/4 = 21/4$$
$$\vdots$$

In general, notice that the first k terms start with a and end with ar^{k-1}. It would be nice to have a simple formula for this expression. To find it we write

$$S_k = a + ar + ar^2 + \cdots + ar^{k-1}$$
$$rS_k = \phantom{a + {}} ar + ar^2 + \cdots + ar^{k-1} + ar^k$$
$$S_k - rS_k = a - ar^k$$
$$(1 - r)S_k = a(1 - r^k)$$
$$S_k = \frac{a(1 - r^k)}{1 - r}$$

Let us use this formula to compute S_3 given above.

$$S_3 = \frac{3(1 - (1/2)^3)}{1 - 1/2} = \frac{3(7/8)}{1/2} = 21/4$$

It is interesting to follow this a few steps further. Let us compute the values of S_k for increasing values of k. We shall write the results

$$S_1 = 3,\ S_2 = 4\tfrac{1}{2},\ S_3 = 5\tfrac{1}{4},\ S_4 = 5\tfrac{5}{8},\ S_5 = 5\tfrac{13}{16},\ S_6 = 5\tfrac{29}{32},\ \ldots.$$

It certainly appears that as k gets very large, S_k is approaching the value 6. This is because as k becomes very large, $(1/2)^k$ becomes very small. Thus, when $k = 10$, $(1/2)^{10}$ is about 0.001. Similarly, $(1/2)^{20}$ is about 0.000001. We describe this behavior by saying that $(1/2)^k$ approaches zero as k approaches infinity.

In general, if r is between -1 and $+1$, then for large values of k, r^k will approach zero. Hence, we have

$$S_k = \frac{a(1 - r^k)}{1 - r}$$

approaches

$$S = \frac{a}{1 - r}$$

as k approaches infinity. We shall call

$$S = \frac{a}{1 - r}$$

the sum of the *infinite geometric progression*. This is the value which S_k approaches for large values of k, but remember that the formula is nonsense unless $-1 < r < 1$.

In the preceding example, we have

$$S = \frac{3}{1 - 1/2} = 6$$

Some further examples follow.

Example 1 3, -12, 48 are the first three terms of a geometric progression. Find r, find the sixth term, and find the sum of the first six terms.

We have $a = 3$, $ar = -12$; thus $r = -4$. The sixth term is $ar^5 = 3(-4)^5 = -3{,}072$. The sum of the first six terms is

$$S_6 = \frac{a(1 - r^6)}{1 - r} = \frac{3(1 - (-4)^6)}{1 - (-4)} = -2{,}457$$

If we compute $S = a/(1 - r) = 3/5$ as the sum of the infinite progression, we see that the result is nonsense.

Example 2 In a geometric progression, the first term is 3 and the fourth term is 8/9. Find the second and third terms and the sum of the infinite progression.

We have $a = 3$, $ar^3 = 8/9$. Thus,

$$r^3 = 8/27 \qquad r = 2/3$$

Hence the progression goes

$$3, \ 2, \ 4/3, \ 8/9, \ \ldots$$

and

$$S = \frac{3}{1 - 2/3} = 9$$

EXERCISES

1. Sum the first 10 terms of the progression 4, 10, 25, ... , .

2. Find the eighth term of the progression 4, 4/9, 4/81, . . . , . Find the sum of the first 15 terms and the infinite sum.

3. The first two terms of a geometric progression are 6 and -2. Find the common ratio, the twelfth term, the sum of the first twenty terms, and the sum of the infinite progression.

4. The numbers 4, x, 16 are in geometric progression. Find the possible values of x.

5. The numbers x, 8, x^2 are in geometric progression. Find the possible values of x.

6. The first term of a geometric progression is 162 and the fifth is 32. Find the possible values of r and the corresponding sums of infinite progression.

7. The first term of an infinite geometric progression is 6 and the sum is 7. Find r and the first four terms.

8. The first five terms of a geometric progression sum to 5. The infinite sum is 7; find the first four terms.

9. The numbers 4, x, y, z, 324 form a geometric progression. Find x, y, z.

10. The general term of a sequence is $u_k = 2 + 4(k - 1) + 3^{k-1}$. Find the eighteenth term and the sum of the first eighteen terms.

11. Repeat exercise 10 for the sequence whose kth term is $u_k = 5 - 6k - 7(1/3)^{k+1}$.

4.4 Fixed-Percentage Depreciation

The last common form of depreciation is the fixed-percentage method. In this technique, it is assumed that an item depreciates in each year by a certain percentage of its value at the beginning of the year. For example, suppose that we have an item valued when new at $1,000 and that it loses 20% of its value each year. In the first year it loses $200, leaving a new value of $800. In its second year it loses 20% of $800 or $160, leaving a new value of $640. Continuing in this manner, we generate Table 3 for the first five years.

Table 3

End of Year Numbered	Amount Depreciated	Value of Asset
0	0	$1,000.00
1	$200.00	800.00
2	160.00	640.00
3	128.00	512.00
4	102.40	409.60
5	81.92	327.68

The depreciation is rapid at first but slows down quickly after the first few years. In order to find a general formula for this process, let us introduce some notation. Let the initial value of the asset be A, the fraction depreciated in each year be d, and let $r = 1 - d$. Now in the first year the amount of depreciation is Ad, and the new value is $A - Ad = A(1 - d) = Ar$. In the second year, the amount depreciated is Ard, and the new value becomes $Ar - Ard = Ar(1 - d) = Ar^2$. Continuing, it is easy to see that at the end of the kth year the value of the asset will be Ar^k. That is, the value of the asset forms a geometric progression.

In order to determine the value of d, we proceed as follows. If the initial value is A and the salvage value is S after k years, then we must have $S = Ar^k$. In other words, $r^k = S/A$ and $r = \sqrt[k]{S/A}$.

As an example, suppose that a new car costs $2,430 and will be worth $480 in four years. Here we have $A = \$2,430$ and $S = \$480$.

Since $k = 4$, $r = \sqrt[4]{480/2{,}430} = \sqrt[4]{16/81} = 2/3$. Since $r = 2/3$, $d = 1/3$. That is, the depreciation rate is $33\frac{1}{3}\%$. Now unless you are very lucky, the kth root of S/A will not work out to be a very simple number. In fact, generally you will need logarithms or perhaps a good desk calculator to find the value of r by this method, which would seem to limit its practical application. However, an alternative method for determining r is used in general accounting practice.

This method is called *double-declining balance*. In this method, you ignore salvage value in the calculation of r. The depreciation rate is taken to be twice the straight-line rate. For example, if depreciation is taken over a 20-year period, the straight-line depreciation would be 5% per year and hence the double-declining balance rate would be $d = 10\%$ applied to the balance remaining at the end of each year.

Let us make that more precise with a specific case. Suppose that we have an asset worth \$100,000 which will depreciate to \$20,000 over 20 years. The total write-off will be \$80,000, which in straight line amounts to \$4,000 per year. For the fixed-percentage method, we use 10% per year but we apply it to the balance remaining at the end of the year. Table 4 shows how the depreciation table starts.

Table 4

End of Year Numbered	Amount Depreciated	Value of Asset
0	0	\$100,000.00
1	\$10,000.00	90,000.00
2	9,000.00	81,000.00
3	8,100.00	72,900.00
	$\vdots$	
15	2,287.68	20,589.11

In the sixteenth year the value of the asset would fall below the salvage value of \$20,000. This is not allowed for tax purposes. Therefore, it is usual at some point—any convenient time—to switch over to straight-line depreciation. In this case let us assume that it is done in year 16. Therefore, we must depreciate the remaining excess over salvage value, \$589.11, over the last five years at a rate of \$117.82 per year.

Consider one last example. An asset valued at \$1,000 and having a \$50 salvage value is to be depreciated over five years. If the double-declining balance method is used, then $d = 0.4$. At the end of 5 years, the asset is valued at $1{,}000(0.6)^5 = \$77.76$, which is more than the salvage value. Therefore, the decision is made to switch to straight line after three years. Table 5 shows the entire depreciation table.

Table 5

End of Year Numbered	Amount Depreciated	Value of Asset
0	0	$1,000.00
1	$400.00	600.00
2	240.00	360.00
3	144.00	216.00
4	83.00	133.00
5	83.00	50.00

EXERCISES

1. Repeat Exercise 1, Section 4.2, using double-declining balance depreciation.

2. For the house and land described in Exercise 2, Section 4.2, find the first five years of a double-declining balance depreciation table.

3. An asset will depreciate from $32,000 new to a scrap value of $1,000 over a five-year period. Find the fixed percent depreciation rate that will yield the exact scrap value. Construct the depreciation table and compare it to the straight-line, sum-of-integers, and double-declining balance depreciation tables for the same data.

4. Repeat Exercise 4, Section 4.2, for double-declining balance depreciation.

5. An asset worth $21,000 with a scrap value of $1,000 is to be depreciated over ten years. Find the depreciation using the double-declining balance method. We see that the scrap value works out to be too high by this method. Therefore, assume that after the fourth year a changeover to straight-line is made to depreciate the remaining balance and end at the proper value. Construct the complete depreciation table using this changeover.

6. Repeat Exercise 5 for an asset depreciated over five years with the changeover made after two years. Compare this table with the simple straight-line table and sum-of-integers table.

7. For used equipment, the Income Tax Bureau allows only the so-called 150% declining balance method rather than double-declining balance. In the 150% method, the write-off is $1\frac{1}{2}$ times the straight-line percentage, but otherwise it is the same as double declining. Repeat Exercise 1 using the 150% method.

8. Repeat Exercise 3 for an asset which depreciates from $81,000 to $1,000 over four years.

9. Repeat Exercise 8 assuming the scrap value is $16,000.

5

Interest and Dated Values

5.1 Simple Interest

Interest is the premium paid by a borrower to a lender for the use of the lender's money. The best-known example of interest is that paid to the depositor by a savings bank. Most bank depositors do not think of themselves as lending money to the bank, but that is in fact what they are doing. The amount of interest to be paid is usually expressed in percentage. That is, the interest rate is the number of dollars to be paid on a $100 loan. Unless some further information is given, the interest percentage is the one-year interest. When we say that a bank pays 5% interest, we mean that it pays $5 for every $100 left on deposit for one full year.

Remember that the symbol % really means 1/100. Thus, 5% written as a fraction is $5/100 = 1/20$, or, written as a decimal, $5\% = 0.05$. We shall first consider simple interest. Under simple interest, if you deposit P dollars for one year at interest rate r, the amount of interest will be Pr. The total value of the deposit at the end of one year will then be

$$S = P + Pr = P(1 + r)$$

For example, $300 deposited in a bank paying 6% interest for one year will amount to

$$S = 300(1 + 6\%)$$
$$= 300(1.06) = \$318$$

Under the simple interest assumption, if the money is on deposit for some time t (measured in years), then the rate of interest is rt. For example, money on deposit for six months (that is, 1/2 year) at rate 6% will earn 3% (that is, 1/2 times 6%) interest.

Example 1   Mr. Jones invests $500 at simple interest 7% for two and one-half years. How much money does he have at the end of that time?

The interest earned is $rt = (7\%)(2.5) = 17.5\%$ of $500, which is $87.50. Therefore, the amount of the investment at the end is $587.50.

In general, the amount will be

$$S = P + Prt$$
$$S = P(1 + rt)$$

where
$$P = \text{Sum invested}$$
$$r = \text{Annual interest rate}$$
$$t = \text{Time in years}$$

Example 2   Mr. Smith paid $9,800 for a note which calls for a payment of $10,000 three months from today. What simple interest did he earn?

The relationship is

$$S = P(1 + rt)$$

and we know

$$S = \$10,000$$
$$P = 9,800$$
$$t = 1/4 \text{ (3 months is 1/4 of a year)}$$

Therefore

$$\$10,000 = 9,800 \left(1 + \frac{1}{4}r\right)$$

$$\frac{100}{98} = 1 + \frac{1}{4}r$$

$$\frac{1}{49} = \frac{1}{4}r$$

$$r = \frac{4}{49}$$

It is usual to express rates as percentage; and unless other instructions are given, we shall always work to the nearest 1/100 of a percent. So,

$$\frac{4}{49} = 0.0816 = 8.16\%$$

to the nearest hundredth of a percent.

Example 3   Mr. Brown wishes to earn 9% per year on his money. How much should he pay for a note which will be worth $1,000 in six months?

Here we know S, r, and t and wish to find P. So we write

$$\$1,000 = P\left(1 + \frac{1}{2} \cdot 9\%\right) = P(1.045)$$

Therefore

$$P = \$1,000/1.045 = \$956.94$$

We have seen three typical business situations. In Example 1, the rate of interest is given. This is the situation for most people, whose only investments are in savings banks or similar institutions. Examples 2 and 3 are typical of many commercial investments. In both cases, the possibility of purchasing a note payable at some future date is being contemplated. In Example 2, the potential purchaser is given a current price and is faced with the problem of determining the yield if he buys. In Example 3, the potential buyer has decided how much return he thinks is fair compensation for his risk in the investment, and he must calculate his offering price. It is precisely by such considerations that investors establish asked and bid prices in a securities market. Naturally, many financial transactions are far more complicated than the three given here. We shall study many of them in the succeeding sections.

EXERCISES

Assume simple interest throughout.

1. Find the total to which the given deposits will grow in the given time.
   (a) $400 at 6% for 1 year.
   (b) $500 at 8% for 6 months.
   (c) $600 at 5% for 27 months.
   (d) $1,000 at 4% for 8 months.

2. How much must be deposited to accumulate to the given amount at the given rate?
   (a) $1,200 after one year at 10%.
   (b) $800 after six months at 6%.
   (c) $900 after eighteen months at 5%.
   (d) $1,000 after twenty months at 9%.

3. If $1,000 left on deposit accumulated to $1,200, what was the annual interest rate if the money was on deposit for:
   (a) 1 year
   (b) 18 months
   (c) 14 months

4. How long must $1,000 be left on deposit to accumulate to $1,500, if the interest is:
   (a) 5%
   (b) 10%
   (c) $7\frac{1}{2}\%$
   (d) $2\frac{1}{4}\%$

5. United States treasury bills are sold at a discount. If a bill due to mature in three months for $10,000 was sold for $9,850, what interest rate would it earn?

6. A bank offers a loan for one year with interest deducted in advance. If on a $100 loan, 10% is deducted in advance, what is the true interest rate? What should be deducted in advance so as to have the true rate be 10% interest?

7. Harry lends Sheldon $50. Sheldon promises to pay back $60 in one month. What interest rate is Sheldon paying?

8. A bank pays 6% per year interest but offers to give you a $20 prize upon deposit of $1,000 to be left for one year. What interest rate are you really getting?

5.2 Compound Interest and Discount

In most investment situations, you have the possibility of reinvesting interest earned at the same rate of return as soon as it is paid. In such a case, the interest itself begins to earn interest. In such a case, you have compound interest. For example, suppose that a bank pays 5% but that interest is credited every quarter. That is, every three months, or four times each year, the bank pays $rt = (5\%)(1/4) = 1\frac{1}{4}\%$ interest. If $100 is left on deposit, after three months, the account contains $100 + \$1.25 = \$101.25$. After the next three months, the account contains $(\$101.25)(1 + 1\frac{1}{4}\%) = (\$101.25)(1.0125) = \$102.51$. After the next three months, the account contains $(\$102.51)(1.0125) = \$103.79$. At the end of the year, the account contains $(\$103.79)(1.0125) = \$105.09$. In other words, the compounding of interest has caused a total yield of $5.09 on $100, or the equivalent of 5.09% simple interest.

Let us introduce some notation. An interest rate stated as j_m will mean the annual rate is as given, and m is the number of times the interest is compounded in each year. For example, $j_6 = 8\%$ means 8% annual interest compounded six times per year. In other words, every two months an interest of $8\%/6 = 1\frac{1}{3}\%$ is paid. This rate, j_m/m, will always be denoted by i. The interval at which it is paid is called an *interest period*. Thus, $j_{12} = 9\%$ means $i = 3/4\%$ paid every month. Again, $j_4 = 5\%$ means interest $i = 1\frac{1}{4}\%$ paid every three months (or quarterly).

Let us now see what a principal P invested at j_m will amount to after n interest periods. Letting $i = j_m/m$, we proceed as follows. After the first interest period, the interest Pi added to the principal P yields $Pi + P = P(1 + i)$. After the second interest period, the interest is $P(1 + i)i$. Added to the new principal $P(1 + i)$, it yields $P(1 + i)i + P(1 + i) = P(1 + i)(1 + i) = P(1 + i)^2$. After the third interest period, the interest is $P(1 + i)^2 i$, which added to the new principal $P(1 + i)^2$, yields $P(1 + i)^2 i + P(1 + i)^2 = P(1 + i)^3$. Continuing in this manner, after n interest periods, the principal P will reach the amount A given by

$$A = P(1 + i)^n$$

or, since

$$i = j_m/m$$

$$A = P(1 + j_m/m)^n$$

For one full year, the amount will be

$$A = P(1 + j_m/m)^m$$

so that the interest is

$$A - P = P(1 + j_m/m)^m - P = P\left[\left(1 + \frac{j_m}{m}\right)^m - 1\right]$$

Therefore, j_m is equivalent to the simple interest rate

$$r = \left(1 + \frac{j_m}{m}\right)^m - 1$$

This rate is called the *effective rate of interest*.

The figure $(1 + i)^n$ is called the *accumulation factor*. Although theoretically it could be computed by hand, the labor of doing so becomes prohibitive. Therefore, some mechanical means is strongly suggested. Table A-1 in the appendix to this book gives the values of $(1 + i)^n$ for a fair range of n values and for most simple values of i.

By use of Table A-1, we can easily answer many questions.

Example 1 Mr. Barry deposits $200 in a bank paying interest $j_4 = 5\%$. How much money will he have in three years?

Since we have $j_4 = 5\%$, $i = 1\frac{1}{4}\%$ and each interest period is three months (four interest periods per year). Therefore, the money will be on deposit for $3 \times 4 = 12$ interest periods and

$$A = \$200\left(1 + 1\frac{1}{4}\%\right)^{12} = \$200(1.160755) = \$232.15$$

Example 2 Mr. Michaels expects to need $3,000 in four and one-half years. He can invest his money at $j_{12} = 7\%$. How much should he invest?

Interest is compounded 12 times per year; therefore 4 $\frac{1}{2}$ years is 54 interest periods and $i = 7/12\%$. Thus, $\$3,000 = P(1 + i)^{54}$.

Looking in Table A-1 for $i = 7/12\%$ and $n = 54$, we see

$$(1 + i)^{54} = 1.369006$$

and

$$P = (3,000)/(1.369006)$$

Now, in order to save division, in Table A-2 we have values of $(1 + i)^{-n}$, called the *discount factor*. Therefore, we could resolve Example 2 as follows:

$$\$3,000 = P(1 + i)^{54}$$

Multiplying both sides of the equation by $(1 + i)^{-54}$ yields

$$P = 3,000(1 + i)^{-54}$$

We now look up $(1 + i)^{-54}$ in Table A-2, for $i = 7/12\%$, yielding

$$P = \$3,000(0.730457) = \$2,191.37$$

Notice that in Example 2, we have a case where we wish to know what should be invested at present to accumulate to a given amount at some later time. This is known as *discounting the amount* and, hence, the term *discount factor*.

It is possible to have problems in which the pertinent information is not contained in the tables in this book. Some techniques for handling such difficulties are discussed in chapter 7. We shall consider one common case here—when the number of interest periods is larger than the largest tabulated value. For example, suppose \$1,000 is left on deposit in an account at $j_4 = 5\%$ for 30 years. The amount accumulated $A = \$1,000(1 + i)^{120}$, where $i = 1\frac{1}{4}\%$. For $1\frac{1}{4}\%$, Table A-1 only goes up to $n = 100$. Therefore, we write $(1 + i)^{120} = (1 + i)^{100}$ $(1 + i)^{20}$. Thus, $A = \$1,000(3.463404)(1.282037) = \$4,440.21$. Naturally, this technique can also be used in discounting.

EXERCISES

1. Mr. Howards deposits \$2,000 in an account paying $j_4 = 6\%$. How much will it grow to in six years?

2. Mr. Johnson deposited a certain sum of money five years ago at $j_{12} = 8\%$. Today it amounts to \$6,000. How much did he deposit?

3. How much will accumulate on the following principals:
   (a) \$300 at $j_{12} = 6\%$ for 22 months
   (b) \$400 at $j_4 = 7\%$ for 27 months
   (c) \$500 at $j_2 = 8\%$ for 30 months

4. How much must be deposited to accumulate:
   (a) \$1,000 at $j_6 = 4\%$ in 14 months
   (b) \$2,000 at $j_{12} = 5\%$ in $3\frac{1}{2}$ years
   (c) \$100 at $j_1 = 6\frac{1}{2}\%$ in 20 years

5. Mr. Josephs deposits $100 in an account at $j_4 = 5\%$ for his newborn son. Thirty-five years later the son withdraws the money. How much does he get?

6. Mrs. Lawrence left a small inheritance to her grandson, which was invested at $j_4 = 4\%$ for forty years. Today it amounts to $7,000. How much was the inheritance?

7. Mrs. Roberts invested $200 at $j_4 = 7\%$ three years ago. One and one-half years ago, she added $300 more. How much does she have now?

8. Mr. Harrison deposited $500 in a bank paying $j_1 = 4\%$. After four years, the bank raised its interest rate to $j_4 = 5\%$. How much was in the account two years later?

9. Mrs. Gold deposited $1,000 in an account paying $j_2 = 3\frac{1}{2}\%$. After seven years, she withdrew $400. How much was in the the account six and one-half years later?

10. Mr. Wooley invested $600 in a note paying $j_{12} = 18\%$. After five years and seven months, the issuer of the note went bankrupt and the note become worthless. How much did Mr. Wooley lose?

5.3 Dated Values

It should be apparent at this stage that identical sums of money payable at different times have different time values. That is, $100 in hand is worth more than $100 to be received in the future. If an investment yielding 8% effective is available, then $100 payable today is worth the same amount as $108 due one year from today. How then do you compare sums of money payable at different times? The answer is that you pick some common date, and find the value of all sums of interest at that date. Of course, in order to do this, it is necessary to know what interest rates are available. The interest rates may vary from investor to investor, depending usually upon the amount of risk that one is willing to assume. Let us take a simple case.

Example 1 You have a chance to buy a note which calls for two payments each of $100. The first is due in one year and the second in two years. If money is worth 7% effective, how much should you pay for this note?

Basically, you are purchasing two $100 payments. The first is due in one year; therefore, you should be willing to pay for it the amount P_1 that will accumulate to $100 in one year at 7%. That is,

$$\$100 = P_1(1 + 7\%)$$
$$P_1 = 100(1 + 7\%)^{-1}$$
$$P_1 = 100(0.934579) = \$93.46$$

The second $100 is due in two years. You should therefore be willing to pay for it the amount P_2 that will accumulate to $100 in two years at 7%. That is,

$$\$100 = P_2(1 + 7\%)^2$$
$$P_2 = \$100(1 + 7\%)^{-2}$$
$$P_2 = \$100 (0.873439) = \$87.34$$

The total value of the investment is $P_1 + P_2 = \$93.46 + 87.34 = \$180.80$.

Actually, we see in this example that the value A of the investment was

$$A = \$100(1 + 7\%)^{-1} + 100(1 + 7\%)^{-2}$$

Let us look at a systematic way of handling problems like this. We draw a "time line" on which we display the amounts involved and the date at which they are due (see figure 1).

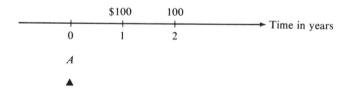

Figure 1

Figure 1 shows the last example. The amount A is shown below the line and the payments that should equal A in value are shown above the line. Time is measured in interest periods, which in this case are years. The $\triangle$ indicates a *focal date* and we compute the values of all amounts at that date. In this diagram 0 is the focal date. All amounts coming after the focal date must be discounted to find their values at that date; all amounts prior to the focal date must have interest accumulated to that date to find their true values. Of course, an amount at the focal date is worth its face value. Thus, in this example, the amount below the line is A at the focal date. The two amounts above the line are worth $\$100(1+7\%)^{-1}$ and $\$100(1+7\%)^{-2}$ when discounted to the focal date. Since the amounts must be equal,

$$A = 100(1+7\%)^{-1} + 100(1+7\%)^{-2}$$

which we solved earlier. Let us look at two more examples.

Example 2   Mr. Hill has \$700 in a bank account paying $j_4 = 6\%$. In six months he intends to withdraw \$300 and two years later he will close the account. How much will he withdraw at that time?

The time diagram is shown in figure 2.

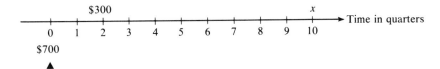

Figure 2

Again we have chosen 0 as the focal date. The equation corresponding to this diagram is

$$700 = 300(1+i)^{-2} + x(1+i)^{-10}$$

where $i = j_4/4 = 1\frac{1}{2}\%$.

Since we wish to solve for x, we write this as

$$x(1+i)^{-10} = 700 - 300(1+i)^{-2}$$

Multiplying by $(1+i)^{10}$ yields

$$x = 700(1+i)^{10} - 300(1+i)^{8}$$

Looking now in Table A-1,

$$x = 700(1.160541) - 300(1.126493) = \$474.43$$

Notice that had we drawn the same time diagram but chosen 10 as the focal date we would have had figure 3. Since the \$700 and \$300 amounts come before the focal date, they must be accumulated up to that date, yielding

$$700(1 + i)^{10} = 300(1 + i)^8 + x$$

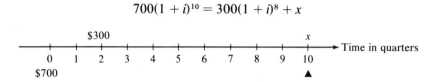

Figure 3

Two remarks are in order here. First, this is the same equation we used earlier, but solving it requires one less step because the focal date has been well-chosen. Second, we see that the $300 due at time 2 has been accumulated from 2 to 10 by multiplying by the accumulation factor $(1 + i)^8$ ($8 = 10 - 2$). That is, the accumulation or discount factor depends on the time from the focal date, not on the choice of numbering. The following example illustrates this principle.

Example 3 Mr. Arthurs deposited $600 two years ago in a bank account paying $j_{12} = 5\%$. Eight months ago he withdrew $400, today he withdrew $100, in three months he will deposit an unknown amount, and in one year he will close the account, withdrawing $500 at that time. What must the unknown deposit be?

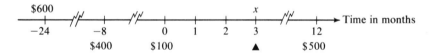

Figure 4

Using 0 as the present, the time diagram is shown in figure 4. Deposits are above the line and withdrawals below. Using 3 as the focal date, we have the equation

$$\underbrace{\$600(1 + i)^{27} + x}_{\text{Values of deposits}} = \underbrace{400(1 + i)^{11} + 100(1 + i)^3 + 500(1 + i)^{-9}}_{\text{Values of withdrawals}}$$

where $i = 5/12\%$
Solving,

$$x = 400(1 + i)^{11} + 100(1 + i)^3 + 500(1 + i)^{-9} - 600(1 + i)^{27}$$

$$x = 400(1.046800) + 100(1.012552) + 500(0.963269)$$
$$- 600(1.118811)$$
$$= \$330.32$$

It is interesting to see what Mr. Arthurs' pass book actually looked like. At the beginning he deposited $600. After 16 interest periods, this had accumulated to $600(1 + i)^{16} = \$641.27$. At that point he withdrew $400, leaving $241.27. This amount accumulated interest for eight interest periods to $241.27(1 + i)^8 = \$249.43$. He then withdrew $100, leaving $149.43. This accumulated interest for three months to $149.43(1 + i)^3 = 151.31$, to which was added 330.32, for a total of $481.63. Finally, this amount accumulates for nine additional months to $481.63(1 + i)^9 = \$500.00$. Although instructive, this long way to do the problem is most inefficient and unnecessary. Simply drawing a time diagram and comparing all amounts at a common focal date incorporates all the information and produces the necessary result.

EXERCISES

1. A contract is available calling for a payment of $1,000 due in 27 months and a payment of $3,000 due in 5 years. If money is worth $j_4 = 8\%$, what is the value of the contract today?

2. A contract at $j_2 = 7\%$ is selling for $5,000 today. It calls for two equal payments, the first due in one year and the second two years later. How much are the payments?

3. Find the cash value of the following set of payments if $j_2 = 6\%$: $200 due 2 years ago, $100 due 3 years 6 months from now, $300 due 4 years from now.

4. Set up and solve an equation to find the value of x at date 3 equivalent to the six payments in figure 5.

Figure 5

5. Write an equation of equivalence only for figure 6, using the focal date indicated. Solve the equation for x if $i = 3\%$ and if $i = 1\frac{1}{2}\%$.

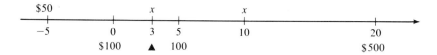

Figure 6

6. I have $1,000 in the bank today at interest $j_4 = 5\%$. I intend to withdraw $200 in 6 months and $400 in one year. I will then empty the account two years from today. How much will I withdraw at that time?

7. A bank account shows deposits of $200 and $500 made 6 months and 9 months ago, respectively, and a $100 withdrawal made 3 months ago. How much is in the account today if interest is $j_4 = 5\%$?

8. A is obligated to pay B $1,000 today and $1,306 3 years from today. A will settle the obligations by making 2 equal payments, the first one year from today and the second 4 years from today. How much should each of these payments be if money is worth $j_2 = 6\%$?

9. A owes B $2,000 due today, $1,000 due 3 years from today, and $1,000 due 5 years from today. At $j_4 = 6\%$ the entire obligation is to be repaid by 2 equal payments: one 2 years from today and the other 4 years from today. How much should each of these payments be?

10. Mr. Shaw owes $6,000 to Mr. Wang due today. Mr. Shaw offers to pay $3,200 next month and $3,000 one year later. If money is worth $j_{12} = 8\%$, should Mr. Wang accept the offer?

5.4 Simple Annuities

A common investment problem involves a sequence of regular payments made at fixed intervals. Suppose that you begin making regular deposits at the end of each quarter into a savings account. Specifically, let the deposits be for $100 and the interest be $j_4 = 5\%$. We then have figure 7.

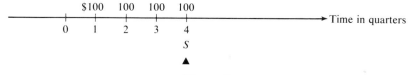

Figure 7

The amount S accumulated at the end of the year is

$$S = 100 + 100(1 + i) + 100(1 + i)^2 + 100(1 + i)^3$$

where $i = 1\frac{1}{4}\%$. Letting $1 + i = t$, we have

$$S = 100 + 100t + 100t^2 + 100t^3$$

$$= 100\,\frac{1 - t^4}{1 - t}$$

since the right-hand side is a geometric progression. Substituting for t its equivalent $(1 + i)$ yields

$$S = 100\,\frac{(1 + i)^4 - 1}{i}$$

Using Table A-1, $S = \$100 \left[\dfrac{1.050945 - 1}{0.0125} \right] = \$407.56$

Notice that by closing the sum before looking in the table, we had to look up only one value instead of three. However, such problems arise so frequently that special tables have been made up for them.

In general, suppose that a contract calls for n payments of amount R dollars, each made at the end of the interest period. Suppose that the interest per interest period is i. Now, the diagram looks like figure 8.

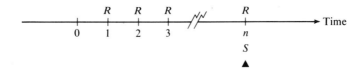

Figure 8

At time n, the total accumulated

$$S = R + R(1 + i) + R(1 + i)^2 + \cdots + R(1 + i)^{n-1}$$

The sum of this geometric progression is:

$$S = R\,\frac{(1 + i)^n - 1}{i}$$

The symbol

$$s_{\overline{n}|\,i} = \frac{(1 + i)^n - 1}{i}$$

read "s angle n at i" is defined as above. We shall refer to this sequence of regular payments at periodic intervals as an *annuity*. The total accumulation at the time the last payment is made is

$$S = R s_{\overline{n}|\,i}$$

where $\qquad R =$ Amount of each payment

$\qquad\qquad n =$ Number of payments

$\qquad\qquad i =$ Interest per interest period

Remember that each payment is assumed to be made at the end of an interest period and that S is the total accumulated at the time that the last payment is made. Let us look at some examples.

Example 1 A man invests $1,000 each month in a fund paying $j_{12} = 9\%$. How much accumulates in three years?

The time diagram is as shown in figure 9. Now, by inspection

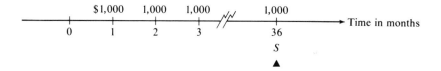

Figure 9

$$S = 1000 s_{\overline{36}|\,i}$$

where $\qquad\qquad i = 3/4\%$

Table A-3 gives values of $s_{\overline{n}|\,i}$. Looking it up, $s_{\overline{36}|\,3/4\%} = 41.152716$, so

$$S = \$1,000(41.152716) = \$4,1152.72$$

Observe that the sum of the deposits is $36,000 (36 payments of $1,000 each), so that the accumulated interest amounts to $5152.72, which looks reasonable.

Example 2 Mr. Howards will need $5,000 in eight years in order to pay off a note due at that time. In order to accumulate the money, he makes regular annual deposits in an account paying 6% effective. How much must each deposit be?

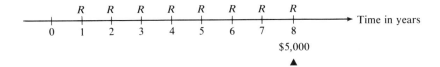

Figure 10

The appropriate time diagram is shown in figure 10. In this case R is unknown, but we still proceed as previously,

$$5,000 = Rs_{\overline{8}|i}$$

where $i = 6\%$. Solving for R

$$R = 5,000/s_{\overline{8}|6\%}$$

We could now look up $s_{\overline{8}|6\%}$ and divide, but for convenience, we have also tabulated $1/s_{\overline{n}|i}$ in Table A-5. Thus, we write

$$R = 5,000(1/s_{\overline{8}|6\%}) = 5,000(0.101036)$$
$$= \$505.18$$

Again, observe that the eight deposits total \$4,041.44 and the remaining \$958.56 is accumulated interest. This also does not seem unreasonable. You should get into the habit of making simple commonsense checks such as these to see if your answer is in the right ball park. If, for example, the sum of the payments you calculated happened to exceed the total amount, you would realize that there must be a mistake.

Let us now consider another type of problem associated with annuities. Suppose that a contract calls for regular payments of amount R at the end of each interest period for n periods. Suppose further that you wish to purchase this contract. How much should you pay for it?

We know that if allowed to accumulate, the n payments would amount to $S = Rs_{\overline{n}|i}$ at the time the last payment is made. The present value of these payments is the value of the amount S discounted n interest periods. Calling the present value A, we have

$$A = S(1 + i)^{-n}$$

Since

$$S = Rs_{\overline{n}|i}$$

$$A = Rs_{\overline{n}|i}(1 + i)^{-n}$$

$$A = R\left[\frac{(1 + i)^n - 1}{i}\right](1 + i)^{-n}$$

$$A = R\left[\frac{1 - (1 + i)^{-n}}{i}\right]$$

We shall define the symbol

$$a_{\overline{n}|i} = \frac{1 - (1 + i)^{-n}}{i}$$

and write

$$A = Ra_{\overline{n}|i}$$

Notice that A was obtained from S by discounting n periods. Since S is the value of the set of payments at time n, A must be the value at time 0, that is, one interest period before the first payment is made. Diagrammatically,

Figure 11

We have tabulated $a_{\overline{n}|i}$ in Table A-4. As you must realize, $1/a_{\overline{n}|i}$ will also come up in problems, but we do not provide a table for this quantity, because it is easy to prove that

$$1/a_{\overline{n}|i} = 1/s_{\overline{n}|i} + i$$

and hence we can simply adjust the values in Table A-5 to cover this case.

Let us look at an example.

Example 3 Mr. Wilson buys a $200 suit from Sam the Tailor. He agrees to pay off the suit by monthly payments for one year at $j_{12} = 6\%$. How much should the payments be?

Figure 12 shows the time line.

Figure 12

Thus $200 is the present value of the set of 12 payments, and we have

$$200 = Ra_{\overline{12}|\,i} \qquad \text{where } i = 1/2\%$$

Therefore

$$R = 200 \left(\frac{1}{a_{\overline{12}|\,i}} \right)$$

Using the relationship given above,

$$R = 200 \left(\frac{1}{s_{\overline{12}|\,i}} + i \right)$$

Looking now in Table A-5

$$R = 200(0.081066 + 0.005) = \$17.21$$

Note: $i = 1/2\% = (0.5)(0.01) = 0.005$

Thus, Mr. Wilson will make 12 payments of $17.21, which will total $206.55. The $200 is the cost of the suit and the $6.55 is interest.

Example 4 We shall look at one of the most common commercial transactions. As a result of the suit sale in Example 3, Mr. Wilson has a suit. Sam the Tailor has a contract calling for 12 monthly payments of $17.21. Now, Sam the Tailor is not in the finance business, so he sells the contract to the EZ Finance Company, which does not care what interest Sam is charging. It wishes to earn $j_{12} = 12\%$ on its money. How much should the EZ Finance Company pay for the contract?

Here we have the situation diagrammed in Figure 13.

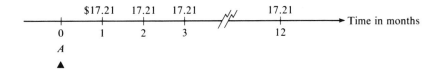

Figure 13

$$A = 17.21 a_{\overline{12}|i} \quad \text{where } i = 1\%$$

Thus $A = 17.21(11.255077) = \$193.70$

The result is that the EZ Finance Company purchases the contract from Sam the Tailor for $193.70. Therefore, Sam receives only $193.70 for a $200 suit, but is relieved of the problems of carrying a time payment customer; he has his money immediately. Mr. Wilson feels that he is paying a most reasonable 6% interest and has his $200 suit. The EZ Finance Company is earning 12% interest but is assuming all the financial risk entailed in a possible default.

EXERCISES

1. Mrs. Allbright will deposit $500 each quarter starting three months from today at $j_4 = 6\%$ in order to send her son to college. If he is going to college six years from now, how much money will be available for him?

2. The day his daughter started college, Mr. Washington decided that starting the next month he would deposit a fixed amount each month in a fund paying $j_{12} = 7\%$ in order to accumulate $30,000 to send her through medical school. Assuming that she will enter medical school in four years, how much must Mr. Washington's deposits be?

3. Mr. Cooperman bought a car from Honest John for $200 per month for 2 years. If Honest John works on a return of $j_{12} = 18\%$, how much was the car worth?

4. Dr. Brown bought an $8,000 car for $1,000 down and 36 monthly payments at $j_{12} = 9\%$. How much must the payments be?

5. The auto dealer from whom Dr. Brown bought his car (see Exercise 4) sold the payment contract to a finance company that

makes $j_{12} = 15\%$ on its money. For how much was the contract sold?

6. Ms. Gillespie borrowed $1,000 to take a vacation. She agreed to pay it back with regular quarterly payments for 1½ years at $j_4 = 8\%$. How much were the payments? If the holder of the contract sold it immediately to a firm that makes only $j_4 = 7\%$, how much was the contract sold for?

7. A sinking fund in which money accumulates interest at $j_4 = 8\%$ is designed to prepare for the extinction of a debt of $10,000 due at the end of 15 years. Find the quarterly payment that must be made into the sinking fund.

8. I lent my brother $1,000 at $j_{12} = 6\%$. He will pay it back by 24 monthly payments starting in one month. How much will each payment be?

9. I deposit $100 each quarter in an account paying $j_4 = 7\%$. How much will accumulate in 6 years?

10. I deposit $100 each quarter in an account paying $j_4 = 8\%$. How much will accumulate in 4 years?

11. I borrowed $1,000 from the bank at $j_{12} = 6\%$. I will repay it by 24 monthly payments starting one month from today. How much will each payment be?

12. Stuart is obligated to pay Watson $258.63 today and $1,000 due 5 years from today. They agree that Stuart may settle the obligation by making 60 equal monthly payments, the first to be made one month from today. Find the monthly payment if settlement is made on the basis that money is worth $j_{12} = 6\%$.

13. A piece of property can be purchased by paying $3,000 down, followed by quarterly payments of $500 each for the next 10 years. Find the equivalent cash value of the property if money is worth $j_4 = 7\%$.

14. Mr. Debt borrowed $1,000 last year and $1,117 today at $j_{12} = 8\%$. Both debts are to be retired by making 15 regular monthly payments, the first due one month from today. What is the monthly payment?

15. Mr. Jones was to pay $1,000 at the end of each year for 6 years. Deviating from this schedule, he pays $2,000 at the end of 2 years and $3,000 at the end of 5 years. What single payment at the end of 6 years will close the transaction if $j_1 = 6\%$?

16. Mr. Jones owes Mr. Brown $1,000 due today and $569.96 due 6 years from today. Jones will settle these obligations by making 72 equal monthly payments, the first to be made one month from today. How much should the monthly payment be if money is worth $j_{12} = 6\%$?

17. Find the dollar amount of each of 2 equal payments after 1 and 2 years which will be equivalent to a 4-year annuity of $100 quarterly with the first $100 due after 1 quarter at $j_4 = 6\%$.

5.5 Amortization

Let us look at some problems involving annuities.

Example 1   Ms. Smith buys a $3,000 car for $500 down and monthly payments for three years at $j_{12} = 8\%$. She misses the first three payments and is threatened with repossession unless she pays in full immediately. How much must she pay?

We have not yet computed the amount of the payments, but it is not necessary. In fact, it is clear that Ms. Smith owes $2,500 plus accrued interest for three months. That is

$$\text{Debt} = 2,500(1 + i)^3$$

where $i = 2/3\%$.

Thus Ms. Smith owes $2,500(1.020134) = \$2,550.33$. Suppose that we had computed Ms. Smith's payments by

$$2,500 = Ra_{\overline{36}|i}$$
$$R = 2,500\left(\frac{1}{a_{\overline{36}|i}}\right)$$
$$R = 2,500(0.024670 + 0.006667)$$
$$= \$78.34$$

Further, suppose that, in fact, that is the information we were given. Thus,

Example 2   Ms. Smith buys a car at $j_{12} = 8\%$ by paying $500 and $78.34 per month for three years. She pays the $500 and then misses the first three payments. The creditor forecloses and demands the total debt. How much must she pay?

Diagrammatically the outstanding debt looks like figure 14.

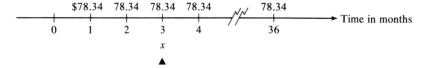

Figure 14

We may evaluate x as the value of the first 3 payments (which form an annuity with last payment at the focal date) plus the value of the last 33 payments (which form an annuity with first payment one interest period after the focal date.) Therefore,

$$x = 78.34s_{\overline{3}|i} + 78.34a_{\overline{33}|i} = 78.34(s_{\overline{3}|i} + a_{\overline{3}|i})$$

where $i = 2/3\%$. Using Tables A-3 and A-4, we arrive at $x = \$2550.25$. Here we see 8¢ worth of round-off error, but actually the answer should be identical to that given earlier.

Notice the difference between Example 2 and Example 3.

Example 3 Ms. Smith makes her down payment and the first three payments on her car and then wishes to pay off the balance of her debt (or refinance it). How much does she owe?

Clearly all that she owes is the remaining 33 payments, commencing in one month, hence

$$\text{Debt} = 78.34a_{\overline{33}|i} = \$2313.71$$

Let us look a little more closely at the last question. In fact, let us look at a larger question. When we make annuity payments, what are they really made up of? We know that part of each payment is interest and part is principal. Actually the portion of the payment which is interest is the interest owed on the outstanding principal for one interest period. The balance is principal repaid. The amount of principal repaid is called the *amortization*. Thus, in the last case, the first payment contains the interest on \$2,500 for one interest period. That is, 2/3% of \$2,500 or \$16.67. The rest of the \$78.34 (\$61.67) is principal. Since \$61.67 principal has been paid, the outstanding principal becomes \$2,500 − 61.67 = \$2,438.33. In the next payment, the interest portion is only 2/3% of \$2,438.33 or \$16.26. This relationship is displayed in an amortization table. The first few lines of the amortization table for Example 3 are as shown in Table 1.

Table 1

Payment Number	Amount of Payment	Interest	Principal Repaid	Principal Outstanding
0	——	——	——	$2500.00
1	$78.34	$16.67	$61.67	2438.33
2	78.34	16.26	62.08	2376.25
3	78.34	15.84	62.50	2313.75

We see that the outstanding principal after three payments is $2,313.75. The 4¢ difference is again due to round-off error.

Let us look at a complete amortization table. Take a very simple case, $1,000 to be repaid in five annual payments at $j_1 = 8\%$. The usual computations yield payments of $250.46.

Table 2

Payment Number	Amount of Payment	Interest	Principal Repaid	Principal Outstanding
0	——	——	——	$1000.00
1	$250.46	$80.00	$170.46	829.54
2	250.46	66.36	184.10	645.44
3	250.46	51.64	198.82	446.62
4	250.46	35.73	214.73	231.89
5	250.44*	18.55	231.89	0
Totals	1252.28	252.28	1000.00	

*Last payment reduced by 2¢ to adjust for round-off error.

Notice that the last payment is determined by adding the interest due on the principal outstanding to the principal outstanding. By doing this, we are assured that any over- or under-payment caused by round-off error is adjusted. Also notice that the total payments should equal the sum of the interest paid and the principal repaid. Of course, the principal repaid must total to the initial principal owed. In this case, the payments total $1,252.28, of which $1,000 is principal and $252.28 is interest.

Let us look at another example in which the payments are chosen for convenience.

Example 4 Joe lends Charlie $400 at $j_{12} = 6\%$. Charlie agrees to repay the loan by $100 payments each month for as long as needed. The amortization table looks like Table 3 ($i = 1/2\%$ each month).

Table 3

Payment Number	Amount of Payment	Interest	Principal Repaid	Principal Outstanding
0	— —	— —	— —	$400.00
1	$100.00	$2.00	$98.00	302.00
2	100.00	1.51	98.49	203.51
3	100.00	1.02	98.98	104.53
4	100.00	.52	99.48	5.05
5	5.08	.03	5.05	0
Totals	$405.08	$5.08	$400.00	

This last method is used very commonly. That is, the payment size is chosen for convenience, and the last payment is a partial payment considerably different from the preceding ones. If the number of payments in the annuity is small, the number of payments and the size of the final partial payment may be determined by writing an amortization table like Table 3. However, it is possible to compute this information directly. Let us look at another example.

Example 5   A debt of $2,000 is to be paid off by $100 monthly payments at $j_{12} = 7\%$ for as long as is necessary. Find the number of full payments and the final partial payment.

Assume that you are lucky enough that the $100 is exactly the right payment. Then there must be an n for which

$$2{,}000 = 100a_{\overline{n}|i} \qquad \text{where } i = 7/12\%$$

Therefore, we seek n so that

$$a_{\overline{n}|i} = 20 \qquad \text{for } i = 7/12\%$$

Looking in Table A-4, we see that

$$a_{\overline{21}|i} = 19.710714$$
$$a_{\overline{22}|i} = 20.590602$$

Thus, 21 payments of $100 will fall short of the necessary amount and 22 payments will be too large. Therefore, we must need the full 21 payments plus a partial payment for the 22nd.

Therefore, our time diagram looks like figure 15.

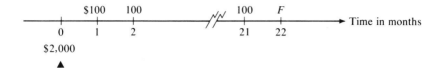

Figure 15

The equation for this diagram is

$$2,000 = 100a_{\overline{21}|\,i} + F(1 + i)^{-22}$$
$$2,000 = 1,971.07 + F(1 + i)^{-22}$$
$$F(1 + i)^{-22} = 28.93$$
$$F = (28.93)(1 + i)^{22}$$
$$F = (28.93)(1.136508) = \$32.88$$

The same type of problem may be encountered where the goal is to accumulate a given sum by payments of given size. The technique for handling this kind of annuity is sketched out in Exercises 11 through 13.

EXERCISES

1. Mr. Smith buys a stereo system worth $600 for $100 down and equal monthly installments for one year at $j_{12} = 7\%$. After missing the first two payments, he decides to refinance the purchase. What is his outstanding debt? What will his new payments be if he refinances at $j_{12} = 8\%$ over eighteen months?

2. Mr. Cox buys a motor boat valued at $10,000, to be purchased by quarterly payments at $j_4 = 8\%$ for five years. What is his outstanding principal after making the first three payments?

3. A building valued at $200,000 is purchased by five annual payments at $j_1 = 5\%$. Write the complete amortization table for this contract.

4. A house is to be paid for by quarterly payments at $j_4 = 7\%$ for ten years. If the house is worth $40,000, what is the outstanding principal after nine years? Write the balance of the amortization table.

5. Mr. Grimes has two outstanding debts. The first, for $10,000, is being paid off quarterly at $j_4 = 6\%$. The second, for $5,000,

is being paid off semiannually at $j_2 = 9\%$. Both contracts run for 10 years. After seven years, Mr. Grimes decides to refinance, so he takes a loan to pay off both notes and agrees to pay monthly for four years at $j_{12} = 8\%$ for this loan. What are the new payments?

6. Mr. Quad owes Ms. Quin $350 which he will pay off with $100 monthly payments at $j_{12} = 5\%$. Write an amortization table for the transaction.

7. The cash value of a motorcycle is $1,200. "Easy Rider," the purchaser, makes monthly payments of $60 for as long as necessary, the first payment being made one month from today. If $j_{12} = 6\%$, find the number of full payments and the final partial payment.

8. A debt of $10,000 with interest at $j_4 = 5\%$ is to be paid by quarterly payments of $200 each. Find the number of full payments and the final partial payment, to be made three months after the last full payment.

9. Mr. Downy deposited $100 every quarter for 10 years. He then began withdrawing $100 every quarter, the first withdrawal being made three months after the last deposit. If interest is paid at 5% compounded quarterly, how many full withdrawals can he make?

10. Mr. Booth borrows $1,000 at $j_2 = 6\%$. The loan will be amortized by semiannual payments of $50 for as long as necessary. Find the number of full payments and the final partial payment.

11. Ms. Grand wishes to accumulate $10,000 by making $500 quarterly deposits in a bank paying $j_4 = 5\%$. Find the number of the payment on which her accumulation first exceeds $10,000.

12. The answer to Exercise 11 is 18. Set up a time diagram for Exercise 11 assuming that 17 full payments are made and that the 18th payment, F, is some unknown final partial payment. Write an equation for F, letting time 17 be the focal date. Solve for F.

13. Suppose Ms. Grand will make her payments annually at $j_1 = 5\%$. Find this accumulation one year later even if no more payments are made. Is a final partial payment needed? If so, how much? If not, why not?

14. Adams can make quarterly deposits of $100 in a fund paying interest at $j_4 = 4\%$. How many full deposits and what final partial payment will it take to accumulate $2,000?

15. A company will make monthly deposits of $300 each into a savings fund earning interest at $j_{12} = 5\%$. How many full deposits of $300 and what final partial deposit will it take to accumulate exactly $18,000?

16. I wish to accumulate $2,000 by making regular quarterly $100 deposits in an account paying $j_4 = 4\%$. How many full payments and what final partial payment will be needed?

5.6 Sinking Funds

The problem of full and final partial payment to accumulate a predetermined amount is most frequently encountered when an organization sets up a *sinking fund*. A sinking fund is a fund into which regular deposits are made to accumulate some amount needed at a given future time. These funds may be needed to retire (i.e., pay off) an outstanding debt or to purchase a piece of equipment or property or for any other business expense.

Example 1 A homeowners' association wants to accumulate $6,000 to replace the community handball court. It is estimated that the construction will be needed in four years. The members are assessed annually for a sinking fund earning $j_1 = 8\%$. How much must the assessment be?

Clearly, we have a simple annuity accumulation problem.

$$\$6,000 = Rs_{\overline{4}|i} \quad \text{where } i = 8\%$$

Therefore,

$$R = \$6,000(1/s_{\overline{4}|i}) = \$1,331.53$$

The growth of the sinking fund may be displayed in a sinking fund table, such as Table 4, similar to an amortization table.

Table 4

Payment Number	Amount Deposited	Interest Accumulated	Total Accumulation
1	$1331.53	——	$1331.53
2	1331.53	106.52	2769.58
3	1331.53	221.57	4322.68
4	1331.51	345.81	6000.00
Totals	5326.10	673.90	——

Notice that the Interest Accumulated column gives the interest earned on the total accumulated up to that point. The total accumulated is increased at each payment time by adding to the previous total the amount deposited and the interest earned. This is exactly what is recorded in a Savings Bank Passbook. Notice also that the last payment is 2¢ smaller than the others, since that is all that is needed to make the $6,000. Finally, notice that the total of the deposits and the interest earned must equal the final total accumulation.

Frequently an organization sets up a sinking fund because it has borrowed money on an agreement calling for it to pay only the interest on the loan each interest period and to repay the principal in a lump sum at the end. In such a case, so as not to be hit with the entire debt in the final year, the company sets aside something each year in a sinking fund.

Example 2 The town of Upton borrows $100,000 to repair its streets and agrees to pay 5% interest every year for 20 years and then repay the $100,000. To accumulate the $100,000, the town makes regular annual deposits in a bank paying $j_1 = 4\%$. How much is the town's annual expense for this loan?

To accumulate $100,000 in twenty years at $j_1 = 4\%$, we have $100,000 = Rs_{\overline{20}|i}$ where $i = 4\%$. Solving, $R = \$3,358.20$. Thus, the town deposits $3,358.20 in a sinking fund. In addition, it pays $5,000 each year in interest. Thus, its total annual expense is $8,358.20.

Let us say that again. If a town (or company) pays interest on a loan and in addition puts deposits in a sinking fund to clear the loan, then its periodic expense is the sum of the two payments. For comparison, suppose that the town had agreed to amortize the $100,000 at $j_1 = 5\%$. That is,

Figure 16

$$100,000 = Ra_{\overline{20}|i} \qquad \text{where } i = 5\%$$
$$R = \$8.024.30$$

Here the town's expense would be less because to amortize is really the same as to pay off the interest and set up a sinking fund at the same interest rate—in this case, 5%. However, this option is not usually available. That is, under normal circumstances, the rate of interest that a company can earn on a sinking fund is less than the rate that must be paid out. In our example, the town must pay 5% interest, but its sinking fund can only earn 4% in interest.

Looked at another way, you should be willing to pay a somewhat higher rate of interest to get a loan that can be amortized. In the last example, if the town could arrange for a $100,000 loan to be amortized at 5½%, it would have about the same annual expense

$$R = 100,000(1/a_{\overline{20}|\,i}) = \$8,367.10$$

EXERCISES

1. Mr. Cortland will need $700 to have his house painted next spring. He sets up a sinking fund in which he will make six monthly payments in a bank paying $j_{12} = 6\%$. Find the size of payments and make a sinking fund table for Mr. Cortland.

2. Ms. White has the same problem as Mr. Cortland (Exercise 1) but she can only afford to make $80 per month payments. Set up a sinking fund table for Ms. White and use it to find the number of full payments and the final partial payment needed.

3. Mr. Schwartz has agreed to buy a newborn race horse when it reaches two years of age. If the agreed-upon price is $15,000, what quarterly deposits must be made at $j_4 = 7\%$ to accumulate the needed funds? Write a sinking fund table for this situation.

4. Mr. Peters borrows $10,000 to open a bakery. The conditions of the loan are such that Mr. Peters will make interest payments at $j_4 = 16\%$ every three months. The principal is to be repaid in one sum at the end of 7 years. Mr. Peters will make equal quarterly deposits throughout the term of the loan into his bank account which pays interest at $j_4 = 6\%$ in order to accumulate the principal. What is the quarterly cost of the debt?

5. For a capital project, a city council needs one million dollars, which they plan to borrow and repay out of taxes over the next thirty years. From one source they can borrow the money and amortize it (by yearly payments for 30 years) at $j_1 = 8\%$. From a second source they can borrow the money by paying the interest every year at $j_1 = 7\frac{1}{2}\%$ and paying the principal at the end of 30 years. If they use the second source, they will provide for the payment of the principal by yearly deposits into a sinking fund that

earns $j_1 = 7\%$. Which source is cheaper to borrow from? By how much yearly?

6. Ms. Gruber wishes to accumulate $10,000 to send her son to medical school in ten years. She begins making quarterly deposits in a fund paying $j_4 = 6\%$. Find the accumulation after the thirty-fourth payment is made and compute the balance of the sinking fund table.

7. Ms. Gruber (Exercise 6), after making 26 payments realizes, that the cost of medical school will be $16,000 not $10,000. To what amount should she increase her payments for the last 14 payments?

8. Ms. Jenkins, Inc., needs $200,000 for plant expansion. It can borrow the money at $j_1 = 9\%$ and amortize the loan over ten years or it can borrow the money at $j_1 = 8\frac{1}{2}\%$ and pay only the interest, repaying the principal in a lump sum at the end of ten years. If the second course of action is adopted, a sinking fund paying $j_1 = 8\%$ will be established to accumulate the $200,000. Find the annual investment cost for each possibility.

5.7 Deferred Annuities

Occasionally a contract calls for annuity payments at regular intervals, with the payments to begin at some future date. Such a contract is called a *deferred annuity*. The simplest way to handle deferred annuity problems is by the method commonly called *lump-and-push*. That is, the value of the annuity payments is lumped at one point. The point chosen is either the time of the last payment (via the $s_{\overline{n}|i}$ formula) or one period before the first payment (via the $a_{\overline{n}|i}$ formula). This value is then pushed, that is, discounted or accumulated, to find its value at the point desired. We illustrate this with an example.

Example 1 A contract calls for 10 monthly payments of $100 each, the first to be made one year from today. How much would you pay for the contract if money is worth $j_{12} = 6\%$?

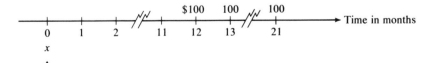

Figure 17

The ten payments have the value $100a_{\overline{10}|i}$ at time 11 (one month before the first payment.) The present value of that amount is $x = 100a_{\overline{10}|i}(1 + i)^{-11}$, where $i = 1/2\%$. Notice we have evaluated the ten payments at a convenient point and then discounted the entire value back to the present time. We could just as easily have lumped at time 21, yielding $100s_{\overline{10}|i}$, and then discounted, giving $x = 100s_{\overline{10}|i}(1 + i)^{-21}$. In both cases,

$$x = \$921.10$$

A similar computation could be made to find the total accumulation in an account in which the last payment of an annuity was made some time ago, and the total has simply been accumulating interest. However, the major advantage of knowing how to handle deferred annuities is that it allows you to calculate annuity values when the number of payments is too many for the tables.

Example 2 Mr. Brown wants to sell a contract calling for $100 monthly payments for 20 years. What is its present value if money is worth $j_{12} = 7\%$?

The time diagram in figure 18 is simple enough.

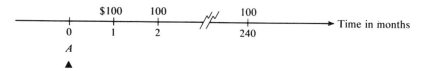

Figure 18

$$A = 100a_{\overline{240}|i} \qquad \text{where } i = 7/12\%$$

Unfortunately, the $a_{\overline{n}|i}$ table only goes up to $n = 150$ for $7/12\%$. Therefore, we cannot just look up the answer. Instead, we think of the contract as calling for a 150-payment annuity plus a 90-payment annuity deferred for 150 interest periods. The value of the first part is

$$A_1 = 100a_{\overline{150}|i}$$

and of the second

$$A_2 = 100a_{\overline{90}|i}(1 + i)^{-150}(i = 7/12\%)$$

Thus

$$A = A_1 + A_2 = 100a_{\overline{150}|i} + 100a_{\overline{90}|i}(1 + i)^{-150} = \$12{,}898.25$$

EXERCISES

1. A contract calls for 12 semiannual payments of $1,000 each, the first due 2 years from today. Find the value of the contract today if money is worth $j_2 = 6\%$.

2. Find the present value of an annuity of $250 monthly if the first payment is made $2\frac{1}{2}$ years from today, the number of payments is 48, and money is worth $j_{12} = 5\%$.

3. A fund is created by semiannual deposits of $500 each for 10 years. How much is in the fund five years after the last deposit, if the fund earns $j_2 = 5\%$?

4. A contract calls for $50 monthly payments for 2 years, followed by $100 monthly payments for 3 more years. Find the present value of the contract if money is worth $j_{12} = 8\%$.

5. A contract calls for 20 quarterly payments of $200 each, followed by 8 quarterly payments of $100 each. If the first $200 payment is due 3 months from today and money is worth $j_4 = 4\%$, what is the value of the contract today?

6. How much should be deposited today in a bank that pays interest at $j_4 = 4\%$ to provide for 45 quarterly withdrawals of $100 each, if the first withdrawal is to be made 4 years and 9 months from today?

7. A contract calls for quarterly payments of $200 for 30 years at $j_4 = 8\%$. Find the present value of the contract.

8. If the contract in Exercise 7 calls for the payment to begin three years from today, what is its present value?

9. A house is purchased on a 15-year mortgage of $30,000. The mortgage is payable monthly at $j_{12} = 8\%$. What are the payments?

10. Repeat Exercise 9 for 20-, 25-, and 30-year mortgages.

11. If the rate on home mortgages is $j_{12} = 6\%$, by how much is the monthly payment reduced by increasing the down payment by $1,000? (Solve for 20-, 25-, and 30-year mortgages.)

12. Repeat Exercise 11 for $j_{12} = 9\%$.

6

Advanced Topics in Finance

6.1 Equivalent Rates

Two different nominal rates are called *equivalent* if they are equal to the same annual effective rate. As you recall, if we have a nominal rate j_m, the interest per interest period $i = j_m/m$ and the effective rate r is given by the equation $1 + r = (1 + i)^m$.

If we have two different nominal rates j_m and j_n and if the rates are equivalent,
then

$$(1 + j_m/m)^m = 1 + r$$

and

$$(1 + j_n/n)^n = 1 + r$$

Therefore,

$$(1 + j_m/m)^m = (1 + j_n/n)^n$$

For example, let us find the quarterly nominal rate equivalent to $j_{12} = 6\%$.

That is, we shall find j_4 such that

$$(1 + j_4/4)^4 = (1 + 6\%/12)^{12}$$

$$(1 + j_4/4)^4 = \left(1 + \frac{1}{2}\%\right)^{12}$$

Taking the 1/4 power of both sides of this equation yields

$$(1 + j_4/4) = \left(1 + \frac{1}{2}\%\right)^3$$

Now solve for j_4,

$$j_4 = 4\left[\left(1 + \frac{1}{2}\%\right)^3 - 1\right]$$

Using Table A-1,

$$j_4 = 4[1.015075 - 1] = 4(0.015075)$$
$$= 0.0603 = 6.03\%$$

Notice that the quarterly nominal rate must be somewhat higher than its monthly equivalent since it is compounded less frequently. This problem could be done using Table A-1. However, consider a problem in which the unknown rate is compounded more times per year than the known rate. For example, find the rate j_6 equivalent to $j_2 = 7\%$. Here we have

$$(1 + j_6/6)^6 = (1 + 7\%/2)^2$$

$$(1 + j_6/6)^6 = \left(1 + 3\frac{1}{2}\%\right)^2$$

To solve for j_6, we must first find the 1/6 power of both sides. Thus,

$$1 + j_6/6 = \left(1 + 3\frac{1}{2}\%\right)^{1/3}$$

$$j_6 = 6\left[\left(1 + 3\frac{1}{2}\%\right)^{1/3} - 1\right]$$

In Table A-6 we have provided values of $(1 + i)^k$ for common fractional values of k. Using this table, we find

$$\left(1 + 3\frac{1}{2}\%\right)^{1/3} = 1.011533$$

Thus

$$j_6 = 6(0.011533) = 0.069198$$

Rounding this to the nearest hundredth percent yields

$$j_6 = 6.92\% \text{ is equivalent to } j_2 = 7\%$$

We see again that the rate compounded more frequently is a lower nominal rate.

EXERCISES

Answer to the hundredth percent.
1. Find the nominal rate j_2 equivalent to $j_{12} = 12\%$.
2. Find the nominal rate compounded monthly that is equivalent to 5% per annum compounded semiannually.
3. Find the nominal rate j_4 equivalent to a yearly effective rate of 5%.
4. Find j_4 equivalent to $j_1 = 6\%$.
5. Find j_4 equivalent to $j_2 = 5\%$.
6. Find the interest rates j_1 and j_{12} equivalent to $j_6 = 6\%$.
7. Find the interest rates j_1 and j_{12} equivalent to $j_4 = 8\%$.
8. Arrange the following rates in order of increasing return:

$$j_1 = 5.12\%, \qquad j_4 = 5\%, \qquad j_{12} = 4.9\%$$

6.2 General Annuities

Suppose that you are faced with an annuity problem in which the needed interest rate is not given in the tables. Usually there is little that you can do other than evaluate the $a_{\overline{n}|i}$ or $s_{\overline{n}|i}$ values directly from the formula by using a calculator or logarithms. However, there is one very special case for which a simple trick will suffice. This is the case in which the interest rate j_m is given and is in the tables, but the payment periods are not the same as the interest periods. For example, if you make monthly deposits in a bank account which pays interest quarterly, the monthly payments form a simple annuity but the proper interest rate will be the interest j_{12} equivalent to the given quarterly rate at the bank. As we have seen from Section 6.1, this rate will in general not be one of the tabulated values. Such a situation is commonly referred to as a *general annuity*.

Let us spell out the notation that will be used for this topic. We let

$m =$ Number of interest periods per year

$p =$ Number of payment periods per year

$j_m =$ Nominal interest rate per interest period

$i = j_m/m$

$j_p =$ Nominal interest rate per payment period equivalent to j_m

$i' = j_p/p$

$n =$ Number of payments

$N =$ Number of interest periods $= \dfrac{nm}{p}$

Thus, we see that i is the interest rate per interest period and i' is the equivalent interest per payment period. The basic assumption is that i is a number that can be found in our tables. The relationship between i and i' is

$$(1 + i')^p = (1 + i)^m$$

which could be written

$$(1 + i') = (1 + i)^{m/p}$$
$$i' = (1 + i)^{m/p} - 1$$

Let us consider the relationship

$$S = Rs_{\overline{n}|i'}$$

which gives the accumulation of n payments made at the end of each payment period. Returning to the definition of $s_{\overline{n}|i'}$, we have

$$s_{\overline{n}|i'} = \frac{(1 + i')^n - 1}{i'}$$

Since

$$(1 + i')^n = (1 + i)^{mn/p} = (1 + i)^N$$

and

$$i' = (1 + i)^{m/p} - 1$$

we have
$$s_{\overline{n}|\,i'} = \frac{(1 + i)^N - 1}{(1 + i)^{m/p} - 1}$$

Therefore, you can compute $s_{\overline{n}|\,i'}$ by using Tables A-1 and A-6. [We note that by multiplying and dividing the last formula by i, the relationship could be reduced to $s_{\overline{n}|\,i'} = s_{\overline{N}|\,i}\,(1/s_{\overline{m/p}|\,i})$; but this would require additional tables of $s_{\overline{k}|\,i}$ for fractional k. In addition, this formula will not work when N has a fractional portion.] Recapping, we have

$$s_{\overline{n}|\,i'} = \frac{(1 + i)^N - 1}{(1 + i)^{m/p} - 1}$$

and similarly, we could show that

$$a_{\overline{n}|\,i'} = \frac{1 - (1 + i)^{-N}}{(1 + i)^{m/p} - 1}$$

Let us look at some examples.

Example 1   A man makes \$100 monthly deposits for ten years in an account paying $j_4 = 5\%$. Find the total accumulation.

We have the time diagram of figure 1.

Figure 1

The appropriate equation is

$$S = 100s_{\overline{120}|\,i'}$$

where i' is the monthly interest rate equivalent to the given $i = 1\frac{1}{4}\%$ quarterly rate.

Since $m = 4$, $p = 12$, $m/p = 1/3$ and $N = nm/p = 120(1/3) = 40$ (40 quarters are the same as 120 months).

$$S = 100\left[\frac{(1 + i)^{40} - 1}{(1 + i)^{1/3} - 1}\right] = 100\left[\frac{0.643619}{0.004149}\right] = \$15,512.63$$

Example 2 A contract calls for semiannual payments of $500 for four years, the first payment to be made six months from today. What is its present value if money is worth $j_{\overline{12}} = 7\%$?

We have an 8-payment annuity, with the relationship $A = 500a_{\overline{8}|\,i'}$, where i' is the semiannual interest equivalent to $i = 7/12\%$ paid monthly. Therefore, $m = 12$, $p = 2$, $m/p = 6$, and $N = nm/p = (8)(6) = 48$ (48 months is the same as 8 half-years). So,

$$A = 500 \left[\frac{1 - (1 + i)^{-48}}{(1 + i)^6 - 1} \right] = 500 \left[\frac{0.243601}{0.035514} \right] = \$3,429.65$$

Example 3 A man intends to make regular monthly deposits in an account earning interest 8% effective. If he wishes to accumulate $8,000 in three years, how large must the deposits be?

Calling the size of payments R, we have

$$8,000 = Rs_{\overline{36}|\,i'}$$

where i' is the monthly interest equivalent to $i = j_1 = 8\%$. Here $m = 1$, $p = 12$, $m/p = 1/12$, and $N = 36(1/12) = 3$. Thus,

$$8,000 = R \left[\frac{(1 + i)^3 - 1}{(1 + i)^{1/12} - 1} \right]$$

Solving for R,

$$R = 8,000 \left[\frac{(1 + i)^{1/12} - 1}{(1 + i)^3 - 1} \right]$$

$$R = 8,000 \left[\frac{0.006434}{0.259712} \right] = \$198.19$$

Example 4 A contract calls for $200 monthly payments for two years, beginning thirteen months from today. If money is worth $j_4 = 6\%$, what is the present value of this contract?

The time diagram for this deferred annuity is figure 2.

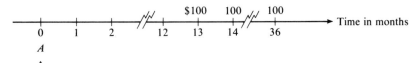

Figure 2

Using the usual technique,

$$A = 100a_{\overline{24}|\,i'} (1 + i')^{-12}$$

Now, $m = 4$, $p = 12$, $m/p = 1/3$, and $N = 8$. Applying our earlier formula to convert $a_{\overline{24}|\,i'}$ and converting the discount factor $(1 + i')^{-12}$ from months to quarters, yields

$$A = 100\left[\frac{1 - (1 + i)^{-8}}{(1 + i)^{1/3} - 1}\right](1 + i)^{-4} \quad \text{where } i = 1\frac{1}{2}\%$$

Finally, looking up all the pertinent data in the tables,

$$A = \$2,126.57$$

Example 5 A contract calls for 25 monthly payments of $200, starting one month from today. If money is worth $j_4 = 5\%$, find the present value of the contract.

The present value is

$$A = 200a_{\overline{25}|\,i'}$$

Since $m = 4$ and $p = 12$, $N = mn/p = 8\frac{1}{3}$,

$$A = 200\left[\frac{1 - (1 + i)^{-8-1/3}}{(1 + i)^{1/3} - 1}\right]$$

To compute $(1 + i)^{-8-1/3}$, we write it as $(1 + i)^{-8}(1 + i)^{-1/3}$. Thus,

$$A = 200\left[\frac{1 - (1 + i)^{-8}(1 + i)^{-1/3}}{(1 + i)^{1/3} - 1}\right] \quad \text{where } i = 1\frac{1}{4}\%$$

Table A-7 provides values of $(1 + i)^{-k}$ for fraction k. Using Tables A-2, A-6, and A-7, yields

$$A = \$4,740.57$$

EXERCISES

1. If a bank pays interest at $j_4 = 5\%$, what should each of 120 equal monthly payments be to accumulate to $10,000 on the date of last deposit if the first payment is made one month from today?

2. A farm is worth $12,000 cash. It is purchased by paying $2,000 down and the balance in quarterly payments for 15 years. What will these payments be if $j_1 = 7\%$?

3. A television set selling for $1,000 cash can be purchased by equal payments made at the end of each semiannual period for 4 years. If $j_4 = 4\%$, find the amount of each semiannual payment.

4. Mr. Bond deposits $1,000 at the end of each year for 5 years into a bank which pays interest at $j_4 = 5\%$. How much will he have in his account just after the fifth payment?

5. Repeat Exercise 4 for interest $j_1 = 5.4\%$. Hint: You will have to work directly from the formula.

6. I deposit $100 each quarter in an account paying $j_2 = 7\%$. How much will accumulate in 6 years?

7. In settlement of a certain debt with interest at $j_{12} = 6\%$, Mrs. Bard agrees to make payment of $200 at the end of each quarter for the next year and a half and a final payment of $100 3 months later. What is the debt?

8. A contract calls for 12 monthly payments of $100 each, the first to be made 37 months from today. Find the cash value of the contract today if money is worth $j_4 = 6\%$.

9. A contract calls for 20 quarterly payments of $200 each, followed by 8 quarterly payments of $100 each. If the first $200 payment is due 3 months from today and money is worth $j_1 = 4\%$, what is the value of the contract today?

10. A contract calls for 45 monthly payments of $100 each, the first due one year from today. Find the value of the contract today if money is worth $j_1 = 6\%$.

11. In order to accumulate $5,000, Mr. Jones makes 40 quarterly deposits in an account paying $j_{12} = 8\%$. What must each deposit be? What if the rate is $j_1 = 8\%$?

12. Mr. Grillo buys a suit listed at $200 for monthly payments for $1\frac{1}{2}$ years. How much should each payment be if money is worth $j_4 = 7\%$?

13. Ms. Gold deposits $5,000 each year in an account paying $j_4 = 6\%$. After making 10 deposits, she leaves the money for 6 more years without making additional deposits. How much has accumulated at that time?

14. Mrs. Rich leaves $100,000 to her favorite niece on her sixteenth birthday. The money is to be invested at $j_2 = 9\%$ until one month after her twenty-first birthday. At that point the niece will start making monthly withdrawals for 15 years. How much will each withdrawal be?

6.3 Perpetuities

An amount A left on deposit will produce interest Ai at the end of every interest period. If a withdrawal of amount R greater than Ai is made, it will eat into the principal. The result will be an annuity of the type considered earlier, terminating when the principal is exhausted. However, if a withdrawal of exactly $R = Ai$ is made at the end of each interest period, no principal will be withdrawn. The result will be the ability to continue making withdrawals for as long as desired. In other words, we have an annuity with an infinite number of payments. This situation is called a *perpetuity*.

The relationship between the payment and present value of a perpetuity is $R = Ai$ or $A = R(1/i)$, where A is the present value and R is the periodic payment. Let us note in passing that for a simple annuity $A = Ra_{\overline{n}|i}$, and

$$a_{\overline{n}|i} = \frac{1 - (1 + i)^{-n}}{i}$$

As n becomes very large, $(1 + i)^{-n} = 1/(1 + i)^n$ approaches zero and $a_{\overline{n}|i}$ approaches $1/i$. Thus, we could really define the perpetuity as an annuity with the number of payments n equal to infinity. Let us look at some simple examples.

Example 1   Mr. Goodwill contributed $20,000 to his alma mater to establish a scholarship fund to last forever. If the money earns 8% effective, how much will the annual award be?

Here we have $i = 8\%$ and $A = \$20,000$; therefore

$$R = 20,000(0.08) = \$1,600$$

That is, the interest on $20,000 for one year is $1,600, which the college can withdraw without touching the principal.

Example 2   If the college invests Mr. Goodwill's money at $j_{12} = 8\%$, how much will the scholarship be?

In this problem the interest rate i is the annual interest equivalent to $j_{12} = 8\%$. That is, $(1 + i')^1 = (1 + i)^{12}$, where $i = 2/3\%$. Hence $i' = (1 + i)^{12} - 1 = 0.083$ and $R = 20,000(0.083) = \$1,660$.

Example 3   Miss White wishes to establish a fund to pay $200 per month for as long as needed. She will invest the fund at $j_{12} = 9\%$. How much must she invest?

We have $R = \$200$ and $i = 3/4\%$. Using $R = Ai$,

$$200 = A(3/4\%)$$
$$200 = A(3/400)$$
$$A = 200(400/3) = \$26,666.67$$

Example 4 A man wishes to establish a fund which will pay $1,000 every five years to redecorate his local church. If the fund will be invested at $j_4 = 8\%$, how large must it be?

We have $R = \$1,000$ but the interest rate for each payment period must be the rate i' payable every five years equivalent to $i = 2\%$ payable quarterly. That is,

$$1 + i' = (1 + 2\%)^{20}$$
$$i' = 0.485947$$

Thus, $\$1,000 = A(0.485947)$

$$A = 1,000/0.485947$$
$$A = \$2,057.84$$

In business applications, perpetuities occur in computing the capitalized cost of an asset. The capitalized cost K is defined to be the initial cost C plus the cost of periodic replacement A.

Example 5 A piece of machinery sells for $10,000. After five years it must be replaced. Its salvage value is $2,000. If money is worth 7% effective, what is the capitalized cost of the machine?

The initial cost $C = \$10,000$. The replacement costs form a perpetuity of $8,000 every five years. The present value of the perpetuity A is $8,000 (1/i')$, where i' is the interest payable for five years equivalent to $j_1 = 7\%$. Thus, $i' = (1 + 7\%)^5 - 1 = 0.402552$ and $A = 8,000/0.402552 = 19,873.21$.

Now,

$$K = C + A = \$29,873.21$$

The periodic investment cost of an asset is defined to be the interest lost on the capitalized cost, usually designated by H.

Thus, in the last example, the cost of the machine is $29,873.21. Since this amount is tied up in the asset, it is not available for investment elsewhere. Hence, the annual investment cost is the earnings lost in one year on $29,873.21. Since money is worth 7% effective, $H = 29,873.21(0.07) = \$2,091.12$.

Summarizing,

$$K = C + A = C + R/i'$$

where

K = Capitalized cost

C = Initial cost

A = Present value of replacement costs

R = Periodic replacement cost

i' = Interest per replacement period

Also

$$H = Ki''$$

where

H = Periodic investment cost

i'' = Interest per investment period

Finally, if the replacement period and the investment period coincide, $i' = i''$ and $H = Ki' = (C + R/i')i' = Ci' + R$. Thus, when the replacement period and investment period coincide, the periodic investment cost is particularly easy to compute.

Example 6 Compare on the basis of annual investment cost the following two machines. Machine A costs $1,000, has no scrap value, and must be replaced every year. Machine B costs $5,000, has $1,000 scrap value, and must be replaced every five years. Assume that money is worth $j_1 = 5\%$.

For Machine A, we have $C = 1,000$ and $R = 1,000$. Since the investment period, interest period, and replacement period all coincide, we have for annual investment cost

$$H = Ci + R = 1,000(5\%) + 1,000 = \$1,050$$

For Machine B, we have $C = 5,000$ and $R = 4,000$. Therefore, the capitalized cost is

$$K = C + R/i' = 5,000 + 4,000/i'$$

where

$$i' = (1 + 5\%)^5 - 1 = 0.276282$$

Thus,

$$K = 19{,}477.96$$

and

$$H = Ki = (19{,}477.96)(0.05) = \$973.90$$

Therefore, the initially more expensive machine is cheaper based on annual investment cost.

EXERCISES

1. A mathematics scholarship pays $500 at the beginning of each year. What amount is required to establish such a scholarship if $j_1 = 5\%$?

2. Repeat Exercise 1 assuming that interest is $j_4 = 5\%$.

3. $10,000 is given to a college today to establish a permanent scholarship. If invested at $j_1 = 6\%$, how much will it provide at the end of each year? How much at $j_2 = 6\%$?

4. Find the present value of a perpetuity with semiannual payments of $1,000 and interest rate $j_2 = 5\%$, if the first payment is made immediately.

5. The XYZ Company uses batteries costing $30 and having a useful life of 2 years. Another model costing $40 with an expected life of 3 years is offered. Which of the two models offers the better investment on the basis of capitalized cost? Assume money is worth 5% effective.

6. Find the capitalized cost and the quarterly investment cost of a machine which costs $15,000 and has a scrap value of $3,000 at the end of 10 years if $j_4 = 4\%$.

7. A machine costs $2,000, has a lifetime of 8 years, and a scrap value of $400 at that time. What is the capitalized cost and annual investment cost of the machine if $j_2 = 5\%$?

8. Find the capitalized cost of a machine that costs $12,000, has

a life of 8 years, and a scrap value of $2,000, if money is worth $j_4 = 4\%$.

9. What sum of money invested at $j_1 = 4\%$ will provide for the construction of a $2,000 tennis court, its reconstruction every 35 years at the same cost, and its annual upkeep of $80?

10. High-Rise College is planning to install new, modern elevators. After careful investigation, Tony, the Dean of Transportation, must decide between the following systems:

    Elevator A costs $5,000 to install and must be overhauled every 2 years at a cost of $300.

    Elevator B costs $8,000 to install and must be overhauled every 4 years at a cost of $400.

    If money is worth $j_2 = 6\%$, find the capitalization for each, and help Tony decide which elevators to install.

11. The cost of a billiard table is $1,200. The table must be recovered every year at a cost of $200. If money is worth $j_1 = 8\%$, find the capitalized cost and annual investment cost of the billiard table.

12. Repeat Exercise 11 if money is worth $j_{12} = 7\%$.

13. Find the capitalized cost of a machine that costs $12,000, has a life of 8 years, and a scrap value of $2,000, if money is worth $j_4 = 4\%$.

14. For the machine in Exercise 13, find the periodic investment cost for each 8-year period. Also, find the annual investment cost and the quarterly investment cost.

6.4 Interpolation

What do you do when the values you seek are not exactly in the table? For example, suppose a sum of money is left on deposit for some given time at an interest rate not given in the tables. How do you find the accumulation? The formula $S = P(1 + i)^n$ is still correct and with a desk calculator may be computed exactly. However, an approximation may be obtained by a technique known as *interpolation*. Interpolation assumes that the curve [in this case $(1 + i)^n$] is actually a straight line, and hence the slope is constant. For example, suppose you wish to find $(1 + 5.8\%)^{10}$. You look at the two values of i that bracket 5.8%

and are tabulated, in this case, 5.5% and 6%. You then make up an interpolation table as below:

i	$(1 + i)^{10}$
5.5	1.7081
5.8	y
6.0	1.7908

Notice that the unknown $(1 + 5.8\%)^{10}$ is marked by y. Also notice that we have rounded the numbers off to four decimal places, because interpolation is an approximation which rarely gives as much as four-place accuracy. Now think of the first-column values as x-values and the second-column values as y-values. Since we are assuming a straight line, the slope (the change of y divided by change of x) must be the same for any pair of points. In particular, using the first and third pairs and first and second pairs of values, we have

$$\frac{1.7908 - 1.7081}{6.0 - 5.5} = \frac{y - 1.7081}{5.8 - 5.5}$$

$$\frac{0.0827}{0.5} = \frac{y - 1.7081}{0.3}$$

$$(0.3)(0.1654) = y - 1.7081$$

$$0.04962 = y - 1.7081$$

$$1.75772 = y$$

Thus $(1 + 5.8\%)^{10} = 1.7577$ by interpolation (by actual computation $(1 + 5.8\%)^{10} = 1.757344$).

Interpolation can be used with any table. Let us see some examples.

Example 1 Find the present value of a $1,000 note payable two years from today if money is worth $j_2 = 7.2\%$.

We have $n = 4$, $i = 3.6\%$, $P = 1,000(1 + 3.6\%)^{-4}$. We interpolate in Table A-2

i	$(1 + i)^{-4}$
3.5	0.8714
3.6	y
4.0	0.8548

$$\frac{0.8548 - 0.8714}{4.0 - 3.5} = \frac{y - 0.8714}{3.6 - 3.5}$$

$$\frac{-.0166}{0.5} = \frac{y - 0.8714}{0.1}$$

$$(-0.0332)(0.1) = y - 0.8714$$

$$0.8681 = y$$

Thus

$$(1 + 3.6\%)^{-4} = 0.8681$$

and
$$P = 868.10$$

Example 2 Find the present value of an annuity calling for 25 monthly payments of $100 each if money is worth $j_{12} = 8.4\%$.

We have

$$A = 100a_{\overline{25}|\,i} \qquad \text{where } i = 0.7\%$$

Now 0.7% falls between 2/3% and 3/4%; therefore we interpolate as

i	$a_{\overline{25}|\,i}$
0.6667	22.9575
0.7000	y
0.7500	22.7188

$$\frac{22.7188 - 22.9575}{0.7500 - 0.6667} = \frac{y - 22.9575}{0.7000 - 0.6667}$$

$$\frac{-0.2387}{0.0833} = \frac{y - 22.9575}{0.0333}$$

$$-(2.8655)(0.0333) = y - 22.9575$$

$$-0.0954 = y - 22.9575$$

$$22.8621 = y$$

Thus

$$A = \$2,286.21$$

One of the more interesting uses of interpolation is to find the time needed for compound interest to amount to a given accumulation.

Example 3 How long will it take for $100 to accumulate to $150 if invested at $j_4 = 8\%$?

We have

$$150 = 100(1 + 2\%)^n$$
$$1.5 = (1 + 2\%)^n$$

Looking in Table A-1 we see that

$$(1 + 2\%)^{20} = 1.485947 \qquad \text{and} \qquad (1 + 2\%)^{21} = 1.515666$$

We shall therefore interpolate for n. Thus,

n	$(1 + 2\%)^n$
20	1.4859
x	1.5000
21	1.5157

$$\frac{1.5157 - 1.4859}{21 - 20} = \frac{1.5000 - 1.4859}{x - 20}$$

We see that the unknown x appears in the denominator of the fraction. We, therefore, cross-multiply to yield

$$(x - 20)(0.0298) = (0.0141)(1)$$
$$x - 20 = \frac{0.0141}{0.0298}$$
$$x = 20.4732$$

We have $x = 20.4732$. What is the number? It is the number of interest periods needed for \$100 to accumulate to \$150. Since each interest period is three months, or one-quarter of a year, we must divide by four to have the result in years. Thus, the time is 5.1183 years. Of course, it is most unusual to express time as a decimal portion of a year. Usually you would convert the 0.1183 years into months by multiplying by twelve. Thus 0.1183 years = (0.1183)(12) months = 1.4196 months.

So far, we have time = 5 years, 1.4196 months.

Again it is usual to convert fractions of a month into days. For this purpose we assume 30 days to a month so that 0.4196 months = (0.4196)(30) days = 12.588 days. We would then say that the time is 5 years, 1 month, 13 days. Of course, we could have carried the 0.588 days out as hours, minutes, and seconds, but from a practical point of view that's a little ridiculous.

In passing, let us note the so-called *rule of 72*. Although not exact, it is roughly true that if you divide 72 by the annual interest in percent, the result will be the number of years it takes for money to double. Thus, at 5%, money will double in about 14 years (72/5 = 14.4); at 6%, money will double in about 12 years (72/6 = 12); and so on. The reader is invited to check this as Exercise 10.

EXERCISES

1. Mr. Lopez deposited $1,000 in a bank paying $j_4 = 5.6\%$ six years ago. Using interpolation, find the approximate value of the investment today.

2. Find the amount to which $2,000 will accumulate in 2½ years at $j_2 = 8.4\%$.

3. Find the present value of a $5,000 note payable in 5 years and paying $j_1 = 7.7\%$.

4. A bank advertises 7.9% effective on 4- to 7-year notes. How much must be deposited to amount to $1,000 in 7 years?

5. Repeat Exercise 4 for a bank which advertises 8.25% and for a bank which advertises 8.17%.

6. A deposit of $200 at $j_{12} = 5.4\%$ amounts now to $450. For how long was it on deposit?

7. Find the amount accumulated by 20 monthly $100 deposits at $j_{12} = 4.8\%$.

8. Find the present value of an annuity of 16 quarterly deposits at $j_4 = 10.5\%$.

9. Find the amount and present value of 30 annual deposits of $500 each at $j_1 = 7.1\%$.

10. Find the time it takes for money to double at 5%, 6%, and 7% effective.

11. Find the times required for $1,000 to accumulate to $1,200 at $j_4 = 5\%$, 6%, and 7%.

6.5 Calculation of Interest Rates

Interpolation is commonly used to estimate the yield rate for investments. Let us look at a simple example.

Example 1   Mr. Jones invested $1,000 in a mutual fund six years ago. Today his investment is worth $1,300. What was the annual effective rate of interest?

The equation is $1,300 = 1,000(1 + i)^6$ where $i = j_1 =$ unknown rate of interest. We see that we seek i so that

$$(1 + i)^6 = 1.3000$$

Looking in Table A-1 for $n = 6$, we find (for i in %):

i	$(1 + i)^6$
4%	1.2653
x	1.3000
$4\frac{1}{2}$	1.3023

We see that if we equate the change in y over the change in x, the unknown will appear in the denominator. Hence, let us equate the reciprocals immediately. Thus,

$$\frac{x - 4}{1.3000 - 1.2653} = \frac{4\frac{1}{2} - 4}{1.3023 - 1.2653}$$

$$\frac{x - 4}{0.0347} = \frac{1/2}{0.0370}$$

$$x = 4 + \frac{(0.0347)/2}{0.0370}$$

$$x = 4.4689$$

To the nearest hundredth percent, $j_1 = 4.47\%$. Consider another example.

Example 2   Mr. Jones is offered a $2,000 note due in $2\frac{1}{2}$ years for $1,600 today. What rate j_4 will this investment yield?

We have $2,000 = 1,600(1 + i)^{10}$ where $i = j_4/4$. Hence,

$$(1 + i)^{10} = 1.2500$$

Again using Table A-1,

i	$(1 + i)^{10}$	j_4
2%	1.2190	8%
x	1.2500	y
$2\frac{1}{2}$	1.2801	10

Notice that, after solving for i, we would have to then multiply by 4 to find j_4. Instead of doing so, we have multiplied both the 2% and 2½% by 4; by using only the last two columns of this interpolation table, we shall interpolate directly for the rate j_4, now represented by y. Thus,

$$\frac{y - 8}{1.2500 - 1.2190} = \frac{10 - 8}{1.2801 - 1.2190}$$

$$\frac{y - 8}{0.0310} = \frac{2}{0.0611}$$

$$y = 8 + \frac{2(0.0310)}{0.0611}$$

$$y = 9.0147$$

Again, to the nearest hundredth percent

$$j_4 = 9.01\%$$

Let us look at an annuity problem.

Example 3   Mr. Garson buys a $200 suit of clothes for $20 down and $20 per month for one year. What interest rate is he paying?

We have not specified whether annual, monthly, quarterly, or some other interest rate is requested. However, since the payments are monthly, it seems natural to seek j_{12}. The time diagram is figure 3.

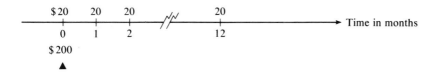

Figure 3

With equation,

$$200 = 20 + 20a_{\overline{12}|\,i}$$

$$180 = 20a_{\overline{12}|\,i}$$

$$9 = a_{\overline{12}|\,i}$$

Using Table A-4 on the next page, we find the values

i	$a_{\overline{12}|i}$	j_{12}
$4\frac{1}{2}\%$	9.1186	54%
x	9.0000	y
5	8.8633	60

As in the last example, we have added a j_{12} column. Using the last two columns to interpolate,

$$\frac{y-54}{9.0000-9.1186} = \frac{60-54}{8.8633-9.1186}$$

$$\frac{y-54}{-0.1186} = \frac{6}{-0.2553}$$

$$y = 54 + \frac{6(0.1186)}{0.2553}$$

$$y = 56.7873$$

Therefore, Mr. Garson is paying $j_{12} = 56.79\%$ interest.

Students frequently wonder how to get a rough idea of the interest rate in an annuity problem so as to avoid extensive searching in the table. A good way to figure is illustrated by the last example. Mr. Garson bought a $200 suit. His total cash outlay was $260 ($20 down + 12 payments of $20.) Therefore, he paid $60 interest. Now, how much did he borrow? Since he paid $20 down, his original debt was $180. We know that when amortizing, the outstanding principal reduces gradually from maximum to zero over the course of the payments. Roughly speaking, the average principal outstanding is the average of $180 and zero, that is, $90. Therefore, Mr. Garson paid $60 interest on a $90 loan, or $66\frac{2}{3}\%$ interest per annum, or a monthly rate of about $5\frac{1}{2}\%$, telling us near where to look in the table. The shortness of the loan period and the magnitude of the interest rate has distorted the accuracy of this approximation for Example 3. Try Example 4.

Example 4 Mr. Jones borrows $1,000, repaying with 60 monthly payments of $20. Find his approximate interest rate.

The total payment is $1,200. Since the loan was $1,000, the interest is $200. The average outstanding principal is $500. Hence, the interest rate is 40% over five years, or 8% per year. We should then look for a monthly rate i of about $2/3\%$.

The exact equation is

$$\$1,000 = 20a_{\overline{60}|\,i}$$
$$50 = a_{\overline{60}|\,i}$$

and a check of Table A-4 shows

$$a_{\overline{60}|\,i} = 49.3184 \text{ for } i = 2/3\%$$

and
$$a_{\overline{60}|\,i} = 50.5020 \text{ for } i = 7/12\%$$

Interpolation yields $j_{12} = 7.42\%$.

EXERCISES

1. Mr. Knox invested $10,000 in stocks 20 years ago. Today the stocks are worth $28,000. By interpolation find the nominal growth rate of the stocks.

2. Interpolate to find the nominal rate j_{12} at which $1,000 will accumulate to $1,500 in 5 years.

3. Find the nominal rate converted semiannually at which $1,000 will accumulate to $1,200 in 5 years, 6 months.

4. Find to the nearest hundredth percent the j_2 rate at which money will double in 15 years.

5. Find the j_4 rate at which $80 will grow to $100 in 3 years.

6. Two thousand dollars is available each quarter for 10 years for deposit into a sinking fund that must contain $100,000 at the date of the last deposit (just after the deposit). What rate, j_4, must be obtained on the fund?

7. A car worth $1,470 is purchased by paying $150 down, followed by monthly payments of $120 for one year. What interest rate compounded monthly does the payment plan include?

8. A piano costing $2,045 can be purchased for $500 down and $100 at the end of each month for 18 months. What rate j_{12} would a purchaser pay?

9. Stuart purchases a car worth $3,100 cash by paying $1,600 down, followed by 12 quarterly payments of $150 each. What rate j_4 is he paying?

10. Just before Christmas, a finance company advertises, "Borrow $150 for a total cost of only $10. You pay the loan in eight easy monthly installments of $20 each, the first one due one month after the loan." What interest rate j_{12} does this finance company realize?

11. A piece of land valued at $10,000 is sold for $2,200 down and 10 annual payments of $1,000. What is the annual interest rate being paid?

6.6 Bonds

One of the most common ways by which large corporations or government bodies raise money is through the issuance of bonds. Briefly, a bond is a contract which calls for regular periodic payments of interest followed by a repayment of principal at some specified future time. Bonds are usually issued in denominations of $1,000 or $5,000, but other amounts are also used. For example, a $1,000 bond might call for an interest payment of $25 every six months for twenty years, followed by the return of the $1,000 on the date of the last interest payment. This date is called the *redemption date* or *date of maturity*. This bond would be issued with the intent that the purchaser would pay $1,000 for the bond. The resulting interest payments would then represent a return of $i = 2\frac{1}{2}\%$ every six months or $j_2 = 5\%$. With the return of capital at maturity, the purchaser would have realized a return of $j_2 = 5\%$ on his $1,000 investment.

It is usual for the issuer of the bond to establish a sinking fund to accumulate the redemption cost at the time of maturity. Alternatively, the issuer may have different redemption dates on different bonds in the issue. The issuer then redeems part of the issue each year, so that from its viewpoint the loan is in effect being amortized. Such an arrangement is called a *serial bond issue*.

However, regardless of the issuer's intent, bonds are sold on the open market. Therefore, as loan rates fluctuate, so will the price one is willing to pay for a bond. In the last example, the bond was issued to yield $j_2 = 5\%$. Suppose, however, that loans of equivalent risk are paying a higher rate, say $j_2 = 6\%$. No one will be willing to pay $1,000 for the bond in question. Therefore, if the holder of the bond wishes to sell it, he will have to sell it at a discount. That is, he will have to sell it for less than the $1,000. In particular, the time diagram for the bond described earlier would be figure 4. If money is worth $j_2 = 6\%$, $i = 3\%$ and the present value of this contract is

$$A = 25a_{\overline{40}|\,i} + 1,000(1 + i)^{-40}$$
$$A = 25(23.114772) + 1,000(0.306557)$$
$$A = \$884.43$$

We see that to yield $j_2 = 6\%$, the bond must be purchased for a discount of \$115.57. Similarly, if interest rates drop, the purchase price of the bond will go up. That is, the bond, in order to yield $j_2 = 4\%$, will sell for a premium, that is, more than \$1,000.

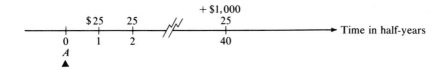

Figure 4

The greatest source of confusion when dealing with bonds is the terminology. To begin, a bond has a "face" or "par" value, usually \$1,000. The periodic payments are usually expressed as a percentage of face. This percentage is called the *bond interest rate*.

Let us introduce some notation. Let

F = Face, or par value, of the bond

C = Redemption price of the bond

n = Number of interest periods until redemption

r = Bond interest rate per payment period

$R = Fr$ = Periodic interest payment

Almost always $C = F$. That is, the bond is redeemed at par or face value. Occasionally, a bond is redeemed at more than face, most commonly when a bond is *callable*. A callable bond is one which the issuer may choose to redeem at some time prior to maturity. Bonds are called when interest rates have dropped so that a new issue can be sold more cheaply to replace them. When a company calls bonds earlier, it usually must pay a penalty to the borrower. In such cases, C may be larger than F.

If P is the price for which a bond can be purchased and i is the yield rate for this purchase price, we have $P = Ra_{\overline{n}|\,i} + C(1 + i)^{-n}$

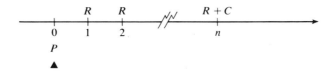

Figure 5

Example 1   A $1,000 bond which pays interest 7%, $m = 2$ will be re-
deemed at 105% of par if called 5 years from now. If the purchaser
wishes to earn $j_2 = 6\%$ when called, for what should it be purchased?

This bond, if called, will pay $35 every 6 months for 5 years and then
be redeemed for $1,050. Hence

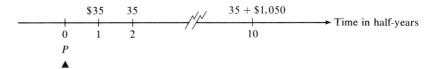

Figure 6

$$P = 35a_{\overline{10}|i} + 1,050(1 + i)^{-10} \qquad \text{where } i = 3\%$$
$$P = 35(8.530203) + 1,050(0.744094)$$
$$P = \$1,079.86$$

We see that with the aid of a time diagram, it is quite easy to find
the purchase price of a bond to yield some predetermined percentage.
This interest rate is called the *yield to maturity*. When bonds are sold
on the market, the price is given and you may wish to compute the
yield to maturity. Large bond rate tables are available which give this
rate exactly. However, an excellent approximation may be obtained
with a method similar to that used for any annuity given in the last
section. The technique is as follows:

The total interest to be paid on the bond is nR, where n is the number of payments remaining and R is the amount of each payment.
To this sum, add the increase in value of the bond from purchase to
maturity, $C - P$. Here, $C - P$ may be negative if the bond is purchased at a premium. Hence,

$$\text{Total return} = nR + C - P$$

Divide this by the number of years to find the annual return. Next
we compute the average value of the investment over the life of the

contract, namely $(P + C)/2$. Dividing annual return by the average value of the investment yields the rate of return per year.

Example 2   A $1,000 bond maturing in 25 years and paying interest 6%, $m = 2$ is offered for sale at $1,050. Find the yield to maturity, if it is redeemed at par.

Over 25 years the bond will pay 50 payments of $30 each, for a total interest of $1,500. In addition, it will lose $50 in value ($P = $1,050, $C = $1,000). Thus, the total return is $1,450.

The annual return is $1,450 ÷ 25 = $58.00. Value of the investment is ($1,050 + $1,000)/2 = $1,025. Therefore, the annual rate of return is $58 ÷ 1,025 = 0.0566$. That is, the yield to maturity is 5.66%.

Example 3   Suppose that the bond in Example 2 were called after 10 years at $1,100. What would the yield be?

Now we have only 20 payments of $30 each, or $600 in interest. In addition, the value of the bond increased $50 ($P = $1,050, C = $1,100). Therefore, total return is $650. The annual return is $65. The average value of the investment is $(1,050 + 1,100)/2 = $1,075$. Hence, the annual rate of return is $65 ÷ 1,075 = 0.06047$, or 6.05%.

Incidentally, the yield rate published with the bond prices in most newspapers is current yield. The current yield is simply the annual interest payment as a percentage of price. Thus, for the bond in Examples 2 and 3, the current yield is $60 ÷ 1,050 = 5.71%$. This figure is of interest to the investor who intends to hold the bond for only a short time and then dispose of it.

Up to this point, we have always assumed that a bond is to be purchased on the day that an interest payment is made and that the payment of that day belongs to the seller. In this way, the time diagram used to derive the formula $P = Ra_{\overline{n}|i} + C(1 + i)^{-n}$ is correct. However, it is most unusual for a bond purchase to be made precisely on an interest date. How do you handle the price of a bond between interest dates? Actually it is very simple. First, calculate the purchase price P_o that would have been paid at the last interest date. Now, let f be the fraction of the interest period that has elapsed since the last interest date. Theoretically, the purchase price P should be $P = P_o(1 + i)^f$. Actually the value of P is usually calculated by assuming simple interest. Thus,

$$P = P_o(1 + fi)$$

Example 4   A bond paying 4%, $m = 2$, with face value $1,000, is redeemable at par on January 1, 1986. For what would it be purchased on March 15, 1973, to yield $j_2 = 7\%$?

Since the bond redemption day is January 1, it must pay interest on January 1 and July 1 each year. Therefore, the last interest date prior to sale was January 1, 1973.

Letting that be time zero,

Figure 7

$$P_0 = 20a_{\overline{26}|i} + 1,000(1 + i)^{-26} \qquad \text{where } i = 3\tfrac{1}{2}\%$$
$$P_0 = 20(16.890352) + 1,000(0.408838)$$
$$P_0 = \$746.65$$

Now, March 15 is 74 days after January 1, assuming 30 days to each month. The number of days in the interest period is 180, under the same assumption.

Therefore $f = 74/180 = 0.41$

$$P = P_0 (1 + fi)$$
$$P = (746.65)[1 + (0.41)(0.035)]$$
$$P = \$757.36$$

Let us extend our previous example. Clearly, as f increases, P will increase from a low of $746.65 when $f = 0$ to a high of $(746.65)(1 + 0.035) = \$772.78$ when $f = 1$. However, when $f = 1$, the next interest payment is made, so that at that moment, the price drops to

$$P = 20a_{\overline{25}|i} + 1,000(1 + i)^{-25}$$
$$P = 20(16.481515) + 1,000(0.423147)$$
$$P = \$752.78$$

That is, the lion's share of the price increase throughout the interest period was due to the fact that an interest payment was coming due. This behavior is typical and causes an artificial up-and-down pattern to bond prices. The prices rise steadily throughout the interest period and drop sharply when the payment is made. To offset this artificiality somewhat, the prices quoted in the newspapers and financial journals omit the portion attributable to the forthcoming payment. For this purpose, the calculation is as follows: If the fraction of the interest period that has elapsed is f, it is assumed the seller owns that fraction of the next payment. Thus, the seller is entitled to fR dollars for his share of the next interest payment. This amount is called the *accrued interest*. The market quotation, Q, is the price less the accrued interest. That is,

$$Q = P - fR$$

or, more significantly to the buyer,

$$P = Q + fR$$

In this way, the quote remains relatively constant from day to day, but the buyer who agrees to pay a given market quotation for a bond must expect a bill for that amount plus the accrued interest. In the last example, $f = 0.41$, $R = \$20$, and $P = \$752.78$. Therefore, the market quote would be

$$Q = 752.78 - (0.41)(20)$$
$$Q = \$744.58$$

Actually, to make matters more confusing, quotes are usually given as percentages of par to the nearest eighth. Thus, $\$744.58$ would appear in the listing as 74½.

EXERCISES

1. A $1,000 bond redeemable at 105, 20 years from today, pays bond interest semiannually at $j_2 = 4\%$. Find the purchase price today to yield the investor $j_2 = 6\%$.

2. The bond of Exercise 1 may be called 12 years from today at 102% of par. What should the purchase price be to guarantee at least $j_2 = 6\%$, if you do not know whether or not it will be called?

3. The city of New York is issuing a $1,000 bond redeemable at par on June 1, 1985, to support free higher education. If the bond interest rate is $j_2 = 7\%$, find the purchase price on June 1, 1975, to yield $j_2 = 6\%$.

4. The bond of Exercise 3 may be called on December 1, 1980, at 106% of par. What should the purchase price be to have a yield of $j_2 = 7\%$ if it is called?

5. A $1,000 bond redeemable at par 17 years from today pays bond interest semiannually at $j_2 = 5\%$. Find the yield rate j_2, if the bond is purchased today for $970.

6. A $1,000 bond pays $30 bond interest on each January 15 and July 15. It will be redeemed at 110% on January 15, 1980. The market quotation on January 15, 1960, was 120. Find the yield rate.

7. An $8,000 bond paying interest at $j_4 = 5\%$ is purchased for $7,400, 15 years before redemption at par. Find the rate of yield (j_4) earned by the purchaser if he holds the bond to maturity.

8. A $1,000 bond redeemable at par 14 years from today pays bond interest annually at $j_1 = 5\%$. Find the yield rate j_1 earned by an investor who buys the bond today for $980.

9. A $1,000 bond pays annual interest at $4\frac{1}{2}\%$ and is redeemable at 102%. Find the yield rate j_1 to an investor who purchases this bond for $900, twelve years before redemption.

10. A $1,000 bond with $30 semiannual coupons is redeemable at par. Find the yield rate j_2, if the bond is bought for $1,030 14 years before redemption.

11. A $1,000 bond paying interest at $j_2 = 6\%$ is redeemable at par on January 1, 1995.
    (a) Find the purchase price on January 1, 1975, to yield an investor $j_2 = 4\%$.
    (b) Find the purchase price on January 10, 1975, to yield an investor $j_2 = 4\%$. (Assume that each month has 30 days.)
    (c) What would the market quotation be?

12. A $1,000 bond paying interest at $j_{12} = 24\%$ is redeemable at par on January 1, 1983.
    (a) Find the purchase price on January 1, 1973, to yield an investor $j_{12} = 12\%$.
    (b) Find the purchase price on January 4, 1973, to yield an investor $j_{12} = 12\%$. (Assume that each month has 30 days.)
    (c) What would the market quotation be?

13. A $1,000 bond, redeemable at par on October 1, 1985, pays bond interest semiannually at $j_2 = 6\%$. Find the purchase price on June 1, 1973, if the bond is to yield $j_2 = 7\%$. What would the market quotation be?

14. A $1,000 bond redeemable at $1,100 on July 1, 1994, pays interest quarterly at $j_4 = 4\%$. What price should a purchaser pay for this bond on September 13, 1974, to yield $j_4 = 6\%$. What would the market quotation be?

15. A $1,000 bond redeemable at par on August 1, 1978, pays bond interest semiannually at $j_2 = 6\%$. Find the purchase price and market quotation of the bond on November 1, 1968, to yield $j_2 = 5\%$.

PART III

Probability

7

Introduction to Probability and Game Theory

7.1 Sets

A set is a well-defined collection of objects—for example, the set of all presidents of the United States, past and present, or the set of whole numbers between 3 and 15, inclusive. Naturally, you would expect that most of the sets in a mathematics book would be sets of numbers. In this book, we shall talk a great deal about sets of numbers, but usually we shall talk about other types of sets. In particular, we shall speak of sets of possible happenings when an experiment is performed. In any case, it is important to know how to describe a set so that it will be well-defined. Perhaps the best way is to list the actual objects in the set. For example, consider the second set described above. For simplicity, let us call this set A. Now, $A = \{3, 4, 5, 6, 7, 8, 9, 10, 11, 12, 13, 14, 15\}$. Note that the curly brackets $\{\ \}$ are used to enclose all the numbers in A. The objects in the set are called *elements* or *points* of the set. We shall use the symbol $\in$ to indicate that an element belongs to a particular set. Thus $6 \in A$, and $17 \notin A$, where the $/$ indicates "not," just as in the symbol $\neq$, for "not equal."

It is sometimes difficult to know whether a collection of objects is well-defined and qualifies as a set. To begin with, you must have in mind some underlying universe from which points can be drawn. Thus, to say, "*B* is the set of all numbers larger than 2," assumes that you are thinking only of numbers which can be compared to 2 in terms of magnitude. In this case, the universe should consist of whole numbers or real numbers but not imaginary or complex numbers. Having decided upon a universe, every element in the universe is either a member of the set or not a member of the set. For example, let *C* be the set of all real numbers which are larger than $\sqrt{198}$. Now consider $7 + \sqrt{50}$: Is this number in *C*? To three decimal places, $\sqrt{198} = 14.071$ and $\sqrt{50} = 7.071$. So, with a limited table of square roots, you really do not know which is larger or if in fact they are equal. Of course, theoretically any two real numbers are comparable in terms of which is greater or smaller, and so the set *C* is well-defined. Nevertheless, there may be more to the innocuous sounding definition of a set than it would first appear. Actually, mathematicians, logicians, and philosophers have devoted many years of effort to the problems involved in this fundamental notion. We shall not. In fact, we shall not discuss set theory at all. We shall, however, use the notation of sets extensively.

How else can we describe a set, other than by listing all its elements or writing a sentence about it? The most common method is to simply write the sentence in mathematical notation, such as $A = \{x : 3 \leq x \leq 15,$ and x is an integer$\}$, read "*A* equals the set of numbers x such that x is greater than or equal to 3 and less than or equal to 15, and x is an integer." Of course, this is the same *A* described in the first paragraph. Note that ":" is read "such that." Having a set *A* and a known universe, one automatically can describe another set, namely, the set of all points not in *A*. We shall symbolize this by *A'* and call it "the complement of *A*". This is stated formally in the following definition.

Definition 1 $A' = \{x : x \notin A\}$ = Complement of *A*.

Suppose the universe is all the whole numbers between 1 and 100 inclusive. If $A = \{3, 4, 5, 6, 7, 8, 9, 10, 11, 12, 13, 14, 15\}$, then $A' = \{1, 2, 16, 17, 18, \ldots, 100\}$. The notation "..." means that the writer has left out something which he expects you to be able to fill in using common sense. Usually this is done to save writing; sometimes it is done because it cannot be avoided. For example, for $U = \{1, 2, 3, \ldots, 100\}$, the dots (or ellipsis) saves the writing of 96 numbers; for $V = \{2, 4, 6, \ldots\}$, V is the set of even positive integers and there is no largest element, so we cannot write them all out. A more complicated example would be $A_2 = \{1, 2\}$, $A_3 = \{1, 2, 3\}$, $A_4 = \{1, 2, 3, 4\}$,   etc,   or, in general, $A_n = \{1, 2, 3, \ldots, n\}$. We know that there is a largest element but we want to have a general expression which will be correct for all possible choices of n.

In the preceding example, it is clear that the elements of A_2 are included among the elements of A_4. When two sets are related in this way, the smaller is said to be a *subset* of the larger or we might say that the larger *contains* the smaller. This relationship is symbolized by $A_2 \subset A_4$. We shall state the following formal definition.

Definition 2 A is a subset of B if whenever $x \in A$, it is also true that $x \in B$.

Some immediate results of this definition are as follows:

1. For every set A, $A \subset A$.
2. If $A \subset B$ and $B \subset C$, then $A \subset C$.
3. If $A \subset B$ and $B \subset A$, then $A = B$.
4. If $A \subset B$, then $B' \subset A'$.

You should try to convince yourself that these are true although perhaps one comment is in order. We have written expressions of the form $A = B$ about two sets, but we have not said what is meant by equality of sets. Perhaps it would be simplest to say that Statement 3 is the definition of equality and let it go at that. But to be perfectly clear, let us say that two sets are equal if they contain exactly the same elements. Thus $\{1, 3, 2\} = \{2, 1, 3\} = \{3, 1, 2\}$, etc.

Suppose we have two sets, A and B. It is possible to form new sets by using the elements of both sets. For example, we define the intersection of A and B as the set of all points common to both sets. The symbol for this is $A \cap B$ and the formal definition follows.

Definition 3 $A \cap B = \{x : x \in A \text{ and also } x \in B\}$.

For example, if $A = \{1, 2, 3, \ldots, 10\}$, $B = \{6, 7, 8, \ldots, 15\}$ and $C = \{12, 13, 14, \ldots, 20\}$, then

$$A \cap B = \{6, 7, 8, 9, 10\}, B \cap C = \{12, 13, 14, 15\}$$

What about $A \cap C$? There are no points common to both A and C. We call such sets *disjoint*. Their intersection is *empty*, that is, it is a set with no elements in it. Such a set is called the *empty set* or *null set* and is identified by the symbol $\varnothing$. Null sets usually arise in one of two ways. The first we have already seen, that is, as the intersection of disjoint sets. The second occurs when a set is described by a mathematical condition which can never be true. For example, $\{x : x^2 = -1$ and x is a real number$\}$ $= \emptyset$. Certain properties of intersections now follow immediately from Definitions 2 and 3:

    5. $A \cap B = B \cap A$.
    6. $A \cap A = A$.
    7. $A \cap U = A$, where U is the universe.
    8. $A \cap \emptyset = \emptyset$.
    9. $A \cap B \subset A$, and $A \cap B \subset B$.
  10. $\emptyset \subset A$, for every set A.

Let us consider another operation involving two sets. The union of A and B is the set of all points in one or the other of the sets or in both. This operation is symbolized $A \cup B$. Thus we have the following Definition.

Definition 4 $A \cup B = \{x : x \in A$ or $x \in B$ or both$\}$.

So, using A, B and C as in the last example, $A \cup B = \{1, 2, 3, \ldots, 15\}$ and $B \cup C = \{6, 7, 8, \ldots, 20\}$. Notice that points which occur in both sets are not written twice in the union. This is so because a point is either in a set or not in a set and indicating it more than once would serve no useful purpose.

Before we list some further properties of complementation, union and intersection, a few remarks about the order of operations should be made. First, the complementation symbol applies only to the set to which it is attached. That is, $A \cap B'$ is the intersection of A with the complement of B. To indicate the complement of the intersection of A and B, one would write $(A \cap B)'$. Here, just as in algebra, the operation within the parentheses is to be performed first. The symbol $A \cap B \cup C$ is unclear, since no agreement has been reached as to which takes precedence, union or intersection. In fact, we shall not reach an agreement, but we will use parentheses in either case. That is, $A \cap (B \cup C) \neq (A \cap B) \cup C$, but at least both sides have a unique interpretation. In order to deduce some of the properties of sets, it is convenient to use a device known as the Venn diagram. In a Venn diagram, the interior of a square is taken to be the universe. Regions bounded by given closed curves are the sets in this universe and intersections and unions have obvious geometric representations. Figure 1 shows Venn diagrams for a number of typical sets which may be encountered. In particular, 1c shows that $A \cup B$ is the union of three disjoint sets, $A \cap B'$, $A \cap B$ and $A' \cap B$. The idea that a set can be partitioned in this way, into a so-called disjoint union of subsets, is quite useful in probability problems.

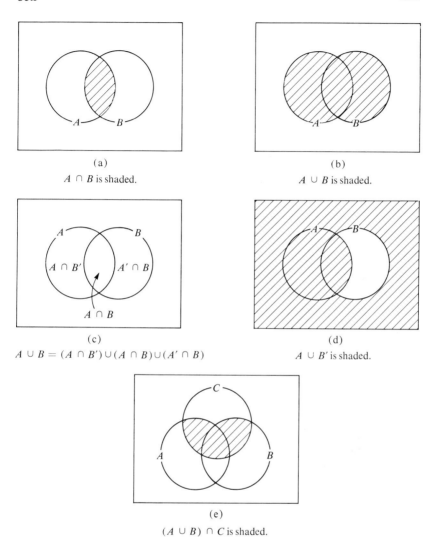

(a)

$A \cap B$ is shaded.

(b)

$A \cup B$ is shaded.

(c)

$A \cup B = (A \cap B') \cup (A \cap B) \cup (A' \cap B)$

(d)

$A \cup B'$ is shaded.

(e)

$(A \cup B) \cap C$ is shaded.

Figure 1

Let us now list some additional simple properties of sets. For unions:

11. $A \cup B = B \cup A$.
12. $A \cup A = A$.
13. $A \cup U = U$, where U is the universe.
14. $A \cup \varnothing = A$.
15. $A \subset A \cup B$, and $B \subset A \cup B$.

For complementation:

16. $(A')' = A$.
17. $U' = \varnothing$, and $\varnothing' = U$.

Finally, some less than obvious results:

18. $A \cap (B \cap C) = (A \cap B) \cap C$, and $A \cup (B \cup C) = (A \cup B) \cup C$, the associative law (which allows us to drop parentheses in cases of multiple union or intersection).
19. $A \cap (B \cup C) = (A \cap B) \cup (A \cap C)$, and $A \cup (B \cap C) = (A \cup B) \cap (A \cup C)$, the distributive laws.
20. $(A \cup B)' = A' \cap B'$, and $(A \cap B)' = A' \cup B'$, DeMorgan's laws.

The last two are not easy to see and you should draw Venn diagrams to convince yourself that they are at least plausible.

Let us look at some simple business examples.

Example 1   A company purchases two mailing lists in use in a direct advertising campaign. The first list contains 150,000 names. The second list contains 200,000 names. However, there is a 65,000 name overlap between the two lists. How many different names do they have?

Refer to figure 1(c). Let A be the set of names on the first list and B be the set of names on the second list. We wish to know the number of names in $A \cup B$. Now $A \cap B$ contains 65,000 names, and hence $A \cap B'$ must have 150,000 − 65,000 = 85,000 names. Similarly, the number in $A' \cap B$ must contain 200,000 − 65,000 = 135,000 names. Thus, the number in $A \cup B = 85,000 + 65,000 + 135,000 = 285,000$ names.

Example 2   Two brokerage firms merge. If the first firm had 30,000 clients, the second firm had 40,000, and the combined firms have 56,000 clients, how many clients deal with both firms?

If we let A be the first firm's clients and B be the second firm's clients, $A \cup B$ is the set of clients of the merged firm. Referring to Example 1, had the two mailing lists been disjoint, we would have expected 350,000 names. There was a "shortage" of 65,000 names represented by the number in $A \cap B$. Similarly, in this case, if the lists were disjoint, we would expect 70,000 names. We are short 14,000. This must be the number in $A \cap B$.

In general, the number in $A \cup B$ = number in A + number in B − number in $A \cap B$.

EXERCISES

1. Given the universe $U = \{-1, 0, 1, 2, 3, 4, 5, 6, 7\}$, $R = \{1, 2, 3, 4\}$, $S = \{-1, 0, 1, 2\}$, $T = \{2, 4, 6\}$, and $X = \{1, 3, 5, 7\}$. Which of the following are true?
   (a) $X \cap T = \varnothing$
   (b) $X \cup T = U$
   (c) $T \cap S \subset R$
   (d) $T \cap S' \subset X$
   (e) $X \cap T' = X$
   (f) $(X \cap T)' = U$
   (g) $R \subset S' \cup T'$
   (h) $S' \subset X \cup T$

In Exercises 2–7, the universe $U = \{1, 2, 3, \ldots, 50\}$, $A = \{1, 2, 3, \ldots, 25\}$, $B = \{10, 11, 12, \ldots, 35\}$ and $C = \{2, 4, 6, \ldots, 50\}$.

2. Find A', B' and C'.

3. Find $A \cap B$, $A \cap C$, $A' \cap C$ and $A' \cap B' \cap C'$.

4. Find $A \cup B$, $A \cup C$, $A' \cup C$, $C' \cup B'$ and $B \cup (A \cap C)$.

5. Find $A \cap (B \cup C)$, $(A \cap B) \cup (A \cap C)$, and verify that the distributive law holds.

6. Repeat Exercise 5 for $A \cup (B \cap C)$ and $(A \cup B) \cap (A \cup C)$.

7. Verify DeMorgan's laws: $(A \cup B)' = A' \cap B'$, and $(A \cap B)' = A' \cup B'$.

8. Construct Venn diagrams to verify the distributive laws and De-Morgan's laws.

9. Let $D = \{-2, -1, 0, 1, 2, 3, 4\}$; find $R = \{y : y = x^2, \text{ for } x \in D\}$.

10. Let $R = \{1, 2, 3, 4, 5, 6\}$; find $D = \{x : x^2 = y, \text{ for } y \in R\}$.

11. Let $D = \{-1, 0, 1, 2, 3, 4, 5\}$; find $E = \{y : x + (1/2)y = 3, \text{ for } x \in D\}$.

12. Find $F = \{(x, y) : x + 2y = 15 \text{ and } x, y \text{ are positive integers}\}$.

13. List all the possible subsets of $H = \{\#\}$. Do the same for $S = \{@, \$\}$ and for $T = \{\%, \phi, \&\}$. (Do not forget the empty set and the set itself!) Can you guess a rule that tells you the number of subsets of a set with n elements?

14. Let A be the set of students who passed the first examination and B be the set of students who passed the second examination. A consists of 25 students, B consists of 18 students and $A \cap B$ contains 13 students. How many students are there in $A \cup B$? How would you describe the sets $A \cap B$ and $A \cup B$ in words?

15. In Exercise 14, suppose that there are 25 students in A, 23 students in B and 29 students in $A \cup B$. How many students passed both exams?

16. A company has 520 employees, of which 333 got a raise, 145 got a promotion, and 67 got both. How many employees got neither a raise nor a promotion?

17. When Smith and Jones merged their two companies, they ended up with 3,500 customers. If 600 customers had dealt with both firms and if 2,800 had dealt with Smith, how many customers were Jones'? How many had been exclusively Jones' customers?

18. An accountant had been covering his embezzlements by attributing the same funds to two different investments. His books showed a total income of $2,000,000, of which $150,000 was as yet unassigned, $1,220,000 was in certificates of deposit, and $790,000 was in Treasury bills. How much had he stolen?

7.2 Relations and Functions

Suppose $A = \{x : 0 \leq x \leq 2\}$ and $B = \{y : 0 \leq y \leq 3\}$. There are various rules by which we may associate elements of A and elements of B. Any specific rule is called a *relation*. For example, the rule $y \leq x$ associates with every $x \in A$ all those elements of B which are less than or equal to x. In this relation there are many y-values associated with each x-value. The set of x-values for which the rule is defined consists of all of the set A. The set of y-values for which the rule is defined consists of a subset of B, namely, $\{y : 0 \leq y \leq 2\}$.

Consider now the rule $y = x^2$. This rule makes sense for all $x \in A$, but in order that the resulting y be an element of B, we must restrict our attention to $D = \{x : 0 \leq x \leq \sqrt{3}\}$. On the other hand, the set of possible y-values is all of B. However, the characteristic of greatest interest in this relation is that to each value of x for which the relation is defined, there is associated exactly one y-value. Such a relation is called a *function*. The set of x-values for which the function is defined is called the *domain* of the function. The set of y-values for which the function is defined is called the *range* of the function. As one allows x to vary, y varies in an exactly predictable fashion. This is so because for every chosen x, precisely one y-value is defined. Therefore, we call x the *independent* variable, y the *dependent* variable, and we say that y is a function of x.

We usually use the following notational conventions. The function is called f (or g, or h, . . .); the set D of possible values of the independent variable is called the *domain* of f. The value of y associated with a given x is denoted by $f(x)$ (read "f of x") and we write the rule as $y = f(x)$. Finally, the set of possible y-values is called the *range* of f. Mathematically, we could describe the range as

$$R = \{y : y = f(x), x \in D\}$$

For example, if the rule is $y = x^{1/2}$ and if we deal only with real numbers, then the largest set that D could be is $D = \{x : x \geq 0\}$, since we cannot take the square root of a negative number. In $f(x)$ notation, we would say that $f(x) = x^{1/2}$. In this case $R = \{y : y \geq 0\}$.

From these examples it would appear that D and f determine R, and this is correct. However, it is also possible that R may determine D to some extent, as we can see from the earlier example, $y = x^2$, where $0 \leq y \leq 3$ forced $0 \leq x \leq \sqrt{3}$.

The principal difference between the independent and dependent variable is as follows: For every x there is associated only one y but for several different x's, $f(x)$ may be the same. For example, if $y = x^2$ and the domain contains positive and negative values, we have $f(-a) = (-a)^2 = a^2$ and $f(a) = a^2$ for every choice of a. That is, each y-value (except 0) is associated with two different x-values.

As you see, if an expression $f(x)$ gives the y-value corresponding to each x-value, then the y corresponding to any specific x can be found by direct substitution.

Example 1 If the relationship between x and y is given by $y = f(x) = x^2 + 3x - 4$, find $f(1)$, $f(0)$, $f(2 + a)$, and $f(x + t)$. Does $f(x + t) = f(x) + f(t)$?

To find $f(1)$, substitute 1 for x wherever it appears. Thus,

$$f(1) = (1)^2 + 3(1) - 4 = 0$$

We find $f(0)$ similarly.

$$f(0) = (0)^2 + 3(0) - 4 = -4$$

In the same manner,

$$f(2 + a) = (2 + a)^2 + 3(2 + a) - 4$$
$$= a^2 + 7a + 6$$

Again,

$$f(x + t) = (x + t)^2 + 3(x + t) - 4$$
$$= x^2 + 2xt + t^2 + 3x + 3t - 4$$

but

$$f(x) + f(t) = (x^2 + 3x - 4) + (t^2 + 3t - 4)$$
$$= x^2 + 3x + t^2 + 3t - 8 \neq f(x + t)$$

If all the (x, y) pairs satisfying a given function or relation are plotted, the resulting picture is called its *graph*. Since for a function each x-value calls for precisely one y-value, the graph of a function will have the characteristic that any vertical line crosses the graph in exactly one point. For example, the graph in Figure 2 is a function but the graph in Figure 3 is not.

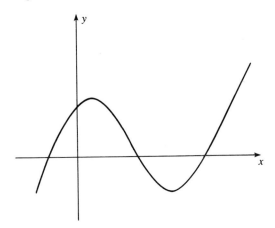

Figure 2

The idea of a graph of a function is really only useful when both the dependent and independent variables are real numbers. In part IV of this text, we shall study some techniques that are helpful in finding the graphs of such functions. However, in this book, functions appear in a variety of guises. One identified as such is the random variable. For the random variable we use a markedly different notation from that given here. In addition, the domain of the random variable is not a set of numbers. It is instead a set of elements in a sample space. Prior to the random variable we encounter the probability measure. This is also a function, but we do not refer to it as such in the text.

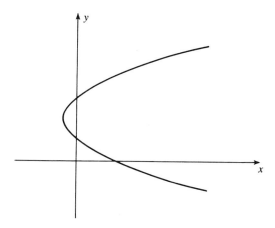

Figure 3

This function has as its domain the space of subsets of the sample space. That is, the points in the domain are sets. We also encounter the objective function for a linear programming problem. This function has as its domain the space of ordered pairs or triples (or n-tuples), depending upon the number of variables. Thus there is almost no limit to the kinds of mathematical spaces upon which functions may be defined.

EXERCISES

1. Classify the following relations between x and y as: (1) y is a function of x, (2) x is a function of y, (3) both, or (4) neither.
   (a) $x + y = 11$
   (b) $x^2 + y = 17$
   (c) $x + y^3 = 3$
   (d) $x^2 + y = 2$
   (e) $x^2 + y^2 = 4$

2. Repeat Exercise 1 for the relations defined by the following tables of values.

(a)

x	y
1	1
2	4
-1	1
-2	4
0	0

(b)

x	y
0	1
1	3
-1	5
-1	7
1	9

(c)

x	y
1	1
2	1
3	1
4	1
5	1

3. Let $y = x + 3$ be the function relating x and y. Let the domain
    be $D = \{x : -1 \leq x \leq 7\}$. Find the range.

4. Repeat Exercise 3 for the function $y = x^2$.

5. Let $w = f(z)$, $f(z) = z - 4$, and let the range of f be $R = \{w : 1 \leq w \leq 17\}$. Find the domain.

6. Repeat Exercise 5 for $f(z) = z^2 + 1$.

7. Plot the relations in Exercise 2.

8. Plot the functions in Exercises 3, 4, 5, and 6.

9. Find a function whose domain is $D = \{x : 0 \leq x \leq 5\}$ and whose
    range is $R = \{y : 1 \leq y \leq 11\}$.

10. Repeat Exercise 9 for $D = \{s : -4 \leq s \leq 4\}$ and $R = \{t : 1/2 \leq t \leq 12\}$.

11. If $f(x) = x^3 + 3x + 1$, find $f(-1), f(0), f(1), f(2)$, and $f(3)$. Plot the
    pairs (x, y) for $x = -1, 0, 1, 2, 3$ and $y = f(x)$. Connect the points
    with a smooth curve to get an idea of the graph of $y = x^3 + 3x + 1$.

12. For $f(t) = t - 1/t$. Find:
    (a) $f(3)$
    (b) $1/f(3)$
    (c) $f(1/2)$
    (d) $1/f(1/2)$
    (e) $f(x)$
    (f) $f(a)$
    (g) $(f(x) + f(a))/2$
    (h) $f(f(1/2))$
    (i) $f(f(t))$.

13. Let $f(x) = x^2$ and $g(t) = t + 3$. Find:
    (a) $f(3)$
    (b) $g(5)$
    (c) $f(1/2)$
    (d) $f(-1) + g(-3)$
    (e) $f(1)g(-2)$
    (f) $f(t)g(x)$
    (g) $f(g(0))$
    (h) $g(f(1))$

14. Using f and g as defined in Exercise 13, find:
    (a) $f(x) - x^2$
    (b) $(g(x) - x) \div 3$

(c) $(f(t) - 2t)g(t)$
(d) $(f(0) - g(0)) \div (f(0) + g(0))$
(e) $f(f(2) + g(2))$
(f) $g(f(x) + g(x))$

7.3 Events and Sets

The origin of the modern theory of probability is reputedly in a question raised by a gambler, the Chevalier de Mere, to the French mathematician and philosopher, Blaise Pascal (1623–1662). The question supposedly concerned how to divide the stakes in a game which is interrupted before completion. As an illustration, consider the following game. Two players, A and B, agree to play a dice game. Each player will roll one die. The one who rolls the higher number will collect as many dollars as the sum of the two dice. Player A rolls his die and gets a two. At this point the game is stopped. Clearly, the situation as it stands seems to favor Player B. If the game can never be resumed, how much should A pay to B? Another way of asking the same question is, How much would a bystander be willing to pay to B for the right of taking his place in the game at this juncture? It seemed to the mathematicians that the fair way to settle the game would be for A to pay to B an amount equal to what he could honestly expect to win on the average whenever this situation occurred. Average value could be obtained as follows: First, assume that the dice are perfect balanced cubes. Then if B were to roll his die a large number of times, one would expect that he would get each of the numbers one, two, three, four, five and six, each about one-sixth of the time.

Table 1 summarizes the results of these outcomes.

Table 1

B's Number	B's Winnings	Fraction of Time
1	−3	1/6
2	0	1/6
3	5	1/6
4	6	1/6
5	7	1/6
6	8	1/6

So we would expect that B will win −3 (i.e., lose 3), 0, 5, 6, 7 or 8 dollars, each about one-sixth of the time. Hence, on the average, B may expect to win $(-3 + 0 + 5 + 6 + 7 + 8)/6 = 23/6$ dollars every time this situation occurs. Note that under no condition can the sum of 23/6 of a dollar actually be the amount won. Nevertheless, this is the *average* value of the game to B and this is the amount for which he should be willing to sell his turn. In the development of the theory of probability, an attempt is made to set up a formal mathematical structure for problems of this type and others of a related nature.

Let us begin by assuming that an experiment is about to be performed. The experiment may be rolling a die, or flipping a coin, or measuring the height of a person selected from names in the telephone book by jabbing a pin into a page or it might be simply observing whether rain will be falling at noon tomorrow in Chicago. However, one characteristic is necessary, that is, the outcome of the experiment must be at least partly determined by chance so that there is no way to predict with certainty the exact outcome. Let us further assume that there are only a finite number of possible outcomes to the experiment. When a coin is flipped, the possible outcomes are "heads" and "tails," assuming that the coin will not land on its edge. Of course, one could observe the angle between some axis on the coin and true north, or one could observe the temperature of the room after the coin is flipped, but these seem to have little bearing in the usual case.

Let us assume that one could write a list of the outcomes of interest. Also, assume that this list is finite, that all the possible outcomes are included and that anything that can occur is described by precisely one item on the list. Such a list is called a set of *elementary outcomes* and the Universe S, composed of these outcomes, is called a *sample space* for the experiment. For example, when a die is rolled, $S = \{1, 2, 3, 4, 5, 6\}$ gives a sample space for the experiment. In measuring the height of a person selected at random, we would not get a sample space as defined above, since one cannot list all the possible heights. If, on the other hand, one agrees to measure to the nearest inch, then we can probably assume that $S = \{1, 2, \ldots, 120\}$ is a reasonable sample space, since people over 10 feet tall are rather scarce.

Of course, one may be interested in something other than an elementary outcome. For example, one may wish to describe the case in which B wins in the game described at the outset. Clearly, B wins if he rolls a three, four, five or six. Letting $W = \{3, 4, 5, 6\}$, we see that the outcome "B wins" can be described by the words "one of the elements in W occurs" or simply "W occurs." W is an example of a composite outcome or "event," that is, an event is a subset of the sample space. An event is said to occur if any element in the event is the outcome of the experiment. Let us look at some simple examples. In rolling two dice, one is usually interested in the sum of the two dice. Therefore, we shall take as the sample space the set $S = \{2, 3, 4, \ldots, 12\}$. The event, "a number divisible by 3 occurs," $= A = \{3, 6, 9, 12\}$. The event, "a number bigger than 5 and smaller than 10 occurs," $= B = \{6, 7, 8, 9\}$.

Common English sentences describing the occurrence or nonoccurrence of certain events now take on their natural set notational interpretation. Thus, if a person says, "I'll bet that a number divisible by 3, falling between 5 and 10, will be rolled," he is betting that A and B will occur simultaneously. That is, in set notation, he is betting on $A \cap B = \{6, 9\}$. Similarly, the statement "a number between 5 and 10 or divisible by 3" is interpreted as $A \cup B = \{3, 6, 7, 8, 9, 12\}$. To say that A does not occur is to refer to A'. Since either A or A' must occur, we say that $A \cup A'$ is a "sure" or "certain" event. That is, $A \cup A' = S$, the sample space, is sometimes referred to as the sure event. Similarly, since A and A' cannot both occur at once, $A \cap A'$ is called the *impossible event*. So, the symbol $\varnothing$, used for the empty set, will signify, in probability theory, an event that cannot occur.

Interestingly, it is possible to construct many different sample spaces for the same experiment. In fact, given any sample space for an experiment, any partition of the sample space into disjoint sets which together encompass all outcomes will serve as a new sample space. For example, suppose an experiment consists of selecting a card from a well-shuffled deck of playing cards. The usual sample space would consist of 52 points identified by suit and rank. Thus, Ca = club ace; Hq = heart queen; S7 = spade seven and Dk = diamond king. However, one could just as easily deal with the sample space $S_1 = \{$Heart, Spade, Diamond, Club$\}$. Certainly any card selected falls into one of these categories. No card falls into two categories simultaneously and so all the conditions for a set of elementary outcomes are satisfied. On the other hand, $S = \{$Heart, Face card, Diamond, Black card$\}$, is not a proper sample space. Any card picked will surely fall into one of the categories, but the Queen of Hearts, for example, falls into two at once. In some problems it is difficult to know whether all possibilities are included or whether they are mutually exclusive. However, in most of what we do this should not offer any difficulty.

EXERCISES

1. Calculate the value to B of the dice game described at the beginning of this section, if A had rolled a 1. Now try it for the other possible numbers that A could have rolled. Find the average of the values for the cases when A rolled 1, 2, 3, 4, 5 and 6. Does this result surprise you?

2. In playing certain board games, two dice are rolled, the sum of the two dice tells how far to move and a roll of doubles gives an extra turn. Write a sample space suitable for the experiment of rolling the dice in these games.

3. A deck consists of ten cards numbered 1 to 10. A card is drawn at random from the deck. Write a sample space for this experiment.

4. Write a sample space consisting of five elements for the experiment in Exercise 3 and such that (a) you think the elementary outcomes are equally likely to occur, and (b) you think the outcomes are not equally likely.

5. A bag contains balls lettered $a, b, \ldots, z$. A ball is chosen at random from the bag. Let the sample space be $S = \{a, b, c, \ldots, z\}$. Write the event, V, a vowel is drawn. Write the event, E, a letter in the word *event* is drawn. How would you express the event $\{e\}$ in terms of E and V? What is the event E or V occurred? What is the event E occurred but V did not?

6. A bag contains four blocks colored red, green, blue and yellow. A block is selected at random. Let the sample space be the four possible colors. Write all possible events for this experiment.

7. A red die and a green die are rolled. It is important to know what numbers turned up on each die. Write a suitable sample space for this experiment.

8. A man has five nails which he is trying to drive into a board. The nails bend easily. He tries each one in turn until he succeeds. What is the sample space showing all possible outcomes for this experiment?

9. For the experiment described in Exercise 8, display the following events: It takes at least three tries to succeed; it takes no more than three tries to succeed; either it works the first time or not at all; it does not work at first but at least one nail is left over.

10. Weather observers in New York and Chicago report either clear weather, rain or snow. Write the set of all possible joint communiques. Write the following events: It is raining in at least one city; it is raining in exactly one of the two cities; the weather is the same in both cities; the weather is not the same in both cities; it is snowing in New York; it is snowing in one city and not in the other.

7.4 Probability Measure

In all of the experiments described and in any other one that may be encountered, it is clear that some events seem to be more likely to occur than others. For example, if $A \subset B$ then whenever A occurs so does B, but B may occur without A doing so. Hence, B is more likely than A. Or, as a matter of experience, gamblers have noted that in rolling two dice, one is far more likely to get a total of seven than of two. In the theory of probability, mathematicians attempt to apply a quantitative measure of likelihood to the possible subsets (events) of a sample space. It would be nice to express these likelihoods in terms of percents. That is, a sure event has 100% chance of occurring and an impossible event has 0% chance of occurrence. However, in order to avoid percent signs, it has been agreed to use numbers on the scale of zero to one. That is, a likelihood of one means certainty and zero means impossibility. (In general probability theory this is not quite true, but it is correct for finite probability theory, which is the only type to be discussed in this section.)

In order to have this measure of likelihood in accordance with intuition, we shall define the "probability" of an event E, $P(E)$, to have the following properties:

1. If E is any event, $0 \leq P(E) \leq 1$.
2. $P(S) = 1$.
3. If $A \cap B = \varnothing$, then $P(A \cup B) = P(A) + P(B)$.

These "Probability Axioms" have a very simple intuitive basis. Axiom 1 simply states that the measure of likelihood shall be scaled from zero to one. Axiom 2 states that the likelihood of a sure event is one and hence fixes the top end of the scale. Axiom 3 says that if two events cannot occur simultaneously, then the probability of one or the other occurring is simply the sum of the probabilities of the events separately occurring. Perhaps a simple example would illustrate this. Let a card be selected from a deck at random. Let H be the event a heart is drawn and D be the event a diamond is drawn. One would suspect that $P(H) = 1/4$ and $P(D) = 1/4$ since there are four suits and no one suit seems more likely to be drawn than the other. Now, $P(\text{Red card}) = P(H \cup D)$. Since H and D are mutually exclusive, by Axiom 3, $P(H \cup D) = P(H) + P(D) = 1/4 + 1/4 = 1/2$. The final result also seems to agree with intuition.

In applying Axiom 3, one must be certain that the events are mutually exclusive. For example, suppose a coin is tossed twice. Let $A =$ a head occurs on the first toss and $B =$ a head occurs on the second toss. Consider $P(\text{Head on either first or second toss}) = P(A \cup B)$. If the coin is fair, it seems reasonable to attach probability $1/2$ to both A and B. If one were now to apply Axiom 3, the result would be $P(A \cup B) = P(A) + P(B) = 1/2 + 1/2 = 1$. This means that in flipping a coin twice, one is certain to get at least one head. Of course, experience tells us that this is not at all the case. The error enters in, because A and B are not mutually exclusive, that is, the probability of getting two heads in a row is not zero. In fact, we shall see a little later that in two independent flips of a fair coin, the probability of getting two heads is $1/4$. We shall also discover how to use this information to obtain a proper result for the preceeding example. However, let us first investigate how one goes about constructing probability measures on the events of a finite sample space.

Let $S = \{s_1, s_2, s_3, \ldots, s_n\}$ be a finite sample space for some experiment. A probability measure may be applied to all the subsets of S as follows: Associate with each point s_j a number p_j which measures the likelihood of s_j. The only restrictions on the p's are

1. $p_j \geq 0$ for all $j = 1, 2, \ldots, n$;
2. $p_1 + p_2 + \cdots + p_n = 1$.

We shall define the probability of any set A, $P(A)$, as the sum of the likelihoods of the points in A. In particular, the probability of the singleton set $\{s_j\}$ is just p_j. Hence, we shall mix our notation and sometimes refer to the likelihood of a point as the probability of the point and thus not really distinguish between the point s and the set $\{s\}$ whose only element is s. To a set theorist this is an unforgivable sin, but for our purposes there will be little chance of confusion.

Suppose, for example, that we have a rather biased coin with a wide edge. In flipping this coin we have three possible outcomes, h, t and e. Let us assign the likelihood $1/2$ to h, $1/3$ to t and $1/6$ to e. The three likelihoods are nonnegative numbers whose sum is 1. This experiment has eight possible events associated with it, namely,

1. H = Heads occurs; $P(H) = 1/2$,
2. T = Tails occurs; $P(T) = 1/3$;
3. E = Coin lands on edge; $P(E) = 1/6$;
4. $H' = \{t, e\}$ = Heads does not occur; $P(H') = 1/3 + 1/6 = 1/2$;
5. $T' = \{h, e\}$ = Tails does not occur; $P(T') = 1/2 + 1/6 = 2/3$;
6. $E' = \{h, t\}$ = The coin does not land on its edge; $P(E') = 1/2 + 1/3 = 5/6$;
7. $S = \{h, t, e\}$ = The coin lands in one of the three possible positions; $P(S) = 1$;
8. $\varnothing$ = The coin lands in none of the three positions; $P(\varnothing) = 0$.

The observant reader will have noticed in this example that the probability of $\varnothing$, the impossible event, is 0. We have remarked earlier that this should be the case, but have not stated it as one of our axioms. We shall prove this as our first result on probability.

THEOREM 1 Let S be the sample space for any experiment; then $P(\varnothing) = 0$.

Proof From Axiom 2, $P(S) = 1$. Now $S \cup \varnothing = S$ and $S \cap \varnothing = \varnothing$, so by Axiom 3, $P(S) = P(S) + P(\varnothing)$. Therefore, $1 = 1 + P(\varnothing)$; $P(\varnothing) = 0$.

The method of this proof may be extended to the following more general result.

THEOREM 2   Let S be the sample space for any experiment and let A be any subset of S; then, $P(A') = 1 - P(A)$.

Proof $A \cup A' = S$ and $A \cap A' = \varnothing$. Hence $1 = P(S) = P(A \cup A')$. Therefore, $1 = P(A) + P(A')$ and $P(A') = 1 - P(A)$.

The reader will note that this theorem does indeed hold for the example discussed above; but he should also realize that the proof does not depend upon the method by which the probability measure is attached to the subsets of S but only upon the three axioms. Let us consider one other well-known result, which deals with the probability of the union of sets which are not disjoint.

THEOREM 3   Let S be the sample space of an experiment and let A and B be any two subsets of S; then $P(A \cup B) = P(A) + P(B) - P(A \cap B)$.

Proof   Referring to figure 1c, p. 205, we can write $A \cup B = A \cup (A' \cap B)$ and $A \cap (A' \cap B) = \varnothing$. Therefore, $P(A \cup B) = P(A) + P(A' \cap B)$. Furthermore, $B = (A \cap B) \cup (A' \cap B)$ and $(A \cap B) \cap (A' \cap B) = \varnothing$. Therefore, $P(B) = P(A \cap B) + P(A' \cap B)$. This gives two basic relationships:

$$P(A \cup B) = P(A) + P(A' \cap B) \qquad \textbf{(1)}$$

$$P(B) = P(A \cap B) + P(A' \cap B) \qquad \textbf{(2)}$$

Subtracting Eq. (2) from Eq. (1), we have

$$P(A \cup B) - P(B) = P(A) - P(A \cap B)$$

or

$$P(A \cup B) = P(A) + P(B) - P(A \cap B)$$

which completes the proof.

How does one go about understanding the intuitive justification of such a result? There is a very nice geometric method for visualizing probabilistic results. Let the sample space be represented by a square of area 1. Let all the events be subregions of this square just as in a Venn diagram. Let the probability of an event be the area of the subregion. Referring to figure 4, we are looking for the area of $A \cup B$. The area of A plus the area of B is clearly larger than the area of $A \cup B$. In fact, it seems obvious that the excess is caused by the fact that we have added in the area of $A \cap B$ twice. Hence, area of $A \cup B$ = area of A + area of B − area of $A \cap B$.

When this type of geometric reasoning is used, it is apparent that if $A \subset B$, then the area of A is less than or equal to the area of B. Thus, we should be able to prove the following theorem.

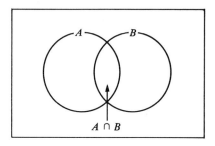

Figure 4

THEOREM 4   Let A and B be events and let $A \subset B$. Then $P(A) \leq P(B)$.

Proof $B = A \cup (A' \cap B)$, where $A \cap (A' \cap B) = \varnothing$. Thus, $P(B) = P(A) + P(A' \cap B)$. Since $P(A' \cap B) \geq 0$, by Axiom 1 it follows that $P(B) \geq P(A)$.

Let us demonstrate the use of some of these theorems with an example. A certain political party is backing three candidates for different offices. Their names are Adams, Bailey and Calhoun. The pollsters tell us that Adams has a 34% chance of winning, Bailey has a 44% chance of winning and there is a 21% chance that both will be elected. What is the probability that at least one will be a winner? Let A be the event Adams wins, and let B be the event Bailey wins. Then

$$P(A) = 0.34 \qquad P(B) = 0.44 \qquad P(A \cap B) = 0.21$$

Therefore,

$$P(A \cup B) = P \text{ (at least one wins)}$$
$$= P(A) + P(B) - P(A \cap B)$$
$$= 0.34 + 0.44 - 0.21 = 0.57$$

Let us assume additionally that the probability that both Bailey and Calhoun are elected is 0.20 and the probability that at least one is elected is 0.79. What is the probability that Calhoun is elected?

Let C be the event that Calhoun is elected. Then

$$P(B \cup C) = P(B) + P(C) - P(B \cap C)$$
$$0.79 = 0.44 + P(C) - 0.20$$
$$P(C) = 0.55$$

Suppose that the probability that all three are simultaneously elected is 0.12. What is the probability that Bailey and Calhoun get elected but Adams does not? Here we are given $P(A \cap B \cap C) = 0.12$ and asked to find $P(A' \cap B \cap C)$. Now $B \cap C = (A \cap B \cap C) \cup (A' \cap B \cap C)$, and $A \cap B \cap C$ and $A' \cap B \cap C$ are disjoint so we can apply Axiom 3 directly:

$$P(B \cap C) = P(A \cap B \cap C) + P(A' \cap B \cap C)$$
$$0.20 = 0.12 + P(A' \cap B \cap C)$$
$$P(A' \cap B \cap C) = 0.08$$

If $P(A \cap B' \cap C) = 0.07$, what is $P(A \cup C)$?

$$P(A \cup C) = P(A) + P(C) - P(A \cap C)$$

and

$$P(A \cap C) = P(A \cap B' \cap C) + P(A \cap B \cap C)$$
$$= 0.07 + 0.12 = .19$$
$$P(A \cup C) = 0.34 + 0.55 - 0.19 = 0.70$$

What is the probability that none are elected? This could be done directly, but figure 5 shows how all the information given previously can be summarized to completely expose the answers to any problems about this example.

The last part of the preceding example really requires finding $P(A \cup B \cup C)$, where A, B and C are not mutually exclusive. There is a general formula for this. In fact, there is a general formula for $P(A_1 \cup A_2 \cup A_3 \ldots \cup A_n)$. For now we content ourselves with the following theorem.

THEOREM 5 $P(A \cup B \cup C) = P(A) + P(B) + P(C) - P(A \cap B) - P(A \cap C) - P(B \cap C) + P(A \cap B \cap C)$.

The proof of this result is the first exercise. However, one may convince oneself of this result geometrically by means of a Venn diagram.

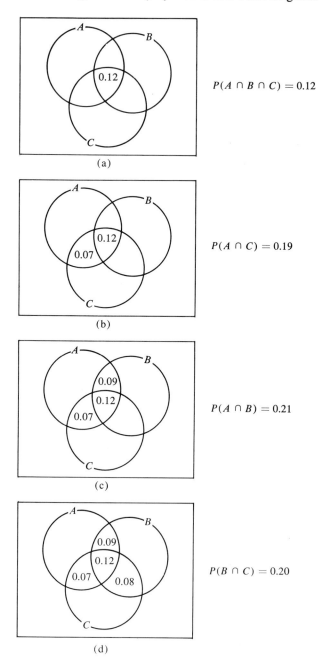

$P(A \cap B \cap C) = 0.12$

(a)

$P(A \cap C) = 0.19$

(b)

$P(A \cap B) = 0.21$

(c)

$P(B \cap C) = 0.20$

(d)

Figure 5

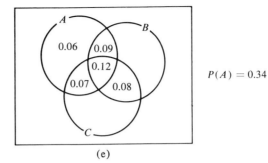

$P(A) = 0.34$

(e)

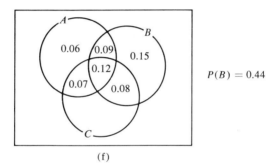

$P(B) = 0.44$

(f)

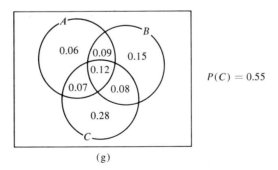

$P(C) = 0.55$

(g)

$P(A \cup B \cup C) = 0.06 + 0.09 + 0.07 + 0.12 + 0.15 + 0.08 + 0.28 = 0.85$

$P(A \cup B \cup C) = 0.85$

$P([A \cup B \cup C]') = 1 - P(A \cup B \cup C) = 0.15$

Figure 5, Cont.

EXERCISES

1. Prove Theorem 5.

2. Referring to Exercise 3, Section 7.3, assume all cards are equally likely. Let X be the number on the card drawn. Let $A = X$ is even and let $B = 2 \leq X < 8$. Find $P(A)$, $P(B)$, $P(A \cap B)$ and $P(A \cup B)$.

3. Referring to Exercise 5, Section 7.3, assume all the letters are equally likely to be drawn. Find $P(V)$, $P(E)$, $P(E \cup V)$ and $P(E \cap V')$.

4. Referring to Exercise 6, Section 7.3, suppose that red is twice as likely as green which is twice as likely as blue which is just as likely as yellow. Find the probabilities of all the events for this sample space.

5. Referring to Exercise 8, Section 7.3, let X be the number of the attempt on which the first success occurs. Suppose $P(X = 1) = 1/3$, $P(X = 2) = 2/9$, $P(X = 3) = 2/9$, $P(X = 4) = 1/9$ and $P(X = 5) = 1/18$. Find the probabilities of all the events in Exercise 9.

6. Of students studying French and English, 95% pass at least one of the courses, 78% pass French and 88% pass English. What percent pass both?

7. George and Harry are unreliable workers; the probability that at least one of them will be out sick is 0.6. The probability that Harry will be out sick is 0.5 and the probability that they will both be out is 0.2. What is the probability that George will be out? What is the probability that neither is sick? What is the probability that exactly one will be sick? What is the probability that George will be sick and Harry will not be?

8. Continuation of Exercise 7. Sam is also unreliable and counting him, one of the three men is out 90% of the time. The probability that only Sam is sick is 0.2. Find the probability that Sam and at least one of the others are out sick.

9. A survey of luncheonettes shows that in addition to conducting their regular business many of them sell reading matter as well. In fact, 1/2 sell newspapers, 23/36 sell magazines, 2/3 sell paperback books, 7/18 sell newspapers and magazines, 1/3 sell magazines and paperbacks, 10/36 sell newspapers and paperbacks, and 1/6 sell all three. (a) What fraction sell no reading matter? (b) What fraction sell only newspapers? (c) What fraction sell exactly one of the three types of reading matter?

10. A recent advertising survey has shown that a person selected at random watches TV commercials with probability 0.8, reads newspaper ads with probability 0.7 and reads magazine ads with probability 0.4. Only 10% of the people do none of these things and 20% do all three. Find the probability that a person selected at random is exposed to exactly two of these three forms of advertising.

11. In a retail store, the owner estimates that his costs amount to $5 per customer. He finds that 30% of the customers buy nothing, 20% spend $3, 20% spend $5, 10% spend $10, 10% spend $20, and 10% spend $30. Find the probability of the following events. The owner makes no money or loses money on a customer. The owner makes at least $10 over expenses on a customer. A customer spends between $5 and $50. How much does the average customer spend? How much does the store owner clear on the average customer?

12. A stock broker surveys his clients to determine which types of securities they would like to receive information about. The result of the survey shows that 60% are interested in stocks, 50% are interested in corporate bonds, 40% are interested in municipal bonds, and 10% are interested in all three. How many are interested in exactly two? If no one is interested in just the combination "stocks and municipals," and 30% are interested exclusively in stocks, draw a Venn diagram showing the complete breakdown of the clients in terms of investment interests.

7.5 Assigning Probabilities

Now that we know how to handle combinations of events given the probabilities of the component parts, there still remains some doubt as to how one begins to assign probability measures to a completely new sample space. Certainly, the most straightforward approach seems to be as follows: Describe and list all the possible elementary outcomes for the experiment and assign to each one a likelihood as described in the preceding section. The difficulty arises in assigning likelihoods in such a way as to mirror reality, that is, to pick the likelihood so that the likelihood of a point s is the fraction of the time that one would really expect s to occur. To be more precise, let us suppose that we are able to repeat an experiment a large number of times under essentially identical conditions and in such a way that the occurrence or nonoccurrence of an event in any trial is totally independent of what happened previously. For example, in flipping a coin, one feels relatively confident that each flip is unaffected by the others, that the result of each flip is random, and that there are no outside influences that could affect the likelihood of a head or a tail.

Now, each time the experiment is performed, there is a sample space $S = \{s_1, s_2, s_3, \ldots, s_k\}$. If the experiment is performed N times, then s_1 will have occurred n_1 times, s_2 will have occurred n_2 times and so on. We would then be able to record the frequency with which each elementary outcome occurred. That is, $f_1 = n_1/N$, $f_2 = n_2/N$, $\ldots$, $f_k = n_k/N$. Note that $n_1 + n_2 + \cdots + n_k = N$, or, in other words, $f_1 + f_2 + \cdots + f_k = 1$. This much can always be done. Whether or not these frequencies mean anything is a philosophical question. However, we do assume that there is some regularity in even a probabilistic universe. We exhibit our faith in this proposition via the so-called Principle of Statistical Regularity. This states that there exist numbers $p_1, p_2, \ldots, p_k$ such that for large values of N, f_j is approximately p_j for $j = 1, 2, 3, \ldots, k$. These p's are the likelihoods of the outcomes $s_1, s_2, \ldots, s_k$. Therefore, when faced with a new experiment, one should perform a large number of trials and measure the frequencies of the possible outcomes. These frequencies may then serve as a first approximation to the likelihoods of the elementary outcomes. One may then define the probability of each event in the sample space.

As a simple example, let us consider rolling a single die. An actual string of outcomes in successive trials yielded 5, 4, 4, 1, 2, 1, 1, 2, 3, 6, 3, 2, 1, 3, 2, 1, 2, 5, 4, 6. We may now display the result of these twenty trials. (See table 2.)

Table 2

20 Trials

No. of 1's = 5	$f_1 = 5/20 = .25$
No. of 2's = 5	$f_2 = 5/20 = .25$
No. of 3's = 3	$f_3 = 3/20 = .15$
No. of 4's = 3	$f_4 = 3/20 = .15$
No. of 5's = 2	$f_5 = 2/20 = .10$
No. of 6's = 2	$f_6 = 2/20 = .10$

Of course, this is a very small number of trials. A second string of twenty yielded 5, 5, 6, 1, 1, 3, 4, 6, 2, 3, 2, 3, 5, 3, 5, 3, 3, 4, 2, 6. The results of combining these with the first group are given in table 3.

Table 3

40 Trials

No. of 1's = 7	$f_1 = 7/40 = .175$
No. of 2's = 8	$f_2 = 8/40 = .200$
No. of 3's = 9	$f_3 = 9/40 = .225$
No. of 4's = 5	$f_4 = 5/40 = .125$
No. of 5's = 6	$f_5 = 6/40 = .150$
No. of 6's = 5	$f_6 = 5/40 = .125$

Continuing, we performed 160 more trials, reaching a total of 200 with the results in table 4.

Table 4

200 Trials

No. of 1's = 27	$f_1 = .135$
No. of 2's = 37	$f_2 = .185$
No. of 3's = 39	$f_3 = .195$
No. of 4's = 28	$f_4 = .140$
No. of 5's = 35	$f_5 = .175$
No. of 6's = 34	$f_6 = .170$

Using these figures, one might say, for example,

$$P[\text{Even number}] = P(E) = P\{2, 4, 6\} = f_2 + f_4 + f_6 = 0.495$$

Of course, there is another point of view. Namely, since a die is totally symmetric, no face should be favored over any other, if it is well made. Therefore, the likelihood of each elementary outcome should be taken to be $1/6$. From this angle, the data collected so far may be viewed as an attempt to ascertain whether the actual die rolled is "fair," that is, whether the real die behaved as a mathematically ideal die should. Answers to questions of this type fall into the province of statistical theory.

Nevertheless, the idea of a mathematically ideal die or fair coin or "perfectly shuffled" deck of cards is pervasive in elementary probability theory. It is expressed as the "Principle of Equal Likelihood." This principle says that in the absence of evidence to the contrary, one should assume that all elementary outcomes have equal likelihood. That is, if an experiment has k possible elementary outcomes, each should be assigned the probability $1/k$ unless experience dictates otherwise. Now,

look back at the table of 200 trials (table 4). Do you think that the frequencies $f_1, f_2, \ldots, f_6$ differ significantly from $1/6 = 0.167$? We will not
attempt an answer here.

Let us consider another example. In rolling two dice, we will record
only the sum of the faces which come up. If we consider our sample space
to be $S = \{2, 3, 4, \ldots, 12\}$ and assign the probability $1/11$ to each point,
we would have a perfectly valid probability measure established in accordance with the principle of equal likelihood. However, gamblers have
ascertained over the centuries that this is a very poor model of reality.
In fact, when two dice are rolled, a total of seven will occur about six
times as often as a total of two. Interestingly enough, this disparity can
be cleared up within the framework of the equal likelihood principle by
choosing the elementary outcomes more critically. To be exact, one should
consider two dice of different color (so that they may be easily distin-
guished) and consider the elementary outcomes to be all possible distinguishable outcomes. That is, calling the dice red and green, there are 36
outcomes, ranging from $(R1, G1)$ to $(R6, G6)$, each of which may be
assigned likelihood $1/36$. We leave the actual listing of all the outcomes to
the reader. As an example, however, $P(\text{Total of the dice is 7}) = P\{(R1, G6),$
$(R2, G5), (R3, G4), (R4, G3), (R5, G2), (R6, G1)\} = 6/36 = 1/6$.

Thus, the equal likelihood method of assigning probabilities is momen-
tarily revived. Still, in flipping biased coins or rolling "loaded" dice, the
principle is of no use. Nevertheless, we shall use it repeatedly. Whenever
we refer to flipping a fair coin, we mean $P(H) = P(T) = 1/2$. Rolling a
fair die means $P(1) = P(2) = \cdots = P(6) = 1/6$. Or, in general, the
phrase, "select an object at random from a set," will mean that all objects
in the set are to be equally likely selections.

EXERCISES

1. List all the outcomes in rolling a red die and a green die. Find the
   probabilities of each of the totals 2, 3, . . . , 12 assuming each elementary outcome has probability $1/36$.

2. List all the outcomes possible when a coin is flipped three times in a
   row. Assuming heads and tails are equally likely, find
   (a) P (Three heads)
   (b) P (At least two tails)
   (c) P (Odd number of heads)
   (d) P (Last flip is heads)
   (e) P (First or last flip is tails)
   (f) P (First and second flip are tails)
   (g) P (At least one head)

3. Flip a penny and a dime simultaneously. Repeat 100 times. Find the frequency of two heads, one head, two tails, head on the penny and tail on the dime.

4. Radioactive decay simulation. Let ten pennies represent ten atomic particles. Flip the ten coins and discard all those that come up heads. Flip the remaining coins again; discard all that come up heads. Continue in this manner until no coins remain. Each flip represents a half-life. The number of flips needed is the number of half-lives until total decay. Repeat the experiment 100 times and find the frequencies of one flip, two flips, etc.

5. A poker player has four hearts and a spade. He discards the spade and draws one card. What is the probability that he ends up with a heart flush? HINT: Since he does not know his opponents' cards, assume all 47 remaining cards are equally likely.

6. A poker player has two pairs. He discards his odd card and draws one. What is the probability that he gets a full house?

7. Continuation of 5 and 6. What is the probability of filling an "inside straight," a straight open at both ends? Drawing to $H5$, $H6$, $H7$, $H8$, what is the probability of ending up with a straight, a flush, or a straight flush?

8. For each section of this text, count the number of exercises. Find the frequency with which each of the numbers 10, 11, and 12 appear.

7.6 Random Variables

In many mathematical applications, it is desirable to be able to describe the outcome of an experiment with a single number rather than verbally. In some cases, this is done automatically. That is, in rolling a die, the elementary outcomes are already represented by the numbers 1, 2, 3, 4, 5, 6. Of course, in any case with a finite number of elementary outcomes, it is possible to number the elements of the sample space $S = \{s_1, s_2, \ldots, s_n\}$ and use the subscript as the numerical description of an outcome. However, whatever means is used, a rule of assignment is defined which assigns to each element in the sample space a real number. Thus, we have a function whose domain is the sample space and whose range is some subset of the real numbers. Such a function is called a *random variable*.

Unfortunately, the standard terminology for random variables is different from the functional notation with which the reader is familiar. We will use s to symbolize a typical point in the sample space, X (or Y or $Z \ldots$)

as the function and x (or y or z . . .) as the values of function. That is, we will write $x = X(s)$. Of course, we could use different notation, but only at the price of making all other books on the subject unintelligible to students who have learned from this one.

Some typical examples of random variables follow.

Example 1   A coin is flipped. We assign 1 to heads and 0 to tails. That is, $X(H) = 1$, $X(T) = 0$. This could be said to be $X(s) =$ number of heads.

Example 2   A coin is flipped four times. Let $X(s) =$ number of heads. Now the range of $X = \{0, 1, 2, 3, 4\}$. For example, $X(H, H, T, H) = 3$.

Example 3   Two dice (one red, one green) are rolled. Let $Y(s) =$ sum of the two dice. Now, range of $Y = \{2, 3, 4, \ldots, 12\}$. For example, $Y(R2, G6) = 8$.

Notice that the outcome of a random variable is random, and one may assign probabilities to it in the natural way. That is, $P(X = x) = P\{s : X(s) = x\}$. For example, in Example 1 $P(X = 1) = 1/2$.

In Example 2, suppose we wanted $P(X = 3)$. That is, the probability of getting three heads in four flips of a fair coin. $P(X = 3) = P(HHHT, HHTH, HTHH, THHH)$. That is, $\{s : X(s) = 3\}$ contains four of the elementary outcomes. The reader may check that there are sixteen all together. Hence, $P(X = 3) = 4/16 = 1/4$.

In order to save writing, we shall use the symbol $p(x)$ for $P(X = x)$. This is called the *probability function*. Thus, associated with each random variable X, there is a probability function, $p(x) = P(X = x)$.

Let us consider Example 3 in some detail. In this case, the range of Y is $\{2, 3, 4, 5, \ldots, 12\}$. The probability function $p(y)$ could be displayed as follows:

y	2	3	4	5	6	7	8	9	10	11	12
$p(y)$	1/36	2/36	3/36	4/36	5/36	6/36	5/36	4/36	3/36	2/36	1/36

Notice the interesting relationship between the random variable and its probability function. The random variable is a function whose domain is the sample space. The range of the random variable is some subset of the real numbers. The probability function is zero except for values of x in the range of the random variable X. Hence, the probability function $p(x)$ need only be defined for the values in the range of X. In this sense, the range of the random variable is the domain of the associated probability function. Note that the sum of the values of $p(y)$ over all y in the range of Y must add up to 1. It is possible to express $p(y)$ as

$$p(y) = \frac{6 - |7 - y|}{36} \qquad y = 2, 3, \ldots, 12$$

When it is not too complicated, we shall try to write $p(x)$ as a formula valid for all suitable values of x. Otherwise we shall use a table.

In addition, any function of a random variable will be a random variable. In the preceding, let $X = (Y - 6)^2$. Range of X is $\{0, 1, 4, 9, 16, 25, 36\}$, where $P(X = 4) = P(Y = 4 \text{ or } Y = 8) = P(Y = 4) + P(Y = 8) = 8/36$, for example. The probability function is

x	0	1	4	9	16	25	36
$p(x)$	5/36	10/36	8/36	6/36	4/36	2/36	1/36

Here is a simulation of a practical problem.

Example 4 A barbershop in an airlines terminal gets most of its business in the last half-hour before major departures. In fact, if we let X be the number of customers who enter the store in that time we have

x	0	1	2	3	4	5
$p(x)$	0.1	0.1	0.3	0.2	0.2	0.1

If the owner is the only barber, and if it takes 15 minutes per haircut, we can let Y be the number of customers turned away. Now $p_Y(y)$ is the following:

y	0	1	2	3
$p_Y(y)$	0.5	0.2	0.2	0.1

Do you see where these numbers came from? There will be no customers turned away ($Y = 0$) when $X = 0$, 1, or 2. Therefore, $p_Y(0) = P(Y = 0) = P(X = 0) + P(X = 1) + P(X = 2) = p(0) + p(1) + p(2) = 0.1 + 0.1 + 0.3$. Similarly, $p_Y(1) = P(X = 3) = p(3) = 0.2$ and so on. If we let Z be the number of customers serviced, then in the same manner we obtain

z	0	1	2
$p_Z(z)$	0.1	0.1	0.8

Suppose that the barber hires an assistant who can work just as fast as the barber. Let T be the number of customers that they can handle jointly. Here

t	0	1	2	3	4
$p_T(t)$	0.1	0.1	0.3	0.2	0.3

Finally, let U be the number of customers handled by the assistant. Assuming that the two barbers divide the customers and that, given a choice, people go to the first barber, we have the following analysis:

If $X =$	0	1	2	3	4	5
then $U =$	0	0	1	1	2	2

Therefore, U has the probability function

u	0	1	2
$p_U(u)$	0.2	0.5	0.3

Does the assistant earn his pay? That depends on how much is charged for a haircut. We shall revisit this example in the next section.

EXERCISES

1. Write the probability function for X in Example 1.

2. Write the probability function for X in Example 2.

3. For the example in Exercise 2, find $P(X \geq 3)$ and $P(1 \leq X < 4)$.

4. Referring to Adams, Bailey and Calhoun in Section 7.4, let $Z =$ number of winners in the election. Find the probability function for Z.

5. Referring to Exercise 4, $Y = 3 - Z =$ number of losers, find the probability function for Y.

6. Referring to Exercise 2, write the probability function for $Y = (X - 2)^2$.

7. A box contains three white balls numbered 1, 2, 3 and three black balls numbered 1, 2, 3. Two balls are drawn at random (simultaneously) from the box. Write all the points in the sample space. Let $X =$ largest number drawn. Find the probability function for X. Let $Y =$ the number on the highest numbered white ball drawn. Find the probability function for Y.

8. Referring to Exercise 7, let $Z =$ sum of all white ball numbers minus the sum of all black ball numbers drawn. Find the probability function for Z.

9. Referring to Exercise 7, let W = difference between the numbers drawn. Find the probability function for W.

10. The probability that k customers enter a store is equal to c/k. If k may be 1, 2, 3, or 4, find c. Let X be the number of customers. Write out the probability function for X. Let $Y = |X - 2|$. Find the probability function for Y.

11. In a certain card game, each card counts its number, with aces counting one and pictures 10 points. Find the probability function for X = the number of points drawn, if all cards are equally likely to be drawn.

12. An auto agency has weekly overhead of $500. It purchases cars for $3,000 each and sells them for $4,500. If it orders only as many cars as it needs and X = the weekly demand is distributed as below, find the probability function for Y = weekly profit.

x	0	1	2	3	4
$p(x)$	0.40	0.30	0.20	0.05	0.05

13. If the overhead costs in Exercise 12 go up to $1,500 and the selling price of a car must be reduced to $3,800 in order to stimulate sales, find the new distribution of Y. What is the probability of at least breaking even?

14. (Continuation of Exercise 8, Section 7.5) For each section of this text count the number of exercises. If a section is selected at random and E = number of exercises for the section, find the probability function for E.

7.7 Expected Values

We are now in a position to formalize the concept with which this chapter began. That is, what is the expected outcome of a random experiment? Suppose that a random variable X has k possible values, $x_1, x_2, \ldots, x_k$ with $p(x_1) = p_1, p(x_2) = p_2, \ldots, p(x_k) = p_k$. Suppose further that the experiment is performed N times and that x_1 is the outcome n_1 times, x_2 is the outcome n_2 times and so on. The average value of the outcomes will be given by the sum of all the outcomes, $n_1x_1 + n_2x_2 + \cdots + n_kx_k$ divided by N, the number of trials. Hence,

$$\text{Average} = [n_1x_1 + n_2x_2 + \cdots + n_kx_k] \div N$$

$$= x_1\frac{n_1}{N} + x_2\frac{n_2}{N} + \cdots + x_k\frac{n_k}{N}$$

$$= x_1f_1 + x_2f_2 + \cdots + x_kf_k$$

where $f_1, f_2, \ldots, f_k$ are the frequencies of occurrence of the various values. Now these frequencies should be approximately equal to the corresponding probabilities. Hence, we expect that over a large number of trials the average value of X will be $x_1 p_1 + x_2 p_2 + \cdots + x_k p_k$. We will symbolize this value by $E(X)$, called the *expected value of X*; that is, $E(X) = x_1 p_1 + x_2 p_2 + \cdots + x_k p_k$.

For example, let $X =$ the outcome in rolling one die. The possible values of X are (1, 2, 3, 4, 5, 6). The corresponding probabilities are all $1/6$. Hence, $E(X) = 1(1/6) + 2(1/6) + 3(1/6) + 4(1/6) + 5(1/6) + 6(1/6) = 21/6 = 3\frac{1}{2}$. Does this mean that when we roll a die we can expect to roll a $3\frac{1}{2}$? Of course not! In fact, we can never roll $3\frac{1}{2}$. But in a large number of rolls, the average of all the rolls should be close to $3\frac{1}{2}$. Consider the 200 trial run given on page 227. We have 27 ones totaling 27, 37 twos totaling 74, 39 threes totaling 117, etc. The grand total is 709. Dividing by 200, the total number of rolls, we find that the average value is 3.545, which is fairly close to 3.5.

Alternatively, we could have computed the average by taking $x_1 f_1 + x_2 f_2 + \cdots + x_6 f_6 = 1(.135) + 2(.185) + 3(.195) + 4(.140) + 5(.175) + 6(.170)$, but it was easier to work with whole numbers.

Since expressions of the previous kind occur frequently in probability, it is convenient to introduce some notation which will save considerable writing. We will use the symbol **x** to stand for the vector

$$(x_1, x_2, \ldots, x_k)$$

We will symbolize the column vector of probabilities by

$$\mathbf{p} = \begin{pmatrix} p_1 \\ p_2 \\ \vdots \\ p_k \end{pmatrix}$$

Using this notation, we have

$$E(X) = \mathbf{xp} = x_1 p_1 + x_2 p_2 + \cdots + x_k p_k$$

where **x** is the row vector of possible values and **p** is the column vector of the corresponding probabilities.

For the actual average value of X in the 200-trial experiment, we have

$$\text{Average} = \mathbf{xf}$$

$$= (1, 2, 3, 4, 5, 6) \begin{pmatrix} .135 \\ .185 \\ .195 \\ .140 \\ .175 \\ .170 \end{pmatrix}$$

where, of course, **f** is the "frequency vector."

Let us try some other examples.

Example 1   A coin is flipped three times. Let X = number of heads. Here

$$\mathbf{x} = (0, 1, 2, 3) \qquad \mathbf{p} = \begin{pmatrix} 1/8 \\ 3/8 \\ 3/8 \\ 1/8 \end{pmatrix}$$

$$E(X) = \mathbf{xp} = (0, 1, 2, 3) \begin{pmatrix} 1/8 \\ 3/8 \\ 3/8 \\ 1/8 \end{pmatrix}$$

$$= 0(1/8) + 1(3/8) + 2(3/8) + 3(1/8) = 12/8 = 1\tfrac{1}{2}$$

So we should average $1\tfrac{1}{2}$ heads out of three flips.

Example 2   Two dice are rolled. Y = sum of the faces.

$$\mathbf{y} = (2, 3, 4, \ldots, 12) \qquad \mathbf{p} = \begin{pmatrix} 1/36 \\ 2/36 \\ \vdots \\ 1/36 \end{pmatrix}$$

$$E(Y) = \mathbf{yp} = 7$$

The reader should check this one out. Also note that the expected sum on two dice is simply twice the expected value of a single die!

Interestingly enough, in Example 1, $E(X)$ is a number which X can never equal, and in Example 2, $E(Y)$ is the most likely value possible. This simply indicates that the expected value may or may not be a value which will come up frequently.

Since functions of random variables will be random variables themselves, it is possible to discuss the expected value of $Y = g(X)$. We may represent this as $E[g(X)]$, or simply $E(Y)$. The computation of this quantity may be carried out by finding the probability function for Y, $p_Y(y)$ and computing the expected value in the usual way or by simply finding the product

$$(g(x_1), g(x_2), \ldots, g(x_k)) \begin{pmatrix} p_1 \\ p_2 \\ \vdots \\ p_k \end{pmatrix}$$

For example, in rolling a die, let $Y = (X - 3)^2$ where X is the number which appears. We now have

$$\mathbf{y} = (0, 1, 4, 9)$$

with corresponding probability vector

$$\mathbf{p}_Y = \begin{pmatrix} 1/6 \\ 1/3 \\ 1/3 \\ 1/6 \end{pmatrix}$$

and

$$E(Y) = (0, 1, 4, 9) \begin{pmatrix} 1/6 \\ 1/3 \\ 1/3 \\ 1/6 \end{pmatrix}$$

$$= 0(1/6) + 1(1/3) + 4(1/3) + 9(1/6) = 19/6 = 3\tfrac{1}{6}$$

Alternatively

$$E(g(X)) = ((-2)^2, (-1)^2, 0^2, 1^2, 2^2, 3^2) \begin{pmatrix} 1/6 \\ 1/6 \\ 1/6 \\ 1/6 \\ 1/6 \\ 1/6 \end{pmatrix}$$

$$= 4(1/6) + 1(1/6) + 0(1/6) + 1(1/6) + 4(1/6) + 9(1/6)$$
$$= 19/6 = 3\tfrac{1}{6}$$

Usually we shall use the latter method to avoid having to compute a new probability function.

In business and economic decision making, the expected value usually plays a critical role. Let us look at a simple example.

Example 2 A record store sells records for $4.50 regularly and $3.80 when on sale. Letting $X =$ number of records sold, the store has found that the probabilities that a customer will buy X records are given by the probability functions $p(x)$ regularly and $q(x)$ when on sale. The two probability functions are as shown.

x	$p(x)$	$q(x)$
0	0.2	0.1
1	0.4	0.3
2	0.2	0.2
3	0.1	0.2
4	0.1	0.2

Does it pay to hold a sale?

Letting Y be the money spent by a customer, then under regular conditions, Y may equal 0, 4.5, 9, 13.5, or 18, according to whether X is 0, 1, 2, 3, or 4, and

$$E(Y) = 0(0.2) + 4.5(0.4) + 9(0.2) + 13.5(0.1) + 18(0.1)$$
$$= 6.75$$

Alternatively, we could say that the expected amount taken in is $4.50 times the expected number of records sold, or $E(Y) = 4.5E(X)$. Thus,

$$E(X) = 0(0.2) + 1(0.4) + 2(0.2) + 3(0.1) + 4(0.1)$$
$$= 1.5$$

and

$$E(Y) = 4.5(1.5) = 6.75$$

When a sale is held, $E(Y) = 3.8E(X)$, where $E(X)$ must be computed using the probability function $q(x)$. That is,

$$E(X) = 0(0.1) + 1(0.3) + 2(0.2) + 3(0.2) + 4(0.2)$$
$$= 2.1$$

and

$$E(Y) = 3.8(2.1) = 7.98$$

Hence, on a sale, the average customer will buy 2.1 records rather than 1.5 records and the average amount spent per customer will go up $1.23. In short, if the criterion is amount of total receipts, it pays to have a sale.

For a more complicated case, let us look again at the barber shop example begun in the last section.

Example 3 Suppose that the barber charges $3 for a haircut. If he could handle all his customers, then his expected number of customers would be $E(X) = 0(0.1) + 1(0.1) + 2(0.3) + 3(0.2) + 4(0.2) + 5(0.1) = 2.3$. His expected income would be $3E(X) = 6.9$ or $6.90 per half-hour. This is the best that can be hoped for.

Recall that Z was defined to be the number of customers that the barber can handle single-handed. Thus, without an assistant, his expected income is

$$3E(Z) = 3[0(0.1) + 1(0.1) + 2(0.8)] = 5.1 = \$5.10$$

Suppose that his assistant gets paid $5 per hour. Does it pay to hire him?

The random variable T is the number that he and his assistant can handle together. We see that with the assistant, his expected net income is $3E(T) - 2.5$, since the assistant gets $2.50 per half hour. Computing,

$$3E(T) - 2.5 = 3[0(0.1) + 1(0.1) + 2(0.3) + 3(0.2) + 4(0.3)] - 2.5$$
$$= 3(2.5) - 2.5 = 7.5 - 2.5 = 5.0 \text{ or } \$5.00$$

Therefore, although he has only a 10% chance of turning away a customer, he makes less money with an assistant. In fact, the most that the owner can afford to pay the assistant is $2.40 per half-hour. So, instead, the owner offers to put the assistant on commission, that is, pay him c dollars per haircut. We had defined U to be the number of customers that the assistant will handle. The assistant's expected earnings under this plan is

$$cE(U) = c[0(0.2) + 1(0.5) + 2(0.3)] = 1.1c$$

Therefore, the assistant must insist on $1.1c = 2.4$, $c = 2.4/1.1 = \$2.18$ per haircut, if he is to receive the maximum that his employer is really capable of paying.

Sometimes you can use the expected value to deduce information about probabilities.

Example 4 Suppose that U.S. Government securities are paying 6% per annum. A certain "risky" venture is paying 12%. We may assume that the U.S. security is 100% safe. Hence, after one year, the expected value of a $100 security is $106. In the risky venture, there is a probability p that the venture will fail and be worth nothing at the end of the year. We can estimate the investor's opinion of the value of p by assuming that the expected value of the investment must be the same as the return one could get on a "sure thing." Letting V be the value of the venture when $100 is invested, we have that $V = 0$ with probability p and $V = 112$ with probability $1 - p$. Now,

$$E(V) = 0(p) + 112(1 - p) = 112 - 112p$$

which must equal 106. In other words,

$$112 - 112p = 106$$
$$6 = 112p$$
$$p = 6/112 = 0.054$$

In other words, if a safe investment pays 6% for one year, then a 12% return implies that there is about a 5.4% probability of default.

Let us see how vector algebra can be applied to problems involving expected value. Suppose X is a random variable, $Y = f(X)$ and $Z = g(X)$. Suppose we wish to find $E[af(X) + bg(X)]$. Let

$$\mathbf{y} = [f(x_1), f(x_2), \ldots, f(x_k)]$$

and

$$\mathbf{z} = [g(x_1), g(x_2), \ldots, g(x_k)]$$

Now

$$E[af(X) + bg(X)] = (a\mathbf{y} + b\mathbf{z})\mathbf{p}$$
$$= (a\mathbf{y})\mathbf{p} + (b\mathbf{z})\mathbf{p} = a(\mathbf{yp}) + b(\mathbf{zp})$$
$$= aE(Y) + bE(Z) = aE[f(X)] + bE[g(X)]$$

For example, suppose a bag contains four balls numbered 1, 2, 3, 4. A ball is chosen at random and X is the number of the ball. Now

$$\mathbf{x} = (1, 2, 3, 4) \qquad \mathbf{p} = \begin{pmatrix} 1/4 \\ 1/4 \\ 1/4 \\ 1/4 \end{pmatrix}$$

$$E(X) = (1, 2, 3, 4)\begin{pmatrix} 1/4 \\ 1/4 \\ 1/4 \\ 1/4 \end{pmatrix} = 1/4 + 1/2 + 3/4 + 1 = 2\tfrac{1}{2}$$

Suppose one wished to know $E(X^2 + 2X)$. We would write

$$E(X^2 + 2X) = E(X^2) + 2E(X)$$

$$= (1, 4, 9, 16)\begin{pmatrix} 1/4 \\ 1/4 \\ 1/4 \\ 1/4 \end{pmatrix} + 2(2\tfrac{1}{2})$$

$$= 1/4 + 1 + 9/4 + 4 + 5 = 12\tfrac{1}{2}$$

What about $E[(X + 1)^2]$? This would be

$$E[X^2 + 2X + 1] = 12\tfrac{1}{2} + E(1)$$

What is $E(1)$? We could work indirectly, letting

$$(X + 1)^2 = Y \qquad y = (4, 9, 16, 25)$$

$$E(Y) = (4, 9, 16, 25)\begin{pmatrix} 1/4 \\ 1/4 \\ 1/4 \\ 1/4 \end{pmatrix} = 1 + 9/4 + 4 + 25/4 = 13\tfrac{1}{2}$$

Therefore, $13\tfrac{1}{2} = 12\tfrac{1}{2} + E(1)$ and $E(1) = 1$. It would be nice if this were always the case, and it is. In fact, let c be any constant. Now for all values of X, c is equal to c; hence

$$E(c) = cp_1 + cp_2 + \cdots + cp_k$$
$$= c(p_1 + p_2 + \cdots + p_k) = c(1) = c$$

since the sum of the probabilities is always one.

As a last example, let us consider the following example: A biased coin lands heads with probability 0.5, tails with probability 0.3 and edge with probability 0.2. Suppose we agree to the following game: If heads comes up, you pay me \$2; if edge comes up, you pay me \$1; and if tails comes up, you pay me nothing. Letting X be the amount which you pay, then $x = (2, 1, 0)$ and

$$E(X) = (2, 1, 0)\begin{pmatrix} .5 \\ .2 \\ .3 \end{pmatrix} = 1.2$$

If I pay you \$1.20 to persuade you to play, then the payoffs would be $Y = X - 1.2$ and $E[X - 1.2] = E(X) - 1.2 = 1.2 - 1.2 = 0$. Thus we have a fair game. That is, on the average we both expect to break even.

EXERCISES

1. Calculate the expected number of heads in one flip of a fair coin, two flips, three flips, four flips. Can you guess a general formula?

2. In a state lottery, tickets cost 50¢. Out of every million tickets, one is worth \$50,000, ten are worth \$5,000, 100 are worth \$500, 1,000 are worth \$50 and the rest are worth nothing. Find the expected value of a ticket.

3. In roulette, there are eighteen red numbers, eighteen black numbers and two green numbers. If you bet on red, you win \$1.00 if red comes up; you lose \$1.00 otherwise. All numbers are equally likely to come up. Find the expected value of your bet.

4-14. Find the expected values of all the random variables given in Exercises 4 through 14 in the last section (Section 7.6).

15. Two fair dice are rolled. Let X be the sum of the uppermost faces. Find $E[(X - 7)^2]$ directly and by expanding $(X - 7)^2$ and applying the properties of expectation.

16. Repeat Exercise 6, by expanding $(X - 2)^2$ and using the properties of expectation.

17. A man who drives to work in New York City has his choice of putting his car in a parking lot and paying \$4.00 for the day or parking illegally. Sometimes when he parks illegally, he gets a \$15.00 parking ticket. What must the probability of being ticketed be for it to pay to use the parking lot?

18. Given $E(X) = 1$, $E(X^2) = 3$ and $E(X^3) = 2$, find $E[(X - 1)^3]$.

19. Given $E[(X + 3)^2] = 19$ and $E(X) = -1$, find $E(X^2)$.

20. Given $E[(X + 3)^2] = 19$ and $E[(X - 3)^2] = 3$, find $E(X^2)$ and $E(X)$.

21. An item costs \$20 to manufacture and sells for \$38. Of the items produced, 10% are very poorly made and must be replaced by a specially made substitute that costs \$25. The original must be junked. Another 15% must be repaired at a cost to the seller of \$15. The rest are perfect. What is the expected profit per sale?

22. For the manufacturer in Exercise 21, the cost of inspection would be $2 per item. As a result of inspection, no very poorly made items will be produced and the number needing repair will be reduced to 10%. Does it pay to inspect? How much should the seller be willing to pay for inspection?

23. Suppose that the barber in the text must pay his assistant $6 per hour. How much must the barber charge for a haircut so that his earnings will be the same with or without an assistant? How much will these earnings be?

7.8 Variance

As we have seen, the expected value of a random variable is the weighted average of the points in its range. The probabilities play the roles of the weights and hence the more likely a value is, the more heavily it is counted in finding the average. For this reason, $E(X)$ is usually called the *mean* of X and is thought of as the center about which observations of X will distribute themselves. Of course, the mean alone does not really give that much information. Consider, for example, the following probability functions:

x	$p_1(x)$	$p_2(x)$	$p_3(x)$
1	.2	.4	.05
2	.2	.1	.1
3	.2	0	.7
4	.2	.1	.1
5	.2	.4	.05

For each of the probability functions $p_1(x)$, $p_2(x)$ and $p_3(x)$ the mean is 3. In each case, the probabilities are symmetrically distributed about the mean. Nevertheless, one would expect quite different behavior if observations were made of random variables having these probability functions. For $p_1(x)$, one would expect about equal numbers of observations of all five of the values 1, 2, 3, 4, 5. In the second case, $p_2(x)$, most of the observations should be ones and fives, far from the mean. In the third case, most observations should be right at the mean. In this section, we shall describe a measurement called the *variance* which describes how spread out the observations are expected to be.

To fix the ideas, let us denote the expected value or mean of the random variable X by μ (the Greek letter mu). The mean is in some sense the central point about which observations of X will distribute. For short, we say "μ is the center of the distribution." We are interested in measuring the spread of the distribution. Since $X - \mu$ is the difference between X and its mean, one might wish to find the average or expected value of this quantity. However, $E[X - \mu] = E(X) - \mu = \mu - \mu = 0$. So this gives no information. A better choice might be $E[|X - \mu|]$. The absolute value eliminates negative numbers and hence avoids having the average come out zero. However, absolute values are algebraically annoying. So instead we use $E[(X - \mu)^2]$. This measurement is called the *variance* of X. It is abbreviated Var(X). Var(X) has the drawback that it involves square units. That is, if X is measured in feet, Var(X) would be in square feet. Therefore, many people prefer to use $\sqrt{\text{Var}(X)}$. This expression is called the "standard deviation of X." It is usually denoted by σ (the Greek letter sigma). Accordingly, the variance is denoted by σ^2. Summarizing, we have

$$\mu = E(X) \tag{1}$$

$$\sigma^2 = \text{Var}(X) = E[(X - \mu)^2] \tag{2}$$

$$\sigma = \text{SD}(X) = \sqrt{\text{Var}(X)} \tag{3}$$

Let us now contrast the three distributions given at the beginning of this section. For the distribution $p_1(x)$ we have,

$$\text{Var}(X) = E[(X - \mu)^2] = E[(X - 3)^2]$$
$$= (-2)^2(0.2) + (-1)^2(0.2) + 0^2(0.2) + (1)^2(0.2) + (2)^2(0.2) = 2$$

and

$$\sigma = \sqrt{2}$$

For the distribution $p_2(x)$,

$$\text{Var}(X) = (-2)^2(0.4) + (-1)^2(0.1) + (1)^2(0.1) + (2)^2(0.4)$$
$$= 1.6 + 0.1 + 0.1 + 1.6 = 3.4$$

and

$$\sigma = \sqrt{3.4}$$

Finally, for $p_3(x)$,

$$\text{Var}(X) = (-2)^2(0.05) + (-1)^2(0.1) + 0^2(0.7) + (1)^2(0.1) + (2)^2(0.05)$$
$$= 0.2 + 0.1 + 0 + 0.1 + 0.2 = 0.6$$

and

$$\sigma = \sqrt{0.6}$$

It is easy to see that the more spread out distribution, the larger the variance. Let us consider another example. Suppose we have the following distribution:

x	1	2	3	4	5	6	7	8
$p_4(x)$	.3	.2	.1	.05	.05	.1	.1	.1

In this case, $E(X) = 0.3 + 0.4 + 0.3 + 0.2 + 0.25 + 0.6 + 0.7 + 0.8 = 3.55$. To compute $E[(X - 3.55)^2]$ now would be quite a nuisance. However, there is a very nice little identity which can ease the task. Remembering that μ is a constant, we can say

$$\begin{aligned} \text{Var}(X) = E[(X - \mu)^2] &= E[X^2 - 2\mu X + \mu^2] \\ &= E(X^2) - 2\mu E(X) + E(\mu^2) \\ &= E(X^2) - 2\mu\mu + \mu^2 \\ &= E(X^2) - 2\mu^2 + \mu^2 = E(X^2) - \mu^2 \end{aligned}$$

Thus, in general, $\text{Var}(X) = E(X^2) - \mu^2$. Notice, $E(X^2) \neq [E(X)]^2$. Now, in our last example,

$$\begin{aligned} E(X^2) = \ &1^2(0.3) + 2^2(0.2) + 3^2(0.1) + 4^2(0.05) + 5^2(0.05) + 6^2(0.1) \\ &+ 7^2(0.1) + 8^2(0.1) \\ = \ &18.95 \end{aligned}$$

Hence,

$$\begin{aligned} \text{Var}(X) = 18.95 - \mu^2 &= 18.95 - (3.55)^2 \\ &= 18.95 - 12.6025 = 6.3475 \end{aligned}$$

With the aid of this last identity, we have a very nice way to compute the variance. We feel that the variance should measure the spread of the distribution. The question is, in what sense? A very famous inequality discovered by Chebyschev provides a partial answer. In words it says that the probability of having an observation more than k standard deviations away from μ is less than $1/k^2$. That is, the probability that an observation is more than two standard deviations from μ is less than $1/4$. An observation more than three standard deviations from μ occurs less than $1/9$ of the time and so on.

Another way of saying this is to say that the probability of an observation falling between $\mu - k\sigma$ and $\mu + k\sigma$ is at least $1 - 1/k^2$. Or in symbols,

$$P[\mu - k\sigma \leq X \leq \mu + k\sigma] \geq 1 - 1/k^2$$

Let us reconsider the three examples we have for the case $k = 2$. For $p_1(x)$, $\sigma = \sqrt{2} \approx 1.4$ and $\mu = 3$. Chebyschev's inequality says

$$P[3 - 2.8 \leq X \leq 3 + 2.8] \geq 1 - 1/4$$
$$P[0.2 \leq X \leq 5.8] \geq 3/4$$

In fact, X is always between 1 and 5. Hence,

$$P[0.2 \leq X \leq 5.8] = 1 \geq 3/4$$

The case $p_2(x)$ gives similar results. For the case $p_3(x)$, $\sigma = \sqrt{0.6} \approx 0.77$, $\mu = 3$. The inequality gives

$$P[3 - 1.54 \leq X \leq 3 + 1.54] \geq 3/4$$
$$P[1.46 \leq X \leq 4.54] \geq 3/4$$

Now,

$$P[1.46 \leq X \leq 4.54] = P[X = 2, 3, 4] = 0.9 \geq 3/4$$

as predicted.

Finally, for $p_4(x)$, $\sigma = \sqrt{6.3475} \approx 2.52$, $\mu = 3.55$. The case $k = 2$ would again yield a true probability of 1, so let us try $k = 1.5$. Chebyschev's inequality states

$$P[3.55 - (1.5)(2.52) \leq X \leq 3.55 + (1.5)(2.52)] \geq 1 - 1/(1.5)^2$$
$$P[-0.23 \leq X \leq 7.33] \geq 0.56$$

In fact,

$$P[-0.23 \leq X \leq 7.33] = P(X \neq 8)$$
$$= 1 - P(X = 8) = 1 - 0.1 = 0.9 \geq 0.56$$

In every case, Chebyschev's inequality, although correct, does not give very precise values for the probability. Nevertheless, it gives an upper bound which is correct for *every* probability distribution. The proof of this remarkable result may be found in most books on probability theory. A simple proof may be found in Shane, *Finite Mathematics, An Integrated Approach*, Charles E. Merrill, 1974, p. 235.

EXERCISES

1. Let X be the number which appears when a fair die is rolled. Find Var(X).

2. Find the variance of the random variable X described in Exercise 18, Section 7.7.

3. (a) Find the variance of X described in Exercise 19, Section 7.7.
   (b) Find Var(X) for X described in Exercise 20, Section 7.7.

4-14. Find the variances of the random variables whose expectations were found in Exercises 4 through 14 of Section 7.7.

Properties of Variance:

15. Let X be a random variable, with range $\{1, 2, \ldots, 8\}$ and let $p(x) = x/36$. Find $E(X)$ and Var(X).

16. For X in Exercise 15, compare the Chebyschev probability upper bound with the true probability for

$$P[\mu - k\sigma \leq X \leq \mu + k\sigma] \qquad \text{for } k = 1\,\tfrac{1}{2},\, 2,\, 2\,\tfrac{1}{2}$$

17. A card is drawn from a standard deck. Let X be the number of the card where all pictures are 10 and aces are 11. Find the probability function for X, $E(X)$ and Var(X). Now repeat Exercise 16 for this random variable.

18. If SD(X) measures spread, then doubling X should double SD(X). Show that if $Y = 2X$, Var(Y) = 4 Var(X) and hence SD(Y) = 2 SD(X).

19. Repeat Exercise 18 for $Y = -2X$.

20. Show that if c is any constant, Var(cX) = c^2Var(X), and hence SD(cX) = $|c|$SD(X).

21. Show that Var($X + b$) = Var(X) for any constant b. (This makes sense, since adding a constant to all values of X should not change the spread.)

7.9 Games of Strategy

We began this chapter with a discussion of a simple gambling game. Like many such games, this one involved pure chance with no strategic considerations. In this section, we shall discuss some competitive games which do not involve any chance. Of course, most games which are really of interest involve elements of both skill and chance. Real games of this type are far too complicated to be analyzed here.

We shall deal with a very special kind of game. To begin with, we shall always consider two-player games in which each player has only a finite number of possible plays. To be specific, let us say that Player I has m possible plays and Player II has n possible plays. Each player makes his play without the other knowing what he will do. When Player I picks his ith play and Player II picks his jth play, there results a "payoff" g_{ij} from Player II to Player I. Of course, g_{ij} may be negative, indicating that Player II is the winner. We may display the collection of outcomes as a matrix G. The entries in G will be the numbers g_{ij} arranged as follows: Numbering the rows of G, $1, 2, \ldots, m$ from top to bottom and the columns $1, 2, \ldots, n$ from left to right, then g_{ij} is the entry in Row i, Column j. For example,

$$G = \begin{pmatrix} -1 & 2 & 3 \\ 1 & -4 & 5 \end{pmatrix}$$

In this case, $m = 2$, $n = 3$, and G is a 2×3 matrix. The first player has two possible plays and the second player has three possible plays. If Player I plays his first possibility and Player II plays his third possibility, the payoff is g_{13}, the entry in Row 1 and Column 3, namely, 3. Thus, in this case Player II pays three units to Player I.

Let us now look at a simple (2×2) matrix game. Suppose each player has two cards; Player I has a red 1 and a black 6. Player II has a red 3 and a black 1. Each player plays a card. If the colors match, Player I wins the sum of the numbers played. Otherwise, Player II does. The payoff matrix for this game is

$$G = \begin{pmatrix} 4 & -2 \\ -9 & 7 \end{pmatrix} \begin{matrix} R1 \\ B6 \end{matrix}$$
$$ R3 \quad B1$$

Now Player I would like to play $B6$ where he might win 7 units but he opens himself up to a loss of 9 units if his opponent guesses correctly. Similarly, $R1$ may offer both rewards and penalties. Therefore, Player I must avoid falling into any pattern of play in repetitions of the game for fear that his opponent may discover the pattern. Accordingly, Player I decides to play his cards randomly. To start, he may try playing each card $1/2$ of the time. Thus, when his opponent plays $R3$, Player I expects to win

$$v_1 = (1/2)(4) + (1/2)(-9) = -2\tfrac{1}{2}$$

When his opponent plays $B1$, Player I expects to win

$$v_2 = (1/2)(-2) + (1/2)(7) = +2\tfrac{1}{2}$$

We may write this in matrix notation as

$$(1/2,\ 1/2)\begin{pmatrix} 4 & -2 \\ -9 & 7 \end{pmatrix} = (-2\tfrac{1}{2},\ 2\tfrac{1}{2})$$

If Player I chooses to play $R1$ with probability $1/3$ and the other card with probability $2/3$, we arrive at

$$(1/3,\ 2/3)\begin{pmatrix} 4 & -2 \\ -9 & 7 \end{pmatrix} = (-14/3,\ 12/3)$$

In this way, Player I increases his possible winnings but also his possible losses! Game theorists, being conservative, would prefer $(1/2,\ 1/2)$ where the possible losses are minimized.

Now, in general, let $\mathbf{p} = (p,\ 1 - p)$ be the vector of probabilities with which Player I chooses his plays; p may be any number between 0 and 1. Now

$$(v_1,\ v_2) = (p,\ 1 - p)\begin{pmatrix} 4 & -2 \\ -9 & 7 \end{pmatrix}$$

$$(v_1,\ v_2) = (4p - 9 + 9p,\ -2p + 7 - 7p)$$

$$(v_1,\ v_2) = (13p - 9,\ 7 - 9p)$$

Thus,

$$v_1 = 13p - 9 \quad \text{and} \quad v_2 = 7 - 9p$$

Plotting these two equations, we get two intersecting straight lines (figure 6). They intersect at $p = 8/11$, $v_1 = v_2 = 5/11$. For values of $p < 8/11$, v_2 is greater than v_1 and for $p > 8/11$ the opposite is true. The conservative game theorist looks at the smaller possible value for each value of p, which represents the minimum possible expected winnings (which is sometimes negative). The graph of minimum possible winnings plotted versus p is indicated by the heavy broken line in figure 7. Clearly, Player I should pick p so as to hit the high point on this graph. But this is precisely the point of intersection of the two original lines. That is, the optimal value of p must be where $v_1 = v_2$. Hence we must solve

$$\mathbf{p}G = (v,\ v) \quad \text{where } \mathbf{p} = (p,\ 1 - p)$$

and **G** is the (2×2) payoff matrix. Of course, the resulting v is the expected winnings of Player I. This is called the *value of the game to Player I*.

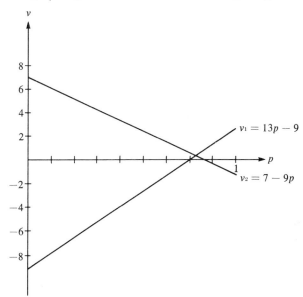

Figure 6

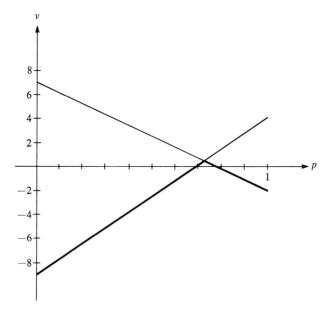

Figure 7

Let us now look at the game from Player II's point of view. He also must play randomly and his strategy may be represented by the column vector

$$\mathbf{q} = \begin{pmatrix} q \\ 1 - q \end{pmatrix}$$

where q is the probability with which he plays the first column. The product

$$\mathbf{Gq} = \begin{pmatrix} 4 & -2 \\ -9 & 7 \end{pmatrix} \begin{pmatrix} q \\ 1 - q \end{pmatrix} = \begin{pmatrix} 4q - 2 + 2q \\ -9q + 7 - 7q \end{pmatrix} = \begin{pmatrix} w_1 \\ w_2 \end{pmatrix}$$

yields the vector of expected values to Player II assuming that Player I plays Row 1 or Row 2. So we have

$$w_1 = 6q - 2$$
$$w_2 = -16q + 7$$

and plotting these two lines, we see that they intersect at $q = 9/22$, $w_1 = w_2 = 5/11$. Figure 8 shows these two lines. Remembering that the values of w represent the amount that Player II loses, we realize that he must always worry about the larger of the two possible values. The heavy line in figure 9 shows the graph of the larger value of w versus q. Surely Player II must aim for the low point on this graph, which is again the point of

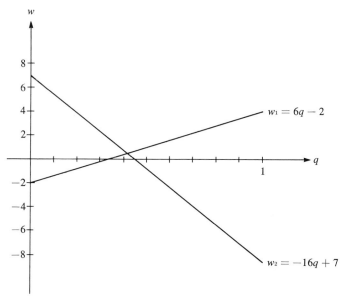

Figure 8

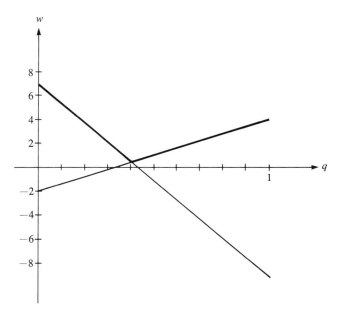

Figure 9

intersection of the two original lines. Hence, Player II's strategy must be arrived at by solving

$$\mathbf{Gq} = \begin{pmatrix} w \\ w \end{pmatrix}$$

Here we would call w the *value of the game to Player II.* By now the reader has observed that in this case $v = w = 5/11$. This is not a coincidence. It follows from the fact that the associative law holds for multiplication of matrices. That is,

$$(\mathbf{pG})\mathbf{q} = \mathbf{p}(\mathbf{Gq})$$

Hence,

THEOREM 6 Let **G** be a (2×2) game matrix and suppose there are solutions to

$$\mathbf{pG} = (v, v) \quad \text{and} \quad \mathbf{Gq} = \begin{pmatrix} w \\ w \end{pmatrix}$$

Then $v = w$.

Proof By the associative law

$$(\mathbf{pG})\mathbf{q} = \mathbf{p}(\mathbf{Gq})$$

Therefore,

$$(v, v)\begin{pmatrix} q \\ 1 - q \end{pmatrix} = (p, 1 - p)\begin{pmatrix} w \\ w \end{pmatrix}$$

$$vq + v(1 - q) = pw + w(1 - p)$$

$$vq + v - vq = pw + w - pw$$

$$v = w$$

In summary, if **G** is a (2 × 2) game matrix, the optimal strategies of the two players may be sought by solving the equations

$$(p, 1 - p)\mathbf{G} = (v, v)$$

and

$$\mathbf{G}\begin{pmatrix} q \\ 1 - q \end{pmatrix} = \begin{pmatrix} v \\ v \end{pmatrix}$$

The vector $\mathbf{p} = (p, 1 - p)$ gives the first player's strategy, $\mathbf{q} = \begin{pmatrix} q \\ 1 - q \end{pmatrix}$ gives the second player's strategy and v gives the "value of the game." Finding $\mathbf{p}$, $\mathbf{q}$ and v is called *solving the game*. Now it is possible that these equations do not submit to a solution with p and q between zero and one. In such cases another approach must be found, and we shall find it in the next section.

However, let us first go back one step. If the first player plays $\mathbf{p}$, then $\mathbf{pG} = \mathbf{v} = (v_1, v_2)$ gives the values of the game to the first player. The value v_1 assumes that player two plays only Column 1 and the value v_2 assumes that he plays only Column 2. If the second player plays any mixed strategy $\mathbf{q}$, then the value of the game will be $\mathbf{vq} = \mathbf{pGq}$. In particular, this gives the startling result that if one player plays his optimal strategy, it does not matter what the other player does. Thus, if player one's strategy satisfies $\mathbf{pG} = (v, v)$, then

$$\mathbf{pGq} = (v, v) \begin{pmatrix} q \\ 1 - q \end{pmatrix}$$

$$= vq + v - vq = v$$

regardless of q! Again, in the next section, we shall see examples of games in which deviation from the optimal strategy by either player will cause that player to be penalized.

EXERCISES

1. Let $G = \begin{pmatrix} a & b \\ c & d \end{pmatrix}$, $\mathbf{p} = (p_1, p_2)$, and $\mathbf{q} = \begin{pmatrix} q_1 \\ q_2 \end{pmatrix}$. Show that $(\mathbf{p}G)\mathbf{q} = \mathbf{p}(G\mathbf{q})$.

2. Find the optimal strategies and the value of the game if

   (a) $G = \begin{pmatrix} -1 & 2 \\ 1 & -3 \end{pmatrix}$

   (b) $G = \begin{pmatrix} 4 & 1 \\ 4 & 6 \end{pmatrix}$

   (c) $G = \begin{pmatrix} -1 & -2 \\ -3 & 0 \end{pmatrix}$

3. Two competing route salesmen may go to either street 1 or 2 each day. Credit the first salesman with 8 points if only he goes to street 1. Credit him with 5 points if only he goes to street 2. If both go to the same street, credit him with 0. The second salesman's only interest is in holding down the first salesman's winnings. Find the optimal strategies for both players.

4. On a certain hedge investment, a stock buyer can plan for the price to go up or down. If he plans correctly, he will gain $1,000. If he plans for a rise and the price falls, he will make $100. If he plans for a fall and the price rises, he will make $300. In such a situation, the conservative way to figure is that the market is a malevolent competitor that is doing its best to defeat you. Under that assumption, find the optimal investment strategy.

5. Suppose we play the same game as in the text but let the payoff be the product of the numbers. Write the payoff matrix and solve the game.

6. Joe Namath may call for a "pass play" or a "running play." The defense may prepare for a pass or a run. If the defense guesses wrong, Joe's team gains 20 yards on a pass or 10 yards on a run. If the defense guesses right, Joe's team gains nothing on a pass and 2 yards on a run. Write this as a matrix game and solve.

7. Suppose that the investor in Exercise 4 is really not sure of the values of his payoff matrix and thus cannot compute his optimal strategy. Instead, he plays each possibility with probability 1/2.

Find the value of the game as a function of q, the probability that the price will go up. Show that for certain values of q, he does worse than he would in the optimal case and for certain values he does better.

8. Repeat Exercise 7 for the football example in Exercise 5, assuming that Namath passes two-thirds of the time.

7.10 Row and Column Dominance: Saddle Points

Suppose we have a game payoff matrix

$$G = \begin{pmatrix} 3 & 5 \\ 1 & 7 \end{pmatrix}$$

We try our standard method of attack, seeking the first player's strategy,

$$(p, 1 - p)\begin{pmatrix} 3 & 5 \\ 1 & 7 \end{pmatrix} = (v, v)$$

$$3p + 1 - p = v$$

$$5p + 7 - 7p = v$$

Equating the lefthand sides of these equations, we obtain

$$2p + 1 = 7 - 2p$$

$$4p = 6$$

$$p = 1\tfrac{1}{2}$$

Of course, $p = 1\tfrac{1}{2}$ is impossible since p, being a probability measurement, cannot exceed 1. Something must be wrong. Let us look at G more closely. From the first player's point of view it seems that a random strategy is necessary. However, let us take the second player's viewpoint. He sees that if Player I plays Row 1, he should play Column 1, since he loses three instead of five. If Player I plays Row 2, Player II should still play Column 1, since he loses one instead of seven. Thus, the second player will never play Column 2. Accordingly, we may as well strike Column 2 from consideration. Now Player I looks at the payoff matrix, seeing

$$G = \begin{pmatrix} 3 & \cancel{5} \\ 1 & \cancel{7} \end{pmatrix}$$

Surely, he will now choose to always play Row 1 since this gains him three units instead of one. Thus, the first player's strategy is $\mathbf{p} = (1, 0)$, the second player's strategy is $\mathbf{q} = \begin{pmatrix} 1 \\ 0 \end{pmatrix}$ and the value of the game is three.

The idea here is that neither player will select a play if there is another one available which always gives better results. Formally we will say that $\mathbf{u} = (u_1, u_2, \ldots, u_k)$ dominates $\mathbf{v} = (v_1, v_2, \ldots, v_k)$ if $u_1 \geq v_1, u_2 \geq v_2, \ldots,$ $u_k \geq v_k$, with a similar definition for column vectors. Now, we have two rules for analysis of payoff matrices:

1. We may strike out any column which dominates any other column (since Player II will never choose it).
2. We may strike out any row which is dominated by any other (since Player I will never choose it).

Sometimes application of these two rules may simplify a complicated looking game. For example,

$$G = \begin{pmatrix} 1 & 3 & 5 \\ 2 & 4 & 2 \\ -1 & 0 & -2 \\ -2 & 5 & -3 \end{pmatrix}$$

Inspecting **G**, we first check the rows. We see that Row 3 is dominated by Rows 1 and 2 and hence may be struck out, leaving

$$G = \begin{pmatrix} 1 & 3 & 5 \\ 2 & 4 & 2 \\ \overline{-1} & \overline{0} & \overline{-2} \\ -2 & 5 & -3 \end{pmatrix}$$

There are now no more row dominances. Let us look at the columns. We see that Column 2 dominates Column 1, leaving

$$G = \begin{pmatrix} 1 & 3 & 5 \\ 2 & 4 & 2 \\ \overline{-1} & \overline{0} & \overline{-2} \\ -2 & 5 & -3 \end{pmatrix}$$

In the reduced payoff matrix, Row 4 is now dominated by Rows 1 and 2; hence

$$G = \begin{pmatrix} 1 & 3 & 5 \\ 2 & 4 & 2 \\ \overline{-1} & \overline{0} & \overline{-2} \\ \overline{-2} & \overline{5} & \overline{-3} \end{pmatrix}$$

Here Column 3 dominates Column 1

$$G = \begin{pmatrix} 1 & 3 & 5 \\ 2 & 4 & 2 \\ -1 & 0 & -2 \\ -2 & 5 & -3 \end{pmatrix}$$

and finally Row 2 dominates Row 1, leaving

$$G = \begin{pmatrix} 1 & 3 & 5 \\ 2 & 4 & 2 \\ -1 & 0 & -2 \\ -2 & 5 & -3 \end{pmatrix}$$

Thus, Player I's strategy is $\mathbf{p} = (0, 1, 0, 0)$. Player II's strategy is

$$\mathbf{q} = \begin{pmatrix} 1 \\ 0 \\ 0 \end{pmatrix} \quad \text{and} \quad v = 2$$

In both of these cases, we have what is known as a pure strategy. That is, each player is logically able to select only one play and no randomization is needed. There is another type of game which leads to a pure strategy solution. It is typified by the following example:

$$G = \begin{pmatrix} 5 & -2 & -1 \\ 3 & 2 & 1 \\ -3 & 5 & -1 \end{pmatrix}$$

Player I makes a list of the worst that can happen to him if he plays pure strategies:

	Worst Possibility
Row 1	−2
Row 2	1
Row 3	−3

From a pessimistic point of view, all he can guarantee by any mixed strategy is a weighted average of these numbers. Therefore, the best he can hope for is a payoff of 1 unit.

Player II lists the worst that can happen to him if he plays pure strategies:

Worst Possibility

Column 1	5
Column 2	5
Column 3	1

Again figuring conservatively, the best he can hope for is a payoff of one unit. Accordingly, Player I will play Row 2 always and Player II will play Column 3 always and if either player deviates he will lose out. The crucial factor is that g_{23} is simultaneously the smallest element in its row and the largest element in its column. Such a point is called a *saddle* point. To check for a saddle point, simply circle the smallest element in each row, put a box around the largest element in each column and if any number is both circled and boxed, it is a saddle point. Thus

$$G = \begin{pmatrix} \boxed{5} & \boxed{-2} & -1 \\ 3 & 2 & \boxed{1} \\ \boxed{-3} & \boxed{5} & -1 \end{pmatrix}$$

If g_{ij} is a saddle point, then Player I must play Row i, Player II must play Column j and $v = g_{ij}$.

Incidentally, it is possible to have two (or more) saddle points, in which case any mixture of the possible pure strategies is equally good. Hence, we should proceed as follows to analyze an arbitrary game:

1. Check for saddle points.
2. If no saddle, check for and strike out any dominated rows or dominating columns.
3. Use a random strategy on the reduced payoff matrix, if necessary.

For example,

$$G = \begin{pmatrix} -1 & 3 & 1 \\ 1 & 2 & -1 \\ -2 & 4 & -2 \end{pmatrix}$$

Checking for saddle points, we have

$$G = \begin{pmatrix} \boxed{-1} & 3 & \boxed{1} \\ \boxed{1} & 2 & \boxed{-1} \\ \boxed{-2} & \boxed{4} & \boxed{-2} \end{pmatrix}$$

We see that there is no saddle point but that we may strike Column 2, and having done so, we may strike Row 3:

$$G = \begin{pmatrix} -1 & 3 & 1 \\ 1 & 2 & -1 \\ -2 & 4 & -2 \end{pmatrix}$$

The remaining payoff matrix is

$$G' = \begin{pmatrix} -1 & 1 \\ 1 & -1 \end{pmatrix}$$

We must now try a random strategy:

$$(p, 1 - p)\begin{pmatrix} -1 & 1 \\ 1 & -1 \end{pmatrix} = (v, v)$$

Thus,

$$-p + 1 - p = v$$
$$p - 1 + p = v$$

yielding

$$-2p + 1 = 2p - 1$$
$$2 = 4p$$
$$1/2 = p$$

and hence $v = 0$. Similarly, Player II's strategy will yield $q = 1/2$. Thus, we finally arrive at a solution to G:

$$\mathbf{p} = (1/2, 1/2, 0) \qquad \mathbf{q} = \begin{pmatrix} 1/2 \\ 0 \\ 1/2 \end{pmatrix}$$

and

$$v = 0$$

EXERCISES

1. Show that if for $\mathbf{G} = \begin{pmatrix} a & b \\ c & d \end{pmatrix}$ pure strategies can be arrived at by row and column dominance, then the resulting solution is also a saddle point, and conversely.

2. Solve the following games:

(a) $\mathbf{G} = \begin{pmatrix} -1 & 1 \\ -3 & 0 \end{pmatrix}$

(b) $\mathbf{G} = \begin{pmatrix} 1 & 0 & 3 \\ 2 & 1 & 1 \end{pmatrix}$

(c) $\mathbf{G} = \begin{pmatrix} 1 & -2 & -3 & 4 \\ 1 & -1 & 0 & 2 \\ 1 & -3 & 4 & -5 \end{pmatrix}$

3. Solve the following games:

(a) $\mathbf{G} = \begin{pmatrix} 2 & 8 & 3 & 4 \\ 4 & 3 & 4 & 4 \\ 6 & 6 & 5 & 5 \\ 7 & 8 & 6 & 5 \end{pmatrix}$

(b) $\mathbf{G} = \begin{pmatrix} 1 & 2 & 2 \\ 2 & 1 & 3 \\ 1 & -1 & -2 \end{pmatrix}$

4. Solve the following games:

(a) $\mathbf{G} = \begin{pmatrix} -3 & 1 & -2 \\ 5 & 4 & 2 \\ 0 & 3 & 3 \end{pmatrix}$

(b) $\mathbf{G} = \begin{pmatrix} -3 & 1 & -2 \\ 5 & 4 & 4 \\ 0 & 3 & 3 \end{pmatrix}$

5. Consider the card game in which the payoff to Player I is the product of the numbers if the colors match or to Player II if they do not match. Suppose Player I has a black 2, a black 3 and a red 3, and Player II has a black 1, a black 2 and a black 3. Find the payoff matrix and solve the game.

6. Mike suggests the following game to Harry: Each will pick a number 1, 2 or 3. If the numbers match Harry wins $1. For nonmatching numbers, if either player plays a 3, he loses $1. If either player plays a 2, Mike wins $1. Should Harry agree to play? What is the best strategy for each player?

7. A man holds a stock worth $100 which he may hold or sell. If he holds and the stock goes up, he will make $10. If he holds and it goes down, he will lose $5. If he sells, his gain will be zero regardless of what the stock does. Consider this as a two-player

game, man against stock market, and find the optimal solution for the man. If q is the probability that the stock will go up, for what values of q will it pay the man to hold?

7.11 Larger Games

Let us consider some other possible payoff matrices. Let us assume that all the advantages of row and column domination have been realized and we are left with a $2 \times n$ game. It appears that Player II may select a mixed strategy which involves all n of his possible plays. However, it can be shown that his optimum strategy will turn out to use only two columns. So, for example,

$$G = \begin{pmatrix} 1 & -1 & 3 \\ 3 & 4 & 0 \end{pmatrix}$$

Looking at only Column 1 and 2, we have

$$G_1 = \begin{pmatrix} 1 & -1 \\ 3 & 4 \end{pmatrix}$$

For this game, there is a saddle point, so the best strategy is

$$q_1 = \begin{pmatrix} 0 \\ 1 \end{pmatrix} \quad \text{and} \quad v_1 = 3$$

Looking at Columns 1 and 3, we have

$$G_2 = \begin{pmatrix} 1 & 3 \\ 3 & 0 \end{pmatrix}$$

with optimal strategy $q_2 = \begin{pmatrix} 3/5 \\ 2/5 \end{pmatrix}$ and $v_2 = 9/5$. Looking at Columns 2 and 3, we have

$$G_3 = \begin{pmatrix} -1 & 3 \\ 4 & 0 \end{pmatrix}$$

which has optimal strategy, $q_3 = \begin{pmatrix} 3/8 \\ 5/8 \end{pmatrix}$ and $v_3 = 3/2$.

From Player II's point of view, the best result is from G_3, where $v_3 = 3/2$, which is smaller than either 9/5 or 3. Hence, the best strategy for Player II is to play only Columns 2 and 3, so his best strategy is

$$q = \begin{pmatrix} 0 \\ 3/8 \\ 5/8 \end{pmatrix}$$

Knowing this, Player I seeks his optimal strategy based only on G_3 and gets $p = (1/2, 1/2)$. Of course, $m \times 2$ games may be handled in an analogous manner, as we shall see in the following example.

Let us look at an application of game theory to the planning of an investment portfolio. The manager of the portfolio is undecided as to how to divide his funds between growth stocks, blue chips, and gold. In a bull market, he would like to be fully invested in growth stocks; and in a bear market, he would like to be fully into gold. In fact, he displays his possible gains and losses in thousands of dollars as below:

	Bull market	Bear market
All blue chips	+5	−5
All growth	+15	−30
All gold	−20	+20

The manager now assumes that the market is his opponent and will do its best to defeat him. Of course, the manager does not really believe that the market is out to get him. However, if he plans for the worst, any other behavior of the market may improve his results. We now have a 3×2 game. Considering only Rows 1 and 2, we have

$$G_1 = \begin{pmatrix} 5 & -5 \\ 15 & -30 \end{pmatrix}$$

where -5 is a saddle point. Considering Rows 1 and 3, we have

$$G_2 = \begin{pmatrix} 5 & -5 \\ -20 & 20 \end{pmatrix}$$

which has optimal strategy $p_2 = (4/5, 1/5)$, $v_2 = 0$. Considering Rows 2 and 3, we have

$$G_3 = \begin{pmatrix} 15 & -30 \\ -20 & 20 \end{pmatrix}$$

which has optimal strategy $p_3 = (8/17, 9/17)$, $v_3 = -60/17$. Clearly, the best that the manager can hope for is to play only Rows 1 and 3. That is, he should play $p = (4/5, 0, 1/5)$. In financial terms, this means that he should put 80% of his funds into blue chips and 20% into gold. In this way, he will break even no matter what the market does. Is there no way that he can make money? Of course there is, but it depends on his being able to predict accurately the fractions of the time that the market will be bull and bear. If one can make accurate predictions, then there are different values for which each of the pure strategies is best. Instructions for completing this analysis are given in Exercise 6 at the end of this section.

Finally, let us consider a 3×3 matrix game without a saddle point. Let us suppose that the 3×3 game cannot be reduced by row or column dominances. Suppose further that all of the payoffs are positive. If not, just add a constant to every entry in the game matrix so as to make every entry nonnegative. For example, let

$$\mathbf{G}' = \begin{pmatrix} 2 & 0 & 1 \\ -1 & 1 & 0 \\ 3 & 0 & -1 \end{pmatrix}$$

In order to have all entries nonnegative, add $+1$ to every entry, producing the new game

$$\mathbf{G} = \begin{pmatrix} 3 & 1 & 2 \\ 0 & 2 & 1 \\ 4 & 1 & 0 \end{pmatrix}$$

The only difference between $\mathbf{G}'$ and $\mathbf{G}$ is that the value of $\mathbf{G}$ is 1 more than the value of $\mathbf{G}'$. Accordingly, if we can solve $\mathbf{G}$, the value of $\mathbf{G}'$ is easily attained, and the optimal strategies will be the same. We assume that $\mathbf{G}$ has some value v. Now let the second player's strategy be

$$\mathbf{q} = \begin{pmatrix} q_1 \\ q_2 \\ q_3 \end{pmatrix}$$

Then,

$$\mathbf{Gq} = \begin{pmatrix} 3 & 1 & 2 \\ 0 & 2 & 1 \\ 4 & 1 & 0 \end{pmatrix}\begin{pmatrix} q_1 \\ q_2 \\ q_3 \end{pmatrix} = \begin{pmatrix} 3q_1 + q_2 + 2q_3 \\ 2q_2 + q_3 \\ 4q_1 + q_2 \end{pmatrix} = \begin{pmatrix} v_1 \\ v_2 \\ v_3 \end{pmatrix}$$

The values v_1, v_2, and v_3 give the values of the game to the second player, assuming that the first player plays each of his possible pure strategies. Therefore, none of these values may exceed the value of the game; thus, $v_1 \leq v$, $v_2 \leq v$, $v_3 \leq v$. In other words,

$$3q_1 + q_2 + 2q_3 \leq v$$
$$2q_2 + q_3 \leq v$$
$$4q_1 + q_2 \qquad \leq v$$

Since every payoff in the game is positive, v must be positive. Therefore, divide each inequality by v and let $x = q_1/v$, $y = q_2/v$, $z = q_3/v$. We now have

$$3x + y + 2z \leq 1$$
$$2y + z \leq 1$$
$$4x + y \qquad \leq 1$$

Moreover, $x + y + z = q_1/v + q_2/v + q_3/v = (q_1 + q_2 + q_3)/v = 1/v$. Since Player II is trying to minimize v, he is trying to maximize $1/v$. Therefore, since $1/v = x + y + z$, we have reduced the problem of finding the column player's strategy to solving the linear programming problem

Maximize: $P = x + y + z$

Subject to: $3x + y + 2z \leq 1$
$$2y + z \leq 1$$
$$4x + y \qquad \leq 1$$
$$x, y, z \geq 0$$

By similar reasoning, you can show that the problem of finding the first player's strategy will reduce to solving the dual of this problem. Hence, solving by the simplex procedure will completely solve the game. The appropriate simplex tableau is

x	y	z	r	s	t	P	
3	1	2	1	0	0	0	1
0	2	1	0	1	0	0	1
④	1	0	0	0	1	0	1
−1	−1	−1	0	0	0	1	0

Notice that in the upper lefthand corner is the original game matrix. Also notice that we have circled the pivotal element with which to begin the simplex. Of course, we could have chosen any of the first

three columns with which to have begun the procedure. After three
cycles of the simplex, the tableau reduces to

x	y	z	r	s	t	P	
0	0	1	8/15	−1/15	−9/20	0	1/15
0	1	0	−4/15	4/15	1/5	0	7/15
1	0	0	1/15	−1/15	1/5	0	2/15
0	0	0	1/3	1/3	0	1	2/3

Here, we can read off the solution; $x = 2/15$, $y = 7/15$, $z = 1/15$, and
$P = 2/3$. Since $P = 2/3$, $v = 3/2$. Finally, $q_1 = xv = (2/15)(3/2) = 2/10$,
$q_2 = yv = 7/10$, $q_3 = zv = 1/10$. Similarly, the solution to the dual is
$x = 1/3$, $y = 1/3$, $z = 0$, and $p_1 = xv = 1/2$, $p_2 = yv = 1/2$, $p_3 = zv = 0$.
We thus have arrived at the solution,

$$\mathbf{p} = (0.5 \quad 0.5 \quad 0), \mathbf{q} = \begin{pmatrix} 0.1 \\ 0.7 \\ 0.2 \end{pmatrix}, v = 1.5$$

Actually, solution by the simplex procedure will work for any $m \times n$
game that does not have a saddle point!

In closing, let us make one final observation about this example. It
turned out that the row player's strategy involved using only the first
and second rows. Knowing this, the second player could reinvestigate
the game, thinking of it as a 2×3 game, by striking out the last row.
Doing so would allow us to solve by the technique described at the
beginning of this section and should yield a strategy for the second
player which involves the use of only two columns. The reader is
asked to do this in Exercise 7 at the end of this section. In addition,
the reader is asked to show that starting the simplex at a different
column would have led to this simpler solution directly.

EXERCISES

1. Solve the following games:

(a) $\begin{pmatrix} 1 & -1 & 4 & 2 \\ 2 & 3 & 1 & 0 \end{pmatrix}$

(b) $\begin{pmatrix} 1 & -2 & 4 \\ -1 & 2 & 0 \\ -1 & 1 & -1 \\ 3 & 0 & -3 \end{pmatrix}$

2. Player I has a black 2, a black 3 and a red 3. Player II has a red 1, a black 2 and a black 3. Each player plays a card. If the colors match, the payoff to Player I is the sum of the numbers; if not, the payoff is to Player II. Find the payoff matrix and solve.

3. The two players have the same cards as in Exercise 2. However, the payoff to Player I is the sum of the numbers if the colors match and the positive difference if they do not. Find the payoff matrix and solve the game.

4. Joe and Sam agree to the following game. Each will pick a number 1, 2 or 3. If the numbers do not match, Sam wins $1. If both pick 1, no one wins and if they match 2's or 3's, Joe wins $3. Find the best strategies for both players.

5. Solve the following matrix games:

(a) $\mathbf{G} = \begin{pmatrix} 7 & 5 \\ 8 & 4 \\ 7 & 4 \\ 1 & 2 \\ 2 & 9 \end{pmatrix}$

(b) $\mathbf{G} = \begin{pmatrix} 5 & 3 \\ 7 & 5 \\ 0 & 2 \\ 4 & 4 \end{pmatrix}$

(c) $\mathbf{G} = \begin{pmatrix} 0 & 1 & 3 & 6 \\ 9 & 4 & 0 & 6 \end{pmatrix}$

(d) $\mathbf{G} = \begin{pmatrix} 5 & 5 & 6 \\ 1 & 1 & 0 \\ 8 & 3 & 9 \end{pmatrix}$

(e) $\mathbf{G} = \begin{pmatrix} 9 & 1 & 6 \\ 7 & 6 & 8 \\ 7 & 9 & 8 \end{pmatrix}$

(f) $\mathbf{G} = \begin{pmatrix} 0 & 1 & -7 & 9 \\ 5 & 0 & 4 & 3 \\ 9 & 4 & 3 & 4 \end{pmatrix}$

(g) $\mathbf{G} = \begin{pmatrix} 3 & 6 & 1 & 5 \\ 9 & 0 & 8 & 0 \\ 7 & 5 & 2 & 6 \\ 7 & 7 & 9 & 5 \end{pmatrix}$

6. Consider the investment portfolio example in the text. Let q be the probability that the market will be bullish. From the statement of the problem, it is clear that when q is small (near zero), one would wish to be invested in gold. When q is large (near one), one would wish to be in growth stocks. Find the values of the game to the investor as a function of q for each of the three pure strategies. Call these values w_1, w_2, w_3. Plot each of these on the same set of axes. You will see that there are values q_1 and q_2 such that for $0 < q < q_1$, w_3 is best; for $q_1 < q < q_2$, w_2 is best; and for $q_2 < q < 1$, w_1 is best. Find q_1 and q_2 and interpret in financial terms.

7. Solve the 3×3 game solved in the text by the simplex method, using the third column to find the pivot element for the first row reduction. Re-solve the game by using the fact that it is known that the first player will never play Row 3, and so the game is really 2×3. Do not use the simplex technique for this second solution. Show that one of the optimal strategies obtained in this way is the same as the strategy produced by the simplex procedure.

8. The value of the game G solved in the text is 3/2. This should be 1 more than the value of the game G' from which it was derived. Solve the game G' directly and show that its value is 1/2.

9. The first player has a Red 1, a Red 2, and a Black 1. The second player has a Red 1 and a Red 2, and a Black 1 and a Black 2. Each player plays a card. The payoff is the sum of the numbers played. The first player wins if the colors match; the second player wins if they are different. Find the optimal strategies and the value of the game.

8

Conditional Probability

8.1 Introduction

In many probability problems, one is asked to find the probability of some event B given that another event A has already occurred. We shall use the symbol $P(B \mid A)$, which is read "the probability of B given A," to stand for this measure. Sometimes the given is stated explicitly, but other times it must be deduced. For example, in a math course, seven girls passed, three girls failed, nine boys passed and four boys failed. The makeup of the class may be tabulated as

	P	F
B	9	4
G	7	3

Let us ask some simple questions. If a student is chosen at random, what is the probability that the student is a boy? The answer is easy, $P(B) = 13/23$. If a boy is chosen at random, what is the probability that he failed? Here we really have $P(F \mid B) = 4/13$, since we look only at that portion of the sample space which is composed of boys. Let us try the following:

If a student is chosen at random, what is the probability that it is a boy who failed? Here we have $P(F \cap B) = 4/23$. Note the relationship

$$P(F \cap B) = P(B)P(F \mid B) \quad \text{or} \quad P(F \mid B) = \frac{P(F \cap B)}{P(B)}$$

If we think of probability as area in a Venn diagram, then we would want to say that the $P(F \mid B)$ is that fraction of the area of B which is also in F, leading us again to

$$P(F \mid B) = \frac{P(F \cap B)}{P(B)}$$

Let us take this formula as the definition of conditional probability.

Definition 1 $P(B \mid A) = P(B \cap A)/P(A)$ if $P(A) \neq 0$.

Interestingly, this formula is commonly used in the form $P(A \cap B) = P(A)P(B \mid A)$. For example, two cards are chosen at random from an ordinary deck of playing cards. What is the probability that both are hearts? Let $A =$ the first card is a heart and $B =$ the second card is a heart. We want $P(A \cap B)$. We write $P(A \cap B) = P(A)P(B \mid A)$. Now, $P(A) = 13/52$; $P(B \mid A) = 12/51$ since one card is used up and it is a heart. Hence $P(A \cap B) = 13/52 \cdot 12/51 = 1/17$.

Another common use of conditional probability is in computing the probability of complicated events which may be broken down into a collection of disjoint events. To be precise let $B_1, B_2, \ldots, B_k$ be a collection of k events having the following properties:

$$B_1 \cup B_2 \cup \ldots \cup B_k = S \tag{1}$$
$$B_i \cap B_j = \emptyset \quad \text{if } i \neq j \tag{2}$$

That is, the B's are disjoint events which together make up the whole sample space. Now, let A be any event; the subsets $A \cap B_1, A \cap B_2, \ldots, A \cap B_k$ partition A into disjoint events whose union is A. That is,

$$A = (A \cap B_1) \cup (A \cap B_2) \cup \ldots \cup (A \cap B_k) \tag{3}$$
$$(A \cap B_i) \cap (A \cap B_j) = \emptyset \quad \text{if } i \neq j \tag{4}$$

Thus, we can write

$$P(A) = P(A \cap B_1) + P(A \cap B_2) + \cdots + P(A \cap B_k)$$

and applying the conditional probability formula, we have

$$P(A) = P(A \mid B_1)P(B_1) + P(A \mid B_2)P(B_2) + \cdots + P(A \mid B_k)P(B_k)$$

Let us consider an example of the application of this formula. Suppose we have three urns with contents as shown:

Urn I	Urn II	Urn III
5 red balls	4 red balls	1 red ball
3 white balls	1 white ball	9 white balls

Let us refer to this as Urn Model A. An urn is chosen at random and a ball is selected from the urn at random. What is the probability that the ball is red? One might be tempted to say that there are 23 balls all together and 10 are red and hence the probability is $10/23$. However, let us take a closer look. Let

$$R = \text{A red ball is chosen.}$$
$$U_1 = \text{Urn I is chosen.}$$
$$U_2 = \text{Urn II is chosen.}$$
$$U_3 = \text{Urn III is chosen.}$$

Now,

$$P(U_1) = P(U_2) = P(U_3) = 1/3$$
$$P(R \mid U_1) = 5/8 \quad P(R \mid U_2) = 4/5 \quad \text{and} \quad P(R \mid U_3) = 1/10$$

Our partitioning formula would say

$$P(R) = P(R \mid U_1)P(U_1) + P(R \mid U_2)P(U_2) + P(R \mid U_3)P(U_3)$$
$$= 5/8 \cdot 1/3 + 4/5 \cdot 1/3 + 1/10 \cdot 1/3 = 5/24 + 4/15 + 1/30$$
$$= 61/120$$

An interesting question is the following: With the same set-up as previously, a red ball is chosen. What is the probability that it came from Urn III? Here we want $P(U_3 \mid R)$. Our definition says

$$P(U_3 \mid R) = \frac{P(U_3 \cap R)}{P(R)}$$

$P(R)$ was just found. $P(U_3 \cap R)$ may be found by

$$P(U_3 \cap R) = P(R \cap U_3) = P(U_3)P(R \mid U_3) = 1/3 \cdot 1/10 = 1/30$$

Hence,

$$P(U_3 \mid R) = (1/30) \div (61/120)$$
$$= 1/30 \cdot 120/61 = 4/61$$

In other words, the information that a red ball was selected has dropped the probability that Urn III was selected from 1/3 to less than 1/15! This is intuitively reasonable due to the extreme unlikeliness of picking a red ball from Urn III.

Perhaps the simplest way to visualize problems of the preceding type is through the use of "tree diagrams." In a tree diagram, one starts at some point and draws branches indicating each of the possible outcomes of the first stage of the experiment. Thus figure 1 shows the start of a tree diagram for the urn problem. The numbers on the branches are the probabilities of the outcomes. Now, from each terminus, again draw branches for each possibility. Figure 2 shows the completed tree diagram. The numbers on the second set of branches give the probabilities of those branches given their starting points. Thus, $5/8 = P(R \mid U_1)$, and so on. Notice the following points:

1. The sum of the probabilities of all branches emanating from any point is one.
2. The probability of any sequence of outcomes from start to a given terminus is the product of the probabilities along the branch.

Naturally, this process can be extended to multistage experiments.

Most of the properties of conditional probability can be exhibited nicely by urn models. In addition, many problems can be translated into

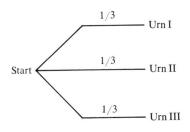

Figure 1

urn models. For example, ten men and five women volunteer for a special job. Two people are selected at random to do the job. What is the probability that the second person is a woman? This problem may be restated as Urn Model *B*. An urn contains ten black balls and five red balls. Two balls are drawn at random. What is the probability that the second ball is red? A tree provides the answer easily. Referring to figure 3, we find

$$P(R_2) = P(R_1 - R_2) + P(B_1 - R_2)$$
$$= 1/3 \cdot 4/14 + 2/3 \cdot 5/14 = 4/42 + 10/42 = 14/42 = 1/3$$

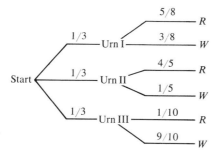

Figure 2

It was obvious that $P(R_1) = 1/3$ but should $P(R_2) = 1/3$? Think not of balls in an urn but of five red and ten black cards with identical backs, well-shuffled and laid out face down. If a card is turned over, what is the probability that it is red? The answer must be $1/3$ whether it is the first card in line, or the second or the last. The same is true in drawing balls from an urn. Of course, if you know the color of the first one drawn, then the probabilities on the second one change. Conversely, knowledge about the second ball changes the probabilities on the first one.

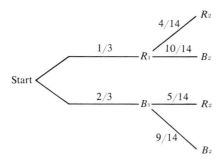

Figure 3

EXERCISES

1. In the Urn Model B example in the text, find the following:
   (a) the probability that the last ball picked is red;
   (b) the probability that the last ball picked is red given that the first one picked is red;
   (c) the probability that the first picked was red given that the last picked was red.

2. A scientist is running rats through a maze. If he ever succeeds, the probability of his succeeding again is 0.9. If he fails, the probability of succeeding is given by $k/10$ where k is the number of the trial, that

is, 1/10 on the first time, 2/10 on the second, and so on. Draw a tree diagram for a rat with four tries at the maze. Find

(a) the probability that the rat ever makes it;

(b) the probability that the rat makes it on the last try;

(c) the probability that the rat only makes it on his last try.

3. Find the probability that three cards drawn at random from a deck are all hearts. Find the probability of drawing a heart flush in five-card poker. Find the probability of drawing any flush.

4. A class consists of ten men and nine women. One-half of the men and one-third of the women smoke. What is the probability that a person chosen at random smokes? What is the probability that a smoker chosen at random is a woman?

5. There are two jars of nuts on a table. One contains ten peanuts and six cashews. The other contains five peanuts and twenty cashews. A jar is picked at random and a nut selected from the jar. What is the probability that it is a peanut? Another nut is chosen from the same jar; if the first nut was a peanut, what is the probability that the second nut is a peanut? If two peanuts were selected, what is the probability that they were selected from the second jar?

6. A poker player has two aces, two kings and a jack. He discards the jack and picks a card. What is the probability that he ends up with a full house?*

7. A jar contains four nickels and two dimes. Four coins are chosen successively at random. Find

(a) the probability that the total drawn is 30¢;

(b) the probability that the first two coins drawn total more money than the last two;

(c) the probability that the coins alternate in denomination.

8. A box contains ten tags numbered 1, 2, 3, . . . , 10. Arthur draws a tag numbered 7 and keeps it. Now Sue picks a tag. What is the probability that Sue's number is higher than Arthur's?

9. The probability that I am late is 1/3. The probability of getting caught in the rain is 1/4. The probability of being late if I am caught in the rain is 1/2. Find

(a) the probability of being late and caught in the rain;

---

* A full house is a five-card poker hand consisting of three cards of one denomination and two cards of another.

(b) the probability of being late and not caught in the rain;
(c) the probability of being late or caught in the rain;
(d) the probability that I was caught in the rain given that I am late.

10. $P(A \mid B) = 1/2$, $P(A) = 1/6$ and $P(B \mid A) = 1/12$. Find $P(B)$.

11. $P(A \cup B) = 2/3$, $P(A) = 1/2$, $P(B) = 7/12$. Find $P(B \mid A)$ and $P(A \mid B)$.

12. The Andrews Appliance Center has always bought from ABC Suppliers and found that it has 5% of its sales returned as defective. This month it bought 20% of its supplies from DEF Suppliers and found that 8% of the total sales were returned as defective. What percentage of DEF Suppliers' appliances were defective?

13. The Third National Bank is considering opening a branch office. They take a survey of pedestrians passing the proposed site and find that 10% of them already bank at Third National. Of this group, 95% say that they would use the new branch. Of the other people, 40% say that they would open an account if the bank were located conveniently. What percentage of the pedestrians could they count upon as customers?

8.2 Bayes' Theorem

Normally when one constructs a tree, one starts at the first stage and builds towards the end, using conditional probabilities. Sometimes, however, it is required to find the first probabilities conditioned upon knowledge of the latter stages. The formula by which one works backward in this way is called *Bayes' theorem*. We have actually used this theorem in the last section without naming it. The theorem supposes that an event A is attained on the second (or later) stage of an experiment and can be reached via k events $B_1, B_2, \ldots, B_k$ on the first stage. It is assumed that the B's form a partition of S, so that

$$P(A) = P(A \mid B_1)P(B_1) + P(A \mid B_2)P(B_2) + \cdots + P(A \mid B_k)P(B_k)$$

The values $P(B_1), P(B_2), \ldots, P(B_k)$ are assumed to be known. Now, if A occurs, what is $P(B_j \mid A)$ where $j = 1, 2, \ldots, k$? The answer is

$$P(B_j \mid A) = \frac{P(A \cap B_j)}{P(A)} = \frac{P(A \mid B_j)P(B_j)}{P(A)} \qquad j = 1, 2, \ldots, k$$

where $P(A)$ is given above. The numerator of the fraction is simply the probability of the branch $B_j - A$ on the tree for the experiment.

Many statisticians like to reason in this Bayesian fashion. That is, they assume values for $P(B_1)$, $P(B_2)$, . . . , $P(B_k)$ which they believe are good guesses based on past experience. These are called *a priori* or *prior* probabilities. After the experiment is performed, the computed $P(B_1 \mid A)$, $P(B_2 \mid A)$, . . . , $P(B_k \mid A)$ are now called the *a posteriori* or *posterior* probabilities. If another experiment is run, they will use these new probabilities as the prior probabilities. For example, let us try Urn Model C. Urn 1 contains one red and nine black balls. Urn II contains seven red and three black balls. An urn is chosen at random. A ball is chosen from the urn and it is red. What is the probability that Urn I was chosen? From figure 4,

$$P(U_1 \mid R) = \frac{P(U_1 \cap R)}{P(R)} = \frac{(0.5)(0.1)}{(0.5)(0.1) + (0.5)(0.7)} = \frac{0.05}{0.40} = \frac{1}{8}$$

Now, it must be that $P(U_2 \mid R) = 7/8$.

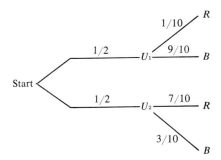

Figure 4

Suppose that we now replace the ball, shake up the urn and draw again. Suppose the ball is again red. What is the probability that Urn I was chosen? In figure 5, we have the same diagram except that the prior probabilities of the urns have been adjusted to take into account the previous information. Now,

$$P(U_1 \mid R) = \frac{P(U_1 \cap R)}{P(R)} = \frac{(1/8)(1/10)}{(1/8)(1/10) + (7/8)(7/10)} = \frac{1}{50}$$

Therefore, $P(U_2 \mid R) = 49/50$.

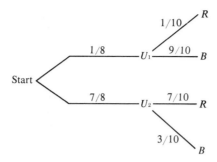

Figure 5

Interestingly, we could have considered this problem as two draws from the urn starting with the original prior, as shown in figure 6. From this diagram we see

$$P(U_1 \mid R - R) = \frac{P(U_1 - R - R)}{P(R - R)} = \frac{(0.5)(0.1)(0.1)}{(0.5)(0.1)(0.1) + (0.5)(0.7)(0.7)}$$

$$= \frac{0.005}{0.005 + 0.245} = \frac{1}{50}$$

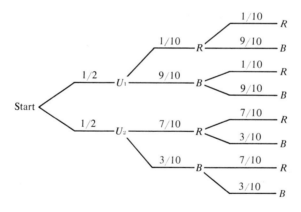

Figure 6

EXERCISES

1. Urn I contains six white and three green balls. Urn II contains two white balls and seven green balls. An urn is chosen at random and a ball is chosen from it at random. Given that the ball was white, find the posterior probabilities of selecting the two urns.

2. Box 1 contains five slips with the number 1 and three with the number 2. Box 2 contains six slips with the number 1 and six with the number 2. A box is chosen at random and a slip selected from the box. The number on the slip tells which box to pick the next slip from. If the second slip is numbered 2, find the probability that the first slip was numbered 1. Find the probability that the first box chosen was number 1. (Draw a tree diagram.)

3. In a good teacher's math class, 10% of the students fail. In a bad teacher's math class, 20% of the students fail. Only 5% of the teachers are bad teachers. If a student selected at random passed math, what is the probability that he had a good teacher?

4. The probability that a willow will wither if it is watered is 1/3. The probability that a willow will wither if it is not watered is 1/2. The probability that Walter will water the willow is 3/4. The willow withered. What is the probability that Walter watered it?

5. Of all potatoes, 1/4 are small, 1/4 are large and 1/2 are medium-sized. Of small potatoes, 10% are rotten; of medium potatoes, 15% are rotten; and of large potatoes, 40% are rotten. If a potato chosen at random is rotten, find the posterior probabilities of its possible sizes.

6. An observation is made of a random variable which may be distributed according to $p_1(x)$, $p_2(x)$ or $p_3(x)$, given in Section 7.8. A priori, all three distributions are equally likely. The value observed is $x = 5$. Find the posterior probabilities of the three distributions.

7. Continuation of 6. A second observation is made and it is $x = 4$. What are the posterior probabilities of the three distributions now?

8. (a) Assuming that the first observation was $x = 3$, repeat Exercise 6.
   (b) Another observation is made, again $x = 3$. What are now the posterior probabilities?

9. Three different loan examiners review applications in a large bank. Each reviews one-third of the applications. Mr. Able rejects 25%, Mr. Black rejects 40% and Mrs. Charles rejects 60% of those considered. Miss Wilson's application was rejected. What is the probability that the decision was made by Mrs. Charles?

10. A manufacturer deals with three different suppliers. From source A, he receives 50% of his goods; from source B, he receives 30% of his goods; from source C, he receives 20% of his goods. From these sources, 3%, 2%, and 6% respectively of the goods are defective. If a piece of goods selected at random is defective,

what is the probability that it came from source C? If a second piece from the same source is selected and is also defective, what is the probability that *it* was provided by source C?

11. A loan association classifies borrowers as prime risk, low risk, and high risk. Sixty percent of its loans go to prime risk borrowers, who have a 1% default rate. Thirty percent go to low risk borrowers, who have a 2% default rate. If its overall default rate is 5%, what is the default rate among high risk borrowers? What is the probability that a defaulter was a high risk customer?

8.3 Independence

Let us reconsider Urn Model C. Recall that Urn I contains one red ball and nine black balls, Urn II contains seven red and three black balls. A ball chosen from an urn selected at random is red. The posterior probabilities of U_1 and U_2 are $1/8$ and $7/8$, respectively. Suppose a second ball is drawn without replacement and it is red. According to our analysis of Urn Model B, the probability of R_2 and R_1 is the same. Hence, we have a tree as shown in figure 7a.

From the diagram, $P(R_2) = 1/80 + 49/80 = 5/8$ and

$$P(U_1 \mid R_2) = \frac{P(U_1 \cap R_2)}{P(R_2)} = \frac{1/80}{5/8} = \frac{1}{50}$$

However, clearly since both picks were red, the posterior probability of U_1 must be zero since U_1 had only one red ball and the sampling was done without replacement. The difficulty is caused by the fact that $P(R_2 \mid R_1) \neq P(R_2)$. The correct tree is shown in figure 7b. When the sampling was with replacement, $P(R_2 \mid R_1) = P(R_2)$, that is, knowing that R_1 occurred did not change the probability of R_2 occurring. We express this idea by saying that R_2 is independent of R_1. So if A is independent of B, then $P(A \mid B) = P(A)$. In general, $P(A \mid B) = P(A \cap B)/P(B)$. If we have independence, then $P(A) = P(A \cap B)/P(B)$, or

$$P(A \cap B) = P(A)P(B)$$

In this form, the expression is symmetric in A and B. That is, if A is independent of B, then B is independent of A. Therefore, we shall take as a definition the following.

Definition 2 A and B are called independent if $P(A \cap B) = P(A)P(B)$.

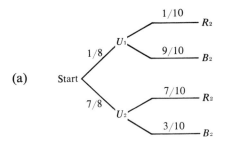

(a)

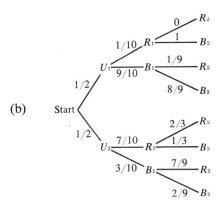

(b)

$$P(U_1 \mid R_2) = \frac{P(U_1 \cap R_2)}{P(R_2)} = \frac{0}{2/5} = 0$$

Figure 7

Of course, if in a description of an experiment different events appear to be totally unrelated, we may use this definition to compute probabilities. For example, two fair coins are flipped. What is the probability that both come up heads? Let H_1 be the event "the first coin is heads," and H_2 be the event "the second coin is heads." Certainly, the outcome on one coin should not affect the other. Hence, $P(H_1 \cap H_2) = P(H_1)P(H_2) = (1/2)$ $(1/2) = 1/4$.

It is interesting that given three events A, B and C, it is possible that C is independent of A, and C is independent of B but C is *not* independent of $A \cap B$. For example, a box contains four cards. One card is blue, one card is green, one card is red and the last card is paisley—red, green and blue. A card is drawn at random. Let B = a card with blue on it; G = a card with green on it; and R = a card with red on it. Now, $P(R) = P(G) =$

$P(B) = 1/2$. R is independent of both G and B, since $P(R \cap G) = 1/4 = P(R)P(G)$ and $P(R \cap B) = 1/4 = P(R)P(B)$. But $P(R \mid B \cap G) = 1$ since given B and G, the only possible draw is the paisley card and so R must also have occurred. In addition, B and G are also independent. Therefore, the events B, G and R would be called *pairwise independent* but you would surely not want to say they form an independent threesome. Accordingly, we have the following definition.

Definition 3 A collection of events $A_1, A_2, \ldots, A_k$ are called *independent* if for every possible subcollection, the probability of the intersection is the product of the probabilities. For example, A_1, A_2, A_3 and A_4 are called independent only if they are pairwise independent and, in addition,

$$P(A_1 \cap A_2 \cap A_3) = P(A_1)P(A_2)P(A_3)$$

$$P(A_1 \cap A_2 \cap A_4) = P(A_1)P(A_2)P(A_4)$$

$$P(A_1 \cap A_3 \cap A_4) = P(A_1)P(A_3)P(A_4)$$

$$P(A_2 \cap A_3 \cap A_4) = P(A_2)P(A_3)P(A_4)$$

$$P(A_1 \cap A_2 \cap A_3 \cap A_4) = P(A_1)P(A_2)P(A_3)P(A_4)$$

Earlier we asked what the probability of getting at least one head would be. We are now in a position to answer that question. The probability of at least one head is expressed as $P(H_1 \cup H_2) = P(H_1) + P(H_2) - P(H_1 \cap H_2) = 1/2 + 1/2 - 1/4 = 3/4$. Alternatively, we could say $P(\text{at least one head}) = 1 - P(\text{no heads})$. $P(\text{no heads}) = P(T_1 \cap T_2)$. Now since the two flips are independent, T_1 and T_2 are independent. Therefore, $P(T_1 \cap T_2) = P(T_1)P(T_2) = (1/2)(1/2) = 1/4$, and we again reach the result that the probability of at least one head is $3/4$. By the way, it is generally true that if A and B are independent, so also are A' and B', A' and B, and A and B'. The reader is asked to prove this in Exercise 4. In this case, of course, T_1 is the same as H_1' and T_2 is the same as H_2'.

Of course, tree diagrams for sequences of independent events are particularly simple to construct. Consider the following case: It has been found that 80% of all children exposed to chicken pox will come down with the disease. If three children are exposed to the infection, what is the probability that exactly two will contract it? Let C_1 be the event "the first child contracts the disease," C_1' be the event "the first child does not get sick" and so on for C_2, C_2', C_3 and C_3'. Figure 8 shows the tree diagram for this situation and

$$P(\text{Exactly 2}) = P(C_1 - C_2' - C_3) + P(C_1 - C_2 - C_3') + P(C_1' - C_2 - C_3)$$

$$= (0.8)(0.2)(0.8) + (0.8)(0.8)(0.2) + (0.2)(0.8)(0.8)$$

$$= (3)(0.2)(0.8)(0.8) = 0.384$$

This is an example of a so-called binomial distribution which results from independent repetition of trials in which the outcomes can be classified as either "success" or "failure." We shall discuss the general problem in Section 9.5.

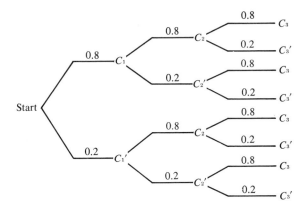

Figure 8

Let us look at one last example. A company is about to launch a large advertising campaign. It figures that a television ad will reach 60% of the target population and a direct mail ad will reach 50% of the target population. If the two possibilities are independent, what percentage of the population will see at least one ad? Letting T = see the television ad and M = see the mailing ad, then

$$P(\text{at least one}) = P(T \cup M) = P(T) + P(M) - P(T \cap M)$$

Since T and M are independent, $P(T \cap M) = P(T)P(M)$. Hence $P(\text{at least one}) = 0.60 + 0.50 - (0.60)(0.50) = 0.80$. In other words, the campaign will reach 80% of the target population.

EXERCISES

1. A and B are independent events, $P(A) = 0.7$, $P(B) = 0.8$. What is $P(A \cap B)$?

2. A and B are independent events, $P(A) = 0.6$ and $P(A \cap B) = 0.2$. What is $P(A \cup B)$?

3. A and B are independent events, $P(A \cup B) = 0.8$ and $P(A) = 0.6$. What is $P(B)$?

4. Show that if A and B are independent, then so are A and B', A' and B, and A' and B'.

5. A and B are independent events, $P(A \cup B) = 0.76$ and $P(A \cup B') = 0.94$. Find $P(A)$ and $P(B)$.

6. $P(A \cup B) = 0.8$, $P(A) = 0.7$ and $P(B) = 0.6$. Are A, B independent? Why or why not?

7. An urn contains six white and three red balls. Three balls are chosen successively at random. Draw tree diagrams for this situation assuming first that the drawing is without replacement and second with replacement. Compare the probabilities of drawing three red balls under the two assumptions.

8. The probability that a man is shorter than 64 inches is $1/3$. Find the probability that of four men chosen at random, exactly two are shorter than 64 inches.

9. Use the information in Exercise 8 to find the probability that at least one man out of four is shorter than 64 inches.

10. A, B and C are independent events. $P(A \cap B \cap C) = 0.2$, $P(A) = 0.8$ and $P(A \cap B) = 0.6$. Find $P(B)$, $P(C)$, $P(B \cap C)$, $P(A \cap C)$ and $P(A \cup B \cup C)$.

11. Mr. Able, Mr. Black and Mr. Clark check their hats. The hat check operator gives them back randomly. What is the probability that at least one man gets his own hat back? Are the events "Mr. Able gets his hat back" and "Mr. Black gets his hat back" independent? Explain.

12. To demonstrate the advantage of multiple information channels, consider the following. The probability that a message is conveyed accurately is 0.90. If two independent channels are used to send the same message, what is the probability that at least one message comes through correctly?

13. A player is to play three games against two opponents, who will take turns playing. Thus, the first opponent he plays will play two games and the other only one game. The probability of beating the stronger of the two opponents is $1/3$. The probability of beating the weaker is $1/2$. If the player's object is to win two games in a row, who should he choose to play first? (Assume that the outcomes of successive games are independent.)

14. An airplane engine has probability 0.2 of failing. If failures of different engines are independent, which is safer, a two-engine plane that can fly only if both engines function or a four-engine plane that can fly on three out of four engines?

8.4 Stochastic Processes

Let us consider the following learning model. A scientist is training a rat
to run through a maze. The probability of the rat being successful is
$(k + 1)/(n + 2)$ where n is the number of times the rat has tried the maze
and k is the number of times the rat has succeeded. Figure 9 shows a tree
diagram for three trials.

Let X_1 = number of successes after one trial. The range of X_1 is $\{0, 1\}$.
The probability function for X_1, $p_1(x)$ is given by

x	$p_1(x)$
0	1/2
1	1/2

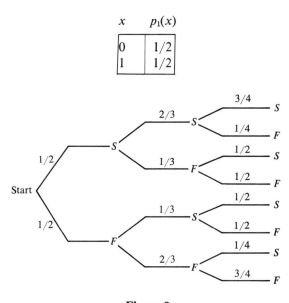

Figure 9

Let X_2 = number of successes after two trials. The range of X_2 is $\{0, 1, 2\}$.
The probability function for X_2, $p_2(x)$ is given by

x	$p_2(x)$
0	1/3
1	1/3
2	1/3

Do you think that it is generally true that X_r would have range
$\{0, 1, 2, \ldots, r\}$ and that $p_r(j) = 1/(r + 1)$ for $j = 0, 1, 2, \ldots, r$? Could
you prove it? It happens to be true. More importantly, we have here an
example of a sequence of random variables, $X_1, X_2, \ldots, X_r, \ldots$. Each

random variable has a probability distribution, and the distribution depends upon the number of the trial. If we think of the number of trials as measuring time passing, then the different probability distributions may be thought of as a single distribution which varies as a function of time. In this case, the probability of having j successes in r tries is $1/(r + 1)$ and the distribution as a function of time is very simple. Such a mathematical structure is called a *stochastic process*.

Let us take another urn model as an example. Urn I contains eight tags numbered 1 and eight tags numbered 2. Urn II contains four tags numbered 1 and twelve tags numbered 2. To start the process, a tag is selected at random from Urn I. The number on the tag is noted. For the second step, a tag is chosen from the urn whose number was on the first tag and so on. A tag once chosen is not replaced in the urn. The process ends when there are no tags left to be selected in the appropriate urn. At each step the possible numbers that may be drawn are 1 and 2. We shall refer to these as the "states" of the process. By means of a tree diagram, the reader should ascertain that on the first pick, P(State 1) = 1/2 and P(State 2) = 1/2. On the second pick, P(State 1) = 43/120 and P(State 2) = 77/120, etc.

Let us take a second learning model as an example of a stochastic process. Again, suppose a scientist is training a rat to run a maze. The probability that the rat does not succeed on a given trial is $1/2^{k+1}$ where k is the number of previous successes. A tree diagram would look like figure 10 for the first few trials. As in the first example, we let the "state" of the process at the rth step be X_r = number of successes in r attempts.

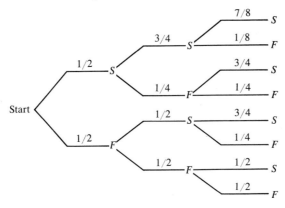

Figure 10

Now, the difference between this last model and the preceding two is that if one is told the state of the process at the rth step, then one can say exactly the possible states on the $(r + 1)$st step and the probabilities of entering into each of these states independent of r and of how the state X_r was reached. That is, if you are told that the rat has had four previous successes, the probability of having four successes after the next trial is $1/2^5 = 1/32$ and the probability of having five successes is $31/32$; and nothing else is possible regardless of how many steps have passed. This type of process is called a *Markov process* or *Markov chain*. In the first learning model, it would be necessary to know not only the number of successes, but also how long the process has been going on. In the urn model, if you were told that the process was in State 2, you would have no idea what the probabilities of going into State 1 or State 2 are without having a good deal of knowledge about the history of the process. In other words, a Markov process may be thought of as a filmstrip which is running on. You observe one frame of the strip without seeing any others and yet you are able to state with absolute assurance the likelihoods of everything that may be on the next frame. Strangely enough, this "memoryless" process can be used as a model for all kinds of practical problems.

The only thing annoying about our second learning model is that there is no limit to the number of possible states (i.e., number of possible successes) if the process goes on long enough. Thus, we would have to say that the number of possible states is infinite, which causes difficulties. Hence, in the next section, we shall discuss Markov processes, in which there are only a fixed number of possible states. These so-called finite Markov chains turn out to have vast applications, of which only a few will be indicated.

EXERCISES

1. As a miniature version of the urn model with numbered tags, suppose the first urn contains one tag numbered 1 and one tag numbered 2, and the second urn contains one number 1 and two number 2's.
    (a) Assuming that the first pick is from·Urn I, construct a tree diagram showing all possibilities.
    (b) What is the probability that the final pick is a 1?
    (c) What is the probability that the third pick is a 1?
    (d) What is the expected number of picks? What is the probability that the second pick was a 1 given that the third pick was a 2?

2. Assuming that the first pick is from Urn II, repeat Exercise 1.

3. Assuming that the first urn to be picked from is selected at random, repeat Exercise 1.

4. Consider a learning model in which the probability of a failure is $1/(k + 2)$ where k is the number of successes previously. Draw a tree diagram for the first three trials. What are the probabilities of none,

one, two and three successes? What is the expected number of successes? What is the probability that there was a success on the first trial given that there was a success on the third?

5. Repeat Exercise 4 for both learning models given in the text.

6. For the first learning model in the text, suppose the process ends with the third success. What is the probability that the process ends in four steps? What is the probability that the process ends in less than five steps?

7. Repeat Exercise 6 for the second learning model in the text.

8. Repeat Exercise 6 for the model in Exercise 4.

9. As an example of a process with a short memory, consider the following: For a hockey team a win represents two points; a tie, one point; and a loss, no points. If the team has just won a game, it has probability $1/2$ of winning, $1/4$ of tying and $1/4$ of losing. If it has just lost, the probabilities are $1/4$ of winning, $1/4$ of tying and $1/2$ of losing. If it has just tied, the probabilities are $1/3$ for each. Draw a tree for a three-game series following a tie.
   (a) Given that the first game was won, what is the probability of winning one out of the next two?
   (b) Given that the team won one out of the last two, what is the probability that it won the first game?
   (c) If the team won the first game, what is the expected number of wins in the next two?

10. Here is a simple queueing problem. In each 5-minute period, there is a probability of 0.7 that a customer will enter a store. It takes the single server 10 minutes to handle each customer, who then departs. Find the expected number of customers in the store 5 minutes after it opens, 10 minutes after it opens, and 15 minutes after it opens.

11. Follow the directions of Exercise 10 for the first two 5-minute periods, but assume that there is a 40% probability that a customer can be serviced in 5 minutes and a 60% probability that it takes 10 minutes.

12. Let us look at a traffic control problem. It is found that at a certain traffic light during the rush hour only 3 cars can get through on the green. The number of cars arriving when it is red is a random variable X whose distribution is given in the table. Find the number of cars expected to be still waiting after one complete red-green cycle, after 2 cycles, and after 3 cycles.

x	2	3	4
$p(x)$	0.1	0.2	0.7

13. Follow the directions of Exercise 12 for the first 2 cycles, assuming in addition that there is a 60% probability that the intersection will be blocked by cross traffic when the light is green.

8.5 Finite Markov Chains

At the end of the last section we defined a finite Markov chain. Let us review that definition. To begin, a finite Markov chain is a stochastic process having a finite number of states, say $s_1, s_2, \ldots, s_k$. At each step in the process there are probabilities of going from the existing state into other states. These we shall call *transition* probabilities. In addition, the process has no memory, that is, given that the process is in state s_i, the probability of its going into state s_j, on the next step, is p_{ij}; and p_{ij} is independent of the history of the process. Thus, all the information about the process is given by the numbers p_{ij}; $i = 1, 2, \ldots, k, j = 1, 2, \ldots, k$. As you can guess from the notation, we shall display the p_{ij}'s as a matrix **P**, called the *transition* matrix. A typical 4×4 transition matrix might be

$$\mathbf{P} = \begin{pmatrix} 1/2 & 1/4 & 1/8 & 1/8 \\ 1/3 & 1/3 & 0 & 1/3 \\ 1/4 & 1/2 & 0 & 1/4 \\ 1 & 0 & 0 & 0 \end{pmatrix}$$

Let us try to ascertain the meanings of some of these numbers. Take the first row. These are the numbers $p_{11}, p_{12}, p_{13}, p_{14}$. They represent the probabilities of going from state s_1 into s_1, s_2, s_3 and s_4 respectively. Notice that these fractions add up to one since all the possible transitions from s_1 are covered. Since the other rows cover the possible transitions from s_2, s_3 and s_4, the sums of these rows must also be one. This is, of course, generally true for the rows of any transition matrix. We see that $p_{23} = 0$, which means that it is impossible to get from state s_2 to state s_3. Also, $p_{41} = 1$ and $p_{42} = p_{43} = p_{44} = 0$. Thus, whenever this process reaches state s_4, it must go into s_1 on the next step.

Let us note that any transition matrix must have the same number of rows as it has columns. Such a matrix is called a *square* matrix. We shall take the following definition.

Definition 4 Every square matrix with nonnegative entries and such that the sum of the numbers in each row is one shall be called a *stochastic* matrix and it represents the transition matrix for some Markov process.

Consider the given matrix **P**. Suppose that at the kth step we are told that $P(s_1) = 1/2$, $P(s_2) = 1/4$, $P(s_3) = 1/6$ and $P(s_4) = 1/12$. What are the probabilities of these states on the $(k + 1)$st step? Let us draw a tree (figure 11). We now can read

$$P(s_1) = (1/2)(1/2) + (1/4)(1/3) + (1/6)(1/4) + (1/12)(1)$$

If we had written the original probabilities of s_1, s_2, s_3 and s_4 as a vector

$$\mathbf{v} = (1/2, 1/4, 1/6, 1/12)$$

we see that the probability of being in state s_1 on the next step is the product of **v** with the first column of **P**. Similarly, the product of **v** with

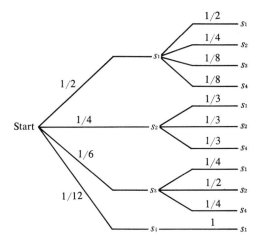

Figure 11

the second column of **P** is the new probability of s_2, and so on. Hence the product **vP** gives a row vector, the entries of which are the probabilities of being in the various states on the next step. Let us denote by $\mathbf{v}_0$ the initial vector of probabilities. Now, $\mathbf{v}_1 = \mathbf{v}_0\mathbf{P}$ is the vector of probabilities on the next step. Similarly, $\mathbf{v}_2 = \mathbf{v}_1\mathbf{P} = (\mathbf{v}_0\mathbf{P})\mathbf{P}$ is the vector of probabilities after two steps and so forth.

In general, let **P** be the transition matrix for a k state Markov process. That is,

$$\mathbf{P} = \begin{pmatrix} p_{11} & p_{12} & \cdots & p_{1k} \\ p_{21} & p_{22} & \cdots & p_{2k} \\ \vdots & & & \vdots \\ p_{k1} & p_{k2} & \cdots & p_{kk} \end{pmatrix}$$

Let $v_0 = (a_1, a_2, \ldots, a_k)$ be the vector of probabilities of the states at some given time. Let $v_1 = (b_1, b_2, \ldots, b_k)$ be the vector of probabilities on the next step. That is, $b_j = P(s_j$ after one step). To calculate b_j we write

$$b_j = P(s_j \mid s_1 \text{ now})P(s_1 \text{ now}) + P(s_j \mid s_2 \text{ now})P(s_2 \text{ now})$$
$$+ \cdots + P(s_j \mid s_k \text{ now})P(s_k \text{ now})$$
$$= P(\text{going from } s_1 \text{ to } s_j)a_1 + P(\text{going from } s_2 \text{ to } s_j)a_2$$
$$+ \cdots + P(\text{going from } s_k \text{ to } s_j)a_k$$
$$= a_1 p_{1j} + a_2 p_{2j} + \cdots + a_k p_{kj}$$

Thus, b_j is the product of v_0 and the jth column of P. But this is true for $b_1, b_2, \ldots, b_k$. Therefore

$$v_0 P = v_1$$

Take another example. Suppose we classify people by whether they own luxury cars (State 1), intermediate priced cars (State 2), and economy cars (State 3). Now most people try to move upwards, so each year there is a possible transition from state to state. We let

$$P = \begin{pmatrix} .7 & .3 & 0 \\ .5 & .3 & .2 \\ 0 & .5 & .5 \end{pmatrix}$$

give the probabilities of the transitions in any one year. An independent survey shows that this year 60% of the population own economy cars, 30% own intermediate cars and 10% own luxury cars. If the transition probabilities remain stable, what will the percentages look like in two years? Now, $v_0 = (0.1, 0.3, 0.6)$. (Note "luxury" is State 1.) After one year we have,

$$v_1 = v_0 P = (.1, .3, .6) \begin{pmatrix} .7 & .3 & 0 \\ .5 & .3 & .2 \\ 0 & .5 & .5 \end{pmatrix}$$
$$= (.22, .42, .36)$$

After two years we have

$$v_2 = v_1 P = (.22, .42, .36) \begin{pmatrix} .7 & .3 & 0 \\ .5 & .3 & .2 \\ 0 & .5 & .5 \end{pmatrix}$$
$$= (.364, .372, .264)$$

Thus, we see a marked trend away from economy and toward luxury! (This is a hypothetical example.)

It would be nice to know if there is some way to get from v_0 to v_2 directly without passing through v_1. That is, we would like to produce a matrix $P^{(2)}$ which gives the two-step transition probabilities. Mathematically, $v_2 = v_0 P^{(2)}$ would give the same result as $v_2 = v_1 P = (v_0 P)P$. In other words, $v_0 P^{(2)} = (v_0 P)P = v_0 P^2$. That is,

$$P^{(2)} = P^2$$

More generally, let

$$P^{(n)} = \begin{pmatrix} a_{11} & a_{12} & \cdots & a_{1k} \\ a_{21} & a_{22} & \cdots & a_{2k} \\ \vdots & & & \vdots \\ a_{k1} & a_{k2} & \cdots & a_{kk} \end{pmatrix}$$

be the n-step transition matrix and let

$$P^{(m)} = \begin{pmatrix} b_{11} & b_{12} & \cdots & b_{1k} \\ b_{21} & b_{22} & \cdots & b_{2k} \\ \vdots & & & \vdots \\ b_{k1} & b_{k2} & \cdots & b_{kk} \end{pmatrix}$$

be the m-step transition matrix for the process. Let us try to find $P^{(n+m)}$, the $(n + m)$-step transition matrix. Let the entry in the ith row and jth column of $P^{(n+m)}$ be c_{ij}. Now, c_{ij} is the probability that if we are now in state s_i we will be in state s_j in $n + m$ steps. The tree diagram of figure 12 shows the possible ways this can occur.

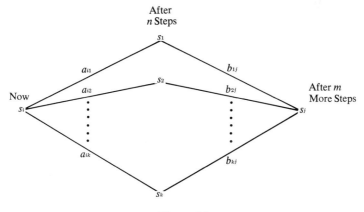

Figure 12

The probability of going from s_i to s_j is just the sum of the probabilities of each branch,

$$c_{ij} = a_{i1}b_{1j} + a_{i2}b_{2j} + \cdots + a_{ik}b_{kj}$$

Thus, c_{ij} is the product of the ith row of $\mathbf{P}^{(n)}$ and the jth column of $\mathbf{P}^{(m)}$. That is,

$$\mathbf{P}^{(n+m)} = \mathbf{P}^{(n)}\mathbf{P}^{(m)}$$

In particular, $\mathbf{P}^{(2)} = \mathbf{PP}$, $\mathbf{P}^{(3)} = \mathbf{P}^{(2)}\mathbf{P} = \mathbf{PP}^{(2)}$, $\mathbf{P}^{(4)} = \mathbf{PP}^{(3)} = \mathbf{P}^{(2)}\mathbf{P}^{(2)} = \mathbf{P}^{(3)}\mathbf{P}^{(1)}$, and so forth. Hence, we are justified in writing $\mathbf{P}^n$ for $\mathbf{P}^{(n)}$. That is, the n-step transition matrix is the nth power of $\mathbf{P}$, assuming that we perform the multiplications according to the rules set forth in the definition of matrix products. Going back to our last example, we see that

$$\mathbf{P} = \begin{pmatrix} .7 & .3 & 0 \\ .5 & .3 & .2 \\ 0 & .5 & .5 \end{pmatrix}$$

$$\mathbf{P}^2 = \mathbf{PP} = \begin{pmatrix} .7 & .3 & 0 \\ .5 & .3 & .2 \\ 0 & .5 & .5 \end{pmatrix}\begin{pmatrix} .7 & .3 & 0 \\ .5 & .3 & .2 \\ 0 & .5 & .5 \end{pmatrix}$$

$$\mathbf{P}^2 = \begin{pmatrix} .64 & .30 & .06 \\ .50 & .34 & .16 \\ .25 & .40 & .35 \end{pmatrix}$$

Also,

$$\mathbf{P}^3 = \mathbf{P}^2\mathbf{P} = \begin{pmatrix} .64 & .30 & .06 \\ .50 & .34 & .16 \\ .25 & .40 & .35 \end{pmatrix}\begin{pmatrix} .7 & .3 & 0 \\ .5 & .3 & .2 \\ 0 & .5 & .5 \end{pmatrix}$$

$$= \begin{pmatrix} .598 & .312 & .090 \\ .520 & .332 & .148 \\ .375 & .370 & .255 \end{pmatrix}$$

Checking this out with all the decimals is annoying, but since probabilities must be numbers between zero and one, the alternative is fractions, which are even less appetizing. Nevertheless, the reader should check that

1. each matrix shown is a transition matrix as predicted;
2. $\mathbf{P}^2\mathbf{P} = \mathbf{PP}^2$, that is, $\mathbf{P}^3$ is well defined.

Let us look at one final example. A small company is about to start an aggressive and expensive promotional campaign of 8 weeks duration. Preliminary field studies show that in each week it will pick up 3% of its competitor's customers and lose none of its own as a result.

One executive argues that 3% is so small that it is not worth the expense. A second executive says that 3% per week for 8 weeks is 24%, and hence they will increase their share of the market from its current 10% to 34%. Who is correct?

Let a customer be in state 1 if he is one of the company's customers and in state 2 if he is a competitor's customer. The transition matrix is

$$P = \begin{pmatrix} 1 & 0 \\ 0.03 & 0.97 \end{pmatrix}$$

and

$$v_0 = (0.1 \quad 0.9)$$

Now,

$$P^2 = \begin{pmatrix} 1 & 0 \\ 0.0591 & 0.9409 \end{pmatrix}$$

$$P^4 = P^2P^2 = \begin{pmatrix} 1 & 0 \\ 0.1147 & 0.8853 \end{pmatrix}$$

$$P^8 = P^4P^4 = \begin{pmatrix} 1 & 0 \\ 0.2163 & 0.7837 \end{pmatrix}$$

Finally, $v_8 = v_0 P^8 = (0.2947 \quad 0.7053)$

Thus, the first executive is too pessimistic and the second is too optimistic. Actually, at the end of the campaign, the company will have about 29% of the market, for an increase of 19%.

EXERCISES

1. Determine which of the following are transition matrices.

(a) $P = \begin{pmatrix} 0 & 1/2 \\ 1/3 & 2/3 \end{pmatrix}$

(b) $P = \begin{pmatrix} 0 & 1 \\ 1 & 0 \end{pmatrix}$

(c) $P = \begin{pmatrix} .5 & .3 & .2 \\ -.1 & .8 & .3 \\ 0 & .5 & .5 \end{pmatrix}$

(d) $P = \begin{pmatrix} .1 & .1 & .8 \\ 0 & 1 & 0 \\ .3 & 0 & .7 \end{pmatrix}$

2.   Sue is a creature of habit. She eats only hamburgers or chicken salad for lunch. If she ate a hamburger yesterday, the probability is 0.8 that she will have chicken salad today. If she had chicken salad yesterday, there is a 50% probability that she will eat a hamburger today. Monday she had a hamburger. Find the probability that she will have a hamburger Wednesday by

   (a)   drawing a tree diagram starting from Monday;

   (b)   expressing Sue's luncheon habits as a Markov transition matrix; computing the probabilities of her Tuesday lunch choice; and using that to compute her Wednesday probabilities;

   (c)   finding the two-step transition matrix and using it to compute Wednesday's probabilities directly.

3.   Debby always lunches with Sue. Unlike Sue, she sometimes eats tuna fish. Letting $s_1 = $ hamburger, $s_2 = $ chicken salad and $s_3 = $ tuna fish, the transition probabilities for Debby's lunch are given by

$$\mathbf{P} = \begin{pmatrix} .2 & .6 & .2 \\ .5 & 0 & .5 \\ .7 & .3 & 0 \end{pmatrix}$$

   If Debby flips a coin to decide between chicken salad and tuna fish on Wednesday, find the probability that she will eat fish on Friday. Find the probabilities of each state on Saturday.

4.   Jo, Ed and Howie share the job of bringing the boss bad news. No one goes twice in a row. If Howie went last, Ed is a gentleman and goes twice as often as Jo. Howie is cowardly, so if Ed went last, Jo goes three times as often as Howie. When the choice is between Howie and Ed, each goes equally often.

   (a)   Express this situation as a Markov process and write the transition matrix.

   (b)   The first time bad news came in, the three of them drew straws to see who would go. Find the probabilities of who went on the next occasion.

   (c)   Find the probabilities on the fourth occasion.

5.   Returning to Exercise 2, the probability of hamburger and chicken salad on Monday is (5/13, 8/13) for Sue. What are the probabilities on Tuesday? Wednesday? Three weeks from Sunday?

6.   Students at Baruch College hate math but never give up. Each student must complete Math 1 and Math 2 but 1/3 fail each course. Those who fail Math 1 repeat it; those who pass take Math 2. Those

who fail Math 2 repeat it; those who pass go into a state of taking no Math. Express this situation as a Markov process. If 100% of all entering freshmen are enrolled in Math 1, what percent are still taking Math in their fourth semester?

7. In a town 40% of the workers are laborers and 60% are professionals. One-half of the laborers' sons are laborers and the remainder become professionals. It is three times as likely that the son of a professional will be a professional than a laborer. After two generations, what portion of the townsfolk are professionals?

8. There are four soap companies competing for a share of the market. Right now, Brand A has 50% of the market, Brand B has 30% and Brand C and D split the remainder equally. Each week people may change brands with the following type of behavior: Brand A retains 10% of its users and the rest divide equally among the other brands. Brand B retains none of its users who divide equally between A and C. Brand C and D users divide equally among all four brands. Write the transition matrix for this process and find the market distribution after two weeks.

9. The cigarette company that manufactures Brand C starts an aggressive advertising campaign. The results of this campaign are such that of people smoking Brand C in a given week, 80% continue to smoke it the following week; of those not smoking Brand C in a given week, 40% are won over to Brand C.
   (a) Determine the transition matrix representing the above situation.
   (b) If the probability that any person chosen at random smokes Brand C today is $1/10$, what is the probability that this person will smoke Brand C one week from now? Two weeks from now?

10. A final exam is given each term in finite math. The final exam is either very easy or slightly difficult (but not both). The probability that if it is easy this term, it will be easy next term is 0.4, whereas if it was slightly difficult one term, then it will be very easy the following term with probability 0.8.
    (a) Determine a transition matrix describing the above process.
    (b) Find the probability that the exam will be very easy next term if it is very easy this term.
    (c) If the probability that the exam will be easy this term is $1/4$, what is the probability it will be very easy next term?

8.6 Regular Markov Chains

In Exercise 5 of the last section, we saw an interesting example. In that case, we found that if $\mathbf{v}_0 = (5/13, 8/13)$, then $\mathbf{v}_1 = \mathbf{v}_0$ and hence $\mathbf{v}_2 = \mathbf{v}_1 = \mathbf{v}_0$ or, in general, $\mathbf{v}_n = \mathbf{v}_0$. That is, the probabilities of the two states remain constant from step to step. This type of behavior is called *equilibrium*. A good question now is, How does one find the equilibrium position of a Markov process? The answer is surprisingly simple. If $\mathbf{w}$ is the initial vector of probabilities and if after one step the vector of probabilities is again $\mathbf{w}$, then $\mathbf{w}P = \mathbf{w}$. Thus, suppose

$$P = \begin{pmatrix} .6 & .4 \\ .8 & .2 \end{pmatrix}$$

Let $\mathbf{w} = (w_1, w_2)$ and try to solve

$$\mathbf{w}P = \mathbf{w}$$

We have

$$(w_1, w_2)\begin{pmatrix} .6 & .4 \\ .8 & .2 \end{pmatrix} = (w_1, w_2)$$

or

$$(0.6)w_1 + (0.8)w_2 = w_1$$
$$(0.4)w_1 + (0.2)w_2 = w_2$$

It pays to multiply both equations by 10 to eliminate decimals, leaving

$$6w_1 + 8w_2 = 10w_1$$
$$4w_1 + 2w_2 = 10w_2$$

The first equation is simply

$$8w_2 = 4w_1$$

and the second equation is the same! So we really have one equation in two unknowns. However, we also know that $w_1 + w_2 = 1$, since the w's are probabilities. Substituting $w_2 = 1 - w_1$ yields

$$8(1 - w_1) = 4w_1$$
$$8 = 12w_1$$
$$w_1 = 2/3 \qquad w_2 = 1/3$$

Hence, $\mathbf{w} = (2/3, 1/3)$ is the vector of equilibrium probabilities.
  Let us look at another aspect of this equilibrium vector. Using, as before,

$$\mathbf{P} = \begin{pmatrix} .6 & .4 \\ .8 & .2 \end{pmatrix}$$

$$\mathbf{P}^2 = \begin{pmatrix} .6 & .4 \\ .8 & .2 \end{pmatrix}\begin{pmatrix} .6 & .4 \\ .8 & .2 \end{pmatrix} = \begin{pmatrix} .68 & .32 \\ .64 & .36 \end{pmatrix}$$

$$\mathbf{P}^4 = \begin{pmatrix} .68 & .32 \\ .64 & .36 \end{pmatrix}\begin{pmatrix} .68 & .32 \\ .64 & .36 \end{pmatrix} = \begin{pmatrix} .6672 & .3328 \\ .6656 & .3344 \end{pmatrix}$$

$$\mathbf{P}^8 = \begin{pmatrix} .6672 & .3328 \\ .6656 & .3344 \end{pmatrix}\begin{pmatrix} .6672 & .3328 \\ .6656 & .3344 \end{pmatrix}$$

$$= \begin{pmatrix} .66666752 & .33333248 \\ .66666596 & .33333504 \end{pmatrix}$$

It should not be hard to convince yourself that as n gets very large, $\mathbf{P}^n$
approaches

$$\mathbf{Q} = \begin{pmatrix} 2/3 & 1/3 \\ 2/3 & 1/3 \end{pmatrix}$$

That is, the rows of $\mathbf{P}^n$ both approach $\mathbf{w}$, the equilibrium vector. Moreover,
let $\mathbf{v}_0 = (a, 1 - a)$ be the initial vector, and

$$\mathbf{v}_0\mathbf{Q} = (a, 1 - a)\begin{pmatrix} 2/3 & 1/3 \\ 2/3 & 1/3 \end{pmatrix}$$

$$= [(2/3)\, a + (2/3)\, (1 - a), (1/3)\, a + (1/3)\, (1 - a)]$$

$$= (2/3, 1/3)$$

That is, no matter what the initial probability vector, after a large number
of steps, the process will approach its equilibrium position! Now, this is
not true for all Markov processes. To take an extreme example, let

$$\mathbf{P} = \begin{pmatrix} 0 & 1 \\ 1 & 0 \end{pmatrix}$$

Now, $\mathbf{w} = (1/2, 1/2)$ is the equilibrium vector. However, let $\mathbf{v}_0 = (1/3, 2/3)$. Then, $\mathbf{v}_1 = (2/3, 1/3)$; $\mathbf{v}_2 = (1/3, 2/3)$; $\mathbf{v}_3 = (2/3, 1/3)$ and so
on. The process oscillates back and forth, never settling down toward the
equilibrium status. However, most processes do tend to stabilize. In
particular, we have the following definition.

Definition 5   Let P be a $(k \times k)$ transition matrix. If for some number n, P^n has no zero entries, then the process is called *regular*.

For a regular process, it can be shown that
1.   There exists a probability vector $\mathbf{w} = (w_1, w_2, \ldots, w_k)$ such that $\mathbf{w}P = \mathbf{w}$.
2.   The rows of P^n all approach $\mathbf{w}$ as n gets large.
3. $\mathbf{v}_0 P^n$ approaches $\mathbf{w}$ regardless of $\mathbf{v}_0$.

Let us take one more example. There are three competing brands of cigars on the market. The most expensive is Swankismoke; the middle-priced brand is called Puffo; and the cheapest is called El Ropo. Each week, 20% of the El Ropo smokers buy Puffo instead. The rest buy El Ropo again. Twenty percent of the Puffo smokers buy El Ropo and 30% buy Swankismoke. The rest buy Puffo. Sixty percent of the Swankismoke users switch to Puffo and the rest are loyal to Swankismoke. Letting $s_1 =$ Swankismoke, $s_2 =$ Puffo and $s_3 =$ El Ropo, the transition matrix is:

$$P = \begin{pmatrix} .4 & .6 & 0 \\ .3 & .5 & .2 \\ 0 & .2 & .8 \end{pmatrix}$$

Now $P^2 = PP$

$$P^2 = \begin{pmatrix} .4 & .6 & 0 \\ .3 & .5 & .2 \\ 0 & .2 & .8 \end{pmatrix} \begin{pmatrix} .4 & .6 & 0 \\ .3 & .5 & .2 \\ 0 & .2 & .8 \end{pmatrix}$$

$$= \begin{pmatrix} .34 & .54 & .12 \\ .27 & .47 & .26 \\ .06 & .26 & .68 \end{pmatrix}$$

Since P^2 has no zero entries, P is a regular transition matrix. The equilibrium vector

$$\mathbf{w} = (w_1, w_2, w_3)$$

is found by solving

$$\mathbf{w}P = \mathbf{w}$$

$$(w_1, w_2, w_3) \begin{pmatrix} .4 & .6 & 0 \\ .3 & .5 & .2 \\ 0 & .2 & .8 \end{pmatrix} = (w_1, w_2, w_3)$$

$$0.4w_1 + 0.3w_2 \qquad\qquad = w_1$$
$$0.6w_1 + 0.5w_2 + 0.2w_3 = w_2$$
$$0.2w_2 + 0.8w_3 = w_3$$

Again multiplying through by 10, we have

$$4w_1 + 3w_2 \qquad\quad = 10w_1$$
$$6w_1 + 5w_2 + 2w_3 = 10w_2$$
$$2w_2 + 8w_3 = 10w_3$$
$$-6w_1 + 3w_2 \qquad\quad = 0$$
$$6w_1 - 5w_2 + 2w_3 = 0$$
$$2w_2 - 2w_3 = 0$$

This really gives us four equations in three unknowns, since

$$w_1 + w_2 + w_3 = 1$$

Writing the four equations in matrix form, we proceed to our usual triangularization:

$$\begin{pmatrix} -6 & 3 & 0 & \vdots & 0 \\ 6 & -5 & 2 & \vdots & 0 \\ 0 & 2 & -2 & \vdots & 0 \\ 1 & 1 & 1 & \vdots & 1 \end{pmatrix} \sim \begin{pmatrix} 1 & -1/2 & 0 & \vdots & 0 \\ 6 & -5 & 2 & \vdots & 0 \\ 0 & 2 & -2 & \vdots & 0 \\ 1 & 1 & 1 & \vdots & 1 \end{pmatrix}$$

$$\sim \begin{pmatrix} 1 & -1/2 & 0 & \vdots & 0 \\ 0 & -2 & 2 & \vdots & 0 \\ 0 & 2 & -2 & \vdots & 0 \\ 0 & 3/2 & 1 & \vdots & 1 \end{pmatrix} \sim \begin{pmatrix} 1 & -1/2 & 0 & \vdots & 0 \\ 0 & 1 & -1 & \vdots & 0 \\ 0 & 1 & -1 & \vdots & 0 \\ 0 & 3/2 & 1 & \vdots & 1 \end{pmatrix}$$

$$\sim \begin{pmatrix} 1 & -1/2 & 0 & \vdots & 0 \\ 0 & 1 & -1 & \vdots & 0 \\ 0 & 0 & 0 & \vdots & 0 \\ 0 & 0 & 5/2 & \vdots & 1 \end{pmatrix}$$

Back substituting yields $(5/2)w_3 = 1$, $w_3 = 2/5$; $w_2 - w_3 = 0$; $w_2 = 2/5$; and $w_1 - (1/2)w_2 = 0$; $w_1 = 1/5$. Thus, $\mathbf{w} = (0.2, 0.4, 0.4)$. That is, regardless of the original shares of the market, in the long run 20% of the smokers will buy Swankismoke and the remaining 80% of the market will be divided evenly between Puffo and El Ropo!

EXERCISES

1. Referring to Exercise 1, Section 8.5, find the equilibrium vectors for each transition matrix. Which matrices are regular?

2. A billing office finds that in 25% of all accounts for which a bill is due in one month, a bill is also due the next month. For those accounts for which no bill is due in one month, no

bill is due in 50% of the cases in the next month. Find the long-run percentage of accounts in which a bill will be due in a given month.

3. Referring to Exercise 3, Section 8.5, find the percentage of the time that Debby will eat tuna fish in the long run.

4. Find the equilibrium probabilities for Jo, Ed, and Howie in Exercise 4, Section 8.5.

5. In a car rental agency, a car may be in one of three states. It may be in the shop for preparation before renting. It may be in the lot waiting to be rented. It may be out rented. Half the cars that are out rented in any day are returned and in the shop the next day and half are still out. Every car in the shop in any day is on the lot the next day. Sixty percent of the cars on the lot in one day are rented on the next day, and the rest remain in the lot. Set up the transition matrix for this process. Show that it is regular and find the long-run percentage of the time that a car is in use.

6. Referring to Exercise 6, Section 8.5, find the equilibrium position for this process. Is this a regular process? Find P^2, P^4 and P^8. Does the process appear to approach its equilibrium position?

7–10. Find the long-run state probabilities for the processes in Exercises 7–10, Section 8.5.

11. Given

$$P = \begin{pmatrix} 1/2 & 1/2 & 0 & 0 \\ 0 & 1/3 & 2/3 & 0 \\ 0 & 0 & 1/3 & 2/3 \\ 1 & 0 & 0 & 0 \end{pmatrix}$$

Is P regular? Find its equilibrium vector.

8.7 Absorbing Markov Chains

At Metropolitan College every student must pass basic mathematics. Fully one-half of the students in the course fail each term but no one gives up. Accordingly, we have a Markov process with two states, s_1 = taking basic math, s_2 = finished basic math. The transition matrix for the process is

$$P = \begin{pmatrix} 1/2 & 1/2 \\ 0 & 1 \end{pmatrix}$$

Since everyone starts off taking basic math, the probability of being in State 1 initially is 1 and of being in State 2 initially is 0. Hence,

$$\mathbf{v}_0 = (1, 0)$$

Now,

$$\mathbf{v}_1 = \mathbf{v}_0 P = (1/2,\ 1/2)$$
$$\mathbf{v}_2 = \mathbf{v}_1 P = ((1/2)^2,\ 1 - (1/2)^2)$$
$$\mathbf{v}_3 = \mathbf{v}_2 P = ((1/2)^3,\ 1 - (1/2)^3)$$
$$\vdots$$

We see that the probabilities of being in state 1 form a geometric progression with $a = 1$ and $r = 1/2$.

In planning schedules, we must know how many students are expected to be taking the course in any given term. Let us suppose that the school admits 1,000 students each term. Let S_k be the expected number of students taking the course in the kth term. Thus,

$$S_1 = 1,000$$
$$S_2 = 1,000 + (1/2)S_1 = 1,000 + 500$$
$$S_3 = 1,000 + (1/2)S_2 = 1,000 + (1/2)(1,000 + 500)$$
$$= 1,000 + 500 + 250$$
$$S_4 = 1,000 + (1/2)S_3 = 1,000 + 500 + 250 + 125$$
$$\vdots$$
$$S_k = a + ar + ar^2 + \cdots + ar^{k-1} \quad \text{where } a = 1,000,\ r = 1/2$$

We see that S_k is the sum of the first k terms of the geometric progression. Thus

$$S_k = \frac{a(1 - r^k)}{1 - r}$$

with $a = 1,000,\ r = 1/2$,

$$S_k = \frac{1000(1 - (1/2)^k)}{1/2} = 2000(1 - (1/2)^k)$$

Let us look at our basic math Markov process again. We have

$$\mathbf{v}_k = [(1/2)^k,\ 1 - (1/2)^k] = (p_k, q_k)$$

As k becomes large, p_k approaches zero and q_k approaches one. Since q_k is the probability that a student has completed basic math after k terms, this says that the probability of eventually completing the course approaches one. Or in other words, if the student remains long enough, he is virtually certain to pass. Of course, an interesting question is, How long should one expect it to take? That is, how many terms will it take the average student to complete the course? If we denote this number by N, then $N = E(X)$ where X is the number of trials needed to pass the course. Now, we have never found the expected value of a random variable which can take on an infinite number of possible values. However, it turns out that the same formula will work, that is,

$$E(X) = 1p_1 + 2p_2 + 3p_3 + \cdots$$

Believe it or not, this can be evaluated. To do so, we note that if $r = 1/2$, the sum of the infinite geometric progression is

$$S = \frac{a}{1 - r} = 2a$$

Now,

$$E(X) = p_1 + 2p_2 + 3p_3 + 4p_4 + \cdots$$
$$E(X) = (1/2) + 2(1/2)^2 + 3(1/2)^3 + 4(1/2)^4 + \cdots$$
$$\begin{aligned} E(X) = (1/2) &+ (1/2)^2 + (1/2)^3 + (1/2)^4 + \cdots \\ &+ (1/2)^2 + (1/2)^3 + (1/2)^4 + \cdots \\ &\qquad\quad + (1/2)^3 + (1/2)^4 + \cdots \\ &\qquad\qquad\qquad + (1/2)^4 + \cdots \\ &\qquad\qquad\qquad\qquad\qquad \vdots \end{aligned}$$

In the last equation, each line is a geometric progression with $r = 1/2$. In the first line $a = 1/2$, in the second $a = (1/2)^2$, and so on. Hence

$$E(X) = 2(1/2) + 2(1/2)^2 + 2(1/2)^3 + \cdots$$

which is a geometric progression with $r = 1/2$ and $a = 1$. Thus, $E(X) = 2(1) = 2$. That is, the average student will spend two terms taking basic math. Intuitively, this seems correct. If there is a 50% chance of passing each time he tries, then the average person should pass in two tries.

Actually we can attack this problem without resorting to the infinite progression. Let N be the number of trials a student is expected to take. Since everyone starts in State 1, we can say that N is equal to 1 plus the average number of additional trials needed. Now 1/2 the students pass and need no more tries. The remaining 1/2 start over and need an average of N more trials. Hence,

$$N = 1 + (1/2)(0) + (1/2)N$$
$$N = 1 + (1/2)N$$
$$(1/2)N = 1$$
$$N = 2$$

Please notice that in this hypothetical example, the student who is repeating the course has no more chance of passing than the newcomer.

This type of Markov chain is characterized by the existence of an *absorbing state*, that is, a state which once entered is never left. In this case, s_2 is an absorbing state. It is easily recognized by the fact that the entry in Row 2, Column 2 of the transition matrix is a 1. Since there is a nonzero probability that the process enters s_2 and there is no probability of ever leaving it, eventually the process must end in State 2.

Now suppose that in order to reduce the number of failures in basic math, Metropolitan College divides the one-semester course into two one-semester courses, allowing more time for study. Thus, we have Math I and Math II. Further, suppose that in each course 1/3 of the students fail and have to repeat. Using the obvious notation, we have as the transition matrix for this process

$$\mathbf{P} = \begin{pmatrix} 1/3 & 2/3 & 0 \\ 0 & 1/3 & 2/3 \\ 0 & 0 & 1 \end{pmatrix}$$

Furthermore, suppose that an exemption examination is given to entering students, on the basis of which a student may be placed in Math I or in Math II or he may be excused from math. This gives as an initial probability vector

$$\mathbf{v}_0 = (p_1, p_2, p_3)$$

which shows the likelihoods that an entering student selected at random is in s_1, s_2 or s_3, respectively. This new situation raises a series of questions. For example,

1. Since we now have two nonabsorbing states, is there still probability 1 that the process will be absorbed in s_3?
2. Assuming that it must be absorbed in s_3, what is the expected number of steps until absorption?
3. What is the expected number of times that the process will be in s_1 and s_2 given that it starts in s_1? Given that it starts in s_2?

To answer these questions, consider the matrix **P**. The four elements in the upper lefthand section form a matrix:

$$Q = \begin{pmatrix} 1/3 & 2/3 \\ 0 & 1/3 \end{pmatrix}$$

which displays the transition probabilities between the nonabsorbing states s_1 and s_2. The largest entry in Q is $2/3$. Therefore, after one step the probability that the process will be in s_1 or s_2 is at most $2/3$. After two steps, this probability will be at most $(2/3)^2$; after three steps $(2/3)^3$ and so on. Since the nth power of $2/3$ rapidly tends to zero, the process must eventually be absorbed in s_3.

Now let n_{ij} be the expected number of steps during which the process will be in state s_j given that it starts in state s_i, that is,

$$n_{11} = \text{time spent in } s_1, \text{ given we start in } s_1$$
$$n_{12} = \text{time spent in } s_2, \text{ given we start in } s_1$$
$$n_{21} = \text{time spent in } s_1, \text{ given we start in } s_2$$
$$n_{22} = \text{time spent in } s_2, \text{ given we start in } s_2$$

Let

$$N = \begin{pmatrix} n_{11} & n_{12} \\ n_{21} & n_{22} \end{pmatrix}$$

We may now write

$$N = I + QN$$

analogously to the previous example. Why should this be so? Suppose $u_0 = (p_1, p_2)$ gives the initial probabilities of s_1 and s_2. Then u_0N gives the expected number of times spent in s_1 and s_2. However, suppose one step has passed. Now the probabilities of the two states is given by u_0Q and the expected number of remaining times in the two states becomes $(u_0Q)N$. Logically, the total number of times spent in a state = number of times spent in that state on the first step + number of times spent in that state on the remaining trials. Now, the expected number of times spent in a given state on the first step is simply equal to the probability of being in that state on the first step. Hence

$$u_0N = u_0 + (u_0Q)N$$

That is,

$$u_0N = u_0(I + QN)$$

But this is true for every possible u_0 and hence

$$N = I + QN$$

Solving for **N**, we obtain

$$\mathbf{N} - \mathbf{QN} = \mathbf{I}$$
$$(\mathbf{I} - \mathbf{Q})\mathbf{N} = \mathbf{I}$$
$$\mathbf{N} = (\mathbf{I} - \mathbf{Q})^{-1}$$

assuming that $(\mathbf{I} - \mathbf{Q})^{-1}$ exists (which it always will for an absorbing chain). For the case in question,

$$\mathbf{I} - \mathbf{Q} = \begin{pmatrix} 1 & 0 \\ 0 & 1 \end{pmatrix} - \begin{pmatrix} 1/3 & 2/3 \\ 0 & 1/3 \end{pmatrix} = \begin{pmatrix} 2/3 & -2/3 \\ 0 & 2/3 \end{pmatrix}$$
$$= (2/3)\begin{pmatrix} 1 & -1 \\ 0 & 1 \end{pmatrix}$$

and

$$\mathbf{N} = (\mathbf{I} - \mathbf{Q})^{-1} = (3/2)\begin{pmatrix} 1 & 1 \\ 0 & 1 \end{pmatrix} = \begin{pmatrix} 3/2 & 3/2 \\ 0 & 3/2 \end{pmatrix}$$

Thus, given that the process starts in s_1, we may expect that it will stay in s_1 for 1.5 steps and in s_2 for 1.5 steps. If it starts in s_2 we expect it to spend zero steps in s_1 and 1.5 steps in s_2. The zero steps in s_1 must be correct since there is no way to go from s_2 into s_1 in this example. Clearly the expected number of steps until absorption is three if we start in s_1 and 1.5 if we start in s_2. That is, the expected numbers of steps until absorption are the sums of the rows of **N**. We know from past examples that this is simply **NU** where U is a column vector of all ones. Thus,

$$\mathbf{t} = \mathbf{NU}$$

gives the expected numbers of steps until absorption starting from each of the nonabsorbing states.

An interesting sidelight is the question, Does this new math-sequence really help the student to finish earlier? Not the student who starts at the beginning. Although his probability of failure has been reduced from 1/2 to 1/3, he now expects to need three terms to finish the sequence, whereas he expected before to need only two terms. However, on the average the student may be better off if enough are able to start in s_2 or s_3 after the placement examination.

Let us further complicate the model under consideration. Suppose it is found that 10% of all students drop out of school each semester while taking Math I and II, never to return. We let

s_1 = taking Math I

s_2 = taking Math II

s_3 = completed mathematics

s_4 = dropped out before completing mathematics

Statistics show the transition matrix to be

$$\mathbf{P} = \begin{pmatrix} .3 & .6 & 0 & .1 \\ 0 & .3 & .6 & .1 \\ 0 & 0 & 1 & 0 \\ 0 & 0 & 0 & 1 \end{pmatrix}$$

Now, we may visualize **P** as

$$\mathbf{P} = \begin{pmatrix} \mathbf{Q} & \mathbf{R} \\ \mathbf{Z} & \mathbf{I} \end{pmatrix}$$

where **Q** gives transition probabilities between nonabsorbing states and **R** gives transition probabilities from nonabsorbing to absorbing states. A reasonable question to ask at this point is, What are the probabilities of eventual absorption in each of the absorbing states?

Let **B** be a matrix giving the probabilities of absorption in s_3 and s_4 given that the process starts in s_1 and s_2, that is,

$$\mathbf{B} = \begin{pmatrix} b_{13} & b_{14} \\ b_{23} & b_{24} \end{pmatrix}$$

where b_{ij} is the probability of absorption in State j having started in State i. Now the probability of eventual absorption must be equal to the probability of immediate absorption plus the probability of transition to another nonabsorbing state, followed by eventual absorption. Thus, for example,

$$b_{14} = 0.1 + (0.3)b_{14} + (0.6)b_{24}$$

| Immediate absorption | Remain in s_1 followed by eventual absorption | Transition to s_2 followed by eventual absorption |

Written in matrix form, this relationship becomes

$$B = R + QB$$
$$B - QB = R$$
$$(I - Q)B = R$$
$$B = (I - Q)^{-1}R$$

Since $(I - Q)^{-1} = N$, we have finally

$$B = NR$$

Summarizing, if we have an absorbing Markov chain, we first will write its transition matrix in the form

$$P = \begin{pmatrix} Q & R \\ Z & I \end{pmatrix}$$

To do this, we may have to renumber the states so that all the absorbing states are last. We next find the "fundamental matrix," $N = (I - Q)^{-1}$. Then N gives the expected times in each nonabsorbing state, $t = NU$ gives the expected times until absorption and $B = NR$ gives the probabilities of absorption in the several absorbing states. Thus, taking our current example, we have

$$P = \begin{pmatrix} .3 & .6 & 0 & .1 \\ 0 & .3 & .6 & .1 \\ 0 & 0 & 1 & 0 \\ 0 & 0 & 0 & 1 \end{pmatrix}$$

$$Q = \begin{pmatrix} .3 & .6 \\ 0 & .3 \end{pmatrix} \qquad I - Q = \begin{pmatrix} .7 & -.6 \\ 0 & .7 \end{pmatrix}$$

$$N = (I - Q)^{-1} = (10/7) \begin{pmatrix} 1 & 6/7 \\ 0 & 1 \end{pmatrix}$$

$$B = NR = (10/7) \begin{pmatrix} 1 & 6/7 \\ 0 & 1 \end{pmatrix} \begin{pmatrix} 0 & 1/10 \\ 6/10 & 1/10 \end{pmatrix}$$

$$B = \begin{pmatrix} 36/49 & 13/49 \\ 6/7 & 1/7 \end{pmatrix}$$

Analyzing these matrices, we draw the following conclusions: Reading the first line of B, we see that of students starting in Math I, 36/49, or about 73%, will be absorbed in the first absorbing state. That is, they will finish the sequence. The remaining 13/49, about 27%, will drop out before finishing. For students who begin in Math II, these probabilities are 6/7 (86%) and 1/7 (14%), respectively. From the matrix $\mathbf{N}$, we get the following information: Students who start in Math I may expect to spend 10/7 or 1.43 semesters in Math I and 60/49 or 1.22 semesters in Math II on the average. Thus, students starting in Math I may expect to average 2.65 semesters in mathematics courses before either finishing up or dropping out of school. For students starting in Math II, we see no terms spent in Math I and 10/7 terms spent in Math II. Of course, among nondropouts the average time until absorption is somewhat longer. Remember, we take into account no relationship between course failure and dropout likelihood. A more realistic model would include such input. In fact, a more realistic model would almost surely not be a Markov process. Nevertheless, a Markov process does give a simple and fairly accurate approximation.

In the analysis of absorbing chains, we have ignored the role of the initial probabilities of the various states. That is, $\mathbf{N}$, $\mathbf{t}$ and $\mathbf{B}$ do not take the initial probabilities into account. To do so, recall that the ith row of $\mathbf{N}$ gives the expected times spent in each nonabsorbing state, assuming that the process starts in each nonabsorbing state. Again, n_{ij} is the expected time spent in s_j given that the process starts in s_i. Hence, if $\mathbf{v}_0 = (p_1, p_2, \ldots, p_k)$ gives the initial probabilities of the nonabsorbing states, then $\mathbf{v}_0\mathbf{N}$ gives the average time spent in each nonabsorbing state. Similarly, $\mathbf{v}_0\mathbf{t}$ yields the average time until absorption, and $\mathbf{v}_0\mathbf{B}$ gives the probability of ending in each of the absorbing states.

EXERCISES

1. Referring to the first basic math course at Metropolitan College as described in the text, suppose that the school only admits new students in the fall semester. If the entering class is 1,000 students, find the numbers expected to be in basic math in the fall semester and spring semester for the first three years. Find the long-run expected numbers.

2. Referring to the first basic math course at Metropolitan College as described in the text, suppose the fail rate is reduced to 1/3. Find $\mathbf{v}_k$ and find the long-run expected number in the course if 1,000 students are admitted to the college each semester.

3. Repeat Exercise 1, if the fail rate is 1/3.

4. Consider the four-state model in the text. How long does the average student stay in math if
   (a) all students start in Math I?
   (b) half the students start in Math I and half in Math II?
   (c) 4/5 start in Math I and 1/5 in Math II?
   (d) 1/3 start in each Math I and Math II and 1/3 exempt math?

5. Consider the four-state model in the text. What percent of the students finish math and what percent drop out under each of initial conditions described in Exercise 4?

6. Given

$$P = \begin{pmatrix} .8 & .1 & 0 & .1 & 0 \\ .4 & 0 & .4 & .1 & .1 \\ .6 & .1 & .1 & .1 & .1 \\ 0 & 0 & 0 & 1 & 0 \\ 0 & 0 & 0 & 0 & 1 \end{pmatrix}$$

   find
   (a) the expected times until absorption starting from s_1, s_2 and s_3;
   (b) the probability of absorption in s_4 and s_5 starting from each non-absorbing state.

7. A particle moves along the x-axis moving 1 unit to the left with probability 1/2 or 1 unit to the right with probability 1/2 on each step. The particle may start at Point 2 or 3. If it reaches 1 or 4 it gets absorbed.
   (a) Write a transition matrix for the process.
   (b) Put the matrix in standard form.
   (c) Analyze the process.
   (This is called a *random walk with absorbing boundaries*.)

8. Repeat Exercise 7 for the case where absorption is at 1 and 5 and the process may start at 2, 3 or 4.

9. Figure 13 shows a maze in which a mouse is placed. The mouse may be placed in Compartment 1, 2 or 3. He selects doors randomly, changing locations every second. If he goes through any exit, the process ends. Set up the transition matrix for this as a Markov process and analyze in terms of number of seconds expected to take until escape and likelihood of escape through each exit.

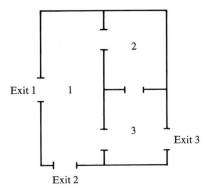

Figure 13

10. Repeat Exercise 9 for the mazes in figure 14.

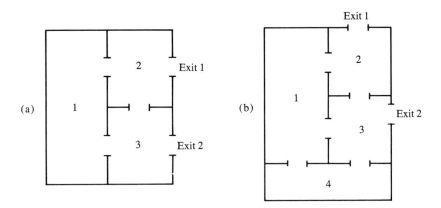

Figure 14

Analyze the Markov chains having the following transition matrices:

(a) $\begin{pmatrix} 1/4 & 3/4 \\ 0 & 1 \end{pmatrix}$

(b) $\begin{pmatrix} 1/2 & 1/4 & 1/4 \\ 1/4 & 1/4 & 1/2 \\ 0 & 0 & 1 \end{pmatrix}$

(c) $\begin{pmatrix} 1/4 & 1/4 & 1/4 & 1/4 \\ 1/4 & 1/2 & 0 & 1/4 \\ 0 & 0 & 1 & 0 \\ 0 & 0 & 0 & 1 \end{pmatrix}$

12. There are 2 loan officers working in a bank. The first officer makes decisions on 60% of the cases that come to him and passes the balance on to the second officer. The second officer makes decisions on 75% of the cases that reach him and passes the balance back to the first officer. If all cases go to the first officer first, find the expected number of times that an application is considered prior to a decision being made.

13. Here is an example of Markov analysis applied to government planning. The Small Business Administration finds that in any year it can classify the companies to whom it makes loans as being in 1 of 4 states. The first is needing minor assistance, the second is needing major assistance, the third is independent and operating successfully, and the fourth is having failed. They find that calling these states respectively s_1, s_2, s_3, and s_4, the transition probabilities are given by

$$P = \begin{pmatrix} 0.7 & 0.1 & 0.1 & 0.1 \\ 0.5 & 0.4 & 0 & 0.1 \\ 0 & 0 & 1 & 0 \\ 0 & 0 & 0 & 1 \end{pmatrix}$$

What is the average number of years that a company initially needing major assistance will remain an active concern of the S.B.A.? What is the probability that a company initially needing major assistance will succeed? If 70% of the businesses coming to the S.B.A. need major assistance and 30% need minor assistance, what percentage of the companies aided will fail? (Notice that the original figures do not look so bad. In fact, a proponent of the agency could say honestly that in one year only 10% of the companies needing major assistance will fail. Nevertheless, if these were real figures, the government might have to do some inquiring about the effectiveness of the program.)

9

Combinatorics

9.1 The Multiplication Principle

In this section we shall try to answer some problems involving counting. Suppose, for example, that a student must study one science and one foreign language to complete his degree requirements. He may choose biology, chemistry or physics as the science, and French, Spanish, German or Russian as the language. How many options does he have? All the possibilities can be exposed as shown below:

	French (F)	Spanish (S)	German (G)	Russian (R)
Biology (B)	(B, F)	(B, S)	(B, G)	(B, R)
Chemistry (C)	(C, F)	(C, S)	(C, G)	(C, R)
Physics (P)	(P, F)	(P, S)	(P, G)	(P, R)

Here we have listed all the possible pairs and see that they are twelve in number. In general, suppose an operation requires two actions. If there are n choices for the first action and m choices for the second action, then the display of possibilities would be an $n \times m$ table similar to the 3×4 table above. Clearly this display would have mn entries. This counting rule is called the *multiplication principle*.

Let us try to apply this principle to some simple examples. How many two-digit numbers between 30 and 70 can be formed using the digits 2, 3, 4, 5, 6, 7, 8? For the first digit we may choose 3, 4, 5 or 6. Therefore, there are four ways to pick the first digit. For the second digit we may choose any of the seven numerals 2, 3, 4, 5, 6, 7, 8. Thus, the total number of possible numbers is $4 \times 7 = 28$. How many may be formed if we may not use the same digit twice? In this case, we may choose the first digit in four ways. Whichever of the four digits is used, there remain six ways to choose the second digit; thus the total is $4 \times 6 = 24$. Now this is not quite the same as the two other examples. In counting the possible course options, we had four choices of language for each choice of a science, and we had a 3×4 table. In this example, for each choice of first digit we have six choices for the second digit, but not the same six choices in each case. In fact, we are really using multiplication as a shortcut for addition. That is, we are saying that beginning with 3 there are six possibilities:

$$32, 34, 35, 36, 37, 38$$

Beginning with 4 there are six possibilities:

$$42, 43, 45, 46, 47, 48$$

and so on for numbers beginning with 5 or 6. Nevertheless, the principle continues to apply because for each of the four possible first choices, there are six possible second choices.

On the other hand, suppose we wished to count only the odd numbers possible. Then, beginning with 3 we could form only 35 and 37, that is, two numbers. Beginning with 4 we have three numbers 43, 45 and 47; beginning with 5, 53 and 57; and beginning with 6, 63, 65 and 67. Thus, the total number of possibilities is ten. The procedure just applied is usually referred to as the *addition principle* and says simply that if A and B are disjoint sets, then the number of elements in $A \cup B$ is the sum of the number of elements in A and the number in B. Here we have automatically extended this principle to four disjoint sets, namely,

A = set of odd numbers beginning with 3

B = set of odd numbers beginning with 4

C = set of odd numbers beginning with 5

D = set of odd numbers beginning with 6

The multiplication principle can also be extended to more than two actions. Thus, the number of three-digit numbers between 300 and 600 that can be formed using 2, 3, 4, 5, 6, 7, 8 without repeating any digit is found as follows: The first digit may be chosen in three ways (3, 4 or 5). The second digit may now be chosen in six ways. Thus, the first two digits may be chosen in $3 \times 6 = 18$ ways. Now, the third digit may be chosen in five ways (since two digits have been used). Thus, the three digits may be chosen in $18 \times 5 = 3 \times 6 \times 5 = 90$ ways.

Sometimes we can combine the multiplication and addition principles. Thus, in the preceding example, count the number of odd three-digit numbers. In this case, it is easier to count by picking the second digit last. So, for the first digit we may select 3, 4 or 5. If the first digit is 3, then the last digit may be chosen in two ways (5 or 7) and the second digit may be chosen as any of the five remaining digits. Hence, we may choose $2 \times 5 = 10$ numbers starting with 3. If the first digit is 4, we may pick the last digit in three ways (3, 5 or 7) and the second digit in five ways. Hence, there are $3 \times 5 = 15$ numbers starting with 4. If the first digit is 5, then there are again $2 \times 5 = 10$ possibilities. Hence, the total number of possibilities is $10 + 15 + 10 = 35$.

One of the standard applications of the multiplication principle is in counting *permutations*. A permutation is simply a rearrangement. How many permutations (i.e., rearrangements) are there of the letters *CAT*? We can write them down:

$$CAT, CTA; TAC, TCA; ACT, ATC$$

six permutations. Note the count: The first letter can be chosen in three ways; the second in two ways and then the last can be chosen in only one way. Hence, we may count by the multiplication principle, $3 \times 2 \times 1 = 6$.

In general, the number of ways of "permuting" or rearranging n objects may be found by the multiplication principle. If we have n objects, we have n choices for the first position, we then have $n - 1$ choices for the second, $n - 2$ choices for the third and so on. Thus, the number of permutations of n objects is $n(n - 1)(n - 2) \ldots (3)(2)(1)$ which we shall call n *factorial*, symbolized $n!$ Thus

$$3! = 3 \cdot 2 \cdot 1 = 6$$

$$4! = 4 \cdot 3 \cdot 2 \cdot 1 = 24$$

$$5! = 5 \cdot 4 \cdot 3 \cdot 2 \cdot 1 = 120$$

Notice that $4! = 4(3!)$, $5! = 5(4!)$ or, in general, $n! = n(n - 1)!$ In order for this to be true for all n, we define $0! = 1$. In summary, the number of possible orderings of n objects is $n! = n(n - 1) \ldots (3)(2)(1)$ and $0! = 1$ by definition.

EXERCISES

1. A club has twelve members. In how many ways may a president and a vice-president be selected?

2. On a dinner menu there is a choice of five entrees, three soups and four desserts. How many different complete dinners may be selected?

3. A club consists of seven men and ten women. In how many ways may a president and a vice-president be selected if the president must be a woman? How many if the president must be a woman and the vice-president a man?

4. In the club described in Exercise 3, a president, a vice-president and a secretary are to be selected. In how many ways can this be done if the president must be a man? If the president and vice-president must be of opposite sex? If exactly one officer is a man?

5. A class consists of six boys and eight girls. In how many ways may the class line up?

6. For the class in Exercise 5, how many lineups are possible if a boy must be at the head of the line? If a boy must be at the foot of the line and a girl at the head?

7. For the class in Exercise 5, how many lineups are possible if all the girls must be together and all the boys must be together?

8. How many arrangements of the letters in the word *ambidextrous* are possible? How many if the first letter must be A? How many if the first letter must be a vowel? How many if the first and last letters must be vowels?

9. A license plate consists of a letter followed by four numerals. How many license plates can be formed?

10. A license plate consists of four numbers and one letter. How many possible plates are there? How many if the first symbol cannot be zero or the letter O?

11. What is the remainder when $12! + 1$ is divided by 9?

12. There are 20 teachers in a math department. A student is asked to indicate his favorite and his least favorite. In how many ways is this possible?

13. A house has 4 doors and 12 windows. In how many ways can a burglar rob the house if he
    (a) Enters through a window and exits through a door?

(b) Exits through the same facility he entered?

(c) Exits through a different facility than the one he entered?

(d) Exits through a different kind of facility than the kind through which he entered?

14. A person has 3 pairs of shoes, 8 pairs of socks, 4 pairs of slacks, and 9 sweaters. How many outfits are possible?

15. An automobile manufacturer produces 3 different models. A and B can come in any of 3 body styles; C can come in only 2. Each car can come in either black or in green. How many distinguishable car types are possible?

16. There are 3 airlines flying between New York and Miami, 4 between Miami and Los Angeles, and 5 between Los Angeles and New York. How many triangular round trips beginning and ending in New York are possible?

17. How many arrangements of 10 men and 10 women in a line are possible if men and women must alternate?

9.2 Combinations and Permutations

Let us consider the following type of problem. Given three letters CAT, in how many ways may we select a pair without regard to order? We may take CA, CT or AT. The pair AC is for this purpose the same as CA. The answer is then three. We shall use the symbol $\binom{3}{2}$ to mean the number of ways of selecting two objects out of three. In general, $\binom{n}{r}$ stands for the number of ways of selecting r objects out of n. Thus, if one were asked how many five-member committees can be selected from a group of twelve people, the answer would be $\binom{12}{5}$. Unfortunately, although we know that $\binom{3}{2} = 3$, we do not know what $\binom{12}{5}$ equals. Let us find out.

To begin, let us note that $\binom{12}{1}$ is the number of ways of picking one item out of twelve and that number is certainly 12. In fact, for any n,

$$\binom{n}{1} = n$$

Now returning to our committee, suppose we wish to have a committee of five, of which one person is the chairman. We could think of this as a two-stage operation. First, we select a chairman; there are twelve ways to do this. Then the chairman selects the other four members out of the remaining eleven people, and there are $\binom{11}{4}$ ways to do this. Thus, the total number of ways of selecting a committee with chairman is $12\binom{11}{4}$. Alternately, we could pick the five members of the committee (there are $\binom{12}{5}$ ways to do this) and have them select their own chairman (which can be done in five ways). Thus, the total number of ways of picking the committee is $5\binom{12}{5}$. We thus have the relationship

$$12\binom{11}{4} = 5\binom{12}{5}$$

In general, for picking a committee of size r with a chairman from a group of size n, we have

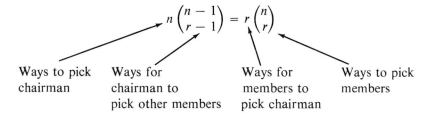

$$n\binom{n-1}{r-1} = r\binom{n}{r}$$

| Ways to pick chairman | Ways for chairman to pick other members | Ways for members to pick chairman | Ways to pick members |

We may rewrite this as

$$\binom{n}{r} = \frac{n}{r}\binom{n-1}{r-1}$$

Therefore,

$$\binom{12}{5} = \frac{12}{5}\binom{11}{4}$$

$$= \frac{12}{5} \cdot \frac{11}{4}\binom{10}{3}$$

$$= \frac{12}{5} \cdot \frac{11}{4} \cdot \frac{10}{3}\binom{9}{2}$$

$$= \frac{12}{5} \cdot \frac{11}{4} \cdot \frac{10}{3} \cdot \frac{9}{2}\binom{8}{1}$$

Since $\binom{n}{1} = n$, $\binom{8}{1} = 8$, and we have

$$\binom{12}{5} = \frac{12 \cdot 11 \cdot 10 \cdot 9 \cdot 8}{5 \cdot 4 \cdot 3 \cdot 2 \cdot 1} = 792$$

There are 792 possible committees of size five that can be chosen from a group of twelve people.

In general,

$$\binom{n}{r} = \frac{n}{r}\binom{n-1}{r-1} = \frac{n(n-1)}{r(r-1)}\binom{n-2}{r-2} = \cdots$$

$$= \frac{n(n-1)(n-2)\ldots(n-r+1)}{r(r-1)(r-2)\ldots(1)}$$

Notice that the denominator of this fraction is $r!$ and the numerator is the product of r numbers counting down from n. Also, notice that $12! = 12 \cdot 11 \cdot 10 \cdot 9 \cdot 8 \cdot 7!$, so we could write

$$\binom{12}{5} = \frac{12 \cdot 11 \cdot 10 \cdot 9 \cdot 8 \cdot 7!}{5!7!} = \frac{12!}{5!7!}$$

and, in general,

$$\binom{n}{r} = \frac{n!}{r!(n-r)!}$$

The symbol representing the number of ways of selecting r objects out of a group size n is called *the number of combinations of n objects taken r at a time*. It may be interpreted as the number of different subsets of r objects which may be chosen from a set of n objects. Interestingly, there is yet another interpretation. Suppose we have r red balls and $n - r$ white balls to be arranged in a row. How many distinguishable arrangements are possible? Two arrangements obtained by simply interchanging the locations of two balls of the same color would not be distinguishable. Thus, we may think of the problem as follows: There are n possible locations. Of them, r must be occupied by red balls. Hence, the number of arrangements is simply the number of ways of selecting r locations out of the n possible ones.

Thus, for example, the number of distinguishable arrangements of five A's and six B's in a row is

$$\binom{11}{5} = \frac{11!}{5!6!} = \frac{11 \cdot 10 \cdot 9 \cdot 8 \cdot 7}{5 \cdot 4 \cdot 3 \cdot 2 \cdot 1} = 462$$

This reasoning may be extended. For example, how many distinguishable arrangements are there of the letters AAA, BB, CC? First, we pick three locations for the A's. This may be done in $\binom{7}{3}$ ways. Next we pick two of the remaining four locations for the B's. This may be done in $\binom{4}{2}$ ways. The C locations are now forced on us. Thus, by the multiplication principle, the number of possible arrangements is

$$\binom{7}{3}\binom{4}{2} = \frac{7!}{3!4!} \cdot \frac{4!}{2!2!} = \frac{7!}{3!2!2!}$$

which is frequently written $\binom{7}{3,\,2,\,2}$ and is called a *multinomial coefficient*. Incidentally, $\binom{7}{3,\,2,\,2} = 210$.

This could again be generalized. A professor decided to give four A's, three B's, seven C's, one D, and five F's to a class of twenty students. The number of possible ways of doing this would be

$$\binom{20}{4,\,3,\,7,\,1,\,5} = \frac{20!}{4!3!7!1!5!}$$

which is about 28 billion ways. The reasoning for this is as shown.

$$\text{Ways to pick } A \text{ students, 4 out of 20} = \binom{20}{4}$$

$$\text{Ways to pick } B \text{ students, 3 out of remaining 16} = \binom{16}{3}$$

$$\text{Ways to pick } C \text{ students, 7 out of remaining 13} = \binom{13}{7}$$

$$\text{Ways to pick } D \text{ students, 1 out of remaining 6} = \binom{6}{1}$$

$$\text{Ways to pick } F \text{ students, 5 out of remaining 5} = \binom{5}{5}$$

$$\text{Total number} = \binom{20}{4}\binom{16}{3}\binom{13}{7}\binom{6}{1}\binom{5}{5}$$

which reduces to the previous result. Notice that $\binom{5}{5} = \frac{5!}{0!5!} = 1$.

It is not hard to see that, in general, if there are k different kinds of objects, r_1 of the first kind, r_2 of the second kind, etc., and if the total number of objects is n, then the number of distinguishable arrangements is

$$\binom{n}{r_1, r_2, \ldots, r_k} = \frac{n!}{r_1! r_2! \ldots r_k!}$$

When all the objects are different, $r_1 = r_2 = \cdots = r_k = 1$ and this expression reduces to $n!$, the number of permutations that we had earlier.

As a last type of count, let us consider the problem of selecting groups of r objects out of n where order counts. For example, how many different ways are there of selecting officers, president, vice-president, secretary and treasurer, from a club with twelve members? The simplest way to look at this is to say, There are twelve ways to pick a president, eleven ways to then pick a vice-president, ten ways to then pick a secretary and nine ways to pick a treasurer. Thus, the total is $12 \cdot 11 \cdot 10 \cdot 9 = 11,880$. Another way to count this is to say that there are $\binom{12}{4}$ ways to pick the officers and then 4! ways to arrange them by rank. This yields

$$\binom{12}{4} 4! = \frac{12!}{8!4!} 4! = \frac{12!}{8!} = (12)(11)(10)(9)$$

again! This number is referred to as the *number of permutations of twelve objects taken four at a time*, and is symbolized $(12)_4$. In general,

$$(n)_r = \binom{n}{r} r!$$

If you prefer, you may write this

$$(n)_r = \frac{n!}{(n-r)!} \quad \text{or} \quad (n)_r = n(n-1)(n-2)\ldots(n-r+1)$$

However, this is a case where it is easier to do it than to write it.

EXERCISES

1. A rummy hand consists of seven cards dealt from a 52-card deck. How many different rummy hands can a player be dealt?

2. An automobile dealer wants to arrange a Toyota, a Ford, a Plymouth, and a Batmobile along a straight curb in order to take publicity pictures. In how many distinct ways can the cars be arranged for the pictures?

3. A student's major department offers six different courses, while his minor department offers five different courses. In how many different ways can a student choose a program consisting of three courses

from his major department and two courses from his minor department?

4. Four of six people will be chosen to ride in a motorboat. One of the six owns the boat and must drive it. Find the number of possible seating arrangements for the ride.

5. A woman has five sons and four daughters. She chooses four sons and two daughters to help with the housework. In how many different ways can she do this?

6. A social studies teacher has a list of five different history books and seven different geography books, from which each student must choose three history books and five geography books to read. In how many ways can a student choose his reading assignment?

7. (a) In how many distinct ways can the letters in the word *calculus* be arranged?
   (b) How many arrangements can be formed from the letters of the word *Tennessee*, taken all at a time?
   (c) Find the number of different permutations which can be formed from the letters of the word *Cincinnati*, taken all at a time.

8. From a group of nine men and seven women a committee of five is to be chosen. Find the number of such committees containing exactly three men.

9. In how many different ways can six books be placed on a shelf so that two particular books are next to each other?

10. How many committees, each consisting of four men and three women, can be selected from a group of six men and seven women?

11. How many different permutations of the letters *ABCdefg* can be formed if each must begin and end with a capital letter and all the letters are used in each permutation?

12. How many committees of five can be formed from a group of six Democrats and three Republicans if each committee is to have at least four Democrats?

13. A signal is formed by placing nine flags in a vertical line on a flagpole. How many different signals of nine flags each can be formed from four red, three blue, and two white flags?

14. (a) How many different permutations can be formed from the letters of the word *perennial*, taken all at a time?
   (b) How many different permutations can be formed from the letters of the word *assassins*, taken all at a time?

15. A man has a penny, nickle, dime, quarter, half dollar, and silver dollar.
    (a) He chooses 3 coins at random. How many sums are possible?
    (b) If he takes a selection of any size, how many sums are possible?

16. A ceremony is to include 7 speeches and 6 musical selections.
    (a) How many programs are possible?
    (b) How many programs are possible if speeches and musical selections are to be alternated?
    (c) Repeat (b) if there are 6 speeches and 6 musical selections.

17. There are 9 boys and 8 girls willing to serve on a committee. How many 7-member committees are possible if a committee is to contain:
    (a) 3 boys and 4 girls?
    (b) At least one member of both sexes?

18. A woman is packing ski sweaters and pants for a trip. She owns 7 sweaters and 4 pairs of pants. How many ways can she pack if she is to include the same number of sweaters as pants?

9.3 Binomial Formula

Let us consider some properties of the combination symbol $\binom{n}{r}$. To begin, we state the following.

Property 1 $\binom{n}{r} = \binom{n}{n-r}$.

This follows from directly substituting $n - r$ for r in the formula. Thus

$$\binom{n}{n-r} = \frac{n!}{[n-(n-r)]!(n-r)!} = \frac{n!}{r!(n-r)!} = \binom{n}{r}$$

Alternatively, one could simply realize that every time a group of size r is selected from n objects, there remains a group of size $n - r$. Thus, there are just as many ways of selecting size r groups as size $n - r$ groups.

Property 2 $\binom{n}{0} = \binom{n}{n} = 1$.

This, of course, is simply obtained by substituting $r = 0$ and remembering that $0! = 1$.

Property 3 $\binom{n-1}{r} + \binom{n-1}{r-1} = \binom{n}{r}$.

This could be proved by algebra but there is a nice combinatoric argument for it. Suppose you are one of a group of n people from which a committee of size r is to be chosen. The total number of possible committees is $\binom{n}{r}$. These can be divided into those of which you are a member and those of which you are not a member. There are $\binom{n-1}{r}$ ways of choosing the committee when you are not a member since all r people must be chosen from the $n - 1$ others. If you are a member, then you need select only $r - 1$ other members and the number of ways of doing this is $\binom{n-1}{r-1}$.

Since these two possibilities exhaust the ways in which committees can be formed, we have

$$\binom{n}{r} = \binom{n-1}{r-1} + \binom{n-1}{r}$$

Using this relationship and $\binom{n}{0} = \binom{n}{n} = 1$, we may generate these coefficients via the so-called Pascal's triangle shown below:

```
              1                     Row 0
            1   1                   Row 1
          1   2   1                 Row 2
        1   3   3   1               Row 3
      1   4   6   4   1             Row 4
    1   5  10  10   5   1           Row 5
                :
```

In each row, the first and last numbers are 1 and each other number is the sum of the two adjacently above it. Now, the fourth row gives $\binom{3}{r}$, $\binom{3}{0} = 1$, $\binom{3}{1} = 3$, $\binom{3}{2} = 3$, $\binom{3}{3} = 1$. The fourth row is

$$\binom{4}{0} = 1 \qquad \binom{4}{1} = \binom{3}{0} + \binom{3}{1} = 1 + 3 = 4$$

$$\binom{4}{2} = \binom{3}{1} + \binom{3}{2} = 3 + 3 = 6$$

and so on. Furthermore, we can use these numbers to generate the expansion of $(x + y)^n$. Since $x + y$ is a binomial, the formula for $(x + y)^n$ is called the *binomial* formula. We may generate this as follows: Consider $(1 + t)^n$:

$$(1 + t)^2 = 1 + 2t + t^2 \quad \text{and} \quad (1 + t)^3 = 1 + 3t + 3t^2 + t^3$$

can be worked out longhand. Notice that the coefficients of the powers of t are the entries in Row 2 and Row 3 of Pascal's triangle.

Now $(1 + t)^{n-1}$ must be a polynomial of order t^{n-1}; thus

$$(1 + t)^{n-1} = a_0 + a_1 t + a_2 t^2 + \cdots + a_{n-1} t^{n-1}$$

Multiplying by $(1 + t)$, we have

$$
\begin{aligned}
(1 + t)^n &= (1 + t)(a_0 + a_1 t + a_2 t^2 + \cdots + a_{n-1} t^{n-1}) \\
&= a_0 + a_1 t + a_2 t^2 + \cdots + a_{n-1} t^{n-1} \\
&\quad + a_0 t + a_1 t^2 + \cdots + a_{n-2} t^{n-1} + a_{n-1} t^n \\
&= a_0 + (a_1 + a_0)t + (a_2 + a_1)t^2 + \cdots \\
&\qquad\qquad\qquad\qquad + (a_{n-1} + a_{n-2})t^{n-1} + a_{n-1} t^n
\end{aligned}
$$

Thus, we see that the coefficients of $(1 + t)^n$ start with a_0 and end with a_{n-1} unchanged for each n. Since for $n = 2$ and 3 the first and last are both 1, that must be so for all n. Furthermore, the coefficients of the powers of t in $(1 + t)^n$ are the sums of adjacent pairs of coefficients from the expansion of $(1 + t)^{n-1}$. Starting from $n = 2$, we can then generate these so-called binomial coefficients via Pascal's triangle exactly as we did $\binom{n}{r}$. We start with the same values for $n = 2$ and $n = 3$. Hence, they must be the identical numbers. Thus, we may write

$$(1 + t)^n = \binom{n}{0} + \binom{n}{1} t + \binom{n}{2} t^2 + \cdots + \binom{n}{n} t^n$$

Letting $t = y/x$, we have $x^n(1 + t)^n$ is

$$x^n \left(1 + \frac{y}{x}\right)^n = x^n \left[\binom{n}{0} + \binom{n}{1} \frac{y}{x} + \binom{n}{2} \frac{y^2}{x^2} + \cdots + \binom{n}{n} \frac{y^n}{x^n}\right]$$

$$(x + y)^n = \binom{n}{0} x^n + \binom{n}{1} x^{n-1}y + \binom{n}{2} x^{n-2}y^2 + \cdots + \binom{n}{n} y^n$$

This last is the binomial formula. For example, from Pascal's triangle, the coefficients for $(x + y)^4$ are 1, 4, 6, 4, 1 and the expansion is

$$(x + y)^4 = x^4 + 4x^3y + 6x^2y^2 + 4xy^3 + y^4$$

More difficult problems are also possible. Thus,

$$(2x - 3y)^4 = 16x^4 - 96x^3y + 216x^2y^2 - 216xy^3 + 81y^4$$

is obtained by substituting $2x$ for x and $-3y$ for y in the formula.

Of course, by using this formula, one could find a particular term in the expansion without computing all the terms. For example, find the fifth term of $(x + 2y)^{13}$. The first term involves $x^{13}y^0$; second, $x^{12}y^1$; and the fifth, x^9y^4. Notice that the power of x and the power of y must sum to n (in this case 13). Therefore, the fifth term is

$$\binom{13}{4} x^9(2y)^4 = 715x^9(16y^4) = 11{,}440x^9y^4$$

Similarly, the coefficient of x^3y^8 in the expansion of $(2x - y)^{11}$ may be found by realizing that to have y^8 the term must be

$$\binom{11}{8}(2x)^3(-y)^8 = \binom{11}{8} 2^3(-1)^8x^3y^8$$
$$= 528x^3y^8$$

Hence, the coefficient is 528.

EXERCISES

1. Write out Rows 0 to 12 of Pascal's triangle.

2. Use the result of Exercise 1 to compute $(x + y)^{10}$.

3. Use the result of Exercise 1 to compute $(2x - y/2)^6$.

4. Compute $(x - 1/x)^7$.

5. Find the coefficient of x^2y^5 in the expansion of $(3x - y/3)^7$.

6. Find the coefficient of x^6y^3 in the expansion of $(x^2 + y)^6$.

7. Find the coefficient of x in the expansion of $(x^2 - 2/x)^8$.

8. Find and simplify the fifth term only in the expansion of $(2x - 3y)^9$.

9. Find and simplify the fifth term only in the expansion of $(2x - y^2/2)^6$.

10. Find and simplify the sixth term in the expansion of $(a^2 + 1/a^2)^{10}$.

11. Write the first four terms of the expansion of $(x/y - y/2x^2)^8$ and simplify each term.

12. Find and simplify the middle term in the expansion of $(y^2 - 1/2)^8$.

13. Write and simplify the middle term *only* in the expansion of $(2/x - x^2/2)^8$.

14. Write and simplify the middle term *only* in the expansion of $(a/x^2 + x/a^2)^{10}$.

9.4 Counting and Probabilities

The most basic type of probability problem involves probability spaces having N elementary outcomes, all of which are equally likely. That is, S consists of N points, each having likelihood $1/N$. Now if $E \subset S$ is any event, then

$$P(E) = k(1/N)$$

where k is the number of elements of E. Since

$$k(1/N) = k/N$$

this is expressed by saying

$$P(E) = \frac{\text{number of outcomes favorable to } E}{\text{total number of possible outcomes}}$$

This is only valid when all N possible outcomes are equally likely.

This rule is relatively simple to apply when the counting of possibilities is simple to do. Thus, you are part of a class of twenty students, from which one will be selected to put a problem on the blackboard. What is the probability that you are chosen? In this case, $N = 20$, $k = 1$ and $P(\text{You}) = 1/20$. Now, suppose that three students will be chosen. What is the probability that you are one of the three? In this case $N = \binom{20}{3}$, the number of ways of choosing three out of twenty. The number of possible sets which do not include you is $\binom{19}{3}$. Thus,

$$P(\text{Not You}) = \binom{19}{3} \Big/ \binom{20}{3} = \frac{19 \cdot 18 \cdot 17}{3 \cdot 2 \cdot 1} \div \frac{20 \cdot 19 \cdot 18}{3 \cdot 2 \cdot 1} = \frac{17}{20}$$

and

$$P(\text{You}) = 1 - P(\text{Not You}) = 1 - \frac{17}{20} = \frac{3}{20}$$

Examples may be even more difficult. Suppose one is dealt a poker hand of five cards from a standard deck. What is the probability of having a "full house"? (A full house is three cards of one denomination and two cards of another denomination.) The number of possible poker hands is $\binom{52}{5}$. The number of possible full houses is more difficult to count. First, there are thirteen possible ways to choose the denomination for the three-some and $\binom{4}{3}$ to pick the three cards of that denomination. There are then twelve ways to choose the denomination of the pair and $\binom{4}{2}$ to pick the two cards of that denomination. Thus

$$P(\text{Full House}) = \frac{(13) \cdot \binom{4}{3} \cdot (12) \cdot \binom{4}{2}}{\binom{52}{5}} = \frac{6}{4{,}165}$$

or about one chance in 700.

A deceptively simple problem follows. There are tickets numbered 1, 2, 3, . . . , 1,000 in a lottery. Four tickets are drawn successively. What is the probability that they are in increasing order? Notice, we did not say in sequence. Thus, 3, 11, 78, 651 are in increasing order although not in sequence. In this case, whatever the four numbers be, there are 4! possible arrangements. Since only one such can be the proper order, the proba-bility is $1/4! = 1/24$.

Consider another example. An assembly line produces 2,000 items of which 600 are faulty. Twenty items are selected at random. What is the probability that exactly five are defective? The number of possible draw-ings is $\binom{2{,}000}{20}$, since we must pick twenty out of 2,000. Letting X be the number of defectives, to have $X = 5$, we must pick five out of the 600 faulty items. This can be done in $\binom{600}{5}$ ways. We must pick the remaining fifteen out of the 1,400 good items. This can be done in $\binom{1{,}400}{15}$ ways. Thus, the number of favorable outcomes to the event "$X = 5$" is $\binom{600}{5} \cdot \binom{1{,}400}{15}$ and

$$P(X = 5) = \frac{\binom{600}{5} \cdot \binom{1{,}400}{15}}{\binom{2{,}000}{20}}$$

This would work out to be about 18%.

We have here an example of a so-called hypergeometric distribution. The population consists of N objects (in this case 2,000). There are D items of interest (in this case the 600 defectives). There are $N - D$ remaining items. From the population, n items are chosen and X is the number of items of interest. By the same reasoning as above, we obtain

$$P(X = k) = \frac{\binom{D}{k}\binom{N - D}{n - k}}{\binom{N}{n}}$$

Naturally, there are certain values of k which cannot occur. In the preceding example, even if we had drawn 700 items ($n = 700$), we could still not draw more than 600 defectives. However, if we tried to substitute $k = 625$

$$P(X = 625) = \frac{\binom{600}{625}\binom{1,400}{75}}{\binom{2,000}{700}}$$

we see the expression $\binom{600}{625}$. This is the number of ways of drawing 625 items out of 600, which is certainly nonsense. If we just interpret any nonsensical binomial coëfficient to be zero, the hypergeometric formula will automatically prevent us from asking incorrect questions.

EXERCISES

1. Six married couples are seated at random at a straight banquet table. What is the probability that Mr. and Mrs. A sit next to each other?

2. What is the probability of drawing four-of-a-kind in a five-card poker hand?

3. What is the probability that a bridge hand of thirteen cards will have flat distribution (four cards of one suit and three of each other)?

4. (a) A committee of four persons is selected from among five women and six men. What is the probability that the committee will consist of three men and one woman?

   (b) A bag contains five white and three red balls. If three balls are taken together at random, what is the probability that two are white and one is red?

   (c) An urn contains seven red and four black balls. If three balls are drawn together, what is the probability that two are red and one is black?

5. (a) Box *A* contains 100 bulbs, sixty of which are defective, while Box *B* contains 100 bulbs ten of which are defective. A box is chosen at random and three bulbs are drawn at random from the box. Compute the probability that one bulb is defective.

   (b) If one defective bulb has been drawn, what is the probability that it came from Box *B*?

6. (a) A box contains five red, four white and three black balls. If two balls are drawn simultaneously, what is the probability that both are white?

   (b) What is the probability that at least two are white if four balls are drawn?

   (c) What is the probability that exactly two are white and two are red if five are drawn?

7. Five different books are to be placed randomly on a shelf. What is the probability that two certain books will be next to each other?

8. A box contains ten flashbulbs, two of which are defective. Four bulbs are drawn. Let X be the number of defectives. Find the $P(X = 0)$, $P(X = 1)$, $P(X = 2)$ and the expected value of X.

9. For the situation in Exercise 6, find the expected number of red balls drawn in three picks.

10. From a group of six Democrats and eight Republicans, five people are selected at random. What is the probability that a majority of the five are Republicans?

11. Six couples line up in a row. What is the probability that the line alternates men and women?

12. An urn contains four white and two black balls. Three balls are chosen at random. For every black ball drawn, one additional ball is drawn. What is the expected value of the total number of black balls drawn?

13. Here is an application to quality control. A certain machine turns out 2% defectives when it is operating properly and 20% defectives when operating improperly. It operates properly 80% of the time. From a run of 100 items, 2 are selected and tested. Both are defective. Use Bayes' Theorem to find the probability that the machine is operating improperly.

14. For the machine in Exercise 13, the decision is made that the machine will be sent for repairs whenever one or both of the 2 tested items is found to be defective. What is the probability that the machine will be sent for repair when it is actually working well? What is the probability that it will not be sent for repair when repair is actually needed?

9.5 The Binomial Distribution

Let us consider another random variable closely associated with the hypergeometric. Suppose we have an experiment in which there are two possible outcomes, success and failure. For example, in flipping a coin we might call heads a success and tails a failure. Suppose the probability of a success is p. The probability of a failure is $q = 1 - p$. Let us have n independent repetitions of the experiment. For each trial we may have success or failure. Let X be the number of successes. We shall use the symbol $b(k; n, p)$ to stand for the probability of exactly k successes, that is,

$$b(k; n, p) = P(X = k)$$

Let us first consider $P(X = 0) = b(0; n, p)$. To have $X = 0$, we must get a string of n failures. The probability of a failure on each trial is q. Since the trials are independent, we may write

$$b(0; n, p) = P(F_1, F_2, F_3, \ldots, F_n) = P(F_1)P(F_2)P(F_3) \ldots P(F_n)$$

$$= \underbrace{q \cdot q \cdot q \cdot \ldots \cdot q}_{n \text{ times}}$$

$$= q^n$$

where the subscripts on the F's indicate the number of the trial. Computing $b(1; n, p)$ we must realize that

$$P(X = 1) = P(S_1, F_2, F_3, \ldots, F_n)$$
$$+ P(F_1, S_2, F_3, \ldots, F_n)$$
$$\vdots$$
$$+ P(F_1, F_2, F_3, \ldots, S_n)$$

That is, the one success may occur on any of the n trials. Again using independence,

$$P(S_1, F_2, F_3, \ldots, F_n) = P(S_1)P(F_2) \ldots P(F_n) = pq^{n-1}$$

and this is the same for all the strings having one success. There are exactly $\binom{n}{1} = n$ ways in which we may have exactly one success in n trials and hence

$$b(1; n, p) = \binom{n}{1} pq^{n-1}$$

Similarly, to compute $P(X = k)$ one must consider all possible strings of kS's and $(n - k)F$'s in a row. There are, of course, $\binom{n}{k}$ of these. Each one has the same probability as

$$S_1, S_2 \ldots S_k, F_{k+1} \ldots F_n$$
$$P(S_1, S_2 \ldots S_k, F_{k+1} \ldots F_n) = P(S_1)P(S_2) \ldots$$
$$P(S_k)P(F_{k+1}) \ldots P(F_n) = p^k q^{n-k}$$

Thus,

$$b(k; n, p) = \binom{n}{k} p^k q^{n-k} \quad \text{for } k = 0, 1, 2, \ldots, n$$

This last expression is called the *binomial probability function*, because each probability is exactly the term in the binomial expansion of $(p + q)^n$. Since $p + q = 1$, it is easy to see that the sum of the probabilities is $1^n = 1$, as it must be.

Binomial probability problems may arise in a variety of guises. The most common involves the repetition of a simple experiment. Thus, a pair of dice is rolled eight times. What is the probability of getting exactly two 7's? On any roll, the probability of a seven is $1/6$. Therefore, we have a binomial problem with $p = 1/6$, $q = 5/6$ and $n = 8$.

$$P(X = 2) = b\left(2; 8, \frac{1}{6}\right) = \binom{8}{2}\left(\frac{1}{6}\right)^2\left(\frac{5}{6}\right)^6 = 0.26$$

These probabilities cannot be easily computed and hence they have been tabulated. A short table of this distribution for $n = 1, 2, \ldots, 20$ is included as Table A-8 in the appendix of this book. Let us take another example. A professional basketball player makes 40% of his shots. Find the probability that out of ten shots he makes, at most, three. In this case, $p = 0.4$, $q = 0.6$, $n = 10$ and we want

$$P(X \leq 3) = b(0; 10, 0.4) + b(1; 10, 0.4) + b(2; 10, 0.4) + b(3; 10, 0.4)$$

Looking these up in the table, we find

$$P(X \leq 3) = 0.0060 + 0.0403 + 0.1209 + 0.2150 = 0.3844$$

Again, the probability that a student passes math is 0.9; find the probability that in a class of eighteen students, precisely sixteen pass. In this case

$$P(X = 16) = b(16; 18, 0.9)$$

A glance at the table shows that no p value over 0.5 is included. Hence, we must let Y be the number of *failures*. Then p will equal 0.1 and to have sixteen pass, we must have two fail; hence

$$P(Y = 2) = b(2; 18, 0.1) = 0.2835$$

In general, in order to use our tables, we must always choose as a "success" the possibility which has the smaller probability, so that p will not exceed $1/2$.

A standard case in which the binomial occurs is *sampling with replacement*. In this situation, a batch of items is to be sampled. Items are selected one by one at random and after each item is inspected, it is returned to the batch and may be chosen again. In this way, if we had, say, 100 items ten of which are defective, on each pick there are always ten defectives and ninety good items available to be chosen. Therefore, on each pick the probability of a defective is 0.1 regardless of what has gone before. If the items are not returned, we have sampling without replacement and we are dealing with the hypergeometric case. However, if in a hypergeometric case, the population is quite large and the sample is small, then for all practical purposes, it makes no difference whether we sample with or without replacement. For example, there are 10,000,000 people eligible to vote in New York State. Of these, 7,000,000 are registered. Twenty eligible voters are selected at random. What is the probability that fewer than seventeen have registered? Let X be the number *not* registered. We want the probability that X is 4 or more. It is easiest to write

$$P(X \geq 4) = 1 - [P(X = 0) + P(X = 1) + P(X = 2) + P(X = 3)]$$

Now actually X has hypergeometric distribution. But twenty voters, more or less, will not really change the fact that the probability of selecting a registered voter is 0.7 and an unregistered voter 0.3. Thus, we may treat X as a binomial with $n = 20$ and $p = 0.3$ and

$$P(X \geq 4) = 1 - b(0; 20, 0.3) - b(1; 20, 0.3) - b(2; 20, 0.3) - b(3; 20, 0.3)$$
$$= 1 - 0.0008 - 0.0068 - 0.0278 - 0.0716 = 0.8930$$

How does this answer strike you? Twenty eligibles are picked at random, there is almost a 90% probability that fewer than seventeen are registered. Let us consider. Seven out of every ten eligible people register to vote. Therefore, out of twenty people, we should expect fourteen to be registered, so it seems likely that the observed number would be less than seventeen.

We just said that we should expect fourteen people to be registered. Is that right? If we flip a fair coin 100 times, how many heads do you expect? If we roll a fair die sixty times, how many 1's do you expect to roll? You should have answered, "50 heads and ten 1's." In fact, what we shall prove is that in n independent trials with success probability p, the expected number of successes is np. In other words, if X is binomial, $E(X) = np$. We may prove this by proceeding from the definition. Remember, if X is a random variable and $P(X = k) = p(k), k = 0, 1, 2, \ldots, n$; then

$$E(X) = 0 \cdot p(0) + 1 \cdot p(1) + 2 \cdot p(2) + \cdots + n \cdot p(n)$$

In the binomial case,

$$E(X) = 0 \cdot b(0; n, p) + 1 \cdot b(1; n, p) + 2 \cdot b(2; n, p) + \cdots + n \cdot b(n; n, p)$$

$$= 0 \binom{n}{0} q^n + 1 \binom{n}{1} pq^{n-1} + 2 \binom{n}{2} p^2 q^{n-2} + \cdots + n \binom{n}{n} p^n$$

Earlier, we derived the binomial coefficients by noting that

$$\binom{n}{k} = \frac{n}{k} \binom{n-1}{k-1} \quad \text{or} \quad k \binom{n}{k} = n \binom{n-1}{k-1}$$

Thus,

$$1 \binom{n}{1} = n \binom{n-1}{0}; 2 \binom{n}{2} = n \binom{n-1}{1}; 3 \binom{n}{3} = n \binom{n-1}{2};$$

$$\cdots n \binom{n}{n} = n \binom{n-1}{n-1}$$

Therefore,

$$E(X) = n \binom{n-1}{0} pq^{n-1} + n \binom{n-1}{1} p^2 q^{n-2}$$

$$+ n \binom{n-1}{2} p^3 q^{n-3} + \cdots + n \binom{n-1}{n-1} p^n$$

Factoring np from each term, we have

$$E(X) = np \left[\binom{n-1}{0} q^{n-1} + \binom{n-1}{1} pq^{n-2} \right.$$

$$\left. + \binom{n-1}{2} p^2 q^{n-3} + \cdots + \binom{n-1}{n-1} p^{n-1} \right]$$

$$= np \cdot (p + q)^{n-1} = np(1) = np$$

By an almost identical proof, we could show that

$$E[(X)(X - 1)] = n(n - 1)p^2$$

and hence

$$n(n - 1)p^2 = E(X^2 - X) = E(X^2) - E(X) = E(X^2) - np$$

So,

$$E(X^2) = n(n - 1)p^2 + np$$

and

$$\text{Var}(X) = E(X^2) - [E(X)]^2$$
$$= n(n - 1)p^2 + np - (np)^2 = np(1 - p) = npq$$

The algebra is a little tricky in that last line, but give it a try.
In summary, we may state the following theorem.

THEOREM 1 Let X be the number of successes in n independent trials for which the probability of a success is p on each trial. Then

$$P(X = k) = \binom{n}{k} p^k q^{n-k} \quad \text{for } k = 0, 1, 2, \ldots, n$$

$$E(X) = np \quad \text{and} \quad \text{Var}(X) = npq$$

where $q = 1 - p$.

As a final example, consider the following. Suppose that one out of every five Bostonians can trace his ancestors to the *Mayflower*. In a sample of 100 Bostonians, we would expect $20 = 100 \cdot 1/5$ to be able to thus trace his ancestors. Calling X the number of such Bostonians in the sample of 100, then $\text{Var}(X) = 100 \cdot 1/5 \cdot 4/5 = 16$ and $\text{SD}(X) = 4$. According to Chebyschev's inequality, the probability that X falls more than three standard deviations from its mean is at most $1/9$. That is, there is at most an 11% probability that in a sample of size 100, X will be fewer than 8 $(20 - 12)$, or more than 32 $(20 + 12)$. Another way of saying this is that there is at least an 89% probability that X falls between 8 and 32. In fact, it is virtually certain that this will happen, as we shall see in the next section.

EXERCISES

1. Let X be a binomial random variable with $n = 14$ and $p = 0.2$. Find $P(X = 2)$, $P(X \leq 2)$, $P(X > 11)$, $P(8 < X \leq 12)$.

2. A biased coin is flipped twelve times. The probability of a head on each flip is 0.4. Find the probabilities of
    (a) exactly six heads;
    (b) more than ten heads;
    (c) less than nine heads;
    (d) no more than two heads;
    (e) no less than eleven heads.

3. For X in Exercise 1, find $E(X)$ and $\mathrm{Var}(X)$.

4. Find the expected number of heads in the experiment described in Exercise 2.

5. The probability that a student selected at random has taken math is 0.7. In a group of fifteen students, how many would you expect to have taken math? What is the probability that ten have taken math? Eleven? What is the most probable number?

6. The probability that a man is tall is $2/5$. What is the probability that of six men chosen at random, at least four are tall? Let X be the number of tall men in the sample. Find $E(X)$ and $\mathrm{Var}(X)$.

7. The probability that the Knickerbockers will beat the Bucks is 0.6. What is the probability that the Knicks will win a seven-game series from the Bucks in four straight games? What is the probability that they will win in five games? Seven games?

8. What is the probability that a World Series between evenly matched teams will go seven games?

9. In a certain city 30% of the people have brown hair, 20% have black hair, 50% have blond hair. Of fourteen people chosen at random from the town, what is the probability that at least three of them have black hair?

10. It is claimed that among all drivers whose cars are equipped with seat belts, 75% use them on long trips. What is the probability that among five cars (equipped with seat belts) which pass through a toll station on a turnpike, three of the drivers are using seat belts?

11. According to one authority, the expected number of seat belt wearers is eight out of ten people. What is the probability that at least twelve out of fourteen people wear seat belts?

12. According to one authority, 75% of all people wear seat belts. According to a second authority, 50% of all people wear seat belts. In a sample of twelve people, five wore seat belts. If originally you thought both authorities equally reliable, how do you now feel about the probabilities of each being correct? HINT: Use Bayes' theorem approach.

13. Continuation of Exercise 13, Section 9.4. A machine is found to turn out 5% defectives on long production runs when operating properly and 25% when operating improperly. It operates properly 80% of the time. Ten items are selected at random for inspection and four are found to be defective. What is the probability that the machine is operating properly?

14. Continuation of Exercise 14, Section 9.4. For the machine in Exercise 13, it has been decided to send the machine for repairs whenever 3 or more defectives are found in a lot of 10. What is the probability that the machine will be sent for repairs when they are not needed? What is the probability that it will not be sent for repairs when it should be?

9.6 The Central Limit Theorem

Let us reconsider the voter registration example: the number of trials, $n = 20$; the probability of not being registered is $p = 0.3$; the expected number of nonregistrants is $E(X) = np = 20(0.3) = 6$ and $SD(X) = \sqrt{npq} = \sqrt{(20)(0.3)(0.7)} = \sqrt{4.2} = 2.05$. According to Chebyschev's inequality, the probability that X falls within two standard deviations of its mean is at least $3/4$, that is,

$$P[6 - 2(2.05) < X < 6 + 2(2.05)] \geq 0.75$$
$$P[1.9 < X < 10.1] \geq 0.75$$
$$P[X = 2, 3, 4, 5, 6, 7, 8, 9, 10] \geq 0.75$$

From the table $P(X = 2) + P(X = 3) + \cdots + P(X = 10) = 0.9753$. Thus, the true probability is over 97% that the binomial random variable will fall within two standard deviations of its expected value. Clearly, Chebyschev's inequality leaves something to be desired in terms of precision.

For the binomial random variable, if n and p are in one's tables, this is not a problem. Good tables for n up to 100 are available in many libraries, and computers can do the computations for larger n or nontabulated values of p. However, it turns out that this is really unnecessary. In the days before electronic computers, many mathematicians searched for a good approximation to the binomial distribution for large values of n. They were so successful in their quest that the need for large binomial tables is virtually nil. Their method involves approximating the binomial probabilities by the area under the familiar bell curve, which is also known as the *normal distribution* or *Gaussian distribution* function. The approximation rule, known as the central limit theorem, has been extended and amplified to cover far more than approximation to the binomial. However, for our purposes we shall only consider this first application.

We notice in Chebyschev's inequality that we measure

$$P(-k\sigma < X - \mu < k\sigma) \quad \text{or} \quad P\left(-k < \frac{X - \mu}{\sigma} < k\right)$$

and we arrive at an estimate which does not depend upon μ, σ or the specific probability distribution. This suggests that the expression

$$Z = \frac{X - \mu}{\sigma}$$

is somehow the right thing to work with. In fact, for $Z = (X - \mu)/\sigma$

$$E(Z) = \frac{1}{\sigma} E(X - \mu) = \frac{1}{\sigma} [E(X) - \mu]$$

$$= \frac{1}{\sigma} (\mu - \mu) = 0$$

Therefore, Z has mean 0 and hence $\text{Var}(Z) = E(Z^2)$:

$$\text{Var}(Z) = E(Z^2) = \frac{1}{\sigma^2} E(X - \mu)^2 = \frac{1}{\sigma^2} \text{Var}(X)$$

$$= \frac{1}{\sigma^2} \cdot \sigma^2 = 1$$

Therefore, Z has mean 0 and standard deviation 1. Such a random variable is called *standardized*. It is convenient to standardize when comparing random variables since their probability functions will then fit the same scale.

If Z is a standardized binomial random variable, then if n is large, $P(Z \leq b)$ is given approximately by the area under the bell curve to the left of b. We shall call this area $\Phi(b)$. (See figure 1.)

A table with which you may compute $\Phi(b)$ is included in the appendix. The values in the table actually give the area under the bell curve between 0 and b. The table is read down and then across. Thus, the area under the curve between 0 and 1.13 is found by reading down to $b = 1.1$ and then across over to the column headed 0.03. The entry in this spot is 0.3708. The area is illustrated in figure 2.

Actually, the bell curve is symmetric with area 1/2 on either side of 0. Hence, $\Phi(1.13) = P(Z \leq 1.13)$ = area between 0 and 1.13 + area to the left of 0 = 0.3708 + 0.5000 = 0.8708. Thus, if b is positive, one finds the

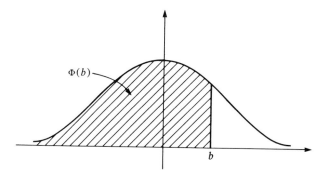

Figure 1

$P(Z \leq b)$ by adding 0.5 to the table entry for that value of b. To find $P(Z \leq -b)$ we also use symmetry as shown in figure 3. The shaded area is 0.3708, the same as between 0 and $+1.13$. Therefore, the left end tail has area $0.5000 - 0.3708 = 0.1292$. Hence

$$P(Z \leq -1.13) = 0.1292$$

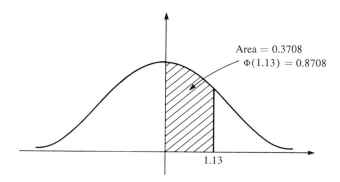

Figure 2

If $a < b$, we may write

$$P(Z \leq b) = P(Z \leq a) + P(a < Z \leq b)$$
$$\Phi(b) = \Phi(a) + P(a < Z \leq b)$$
$$P(a < Z \leq b) = \Phi(b) - \Phi(a)$$

For example, $P(-0.1 < Z \leq 1.26) = \Phi(1.26) - \Phi(-0.1)$:

$$\Phi(1.26) = 0.3962 + 0.5 = 0.8962$$
$$\Phi(-0.1) = 0.5000 - 0.0398 = 0.4602$$

Therefore, $P(-0.1 < Z \leq 1.26) = 0.8962 - 0.4602 = 0.4360$

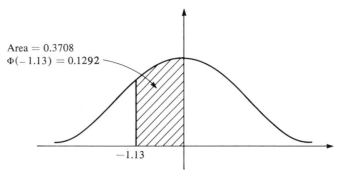

Area = 0.3708
$\Phi(-1.13) = 0.1292$

-1.13

Figure 3

Now, to actually compute binomial probabilities, suppose X is binomial; then to find $P(X = k)$ write it in the form

$$P(X = k) = P[k - (1/2) < X \le k + (1/2)]$$

This is a correct statement since the binomial cannot take on fractional values. Next, standardize

$$P(X = k) = P[k - (1/2) < X \le k + (1/2)]$$
$$= P[k - (1/2) - \mu < X - \mu \le k + (1/2) - \mu]$$
$$= P\left[\frac{k - 1/2 - \mu}{\sigma} < \frac{X - \mu}{\sigma} \le \frac{k + 1/2 - \mu}{\sigma}\right]$$
$$= P\left[\frac{k - 1/2 - \mu}{\sigma} < Z \le \frac{k + 1/2 - \mu}{\sigma}\right]$$
$$= \Phi\left(\frac{k + 1/2 - \mu}{\sigma}\right) - \Phi\left(\frac{k - 1/2 - \mu}{\sigma}\right)$$

where the last equality is only approximate. Remember that $\mu = np$ and $\sigma = \sqrt{npq}$.

Now let us try another problem. A fair coin is flipped sixteen times. The probability of getting eight heads may be looked up in the binomial table:

$$P(X = 8) = b(8; 16, 1/2) = 0.1964$$

Using the normal approximation,

$$\mu = 16(1/2) = 8$$
$$\sigma = \sqrt{(16)(1/2)(1/2)} = 2$$

we obtain

$$P(X = 8) = \Phi \left(\frac{8 + 1/2 - 8}{2} \right) - \left(\frac{8 - 1/2 - 8}{2} \right)$$

$$= \Phi(0.25) - \Phi(-0.25)$$

$$\Phi(0.25) = 0.5000 + 0.0987 = 0.5987$$

$$\Phi(-0.25) = 0.5000 - 0.0987 = 0.4013$$

$$P(X = 8) = 0.5487 - 0.4013 = 0.1974$$

with an error of about one part in two hundred!

Suppose we have $n = 18$, $p = 0.7$ and are to find $P(X \geq 14)$. Here, $P(X \geq 14) = P(X = 14) + P(X = 15) + \ldots$. Since we interpret

$$P[X = 14] \quad \text{as} \quad P[13\frac{1}{2} < X \leq 14\frac{1}{2}]$$
$$P[X = 15] \quad \text{as} \quad P[14\frac{1}{2} < X \leq 15\frac{1}{2}]$$
$$\vdots$$

we shall write

$$P(X \geq 14) = P[X > 13\frac{1}{2}]$$

$$= 1 - P[X \leq 13\frac{1}{2}]$$

$$= 1 - P\left[\frac{X - \mu}{\sigma} \leq \frac{13\frac{1}{2} - \mu}{\sigma} \right]$$

Here $\mu = (18)(0.7) = 12.6$, $\sigma = \sqrt{(18)(0.7)(0.3)} = 1.94$ and

$$P[X \geq 14] = 1 - \Phi \left[\frac{13.5 - 12.6}{1.94} \right] = 1 - \Phi(0.46) = 0.3228$$

As a check, since X is binomial with $n = 18$ and $p = 0.7$, for $X \geq 14$, as earlier we must have $Y = 0, 1, 2, 3, 4$ where Y has $n = 18$ and $p = 0.3$. Thus

$$P[X \geq 14] = b(0; 18, 0.3) + b(1; 18, 0.3) + b(2; 18, 0.3)$$
$$+ b(3; 18, 0.3) + b(4; 18, 0.3)$$

$$= 0.0016 + 0.0126 + 0.0458 + 0.1046 + 0.1681 = 0.3327$$

This time the approximation is not quite as good but remember, it is only intended to be used for large values of n.

EXERCISES

1. Find $\Phi(b)$ for $b = 0.2$, 1.31, -2.2, -1.36.

2. Find b such that $\Phi(b) = 0.6915$, 0.8438, 0.9357, 0.0548, 0.0764, 0.4880.

3. If Z is a standardized binomial variable with large n, find
   (a) $P(1 < Z \le 2.5)$;
   (b) $P(-1 < Z \le 2.5)$;
   (c) $P(-2.2 < Z \le 2.36)$;
   (d) $P(-3 < Z \le 3)$.

4. If Z is a standardized binomial variable with large n, find
   (a) $P(Z > -1.3)$;
   (b) $P(Z > 1.27)$;
   (c) $P(Z \le 1.12)$;
   (d) $P(Z \le -1.76)$.

5. Let X be a random variable with $n = 16$ and $p = 0.2$. Find
   (a) the exact probability that X falls within two standard deviations of its mean (use the binomial tables);
   (b) the Chebyschev bound for the probability of this event;
   (c) the normal approximation to the probability of this event.

6. A fair coin is flipped 100 times. (a) Find, approximately, the probability of getting exactly fifty heads. Find the probability of getting between 45 and 55 heads. (b) If the coin is flipped 10,000 times, find the probability of 5,000 heads and the probability that the number of heads is between 4,500 and 5,500. Interpret your results (between means not including the end points).

7. Repeat Exercise 6, only this time compute the probability that the fraction heads is between 0.49 and 0.51 for 100 flips, 10,000 flips and 1,000,000 flips. Interpret your results.

8. One-third of all television viewers watch "All in the Family." If 1,800 viewers are sampled at random, what is the probability that fewer than 650 watch that show? What is the probability that between 575 and 660 people watch that show?

9. A multiple choice test has fifty questions, each having four possible answers. What is the probability that a student guessing at random will score over 35% on the test?

10. (a) Find b, so that $\Phi(b) = 0.99$.
    (b) The probability that a gunner hits his target is 0.6. If he fires 96 shots, what is the probability that he makes less than 60 hits? 65 hits? 70 hits? For what number of hits is the probability 99%? 95%?

11. The probability that the Orioles will win a baseball game is 0.6. What is the probability that they will win over 100 games in a 162-game season?

12. A tennis critic says that Rod Laver has a 2/3 chance of winning a given point from Arthur Ashe. A record of 120 tie-breaker points between the two shows that Laver has won one-half. What do you think of the critic's judgment?

13. Repeat Exercise 13, Section 9.5, but assume that 100 items have been sampled and 20 have been found defective.

14. Repeat Exercise 14, Section 9.5, assuming that the decision is to send the machine for repairs whenever 18 or more defectives are found in a lot of 100. What if the decision is to send for repairs if 15 or more defectives are found? What do you think a good choice would be?

15. At the end of Section 9.5, we said that out of 100 Bostonians, it was virtually certain that between 8 and 32 of them could trace their ancestry back to the *Mayflower*. Show by the methods of this section that this is true.

PART IV

Calculus

10

Introduction to Mathematical Economics

10.1 Supply, Demand, and Revenue

In elementary economic theory there is a fundamental assumption that, all other things being equal, the supply of a given commodity is a function of the price of the commodity. In particular, it is assumed that as the price of a commodity increases, the producers will be willing to provide more of it and hence the supply will rise. We would thus say that supply is an increasing function of price. In mathematical notation, let x be the number of units of the commodity supplied and p be the price per unit, then $x = S(p)$ says that the amount supplied is a function of price. Now, as p increases, so should x. That is, if $p_2 > p_1$, then $S(p_2) > S(p_1)$. Graphically, this would mean that, plotting x in terms of p, as we move from left to right the graph goes upward.

Although the logic seems to indicate that you should plot x as a function of p, it is normal to plot x on the horizontal axis and p on the vertical axis and consider p as a function of x. For example, if the relationship between amount and price is $2p - 3x = 12$, then solving for x in terms of p yields

$$3x = 2p - 12$$

$$x = \frac{2}{3}p - 4$$

This is a linear supply function. Since the slope is positive, we see that x does increase as p increases. In fact, for every unit increase in price, the supply increases by 2/3 of a unit. Nevertheless, you could just as easily have solved for p in terms of x. Thus,

$$p = \frac{3}{2}x + 6$$

Notice that the relationship between x and p is unchanged. Both increase together. That is, not only is x an increasing function of p, but p is also an increasing function of x. The second form is mathematically just as meaningful as the first and offers the advantage that the x-axis is in its usual horizontal position. One additional constraint is applied to supply equations: neither x nor p can be a negative number.

In our example, the relationship between x and p is

$$2p - 3x = 12 \qquad x \geq 0 \qquad p \geq 0$$

The graph is shown in figure 1.

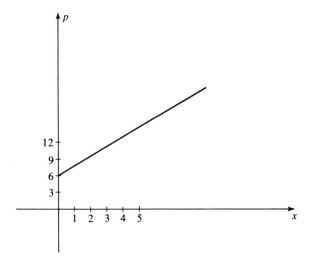

Figure 1

We see that when $x = 0$, $p = 6$. Of course, you should read this the other way: when the price is 6 (or less) there will be no supply. In other words, there is no profit to be made in supplying the commodity for less than a price of 6. This is very typical of a linear supply function, which is of the form

$$p = mx + p_o$$

where p_o is the smallest price for which there will be any supply.

In this rudimentary theory, there is also a relationship between the amount that can be sold and the unit price. This relationship is called the *demand equation*. When written in the form $x = D(p)$, it is called the *demand function*; when written in the form $p = P(x)$, it is called the *price function*. The basic assumption here is that as p increases, x should decrease. That is, as prices rise, fewer sales will be made. In other words, x is a decreasing function of p; symbolically, if $p_2 > p_1$, $D(p_2) < D(p_1)$. Again, not only is x a decreasing function of p, but p is also a decreasing function of x. Again, normally we will plot p as a function of x. We retain the restriction that x and p must be non-negative. A typical demand equation might be

$$2x + 9p = 72 \qquad x \geq 0 \qquad p \geq 0$$

Solving for x,

$$x = 36 - \frac{9}{2}p$$

That is,

$$D(p) = 36 - \frac{9}{2}p$$

Solving for p,

$$p = 8 - \frac{2}{9}x$$

That is,

$$P(x) = 8 - \frac{2}{9}x$$

The graph is shown in figure 2.

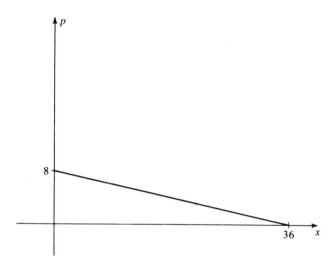

Figure 2

We see two crucial values. When $x = 0$, $p = 8$. This price ($p = 8$) is the highest price possible. If p is greater than 8, there will be no demand. When $p = 0$, $x = 36$. This amount ($x = 36$) is the largest possible demand. Even when the commodity is free, this is the most that can be given away.

If the supply and demand equations are plotted on the same set of axes, the point of intersection is called the *equilibrium position for the market*. It is characterized by the fact that at the equilibrium price, supply will exactly equal demand. If the price rises, there will be an oversupply and a resulting downward adjustment in the market. Similarly, a drop in price will cause a shortage, which will be followed by an upward adjustment. To find the equilibrium point, it is necessary only to solve the supply and demand equations simultaneously. If the equations are not linear, this process may offer some difficulties. However, suppose that our earlier examples referred to the same commodity. We display the behavior in figure 3.

The equilibrium point is $x = 36/31$, $p = 240/31$.

Another economic function closely related to the demand equation is the total revenue function. It is easy to see that if x units are produced at price per unit p, the revenue to the seller is $x \cdot p$. Since the demand and the price are related by the price function $p = P(x)$, we could describe the total revenue function $R(x)$ by

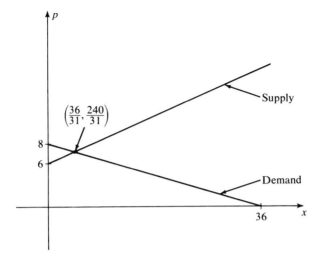

Figure 3

$$R(x) = xP(x)$$

The behavior of this function is almost always the same. When the price is high, x is low. In particular, for p high enough, $x = 0$. In this case $R(x) = 0$. That is, when the price is too high, revenue will be low. When the price is lowered, x will increase. However, again, when the price is zero, $R(x) = 0$. Thus, when the price is too low, revenue will be low. Somewhere between these two points revenue will reach a high point. Methods for finding the maximum revenue point will be discussed later. For now, let us just look at one example.

In our last example, we had

$$P(x) = 8 - \frac{2}{9}x$$

For this example, the total revenue is

$$R(x) = xP(x) = x\left(8 - \frac{2}{9}x\right)$$

$$= 8x - \frac{2}{9}x^2$$

Table 1 shows values for this function and its graph is shown in Figure 4.

Table 1

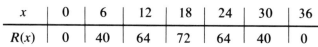

x	0	6	12	18	24	30	36
R(x)	0	40	64	72	64	40	0

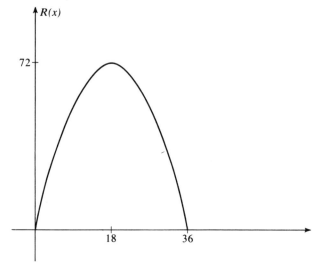

Figure 4

From the graph, it appears that $R(x)$ is maximized at $x = 18$ where $R(18) = 72$. This is, in fact, the case, and the numbers to be plotted were chosen very carefully to illustrate this result. Unfortunately, you will not be this lucky often.

EXERCISES

1. Determine which of the following are supply equations and which demand equations. For the supply equations, find the minimum price for which there will be any supply. For the demand equations, find the maximum possible demand and the maximum price that can be charged.
    (a) $x + 4p = 16$
    (b) $2p - 3x = 16$
    (c) $2p + x = 12$
    (d) $500p + 700x = 11,000$
    (e) $400p - 1,000x = 16,000$

2. Plot the equations in Exercise 1.

3. Follow the directions of Exercise 1 for the following:
   (a) $p = 160 - 10x^2$
   (b) $p = 10 + \sqrt{x}$
   (c) $p = \sqrt{100 - x}$
   (d) $\sqrt{x} + \sqrt{p} = 12$

4. Plot the equations in Exercise 3.

5. Find the linear supply function satisfying the following conditions: The minimum price for which there is any supply is $3. For every dollar increase in price, the supply will go up by 3 units.

6. Repeat Exercise 5 for the following conditions: When the price is $3, there will be no supply. When the price is $10, there will be 600 units supplied.

7. The maximum demand for a certain commodity is 20,000 tons. The highest price for which there is any demand is $40 per ton. If the demand equation is linear, find the demand function and the price function.

8. When the price of a certain commodity is 40¢ per bushel, the demand will be 6 million bushels. If the price increases to 60¢ per bushel, the demand will be for 3 million bushels. If the demand equation is linear, find the demand function and price function, expressing x in millions of bushels.

9. For the following pairs of supply and demand functions, identify which is supply and which is demand. Plot both on the same set of axes and find the market equilibrium point.
   (a) $2p - 3x = 17$
       $2p + x = 30$
   (b) $p + x = 100$
       $2p - 7x = 60$

10. Follow the directions of Exercise 9 for:
    (a) $200p - 600x = 2$
        $100p + x = 200$
    (b) $3p + 15x = 120$
        $p - x = 6$

11. For each of the demand functions in Exercise 1, find the associated total revenue function. Plot the graph of $R(x)$ in terms of x and estimate the point of maximum revenue.

12. Follow the directions of Exercise 11 for all the demand functions in Exercise 3.

13. Follow the directions of Exercise 11 for all the demand equations in Exercises 9 and 10.

14. A dealer in a rare commodity finds that his total revenue is $6,000 when the price is set at $20 and $8,000 when the price is set at $40. If the demand equation is linear, find the demand function, the price function, and the total revenue function.

10.2 Slope of a Curve

By now it is apparent that the way to distinguish between linear supply and demand functions is by observing the slope. That is, the supply function, being an increasing function, must have positive slope; the demand function must have negative slope. If you could define the slope of a curve other than the straight line, the same kind of reasoning could be used. You would not expect the slope of a curve to be constant as it is for straight lines. That is, the value of the slope should vary from point to point. In particular, suppose you were looking at a total revenue function such as the one in the last example in Section 10.1. We would expect the slope to be positive at first as the values of $R(x)$ increase towards the maximum. After passing the maximum point, the function begins to decrease, and you would expect the slope to become negative.

Let us face the problem of defining the slope of a curve. Suppose that we are given a function $y = f(x)$ and that we wish to define the slope at the point with x-coordinate a. That is, we wish the slope at the point $P(a, f(a))$. If we take any neighboring point $Q(b, f(b))$, we could connect the two points by a chord (see figure 5), the slope of which is

$$m_{chord} = \frac{f(b) - f(a)}{b - a}$$

Now visualize b approaching a. That is, let the point Q approach the point P. In this way, we find the slope of a chord between two points arbitrarily close together. In other words, we look at the limiting value of m_{chord} as b approaches a. Some geometric experimentation (see, for example, figure 6) will convince you that for smooth curves, not only will there be a limiting position, but the resulting chord will also appear to be tangent to the curve. In fact, this line of investigation was begun in the effort to define the tangent line to a curve. Therefore, we shall use the terms "slope of the curve" and "slope of the tangent line to the curve" interchangeably.

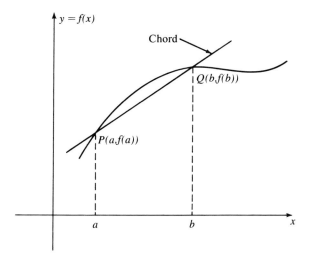

Figure 5

Let us try to solve a problem algebraically. Let $y = x^2 + 1$ and let us try to find the slope at (2,5). Following the intuitive reasoning outlined above, we must take a neighboring point on the curve and then let that point approach (2,5). The easiest way to do this is to let the x-coordinate of the neighboring point be $2 + h$. Now to let this point

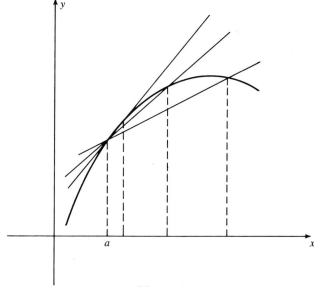

Figure 6

approach the original point, we simply let h approach zero. By the way, we shall read the symbol $\rightarrow$ as "approaches." Thus we would say $h \rightarrow 0$. Now we have $P(2,5), Q(2 + h, f(2 + h))$.

Of course,

$$f(2 + h) = (2 + h)^2 + 1$$

So,

$$m_{chord} = \frac{(2 + h)^2 + 1 - 5}{2 + h - 2}$$

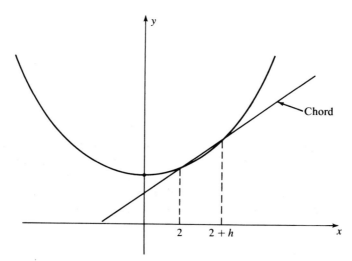

Figure 7

$$m_{chord} = \frac{4 + 4h + h^2 + 1 - 5}{h}$$

$$m_{chord} = \frac{4h + h^2}{h} = 4 + h$$

Here we see that $m_{chord} = 4 + h$. As $h \rightarrow 0$, $m_{chord} \rightarrow 4$. Thus, the limiting value of the slope is 4 and we shall define the slope of $y = x^2 + 1$ at $(2,5)$ to be 4.

Suppose that we wished to compute the slope of $f(x) = x^2 + 1$ at some other points. We could go back and go through the same computations for each point. However, it is easier to do it only once for all points (x,y) on the curve.

Let us take the general point $P(x, x^2 + 1)$ and as a neighboring point $Q(x + h, (x + h)^2 + 1)$. Then

$$m_{chord} = \frac{(x + h)^2 + 1 - (x^2 + 1)}{x + h - x}$$

$$m_{chord} = \frac{x^2 + 2xh + h^2 + 1 - x^2 - 1}{h}$$

$$m_{chord} = \frac{2xh + h^2}{h} = 2x + h$$

Thus, for every x,

$$m_{chord} = 2x + h$$

As $h \to 0$, $m_{chord} \to 2x$. Hence, for each value of x, the slope of $y = x^2 + 1$ is $2x$. Notice that this slope expression is, in fact, a function of x and varies from point to point.

We cannot go on writing sentences to describe this situation every time it arises, so we shall introduce some notation. Given some expression $y = f(x)$, the function which describes the slope at any point (x,y) will be designated $f'(x)$ (read "f prime of x"). So, for example, given

$$y = f(x) = x^2 + 1$$

Then $f'(x) = 2x$

We shall refer to $f'(x)$ as the "derivative function" or just the "derivative" of $f(x)$. Let us look at an example.

Example 1   Find the slope of the curve $y = x^2 + 1$ where $x = -2$ and where $x = 3$. At what point will the slope be zero? Find the equation of the tangent line to the curve at the point where $x = 1/2$.

As we have seen,

$$f(x) = x^2 + 1$$
$$f'(x) = 2x$$

The slope at any point is the value of $f'(x)$ at that point. Thus, where $x = -2$, $f'(-2) = 2(-2) = -4$. That is, the slope is -4.
Where $x = 3$, $f'(3) = 2(3) = 6$, and the slope is 6.
The slope is zero where $f'(x) = 2x = 0$; i.e. at $x = 0$.
Finally, at $x = 1/2$, the slope is $f'(1/2) = 2(1/2) = 1$. In addition, the y-value is $y = f(1/2) = (1/2)^2 + 1 = 5/4$. Thus, we want the line passing through $(1/2, 5/4)$ with slope 1.

In point-slope form, the equation of the tangent line is

$$y - 5/4 = 1(x - 1/2)$$
$$y = x + 3/4$$

The graph of the curve showing some of the tangents is figure 8.

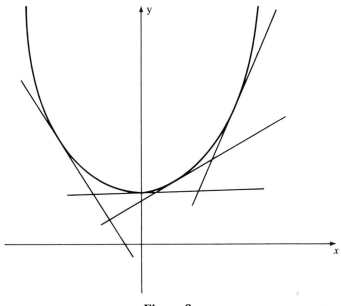

Figure 8

In general, if $y = f(x)$ is the given curve and we let $P(x, f(x))$ be an arbitrary point and $Q(x + h, f(x + h))$ be the neighboring point,

$$m_{chord} = \frac{f(x + h) - f(x)}{h}$$

Formally, we shall say,

Definition 1   If as $h \to 0$, the expression $\dfrac{f(x + h) - f(x)}{h}$ approaches some limiting value (which in general will be different for different values of x), then the limiting value will be designated by $f'(x)$ and will be called the *derivative of $f(x)$*.

Of course, if we have a function $g(x)$, its derivative will be designated $g'(x)$ and so forth. Sometimes, to save writing, we shall just write y' instead of $f'(x)$. That is,

$$y = x^2 + 1, \ y' = 2x$$

Yet another symbol $\dfrac{dy}{dx}$ or dy/dx (read "dee why, dee eks") may be used for the derivative.

EXERCISES

1. Find the slope of the curve $y = x^2 + 3x$ at $(1,4)$.
2. Show that the method given in the text gives the proper slope for the straight line $y = 3x - 5$.
3. Find the slope of $y = x^2 - 3x + 5$ for an arbitrary point (x,y). Find the values of x for which the slope is positive and the values for which it is negative.
4. Repeat Exercise 3 for $y = -x^2 + 6x$.
5. Find $f'(x)$ for $f(x) = x^2 - 7x + 11$.
6. Show that for $f(x) = mx + b, f'(x) = m$.
7. Show that for $f(x) = 7, f'(x) = 0$. Show that the derivative of any constant function is zero.
8. Find $g'(x)$ if $g(x) = 1/x$.
9. Find the equation of the tangent line to $y = x^2 - 4x + 12$ at $(3,9)$.
10. Find the equation of the tangent line to $y = -x^2 - 3x - 12$ at $(-2, -10)$.
11. Find the slope of $y = x^3$ at $x = 2$.
12. Find the equation of the tangent line to $y = x^3$ at $(2,8)$.
13. Find the derivative of $y = x^3$.
14. Find the point at which curve of Exercise 3 has zero slope. Repeat for the curve of Exercise 4.

10.3 Derivatives of Polynomials

The process of finding derivatives is called *differentiation*. The differentiation of simple functions has been done many times in the past, and mathematicians have assembled a collection of formulas that avoid the repeated use of the definition for each problem.

We shall show how to find one general derivative formula. All others shall be stated without proof. The reader is referred to any basic calculus textbook for the proofs.

Let $f(x) = x^n$, where n is any positive integer. That is, $n = 1,2,3,\ldots$. We form the quotient

$$m_{chord} = \frac{f(x + h) - f(x)}{h} = \frac{(x + h)^n - x^n}{h}$$

We expand $(x + h)^n$ by the binomial formula, yielding

$$m_{chord} = \frac{x^n + nx^{n-1}h + \binom{n}{2}x^{n-2}h^2 + \cdots + h^n - x^n}{h}$$

$$m_{chord} = nx^{n-1} + \binom{n}{2}x^{n-2}h + \cdots + h^{n-1}$$

Now every term but the first contains a factor of h, so as $h \to 0$, $m_{chord} \to nx^{n-1}$. Thus we have

Formula 1 If $f(x) = x^n$, $n = 1,2,3,\ldots$, then $f'(x) = nx^{n-1}$.

For example, suppose $f(x) = x^7$. Here we have $n = 7$, so

$$f'(x) = nx^{n-1} = 7x^{7-1} = 7x^6$$

Again, $g(x) = x^{115}$, $g'(x) = 115x^{114}$ and so on.

However, suppose instead of x^n, we had cx^n, where c is a constant. Could we find the derivative? In general, it turns out that the derivative of a constant times a function is just the constant times the derivative.

Formula 2 If $y = cf(x)$, then $y' = cf'(x)$.

For example, let $y = 7x^{11}$. y' is simply 7 times the derivative of x^{11}. Thus

$$y = 7x^{11}$$
$$y' = 7(x^{11})' = 7(11x^{10}) = 77x^{10}$$

Our next rule is particularly simple. It concerns the derivative of a constant function. The graph of $y = c$ is a horizontal straight line, which has slope zero. Therefore, you would expect the derivative to be zero.

Formula 3 If $y = c$, $y' = 0$.

That is, if $f(x) = 12$, $f'(x) = 0$ or if $g(x) = 1,176$, $g'(x) = 0$, etc.

Suppose now that we were faced with a polynomial $P(x) = 5x^3 - 4x^2 + 3x + 11$, could we find $P'(x)$? We know the derivative of each term. To be precise,

$$(5x^3)' = 15x^2$$
$$(-4x^2)' = -8x$$
$$(3x)' = 3$$
$$(11)' = 0$$

(Notice, the derivative of $3x$ is just 3, because x is the same as x^1 and hence has derivative $(1)x^{1-1} = x^0 = 1$. The question is: Can we combine the derivatives of the terms to find the derivative of the sum? The answer is not just yes, it is yes in the easiest way possible! That is, just add them together.

Formula 4 If $y = f(x) + g(x) + \cdots + h(x)$, then $y' = f'(x) + g'(x) + \cdots + h'(x)$.

Thus,

$$P(x) = 5x^3 - 4x^2 + 3x + 11$$
$$P'(x) = 15x^2 - 8x + 3$$

Look back at that last example. The new function $P'(x)$ which we have produced is also a polynomial. It also has a derivative. If we wished we could find the derivative of $P'(x)$. We would denote it $P''(x)$ and call it the *second derivative* of $P(x)$. That is, the derivative of the derivative is the second derivative. In this case

$$P''(x) = 30x - 8$$

We could also have a third derivative,

$$P'''(x) = 30$$

or a fourth derivative,

$$P''''(x) = 0$$

[Actually, for $P''''(x)$ we would usually use the notation $P^{(4)}(x)$.]

There are several possible notations for these "multiple derivatives."

The following listing shows various alternatives for denoting the derivatives of $y = f(x)$.

Original function	y or $f(x)$
First derivative	y' or $f'(x)$ or dy/dx
Second derivative	y'' or $f''(x)$ or d^2y/dx^2
Third derivative	y''' or $f'''(x)$ or d^3y/dx^3
nth derivative	$y^{(n)}$ or $f^{(n)}(x)$ or d^ny/dx^n

Let us look at some examples.

Example 1 Let $f(x) = x^3 - 3x^2$, find the sixth derivative of $f(x)$.

$$f'(x) = 3x^2 - 6x$$
$$f''(x) = 6x - 6$$
$$f'''(x) = 6$$
$$f^{(4)}(x) = 0$$

Since the fourth derivative is zero and zero is a constant, then the fifth and sixth derivatives are both zero. (In fact, all the following derivatives are zero.)

Example 2 Find the equation of the tangent line to $y = x^2 - 7x^4 - 11x^5 + 13$ at $(1,-4)$.

The derivative is

$$y' = 2x - 28x^3 - 55x^4$$

which at $x = 1$ is equal to -81.

Hence the tangent line has slope -81 and passes through $(1, -4)$. Using the point-slope formula, the equation is

$$y - (-4) = -81(x - 1)$$
$$y + 4 = -81x + 81$$
$$y = -81x + 77$$

Example 3 Find the slope of the derivative of $F(x) = 7x^3 - 6x^5$ at $x = 1$.

The derivative is

$$F'(x) = 21x^2 - 30x^4$$

The slope of the derivative is, of course, the second derivative

$$F''(x) = 42x - 120x^3$$

which at $x = 1$ is

$$F''(1) = 42 - 120 = -78$$

EXERCISES

1. Find the first derivative of
   (a) $f(x) = 7x^2 - 6x + 11$
   (b) $g(x) = 15x^3 - 6x^4 - 11x$
   (c) $F(x) = x^{12} + (1/2)x^6 + 10$
   (d) $H(x) = 3x^{11} - 16x^2 + 28$

2. Find the second and third derivatives of the functions in Exercise 1.

3. Find the equation of the tangent line to $y = f(x)$ given in 1(a) at $x = 1$.

4. Repeat Exercise 3, for $F(x)$ in 1(c) at $x = -1$.

5. (a) Find $f'(x)$ for $f(x) = 3x^2 + 1$. Find the equation of the line tangent to $y = 3x^2 + 1$ at the point where $x = 1$.
   (b) Find the equation of the line tangent to $y = 2x^2 - 3x + 5$, at the point where $x = 2$.
   (c) Find the point of intersection of the two lines.

6. For $y = x$, find y'; for $y = x^2$, find y''; for $y = x^3$, find y'''; for $y = x^n$, guess $y^{(n)}$.

7. Find the slope of the second derivative of $y = 3x^2 + 11x^3 - 8x^4$ at $x = -2$.

8. Show that the first derivative of $y = x^2 - 2x + 3$ is positive for $x > 1$ and negative for $x < 1$.

9. For what values of x is $f'(x)$ positive, if $f(x) = x^2 + 12x + 11$? For what x is $f''(x)$ positive?

10. Repeat Exercise 9 for $f(x) = 2x^3 + 9x^2 - 24x$.

10.4 Profit in a Monopoly and Other Optimization Problems

Let us return to our earlier economic considerations. Suppose we have a linear price function $P(x) = 8 - x$. The total revenue function is $R(x) =$

$xP(x) = 8x - x^2$. Now, $R(0) = 0$ and $R(8) = 0$. At some point x_o in the interval $0 \leq x \leq 8$, the total revenue reaches a maximum value. All other things being equal, it is a reasonable goal to wish to maximize revenue. That is, it is interesting to seek x_o. To do so, let us look at the derivative of the revenue function, $R'(x) = 8 - 2x$. When $x = 4$. $R'(4) = 0$. For $x < 4$, $R'(x)$ is positive. That is, the slope of the revenue curve is positive. In other words, as x goes from 0 to 4, the revenue increases. When $x > 4$, $R'(x)$ is negative. That is, the slope of the revenue curve is negative. In other words, as x goes from 4 to 8, the revenue decreases. Thus, the revenue gets greater and greater until x reaches 4 and then starts getting smaller. Clearly, the optimal value is $x_o = 4$. The maximum value of the revenue function is $R(x_o) = R(4) = 16$. The graph of $R(x)$ is shown in figure 9.

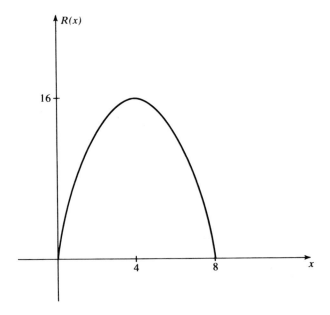

Figure 9

It is not an accident that the maximum value is attained at the point at which the derivative is equal to zero. The zero derivative means a horizontal tangent line. Any time a curve passes smoothly through a high or low point, the tangent line will be horizontal. In figure 10 we illustrate a graph with a number of points at which the derivative will be zero. Notice that A and C are high points (called *relative maxima*) while B and E are low points (called *relative minima*.)

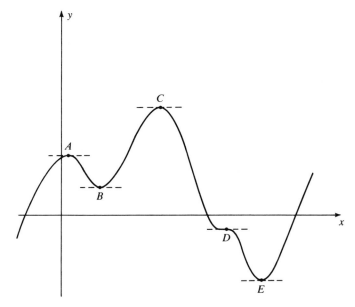

Figure 10

At the point D, the tangent line is also horizontal, but this point is neither a maximum nor a minimum. Therefore, it is possible to have a zero derivative without having an extreme point. However, we do have the following theorem.

THEOREM If $f'(x_o)$ exists and if $f(x)$ reaches a relative maximum or minimum at x_o, then $f'(x_o) = 0$.

The value of this theorem is in its application. If you wish to find the extreme values of a function, the best places to look are places at which the derivative of the function is zero.

Example 1 Let $f(x) = x^2 - 10x + 11$. $f'(x) = 2x - 10$. Now, $f'(x) = 0$ means $2x - 10 = 0$, $x = 5$. Therefore, when $x = 5$, $f(5) = 25 - 50 + 11 = -14$, which is an extreme value of the function. Is it a maximum or a minimum? Actually, it is a minimum, but how do we know?

Since it is possible for $f'(x)$ to be zero at maximum points or minimum points or simply flat spots on a curve that are not extreme points, it would be convenient to have a simple test for such points. One test is available, but it is not foolproof. This test involves the use of the second derivative. The second derivative is the derivative of $f'(x)$.

Hence, if $f''(x)$ is positive, then $f'(x)$ is increasing. Suppose that $f'(x_0) = 0$ and $f''(x_0)$ is positive. Now the slope is zero at x_0 and is increasing as you move from left to right. Therefore, to the left of x_0, the slope is negative; to the right of x_0, the slope is positive.

Thus, the curve must look like figure 11(a) and x_0 must give a minimum value to $f(x)$.

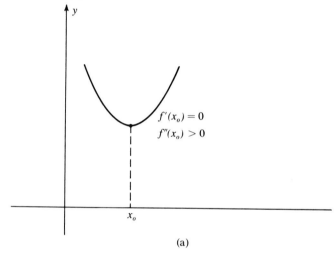

$$f'(x_0) = 0$$
$$f''(x_0) > 0$$

(a)

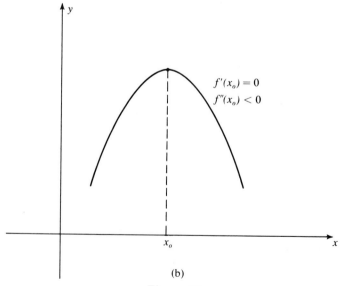

$$f'(x_0) = 0$$
$$f''(x_0) < 0$$

(b)

Figure 11

Similarly, if $f'(x_o) = 0$ and $f''(x_o) < 0$, we have a maximum at x_o. We can summarize this.

THE SECOND DERIVATIVE TEST Suppose that $f'(x_o) = 0$.

> If $f''(x_o) > 0$, then $f(x_o)$ is a relative minimum value for the function f.
> If $f''(x_o) < 0$, then $f(x_o)$ is a relative maximum value for the function f.
> If $f''(x_o) = 0$, the test fails.

Example 2 Analysis of a demand curve. Suppose that price and demand are related by the rule

$$p = P(x) = 8 - 2x - x^2$$

For what values of x and p is this a demand curve?

Since
$$P(x) = 8 - 2x - x^2$$
$$P'(x) = -2 - 2x$$
$$P''(x) = -2$$

The derivative equals zero for $-2 - 2x = 0$, $x = -1$. At $x = -1$, $P''(-1) = -2 < 0$. Therefore, $x = -1$ gives a maximum value of p, $P(-1) = 9$. The curve reaches no minimum. Thus, for all x greater than -1, the values of p are constantly decreasing.

In particular, the curve is a demand curve for the entire portion in the first quadrant. This ranges from $x = 0$ where $p = 8$ to the value of x for which $p = 0$. Now, $p = 0$ means

$$8 - 2x - x^2 = 0$$
$$x^2 + 2x - 8 = 0$$
$$(x + 4)(x - 2) = 0$$
$$x = -4, x = 2$$

Clearly, the value required is $x = 2$. Thus, we have a demand curve for $0 \leq x \leq 2$, in which interval p goes from 8 down to 0.

Example 3 Maximizing revenue. Suppose that price and demand are related by the rule

$$p = P(x) = 4 - 2x - x^2$$

For what x and p is revenue maximized?

The total revenue is

$$R(x) = xP(x) = x(4 - 2x - x^2)$$
$$R(x) = 4x - 2x^2 - x^3$$

Hence,

$$R'(x) = 4 - 4x - 3x^2$$
$$R''(x) = -4 - 6x$$

The revenue is maximum (or minimum) where $R'(x) = 0$. That is,

$$4 - 4x - 3x^2 = 0$$
$$3x^2 + 4x - 4 = 0$$
$$(x + 2)(3x - 2) = 0$$
$$x = -2, x = 2/3$$

Clearly, $x = -2$ makes no sense for an economic problem. In addition, $R''(-2) = 8 > 0$ and $R''(2/3) = -8 < 0$. Thus, at $x = 2/3$, the revenue reaches a maximum. At $x = 2/3$, $P(2/3) = 20/9$ and $R(2/3) = (2/3)P(2/3) = 40/27$.

Example 4 Profit in a monopoly.   Suppose that a monopolist with complete control of a certain commodity finds that the demand equation for this commodity is that given in Example 2,

$$p = 8 - 2x - x^2$$

Suppose further that his production costs are $C(x) = 2 + x$ where x is the number of items produced. (This linear cost function has been discussed in chapter 1. The constant 2 represents overhead cost and the coefficient of x, 1, is the production cost per item.) His profit is his total revenue minus his cost. If we denote profit by $S(x)$, then

$$S(x) = R(x) - C(x)$$
$$S(x) = xP(x) - C(x)$$

In this case,

$$S(x) = x(8 - 2x - x^2) - (2 + x)$$
$$S(x) = 8x - 2x^2 - x^3 - 2 - x$$
$$S(x) = 7x - 2x^2 - x^3 - 2$$

Now to maximize profit, we have

$$S'(x) = 7 - 4x - 3x^2$$
$$S''(x) = -4 - 6x$$

Setting $S'(x) = 0$ yields

$$7 - 4x - 3x^2 = 0$$
$$3x^2 + 4x - 7 = 0$$
$$(3x + 7)(x - 1) = 0$$
$$x = -7/3, \ x = 1$$

Here, again, since $S''(1) = -10 < 0$ is negative, the value $x = 1$ gives a maximum possible profit. To be precise, when $x = 1$, $p = 5$, $R(1) = (1)(5) = 5$, $C(1) = 3$, and $S(1) = 5 - 3 = 2$ is the maximum profit.

In general, the economist uses the term "marginal" to refer to derivatives. Thus, $R'(x)$ is called the *marginal revenue function* and $C'(x)$ is the *marginal cost function*. The profit $S(x)$ is given by

$$S(x) = R(x) - C(x)$$

To maximize profit, you find $S'(x)$ and set it equal to zero, yielding

$$S'(x) = R'(x) - C'(x) = 0$$

or
$$R'(x) = C'(x)$$

This relationship is described by saying that profit is maximized where the marginal revenue equals the marginal cost. Let us look at an example.

Example 5 (a) A monopolist finds that both the price and cost functions are linear. In fact, $P(x) = 100 - x$ and $C(x) = 2 + 3x$. How many units should be produced to maximize profit?

Here,
$$R(x) = (100 - x)x = 100x - x^2$$
$$R'(x) = 100 - 2x$$

and
$$C'(x) = 3$$

Therefore, to maximize profit, let $R'(x) = C'(x)$.

$$100 - 2x = 3$$
$$x = 48.5$$

This value of x yields $p = 51.5$

Example 5(b)   The effect of taxation.   Suppose that the government applies a tax of 0.5 on each unit produced. What production now maximizes profit?

The result of the taxation is to increase the cost by 0.5 times the number of units to yield

$$C(x) = 2 + 3x + 0.5x = 2 + 3.5x$$

and

$$C'(x) = 3.5$$

Thus, profit is maximized by solving

$$100 - 2x = 3.5$$
$$x = 48.25$$

for which

$$p = 51.75$$

Thus we see that the monopolist who is taxed 50¢ per unit passes along a price increase of only 25¢ per unit to the consumer if he wishes to maximize his profits.

Example 5 (c)   What tax rate should the government set in order to maximize tax revenue?

Suppose that the government sets a tax of t dollars per unit. This increases the monopolist's costs to

$$C(x) = 2 + 3x + tx = 2 + (3 + t)x$$

and

$$C'(x) = 3 + t$$

He maximizes profits by solving

$$100 - 2x = 3 + t$$
$$x = 48.5 - (1/2)t$$

Now, the government's tax revenue is

$$T(t) = tx$$
$$= t[48.5 - (1/2)t]$$
$$T(t) = 48.5t - (1/2)t^2$$
$$T'(t) = 48.5 - t$$

Setting $T'(t) = 0$, $t = 48.5$

Thus, the government charges a tax of 48.5 per unit. As a result, the monopolist reduces his production to

$$x = 48.5 - (1/2)t = 48.5 - (1/2)(48.5) = 24.25 \text{ units}$$

which he sells at the price

$$p = 100 - 24.25 = 75.75 \text{ per unit}$$

passing along half the tax to the consumer. Of course, his profit is considerably lower than if he were allowed to operate without interference, but it is the best that he can do.

We conclude this section by looking at one classical problem.

Example 6 A farmer has 400 feet of fencing and wishes to fence off a rectangular field containing as much area as possible. What should the dimensions of the field be?

Suppose the field is x feet by y feet as shown. The total perimeter

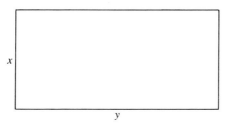

is $2x + 2y = 400$. Therefore

$$y = 200 - x$$

The area of the field is

$$A = xy = x(200 - x) = 200x - x^2$$

In order to maximize the area, find A' and set it equal to zero.

$$A' = 200 - 2x = 0$$

yielding

$$x = 100$$

and

$$y = 200 - x = 200 - 100 = 100$$

Hence, the optimal dimensions are 100×100, i.e., the rectangle is a square. (Notice $A'' = -2 < 0$, so the solution is a maximum as required.) It is not hard to show that in general the largest rectangle for a given perimeter is a square.

EXERCISES

1. For each function, find the values of x at which the first derivative is zero. Apply the second derivative test to determine whether the value of the function is a relative maximum or minimum at the point.
   (a) $f(x) = x^2 + 6$
   (b) $g(x) = 3 - 2x - x^2$
   (c) $F(x) = x^3 - 3x$
   (d) $h(x) = 6 + 12x - x^3$
   (e) $G(x) = x^3 - 6x^2 + 11$

2. Do Exercise 1 for the following:
   (a) $f(x) = x^3 - 3x^2 - 9x$
   (b) $g(x) = 4x^3 + 9x^2 - 12x + 2$
   (c) $F(x) = x^3 - 6x^2 + 3x - 11$
   (d) $G(x) = x^4 - 2x^2$
   (e) $H(x) = x^4 + 4x^3$

3. Find the x and p values for which the following are demand equations.
   (a) $11p = 120 - 2x - x^2$
   (b) $7p = 13 + 24x - 4x^2$
   (c) $32p = 3x^2 - 48x + 192$
   (d) $p = x^2 - 30x + 224$

4. A monopolist finds that demand for his commodity obeys a linear demand equation $p + 2x = 100$ where p is dollars and x,

thousands of units. Find the amount of production that will maximize revenue and find the maximum possible revenue.

5. A diamond dealer finds that the demand for flawless diamonds is governed by $p = 4x - x^2$ where x is carats and p is thousands of dollars.

 (a) Find the set of x values for which this is a possible demand function.

 (b) Find the number of carats to be made available to maximize revenue. What is the price and revenue for this amount?

6. The monopolist of Exercise 4 finds that his cost equation is $C(x) = 2 + 3x$. What should his production be in order to maximize profits?

7. Suppose that the monopolist of Exercise 6 is subjected to a tax of $10 per thousand units. (a) What should his production be in order to maximize profits? (b) What tax should the government impose in order to maximize tax revenues?

8. Repeat Exercises 6 and 7 for a cost function $C(x) = 1 + x + (1/2)x^2$.

9. A dealer in furs finds that when coats sell for $4,000, monthly sales are 6 coats. When the price goes up to $5,000, the demand is for 5 coats.

 (a) Find his price and revenue functions.

 (b) If his overhead is $2,500 per month and his production cost is $1,500 per coat, find his cost function and profit function.

 (c) Find the production that will maximize profit.

 (d) If the government applies a luxury tax of $200 per coat, how does this affect profits?

 (e) What tax should the government impose, if it wishes to maximize tax revenues?

10. A monopolist determines that the cost in cents of producing x units of a certain commodity before government taxes is $C(x) = 90x + 10,000$. However, the government imposes a tax of 10 cents per unit produced. If the demand equation is $x + 100p = 15,000$, where x units are demanded each week when the unit price is p cents, determine the number of units that should be produced for maximum weekly profit. Find the tax rate that should be applied in order to maximize tax revenue.

11. A rectangular field is to be fenced off along the straight bank of a river, and no fencing is required along the river. If 160 feet of

fencing is available, what should the dimensions of the field be in order to have a maximum area?

12. The drawing shows a rectangular window frame with a sash across it. If the total length of frame and sash is 20 feet, what is

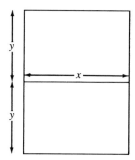

the maximum amount of glass needed to make the window?

13. The sum of twice one number and five times a second number is to be 70. What should the numbers be in order to maximize their product?

14. Express the number 4 as the sum of two positive numbers in such a way that the sum of the first and the square of the second is as small as possible.

10.5 Graphs of Polynomials

In this section we shall discuss the use of the first and second derivative in analyzing the graphs of polynomial functions. The first of these, the linear function, was considered extensively in part I of this text. You might well ask whether real situations actually give rise to such simple functions. In fact, they very rarely do. However, it is possible to approximate a large class of even very complicated functions by polynomials, which are easier to work with.

To begin, the graph of a polynomial function will be a smooth curve. It may have many ups and downs but it will have no breaks, holes, gaps, or even sharp corners. Its derivative and hence its slope will be well-defined at every point. In particular, this means that the graph can have a relative maximum or minimum only at a point where the derivative is zero. Henceforth, we shall refer to such points as "critical points." We shall apply the second derivative test at critical points to determine whether they are relative maxima or minima.

However, let us first see what other information can be garnered from the second derivative. Suppose we have $y = f(x)$ and that over some interval, $f''(x)$ is positive. Thus as we move from left to right the slope of the curve is increasing. Hence, the curve must behave in one of the three ways shown in figure 12.

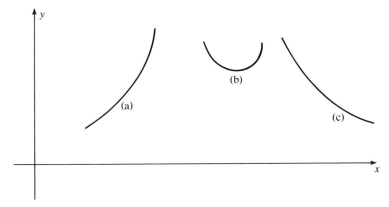

Figure 12

This kind of behavior is called *upward concavity*. In figure 12(a), the curve has positive slope and is concave up; in (c) it has negative slope and is concave up; and in (b) its slope goes from negative to positive, and it is concave up, producing a relative minimum. Similarly, if $f''(x) < 0$ over an interval, the curve must look like one of the curves in figure 13. It will be called *concave down*.

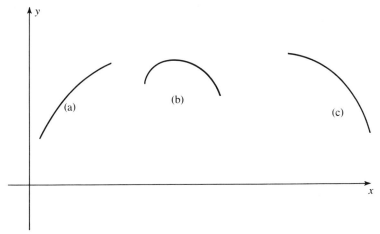

Figure 13

What about a curve that changes concavity? If the curve looks like one in figure 14, then the point at which the concavity changes is called a *point of inflection* or *inflection point*. In order for a curve to go from concave up to concave down (or from down to up), the sign of its second derivative must go from + to − (or − to +). In either case, if the second derivative is well-defined and varies continuously (as it will for any polynomial), then the only way this can happen is for the second derivative to become equal to zero. Hence, inflection points are found at points at which the second derivative equals zero. In summary, the key to plotting polynomials accurately is to find the critical points (where $f'(x)$ is zero) and the points where $f''(x)$ is zero. Bear in mind the following:

1. First derivative rules:
    (a) If $f'(x) > 0$, the function is increasing.
    (b) If $f'(x) < 0$, the function is decreasing.
    (c) $f'(x) = 0$ at a critical point, a possible maximum or minimum value for the function.

2. Second derivative rules:
    (a) If $f''(x) > 0$, the curve is concave up.
    (b) If $f''(x) < 0$, the curve is concave down.
    (c) $f''(x) = 0$ at a possible inflection point.

3. General rules (for polynomials only):
    (a) The curve cannot change direction (going up or down) without having a zero first derivative.
    (b) The curve cannot change concavity without having a zero second derivative.

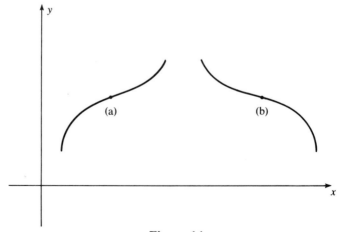

Figure 14

Let us apply these rules to some simple examples. In each case, we shall make a table of x, y, y', and y'' at the important points on the curve.

Example 1 A quadratic. Suppose we are given

$$y = x^2 + 4x - 11$$

We immediately compute

$$y' = 2x + 4$$
$$y'' = 2$$

We determine the critical points

$$2x + 4 = 0$$
$$x = -2$$

Setting $y'' = 0$ yields

$$2 = 0$$

which is impossible. Hence, we have no inflection points.
    Therefore, the only value of interest is $x = -2$, yielding Table 2.

Table 2

x	y	y'	y''
-2	-15	0	2

We see at $(-2, -15)$ that we have a horizontal tangent and the curve has upward concavity. Therefore, $(-2, -15)$ is a relative minimum point. In the vicinity of $(-2, -15)$, the curve must look like figure 15 (a). Since it has no other "turning" points and no changes of concavity, the entire curve must look like figure 15 (b). If you would like to pin it down more closely, plot a few additional points. For example, at $x = 0$, $y = -11$; at $x = 1$, $y = -6$; etc.

Example 2 A cubic. Suppose that we are given

$$y = x^3 + 3x^2 - 9x - 10$$

We compute

$$y' = 3x^2 + 6x - 9$$
$$y'' = 6x + 6$$

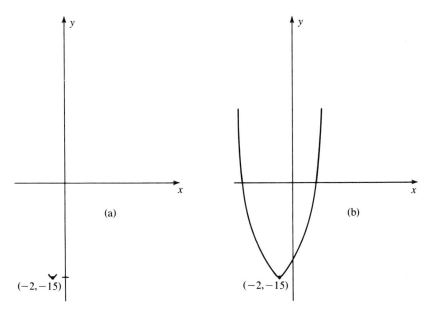

Figure 15

The critical points are found by setting $y' = 0$.

$$3x^2 + 6x - 9 = 0$$
$$x^2 + 2x - 3 = 0$$
$$(x + 3)(x - 1) = 0$$
$$x = -3, \ x = 1$$

The second derivative is zero at

$$6x + 6 = 0, \ x = -1$$

Our table of values is Table 3.

Table 3

x	y	y'	y''
-3	17	0	-12
-1	1	-12	0
1	-15	0	12

We plot these three points in figure 16 (a). The point $(-3, 17)$ is a critical point of downward concavity and hence a maximum. The point $(1, -15)$ is a critical point of upward concavity and hence a minimum. There are no other turning points and the concavity can only change at $(-1, 1)$. Therefore, the completed curve must look like figure 16 (b).

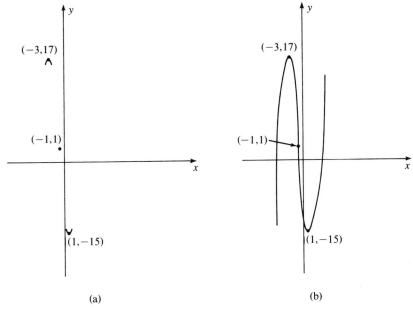

(a)   (b)

Figure 16

Example 3   Another cubic.   Let us consider

$$y = x^3 - 3x^2 + 4x$$
$$y' = 3x^2 - 6x + 4$$
$$y'' = 6x - 6$$

We attempt to find critical points

$$3x^2 - 6x + 4 = 0$$

There are no simple factors to this quadratic, so we apply the quadratic formula

$$x = \frac{6 \pm \sqrt{36 - 48}}{6} = 1 \pm \frac{1}{6}\sqrt{-12}$$

Thus, there are only complex roots. Hence, there are no real turning points to the curve. The only interesting point is where $y'' = 0$,

$$6x - 6 = 0$$
$$x = 1$$

Table 4

x	y	y'	y''
1	2	1	0

Is (1, 2) really an inflection point? Let us check an arbitrary other point on each side. At $x = 2$, $y'' = 6$ and at $x = 0$, $y'' = -6$. Therefore, to the left of $x = 1$, the curve is concave down; to the right, the curve is concave up. The graph has no turning points and has a positive slope at $x = 1$. Hence, it has a positive slope for all x. The graph is shown in figure 17.

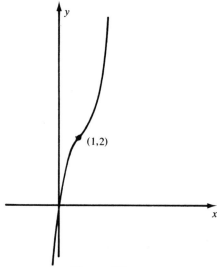

Figure 17

The cubic of Example 2 is very typical. Since the derivative of a cubic is a quadratic, there are at most two real critical points. Hence, the cubic has at most two turning points. Since complex roots come in pairs, if it does not have two turning points, it has none (as in Example 3). Similarly, a quartic has as its derivative a cubic. If the cubic has three real roots, then the curve will have three turning points. However, let us look at the following example.

Example 4   Given

$$y = 4x^3 - x^4$$

We compute

$$y' = 12x^2 - 4x^3$$
$$y'' = 24x - 12x^2$$

To find critical points, set

$$12x^2 - 4x^3 = 0$$
$$3x^2 - x^3 = 0$$
$$x^2(3 - x) = 0$$
$$x = 0, \ x = 3$$

To seek inflection points

$$24x - 12x^2 = 0$$
$$2x - x^2 = 0$$
$$(2 - x)x = 0$$
$$x = 0, \ x = 2$$

We see only three x-values of importance.

Table 5

x	y	y'	y''
0	0	0	0
2	16	16	0
3	27	0	-36

We see that (3, 27) is a critical point with downward concavity and hence a maximum. We see that (2, 16) is a possible inflection point. We see that (0, 0) is a critical point which is also a possible inflection point, since $y'' = 0$. Therefore, the graph so far is shown in figure 18 (a).

To the right of $x = 3$, the curve must remain concave down and continue downward, since there are no more turning points or possible

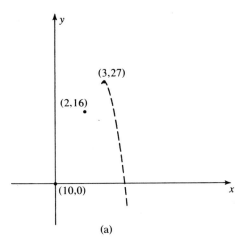

(a)

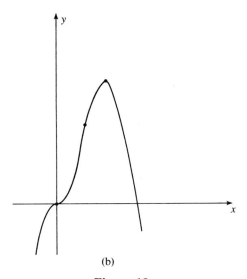

(b)

Figure 18

inflections. This is dotted in figure 18 (a). To check the behavior on
either side of zero, check two extra points.

Table 6

x	y	y'	y''
-1	-5	16	-36
1	3	8	12

We see that curve is concave down and increasing to the left of zero; it is concave up and increasing to the right of zero. Therefore, (2, 16) is an inflection point; (0, 0) is an inflection point at which there is a horizontal tangent; and the graph must look as shown in figure 18 (b).

EXERCISES

Sketch the following curves, showing all relative maxima and minima and locating all inflection points (if any).

1. $y = x^2 + 6x - 3$
2. $y = 6 - x^2$
3. $y = 3 - 4x - 3x^2$
4. $y = 2x^2 - 6x - 11$
5. $y = x^3 - 9x^2 + 24x - 17$
6. $y = 3 + 3x^2 - x^3$
7. $y = x^3$
8. $y = (1/3)x^3 - x^2 - 3x$
9. $y = x^3 + x + 1$
10. $y = x^3 - 3x + 5$
11. $y = -x^3 - 4$
12. $y = x^4 + 4x^3$
13. $y = x^4$
14. $y = x^4 - 2x^2$
15. $y = x^4 - 4x^3 + 4x^2$
16. $y = x^5 - 5x^4$

10.6 Derivative Formulas

As useful as polynomials may be, there are some mathematical functions that have more complicated algebraic formulations. The derivatives of these expressions have also been developed over the years and shall be stated without proof.

Formula 5 If $y = x^n$, then $y' = nx^{n-1}$ where n is any constant. This rule is a direct extension of Formula 1, p. 358, and is applied in the same way.

For example, for fractions:

Given $$y = x^{1/2}$$

$$y' = \frac{1}{2}x^{1/2-1} = \frac{1}{2}x^{-1/2}$$

or for negative numbers:

Given $$y = x^{-3}$$

$$y' = -3x^{-3-1} = -3x^{-4}$$

or even for negative fractions:

Given $$y = x^{-2/3}$$

$$y' = (-2/3)x^{-2/3-1} = (-2/3)x^{-5/3}$$

or for combinations

Given $$y = x^3 + 3/x - 5x^{3/4}$$

First we rewrite $3/x$ using a negative exponent:

$$3/x = 3x^{-1}$$

and $$y = x^3 + 3x^{-1} - 5x^{3/4}$$

and $$y' = 3x^2 + 3(-1)x^{-2} - 5(3/4)x^{-1/4}$$
$$y' = 3x^2 - 3x^{-2} - (15/4)x^{-1/4}$$

or, if you prefer

$$y' = 3x^2 - 3/x^2 - 15/4x^{1/4}$$

Formula 6   The power rule.   If $y = [f(x)]^n$, then $y' = n[f(x)]^{n-1}f'(x)$

For example, given

$$y = (x^3 - 3)^{15}$$

This is of the form $[f(x)]^n$, where $f(x) = (x^3 - 3)$ and $n = 15$. Now $f'(x) = 3x^2$, so

$$y' = 15(x^3 - 3)^{14}(3x^2)$$

One more example,

Given $y = (x^2 + x + 3)^{3/2}$

Then $y' = (3/2)(x^2 + x + 3)^{1/2}(2x + 1)$

Having exhausted all the possibilities involving powers, addition, and subtraction, there are only two other algebraic operations available—products and quotients. Formulas 7 and 8 cover these two cases.

Formula 7 The product rule. If $y = f(x)g(x)$, then $y' = f'(x)g(x) + g'(x)f(x)$.

Notice that the derivative of a product is *not* the product of the derivatives. Let us check this rule by doing an example that can be done in two ways. Consider $y = x^2(2x + 3)$. Think of this as $f(x) = x^2$, $g(x) = 2x + 3$.

Now $f'(x) = 2x$

$g'(x) = 2$

$y' = f'(x)g(x) + g'(x)f(x)$

$y' = 2x(2x + 3) + 2(x^2) = 4x^2 + 6x + 2x^2 = 6x^2 + 6x$

Alternatively, we could multiply out $f(x)$ times $g(x)$, giving

$$y = 2x^3 + 3x^2$$

which can be differentiated as a polynomial to yield

$$y' = 6x^2 + 6x$$

which checks. (Note: Had we just taken $f'(x)g'(x)$, the result would be $(2x)2 = 4x$, which is not correct.)

Another example,

$$y = x^{-3}(x^2 + 1)^{12}$$

Here we have

$f(x) = x^{-3}$

$f'(x) = -3x^{-4}$

$g(x) = (x^2 + 1)^{12}$

$g'(x) = 12(x^2 + 1)^{11}2x = 24x(x^2 + 1)^{11}$

and

$$y' = f'(x)g(x) + g'(x)f(x)$$
$$y' = -3x^{-4}(x^2 + 1)^{12} + 24x(x^2 + 1)^{11}x^{-3}$$

or

$$y' = -3x^{-4}(x^2 + 1)^{12} + 24x^{-2}(x^2 + 1)^{11}$$

Formula 8 The quotient rule.

If $y = \dfrac{f(x)}{g(x)}$, then $y' = \dfrac{f'(x)g(x) - g'(x)f(x)}{[g(x)]^2}$

Here are some examples. Given

$$y = \frac{1 + x^2}{1 - x^2}$$

We have
$$f(x) = 1 + x^2$$
$$f'(x) = 2x$$
$$g(x) = 1 - x^2$$
$$g'(x) = -2x$$
$$y' = \frac{(2x)(1 - x^2) - (-2x)(1 + x^2)}{(1 - x^2)^2}$$

Simplifying

$$y' = \frac{2x - 2x^3 + 2x + 2x^3}{(1 - x^2)^2} = \frac{4x}{(1 - x^2)^2}$$

Let us find y''. We have for y'

$$f(x) = 4x$$
$$f'(x) = 4$$
$$g(x) = (1 - x^2)^2$$
$$g'(x) = 2(1 - x^2)(-2x) = -4x(1 - x^2)$$

So

$$y'' = \frac{4(1 - x^2)^2 - 4x(-4x)(1 - x^2)}{[(1 - x^2)^2]^2}$$

Let us simplify

$$y'' = \frac{4(1 - x^2)^2 + 16x^2(1 - x^2)}{(1 - x^2)^4}$$

$$y'' = \frac{4(1 - x^2) + 16x^2}{(1 - x^2)^3} = 4\left[\frac{1 + 3x^2}{(1 - x^2)^3}\right]$$

EXERCISES

1. Differentiate each of the following:
   (a) $y = x(1 - x^2)^5$
   (b) $y = 10x^5 + \dfrac{1}{x} + 2\sqrt{x} + 2x$
   (c) $y = (2x^2 + 7)^{1/3} - \dfrac{3}{x}$
   (d) $y = \dfrac{(x + 1)^2}{x^3 + 3x}$
   (e) $y = 3x\sqrt{x^2 + 1}$
   (f) $y = (x^3 - 2)^7$
   (g) $y = \dfrac{2x + 3}{3x - 1}$
   (h) $y = 3x^{1/3} - \dfrac{1}{x^2}$
   (i) $y = 2(x^2 - 5x)^5$
   (j) $y = (x^2 + 2)^3(x + 1)^2$
   Remember, the square root is the 1/2 power.

2. Find y' for each of the following:
   (a) $y = \dfrac{x^2 - 3}{(x + 5)^2}$
   (b) $y = 3x\sqrt{x^3 - 2}$
   (c) $y = (2x^2 - 5x + 1)^{50}$
   (d) $y = x(x^2 - 2)^{12}$
   (e) $y = x^3(2x - 1)^4 + \sqrt{2x}$
   (f) $y = \dfrac{(1 - x)^5}{x^2 + 1}$
   (g) $y = \dfrac{(x^2 - 3)^2}{2x}$
   (h) $y = \dfrac{(1 - x)^5}{x^2}$
   (i) $y = x^2(2x - 1)^{50}$
   (j) $y = \dfrac{x}{3 - x^2}$

3. Find all critical points for

   (a) $y = \dfrac{x^2}{x^2 - 1}$

   (b) $y = x + \dfrac{1}{x}$

   (c) $y = \dfrac{x^2 + 1}{x + 1}$

   (d) $y = \dfrac{x^3}{x + 1}$

4. What is the slope of the tangent to the curve $y = (2 + x)/(x^2 - 1)$ at the point $(0, -2)$? What is the equation of the tangent at this point?

5. (a) What is the equation of the tangent line to the curve $y = (x^2 + 1)(x^3 + 3x)$ at the point $(1, 8)$?

   (b) Find the equation of the tangent to the curve $y = (x^2)/(x - 1)$ at $x = 3$.

   (c) Find the equation of the tangent to the curve $f(x) = (x^2 + 1)/(x - 2)$ at $x = -1$.

10.7 Further Optimization Problems

With the aid of our new derivative formulas, it is now possible to expand the class of optimization problems that we can handle. As in Section 10.4, we shall illustrate by means of example. First, we look at some economic problems.

Example 1 A quadratic demand equation. Suppose that we have the demand equation

$$x = 100 - p^2$$

This is a sensible equation for $0 \leq p \leq 10$ when x ranges from 100 down to 0.

Let us try to maximize total revenue. To do so, we must first find the price function by solving for p in terms of x.

$$p^2 = 100 - x \qquad p = \sqrt{100 - x}$$

We have chosen the positive square root in solving for p so as not to have negative price. The total revenue is

$$R(x) = xP(x) = x\sqrt{100 - x}$$

To find $R'(x)$, first write $R(x)$ as

$$R(x) = x(100 - x)^{1/2}$$

Now,

$$R'(x) = (100 - x)^{1/2} + x\left(\frac{1}{2}\right)(100 - x)^{-1/2}(-1)$$

Thus,

$$R'(x) = \sqrt{100 - x} - x/2\sqrt{100 - x}$$

Setting $R'(x) = 0$ yields

$$\sqrt{100 - x} = x/2\sqrt{100 - x}$$

Multiplying through by $2\sqrt{100 - x}$

$$200 - 2x = x$$

$$x = \frac{200}{3}$$

Thus, revenue is maximized at $x = 200/3$, $p = \sqrt{100/3} = 10/\sqrt{3}$, and maximum $R = (200/3)(10/\sqrt{3}) = 2{,}000/3\sqrt{3}$.

Example 2 Minimizing average cost. Suppose that we are given a cost function $C(x)$ which gives the total cost of producing x units of some item. The average cost per unit is then $Q(x) = C(x)/x$. If $C(x)$ is linear, $C(x) = bx + a$. Then a is the overhead cost, and b is the cost of producing a single item. In this case, $Q(x) = b + a/x$. As x increases, $Q(x)$ gets constantly smaller, because the cost of each item is fixed at b and the overhead is divided out over the number produced. Thus, the more you produce, the smaller the portion of the cost attributable to overhead. However, suppose that the cost function is quadratic. For example, let

$$C(x) = 25 + 30x + x^2$$

Now $$Q(x) = C(x)/x = 25/x + 30 + x$$

Let us look at the behavior of this function. We construct a table of values (Table 7). It appears that the average cost decreases steadily until $x = 5$ and then it begins to increase slowly. Therefore, from Table 7, it appears that the average cost is minimized at $x = 5$, $Q(5) = 40$.

Table 7

x	$Q(x)$
1	56.00
2	44.50
3	41.33
4	40.25
5	40.00
6	40.17
7	40.57
8	41.13

Let us check this by using the derivative. First, we rewrite $25/x$ as $25x^{-1}$ to yield

$$Q(x) = 25x^{-1} + 30 + x$$

If we wish to minimize the average cost, we set $Q'(x)$ equal to zero.

$$Q'(x) = -25x^{-2} + 1 = 0$$

$$1 = \frac{25}{x^2}$$

$$x^2 = 25$$

$$x = 5$$

(We ignore the root -5 as having no economic meaning.) Thus, we know that at $x = 5$, $C(5) = 200$, and the average cost is 40 per item.
    Just as a check,

$$Q''(x) = 50x^{-3}$$

and at $x = 5$

$$Q''(5) = 50(5)^{-3} = 50/125 = 2/5$$

is positive. Thus, $(5, 40)$ is indeed the minimum point for $Q(x)$.

Example 3 Minimizing inventory cost. The cost of maintaining an inventory leads to a problem very similar to the average cost problem. Inventory expenses can be divided into three portions: overhead, storage cost, and procurement cost. The overhead cost is a constant, a. The storage cost is a fixed amount b per item, so if x

is the number of items, this cost is bx. The procurement expense is very large for a small number of items and then diminishes quickly. It can usually be closely approximated by c/x. Therefore, the total inventory cost $I(x)$ is

$$I(x) = a + bx + cx^{-1}$$

For example, suppose

$$I(x) = 10 + 2x + 200x^{-1}$$

To minimize the cost of maintaining the inventory, we find $I'(x)$,

$$I'(x) = 2 - 200x^{-2}$$

Setting $I'(x)$ equal to zero yields

$$2 = 200/x^2$$
$$x^2 = 100$$
$$x = 10$$

As above, $I''(10) > 0$, so $(10, 40)$ is indeed a minimum.

In addition to these economic problems, there are a large number of classic problems of a more or less practical nature. All of these problems come down to a standard four-step procedure.
1. Identify the quantity to be maximized (or minimized); call it Q.
2. Express Q as a function of one variable, say x.
3. Find Q'; set it equal to zero; and solve for x.
4. Check that you have the proper extremum and have answered the proper question.
Let us try one.

Example 4   A farmer wishes to fence off a rectangular field with a fence across the middle so as to create two 300 sq ft areas. What is the smallest amount of fencing needed?

Let us draw a diagram.

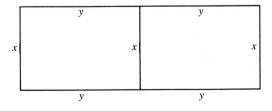

We wish to minimize the length of fence, which from the diagram is

$$Q = 3x + 4y$$

In addition, $xy = 300$; that is, $y = 300/x$. Substituting for y yields

$$Q = 3x + 1{,}200/x$$

We now have Q as a function only of x. Differentiating,

$$Q' = 3 - 1{,}200x^{-2} = 0$$
$$3x^2 = 1{,}200$$
$$x^2 = 400$$
$$x = 20$$

Since $Q''(20) > 0$, this is the desired minimum. For $x = 20$, we have $y = 15$ and the total length of fence is $3(20) + 4(15) = 120$ ft.

EXERCISES

1. Find the minimum average cost for the cost function $C(x) = 9 + 5x + x^2$.

2. Show that, in general, the derivative of the average cost is zero at the point where the marginal cost equals the average cost.

3. Use the result of Exercise 2 to minimize the average cost when $C(x) = 12 + 200x + 3x^2$.

4. Determine which of the following are demand equations and which supply equations. Find the values of x and p for which they are valid.
   (a) $p = 100/(x + 1)$
   (b) $p = (x - 50)/(x + 2)$
   (c) $p^2 + x = 75$
   (d) $p^2 - x^2 = 100$
   (e) $p^2 - x = 100$
   (f) $p^2 + x^2 = 50$

5. Show that the derivative of the revenue function is zero when the marginal price is equal to $-p/x$.

6. Find the maximum revenue for each of the demand equations in Exercise 4.

7. Given a price function $p(x) = 100/(x + 1)$ and a cost function $C(x) = 1 + x$, find the maximum possible profit.

8. Suppose that $P(x) = \sqrt{9 - x} + 3$ and $C(x) = 3x + 1$. Find the maximum possible profit.

9. How would a tax of 3 per unit affect the results of Exercise 8?

10. Find the rectangle of smallest possible perimeter that will contain exactly 100 sq in.

11. A rectangular box with a square base and no top must contain precisely 500 cu in. Find the dimensions that require the smallest amount of material.

12. Find the dimensions of a 500 cc tin can that requires the smallest amount of material to construct.

13. A rectangular box with a square base is made of plywood that costs 50¢ per square foot, except for the top, which is made of beaver board selling for 25¢ per square foot. If the box must contain 20 cu ft, find the dimensions that will minimize the cost.

14. (a) The product of two numbers is 16. Find the numbers if the sum of one number and the square of the other is to be a minimum.

    (b) Find the positive number such that the sum of its square and 16 times the square of its reciprocal is as small as possible.

10.8 Partial Derivatives

So far we have only discussed functions of one variable. However, in real problems it is rare that anything is completely determined by only one variable. For example, in economics, the demand for any item is almost invariably dependent upon its price and the price of all competitive products. The discussion of such economic models is too long and complicated to be included here. What we shall consider is an optimization technique that involves functions of two variables. The generalization to several variables is similar.

To begin, suppose that x and y are both independent variables and that z is a dependent variable which is totally determined by the choice of x and y. We shall say that z is a function of (x, y) and write $z = f(x, y)$. For example, suppose that

$$z = x^2 - 3xy + 7y$$

Now, $f(1, 2) = 1^2 - 3(1)(2) + 7(2) = 9$. Thus, fixing x and y determines z. Of course, $f(2, 1) = 2^2 - 3(2)(1) + 7(1) = 5$, so $f(2, 1) \neq f(1, 2)$. If we were to fix y, at say, $y = 2$, we would have

$$z = f(x, 2) = x^2 - 3(x)(2) + 7(2)$$
$$= x^2 - 6x + 14$$

That is, fixing y, we have z as a function of x alone. If we wished, we could now find the derivative of this function of x. Thus, $z' = 2x - 6$.

More generally, we could simply think of y as being fixed and find the derivative of z with respect to x, which would give us the derivative of z with respect to x for any fixed y. Here we would need some notation, since you could equally well think of fixing x and finding derivatives with respect to y. We shall use the notation $\partial z/\partial x$ or $f_x(x, y)$ to stand for the derivative of z with respect to x with y being considered as a constant. We shall call this the *partial derivative* of f with respect to x. In this case

$$f(x, y) = x^2 - 3xy + 7y$$
$$f_x(x, y) = 2x - 3y$$

At $y = 2$, this reduces to $2x - 6$, as found earlier.

Notice that the derivative of $7y$ is just zero, since y is to be counted as a constant. Similarly, we may define the partial derivative of f with respect to y, using the notation $\partial z/\partial y$ or $f_y(x, y)$. Of course, for $\partial z/\partial y$, we must think of x as a constant.

$$f(x, y) = x^2 - 3xy + 7y$$
$$f_y(x, y) = -3x + 7$$

In many problems, you will have z as a function of two variables and want to find the maximum or minimum value of z. Analogously to the single variable case, relative maxima and minima may be sought at points at which the derivative is zero. For two variables, both derivatives must be zero. Let us take a very simple example.

Example 1   Find the minimum value of

$$z = x^2 + y^2$$

Letting $f(x, y) = x^2 + y^2$, we find

$$f_x(x, y) = 2x \qquad f_y(x, y) = 2y$$

Setting both equal to zero,

$$2x = 0 \qquad 2y = 0$$
$$x = 0 \qquad y = 0$$

Thus, a good candidate for an extreme value is at $(0, 0)$, where $z = 0^2 + 0^2 = 0$.

Now this is actually a minimum as desired, since the sum $x^2 + y^2$ must be greater than zero, except at $(0, 0)$. However, we are in general faced with the same problem we had in the one-variable case — to find a simple test for determining whether a critical point is a maximum or a minimum. For the one-variable case, we proposed a test based on the second derivative. For the two variable problems, there are four possible second derivatives. They are:

1. f_{xx}, or $\partial^2 z/\partial x^2$, obtained by taking two successive partial derivatives with respect to x.
2. f_{yy}, or $\partial^2 z/\partial y^2$, obtained by taking two successive partial derivatives with respect to y.
3. f_{xy}, or $\partial^2 z/\partial y \partial x$, obtained by taking first a partial derivative with respect to x and then differentiating the result with respect to y.
4. f_{yx}, or $\partial^2 z/\partial x \partial y$, obtained by taking first a partial derivative with respect to y and then differentiating the result with respect to x.

Example 2

$$f(x, y) = x^3 - 3x^2y + x^2y^3$$
$$f_x = 3x^2 - 6xy + 2xy^3$$
$$f_{xx} = 6x - 6y + 2y^3$$
$$f_{xy} = -6x + 6xy^2$$
$$f_y = -3x^2 + 3x^2y^2$$
$$f_{yy} = 6x^2y$$
$$f_{yx} = -6x + 6xy^2$$

We observe that $f_{xy} = f_{yx}$ for this case.

For most simple functions, this shall be the case, but examples may be constructed in which $f_{xy} \neq f_{yx}$. Nevertheless, we shall assume that these two *mixed partials* are going to be equal. Under this assumption, we may state the following analogue to the simple second derivative test:

Second Derivative Test for Functions of Two Variables. Suppose that at some point (x_o, y_o), $f_x = 0$ and $f_y = 0$. In addition, $f_{xx}f_{yy} - (f_{xy})^2 > 0$. Then, if $f_{xx} < 0$, (x_o, y_o) is a relative maximum point; if $f_{xx} > 0$, (x_o, y_o) is a relative minimum point. If $f_{xx}f_{yy} - (f_{xy})^2 \le 0$, the test fails. Let us look at some examples.

Example 3 Find the rectangular box of smallest surface area that contains a volume of 1,000 cu in.

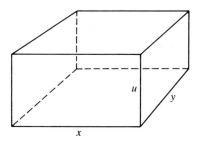

Calling the dimensions of the box x, y, and u, the volume is

$$xyu = 1,000$$

The total surface area z is

$$z = 2xu + 2xy + 2yu$$

Since $u = 1,000/xy$, we may substitute for u and write z as a function of x and y.

$$z = f(x, y) = 2x\left(\frac{1,000}{xy}\right) + 2xy + 2y\left(\frac{1,000}{xy}\right)$$

$$f(x, y) = 2,000y^{-1} + 2xy + 2,000x^{-1}$$

Finding derivatives,

$$f_x = 2y - 2,000x^{-2}$$

$$f_y = -2,000y^{-2} + 2x$$

Setting both f_x and f_y equal to zero yields

$$2y = 2,000x^{-2} \qquad 2x = 2,000y^{-2}$$

$$x^2y = 1,000 \qquad xy^2 = 1,000$$

Since $x^2y = 1{,}000$ and $xy^2 = 1{,}000$, we have $x^2y = xy^2$. We may divide by xy because x or y equal zero makes no sense, thus arriving at $x = y$. Now $x = y$, substituted into any of the above equations, yields

$$x^3 = 1{,}000 \qquad x = 10$$

and back substituting, $x = 10$, $y = 10$, and $u = 10$.

Thus, the required solution is a $10 \times 10 \times 10$ cube. Is this really a minimum? Let us check

$$f_x = 2y - 2{,}000x^{-2} \qquad f_y = -2{,}000y^{-2} + 2x$$
$$f_{xx} = 4{,}000x^{-3} \qquad f_{yy} = 4{,}000y^{-3} \qquad f_{xy} = 2$$

at

$$x = 10 \qquad y = 10$$
$$f_{xx} = 4{,}000(10)^{-3} = 4 > 0$$

Also

$$f_{yy} = 4 \qquad f_{xy} = 2$$

Thus

$$f_{xx} \cdot f_{yy} - (f_{xy})^2 = 4 \cdot 4 - (2)^2 = 12 > 0$$

and the second derivative check yields a clear minimum as desired.

Example 4 Investigate the function $f(x, y) = x^2 - y^2$ for possible maxima and minima.

Find the pertinent derivatives,

$$f_x = 2x \qquad f_y = -2y$$
$$f_{xx} = 2 \qquad f_{yy} = -2 \qquad f_{xy} = 0$$

We see that f_x and f_y are both zero at $(0, 0)$. However, $f_{xx} \cdot f_{yy} - (f_{xy})^2 = -4 < 0$, and the second derivative test fails. Thinking of f as only a function of x, we see f_{xx} is always positive, so that $x = 0$ gives a minimum for all possible y. Similarly f_{yy} is always negative, so that $y = 0$ gives a maximum for all possible x.

What we have here is a saddle point. If $f(x, y)$ represented a pay-off for a game where one player chose x and the other chose y, then we have a saddle point solution analogous to the matrix game solution in chapter 7.

EXERCISES

1. Find f_x and f_y for each of the following:
   (a) $f(x, y) = x(1 - y^2)^5$
   (b) $f(x, y) = 10y^5 + x^{-2} + \sqrt{xy}$
   (c) $f(x, y) = (x^2 - y^2)/(x^2 + y^2)$
   (d) $f(x, y) = \sqrt{x^2 + y^2}$

2. Find f_x and f_y for each of the following:
   (a) $f(x, y) = (x^2 - y^2)/(x^3 + 3xy - y^2)^{10}$
   (b) $f(x, y) = xy/(x^2 - y^2)$
   (c) $f(x, y) = (x - y)\sqrt{x^2 - y^3}$
   (d) $f(x, y) = x^{1/2}/y^{1/2}$

3. Find f_{xx}, f_{yy}, and f_{xy} for each function in Exercise 1.

4. Find f_{xx}, f_{yy}, and f_{xy} for each function in Exercise 2.

5. Find the maximum value of $f(x, y) = 7 - 3x^2 - xy - y^2$.

6. Find the minimum possible value of $f(x, y) = x^2 - 4xy + 8y^2 - 6x + 12y - 11$.

7. Repeat Exercise 6 for $f(x, y) = 3x^2 + 6xy + y^2 - 3x - 4y + 10$.

8. A man was told that postal regulations require that the sum of the length and the girth of a rectangular package not exceed 72 inches. How should the package be designed to have the maximum volume?

9. Continuation of Exercise 8. It turns out that the man was mis-informed. The regulations say "twice the length plus the girth may not exceed 72 inches." What is the best design for a package under this rule?

10. An aquarium is to be built in the form of a rectangular solid with an open top. The base is metal, costing 25¢ per sq in. The sides and back are slate, costing 40¢ per sq in. The front is glass, costing 20¢ per sq in. Find the cheapest aquarium that can be constructed to contain 15,000 cu in.

11

Logarithmic and Exponential Functions

11.1 Continuous Compounding of Interest

In part II of this text, many pages were spent discussing compound interest. We have seen that a nominal rate of interest j compounded m times per year yields $(1 + j/m)^m$ for each dollar invested. We have also seen that the more often the compounding, the greater the accumulation will be. The natural question that arises is, How large can the accumulation possibly be? In other words, as m approaches infinity, is there any limit to this accumulation factor or does it just get larger and larger? Instead of letting m approach infinity, let us make the substitution $h = j/m$ and rewrite the accumulation factor in terms of h instead of m. Since $m = j/h$,

$$(1 + j/m)^m = (1 + h)^{j/h}$$
$$= [(1 + h)^{1/h}]^j$$

Since $h = j/m$, as m becomes very large, h approaches 0. Thus, the question comes down to what happens to $(1 + h)^{1/h}$ as $h \to 0$. It can be shown that a limit does exist. This limit is designated by the letter e and is approximately equal to 2.71828.

The accumulation factor $(1 + j/m)^m = [(1 + h)^{1/h}]^j$. The expression in the square brackets approaches e. Since the accumulation factor is that expression to the j power, the accumulation factor approaches e^j. The value e^j is the maximum accumulation possible at nominal rate j and is referred to as the *accumulation for interest compounded instantaneously*, or continuously, or infinitely often. We shall symbolize this rate by j_∞. This is, of course, the one-year accumulation. The accumulation factor for time n, measured in years, is $(e^j)^n = e^{nj}$. In recent years savings banks have begun to accumulate interest continuously, according to the formula

$$S = Pe^{nj}$$

Since continuous compounding leads inevitably to continuous discounting,

$$P = S/e^{nj} = Se^{-nj}$$

Accordingly, it is convenient to have a table of e^x and e^{-x} (see Table A-10.)

Let us see just how effective compounding continuously can be. Consider a bank that pays interest at 7% compounded continuously ($j_\infty = 7\%$). On $100 deposited for one year, we have $n = 1$ and $j = 0.07$, yielding

$$S = 100e^{(1)(0.07)} = 107.25$$

Thus, 7% compounded continuously amounts to 7.25% effective.

Annuity problems for continuous compounding are handled most easily by finding the proper equivalent interest rates and then proceeding as in part II. For example, a man holds a contract calling for 20 quarterly payments of $100. If money is worth $j_\infty = 5\%$, what is the present value of the contract?

We know that $A = 100a_{\overline{20}|i}$ and i is the quarterly interest equivalent to 5% compounded continuously. The accumulation factor for 5% compounded continuously is $e^{.0125}$, so the interest rate is $i = e^{.0125} - 1 = 0.0126 = 1.26\%$. Remembering that

$$a_{\overline{20}|i} = \frac{1 - (1 + i)^{-20}}{i}$$

we may substitute. Since $1 + i = e^{.0125}$, $(1 + i)^{-20} = e^{(.0125)(-20)} = e^{-0.25} = 0.7788$. Hence $a_{\overline{20}|i} = (1 - 0.7788)/0.0126 = 17.555555$ and $A = \$1,755.56$.

Let us look at one more example. A man holds a note calling for $1,000 to be paid in 40 years. If money is worth 8% compounded continuously, what is the present value of the note? Here we have

$$P = Se^{-nj}$$
$$P = 1,000e^{-(40)(.08)}$$
$$P = 1,000e^{-3.2}$$

Our table contains e^{-3} and e^{-4}, so we could interpolate to find $e^{-3.2} = 0.0435$. However, with such a large difference, it pays to apply the laws of exponents, writing

$$e^{-3.2} = e^{-3}e^{-0.2} = (0.04979)(0.81873) = 0.04076$$

Thus the present value is

$$P = 1,000(0.04076) = \$40.76$$

If the only application of the function e^x were in continuous compounding, it would be of only marginal interest. However, this function is of extreme importance in many areas of theoretical and applied mathematics. We shall refer to $f(x) = e^x$ as the *exponential function*. It has many properties of importance. First, remember that for positive values of x, e^x is an accumulation factor which can never be negative. Since $e^{-x} = 1/e^x$, the function can also never be negative for negative x. Recall also that e is a real number equal to approximately 2.72. Combining these facts with the well-known rules of exponents, we may list the properties of e^x.

1. $e^x > 0$ for all real values of x
2. $e^0 = 1$
3. $e^x > 1$ if $x > 0$
   $e^x < 1$ if $x < 0$
4. $e^a e^b = e^{a+b}$
5. $e^a \div e^b = e^{a-b}$
6. $(e^a)^b = e^{ab}$
7. $e^{-x} = 1/e^x$

In addition, the function $f(x) = e^x$ has a derivative. This derivative is particularly easy to remember.

Formula 9   If $f(x) = e^x$, then $f'(x) = e^x$.

Yes, you read that correctly. The derivative of e^x is e^x. Of course, this also means that the second derivative of e^x is again e^x. Thus, if

$$f(x) = e^x$$
$$f'(x) = e^x$$
$$f''(x) = e^x$$
$$\vdots$$

Since $e^x > 0$ for all x, then $f'(x) > 0$, which means that the function is increasing for all x. Moreover, $f''(x) > 0$, which means that the graph of $y = e^x$ is concave up for all real x. As x becomes large, e^x becomes very large very quickly. Again, since $e^{-x} = 1/e^x$, as x becomes large negative, e^x goes rapidly to zero. A glance at Table A-10 will reinforce these statements. A sketch of $y = e^x$ is shown in Figure 1.

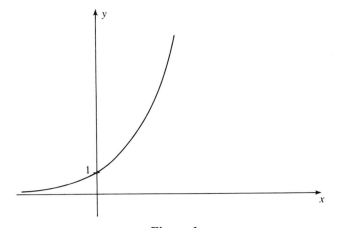

Figure 1

Let us look at some derivative examples.

Example 1   Find y' if $y = x^2 e^x$.

This is a product with $f(x) = x^2$ and $g(x) = e^x$. Thus

$$y' = f'(x)g(x) + g'(x)f(x)$$
$$y' = 2xe^x + (e^x)x^2$$

or

$$y' = xe^x(x + 2)$$

Example 2   Find y' if $y = (e^x + 1)/(e^x + x)$.

This is a quotient, so apply the quotient rule:

$$y' = \frac{(e^x + x)e^x - (e^x + 1)(e^x + 1)}{(e^x + x)^2}$$

$$y' = \frac{e^{2x} + xe^x - e^{2x} - 2e^x - 1}{(e^x + x)^2}$$

or

$$y' = (xe^x - 2e^x - 1)/(e^x + x)^2$$

Of course, we have not considered functions of the form

$$y = e^{f(x)}$$

Here we have another rule:

Formula 10   If $y = e^{f(x)}$, then $y' = e^{f(x)}f'(x)$.

Example 3   Find the first two derivatives of

$$y = e^{x^3}$$

We have something of the form $e^{f(x)}$ with $f(x) = x^3$. Thus, applying the formula,

$$y' = e^{f(x)}f'(x)$$
$$y' = e^{x^3}(3x^2) = 3x^2 e^{x^3}$$

To find y'', we have a product. The first term is $3x^2$ and the second term is e^{x^3}. Combining Formula 10 with the product rule,

$$y'' = 6xe^{x^3} + 3x^2[e^{x^3}(3x^2)]$$

or

$$y'' = 6xe^{x^3} + 9x^4 e^{x^3}$$

or

$$y'' = 3xe^{x^3}(2 + 3x^3)$$

EXERCISES

1.   The number e is defined as the limit of $(1 + h)^{1/h}$ as h approaches zero. This could just as easily be written as the limit of $(1 + 1/n)^n$ as n becomes arbitrarily large. Let

$$a_n = \left(1 + \frac{1}{n}\right)^n$$

Use a desk calculator to find $a_2 = (1 + 1/2)^2$ and $a_{10} = (1 + 1/10)^{10}$. Now find a_{20} and a_{100}. Does a_n appear to be approaching 2.72 as n gets larger?

2. Find the effective rates obtainable by continuous compounding for 3%, 4%, 5%, 6%, and 8%.

3. Mr. Blank deposits \$1,000 in a bank paying 6% interest compounded continuously. What will it amount to after 15 months?

4. Find the present value of \$600 due in two and one-half years if money is worth 9% compounded continuously.

5. Find the accumulation of 15 monthly deposits of \$200 in a bank paying $5\frac{1}{2}\%$ interest compounded continuously.

6. Find the present value of 10 semiannual payments of \$300 each if money is worth 10% compounded continuously.

7. How much must be deposited every month in a bank paying 6% compounded continuously in order to accumulate \$1,000 at the end of one year?

8. Find $f'(x)$ for:
   (a) $f(x) = e^{-3x}$
   (b) $f(x) = xe^x$
   (c) $f(x) = (e^x + 1) \div (e^x - 1)$
   (d) $f(x) = e^{x^2} + 1$
   (e) $f(x) = x^2 e^{x^3}$
   (f) $f(x) = x^2 e^{-x^3}$
   (g) $f(x) = (e^x + 7)^{1/2}$
   (h) $f(x) = (e^{x^2} + x^2)^2$

9. Find $f''(x)$ for each function in Exercise 8.

10. Find the slope of tangent lines as indicated.
    (a) To the curve $y = e^x$ at $x = 0$
    (b) To the curve $y = x^2 e^{-x}$ at $x = 1$
    (c) To the curve $y = (x^2 + 2)e^{-x^2}$ at $x = 0$

11. Find the equations of the tangent lines whose slopes were found in Exercise 10.

12. Find the critical points for each of the following:
    (a) $f(x) = e^x$
    (b) $f(x) = xe^x$

(c) $f(x) = xe^{-x}$

(d) $f(x) = xe^{-x^2}$

(e) $f(x) = x^2 e^{-x^2}$

13. Find f_x and f_y for $f(x, y) = e^{x^2 + y^2}$.

14. Find the minimum possible value for $f(x, y)$ of Exercise 13.

11.2 Logarithms and Exponentials

We have seen how to find the effective rate of interest obtained by compounding some nominal rate continuously. However, suppose that you were interested in the opposite problem. For example, what nominal rate compounded continuously amounts to 8% effective? In other words, solve for j the equation $e^j = 1.08$. We know that the solution must be some number less than 0.08 but we have no idea which one. The solution to this equation is called the "natural logarithm of 1.08" and is written ln 1.08. In Table A-11, we have a listing of the values of ln x. Looking in the table we see that ln 1.08 = 0.07696 = 7.696%. In general, ln x is the solution to the problem, "What power of e is equal to x?" Let us say that again. If $e^a = b$, then $a = $ ln b. That is, e raised to the ln b power is equal to b. For example, the solution to $e^t = 2$ is $t = $ ln 2. In other words, $e^{\ln 2} = 2$.

From the general relationship, $e^{\ln x} = x$, we can derive many properties of this *logarithmic* function. First, note that ln x is only defined for positive x, since all powers of e must be positive. Then note the following seven properties:

1. $e^{\ln x} = x$
2. ln $ab = $ ln $a + $ ln b
3. ln $1 = 0$
4. $\ln(1/b) = -$ln b
5. $\ln(a^b) = b \cdot$ ln a
6. ln $e = 1$
7. ln $e^x = x$

In order to gain practice in the definition, let us try to see why some of these properties are true. Notice that the first property is simply the definition. Let us look at the second property. We know that

$$e^{\ln a} = a \qquad \text{and} \qquad e^{\ln b} = b$$

Therefore,

$$e^{\ln a} e^{\ln b} = ab$$

By the law of exponents,

$$e^{\ln a + \ln b} = ab$$

and since

$$e^{\ln ab} = ab$$

it follows that

$$\ln ab = \ln a + \ln b$$

Property 3 now follows easily from Property 2, since

$$\ln a = \ln(1 \cdot a) = \ln 1 + \ln a$$

Now

$$\ln a = \ln 1 + \ln a$$

and subtracting $\ln a$ from both sides,

$$0 = \ln 1$$

Of course, this one was easy since $\ln 1$ must solve the problem, "e to what power is 1?" and the answer is clearly 0. Property 4 follows 2 and 3 as below:

$$\ln[b(1/b)] = \ln 1 = 0$$
$$\ln b + \ln(1/b) = 0$$

Therefore,

$$\ln(1/b) = -\ln b$$

The remaining properties may be derived in similar manner. However, let us stress again Properties 1 and 7, which state

$$e^{\ln x} = x \qquad \text{and} \qquad \ln e^x = x$$

We see that the two functions undo one another. That is, if we find the natural log of any number x and then find e to that power, we return to the value x. In other words, the exponential function is the antilogarithm. Similarly, if we take e to any power x and then take the logarithm of that number, we arrive back at x. Thus, the log is the anti-exponential. This dual relationship causes us to call the logarithm and exponential *inverse functions*.

Suppose that you wished to know the derivative of $\ln x$. Assuming that the derivative exists and letting $f(x) = \ln x$, we may write

$$e^{f(x)} = x$$

Taking the derivative of both sides, using Formula 10, yields

$$e^{f(x)} f'(x) = 1$$

Since

$$e^{f(x)} = x$$

we have

$$xf'(x) = 1$$

or $$f'(x) = 1/x$$

Thus, we have

Formula 11   If $f(x) = \ln x$, then $f'(x) = 1/x$.

Example 1   If $y = x^2 \ln x$, find y'

This is a product. The first factor is x^2 and the second is $\ln x$. Applying the product rule,

$$y' = x^2(1/x) + 2x \ln x$$

or

$$y' = x + 2x \ln x = x(1 + 2 \ln x)$$

Example 2   Find the critical values of $f(x) = x^4 \ln x$.

Again apply the product rule,

$$f'(x) = x^4(1/x) + 4x^3 \ln x$$

or

$$f'(x) = x^3 + 4x^3 \ln x = x^3(1 + 4 \ln x)$$

Setting $f'(x) = 0$ yields

$$x^3(1 + 4 \ln x) = 0$$

This appears to be zero when $x = 0$, but since $\ln 0$ is undefined, we must eliminate this possibility. Thus, the only possibility is

$$1 + 4 \ln x = 0$$
$$\ln x = -1/4 = -0.25$$

How do you solve $\ln x = -0.25$? We use the relationship $e^{\ln x} = x$, to yield

$$x = e^{\ln x} = e^{-0.25}$$
$$x = 0.7788$$

Thus, the only critical value is $x = 0.7788$. By the way, if we find $f''(x)$, we have

$$f''(x) = 3x^2(1 + 4 \ln x) + x^3(4)(1/x)$$
$$f''(x) = 3x^2(1 + 4 \ln x) + 4x^3$$
$$f''(x) = x^2(3 + 12 \ln x + 4x)$$

At $x = 0.7788$, $\ln x = -0.25$ and

$$f''(0.7788) = (0.7788)^2[3 - 3 + 4(0.7788)] > 0$$

Thus, we see that at the critical point we have a relative minimum, $f(0.7788) = -(0.7788)^3(0.25) = -0.1181$

Let us look at the graph of $y = \ln x$. First we note that $e^0 = 1$, negative powers of e are less than 1, and positive powers of e are greater than 1. Hence,
1. $\ln 1 = 0$
2. $\ln x < 0$ if $x < 1$
3. $\ln x > 0$ if $x > 1$

Now, if
$$y = \ln x$$
$$y' = 1/x$$
$$y'' = -1/x^2$$

Since $\ln x$ is only defined for positive x, then $y' = 1/x > 0$ for all x of interest, so $\ln x$ is an increasing function. Moreover, $y'' = -1/x^2 <$

0, so the graph of $y = \ln x$ is concave down for all x. The graph is shown in figure 2.

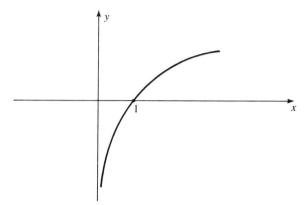

Figure 2

Let us look at some other derivatives. When we dealt with x^n, we next considered $[f(x)]^n$. When we dealt with e^x, we next considered $e^{f(x)}$. Now we have looked at ln x. What about ln $f(x)$? The required derivative formula is similar to the others.

Formula 12   If $y = \ln f(x)$, then $y' = \dfrac{1}{f(x)} f'(x)$ or $y' = f'(x)/f(x)$.

Example 3   Find the tangent line to $y = \ln(x^2 + 1)$ at the point where $x = 2$.

First we need y'. Applying Formula 12 with $f(x) = x^2 + 1$, we have

$$y' = \frac{1}{x^2 + 1}(2x)$$

At $x = 2$, $y' = 4/5 = 0.8$ and $y = \ln 5$. Hence, by the point-slope formula, the equation of the tangent line is

$$y - \ln 5 = 0.8(x - 2)$$

Incidentally, our table of natural logarithms only goes up to $x = 3$. To find ln 5, there are several possibilities. For example,

$$\ln 5 = \ln (2)(2.5)$$
$$= \ln 2 + \ln 2.5$$
$$= 0.69315 + 0.91629 = 1.60944$$

We close this section by noting a very famous result about derivatives. Let us point out the following comparisons:

1. If $y = x^n$, $y' = nx^{n-1}$ and
   if $y = [f(x)]^n$, $y' = n[f(x)]^{n-1}f'(x)$
2. If $y = e^x$, $y' = e^x$ and
   if $y = e^{f(x)}$, $y' = e^{f(x)}f'(x)$
3. If $y = \ln x$, $y' = 1/x$ and
   if $y = \ln f(x)$, $y' = (1/f(x))f'(x)$

These suggest the following general rule:

Formula 13   The chain rule.   If $y = g(u)$ and $u = f(x)$, then $y' = g'(u)f'(x)$. In alternate notation, if $y = g(f(x))$, then $y' = g'(f(x))f'(x)$.

In the first comparison $g(u) = u^n$, in the second $g(u) = e^u$, and in
the third $g(u) = \ln u$. The chain rule gives you no more ability to find
derivatives than you had before. It simply combines Formulas 6, 10,
and 12 into one rule. However, in later work you may encounter other
functions, such as the trigonometric functions sin x, cos x, tan x,
etc. If you are told, for example, that the derivative of sin x is cos x,
then you may apply the chain rule to find the derivative of

$$y = \sin(x^2 + 3x + 1)$$

Thinking of this as sin u where $u = x^2 + 3x + 1$ gives

$$y' = \cos(x^2 + 3x + 1) \cdot (2x + 3)$$

EXERCISES

1. Find the rates j_∞ equivalent to 3%, 4%, 5%, 6%, 7%, and 8%
   effective.

2. Table A-11 gives ln x for a limited selection of values. Use
   Table A-11 and the properties of logarithms to compute
   (a) ln 20
   (b) ln 45
   (c) ln (1/20)
   (d) ln (1/45)
   (e) ln 3.9
   (f) ln (3^{10})
   (g) ln (0.0005)
   (h) ln (0.0000001)

3. Find $f'(x)$ for
   (a) $f(x) = \ln (x + 3)$
   (b) $f(x) = x \ln x$
   (c) $f(x) = \ln (x + 1) \div \ln x$
   (d) $f(x) = \dfrac{\ln (3x + 5)}{x^2 + 1}$
   (e) $f(x) = x^2 \ln (e^x + 2)$
   (f) $f(x) = [\ln x + x^2]^{10}$
   (g) $f(x) = (\ln x)^2 \ln (x^2)$
   (h) $f(x) = e^{(\ln x)^2}$

4. Find $f''(x)$ for each function in Exercise 3.

5. Find the slope of the tangent lines as indicated.
   (a) To the curve $y = \ln x$ at $x = 1$
   (b) To the curve $y = x \ln x$ at $x = e$
   (c) To the curve $y = \ln (x^2 + 2)$ at $x = 0$

6. Find the equations of the tangent lines whose slopes were found in Exercise 5.

7. Find the critical points for each of the following:
   (a) $f(x) = x \ln x$
   (b) $f(x) = \ln x - 2x$
   (c) $f(x) = x^2 \ln x + x^2$

8. Find f_x and f_y for
   (a) $f(x, y) = \ln (x^2 + y^2)$
   (b) $f(x, y) = \ln (e^x + e^y)$
   (c) $f(x, y) = (x^2 + y^2)e^x$
   (d) $f(x, y) = \ln (x^2 y^3)$

9. Find f_{xx}, f_{yy}, and f_{xy} for each of the functions in Exercise 8.

10. Find the minimum possible value for $f(x, y) = \ln (x^2 + y^2 + 7)$.

11.3 Exponential Growth

Suppose we are given $y = f(x)$. We know that $f'(x)$ gives the slope of the curve at the point (x, y). However, there is yet another interpretation of the first derivative. Let the value of x change by amount h. That is, go from x to $x + h$. The value of y changes by amount $f(x + h) - f(x)$. The rate of change of y for unit change in x is then the change in y divided by the change in x or $[f(x + h) - f(x)]/h$. As $h \to 0$, this rate of change approaches $f'(x)$. It is called the *instantaneous rate of change* of y with respect to x. Thus, the derivative is also referred to as the *rate of change*. This is particularly applicable in physics where the position of a moving particle is frequently expressed as a function of time. The derivative is then the rate of change of position, generally referred to as the *velocity*.

In this section we shall be concerned with the function

$$y = Ae^{cx}$$

where A and c are constants.

Finding y', we have

$$y' = Ace^{cx} = c(Ae^{cx}) = cy$$

The equation

$$y' = cy$$

in words says, "the rate of change of y is equal to a constant times y." More simply, it says "the rate of change of y is proportional to y."

In the real world, many processes can be approximated by this simple law. For example:

1. Population growth.   Let $y =$ number of animals (or people) in some population at a given time t. The number of animals of child-bearing age and hence the number of offspring born at any time is some fraction of y. Hence, the rate of change of y is proportional to y. Therefore, $y = Ae^{ct}$, where t is time, describes the population as a function of time.

2. Epidemic spread.   Let $y =$ number of people infected by a communicable disease. Now, the more who have the disease, the more possible carriers there are. Again the rate of change of y is proportional to y. Again, $y = Ae^{ct}$ describes the number of people infected as a function of time.

3. Mechanical failure.   If a large number of mechanical devices of some kind are produced, let y be the number still in use at time t. The number of items which suffer mechanical failure in any time period is proportional to the number still in use. In this case, y is a decreasing function of t; if we want c to be positive, we have $y' = -cy$ which is satisfied by $y = Ae^{-ct}$.

4. Radioactive decay. The decay of atoms of a radioactive substance is exactly analogous to the mechanical failure situation. Hence, if y is the number of particles present at any given time t, $y = Ae^{-ct}$ governs the behavior of y. Since the number of atoms decaying in any time period is a fixed fraction of the number present, then the intensity of radiation is also governed by $y = Ae^{-ct}$.

In all these examples, A has the same meaning: it is the amount present when $t = 0$. That is, if we have $y = Ae^{ct}$, at $t = 0$, $y = Ae^0 = A$. Therefore, it is common to replace A by the symbol y_o. Let us look at some examples.

Example 1 At noon there are 200 plague viruses in a culture medium. At two in the afternoon, there are 700 plague viruses. How many will there be at midnight?

Measuring time in hours starting at noon for $t = 0$, we have

$$y_o = 200$$

and

$$y = 200e^{ct}$$

At $t = 2$, $$y = 700$$

or $$700 = 200e^{2c}$$

$$e^{2c} = 3.5$$

Solving for $2c$,

$$2c = \ln 3.5$$

$$c = \frac{1}{2} \ln 3.5 = 0.6264$$

Thus

$$y = 200e^{(\ln 3.5)t/2}$$

At midnight, $t = 12$ and so

$$y = 200e^{(\ln 3.5)(12)/2}$$
$$y = 200e^{6\ln 3.5}$$

Now we could use ln $3.5 = 1.2528$ and powers of e^x to find y. However, it is easier and more precise to realize that

$$e^{6\ln 3.5} = (e^{\ln 3.5})^6 = (3.5)^6$$

and

$$y = 200(3.5)^6 = 367,653$$

Example 2   The time that it takes for a radioactive substance to decay to half its initial amount is called the *halflife*. Find the relationship between the constant c and the halflife.

Since $y = y_0 e^{-ct}$ let T be the halflife.

Now at T, $$y = \frac{1}{2}y_0$$

and $$\frac{1}{2}y_0 = y_0 e^{-cT}$$

Dividing by y_0

$$\frac{1}{2} = e^{-cT}$$

Taking the natural logarithm of both sides,

$$\ln (1/2) = -cT$$
$$-\ln 2 = -cT$$
$$c = \frac{(\ln 2)}{T}$$

Thus, as the halflife increases, c decreases and vice versa. That is, when c is small, the material decays slowly; when c is large it decays rapidly. For growing populations, a large c indicates rapid growth, and a small c indicates slow growth.

EXERCISES

1.   A wildlife park placed 10 lions on a large range in January, 1968. In January, 1971, the lion population was 28. How many lions will there be in January, 1974?

2. The United States consumption of electric energy in thousands of kilowatt hours was 90,000,000 in 1930 and 140,000,000 in 1940. Assuming an exponential growth law, estimate the 1960 and 1965 consumption. (The actual amounts were 750,000,000 and 1,060,000,000, respectively.)

3. The population of Wyoming was 63,000 in 1890 and 146,000 in 1910. Estimate the 1950 population. (The actual figure was 290,000.)

4. Approximately 4,000 automobiles were produced in the United States in 1900. By 1905, 3,000 were still operating. Assuming an exponential failure law, how many were still running in 1935?

5. The halflife of Potassium 40 is about 1.3 billion years. How long will it take a block of Potassium 40 to decay to 80% of its initial amount?

6. In a recent cholera epidemic, 200 cases were reported on January 15 and 2,000 cases on March 15. Estimate the time of the first case.

7. A company's brochure notes that it tripled its sales from $1,000,000 to $3,000,000 in its first year of operation. If this keeps up, what will sales be after $4\frac{1}{2}$ years?

8. The population of Cleveland dropped from 875,000 to 750,000 between 1960 and 1970. Assuming an exponential reduction of population, estimate the population of Cleveland in 2000. If the shrinkage continues, in what year will Cleveland cease to have any population (i.e. fewer than one person)?

11.4 Elasticity of Demand

Suppose that we are given a demand function in the form $x = D(p)$. It is frequently important to consider the rate of change of demand with respect to price. In symbols, $dx/dp = D'(p)$. If x is expressed in certain demand units and p is expressed in certain price units, then dx/dp is units of demand per unit price. The difficulty with this measurement is that a change of scale may grossly distort the picture. For example, if demand units were changed from tons to pounds, then the value of dx/dp would be multiplied by 2,000. In order to eliminate this kind of distortion, it is convenient to divide by the quantity x/p. Since this quantity is in the same units as dx/dp, the resulting measurement gives the relative rate of change of demand, which is now a unitless quantity. We shall refer to this quantity as the *elasticity of demand* and designate it by E. Thus, given

$$x = D(p)$$

then

$$E = D'(p) \div (x/p)$$

or

$$E = D'(p) \div (D(p)/p) = p\left[\frac{D'(p)}{D(p)}\right]$$

Since $D'(p)/D(p)$ is the derivative of $\ln D(p)$, let $L(p) = \ln D(p)$. We may write

$$E = pL'(p)$$

For example, consider the linear demand function, $x = 100 - 3p$. Now $D(p) = 100 - 3p$, $L(p) = \ln (100 - 3p)$, $L'(p) = -3/(100 - 3p)$, and $E = -3p/(100 - 3p)$. Thus, the elasticity of demand is zero for $p = 0$ and becomes more and more negative as p increases.

Let us continue our analysis of this demand function to see an extended interpretation of E. Let us first look at small values of p. When $p = 1$, $x = 100 - 3(1) = 97$. When $p = 2$, $x = 100 - 3(2) = 94$. Thus, a one-unit change in p causes a 3-unit change in x. However, consider the relative change. A one-unit change in p, from $p = 1$ to $p = 2$, represents a 100% change in price. The 3-unit change in x, from $x = 97$ to $x = 94$, represents a 3/97 or roughly 3% change in demand. Thus, a 100% change in price causes only a 3% change in demand. Thus, the demand is relatively inflexible; to use the term under discussion, it is *inelastic*. On the other hand, look at the change from $p = 30$ to $p = 31$. Here we have a 3% change in price. The corresponding change in x is from 10 to 7, which is a 30% change in demand. Thus, at this end of the price range, a 3% change in price causes a 30% change in demand. Therefore, we would say that the demand is quite elastic.

In fact, there is an interesting lesson to be learned. Let us take the ratio of the relative change in demand to the relative change in price for one-unit change in price and compare the result to E.

At $p = 1$, the relative change in price is $1/1 = 1$, and the relative change in demand is 3/97. The ratio of these two is 3/97, so $1/1 \div 3/97 = 0.031$. Actually the change in demand is negative, so the ratio really should be expressed as -0.031. The value of E is $E = -3(1)/[100 - 3(1)] = -3/97$, which is identical to the ratio of relative change. Again, at $p = 30$, the relative change in price is $1/30$, and the relative change in demand is $3/10$. The ratio is $3/10 \div 1/30 = 9$, which again should really be expressed as -9. The value of E is $E = -3(30)/[100 - 3(30)] = -9$, again identical. Thus, for the linear demand function, the elasticity of demand seems to measure exactly the ratio of percentage change in demand to percentage change in price. Actually, it is not hard to show that this is exactly so for the linear demand function (see Exercise 4).

For the nonlinear demand function, the elasticity of demand E does not give exactly the ratio of percentage change in demand to percentage change in price, but it does give approximately this value. Therefore, the elasticity of demand gives a measurement of relative change of demand for change in price.

Let us take another example. Let $x = D(p) = 6/(p + 1)$ be the demand function. Now $L(p) = \ln 6 - \ln(p + 1)$ and $L'(p) = -1/(p + 1)$. (Notice that $\ln 6$ is a constant which has derivative zero.) Therefore, $E = pL'(p) = -p/(p + 1)$.

Let us see how good an approximation this elasticity formula gives to the relative change ratio. As p goes from $p = 4$ to $p = 5$ (a 25% change in price), x goes from $x = 6/5$ to $x = 1$ (a $-16\frac{2}{3}\%$ change in demand). The relative change ratio is $1/4 \div -1/6 = -2/3 = -0.667$. The value of E at $p = 4$ is $-4/5 = -0.800$. The approximation is fairly good for this case.

There are two particular demand functions of interest when considered from the viewpoint of elasticity. The first is the *generalized hyperbolic demand*,

$$D(p) = k/p^m \qquad (k \text{ and } m \text{ constants})$$

In this case

$$L(p) = \ln k - m \ln p$$
$$L'(p) = -m/p$$

and

$$E = pL'(p) = -m$$

That is, the elasticity of demand is constant.

The second is the *exponential demand function*

$$D(p) = Ae^{-cp} \qquad (A \text{ and } c \text{ constants})$$

In this case

$$L(p) = \ln A - cp$$
$$L'(p) = -c$$

and

$$E = pL'(p) = -cp$$

That is, the elasticity of demand is a simple linear function of p.

EXERCISES

1. Find the elasticity of demand function for each of the following
    demand equations:
    (a) $x = 200 - 4p$
    (b) $x = \sqrt{100 - p}$
    (c) $x = 100e^{-5p}$
    (d) $x = 100/(p + 1)^2$

2. For each of the demand equations in Exercise 1, find the ratio of
    relative demand change to relative price change for a one-unit
    change in price from $p = 2$ to $p = 3$. Compare the result to the
    value of E at $p = 2$.

3. For each of the demand equations in Exercise 1, find the elasticity
    of demand at the point at which revenue is maximized. (Hint:
    Revenue as a function of p is $xp = pD(p)$).

4. Given a general linear demand function $x = mp + b$, let p change
    from p_0 to $p_0 + h$. Show that the ratio of the relative change in
    x to the relative change in p is exactly equal to the elasticity of
    demand at p_0.

5. For the demand equation of Exercise 1(a), let the cost function
    be $C(x) = 1 + 6x$. Find the elasticity of demand at the point of
    maximum profit. Find the effect of a 5% price increase at this
    price on the relative change ratio.

6. Generalization of Exercise 3. Express the revenue function as
    $pD(p)$. Show that the elasticity of demand will be -1 at the point
    at which the marginal revenue is zero.

7. Find the values of x and p for which $x = 31 + 30p - p^2$ is a demand
    equation. Find the elasticity of demand for the extreme values
    of p.

11.5 Optimization Problems

Since we are now familiar with the derivatives of logarithmic and exponential functions, we may consider new types of optimization problems. The first type we shall look at is the exponential demand equation.

Example 1 Suppose $x = 100e^{-2p}$ is the demand equation for some commodity. Find the values of p and x that maximize revenue.

We know that the revenue is the product of x and p. In Chapter 10, we write this as

$$R(x) = xP(x)$$

We could just as easily write total revenue as

$$r(p) = pD(p)$$

and consider revenue as a function of price. Since we have $D(p)$ given, let us use this latter formulation.

$$r(p) = pD(p) = 100pe^{-2p}$$

To maximize revenue, find $r'(p)$ and set it equal to zero.

$$r'(p) = 100e^{-2p} - 200pe^{-2p} = 0$$
$$100e^{-2p}(1 - 2p) = 0$$

Since $100e^{-2p}$ is never equal to zero, we may divide through by this factor, yielding

$$1 - 2p = 0$$
$$p = 1/2$$

At $p = 1/2$, $x = D(1/2) = 100e^{-1} = 36.79$, and $r(1/2) = 18.395$ is the maximum revenue. You may check that $r''(1/2)$ is negative, proving that $r(1/2)$ is indeed a maximum.

Alternatively, we could work with $R(x) = xP(x)$. To do so, we must first solve the demand equation for p in terms of x. This is easy enough to do.

$$x = 100e^{-2p}$$

Take the natural logarithm of both sides, yielding

$$\ln x = \ln 100 - 2p$$
$$2p = \ln 100 - \ln x$$
$$p = \frac{1}{2} \ln 100 - \frac{1}{2} \ln x$$

Now having $\qquad P(x) = \frac{1}{2} \ln 100 - \frac{1}{2} \ln x$

$$R(x) = \left(\frac{1}{2} \ln 100\right) x - \frac{1}{2} x \ln x$$

Proceeding as above,

$$R'(x) = \frac{1}{2} \ln 100 - \frac{1}{2} \ln x - \frac{1}{2} x \left(\frac{1}{x}\right) = 0$$
$$\ln 100 - \ln x - 1 = 0$$
$$\ln x = \ln 100 - 1$$

Taking the antilogarithm of both sides,

$$x = e^{\ln 100 - 1}$$
$$x = e^{\ln 100} e^{-1}$$
$$x = 100 e^{-1}$$

which is the same solution as before.

The number of simple optimization problems involving logarithmic and exponential functions is limited. Such problems generally lead to equations which can only be solved by numerical analysis techniques that fall beyond the scope of this book. However, certain properties of the logarithm make it a great aid in simplifying the computations needed to solve other problems. These properties are:

1. Any expression involving products, quotients, and exponents may be simplified by use of the logarithm.
2. The derivative of $\ln f(x)$ is a very simple one, $f'(x)/f(x)$.
3. The logarithm is an increasing function. Therefore, the value of x which maximizes $f(x)$ also maximizes $\ln f(x)$ and vice versa. Of course, this is also true for minimums. Therefore, in order to find the extreme value of $f(x)$, it is frequently convenient to look instead for the extreme value of $L(x) = \ln f(x)$.

Let us see by some simple examples how the idea in (3) may be used.

Example 2   Find the maximum possible value of $f(x) = xe^{-x}$.

Let $L(x) = \ln f(x) = \ln x - x$. Find the maximum of $L(x)$ by finding $L'(x)$ and setting it equal to zero:

$$L'(x) = \frac{1}{x} - 1 = 0$$

Multiplying through by x,

$$1 - x = 0$$
$$x = 1$$

At $x = 1$, $f(1) = (1)e^{-1} = e^{-1}$. Notice $L''(x) = -x^{-2}$ which is always negative, and hence $x = 1$ does give a maximum.

Example 3   Find the rectangle of maximum area that can be inscribed in a semicircle of radius 4 as shown.

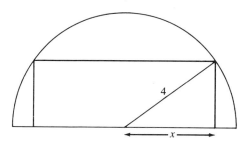

Calling the height of the rectangle y and letting x be as shown, we have the area

$$A = 2xy$$

The relationship between x and y is obtained from the Pythagorean theorem, $x^2 + y^2 = 16$. Therefore, $y = \sqrt{16 - x^2}$. The function to be maximized is

$$f(x) = 2x\sqrt{16 - x^2}$$

Letting $$L(x) = \ln f(x)$$
$$L(x) = \ln 2 + \ln x + \frac{1}{2}\ln(16 - x^2)$$

Proceeding in the routine manner,

$$L'(x) = \frac{1}{x} - \frac{1}{2}\left(\frac{2x}{16-x^2}\right) = 0$$

$$\frac{1}{x} = \frac{x}{16-x^2}$$

$$16 - x^2 = x^2$$

$$2x^2 = 16$$

$$x^2 = 8, \; x = \sqrt{8}$$

If $x = \sqrt{8}$, $y = \sqrt{8}$, and $A = 2\sqrt{8}\sqrt{8} = 16$.

Since x is actually one-half the length of the base, then geometrically the solution is a rectangle twice as long as it is high.

The major advantage of the logarithm here is that it eliminates the need for algebraic manipulation of square roots and the use of the product rule for derivatives.

EXERCISES

1. Find the minimum value of $f(x) = x - \ln x$.

2. Find the maximum revenue possible under the logarithmic demand equation $x = 5 - \ln p$.

3. Find the maximum revenue possible under the exponential demand equation $x = 50e^{-0.2p}$.

4. Find and identify all relative maximum and minimum values for
   (a) $f(x) = x^2 e^{-x}$
   (b) $f(x) = xe^{-x^2}$
   (c) $f(x) = x^k e^{-x}$

5. The probability bell curve introduced in Section 9.6 has equation $y = ce^{-x^2/2}$, where $c = 1/\sqrt{2\pi}$. Find all relative maxima, minima, and points of inflection for this curve.

6. Find the maximum possible revenue if demand is given by $x = 1/(1 + p^2)$.

7. Find two positive numbers x and y such that their sum is 35 and the product $x^2 y^5$ is a maximum.

8. Let the cost function for a certain commodity be $C(x) = 3 + 10x + 10 \ln x$. Find the minimum average cost.

9. Find the minimum value of

$$f(x,y) = e^{x^2+y^2-4x+10y+30}$$

12

Integration

12.1 The Indefinite Integral

Up to this point we have looked at many functions and studied ways to find their derivatives. In this section we shall investigate the inverse process—given a derivative, to find the original function. In some cases this is very simple; in others, it is not so simple. Let us look at a very simple one. Suppose that $f'(x) = 2x$. What is $f(x)$? The answer is obviously $f(x) = x^2$. Or is that the answer? What about $f(x) = x^2 + 3$? Or $f(x) = x^2 - 112$? Or $f(x) = x^2 + c$ where c is any constant? Clearly the last answer is possible, and it includes all the others as special cases. Is there possibly a more general function? The answer to that one is no. The most general antiderivative of $2x$ is $x^2 + c$. In general, let us state without proof:

THEOREM   Let $F(x)$ be any function whose derivative is $f(x)$. Then, the most general antiderivative to $f(x)$ is $F(x) + c$.

For example, given $f(x) = 3x^2$, one obvious antiderivative is x^3, and hence the most general antiderivative is $x^3 + c$.

As is usual mathematically, special notation is introduced to save the trouble of writing a whole sentence to describe a desired operation. Instead of saying, "antiderivative of $f(x)$," we shall write $\int f(x)dx$, which is read "the integral of $f(x)$" or "the indefinite integral of $f(x)$" or "the antiderivative of $f(x)$." An extensive description of the reasons for the choice of this unusual notation may be found in any complete treatment of calculus. However, for our purposes, we may think of the $\int$ (called an *integral sign*) and the dx as book ends holding the function whose antiderivative is to be found.

Let us try to develop some integral formulas by reversing derivative formulas. For example, suppose we wished to know $\int x^4 dx$. Since the derivative is x^4, it is reasonable to look at the function $F(x) = x^5$ as a possible candidate for the antiderivative. However, the derivative of x^5 is $5x^4$. Therefore, we must improve our guess. We wish to eliminate the factor 5, so let us try $(1/5)x^5$ instead of x^5. The derivative of $(1/5)x^5$ is exactly x^4. In other words

$$\int x^4 dx = \frac{1}{5}x^5 + c$$

By similar reasoning,

$$\int x^n dx = \left(\frac{1}{n+1}\right)x^{n+1} + c$$

for any value of n except $n = -1$. Of course, $n = -1$ will not work in this formula because for $n = -1$, $n + 1 = 0$, and you would be dividing by zero. When $n = -1$, you simply recognize that $x^{-1} = 1/x$ and recall that $1/x$ is the derivative of $\ln x$. Therefore $\int x^{-1} dx = \ln x + c$. (To be precise, this is only correct for positive x, since $\ln x$ is not defined for $x \le 0$. See Exercise 10 at the end of this section.) We have then arrived at our first antiderivative formula.

Rule 1.

$$\int x^n dx = \begin{cases} \left(\dfrac{1}{n+1}\right)x^{n+1} + c & \text{if } n \ne -1 \\ \ln x + c & \text{if } n = -1 \end{cases}$$

As a simple example,

$$\int x^{3/2} \, dx = \left(\frac{1}{5/2}\right)x^{5/2} + c$$

$$= \frac{2}{5}x^{5/2} + c$$

To check the correctness of the answer, notice that the derivative of $(2/5)x^{5/2}$ is just $x^{3/2}$.

Our derivative formulas tell us that the derivative of $cf(x)$ is just $cf'(x)$ and that the derivative of $f(x) + g(x) + \cdots + h(x)$ is just $f'(x) + g'(x) + \cdots + h'(x)$. The same results must be true for antiderivatives.

Rule 2.

$$\int cf(x)dx = c \int f(x)dx$$

and

$$\int [f(x) + g(x) + \cdots + h(x)]\, dx = \int f(x)dx + \int g(x)dx + \cdots + \int h(x)dx$$

Example 1 Find $\int (x^2 - 3x^{-1/2} + 7x^{-1} + 4)dx$.

Using Rules 1 and 2, we may do this a piece at a time, as follows:

$$\int x^2 dx = \frac{1}{3}x^3$$

$$\int -3x^{-1/2}dx = -3 \int x^{-1/2}dx = -3(2x^{1/2})$$

$$\int 7x^{-1}dx = 7 \int x^{-1}dx = 7 \ln x$$

$$\int 4dx = 4x$$

We have left off all the arbitrary constants since only the simplest anti-derivative is needed. Now, put the pieces together.

$$\int (x^2 - 3x^{-1/2} + 7x^{-1} + 4)dx = \frac{1}{3}x^3 - 6x^{1/2} + 7 \ln x + 4x + c$$

Notice that at the last step, we have tacked on the arbitrary constant c, giving us the most general answer.

What other derivative rules do we know? The simplest one is that the derivative of e^x is e^x and so,

Rule 3. $\int e^x dx = e^x + c$

How about the product and quotient rule? It is possible that you would recognize that $(x - 1)e^x/x^2$ is exactly the derivative by the quotient rule of e^x/x. Therefore

$$\int \frac{(x - 1)e^x}{x^2} dx = \frac{e^x}{x} + c$$

However, the chance of spotting this is so slim as to make it almost useless to try to use the quotient rule. The product rule has a similar drawback. (The famous method of "integration by parts" does grow out of product rule. For a discussion of this technique, the reader is referred to any standard calculus text.) Does that mean that we are limited to antiderivatives of x^n and e^x? Not quite. We have yet to look at the chain rule for derivatives as a source of antiderivative formulas. Consider, for example,

$$\int 11(x^2 + 1)^{10} \, 2x \, dx$$

It is not hard to see that

$$11(x^2 + 1)^{10} \, 2x$$

is precisely the derivative of

$$(x^2 + 1)^{11} + c$$

obtained by the power or chain rule.

It might be more difficult to recognize in the form $22x(x^2 + 1)^{10}$ but it would still be there. Of course, in general, the derivative of $[f(x)]^n$ is $n[f(x)]^{n-1}f'(x)$; the derivative of $\ln f(x)$ is $f'(x)/f(x)$; and the derivative of $e^{f(x)}$ is $e^{f(x)}f'(x)$. Hence

Rule 4. $\int [f(x)]^n f'(x)dx = \begin{cases} \dfrac{1}{n+1} [f(x)]^{n+1} + c & \text{if } n \neq -1 \\ \ln f(x) + c & \text{if } n = -1 \end{cases}$

and

$$\int e^{f(x)}f'(x)dx = e^{f(x)} + c$$

Let us take some examples.

Example 2

$$\int (x^4 + 5)^{1/2} \, 4x^3 dx$$

Letting $f(x) = x^4 + 5$, we have $f'(x) = 4x^3$, and we recognize that we have $\int [f(x)]^{1/2} f'(x)dx = 2/3 [f(x)]^{3/2} + c$. Thus,

$$\int (x^4 + 5)^{1/2} \, 4x^3 dx = \frac{2}{3}(x^4 + 5)^{3/2} + c$$

You should check this by showing that the derivative of $(2/3)(x^4 + 5)^{3/2}$ is exactly $(x^4 + 5)^{1/2} 4x^3$. Many students ask "What happened to the $4x^3$?" The answer is, "Nothing 'happened' to it." The $4x^3$ is produced by the chain rule in the differentiation process. If we had simply $\int (x^4 + 5)^{1/2} dx$ without the $4x^3$ factor, we would not have had a recognizable derivative.

Example 3 $\int e^{-x^2} x \, dx$

We would like this to look like $\int e^{f(x)} f'(x) dx$, so let $f(x) = -x^2$ and $f'(x) = -2x$. Now we would have the proper form if we only had $-2x$ instead of x multiplying e^{-x^2}. Let us use some trickery. We write

$$\int e^{-x^2} x \, dx = \int e^{-x^2} \left(-\frac{1}{2}\right)(-2) x \, dx$$

(Notice, $(-1/2)(-2) = 1$, so there is no change.) Now, using Rule 2, we may factor out the $-1/2$, yielding

$$\int e^{-x^2} x \, dx = -\frac{1}{2} \int e^{-x^2} (-2x) dx$$

$$= -\frac{1}{2} \int e^{f(x)} f'(x) dx$$

$$= -\frac{1}{2} e^{f(x)} + c$$

$$= -\frac{1}{2} e^{-x^2} + c$$

Example 4 $\int \frac{7x^2}{x^3 + 5} dx$

Letting $f(x) = x^3 + 5$, $f'(x) = 3x^2$. We could make this integral in $\int \frac{f'(x)}{f(x)} dx$ as follows:

$$\int \frac{7x^2}{x^3 + 5} dx = 7 \int \frac{x^2}{x^3 + 5} dx = \frac{7}{3} \int \frac{3x^2}{x^3 + 5} dx$$

$$= \frac{7}{3} \int \frac{f'(x)}{f(x)} dx = \frac{7}{3} \ln f(x) + c$$

$$= \frac{7}{3} \ln (x^3 + 5) + c$$

The presence of the arbitrary constant c arising as a result of anti-differentiation means that just knowing its derivative does not completely determine the function. Accordingly, it is possible to have problems in which there are additional data given which will fully specify the required function. Let us take a simple example.

Example 5 Let $P(x)$ be a polynomial whose derivative is $P'(x) = x^2 - 4x + 9$. Suppose that the curve $y = P(x)$ passes through the point $(1, 12)$. What is $P(x)$?

Since $P'(x) = x^2 - 4x + 9$, the antiderivative is $P(x) = (1/3)x^3 - 2x^2 + 9x + c$. In addition, when $x = 1$, $P(1) = 12$; that is, $1/3 - 2 + 9 + c = 12$, $c = 14/3$, and the solution is $P(x) = (1/3)x^3 - 2x^2 + 9x + (14/3)$.

Consider one final example.

Example 6 A monopolist discovers that his marginal profit function is $S'(x) = 2x - 20$ and his overhead is 21. For what value of x does he start to make a positive profit?

Since $S'(x) = 2x - 20$, the antiderivative is $S(x) = x^2 - 20x + c$.

Of course, at $x = 0$, there are no sales, and hence the "profit" must be a loss equal to overhead. That is,

$$S(0) = -21$$

Therefore $$c = -21$$

and $$S(x) = x^2 - 20x - 21$$

He first makes a positive profit just after $S(x) = 0$. Solving $S(x) = 0$,

$$x^2 - 20x - 21 = 0$$
$$(x - 21)(x + 1) = 0$$
$$x = 21, x = -1$$

We accept the only economically sensible answer, $x = 21$. Therefore, he makes a positive profit for $x > 21$.

EXERCISES

1. Find the indicated antiderivatives:
    (a) $\int x^7 dx$
    (b) $\int x^{-2/3} dx$
    (c) $\int 3x \, dx$

(d) $\int 7e^x dx$

(e) $\int (7 + 5x - e^x)dx$

(f) $\int \frac{1}{x} dx$

2. (a)   Find all possible curves whose slope is given by $2x + 3$ as a function of x.

(b)   Find the specific curve with slope given in (a) and which in addition passes through $(1, -3)$.

3. Repeat Exercise 2 (b) for the curve whose slope is $x^2 - 4x + 5$ and which passes through $(-1, 7)$.

4. (a)   Repeat Exercise 2 (b) for the curve whose slope is $3e^x$ and which passes through $(1, -1)$.

(b)   Follow the directions of (a) for the curve with slope $4/x$ passing through $(4, 6)$.

5. Find the equation $y = f(x)$ satisfying the following conditions: $f''(x) = -2x, f'(2) = 4$, and $f(2) = 6$.

6. Find the equation $y = f(x)$ satisfying the following conditions: $f''(x) = e^{-x}, f'(1) = 1$, and $f(1) = 3$.

7. Given a marginal cost function $C'(x) = 1 + x/5$ and the fact that the overhead cost is 10, find the average cost function and the minimum average cost.

8. Given the marginal revenue for some commodity is $R'(x) = 20 - 2x$, find the price function using the fact that at $x = 0$, the revenue must be zero. What is the highest possible demand for the commodity?

9. Given that the elasticity of demand for some commodity is $E = -1 - p^2$ and given that the demand is for 100 units when $p = 1$, find the demand equation.

10. We know that the derivative of ln x is $1/x$. When x is negative, ln x is not defined but $\ln|x|$ is. In fact, when x is negative, $|x| = -x$ and hence $\ln|x| = \ln(-x)$. Show that for $f(x) = \ln(-x), f'(x) = 1/x$. Hence, the proper antiderivative for $1/x$ is $\ln|x| + c$.

11. Find the indicated antiderivatives:

(a) $\int 2x(x^2 + 1)^{-1/2} dx$

(b) $\int x^2(x^3 - 3)^{1/3} dx$

(c) $\int x^{1/2} e^{x^{3/2}} dx$

(d) $\int x^{-1/2}(x^{1/2} + 1)^{-1} dx$

(e) $\int (3x - 4)^{7/3} dx$

12. Find the indicated antiderivatives:
    (a) $\int x^{1/3}(x^{4/3} - 2)^{7/12}\, dx$
    (b) $\int (x^2 - 3x + 4)^{12}\,(2x - 3)dx$
    (c) $\int (x^3 - 3x)^{-1/4}\,(x^2 - 1)dx$
    (d) $\int \dfrac{e^x}{e^x + 7}\, dx$
    (e) $\int (e^{-x} - 2)(e^{-x} + 2x)^{-1}\, dx$

13. To find $\int 3x(x^3 + 5)^{12}\, dx$, we would like to say $f(x) = x^3 + 5$ and read this integral as $\int [f(x)]^{12} f'(x)dx$. To do so, we must have $f'(x) = 3x^2$.

    Therefore, we write

$$\int 3x(x^3 + 5)^{12}\, dx = \frac{1}{x}\, \int 3x^2(x^3 + 5)^{12}\, dx$$

$$= \frac{1}{x}\left[\frac{1}{13}\,(x^3 + 5)^{13} + c \right]$$

$$= \frac{(x^3 + 5)^{13}}{13x} + \frac{c}{x}$$

Show by taking the derivative that this is *not* the correct antiderivative. What has been done wrong? How could you do the integral properly if you really had to?

14. Given that the derivative of the marginal revenue function for some commodity is $R''(x) = -3$ and that the revenue is zero for $x = 0$ and $x = 300$, find the demand equation.

12.2 The Definite Integral and Fundamental Theorem of Calculus

The problem of finding the area of a region bounded by curves other than straight lines goes back to antiquity. Archimedes discovered a simple formula for the area bounded by a parabolic arc by means of a method now called the "method of total exhaustion." The technique consists of approximating the area repeatedly by polygons getting closer and closer to the desired curve. Newton discovered that the problem of finding the area bounded by a curve was closely related to the derivative and proclaimed this relationship in what is known today as the *fundamental theorem of calculus*. We shall look at a plausibility argument for the correctness of Newton's great discovery. First of all, let us describe the problem that we wish to solve.

Let $y = f(x)$ be a positive function whose graph is a continuous curve. That is, the graph has no holes, breaks, gaps, or jumps. Since the function is assumed to be positive, its graph lies above the x-axis, and hence we may describe a region R by saying that R is the region below the curve and above the x-axis, bounded on the left by a vertical line $x = a$ and on the right by the vertical line $x = b$. (See figure 1.)

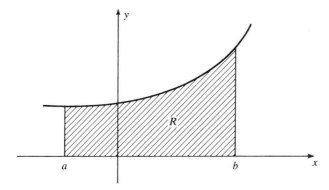

Figure 1

We shall make the fundamental assumption that the area of the region R may be well-defined. Actually, this is not at all obvious, and the largest part of the mathematical theory goes into the means of defining area. However, to continue, if the area of any such region can be defined, then it must have two simple properties. First, the area of a line segment must be zero. Second, let a_1, a_2, and a_3 be any three x-values, $a_1 < a_2 < a_3$. Let A_1 be the area between $x = a_1$ and $x = a_2$, A_2 be the area between $x = a_2$ and $x = a_3$, and A_3 be the total area between $x = a_1$ and $x = a_3$. Then $A_3 = A_1 + A_2$. (See figure 2.) This

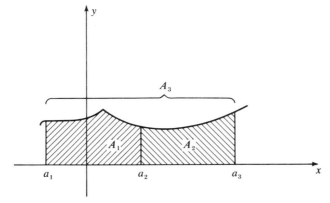

Figure 2

second requirement is just the traditional axiom which states that the whole is equal to the sum of its parts.

Let us now consider the region R between $x=a$ and $x=b$, above the x-axis and below the curve $y=f(x)$. Consider the area between $x = a$ and some arbitrary point x. This area will be a function of x that we shall denote $A(x)$. It is shown in figure 3.

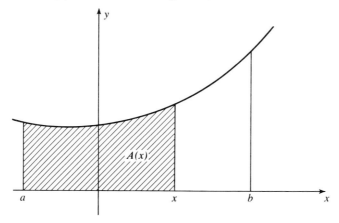

Figure 3

Consider now the area under the curve between x and $x + h$ as shown in figure 4. Calling the region R^* and this area $B(x)$, we have $A(x + h) = A(x) + B(x)$ or $B(x) = A(x + h) - A(x)$.

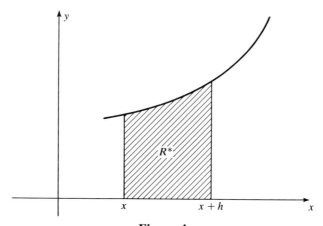

Figure 4

If you draw a horizontal line through the lowest point on $f(x)$ in R^*, it forms a rectangle completely inscribed in R^*. If you draw another horizontal line through the *highest* point on $f(x)$ in R^*, it forms a rectangle completely circumscribing R^*. Thus $B(x)$ falls somewhere between the area of these two rectangles. Hence there must be another horizontal line between the two lines already drawn which completes a rectangle with area exactly equal to $B(x)$. Since $f(x)$ has no gaps or holes, this line must cut the curve at some point $(x^*, f(x^*))$ as shown in figure 5.

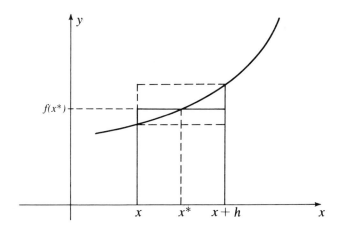

Figure 5

This rectangle has base h and height $f(x^*)$ giving an area $hf(x^*)$. Thus,

$$B(x) = hf(x^*)$$

and

$$B(x) = A(x + h) - A(x)$$

Therefore,

$$A(x + h) - A(x) = hf(x^*)$$

Dividing by h yields

$$\frac{A(x + h) - A(x)}{h} = f(x^*)$$

Letting $h \to 0$, $x^* \to x$ since x^* is trapped between x and $x + h$. Therefore, as $h \to 0$, $f(x^*) \to f(x)$, and the lefthand side of the equation tends to $A'(x)$ by definition. Hence, the relationship between $A(x)$ and $f(x)$ is that $A(x)$ is the antiderivative of $f(x)$.

If we let $F(x)$ be any arbitrary antiderivative of $f(x)$, then $A(x) = F(x) + c$. Now $A(a)$ is the area between a and a; that is, the area of a line segment, which must be zero. Hence, $A(a) = 0 = F(a) + c$, $c = -F(a)$. Thus, $A(x) = F(x) - F(a)$. Finally, the area between $x = a$ and $x = b$ is $A(b) = F(b) - F(a)$.

Therefore, to find the area under a positive function $y = f(x)$, above the x-axis and between $x = a$ and $x = b$, proceed as follows:

1. Find $\int f(x)dx = F(x)$.
2. Find $F(b)$ and $F(a)$.
3. Compute $F(b) - F(a)$.

For example, the area under $y = x^2$ between $x = 1$ and $x = 3$ is shown in figure 6.

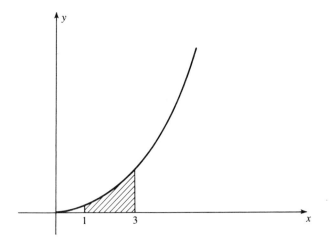

Figure 6

Following the three steps:

1. $\int x^2 dx = (1/3)x^3$; that is $F(x) = (1/3)x^3$.
2. $b = 3$ and $a = 1$, so $F(b) = F(3) = (1/3)(3)^3 = 9$ and $F(a) = F(1) = (1/3)(1)^3 = (1/3)$.
3. The area is $9 - 1/3 = 26/3$.

In order to save some writing, we introduce the following short-hand. First,

$$F(x)\Big|_a^b = F(b) - F(a).$$

The symbol $F(x)\Big|_a^b$ is read "F of x evaluated from a to b." Second,

$$\int_a^b f(x)dx = F(x)\Big|_a^b = F(b) - F(a)$$

where $F(x)$ is the antiderivative of $f(x)$. The symbol $\int_a^b f(x)dx$ is read "the definite integral of f of x from a to b." a is called the *lower limit* of integration and b is called the *upper limit* of integration. Hence, we may now write in one line the area under $y = f(x)$, above the x-axis, and between $x = a$ and $x = b$ is $\int_a^b f(x)dx$.

Example 1 Find the area bounded by $y = 4 - x^2$ and the x-axis.

The graph is shown in figure 7. The region is found under $y = 4 - x^2$, above the x-axis, and between $x = -2$ and $x = 2$. These values are located by finding the x-values for which y is zero. Thus,

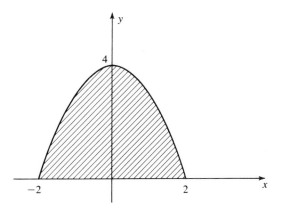

Figure 7

$$\text{Area} = \int_{-2}^2 (4 - x^2)dx = 4x - \frac{1}{3}x^3 \Big|_{-2}^2$$
$$= [4(2) - \frac{1}{3}(2)^3] - [4(-2) - \frac{1}{3}(-2)^3]$$
$$= 32/3$$

Example 2 Evaluate $\int_0^5 (3 - x^3)dx$

$$\int_0^5 (3 - x^3)dx = 3x - \frac{1}{4}x^4 \Big|_0^5$$

$$= [3(5) - \frac{1}{4}(5)^4] - [3(0) - \frac{1}{4}(0)^4]$$

$$= -565/4$$

Notice that the last example yields a negative answer. Clearly, this is not the area under a curve, which cannot be negative. Therefore, there must be some other interpretations for the definite integral which can yield a negative value. A clue to these interpretations is offered by noticing that $y = 3 - x^3$ becomes negative between the limits $x = 0$ and $x = 5$. In the next section, we shall see some of these results.

EXERCISES

1. Find the area under $y = 2x$ between $x = 0$ and $x = 2$ and above the x-axis by the methods of this section. Draw the graph and see that the region is a triangle. Check your result using the formula for area of a triangle.

2. Find the area under $y = 7$ between $x = -1$ and $x = 3$ and above the x-axis by the methods of this section. Draw the graph and see that the region is a rectangle. Check your result using the formula for area of a rectangle.

3. Find the area under $y = 7 - x$ between $x = -2$ and $x = 4$ and above the x-axis by the methods of this section. Draw the graph, and see that the region is a trapezoid. Check your result using the formula for the area of a trapezoid.

4. Find the area under $y = x^3 + x$ and above the x-axis between $x = 1$ and $x = 4$.

5. Find the area under $y = e^x$ between $x = 0$ and $x = \ln 5$ and above the x-axis.

6. Find the area under $y = 3e^{-2x}$ and above the x-axis between $x = -1$ and $x = 3$.

7. Find the area under $y = 1/x$, above the x-axis and between $x = e$ and $x = e^3$.

8. Find the area below $y = x^3 + 1$ and above $y = x$ between $x = 0$ and $x = 3$. (Hint: Draw a picture.)

9. Find the area in the first quadrant bounded above by $y = 8 - 2x^2$.

10. Repeat Exercise 9 for $y = 27 - x^3$.

11. Find the area above the x-axis and below the curve $y = 6 - x - x^2$.

12. Repeat Exercise 11 for $y = -x^2 - 8x - 8$.

13. Evaluate the following definite integrals:

(a) $\displaystyle\int_{-1}^{2} (x^2 + 3x + 5)dx$

(b) $\displaystyle\int_{0}^{7} xe^{x^2}dx$

(c) $\displaystyle\int_{-2}^{5} x(x^2 + 1)^{3/2}dx$

(d) $\displaystyle\int_{1}^{7} (2x + 1)^{-1}dx$

(e) $\displaystyle\int_{1}^{e^4} \frac{1}{x}dx$

(f) $\displaystyle\int_{-1}^{4} (1 - x^2)^4 x\ dx$

(g) $\displaystyle\int_{1}^{\ln 4} (x - e^x)dx$

12.3 Applications to Economics

At the end of the last section, we saw that the definite integral could be defined for functions for which it could not possibly represent the area under a curve. However, let us look at some other possibilities. If $y = f(x)$ is a positive function between $x = a$ and $x = b$, then the area under the curve is the same as the area of a rectangle of base $b - a$ and some height m, as shown in figure 8.

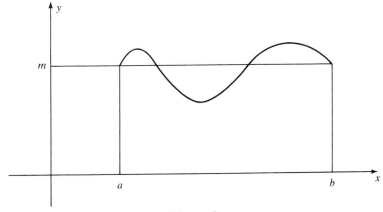

Figure 8

That is, if we replaced $y = f(x)$ by $y = m$, the area would be unchanged. In this sense, we would say that m is the average height of the function. Since

$$m(b - a) = \int_a^b f(x)\, dx$$

we have

$$m = \frac{1}{b - a} \int_a^b f(x)\, dx$$

which is called the *average value of the function over the interval* $a \leq x \leq b$.

Thus, this average value is the average height of a positive function. Suppose that the function becomes negative. Is this interpretation still correct? Let us see. If $y = f(x)$ is reasonably well-behaved, if it becomes negative, there is a smallest value that it reaches on the interval. Let this value be $-B$. Now consider the function $g(x) = f(x) + B$. This new function is nonnegative. Since it exceeds $f(x)$ by B for every x, then its average value should exceed the average value of $f(x)$ by B. In symbols, let the average value of $f(x)$ be m and of $g(x)$ be M. The relationship between these two values is $m + B = M$.

We can find M,

$$M = \frac{1}{b - a} \int_a^b g(x)\, dx$$

Substituting $m + B$ for M, and $f(x) + B$ for $g(x)$,

$$m + B = \frac{1}{b - a} \int_a^b [f(x) + B]\, dx$$

$$m + B = \frac{1}{b - a} \int_a^b f(x)\, dx + \frac{1}{b - a} \int_a^b B\, dx$$

However,

$$\int_a^b B\, dx = Bx \Big|_a^b = Bb - Ba = B(b - a)$$

and so

$$m + B = \frac{1}{b - a} \int_a^b f(x)\, dx + B$$

and

$$m = \frac{1}{b - a} \int_a^b f(x)\, dx$$

Therefore, the average value of $f(x)$ is given by the same formula whether $f(x)$ is positive or negative.

Example 1 Find the average value of $y = x^2 - 1$ on the interval $0 \le x \le 2$.

We have $a = 0$, $b = 2$,

$$m = \frac{1}{2 - 0} \int_0^2 (x^2 - 1)\, dx$$

$$= \frac{1}{2} \left[\frac{1}{3}x^3 - x \right]\Big|_0^2$$

$$= \frac{1}{2} \left(\frac{8}{3} - 2 \right) = 1/3$$

Let us look at two economic applications of the average value. Suppose that we have a supply equation $p = f(x)$ and a demand equation $p = g(x)$ with a market equilibrium point (x_o, p_o). (See figure 9.)

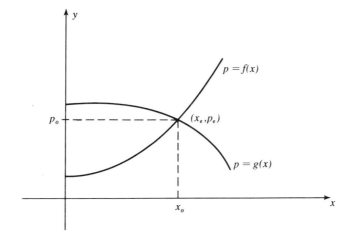

Figure 9

Considering only the demand function, you may reason as follows: If p were greater than p_o, there would be less demand. However, there would be some demand. That is, some consumers would be willing to pay a higher price than the market equilibrium price. To be precise, there would be demand x at the price $g(x)$. Those consumers willing to pay this higher price would feel that they have reaped a benefit of size $g(x) - p_0$. Thus, over the interval 0 to x_0, the average benefit accruing to the consumer would be

$$B = \frac{1}{x_0} \int_0^{x_0} (g(x) - p_0)\, dx$$

Since B is the average price difference 0 to x_0, then the total benefit is $x_0 B$ or

$$CS = \int_0^{x_0} (g(x) - p_0)\, dx$$

which is called the *consumer's surplus*. It is easy to see that

$$\int_0^{x_0} p_0\, dx = p_0 x_0$$

yielding

$$CS = \int_0^{x_0} g(x)\, dx - p_0 x_0$$

In similar fashion, we may look at the supply curve. There are a certain number of suppliers who would be willing to supply the commodity at less than the market price. These suppliers reap a benefit $p_0 - f(x)$. Following analogous reasoning, we define the *producer's surplus* to be

$$PS = p_0 x_0 - \int_0^{x_0} f(x)\, dx$$

(Actually, the assumption that (x_0, p_0) is the market equilibrium point is unessential. We need only assume that (x_0, p_0) is a point on the appropriate demand or supply curve.)

Example 2 Consider the linear supply and demand functions

$$p = 100 - 3x \quad \text{and} \quad p = 5 + 2x$$

Find the consumer's surplus and producer's surplus at the market equilibrium point.

The first equation is demand, $g(x) = 100 - 3x$. The second equation is supply, $f(x) = 5 + 2x$. Solving the two equations simultaneously, we have $(x_0, p_0) = (19, 43)$.

$$CS = \int_0^{19} (100 - 3x)\, dx - (19)(43)$$

$$CS = 100x - \frac{3}{2}x^2 \Big|_0^{19} - 817$$

$$CS = 1900 - \frac{3}{2}(19)^2 - 817 = 541.5$$

and

$$PS = (19)(43) - \int_0^{19} (5 + 2x)\, dx$$

$$PS = 817 - (5x + x^2) \Big|_0^{19}$$

$$PS = 817 - [5(19) + (19)^2] = 361$$

EXERCISES

1. Find the average value of $f(x) = x(x - 1)$ between $x = 0$ and $x = 2$.

2. Consider $y = x(x - 1)$ between $x = 0$ and $x = 1$.
   (a) Graph the curve showing that it is always below the x-axis.
   (b) Graph $y = -x(x - 1)$ and see that this is the same curve, above the x-axis.
   (c) Now $\int_0^1 f(x)\, dx = -\int_0^1 [-f(x)]dx$, and hence $\int_0^1 x(x - 1)\, dx$ is the negative of the area below $y = -x(x - 1)$ and above the x-axis. Hence $\int_0^1 x(x - 1)\, dx$ gives a negative number whose absolute value is the area above the curve $y = x(x - 1)$ and below the x-axis.
   (d) Find the area below the x-axis and above the curve $y = x(x - 1)$.

3. Follow the reasoning of Exercise 2, to find the area bounded by the x-axis and the curve $y = (x + 1)(x - 2)$.

4. (a) Let $f(x)$ be a function with antiderivative $F(x)$. Show that

$$\int_a^c f(x)\, dx = \int_a^b f(x)\, dx + \int_b^c f(x)\, dx$$

(b)   Check this result for $f(x) = x^3$, $a = -1$, $b = 0$, $c = 2$.

(c)   Check this result for $f(x) = x(x - 1)$, $a = 0$, $b = 1$, $c = 2$.

5.   Use the reasoning of Exercise 2 and 4 to interpret in terms of areas

$$\int_0^4 (x^2 - 1) \, dx$$

What can you say, in general, about the integral of a function which is sometimes positive and sometimes negative? What is the total area bounded by the x-axis, $y = x^2 - 1$, and $x = 4$? Hint: Draw a graph.

6.   Find the average value of $f(x) = x - e^x$ between $x = 0$ and $x = 2$.

7.   Find the consumer's surplus and producer's surplus for the demand and supply curves $p = 42 - x$ and $p = 2 + 3x$.

8.   Repeat Exercise 7 for

(a) $p = 100 - x^2$, $p = 3x^2$

(b) $p = 100 - x^2$, $p = 4 + 10x$

(c) $p = 10/(x + 1)$, $p = 4 - 1/(x + 1)$

(d) $p = 10e^{-x}$, $p = e^x$

9.   For the demand function $p = 10 - x$, the price is set by a monopolist so as to maximize revenue. Find the consumer's surplus at this point.

10. Repeat Exercise 9, if the monopolist's demand function is $p = e^{-x}$.

12.4 Applications in Probability

In Section 9.6, we encountered the idea that probabilities can be expressed as areas under a curve. In that section we considered the normal or "bell" curve. We said that the probabilities for a binomial random variable, suitably adjusted, could be expressed in terms of areas under the bell curve. Furthermore, we provided a certain table by which these areas could be computed. To be precise, we wrote

$$P(a < Z \leq b) = \Phi(b) - \Phi(a)$$

where $\Phi(x)$ was tabulated. Now, actually the equation of the bell curve is

$$\phi(x) = \frac{1}{\sqrt{2\pi}} e^{-x^2/2}$$

We could write the area under the curve between $x = a$ and $x = b$ as

$$P(a \le Z \le b) = \int_a^b \left(\frac{1}{\sqrt{2\pi}}\right) e^{-x^2/2}\, dx$$

You might think that with our knowledge of calculus, we could find the antiderivative of $\phi(x)$ and dispense with the use of the table. Unfortunately, this is not true. It is not possible to express the antiderivative of $\phi(x)$ as a simple formula. Hence, we remain with our table.

However, there are many other functions which may serve the same role as the bell curve. That is, there are random variables whose ranges are entire intervals rather than just discrete values. In many cases, the probabilities of events for these variables can be defined as the areas under special curves. Such curves are called *probability density functions*. To be more precise, let $f(x)$ be any function with the following two properties:

1. $f(x) \ge 0$ for all x.
2. The total area under $y = f(x)$ and above the x-axis is 1.

Now, $f(x)$ is a probability density function (*pdf*). Associated with a *pdf* is a random variable X whose distribution is defined by $f(x)$ as follows:

$P(a < X \le b) =$ Area under $f(x)$ between $x = a$ and $x = b$, or, more simply,

$$P(a < X \le b) = \int_a^b f(x)\, dx$$

This type of random variable is called a *continuous random variable*. For a continuous random variable,

$$P(X = c) = \int_c^c f(x)\, dx = 0$$

so the probability of any single point is zero. This leads to a number of interesting observations. First, we have events which are not impossible but which have zero probability. This directly contradicts one of our theorems for discrete random variables. Second, since for any c,

$$P(X = c) = 0$$

for continuous random variables, we have

$$P(a < X \le b) = P(a \le X \le b) = P(a \le X < b) = P(a < X < b)$$

Let us look at one example.

Example 1 Let X be a random variable with associated *pdf.* $f(x) =$ $2x$ for $0 \leq x \leq 1$ and $f(x) = 0$ for all other values of x.

First, we check that this is a *pdf* by noting that $f(x) \geq 0$ for all x and integrating,

$$\int_0^1 f(x) \, dx = \int_0^1 2x \, dx = x^2 \Big|_0^1 = 1$$

as required. We may now calculate probabilities for X, such as

$$P(1/2 < X \leq 1) = \int_{1/2}^1 f(x) \, dx = \int_{1/2}^1 2x \, dx = x^2 \Big|_{1/2}^1 = 3/4$$

Thus, we see that it is much more likely that X falls between 1/2 and 1 than between 0 and 1/2. Of course, for x not between 0 and 1, $f(x)$ is zero; hence the area under the curve is zero and it is impossible to have X fall outside the interval $0 \leq x \leq 1$. Thus, if you were to require $P(X \leq 1/4)$, this would be the same as asking $P(0 \leq X \leq 1/4)$, since $X < 0$ is impossible. Therefore,

$$P(X \leq 1/4) = \int_0^{1/4} 2x \, dx = x^2 \Big|_0^{1/4} = 1/16$$

You might well ask whether or not the expected value of a continuous random variable can be defined. The answer is that it can be. In fact, if we recall that for consumer's surplus, the integral summed up the total benefit accruing to the consumer, we realize that integration is a summation process. Also, recall that we had defined *expectation* as the sum over all possible values of $x_i p(x_i)$. Analogously, let X be a continuous random variable. Let $a \leq x \leq b$ include all x values for which $f(x) \neq 0$. Then we define

$$\mu = E(X) = \int_a^b x f(x) \, dx$$

For our last example, $f(x) = 2x$ for $0 \leq x \leq 1$, hence

$$E(X) = \int_0^1 x(2x) \, dx = \int_0^1 2x^2 \, dx = \frac{2}{3} x^3 \Big|_0^1 = 2/3$$

Similarly,

$$\sigma^2 = Var(X) = \int_a^b (x - \mu)^2 f(x) \, dx$$

which can be reduced to

$$Var(X) = \int_a^b x^2 f(x) \, dx - \mu^2$$

We would define $\int_a^b x^2 f(x) \, dx = E(X^2)$, so that we have the same formula for variance as in part II. Again, for our last example,

$$Var(X) = \int_0^1 x^2(2x) \, dx - (2/3)^2$$
$$= \int_0^1 2x^3 \, dx - (4/9)$$
$$= 1/2 - 4/9 = 1/18$$

We close the discussion by noting that Chebyschev's Inequality continues to hold for these random variables. Consider again our previous example. We have

$$\sigma = \sqrt{Var(X)} = \sqrt{1/18} = 0.236$$

Let us consider

$$P = P(\mu - 2\sigma \le X \le \mu + 2\sigma)$$

According to the inequality, P should exceed 3/4. Actually,

$$P = P(\mu - 2\sigma \le X \le \mu + 2\sigma) = P(0.195 \le X \le 1.139)$$

Now X cannot be larger than 1, hence

$$P = \int_{0.195}^1 2x \, dx = x^2 \Big|_{0.195}^1 = 1 - (0.195)^2 = 0.962$$

which certainly is greater than 3/4.

EXERCISES

1. Show that $f(x) = 3x^2$ for $0 \le x \le 1$ and zero for all other x is a pdf. Let X be the random variable having this pdf. Find $P(0 \le X \le 1/2)$, $P(1/4 \le X \le 1/2)$, $P(2 < X \le 3)$, $P(-1 \le x < 3/4)$, $P(0.8 \le X)$.

2. Let $f(x) = (x \ln 2)^{-1}$ for $2 \le x \le 4$ and zero for all other x. Show

that $f(x)$ is a *pdf*. Find $P(2.2 < X < e)$ for X associated with this *pdf*.

3. (a) Find μ and σ^2 for the random variable of Exercise 1.
    (b) Find μ and σ^2 for the random variable of Exercise 2.

4. Check Chebyschev's Inequality for two standard deviations for
    (a) The random variable in Exercise 1,
    (b) The random variable in Exercise 2.

5. Consider the *pdf* $f(x) = k$(constant) for $a \le x \le b$ and zero for all other x. Find k. Show that the probability the X falls in any subinterval of length L between $x = a$ and $x = b$ is the same regardless of where the interval lies. (This is called a *uniform random variable*.)

6. The uniform random variable on the interval $0 \le x \le 1$ has *pdf* $f(x) = 1$ for $0 \le x \le 1$ and zero for all other x. Find $E(X)$ and $Var(X)$.

7. Verify Chebyschev's Inequality for one, two, and three standard deviations for the uniform random variable in Exercise 6.

8. Let $f(x) = ke^x$ for $-1 \le x \le 1$ and zero for all other x. Find k so that this will be a *pdf*. Find $E(X)$ and $Var(X)$. Find $P(-1/2 \le X < 1/4)$.

9. Let $f(x) = kx^m$ for $0 \le x \le 1$ and zero for all other x. Find k so that this will be a *pdf*. Find $P(X > 1/2)$ as a function of m. What happens to this probability as $m = 1, 2, 3, \ldots$? Find $E(X)$ and $Var(X)$. What happens to them as $m = 1, 2, 3, \ldots$? Plot this *pdf* for some values of m. Can you see why you got your results?

10. The triangular distribution. Let X be a random variable with the following *pdf*: For x not in the interval -1 to $+1$, $f(x) = 0$. For x between -1 and 0, $f(x) = (x + 1)$. For x between 0 and $+1$, $f(x) = (1 - x)$. Plot the *pdf* and show that it is a *pdf*. Find $E(X)$ and $Var(X)$. Verify Chebyschev's Inequality for one, two, and three standard deviations.

11. Let X be a random variable with *pdf*, $f(x) = kx(4 - x)$ for $0 \le x \le 4$ and zero for all other x. Find k. Find $P(1/2 < X < 3)$, $P(0 \le X \le 5)$, $P(1/3 \le X < 5)$. Find $E(X)$ and $Var(X)$.

12.5 The Integral as a Sum

In the preceding sections we have repeatedly referred to the integral as an averaging or summing process. In this section we shall see how the definite integral is really defined and look at some of the implications of the definition. Let us assume that $f(x)$ is a function which is never negative for $a \le x \le b$. Suppose that you wish to know the area under the curve, above the x-axis, and between $x = a$ and $x = b$. Imagine that you do not know the fundamental theorem of calculus or more realistically that you cannot find the antiderivative of $f(x)$ in simple terms. In such a situation it would be natural to try to approximate the area by some simple scheme. The simplest is to approximate by rectangles, as shown in figure 10.

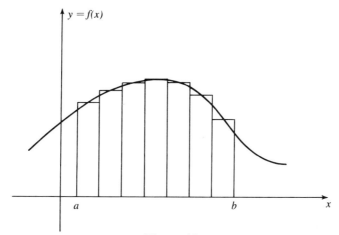

Figure 10

Algebraically, the approximation may be described as follows. Divide the interval into n subintervals. If we are to have n subintervals, there must be $n - 1$ subdivision points between a and b. Designate these points numbered from left to right as $x_1, x_2, \ldots, x_{n-1}$. To be consistent, let a be designated x_0 and let b be labelled x_n. Now, the first interval goes from x_0 to x_1, the second from x_1 to $x_2, \ldots$, the ith from x_{i-1} to $x_i, \ldots$, the last from x_{n-1} to x_n. Let us denote the length of the ith interval by $\Delta_i x = x_i - x_{i-1}$. Now above each subinterval construct a rectangle whose top bar intersects the curve $y = f(x)$ (see figure 11). Call the x-value of the point of intersection t_i. Then the height of the rectangle is $f(t_i)$ and the area of the rectangle is $f(t_i)\Delta_i x$. Now the total area of the rectangles is

$$A = f(t_1)\Delta_1 x + f(t_2)\Delta_2 x + \cdots + f(t_n)\Delta_n x$$

It seems reasonable to expect that if we have many subintervals of small width, the area of the rectangles should closely approximate the

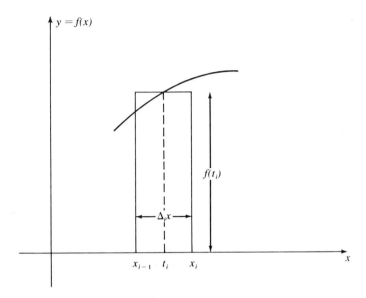

Figure 11

area under the curve. The idea is thus that you should let the number of subintervals approach infinity and the length of each subinterval approach zero. You would then hope that the sum A will tend to some limiting value which will be defined as the area under the curve. However, there are very strange functions for which different choices of subdivision points or interior points would lead to different limiting values. Therefore, the following definition is chosen.

For every possible subdivision and every possible choice of t's in the subintervals, let n go to infinity and let the length of each subinterval go to zero. If A has a limiting value which is the same for every possible subdivision and choice, then this limit is defined to be the definite integral from a to b of $f(x)$ and it is written $\int_a^b f(x)dx$.

Notice that it is extremely difficult to prove that there actually exists a limit that is the same regardless of the choices made. In fact, it is not possible for all functions. However, the chances are very good that you will never have cause to encounter an exception.

Let us take a simple example using this definition to approximate an area.

Example 1   Suppose that you did not have a table of natural logarithms but wished to know ln 2.

We know that $\int_1^2 \frac{1}{x}\,dx = \ln x\Big|_1^2 = \ln 2 - \ln 1 = \ln 2$. Therefore, if we approximate $\int_1^2 \frac{1}{x}\,dx$ we will have approximated $\ln 2$. Let us use 5 subdivisions of equal length. Notice that the definition does not require subdivisions of equal length in the formation of the sum, but this is surely the easiest way. Since the interval from 1 to 2 is of length 1, then each subinterval will be length 0.2. Thus, we take

$$a = x_0 = 1.0$$
$$x_1 = 1.2$$
$$x_2 = 1.4$$
$$x_3 = 1.6$$
$$x_4 = 1.8$$
$$b = x_5 = 2.0$$

Now, $\Delta_i x = 0.2$ for each subinterval. Pick for the t's the midpoint of each interval; that is,

$$t_1 = 1.1, f(t_1) = 1/t_1 = 1/1.1$$
$$t_2 = 1.3, f(t_2) = 1/t_2 = 1/1.3$$
$$t_3 = 1.5, f(t_3) = 1/t_3 = 1/1.5$$
$$t_4 = 1.7, f(t_4) = 1/t_4 = 1/1.7$$
$$t_5 = 1.9, f(t_5) = 1/t_5 = 1/1.9$$

Now,

$$A = f(t_1)\Delta_1 x + f(t_2)\Delta_2 x + f(t_3)\Delta_3 x + f(t_4)\Delta_4 x + f(t_5)\Delta_5 x$$
$$= \frac{1}{1.1}(0.2) + \frac{1}{1.3}(0.2) + \frac{1}{1.5}(0.2) + \frac{1}{1.7}(0.2) + \frac{1}{1.9}(0.2)$$
$$= (0.2)(0.9091 + 0.7692 + 0.6667 + 0.5882 + 0.5263)$$
$$= 0.6919$$

Actually $\ln 2 = 0.6931$, for an error of less than 0.2% using only five subdivisions. More subdivisions would improve the approximation.

Notice that the sum A could just as easily be defined for a function that becomes negative. Of course, the sum would be negative where f is negative. Thus, the integral of a negative function would give a negative number whose absolute value is the area above the curve and below the x-axis.

Example 2 $\displaystyle\int_1^2 (x^2 - 8)dx = \frac{1}{3}x^3 - 8x \Big|_1^2 = -17/3$

Now $y = x^2 - 8$ lies below the x-axis throughout the interval $1 \le x \le 2$. Therefore, $|-17/3| = 17/3$ is the area shown in figure 12.

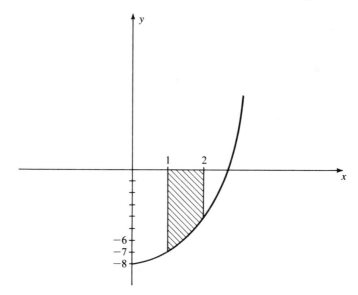

Figure 12

Example 3 Find the area bounded by the x-axis, the y-axis, $y = x^2 - 4$, and $x = 3$.

The graph is shown in figure 13. The total area is composed of the two pieces A_1 and A_2. To find A_1

$$\int_0^2 (x^2 - 4)dx = \frac{1}{3}x^3 - 4x \Big|_0^2 = -16/3$$

Hence, $A_1 = 16/3$. To find A_2

$$\int_2^3 (x^2 - 4)dx = \frac{1}{3}x^3 - 4x \Big|_2^3 = 7/3$$

Hence $A_2 = 7/3$ and the total area is $A_1 + A_2 = 23/3$.

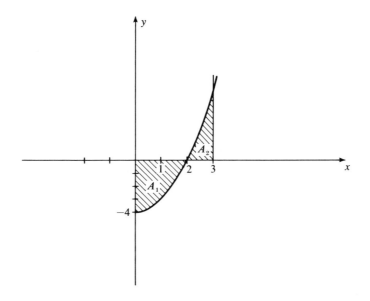

Figure 13

EXERCISES

1. Approximate the area under $y = 3x + 2$ between $x = 0$ and $x = 4$ by using eight equal subdivisions (of length $1/2$) and taking the midpoints of the intervals as the t's. Show that the approximation gives the exact answer, since the graph is a straight line.

2. Repeat Exercise 1 for $y = x^2$ and compute the error in the approximation.

3. Approximate the area under the curve $y = x(\ln x)$ between $x = 2$ and $x = 4$ using five subintervals of equal length. Show that the derivative of $(1/2)x^2(\ln x) - (1/4)x^2$ is $x(\ln x)$. Use this information to check the approximation.

4. Find the area bounded by $y = x^2 - 9$ and the x-axis.

5. Find the area bounded by $x = -2$, $x = 6$, the x-axis, and the curve $y = 5 - 4x - x^2$.

6. Repeat Exercise 5 for the curve $y = 4 - e^x$.

7. For the curve described in Exercise 4, use six subintervals and

any convenient point for t in each to approximate the integral from $x = -2$ to $x = 2$.

8. Use the method in Example 1 to approximate ln 4.

9. Repeat Exercise 8 using ten subintervals.

10. Find the areas bounded by the given curve, the x-axis, and the given vertical lines.

   (a) $y = 4 - x^2$, $x = 0$, and $x = 4$
   (b) $y = x^3 - 8$, $x = 0$, and $x = 3$
   (c) $y = 3 - x^2$, $x = -3$, and $x = 5$
   (d) $y = x^3 - x$, $x = -2$, and $x = 3$

APPENDIX

Tables

Table A-1
Accumulation Factors $(1 + i)^n$

n	$\frac{1}{4}\%$	$\frac{1}{3}\%$	$\frac{5}{12}\%$	$\frac{1}{2}\%$	$\frac{7}{12}\%$	$\frac{2}{3}\%$	n
1	1.0025 0000	1.0033 3333	1.0041 6667	1.0050 0000	1.0058 3333	1.0066 6667	1
2	1.0050 0625	1.0066 7778	1.0083 5069	1.0100 2500	1.0117 0069	1.0133 7778	2
3	1.0075 1877	1.0100 3337	1.0125 5216	1.0150 7513	1.0176 0228	1.0201 3363	3
4	1.0100 3756	1.0134 0015	1.0167 7112	1.0201 5050	1.0235 3830	1.0269 3452	4
5	1.0125 6266	1.0167 7815	1.0210 0767	1.0252 5125	1.0295 0894	1.0337 8075	5
6	1.0150 9406	1.0201 6741	1.0252 6187	1.0303 7751	1.0355 1440	1.0406 7262	6
7	1.0176 3180	1.0235 6797	1.0295 3379	1.0355 2940	1.0415 5490	1.0476 1044	7
8	1.0201 7588	1.0269 7986	1.0338 2352	1.0407 0704	1.0476 3064	1.0545 9451	8
9	1.0227 2632	1.0304 0313	1.0381 3111	1.0459 1058	1.0537 4182	1.0616 2514	9
10	1.0252 8313	1.0338 3780	1.0424 5666	1.0511 4013	1.0598 8865	1.0687 0264	10
11	1.0278 4634	1.0372 8393	1.0468 0023	1.0563 9583	1.0660 7133	1.0758 2732	11
12	1.0304 1596	1.0407 4154	1.0511 6190	1.0616 7781	1.0722 9008	1.0829 9951	12
13	1.0329 9200	1.0442 1068	1.0555 4174	1.0669 8620	1.0785 4511	1.0902 1950	13
14	1.0355 7448	1.0476 9138	1.0599 3983	1.0723 2113	1.0848 3662	1.0974 8763	14
15	1.0381 6341	1.0511 8369	1.0643 5625	1.0776 8274	1.0911 6483	1.1048 0422	15
16	1.0407 5882	1.0546 8763	1.0687 9106	1.0830 7115	1.0975 2996	1.1121 6958	16
17	1.0433 6072	1.0582 0326	1.0732 4436	1.0884 8651	1.1039 3222	1.1195 8404	17
18	1.0459 6912	1.0617 3060	1.0777 1621	1.0939 2894	1.1103 7182	1.1270 4794	18
19	1.0485 8404	1.0652 6971	1.0822 0670	1.0993 9858	1.1168 4899	1.1345 6159	19
20	1.0512 0550	1.0688 2060	1.0867 1589	1.1048 9558	1.1233 6395	1.1421 2533	20
21	1.0538 3352	1.0723 8334	1.0912 4387	1.1104 2006	1.1299 1690	1.1497 3950	21
22	1.0564 6810	1.0759 5795	1.0957 9072	1.1159 7216	1.1365 0808	1.1574 0443	22
23	1.0591 0927	1.0795 4448	1.1003 5652	1.1215 5202	1.1431 3771	1.1651 2046	23
24	1.0617 5704	1.0831 4296	1.1049 4134	1.1271 5978	1.1498 0602	1.1728 8793	24
25	1.0644 1144	1.0867 5344	1.1095 4526	1.1327 9558	1.1565 1322	1.1807 0718	25
26	1.0670 7247	1.0903 7595	1.1141 6836	1.1384 5955	1.1632 5955	1.1885 7857	26
27	1.0697 4015	1.0940 1053	1.1188 1073	1.1441 5185	1.1700 4523	1.1965 0242	27
28	1.0724 1450	1.0976 5724	1.1234 7244	1.1498 7261	1.1768 7049	1.2044 7911	28
29	1.0750 9553	1.1013 1609	1.1281 5358	1.1556 2197	1.1837 3557	1.2125 0897	29
30	1.0777 8327	1.1049 8715	1.1328 5422	1.1614 0008	1.1906 4069	1.2205 9236	30
31	1.0804 7773	1.1086 7044	1.1375 7444	1.1672 0708	1.1975 8610	1.2287 2964	31
32	1.0831 7892	1.1123 6601	1.1423 1434	1.1730 4312	1.2045 7202	1.2369 2117	32
33	1.0858 8687	1.1160 7389	1.1470 7398	1.1789 0833	1.2115 9869	1.2451 6731	33
34	1.0886 0159	1.1197 9414	1.1518 5346	1.1848 0288	1.2186 6634	1.2534 6843	34
35	1.0913 2309	1.1235 2679	1.1566 5284	1.1907 2689	1.2257 7523	1.2618 2489	35
36	1.0940 5140	1.1272 7187	1.1614 7223	1.1966 8052	1.2329 2559	1.2702 3705	36
37	1.0967 8653	1.1310 2945	1.1663 1170	1.2026 6393	1.2401 1765	1.2787 0530	37
38	1.0995 2850	1.1347 9955	1.1711 7133	1.2086 7725	1.2473 5167	1.2872 3000	38
39	1.1022 7732	1.1385 8221	1.1760 5121	1.2147 2063	1.2546 2789	1.2958 1153	39
40	1.1050 3301	1.1423 7748	1.1809 5142	1.2207 9424	1.2619 4655	1.3044 5028	40
41	1.1077 9559	1.1461 8541	1.1858 7206	1.2268 9821	1.2693 0791	1.3131 4661	41
42	1.1105 6508	1.1500 0603	1.1908 1319	1.2330 3270	1.2767 1220	1.3219 0092	42
43	1.1133 4149	1.1538 3938	1.1957 7491	1.2391 9786	1.2841 5969	1.3307 1360	43
44	1.1161 2485	1.1576 8551	1.2007 5731	1.2453 9385	1.2916 5062	1.3395 8502	44
45	1.1189 1516	1.1615 4446	1.2057 6046	1.2516 2082	1.2991 8525	1.3485 1559	45
46	1.1217 1245	1.1654 1628	1.2107 8446	1.2578 7892	1.3067 6383	1.3575 0569	46
47	1.1245 1673	1.1693 0100	1.2158 2940	1.2641 6832	1.3143 8662	1.3665 5573	47
48	1.1273 2802	1.1731 9867	1.2208 9536	1.2704 8916	1.3220 5388	1.3756 6610	48
49	1.1301 4634	1.1771 0933	1.2259 8242	1.2768 4161	1.3297 6586	1.3848 3721	49
50	1.1329 7171	1.1810 3303	1.2310 9068	1.2832 2581	1.3375 2283	1.3940 6946	50

Table A-1 (Cont.)

n	$\frac{1}{4}\%$	$\frac{1}{3}\%$	$\frac{5}{12}\%$	$\frac{1}{2}\%$	$\frac{7}{12}\%$	$\frac{2}{3}\%$	n
51	1.1358 0414	1.1849 6981	1.2362 2022	1.2896 4194	1.3453 2504	1.4033 6325	51
52	1.1386 4365	1.1889 1971	1.2413 7114	1.2960 9015	1.3531 7277	1.4127 1901	52
53	1.1414 9026	1.1928 8277	1.2465 4352	1.3025 7060	1.3610 6628	1.4221 3713	53
54	1.1443 4398	1.1968 5905	1.2517 3745	1.3090 8346	1.3690 0583	1.4316 1805	54
55	1.1472 0484	1.2008 4858	1.2569 5302	1.3156 2887	1.3769 9170	1.4411 6217	55
56	1.1500 7285	1.2048 5141	1.2621 9033	1.3222 0702	1.3850 2415	1.4507 6992	56
57	1.1529 4804	1.2088 6758	1.2674 4946	1.3288 1805	1.3931 0346	1.4604 4172	57
58	1.1558 3041	1.2128 9714	1.2727 3050	1.3354 6214	1.4012 2990	1.4701 7799	58
59	1.1587 1998	1.2169 4013	1.2780 3354	1.3421 3946	1.4094 0374	1.4799 7918	59
60	1.1616 1678	1.2209 9659	1.2833 5868	1.3488 5015	1.4176 2526	1.4898 4571	60
61	1.1645 2082	1.2250 6658	1.2887 0601	1.3555 9440	1.4258 9474	1.4997 7801	61
62	1.1674 3213	1.2291 5014	1.2940 7561	1.3623 7238	1.4342 1246	1.5097 7653	62
63	1.1703 5071	1.2332 4730	1.2994 6760	1.3691 8424	1.4425 7870	1.5198 4171	63
64	1.1732 7658	1.2373 5813	1.3048 8204	1.3760 3016	1.4509 9374	1.5299 7399	64
65	1.1762 0977	1.2414 8266	1.3103 1905	1.3829 1031	1.4594 5787	1.5401 7381	65
66	1.1791 5030	1.2456 2093	1.3157 7872	1.3898 2486	1.4679 7138	1.5504 4164	66
67	1.1820 9817	1.2497 7300	1.3212 6113	1.3967 7399	1.4765 3454	1.5607 7792	67
68	1.1850 5342	1.2539 3891	1.3267 6638	1.4037 5785	1.4851 4766	1.5711 8310	68
69	1.1880 1605	1.2581 1871	1.3322 9458	1.4107 7664	1.4938 1102	1.5816 5766	69
70	1.1909 8609	1.2623 1244	1.3378 4580	1.4178 3053	1.5025 2492	1.5922 0204	70
71	1.1939 6356	1.2665 2015	1.3434 2016	1.4249 1968	1.5112 8965	1.6028 1672	71
72	1.1969 4847	1.2707 4188	1.3490 1774	1.4320 4428	1.5201 0550	1.6135 0217	72
73	1.1999 4084	1.2749 7769	1.3546 3865	1.4392 0450	1.5289 7279	1.6242 5885	73
74	1.2029 4069	1.2792 2761	1.3602 8298	1.4464 0052	1.5378 9179	1.6350 8724	74
75	1.2059 4804	1.2834 9170	1.3659 5082	1.4536 3252	1.5468 6283	1.6459 8782	75
76	1.2089 6291	1.2877 7001	1.3716 4229	1.4609 0069	1.5558 8620	1.6569 6107	76
77	1.2119 8532	1.2920 6258	1.3773 5746	1.4682 0519	1.5649 6220	1.6680 0748	77
78	1.2150 1528	1.2963 6945	1.3830 9645	1.4755 4622	1.5740 9115	1.6791 2753	78
79	1.2180 5282	1.3006 9068	1.3888 5935	1.4829 2395	1.5832 7334	1.6903 2172	79
80	1.2210 9795	1.3050 2632	1.3946 4627	1.4903 3857	1.5925 0910	1.7015 9053	80
81	1.2241 5070	1.3093 7641	1.4004 5729	1.4977 9026	1.6017 9874	1.7129 3446	81
82	1.2272 1108	1.3137 4099	1.4062 9253	1.5052 7921	1.6111 4257	1.7243 5403	82
83	1.2302 7910	1.3181 2013	1.4121 5209	1.5128 0561	1.6205 4090	1.7358 4972	83
84	1.2333 5480	1.3225 1386	1.4180 3605	1.5203 6964	1.6299 9405	1.7474 2205	84
85	1.2364 3819	1.3269 2224	1.4239 4454	1.5279 7148	1.6395 0235	1.7590 7153	85
86	1.2395 2928	1.3313 4532	1.4298 7764	1.5356 1134	1.6490 6612	1.7707 9868	86
87	1.2426 2811	1.3357 8314	1.4358 3546	1.5432 8940	1.6586 8567	1.7826 0400	87
88	1.2457 3468	1.3402 3575	1.4418 1811	1.5510 0585	1.6683 6134	1.7944 8803	88
89	1.2488 4901	1.3447 0320	1.4478 2568	1.5587 6087	1.6780 9344	1.8064 5128	89
90	1.2519 7114	1.3491 8554	1.4538 5829	1.5665 5468	1.6878 8232	1.8184 9429	90
91	1.2551 0106	1.3536 8283	1.4599 1603	1.5743 8745	1.6977 2830	1.8306 1758	91
92	1.2582 3882	1.3581 9510	1.4659 9902	1.5822 5939	1.7076 3172	1.8428 2170	92
93	1.2613 8441	1.3627 2242	1.4721 0735	1.5901 7069	1.7175 9290	1.8551 0718	93
94	1.2645 3787	1.3672 6483	1.4782 4113	1.5981 2154	1.7276 1219	1.8674 7456	94
95	1.2676 9922	1.3718 2238	1.4844 0047	1.6061 1215	1.7376 8993	1.8799 2439	95
96	1.2708 6847	1.3763 9512	1.4905 8547	1.6141 4271	1.7478 2646	1.8924 5722	96
97	1.2740 4564	1.3809 8310	1.4967 9624	1.6222 1342	1.7580 2211	1.9050 7360	97
98	1.2772 3075	1.3855 8638	1.5030 3289	1.6303 2449	1.7682 7724	1.9177 7409	98
99	1.2804 2383	1.3902 0500	1.5092 9553	1.6384 7611	1.7785 9219	1.9305 5925	99
100	1.2836 2489	1.3948 3902	1.5155 8426	1.6466 6849	1.7889 6731	1.9434 2965	100

453

Table A-1 (Cont.)

n	$\frac{1}{4}\%$	$\frac{1}{3}\%$	$\frac{5}{12}\%$	$\frac{1}{2}\%$	$\frac{7}{12}\%$	$\frac{2}{3}\%$	n
101	1.2868 3395	1.3994 8848	1.5218 9919	1.6549 0183	1.7994 0295	1.9563 8585	101
102	1.2900 5104	1.4041 5344	1.5282 4044	1.6631 7634	1.8098 9947	1.9694 2842	102
103	1.2932 7616	1.4088 3395	1.5346 0811	1.6714 9223	1.8204 5722	1.9825 5794	103
104	1.2965 0935	1.4135 3007	1.5410 0231	1.6798 4969	1.8310 7655	1.9957 7499	104
105	1.2997 5063	1.4182 4183	1.5474 2315	1.6882 4894	1.8417 5783	2.0090 8016	105
106	1.3030 0000	1.4229 6931	1.5538 7075	1.6966 9018	1.8525 0142	2.0224 7403	106
107	1.3062 5750	1.4277 1254	1.5603 4521	1.7051 7363	1.8633 0768	2.0359 5719	107
108	1.3095 2315	1.4324 7158	1.5668 4665	1.7136 9950	1.8741 7697	2.0495 3024	108
109	1.3127 9696	1.4372 4649	1.5733 7518	1.7222 6800	1.8851 0967	2.0631 9377	109
110	1.3160 7895	1.4420 3731	1.5799 3091	1.7308 7934	1.8961 0614	2.0769 4840	110
111	1.3193 6915	1.4468 4410	1.5865 1395	1.7395 3373	1.9071 6676	2.0907 9472	111
112	1.3226 6757	1.4516 6691	1.5931 2443	1.7482 3140	1.9182 9190	2.1047 3335	112
113	1.3259 7424	1.4565 0580	1.5997 6245	1.7569 7256	1.9294 8194	2.1187 6491	113
114	1.3292 8917	1.4613 6082	1.6064 2812	1.7657 5742	1.9407 3725	2.1328 9000	114
115	1.3326 1240	1.4662 3202	1.6131 2157	1.7745 8621	1.9520 5822	2.1471 0927	115
116	1.3359 4393	1.4711 1946	1.6198 4291	1.7834 5914	1.9634 4522	2.1614 2333	116
117	1.3392 8379	1.4760 2320	1.6265 9226	1.7923 7644	1.9748 9865	2.1758 3282	117
118	1.3426 3200	1.4809 4327	1.6333 6973	1.8013 3832	1.9864 1890	2.1903 3837	118
119	1.3459 8858	1.4858 7975	1.6401 7543	1.8103 4501	1.9980 0634	2.2049 4063	119
120	1.3493 5355	1.4908 3268	1.6470 0950	1.8193 9673	2.0096 6138	2.2196 4023	120
121	1.3527 2693	1.4958 0212	1.6538 7204	1.8284 9372	2.0213 8440	2.2344 3784	121
122	1.3561 0875	1.5007 8813	1.6607 6317	1.8376 3619	2.0331 7581	2.2493 3409	122
123	1.3594 9902	1.5057 9076	1.6676 8302	1.8468 2437	2.0450 3600	2.2643 2965	123
124	1.3628 9777	1.5108 1006	1.6746 3170	1.8560 5849	2.0569 6538	2.2794 2518	124
125	1.3663 0501	1.5158 4609	1.6816 0933	1.8653 3878	2.0689 6434	2.2946 2135	125
126	1.3697 2077	1.5208 9892	1.6886 1603	1.8746 6548	2.0810 3330	2.3099 1882	126
127	1.3731 4508	1.5259 6858	1.6956 5193	1.8840 3880	2.0931 7266	2.3253 1828	127
128	1.3765 7794	1.5310 5514	1.7027 1715	1.8934 5900	2.1053 8284	2.3408 2040	128
129	1.3800 1938	1.5361 5866	1.7098 1181	1.9029 2629	2.1176 6424	2.3564 2587	129
130	1.3834 6943	1.5412 7919	1.7169 3602	1.9124 4092	2.1300 1728	2.3721 3538	130
131	1.3869 2811	1.5464 1678	1.7240 8992	1.9220 0313	2.1424 4238	2.3879 4962	131
132	1.3903 9543	1.5515 7151	1.7312 7363	1.9316 1314	2.1549 3996	2.4038 6928	132
133	1.3938 7142	1.5567 4341	1.7384 8727	1.9412 7121	2.1675 1044	2.4198 9507	133
134	1.3973 5609	1.5619 3256	1.7457 3097	1.9509 7757	2.1801 5425	2.4360 2771	134
135	1.4008 4948	1.5671 3900	1.7530 0485	1.9607 3245	2.1928 7182	2.4522 6789	135
136	1.4043 5161	1.5723 6279	1.7603 0903	1.9705 3612	2.2056 6357	2.4686 1635	136
137	1.4078 6249	1.5776 0400	1.7676 4365	1.9803 8880	2.2185 2994	2.4850 7379	137
138	1.4113 8214	1.5828 6268	1.7750 0884	1.9902 9074	2.2314 7137	2.5016 4095	138
139	1.4149 1060	1.5881 3889	1.7824 0471	2.0002 4219	2.2444 8828	2.5183 1855	139
140	1.4184 4787	1.5934 3269	1.7898 3139	2.0102 4340	2.2575 8113	2.5351 0734	140
141	1.4219 9399	1.5987 4413	1.7972 8902	2.0202 9462	2.2707 5036	2.5520 0806	141
142	1.4255 4898	1.6040 7328	1.8047 7773	2.0303 9609	2.2839 9640	2.5690 2145	142
143	1.4291 1285	1.6094 2019	1.8122 9763	2.0405 4808	2.2973 1971	2.5861 4826	143
144	1.4326 8563	1.6147 8492	1.8198 4887	2.0507 5082	2.3107 2074	2.6033 8924	144
145	1.4362 6735	1.6201 6754	1.8274 3158	2.0610 0457	2.3241 9995	2.6207 4517	145
146	1.4398 5802	1.6255 6810	1.8350 4588	2.0713 0959	2.3377 5778	2.6382 1681	146
147	1.4434 5766	1.6309 8666	1.8426 9190	2.0816 6614	2.3513 9470	2.6558 0492	147
148	1.4470 6631	1.6364 2328	1.8503 6978	2.0920 7447	2.3651 1117	2.6735 1028	148
149	1.4506 8397	1.6418 7802	1.8580 7966	2.1025 3484	2.3789 0765	2.6913 3369	149
150	1.4543 1068	1.6473 5095	1.8658 2166	2.1130 4752	2.3927 8461	2.7092 7591	150

Table A-1 (Cont.)

n	$\frac{3}{4}\%$	1%	$1\frac{1}{4}\%$	$1\frac{1}{2}\%$	$1\frac{3}{4}\%$	2%	n
1	1.0075 0000	1.0100 0000	1.0125 0000	1.0150 0000	1.0175 0000	1.0200 0000	1
2	1.0150 5625	1.0201 0000	1.0251 5625	1.0302 2500	1.0353 0625	1.0404 0000	2
3	1.0226 6917	1.0303 0100	1.0379 7070	1.0456 7838	1.0534 2411	1.0612 0800	3
4	1.0303 3919	1.0406 0401	1.0509 4534	1.0613 6355	1.0718 5903	1.0824 3216	4
5	1.0380 6673	1.0510 1005	1.0640 8215	1.0772 8400	1.0906 1656	1.1040 8080	5
6	1.0458 5224	1.0615 2015	1.0773 8318	1.0934 4326	1.1097 0235	1.1261 6242	6
7	1.0536 9613	1.0721 3535	1.0908 5047	1.1098 4491	1.1291 2215	1.1486 8567	7
8	1.0615 9885	1.0828 5671	1.1044 8610	1.1264 9259	1.1488 8178	1.1716 5938	8
9	1.0695 6084	1.0936 8527	1.1182 9218	1.1433 8998	1.1689 8721	1.1950 9257	9
10	1.0775 8255	1.1046 2213	1.1322 7083	1.1605 4083	1.1894 4449	1.2189 9442	10
11	1.0856 6441	1.1156 6835	1.1464 2422	1.1779 4894	1.2102 5977	1.2433 7431	11
12	1.0938 0690	1.1268 2503	1.1607 5452	1.1956 1817	1.2314 3931	1.2682 4179	12
13	1.1020 1045	1.1380 9328	1.1752 6395	1.2135 5244	1.2529 8950	1.2936 0663	13
14	1.1102 7553	1.1494 7421	1.1899 5475	1.2317 5573	1.2749 1682	1.3194 7876	14
15	1.1186 0259	1.1609 6896	1.2048 2918	1.2502 3207	1.2972 2786	1.3458 6834	15
16	1.1269 9211	1.1725 7864	1.2198 8955	1.2689 8555	1.3199 2935	1.3727 8571	16
17	1.1354 4455	1.1843 0443	1.2351 3817	1.2880 2033	1.3430 2811	1.4002 4142	17
18	1.1439 6039	1.1961 4748	1.2505 7739	1.3073 4064	1.3665 3111	1.4282 4625	18
19	1.1525 4009	1.2081 0895	1.2662 0961	1.3269 5075	1.3904 4540	1.4568 1117	19
20	1.1611 8414	1.2201 9004	1.2820 3723	1.3468 5501	1.4147 7820	1.4859 4740	20
21	1.1698 9302	1.2323 9194	1.2980 6270	1.3670 5783	1.4395 3681	1.5156 6634	21
22	1.1786 6722	1.2447 1586	1.3142 8848	1.3875 6370	1.4647 2871	1.5459 7967	22
23	1.1875 0723	1.2571 6302	1.3307 1709	1.4083 7715	1.4903 6146	1.5768 9926	23
24	1.1964 1353	1.2697 3465	1.3473 5105	1.4295 0281	1.5164 4279	1.6084 3725	24
25	1.2053 8663	1.2824 3200	1.3641 9294	1.4509 4535	1.5429 8054	1.6406 0599	25
26	1.2144 2703	1.2952 5631	1.3812 4535	1.4727 0953	1.5699 8269	1.6734 1811	26
27	1.2235 3523	1.3082 0888	1.3985 1092	1.4948 0018	1.5974 5739	1.7068 8648	27
28	1.2327 1175	1.3212 9097	1.4159 9230	1.5172 2218	1.6254 1290	1.7410 2421	28
29	1.2419 5709	1.3345 0388	1.4336 9221	1.5399 8051	1.6538 5762	1.7758 4469	29
30	1.2512 7176	1.3478 4892	1.4516 1336	1.5630 8022	1.6828 0013	1.8113 6158	30
31	1.2606 5630	1.3613 2740	1.4697 5853	1.5865 2642	1.7122 4913	1.8475 8882	31
32	1.2701 1122	1.3749 4068	1.4881 3051	1.6103 2432	1.7422 1349	1.8845 4059	32
33	1.2796 3706	1.3886 9009	1.5067 3214	1.6344 7918	1.7727 0223	1.9222 3140	33
34	1.2892 3434	1.4025 7699	1.5255 6629	1.6589 9637	1.8037 2452	1.9606 7603	34
35	1.2989 0359	1.4166 0276	1.5446 3587	1.6838 8132	1.8352 8970	1.9998 8955	35
36	1.3086 4537	1.4307 6878	1.5639 4382	1.7091 3954	1.8674 0727	2.0398 8734	36
37	1.3184 6021	1.4450 7647	1.5834 9312	1.7347 7663	1.9000 8689	2.0806 8509	37
38	1.3283 4866	1.4595 2724	1.6032 8678	1.7607 9828	1.9333 3841	2.1222 9879	38
39	1.3383 1128	1.4741 2251	1.6233 2787	1.7872 1025	1.9671 7184	2.1647 4477	39
40	1.3483 4861	1.4888 6373	1.6436 1946	1.8140 1841	2.0015 9734	2.2080 3966	40
41	1.3584 6123	1.5037 5237	1.6641 6471	1.8412 2868	2.0366 2530	2.2522 0046	41
42	1.3686 4969	1.5187 8989	1.6849 6677	1.8688 4712	2.0722 6624	2.2972 4447	42
43	1.3789 1456	1.5339 7779	1.7060 2885	1.8968 7982	2.1085 3090	2.3431 8936	43
44	1.3892 5642	1.5493 1757	1.7273 5421	1.9253 3302	2.1454 3019	2.3900 5314	44
45	1.3996 7584	1.5648 1075	1.7489 4614	1.9542 1301	2.1829 7522	2.4378 5421	45
46	1.4101 7341	1.5804 5885	1.7708 0797	1.9835 2621	2.2211 7728	2.4866 1129	46
47	1.4207 4971	1.5962 6344	1.7929 4306	2.0132 7910	2.2600 4789	2.5363 4351	47
48	1.4314 0533	1.6122 2608	1.8153 5485	2.0434 7829	2.2995 9872	2.5870 7039	48
49	1.4421 4087	1.6283 4834	1.8380 4679	2.0741 3046	2.3398 4170	2.6388 1179	49
50	1.4529 5693	1.6446 3182	1.8610 2237	2.1052 4242	2.3807 8893	2.6915 8803	50

Table A-1 (Cont.)

n	$\frac{3}{4}\%$	1%	$1\frac{1}{4}\%$	$1\frac{1}{2}\%$	$1\frac{3}{4}\%$	2%	n
51	1.4638 5411	1.6610 7814	1.8842 8515	2.1368 2106	2.4224 5274	2.7454 1979	51
52	1.4748 3301	1.6776 8892	1.9078 3872	2.1688 7337	2.4648 4566	2.8003 2819	52
53	1.4858 9426	1.6944 6581	1.9316 8670	2.2014 0647	2.5079 8046	2.8563 3475	53
54	1.4970 3847	1.7114 1047	1.9558 3279	2.2344 2757	2.5518 7012	2.9134 6144	54
55	1.5082 6626	1.7285 2457	1.9802 8070	2.2679 4398	2.5965 2785	2.9717 3067	55
56	1.5195 7825	1.7458 0982	2.0050 3420	2.3019 6314	2.6419 6708	3.0311 6529	56
57	1.5309 7509	1.7632 6792	2.0300 9713	2.3364 9259	2.6882 0151	3.0917 8859	57
58	1.5424 5740	1.7809 0060	2.0554 7335	2.3715 3998	2.7352 4503	3.1536 2436	58
59	1.5540 2583	1.7987 0960	2.0811 6676	2.4071 1308	2.7831 1182	3.2166 9685	59
60	1.5656 8103	1.8166 9670	2.1071 8135	2.4432 1978	2.8318 1628	3.2810 3079	60
61	1.5774 2363	1.8348 6367	2.1335 2111	2.4798 6807	2.8813 7306	3.3466 5140	61
62	1.5892 5431	1.8532 1230	2.1601 9013	2.5170 6609	2.9317 9709	3.4135 8443	62
63	1.6011 7372	1.8717 4443	2.1871 9250	2.5548 2208	2.9831 0354	3.4818 5612	63
64	1.6131 8252	1.8904 6187	2.2145 3241	2.5931 4442	3.0343 0785	3.5514 9324	64
65	1.6252 8139	1.9093 6649	2.2422 1407	2.6320 4158	3.0884 2574	3.6225 2311	65
66	1.6374 7100	1.9284 6015	2.2702 4174	2.6715 2221	3.1424 7319	3.6949 7357	66
67	1.6497 5203	1.9477 4475	2.2986 1976	2.7115 9504	3.1974 6647	3.7688 7304	67
68	1.6621 2517	1.9672 2220	2.3273 5251	2.7522 6896	3.2534 2213	3.8442 5050	68
69	1.6745 9111	1.9868 9442	2.3564 4442	2.7935 5300	3.3103 5702	3.9211 3551	69
70	1.6871 5055	2.0067 6337	2.3858 9997	2.8354 5629	3.3682 8827	3.9995 5822	70
71	1.6998 0418	2.0268 3100	2.4157 2372	2.8779 8814	3.4272 3331	4.0795 4939	71
72	1.7125 5271	2.0470 9931	2.4459 2027	2.9211 5796	3.4872 0990	4.1611 4038	72
73	1.7253 9685	2.0675 7031	2.4764 9427	2.9649 7533	3.5482 3607	4.2443 6318	73
74	1.7383 3733	2.0882 4601	2.5074 5045	3.0094 4996	3.6103 3020	4.3292 5045	74
75	1.7513 7486	2.1091 2847	2.5387 9358	3.0545 9171	3.6735 1098	4.4158 3546	75
76	1.7645 1017	2.1302 1975	2.5705 2850	3.1004 1059	3.7377 9742	4.5041 5216	76
77	1.7777 4400	2.1515 2195	2.6026 6011	3.1469 1674	3.8032 0888	4.5942 3521	77
78	1.7910 7708	2.1730 3717	2.6351 9336	3.1941 2050	3.8697 6503	4.6861 1991	78
79	1.8045 1015	2.1947 6754	2.6681 3327	3.2420 3230	3.9374 8592	4.7798 4231	79
80	1.8180 4398	2.2167 1522	2.7014 8494	3.2906 6279	4.0063 9192	4.8754 3916	80
81	1.8316 7931	2.2388 8237	2.7352 5350	3.3400 2273	4.0765 0378	4.9729 4794	81
82	1.8454 1691	2.2612 7119	2.7694 4417	3.3901 2307	4.1478 4260	5.0724 0690	82
83	1.8592 5753	2.2838 8390	2.8040 6222	3.4409 7492	4.2204 2984	5.1738 5504	83
84	1.8732 0196	2.3067 2274	2.8391 1300	3.4925 8954	4.2942 8737	5.2773 3214	84
85	1.8872 5098	2.3297 8997	2.8746 0191	3.5449 7838	4.3694 3740	5.3828 7878	85
86	1.9014 0536	2.3530 8787	2.9105 3444	3.5981 5306	4.4459 0255	5.4905 3636	86
87	1.9156 6590	2.3766 1875	2.9469 1612	3.6521 2535	4.5237 0584	5.6003 4708	87
88	1.9300 3339	2.4003 8494	2.9837 5257	3.7069 0723	4.6028 7070	5.7123 5402	88
89	1.9445 0865	2.4243 8879	3.0210 4948	3.7625 1084	4.6834 2093	5.8266 0110	89
90	1.9590 9246	2.4486 3267	3.0588 1260	3.8189 4851	4.7653 8080	5.9431 3313	90
91	1.9737 8565	2.4731 1900	3.0970 4775	3.8762 3273	4.8487 7496	6.0619 9579	91
92	1.9885 8905	2.4978 5019	3.1357 6085	3.9343 7622	4.9336 2853	6.1832 3570	92
93	2.0035 0346	2.5228 2869	3.1749 5786	3.9933 9187	5.0199 6703	6.3069 0042	93
94	2.0185 2974	2.5480 5698	3.2146 4483	4.0532 9275	5.1078 1645	6.4330 3843	94
95	2.0336 6871	2.5735 3755	3.2548 2789	4.1140 9214	5.1972 0324	6.5616 9920	95
96	2.0489 2123	2.5992 7293	3.2955 1324	4.1758 0352	5.2881 5429	6.6929 3318	96
97	2.0642 8814	2.6252 6565	3.3367 0716	4.2384 4057	5.3806 9699	6.8267 9184	97
98	2.0797 7030	2.6515 1831	3.3784 1600	4.3020 1718	5.4748 5919	6.9633 2768	98
99	2.0953 6858	2.6780 3349	3.4206 4620	4.3665 4744	5.5706 6923	7.1025 9423	99
100	2.1110 8384	2.7048 1383	3.4634 0427	4.4320 4565	5.6681 5594	7.2446 4612	100

Table A-1 (Cont.)

n	2½%	3%	3½%	4%	4½%	5%	n
1	1.0250 0000	1.0300 0000	1.0350 0000	1.0400 0000	1.0450 0000	1.0500 0000	1
2	1.0506 2500	1.0609 0000	1.0712 2500	1.0816 0000	1.0920 2500	1.1025 0000	2
3	1.0768 9063	1.0927 2700	1.1087 1788	1.1248 6400	1.1411 6613	1.1576 2500	3
4	1.1038 1289	1.1255 0881	1.1475 2300	1.1698 5856	1.1925 1860	1.2155 0625	4
5	1.1314 0821	1.1592 7407	1.1876 8631	1.2166 5290	1.2461 8194	1.2762 8156	5
6	1.1596 9342	1.1940 5230	1.2292 5533	1.2653 1902	1.3022 6012	1.3400 9564	6
7	1.1886 8575	1.2298 7387	1.2722 7926	1.3159 3178	1.3608 6183	1.4071 0042	7
8	1.2184 0290	1.2667 7008	1.3168 0904	1.3685 6905	1.4221 0061	1.4774 5544	8
9	1.2488 6297	1.3047 7318	1.3628 9735	1.4233 1181	1.4860 9514	1.5513 2822	9
10	1.2800 8454	1.3439 1638	1.4105 9876	1.4802 4428	1.5529 6942	1.6288 9463	10
11	1.3120 8666	1.3842 3387	1.4599 6972	1.5394 5406	1.6228 5305	1.7103 3936	11
12	1.3448 8882	1.4257 6089	1.5110 6866	1.6010 3222	1.6958 8143	1.7958 5633	12
13	1.3785 1104	1.4685 3371	1.5639 5606	1.6650 7351	1.7721 9610	1.8856 4914	13
14	1.4129 7382	1.5125 8972	1.6186 9452	1.7316 7645	1.8519 4492	1.9799 3160	14
15	1.4482 9817	1.5579 6742	1.6753 4883	1.8009 4351	1.9352 8244	2.0789 2818	15
16	1.4845 0562	1.6047 0644	1.7339 8604	1.8729 8125	2.0223 7015	2.1828 7459	16
17	1.5216 1826	1.6528 4763	1.7946 7555	1.9479 0050	2.1133 7681	2.2920 1832	17
18	1.5596 5872	1.7024 3306	1.8574 8920	2.0258 1652	2.2084 7877	2.4066 1923	18
19	1.5986 5019	1.7535 0605	1.9225 0132	2.1068 4918	2.3078 6031	2.5269 5020	19
20	1.6386 1644	1.8061 1123	1.9897 8886	2.1911 2314	2.4117 1402	2.6532 9771	20
21	1.6795 8185	1.8602 9457	2.0594 3147	2.2787 6807	2.5202 4116	2.7859 6259	21
22	1.7215 7140	1.9161 0341	2.1315 1158	2.3699 1879	2.6336 5201	2.9252 6072	22
23	1.7646 1068	1.9735 8651	2.2061 1448	2.4647 1554	2.7521 6635	3.0715 2376	23
24	1.8087 2595	2.0327 9411	2.2833 2849	2.5633 0416	2.8760 1383	3.2250 9994	24
25	1.8539 4410	2.0937 7793	2.3632 4498	2.6658 3633	3.0054 3446	3.3863 5494	25
26	1.9002 9270	2.1565 9127	2.4459 5856	2.7724 6978	3.1406 7901	3.5556 7269	26
27	1.9478 0002	2.2212 8901	2.5315 6711	2.8833 6858	3.2820 0956	3.7334 5632	27
28	1.9964 9502	2.2879 2768	2.6201 7196	2.9987 0332	3.4296 9999	3.9201 2914	28
29	2.0464 0739	2.3565 6551	2.7118 7798	3.1186 5145	3.5840 3649	4.1161 3560	29
30	2.0975 6758	2.4272 6247	2.8067 9370	3.2433 9751	3.7453 1813	4.3219 4238	30
31	2.1500 0677	2.5000 8035	2.9050 3148	3.3731 3341	3.9138 5745	4.5380 3949	31
32	2.2037 5694	2.5750 8276	3.0067 0759	3.5080 5875	4.0899 8104	4.7649 4147	32
33	2.2588 5086	2.6523 3524	3.1119 4235	3.6483 8110	4.2740 3018	5.0031 8854	33
34	2.3153 2213	2.7319 0530	3.2208 6033	3.7943 1634	4.4663 6154	5.2533 4797	34
35	2.3732 0519	2.8138 6245	3.3335 9045	3.9460 8899	4.6673 4781	5.5160 1537	35
36	2.4325 3532	2.8982 7833	3.4502 6611	4.1039 3255	4.8773 7846	5.7918 1614	36
37	2.4933 4870	2.9852 2668	3.5710 2543	4.2680 8986	5.0968 6049	6.0814 0694	37
38	2.5556 8242	3.0747 8348	3.6960 1132	4.4388 1345	5.3262 1921	6.3854 7729	38
39	2.6195 7448	3.1670 2698	3.8253 7171	4.6163 6599	5.5658 9908	6.7047 5115	39
40	2.6850 6384	3.2620 3779	3.9592 5972	4.8010 2063	5.8163 6454	7.0399 8871	40
41	2.7521 9043	3.3598 9893	4.0978 3381	4.9930 6145	6.0781 0094	7.3919 8815	41
42	2.8209 9520	3.4606 9589	4.2412 5799	5.1927 8391	6.3516 1548	7.7615 8756	42
43	2.8915 2008	3.5645 1677	4.3897 0202	5.4004 9527	6.6374 3818	8.1496 6693	43
44	2.9638 0808	3.6714 5227	4.5433 4160	5.6165 1508	6.9361 2290	8.5571 5028	44
45	3.0379 0328	3.7815 9584	4.7023 5855	5.8411 7568	7.2482 4843	8.9850 0779	45
46	3.1138 5086	3.8950 4372	4.8669 4110	6.0748 2271	7.5744 1961	9.4342 5818	46
47	3.1916 9713	4.0118 9503	5.0372 8404	6.3178 1562	7.9152 6849	9.9059 7109	47
48	3.2714 8956	4.1322 5188	5.2135 8898	6.5705 2824	8.2714 5557	10.4012 6965	48
49	3.3532 7680	4.2562 1944	5.3960 6459	6.8333 4937	8.6436 7107	10.9213 3313	49
50	3.4371 0872	4.3839 0602	5.5849 2686	7.1066 8335	9.0326 3627	11.4673 9979	50

Table A-1 (Cont.)

n	2½%	3%	3½%	4%	4½%	5%	n
51	3.5230 3644	4.5154 2320	5.7803 9930	7.3909 5068	9.4391 0490	12.0407 6978	51
52	3.6111 1235	4.6508 8590	5.9827 1327	7.6865 8871	9.8638 6463	12.6428 0826	52
53	3.7013 9016	4.7904 1247	6.1921 0824	7.9940 5226	10.3077 3853	13.2749 4868	53
54	3.7939 2491	4.9341 2485	6.4088 3202	8.3138 1435	10.7715 8677	13.9386 9611	54
55	3.8887 7303	5.0821 4859	6.6331 4114	8.6463 6692	11.2563 0817	14.6356 3092	55
56	3.9859 9236	5.2346 1305	6.8653 0108	8.9922 2160	11.7628 4204	15.3674 1246	56
57	4.0856 4217	5.3916 5144	7.1055 8662	9.3519 1046	12.2921 6993	16.1357 8309	57
58	4.1877 8322	5.5534 0098	7.3542 8215	9.7259 8688	12.8453 1758	16.9425 7224	58
59	4.2924 7780	5.7200 0301	7.6116 8203	10.1150 2635	13.4233 5687	17.7897 0085	59
60	4.3997 8975	5.8916 0310	7.8780 9090	10.5196 2741	14.0274 0793	18.6791 8589	60
61	4.5097 8449	6.0683 5120	8.1538 2408	10.9404 1250	14.6586 4129	19.6131 4519	61
62	4.6225 2910	6.2504 0173	8.4392 0793	11.3780 2900	15.3182 8014	20.5938 0245	62
63	4.7380 9233	6.4379 1379	8.7345 8020	11.8331 5016	16.0076 0275	21.6234 9257	63
64	4.8565 4464	6.6310 5120	9.0402 9051	12.3064 7617	16.7279 4487	22.7046 6720	64
65	4.9779 5826	6.8299 8273	9.3567 0068	12.7987 3522	17.4807 0239	23.8399 0056	65
66	5.1024 0721	7.0348 8222	9.6841 8520	13.3106 8463	18.2673 3400	25.0318 9559	66
67	5.2299 6739	7.2459 2868	10.0231 3168	13.8431 1201	19.0893 6403	26.2834 9037	67
68	5.3607 1658	7.4633 0654	10.3739 4129	14.3968 3649	19.9483 8541	27.5976 6488	68
69	5.4947 3449	7.6872 0574	10.7370 2924	14.9727 0995	20.8460 6276	28.9775 4813	69
70	5.6321 0286	7.9178 2191	11.1128 2526	15.5716 1835	21.7841 3558	30.4264 2554	70
71	5.7729 0543	8.1553 5657	11.5017 7414	16.1944 8308	22.7644 2168	31.9477 4681	71
72	5.9172 2806	8.4000 1727	11.9043 3624	16.8422 6241	23.7888 2066	33.5451 3415	72
73	6.0651 5876	8.6520 1778	12.3209 8801	17.5159 5290	24.8593 1759	35.2223 9086	73
74	6.2167 8773	8.9115 7832	12.7522 2259	18.2165 9102	25.9779 8688	36.9835 1040	74
75	6.3722 0743	9.1789 2567	13.1985 5038	18.9452 5466	27.1469 9629	38.8326 8592	75
76	6.5315 1261	9.4542 9344	13.6604 9964	19.7030 6485	28.3686 1112	40.7743 2022	76
77	6.6948 0043	9.7379 2224	14.1386 1713	20.4911 8744	29.6451 9862	42.8130 3623	77
78	6.8621 7044	10.0300 5991	14.6334 6873	21.3108 3494	30.9792 3256	44.9536 8804	78
79	7.0337 2470	10.3309 6171	15.1456 4013	22.1632 6834	32.3732 9802	47.2013 7244	79
80	7.2095 6782	10.6408 9056	15.6757 3754	23.0497 9907	33.8300 9643	49.5614 4107	80
81	7.3898 0701	10.9601 1727	16.2243 8835	23.9717 9103	35.3524 5077	52.0395 1312	81
82	7.5745 5219	11.2889 2079	16.7922 4195	24.9306 6267	36.9433 1106	54.6414 8878	82
83	7.7639 1599	11.6275 8842	17.3799 7041	25.9278 8918	38.6057 6006	57.3735 6322	83
84	7.9580 1389	11.9764 1607	17.9882 6938	26.9650 0475	40.3430 1926	60.2422 4138	84
85	8.1569 6424	12.3357 0855	18.6178 5881	28.0436 0494	42.1584 5513	63.2543 5344	85
86	8.3608 8834	12.7057 7981	19.2694 8387	29.1653 4914	44.0555 8561	66.4170 7112	86
87	8.5699 1055	13.0869 5320	19.9439 1580	30.3319 6310	46.0380 8696	69.7379 2467	87
88	8.7841 5832	13.4795 6180	20.6419 5285	31.5452 4163	48.1098 0087	73.2248 2091	88
89	9.0037 6228	13.8839 4865	21.3644 2120	32.8070 5129	50.2747 4191	76.8860 6195	89
90	9.2288 5633	14.3004 6711	22.1121 7595	34.1193 3334	52.5371 0530	80.7303 6505	90
91	9.4595 7774	14.7294 8112	22.8861 0210	35.4841 0668	54.9012 7503	84.7668 8330	91
92	9.6960 6718	15.1713 6556	23.6871 1568	36.9034 7094	57.3718 3241	89.0052 2747	92
93	9.9384 6886	15.6265 0652	24.5161 6473	38.3796 0978	59.9535 6487	93.4554 8884	93
94	10.1869 3058	16.0953 0172	25.3742 3049	39.9147 9417	62.6544 7529	98.1282 6328	94
95	10.4416 0385	16.5781 6077	26.2623 2856	41.5113 8594	65.4707 9168	103.0346 7645	95
96	10.7026 4395	17.0755 0559	27.1815 1006	43.1718 4138	68.4169 7730	108.1864 1027	96
97	10.9702 1004	17.5877 7076	28.1328 6291	44.8987 1503	71.4957 4128	113.5957 3078	97
98	11.2444 6530	18.1154 0388	29.1175 1311	46.6946 6363	74.7130 4964	119.2755 1732	98
99	11.5255 7693	18.6588 6600	30.1366 2607	48.5624 5018	78.0751 3687	125.2392 9319	99
100	11.8137 1635	19.2186 3198	31.1914 0798	50.5049 4818	81.5885 1803	131.5012 5785	100

Table A-1 (Cont.)

n	5½%	6%	6½%	7%	7½%	8%	n
1	1.0550 0000	1.0600 0000	1.0650 0000	1.0700 0000	1.0750 0000	1.0800 0000	1
2	1.1130 2500	1.1236 0000	1.1342 2500	1.1449 0000	1.1556 2500	1.1664 0000	2
3	1.1742 4138	1.1910 1600	1.2079 4963	1.2250 4300	1.2422 9688	1.2597 1200	3
4	1.2388 2465	1.2624 7696	1.2864 6635	1.3107 9601	1.3354 6914	1.3604 8896	4
5	1.3069 6001	1.3382 2558	1.3700 8666	1.4025 5173	1.4356 2933	1.4693 2808	5
6	1.3788 4281	1.4185 1911	1.4591 4230	1.5007 3035	1.5433 0153	1.5868 7432	6
7	1.4546 7916	1.5036 3026	1.5539 8655	1.6057 8148	1.6590 4914	1.7138 2427	7
8	1.5346 8651	1.5938 4807	1.6549 9567	1.7181 8618	1.7834 7783	1.8509 3021	8
9	1.6190 9427	1.6894 7896	1.7625 7039	1.8384 5921	1.9172 3866	1.9990 0463	9
10	1.7081 4446	1.7908 4770	1.8771 3747	1.9671 5136	2.0610 3156	2.1589 2500	10
11	1.8020 9240	1.8982 9856	1.9991 5140	2.1048 5195	2.2156 0893	2.3316 3900	11
12	1.9012 0749	2.0121 9647	2.1290 9624	2.2521 9159	2.3817 7960	2.5181 7012	12
13	2.0057 7390	2.1329 2826	2.2674 8750	2.4098 4500	2.5604 1307	2.7196 2373	13
14	2.1160 9146	2.2609 0396	2.4148 7418	2.5785 3415	2.7524 4405	2.9371 9362	14
15	2.2324 7649	2.3965 5819	2.5718 4101	2.7590 3154	2.9588 7735	3.1721 6911	15
16	2.3552 6270	2.5403 5168	2.7390 1067	2.9521 6375	3.1807 9315	3.4259 4264	16
17	2.4848 0215	2.6927 7279	2.9170 4637	3.1588 1521	3.4193 5264	3.7000 1805	17
18	2.6214 6627	2.8543 3915	3.1066 5438	3.3799 3228	3.6758 0409	3.9960 1950	18
19	2.7656 4691	3.0255 9950	3.3085 8691	3.6165 2754	3.9514 8940	4.3157 0106	19
20	2.9177 5749	3.2071 3547	3.5236 4506	3.8696 8446	4.2478 5110	4.6609 5714	20
21	3.0782 3415	3.3995 6360	3.7526 8199	4.1405 6237	4.5664 3993	5.0338 3372	21
22	3.2475 3703	3.6035 3742	3.9966 0632	4.4304 0174	4.9089 2293	5.4365 4041	22
23	3.4261 5157	3.8197 4966	4.2563 8573	4.7405 2986	5.2770 9215	5.8714 6365	23
24	3.6145 8990	4.0489 3464	4.5330 5081	5.0723 6695	5.6728 7406	6.3411 8074	24
25	3.8133 9235	4.2918 7072	4.8276 9911	5.4274 3264	6.0983 3961	6.8484 7520	25
26	4.0231 2893	4.5493 8296	5.1414 9955	5.8073 5292	6.5557 1508	7.3963 5321	26
27	4.2444 0102	4.8223 4594	5.4756 9702	6.2138 6763	7.0473 9371	7.9880 6147	27
28	4.4778 4307	5.1116 8670	5.8316 1733	6.6488 3836	7.5759 4824	8.6271 0639	28
29	4.7241 2444	5.4183 8790	6.2106 7245	7.1142 5705	8.1441 4436	9.3172 7490	29
30	4.9839 5129	5.7434 9117	6.6143 6616	7.6122 5504	8.7549 5519	10.0626 5689	30
31	5.2580 6861	6.0881 0064	7.0442 9996	8.1451 1290	9.4115 7683	10.8676 6944	31
32	5.5472 6238	6.4533 8668	7.5021 7946	8.7152 7080	10.1174 4509	11.7370 8300	32
33	5.8523 6181	6.8405 8988	7.9898 2113	9.3253 3975	10.8762 5347	12.6760 4964	33
34	6.1742 4171	7.2510 2528	8.5091 5950	9.9781 1354	11.6919 7248	13.6901 3361	34
35	6.5138 2501	7.6860 8679	9.0622 5487	10.6765 8148	12.5688 7042	14.7853 4429	35
36	6.8720 8538	8.1472 5200	9.6513 0143	11.4239 4219	13.5115 3570	15.9681 7184	36
37	7.2500 5008	8.6360 8712	10.2786 3603	12.2236 1814	14.5249 0088	17.2456 2558	37
38	7.6488 0283	9.1542 5235	10.9467 4737	13.0792 7141	15.6142 6844	18.6252 7563	38
39	8.0694 8699	9.7035 0749	11.6582 8595	13.9948 2041	16.7853 3858	20.1152 9768	39
40	8.5133 0877	10.2857 1794	12.4160 7453	14.9744 5784	18.0442 3897	21.7245 2150	40
41	8.9815 4076	10.9028 6101	13.2231 1938	16.0226 6989	19.3975 5689	23.4624 8322	41
42	9.4755 2550	11.5570 3267	14.0826 2214	17.1442 5678	20.8523 7366	25.3394 8187	42
43	9.9966 7940	12.2504 5463	14.9979 9258	18.3443 5475	22.4163 0168	27.3666 4042	43
44	10.5464 9677	12.9854 8191	15.9728 6209	19.6284 5959	24.0975 2431	29.5559 7166	44
45	11.1265 5409	13.7646 1083	17.0110 9813	21.0024 5176	25.9048 3863	31.9204 4939	45
46	11.7385 1456	14.5904 8748	18.1168 1951	22.4726 2338	27.8477 0153	34.4740 8534	46
47	12.3841 3287	15.4659 1673	19.2944 1278	24.0457 0702	29.9362 7915	37.2320 1217	47
48	13.0652 6017	16.3938 7173	20.5485 4961	25.7289 0651	32.1815 0008	40.2105 7314	48
49	13.7838 4948	17.3775 0403	21.8842 0533	27.5299 2997	34.5951 1259	43.4274 1899	49
50	14.5419 6120	18.4201 5427	23.3066 7868	29.4570 2506	37.1897 4603	46.9016 1251	50

Table A-2
Discount Factors $(1 + i)^{-n}$

n	$\frac{1}{4}\%$	$\frac{1}{3}\%$	$\frac{5}{12}\%$	$\frac{1}{2}\%$	$\frac{7}{12}\%$	$\frac{2}{3}\%$	n
1	0.9975 0623	0.9966 7774	0.9958 5062	0.9950 2488	0.9942 0050	0.9933 7748	1
2	0.9950 1869	0.9933 6652	0.9917 1846	0.9900 7450	0.9884 3463	0.9867 9882	2
3	0.9925 3734	0.9900 6630	0.9876 0345	0.9851 4876	0.9827 0220	0.9802 6373	3
4	0.9900 6219	0.9867 7704	0.9835 0551	0.9802 4752	0.9770 0302	0.9737 7192	4
5	0.9875 9321	0.9834 9871	0.9794 2457	0.9753 7067	0.9713 3688	0.9673 2310	5
6	0.9851 3038	0.9802 3127	0.9753 6057	0.9705 1808	0.9657 0361	0.9609 1699	6
7	0.9826 7370	0.9769 7469	0.9713 1343	0.9656 8963	0.9601 0301	0.9545 5330	7
8	0.9802 2314	0.9737 2893	0.9672 8308	0.9608 8520	0.9545 3489	0.9482 3175	8
9	0.9777 7869	0.9704 9395	0.9632 6946	0.9561 0468	0.9489 9907	0.9419 5207	9
10	0.9753 4034	0.9672 6972	0.9592 7249	0.9513 4794	0.9434 9534	0.9357 1398	10
11	0.9729 0807	0.9640 5620	0.9552 9211	0.9466 1487	0.9380 2354	0.9295 1720	11
12	0.9704 8187	0.9608 5335	0.9513 2824	0.9419 0534	0.9325 8347	0.9233 6145	12
13	0.9680 6171	0.9576 6115	0.9473 8082	0.9372 1924	0.9271 7495	0.9172 4648	13
14	0.9656 4759	0.9544 7955	0.9434 4978	0.9325 5646	0.9217 9779	0.9111 7200	14
15	0.9632 3949	0.9513 0852	0.9395 3505	0.9279 1688	0.9164 5182	0.9051 3775	15
16	0.9608 3740	0.9481 4803	0.9356 3657	0.9233 0037	0.9111 3686	0.8991 4346	16
17	0.9584 4130	0.9449 9803	0.9317 5426	0.9187 0684	0.9058 5272	0.8931 8886	17
18	0.9560 5117	0.9418 5851	0.9278 8806	0.9141 3616	0.9005 9922	0.8872 7371	18
19	0.9536 6700	0.9387 2941	0.9240 3790	0.9095 8822	0.8953 7619	0.8813 9772	19
20	0.9512 8878	0.9356 1071	0.9202 0372	0.9050 6290	0.8901 8346	0.8755 6065	20
21	0.9489 1649	0.9325 0236	0.9163 8544	0.9005 6010	0.8850 2084	0.8697 6224	21
22	0.9465 5011	0.9294 0435	0.9125 8301	0.8960 7971	0.8798 8815	0.8640 0222	22
23	0.9441 8964	0.9263 1663	0.9087 9636	0.8916 2160	0.8747 8524	0.8582 8035	23
24	0.9418 3505	0.9232 3916	0.9050 2542	0.8871 8567	0.8697 1192	0.8525 9638	24
25	0.9394 8634	0.9201 7192	0.9012 7013	0.8827 7181	0.8646 6802	0.8469 5004	25
26	0.9371 4348	0.9171 1487	0.8975 3042	0.8783 7991	0.8596 5338	0.8413 4110	26
27	0.9348 0646	0.9140 6798	0.8938 0623	0.8740 0986	0.8546 6782	0.8357 6931	27
28	0.9324 7527	0.9110 3121	0.8900 9749	0.8696 6155	0.8497 1117	0.8302 3441	28
29	0.9301 4990	0.9080 0453	0.8864 0414	0.8653 3488	0.8447 8327	0.8247 3617	29
30	0.9278 3032	0.9049 8790	0.8827 2611	0.8610 2973	0.8398 8394	0.8192 7434	30
31	0.9255 1653	0.9019 8130	0.8790 6335	0.8567 4600	0.8350 1303	0.8138 4868	31
32	0.9232 0851	0.8989 8468	0.8754 1578	0.8524 8358	0.8301 7037	0.8084 5896	32
33	0.9209 0624	0.8959 9802	0.8717 8335	0.8482 4237	0.8253 5580	0.8031 0492	33
34	0.9186 0972	0.8930 2128	0.8681 6599	0.8440 2226	0.8205 6914	0.7977 8635	34
35	0.9163 1892	0.8900 5444	0.8645 6365	0.8398 2314	0.8158 1025	0.7925 0299	35
36	0.9140 3384	0.8870 9745	0.8609 7624	0.8356 4492	0.8110 7896	0.7872 5463	36
37	0.9117 5445	0.8841 5028	0.8574 0373	0.8314 8748	0.8063 7510	0.7820 4102	37
38	0.9094 8075	0.8812 1290	0.8538 4604	0.8273 5073	0.8016 9853	0.7768 6194	38
39	0.9072 1272	0.8782 8528	0.8503 0311	0.8232 3455	0.7970 4907	0.7717 1716	39
40	0.9049 5034	0.8753 6739	0.8467 7488	0.8191 3886	0.7924 2659	0.7666 0645	40
41	0.9026 9361	0.8724 5920	0.8432 6129	0.8150 6354	0.7878 3091	0.7615 2959	41
42	0.9004 4250	0.8695 6066	0.8397 6228	0.8110 0850	0.7832 6188	0.7564 8635	42
43	0.8981 9701	0.8666 7175	0.8362 7779	0.8069 7363	0.7787 1935	0.7514 7650	43
44	0.8959 5712	0.8637 9245	0.8328 0776	0.8029 5884	0.7742 0316	0.7464 9984	44
45	0.8937 2281	0.8609 2270	0.8293 5212	0.7989 6402	0.7697 1317	0.7415 5613	45
46	0.8914 9407	0.8580 6249	0.8259 1083	0.7949 8907	0.7652 4922	0.7366 4516	46
47	0.8892 7090	0.8552 1179	0.8224 8381	0.7910 3390	0.7608 1115	0.7317 6672	47
48	0.8870 5326	0.8523 7055	0.8190 7102	0.7870 9841	0.7563 9883	0.7269 2058	48
49	0.8848 4116	0.8495 3876	0.8156 7238	0.7831 8250	0.7520 1209	0.7221 0654	49
50	0.8826 3457	0.8467 1637	0.8122 8785	0.7792 8607	0.7476 5079	0.7173 2437	50

From MATHEMATICS OF FINANCE by Frank Ayres. Copyright © 1963 by McGraw-Hill, Inc. Used with permission of McGraw-Hill Book Company.

Table A-2 (Cont.)

n	$\frac{1}{4}\%$	$\frac{1}{3}\%$	$\frac{5}{12}\%$	$\frac{1}{2}\%$	$\frac{7}{12}\%$	$\frac{2}{3}\%$	n
51	0.8804 3349	0.8439 0336	0.8089 1736	0.7754 0902	0.7433 1479	0.7125 7388	51
52	0.8782 3790	0.8410 9969	0.8055 6086	0.7715 5127	0.7390 0393	0.7078 5485	52
53	0.8760 4778	0.8383 0534	0.8022 1828	0.7677 1270	0.7347 1808	0.7031 6707	53
54	0.8738 6312	0.8355 2027	0.7988 8957	0.7638 9324	0.7304 5708	0.6985 1033	54
55	0.8716 8391	0.8327 4446	0.7955 7468	0.7600 9277	0.7262 2079	0.6938 8444	55
56	0.8695 1013	0.8299 7787	0.7922 7354	0.7563 1122	0.7220 0907	0.6892 8918	56
57	0.8673 4178	0.8272 2047	0.7889 8610	0.7525 4847	0.7178 2178	0.6847 2435	57
58	0.8651 7883	0.8244 7222	0.7857 1230	0.7488 0445	0.7136 5877	0.6801 8975	58
59	0.8630 2128	0.8217 3311	0.7824 5208	0.7450 7906	0.7095 1990	0.6756 8518	59
60	0.8608 6911	0.8190 0310	0.7792 0539	0.7413 7220	0.7054 0504	0.6712 1044	60
61	0.8587 2230	0.8162 8216	0.7759 7217	0.7376 8378	0.7013 1404	0.6667 6534	61
62	0.8565 8085	0.8135 7026	0.7727 5237	0.7340 1371	0.6972 4677	0.6623 4968	62
63	0.8544 4474	0.8108 6737	0.7695 4593	0.7303 6190	0.6932 0308	0.6579 6326	63
64	0.8523 1395	0.8081 7346	0.7663 5279	0.7267 2826	0.6891 8285	0.6536 0588	64
65	0.8501 8848	0.8054 8850	0.7631 7291	0.7231 1269	0.6851 8593	0.6492 7737	65
66	0.8480 6831	0.8028 1246	0.7600 0621	0.7195 1512	0.6812 1219	0.6449 7752	66
67	0.8459 5343	0.8001 4531	0.7568 5266	0.7159 3544	0.6772 6150	0.6407 0614	67
68	0.8438 4382	0.7974 8702	0.7537 1219	0.7123 7357	0.6733 3372	0.6364 6306	68
69	0.8417 3947	0.7948 3756	0.7505 8476	0.7088 2943	0.6694 2872	0.6322 4807	69
70	0.8396 4037	0.7921 9690	0.7474 7030	0.7053 0291	0.6655 4637	0.6280 6100	70
71	0.8375 4650	0.7895 6502	0.7443 6876	0.7017 9394	0.6616 8653	0.6239 0165	71
72	0.8354 5786	0.7869 4188	0.7412 8009	0.6983 0243	0.6578 4908	0.6197 6985	72
73	0.8333 7442	0.7843 2745	0.7382 0424	0.6948 2829	0.6540 3388	0.6156 6542	73
74	0.8312 9618	0.7817 2171	0.7351 4115	0.6913 7143	0.6502 4087	0.6115 8816	74
75	0.8292 2312	0.7791 2463	0.7320 9078	0.6879 3177	0.6464 6973	0.6075 3791	75
76	0.8271 5523	0.7765 3618	0.7290 5306	0.6845 0923	0.6427 2053	0.6035 1448	76
77	0.8250 9250	0.7739 5632	0.7260 2794	0.6811 0371	0.6389 9307	0.5995 1769	77
78	0.8230 3491	0.7713 8504	0.7230 1537	0.6777 1513	0.6352 8723	0.5955 4738	78
79	0.8209 8246	0.7688 2230	0.7200 1531	0.6743 4342	0.6316 0288	0.5916 0336	79
80	0.8189 3512	0.7662 6807	0.7170 2770	0.6709 8847	0.6279 3990	0.5876 8545	80
81	0.8168 9289	0.7637 2233	0.7140 5248	0.6676 5022	0.6242 9816	0.5837 9350	81
82	0.8148 5575	0.7611 8505	0.7110 8960	0.6643 2858	0.6206 7754	0.5799 2732	82
83	0.8128 2369	0.7586 5619	0.7081 3902	0.6610 2346	0.6170 7792	0.5760 8674	83
84	0.8107 9670	0.7561 3574	0.7052 0069	0.6577 3479	0.6134 9917	0.5722 7159	84
85	0.8087 7476	0.7536 2366	0.7022 7454	0.6544 6248	0.6099 4118	0.5684 8171	85
86	0.8067 5787	0.7511 1993	0.6993 6054	0.6512 0644	0.6064 0382	0.5647 1693	86
87	0.8047 4600	0.7486 2451	0.6964 5863	0.6479 6661	0.6028 8698	0.5609 7709	87
88	0.8027 3915	0.7461 3739	0.6935 6876	0.6447 4290	0.5993 9054	0.5572 6201	88
89	0.8007 3731	0.7436 5853	0.6906 9088	0.6415 3522	0.5959 1437	0.5535 7153	89
90	0.7987 4046	0.7411 8790	0.6878 2495	0.6383 4350	0.5924 5836	0.5499 0549	90
91	0.7967 4859	0.7387 2548	0.6849 7090	0.6351 6766	0.5890 2240	0.5462 6374	91
92	0.7947 6168	0.7362 7125	0.6821 2870	0.6320 0763	0.5856 0636	0.5426 4610	92
93	0.7927 7973	0.7338 2516	0.6792 9829	0.6288 6331	0.5822 1014	0.5390 5241	93
94	0.7908 0273	0.7313 8720	0.6764 7962	0.6257 3464	0.5788 3361	0.5354 8253	94
95	0.7888 3065	0.7289 5735	0.6736 7265	0.6226 2153	0.5754 7666	0.5319 3629	95
96	0.7868 6349	0.7265 3556	0.6708 7733	0.6195 2391	0.5721 3918	0.5284 1353	96
97	0.7849 0124	0.7241 2182	0.6680 9361	0.6164 4170	0.5688 2106	0.5249 1410	97
98	0.7829 4388	0.7217 1610	0.6653 2143	0.6133 7483	0.5655 2218	0.5214 3785	98
99	0.7809 9140	0.7193 1837	0.6625 6076	0.6103 2321	0.5622 4243	0.5179 8462	99
100	0.7790 4379	0.7169 2861	0.6598 1155	0.6072 8678	0.5589 8171	0.5145 5426	100

Table A-2 (Cont.)

n	$\frac{1}{4}\%$	$\frac{1}{3}\%$	$\frac{5}{12}\%$	$\frac{1}{2}\%$	$\frac{7}{12}\%$	$\frac{2}{3}\%$	n
101	0.7771 0104	0.7145 4679	0.6570 7374	0.6042 6545	0.5557 3989	0.5111 4661	101
102	0.7751 6313	0.7121 7288	0.6543 4730	0.6012 5915	0.5525 1688	0.5077 6154	102
103	0.7732 3006	0.7098 0686	0.6516 3216	0.5982 6781	0.5493 1255	0.5043 9888	103
104	0.7713 0180	0.7074 4869	0.6489 2829	0.5952 9136	0.5461 2681	0.5010 5849	104
105	0.7693 7836	0.7050 9837	0.6462 3565	0.5923 2971	0.5429 5955	0.4977 4022	105
106	0.7674 5971	0.7027 5585	0.6435 5417	0.5893 8279	0.5398 1065	0.4944 4393	106
107	0.7655 4584	0.7004 2111	0.6408 8382	0.5864 5054	0.5366 8002	0.4911 6946	107
108	0.7636 3675	0.6980 9413	0.6382 2455	0.5835 3288	0.5335 6754	0.4879 1669	108
109	0.7617 3242	0.6957 7488	0.6355 7632	0.5806 2973	0.5304 7312	0.4846 8545	109
110	0.7598 3284	0.6934 6334	0.6329 3907	0.5777 4102	0.5273 9664	0.4814 7561	110
111	0.7579 3799	0.6911 5947	0.6303 1277	0.5748 6669	0.5243 3800	0.4782 8703	111
112	0.7560 4787	0.6888 6326	0.6276 9736	0.5720 0666	0.5212 9710	0.4751 1957	112
113	0.7541 6247	0.6865 7468	0.6250 9281	0.5691 6085	0.5182 7383	0.4719 7308	113
114	0.7522 8176	0.6842 9370	0.6224 9906	0.5663 2921	0.5152 6810	0.4688 4743	114
115	0.7504 0575	0.6820 2030	0.6199 1608	0.5635 1165	0.5122 7980	0.4657 4248	115
116	0.7485 3441	0.6797 5445	0.6173 4381	0.5607 0811	0.5093 0884	0.4626 5809	116
117	0.7466 6774	0.6774 9613	0.6147 8222	0.5579 1852	0.5063 5510	0.4595 9413	117
118	0.7448 0573	0.6752 4531	0.6122 3126	0.5551 4280	0.5034 1849	0.4565 5046	118
119	0.7429 4836	0.6730 0198	0.6096 9088	0.5523 8090	0.5004 9891	0.4535 2695	119
120	0.7410 9562	0.6707 6608	0.6071 6104	0.5496 3273	0.4975 9627	0.4505 2346	120
121	0.7392 4750	0.6685 3763	0.6046 4170	0.5468 9824	0.4947 1046	0.4475 3986	121
122	0.7374 0399	0.6663 1657	0.6021 3281	0.5441 7736	0.4918 4138	0.4445 7602	122
123	0.7355 6508	0.6641 0289	0.5996 3434	0.5414 7001	0.4889 8895	0.4416 3181	123
124	0.7337 3075	0.6618 9657	0.5971 4623	0.5387 7612	0.4861 5305	0.4387 0710	124
125	0.7319 0100	0.6596 9758	0.5946 6844	0.5360 9565	0.4833 3361	0.4358 0175	125
126	0.7300 7581	0.6575 0590	0.5922 0094	0.5334 2850	0.4805 3051	0.4329 1565	126
127	0.7282 5517	0.6553 2149	0.5897 4367	0.5307 7463	0.4777 4367	0.4300 4866	127
128	0.7264 3907	0.6531 4434	0.5872 9660	0.5281 3396	0.4749 7300	0.4272 0065	128
129	0.7246 2750	0.6509 7443	0.5848 5969	0.5255 0643	0.4722 1839	0.4243 7151	129
130	0.7228 2045	0.6488 1172	0.5824 3288	0.5228 9197	0.4694 7976	0.4215 6110	130
131	0.7210 1791	0.6466 5620	0.5800 1615	0.5202 9052	0.4667 5701	0.4187 6930	131
132	0.7192 1986	0.6445 0784	0.5776 0944	0.5177 0201	0.4640 5005	0.4159 9600	132
133	0.7174 2629	0.6423 6662	0.5752 1273	0.5151 2637	0.4613 5879	0.4132 4106	133
134	0.7156 3720	0.6402 3251	0.5728 2595	0.5125 6356	0.4586 8314	0.4105 0436	134
135	0.7138 5257	0.6381 0549	0.5704 4908	0.5100 1349	0.4560 2301	0.4077 8579	135
136	0.7120 7239	0.6359 8554	0.5680 8207	0.5074 7611	0.4533 7830	0.4050 8522	136
137	0.7102 9664	0.6338 7263	0.5657 2488	0.5049 5135	0.4507 4893	0.4024 0254	137
138	0.7085 2533	0.6317 6674	0.5633 7748	0.5024 3916	0.4481 3481	0.3997 3762	138
139	0.7067 5843	0.6296 6785	0.5610 3981	0.4999 3946	0.4455 3585	0.3970 9035	139
140	0.7049 9595	0.6275 7593	0.5587 1185	0.4974 5220	0.4429 5197	0.3944 6061	140
141	0.7032 3785	0.6254 9096	0.5563 9354	0.4949 7731	0.4403 8306	0.3918 4829	141
142	0.7014 8414	0.6234 1292	0.5540 8485	0.4925 1474	0.4378 2906	0.3892 5327	142
143	0.6997 3480	0.6213 4178	0.5517 8574	0.4900 6442	0.4352 8987	0.3866 7543	143
144	0.6979 8983	0.6192 7752	0.5494 9618	0.4876 2628	0.4327 6541	0.3841 1467	144
145	0.6962 4921	0.6172 2012	0.5472 1611	0.4852 0028	0.4302 5558	0.3815 7086	145
146	0.6945 1292	0.6151 6955	0.5449 4550	0.4827 8635	0.4277 6031	0.3790 4390	146
147	0.6927 8097	0.6131 2580	0.5426 8432	0.4803 8443	0.4252 7952	0.3765 3368	147
148	0.6910 5334	0.6110 8884	0.5404 3252	0.4779 9446	0.4228 1311	0.3740 4008	148
149	0.6893 3001	0.6090 5864	0.5381 9006	0.4756 1637	0.4203 6100	0.3715 6299	149
150	0.6876 1098	0.6070 3519	0.5359 5690	0.4732 5012	0.4179 2312	0.3691 0231	150

Table A-2 (Cont.)

n	$\frac{3}{4}\%$	1%	$1\frac{1}{4}\%$	$1\frac{1}{2}\%$	$1\frac{3}{4}\%$	2%	n
1	0.9925 5583	0.9900 9901	0.9876 5432	0.9852 2167	0.9828 0098	0.9803 9216	1
2	0.9851 6708	0.9802 9605	0.9754 6106	0.9706 6175	0.9658 9777	0.9611 6878	2
3	0.9778 3333	0.9705 9015	0.9634 1833	0.9563 1699	0.9492 8528	0.9423 2233	3
4	0.9705 5417	0.9609 8034	0.9515 2428	0.9421 8423	0.9329 5851	0.9238 4543	4
5	0.9633 2920	0.9514 6569	0.9397 7706	0.9282 6033	0.9169 1254	0.9057 3081	5
6	0.9561 5802	0.9420 4524	0.9281 7488	0.9145 4219	0.9011 4254	0.8879 7138	6
7	0.9490 4022	0.9327 1805	0.9167 1593	0.9010 2679	0.8856 4378	0.8705 6018	7
8	0.9419 7540	0.9234 8322	0.9053 9845	0.8877 1112	0.8704 1157	0.8534 9037	8
9	0.9349 6318	0.9143 3982	0.8942 2069	0.8745 9224	0.8554 4135	0.8367 5527	9
10	0.9280 0315	0.9052 8695	0.8831 8093	0.8616 6723	0.8407 2860	0.8203 4830	10
11	0.9210 9494	0.8963 2372	0.8722 7746	0.8489 3323	0.8262 6889	0.8042 6304	11
12	0.9142 3815	0.8874 4923	0.8615 0860	0.8363 8742	0.8120 5788	0.7884 9318	12
13	0.9074 3241	0.8786 6260	0.8508 7269	0.8240 2702	0.7980 9128	0.7730 3253	13
14	0.9006 7733	0.8699 6297	0.8403 6809	0.8118 4928	0.7843 6490	0.7578 7502	14
15	0.8939 7254	0.8613 4947	0.8299 9318	0.7998 5150	0.7708 7459	0.7430 1473	15
16	0.8873 1766	0.8528 2126	0.8197 4635	0.7880 3104	0.7576 1631	0.7284 4581	16
17	0.8807 1231	0.8443 7749	0.8096 2602	0.7763 8526	0.7445 8605	0.7141 6256	17
18	0.8741 5614	0.8360 1731	0.7996 3064	0.7649 1159	0.7317 7990	0.7001 5937	18
19	0.8676 4878	0.8277 3992	0.7897 5866	0.7536 0747	0.7191 9401	0.6864 3076	19
20	0.8611 8985	0.8195 4447	0.7800 0855	0.7424 7042	0.7068 2458	0.6729 7133	20
21	0.8547 7901	0.8114 3017	0.7703 7881	0.7314 9795	0.6946 6789	0.6597 7582	21
22	0.8484 1589	0.8033 9621	0.7608 6796	0.7206 8763	0.6827 2028	0.6468 3904	22
23	0.8421 0014	0.7954 4179	0.7514 7453	0.7100 3708	0.6709 7817	0.6341 5592	23
24	0.8358 3140	0.7875 6613	0.7421 9707	0.6995 4392	0.6594 3800	0.6217 2149	24
25	0.8296 0933	0.7797 6844	0.7330 3414	0.6892 0583	0.6480 9632	0.6095 3087	25
26	0.8234 3358	0.7720 4796	0.7239 8434	0.6790 2052	0.6369 4970	0.5975 7928	26
27	0.8173 0380	0.7644 0392	0.7150 4626	0.6689 8574	0.6259 9479	0.5858 6204	27
28	0.8112 1966	0.7568 3557	0.7062 1853	0.6590 9925	0.6152 2829	0.5743 7455	28
29	0.8051 8080	0.7493 4215	0.6974 9978	0.6493 5887	0.6046 4697	0.5631 1231	29
30	0.7991 8690	0.7419 2292	0.6888 8867	0.6397 6243	0.5942 4764	0.5520 7089	30
31	0.7932 3762	0.7345 7715	0.6803 8387	0.6303 0781	0.5840 2716	0.5412 4597	31
32	0.7873 3262	0.7273 0411	0.6719 8407	0.6209 9292	0.5739 8247	0.5306 3330	32
33	0.7814 7158	0.7201 0307	0.6636 8797	0.6118 1568	0.5641 1053	0.5202 2873	33
34	0.7756 5418	0.7129 7334	0.6554 9429	0.6027 7407	0.5544 0839	0.5100 2817	34
35	0.7698 8008	0.7059 1420	0.6474 0177	0.5938 6608	0.5448 7311	0.5000 2761	35
36	0.7641 4896	0.6989 2495	0.6394 0916	0.5850 8974	0.5355 0183	0.4902 2315	36
37	0.7584 6051	0.6920 0490	0.6315 1522	0.5764 4309	0.5262 9172	0.4806 1093	37
38	0.7528 1440	0.6851 5337	0.6237 1873	0.5679 2423	0.5172 4002	0.4711 8719	38
39	0.7472 1032	0.6783 6967	0.6160 1850	0.5595 3126	0.5083 4400	0.4619 4822	39
40	0.7416 4796	0.6716 5314	0.6084 1334	0.5512 6232	0.4996 0098	0.4528 9042	40
41	0.7361 2701	0.6650 0311	0.6009 0206	0.5431 1559	0.4910 0834	0.4440 1021	41
42	0.7306 4716	0.6584 1892	0.5934 8352	0.5350 8925	0.4825 6348	0.4353 0413	42
43	0.7252 0809	0.6518 9992	0.5861 5656	0.5271 8153	0.4742 6386	0.4267 6875	43
44	0.7198 0952	0.6454 4546	0.5789 2006	0.5193 9067	0.4661 0699	0.4184 0074	44
45	0.7144 5114	0.6390 5492	0.5717 7290	0.5117 1494	0.4580 9040	0.4101 9680	45
46	0.7091 3264	0.6327 2764	0.5647 1397	0.5041 5265	0.4502 1170	0.4021 5373	46
47	0.7038 5374	0.6264 6301	0.5577 4219	0.4967 0212	0.4424 6850	0.3942 6836	47
48	0.6986 1414	0.6202 6041	0.5508 5649	0.4893 6170	0.4348 5848	0.3865 3761	48
49	0.6934 1353	0.6141 1921	0.5440 5579	0.4821 2975	0.4273 7934	0.3789 5844	49
50	0.6882 5165	0.6080 3882	0.5373 3905	0.4750 0468	0.4200 2883	0.3715 2788	50

Table A-2 (Cont.)

n	3/4%	1%	1 1/4%	1 1/2%	1 3/4%	2%	n
51	0.6831 2819	0.6020 1864	0.5307 0524	0.4679 8491	0.4128 0475	0.3642 4302	51
52	0.6780 4286	0.5960 5806	0.5241 5332	0.4610 6887	0.4057 0492	0.3571 0100	52
53	0.6729 9540	0.5901 5649	0.5176 8229	0.4542 5505	0.3987 2719	0.3500 9902	53
54	0.6679 8551	0.5843 1336	0.5112 9115	0.4475 4192	0.3918 6947	0.3432 3433	54
55	0.6630 1291	0.5785 2808	0.5049 7892	0.4409 2800	0.3851 2970	0.3365 0425	55
56	0.6580 7733	0.5728 0008	0.4987 4461	0.4344 1182	0.3785 0585	0.3299 0613	56
57	0.6531 7849	0.5671 2879	0.4925 8727	0.4279 9194	0.3719 9592	0.3234 3738	57
58	0.6483 1612	0.5615 1365	0.4865 0594	0.4216 6694	0.3655 9796	0.3170 9547	58
59	0.6434 8995	0.5559 5411	0.4804 9970	0.4154 3541	0.3593 1003	0.3108 7791	59
60	0.6386 9970	0.5504 4962	0.4745 6760	0.4092 9597	0.3531 3025	0.3047 8227	60
61	0.6339 4511	0.5449 9962	0.4687 0874	0.4032 4726	0.3470 5676	0.2988 0614	61
62	0.6292 2592	0.5396 0358	0.4629 2222	0.3972 8794	0.3410 8772	0.2929 4720	62
63	0.6245 4185	0.5342 6097	0.4572 0713	0.3914 1669	0.3352 2135	0.2872 0314	63
64	0.6198 9266	0.5289 7126	0.4515 6259	0.3856 3221	0.3294 5587	0.2815 7170	64
65	0.6152 7807	0.5237 3392	0.4459 8775	0.3799 3321	0.3237 8956	0.2760 5069	65
66	0.6106 9784	0.5185 4844	0.4404 8173	0.3743 1843	0.3182 2069	0.2706 3793	66
67	0.6061 5170	0.5134 1429	0.4350 4368	0.3687 8663	0.3127 4761	0.2653 3130	67
68	0.6016 3940	0.5083 3099	0.4296 7277	0.3633 3658	0.3073 6866	0.2601 2873	68
69	0.5971 6070	0.5032 9801	0.4243 6817	0.3579 6708	0.3020 8222	0.2550 2817	69
70	0.5927 1533	0.4983 1486	0.4191 2905	0.3526 7692	0.2968 8670	0.2500 2761	70
71	0.5883 0306	0.4933 8105	0.4139 5462	0.3474 6495	0.2917 8054	0.2451 2511	71
72	0.5839 2363	0.4884 9609	0.4088 4407	0.3423 3000	0.2867 6221	0.2403 1874	72
73	0.5795 7681	0.4836 5949	0.4037 9661	0.3372 7093	0.2818 3018	0.2356 0661	73
74	0.5752 6234	0.4788 7078	0.3988 1147	0.3322 8663	0.2769 8298	0.2309 8687	74
75	0.5709 7999	0.4741 2949	0.3938 8787	0.3273 7599	0.2722 1914	0.2264 5771	75
76	0.5667 2952	0.4694 3514	0.3890 2506	0.3225 3793	0.2675 3724	0.2220 1737	76
77	0.5625 1069	0.4647 8726	0.3842 2228	0.3177 7136	0.2629 3586	0.2176 6408	77
78	0.5583 2326	0.4601 8541	0.3794 7879	0.3130 7523	0.2584 1362	0.2133 9616	78
79	0.5541 6701	0.4556 2912	0.3747 9387	0.3084 4850	0.2539 6916	0.2092 1192	79
80	0.5500 4170	0.4511 1794	0.3701 6679	0.3038 9015	0.2496 0114	0.2051 0973	80
81	0.5459 4710	0.4466 5142	0.3655 9683	0.2993 9916	0.2453 0825	0.2010 8797	81
82	0.5418 8297	0.4422 2913	0.3610 8329	0.2949 7454	0.2410 8919	0.1971 4507	82
83	0.5378 4911	0.4378 5063	0.3566 2547	0.2906 1531	0.2369 4269	0.1932 7948	83
84	0.5338 4527	0.4335 1547	0.3522 2268	0.2863 2050	0.2328 6751	0.1894 8968	84
85	0.5298 7123	0.4292 2324	0.3478 7426	0.2820 8917	0.2288 6242	0.1857 7420	85
86	0.5259 2678	0.4249 7350	0.3435 7951	0.2779 2036	0.2249 2621	0.1821 3157	86
87	0.5220 1169	0.4207 6585	0.3393 3779	0.2738 1316	0.2210 5770	0.1785 6036	87
88	0.5181 2575	0.4165 9985	0.3351 4843	0.2697 6666	0.2172 5572	0.1750 5918	88
89	0.5142 6873	0.4124 7510	0.3310 1080	0.2657 7997	0.2135 1914	0.1716 2665	89
90	0.5104 4043	0.4083 9119	0.3269 2425	0.2618 5218	0.2098 4682	0.1682 6142	90
91	0.5066 4063	0.4043 4771	0.3228 8814	0.2579 8245	0.2062 3766	0.1649 6217	91
92	0.5028 6911	0.4003 4427	0.3189 0187	0.2541 6990	0.2026 9057	0.1617 2762	92
93	0.4991 2567	0.3963 8046	0.3149 6481	0.2504 1369	0.1992 0450	0.1585 5649	93
94	0.4954 1009	0.3924 5590	0.3110 7636	0.2467 1300	0.1957 7837	0.1554 4754	94
95	0.4917 2217	0.3885 7020	0.3072 3591	0.2430 6699	0.1924 1118	0.1523 9955	95
96	0.4880 6171	0.3847 2297	0.3034 4287	0.2394 7487	0.1891 0190	0.1494 1132	96
97	0.4844 2850	0.3809 1383	0.2996 9666	0.2359 3583	0.1858 4953	0.1464 8169	97
98	0.4808 2233	0.3771 4241	0.2959 9670	0.2324 4909	0.1826 5310	0.1436 0950	98
99	0.4772 4301	0.3734 0832	0.2923 4242	0.2290 1389	0.1795 1165	0.1407 9363	99
100	0.4736 9033	0.3697 1121	0.2887 3326	0.2256 2944	0.1764 2422	0.1380 3297	100

Table A-2 (Cont.)

n	2½%	3%	3½%	4%	4½%	5%	n
1	0.9756 0976	0.9708 7379	0.9661 8357	0.9615 3846	0.9569 3780	0.9523 8095	1
2	0.9518 1440	0.9425 9591	0.9335 1070	0.9245 5621	0.9157 2995	0.9070 2948	2
3	0.9285 9941	0.9151 4166	0.9019 4271	0.8889 9636	0.8762 9660	0.8638 3760	3
4	0.9059 5064	0.8884 8705	0.8714 4223	0.8548 0419	0.8385 6134	0.8227 0247	4
5	0.8838 5429	0.8626 0878	0.8419 7317	0.8219 2711	0.8024 5105	0.7835 2617	5
6	0.8622 9687	0.8374 8426	0.8135 0064	0.7903 1453	0.7678 9574	0.7462 1540	6
7	0.8412 6524	0.8130 9151	0.7859 9096	0.7599 1781	0.7348 2846	0.7106 8133	7
8	0.8207 4657	0.7894 0923	0.7594 1156	0.7306 9021	0.7031 8513	0.6768 3936	8
9	0.8007 2836	0.7664 1673	0.7337 3097	0.7025 8674	0.6729 0443	0.6446 0892	9
10	0.7811 9840	0.7440 9391	0.7089 1881	0.6755 6417	0.6439 2768	0.6139 1325	10
11	0.7621 4478	0.7224 2128	0.6849 4571	0.6495 8093	0.6161 9874	0.5846 7929	11
12	0.7435 5589	0.7013 7988	0.6617 8330	0.6245 9705	0.5896 6386	0.5568 3742	12
13	0.7254 2038	0.6809 5134	0.6394 0415	0.6005 7409	0.5642 7164	0.5303 2135	13
14	0.7077 2720	0.6611 1781	0.6177 8179	0.5774 7508	0.5399 7286	0.5050 6795	14
15	0.6904 6556	0.6418 6195	0.5968 9062	0.5552 6450	0.5167 2044	0.4810 1710	15
16	0.6736 2493	0.6231 6694	0.5767 0591	0.5339 0818	0.4944 6932	0.4581 1152	16
17	0.6571 9506	0.6050 1645	0.5572 0378	0.5133 7325	0.4731 7639	0.4362 9669	17
18	0.6411 6591	0.5873 9461	0.5383 6114	0.4936 2812	0.4528 0037	0.4155 2065	18
19	0.6255 2772	0.5702 8603	0.5201 5569	0.4746 4242	0.4333 0179	0.3957 3396	19
20	0.6102 7094	0.5536 7575	0.5025 6588	0.4563 8695	0.4146 4286	0.3768 8948	20
21	0.5953 8629	0.5375 4928	0.4855 7090	0.4388 3360	0.3967 8743	0.3589 4236	21
22	0.5808 6467	0.5218 9250	0.4691 5063	0.4219 5539	0.3797 0089	0.3418 4987	22
23	0.5666 9724	0.5066 9175	0.4532 8563	0.4057 2633	0.3633 5013	0.3255 7131	23
24	0.5528 7535	0.4919 3374	0.4379 5713	0.3901 2147	0.3477 0347	0.3100 6791	24
25	0.5393 9059	0.4776 0557	0.4231 4699	0.3751 1680	0.3327 3060	0.2953 0277	25
26	0.5262 3472	0.4636 9473	0.4088 3767	0.3606 8923	0.3184 0248	0.2812 4073	26
27	0.5133 9973	0.4501 8906	0.3950 1224	0.3468 1657	0.3046 9137	0.2678 4832	27
28	0.5008 7778	0.4370 7675	0.3816 5434	0.3334 7747	0.2915 7069	0.2550 9364	28
29	0.4886 6125	0.4243 4636	0.3687 4815	0.3206 5141	0.2790 1502	0.2429 4632	29
30	0.4767 4269	0.4119 8676	0.3562 7841	0.3083 1867	0.2670 0002	0.2313 7745	30
31	0.4651 1481	0.3999 8715	0.3442 3035	0.2964 6026	0.2555 0241	0.2203 5947	31
32	0.4537 7055	0.3883 3703	0.3325 8971	0.2850 5794	0.2444 9991	0.2098 6617	32
33	0.4427 0298	0.3770 2625	0.3213 4271	0.2740 9417	0.2339 7121	0.1998 7254	33
34	0.4319 0534	0.3660 4490	0.3104 7605	0.2635 5209	0.2238 9589	0.1903 5480	34
35	0.4213 7107	0.3553 8340	0.2999 7686	0.2534 1547	0.2142 5444	0.1812 9029	35
36	0.4110 9372	0.3450 3243	0.2898 3272	0.2436 6872	0.2050 2817	0.1726 5741	36
37	0.4010 6705	0.3349 8294	0.2800 3161	0.2342 9685	0.1961 9921	0.1644 3563	37
38	0.3912 8492	0.3252 2615	0.2705 6194	0.2252 8543	0.1877 5044	0.1566 0536	38
39	0.3817 4139	0.3157 5355	0.2614 1250	0.2166 2061	0.1796 6549	0.1491 4797	39
40	0.3724 3062	0.3065 5684	0.2525 7247	0.2082 8904	0.1719 2870	0.1420 4568	40
41	0.3633 4695	0.2976 2800	0.2440 3137	0.2002 7793	0.1645 2507	0.1352 8160	41
42	0.3544 8483	0.2889 5922	0.2357 7910	0.1925 7493	0.1574 4026	0.1288 3962	42
43	0.3458 3886	0.2805 4294	0.2278 0590	0.1851 6820	0.1506 6054	0.1227 0440	43
44	0.3374 0376	0.2723 7178	0.2201 0231	0.1780 4635	0.1441 7276	0.1168 6133	44
45	0.3291 7440	0.2644 3862	0.2126 5924	0.1711 9841	0.1379 6437	0.1112 9651	45
46	0.3211 4576	0.2567 3653	0.2054 6787	0.1646 1386	0.1320 2332	0.1059 9668	46
47	0.3133 1294	0.2492 5876	0.1985 1968	0.1582 8256	0.1263 3810	0.1009 4921	47
48	0.3056 7116	0.2419 9880	0.1918 0645	0.1521 9476	0.1208 9771	0.0961 4211	48
49	0.2982 1576	0.2349 5029	0.1853 2024	0.1463 4112	0.1156 9158	0.0915 6391	49
50	0.2909 4221	0.2281 0708	0.1790 5337	0.1407 1262	0.1107 0965	0.0872 0373	50

Table A-2 (Cont.)

n	2½%	3%	3½%	4%	4½%	5%	n
51	0.2838 4606	0.2214 6318	0.1729 9843	0.1353 0059	0.1059 4225	0.0830 5117	51
52	0.2769 2298	0.2150 1280	0.1671 4824	0.1300 9672	0.1013 8014	0.0790 9635	52
53	0.2701 6876	0.2087 5029	0.1614 9589	0.1250 9300	0.0970 1449	0.0753 2986	53
54	0.2635 7928	0.2026 7019	0.1560 3467	0.1202 8173	0.0928 3683	0.0717 4272	54
55	0.2571 5052	0.1967 6717	0.1507 5814	0.1156 5551	0.0888 3907	0.0683 2640	55
56	0.2508 7855	0.1910 3609	0.1456 6004	0.1112 0722	0.0850 1347	0.0650 7276	56
57	0.2447 5956	0.1854 7193	0.1407 3433	0.1069 3002	0.0813 5260	0.0619 7406	57
58	0.2387 8982	0.1800 6984	0.1359 7520	0.1028 1733	0.0778 4938	0.0590 2291	58
59	0.2329 6568	0.1748 2508	0.1313 7701	0.0988 6282	0.0744 9701	0.0562 1230	59
60	0.2272 8359	0.1697 3309	0.1269 3431	0.0950 6040	0.0712 8901	0.0535 3552	60
61	0.2217 4009	0.1647 8941	0.1226 4184	0.0914 0423	0.0682 1915	0.0509 8621	61
62	0.2163 3179	0.1599 8972	0.1184 9453	0.0878 8868	0.0652 8148	0.0485 5830	62
63	0.2110 5541	0.1553 2982	0.1144 8747	0.0845 0835	0.0624 7032	0.0462 4600	63
64	0.2059 0771	0.1508 0565	0.1106 1591	0.0812 5803	0.0597 8021	0.0440 4381	64
65	0.2008 8557	0.1464 1325	0.1068 7528	0.0781 3272	0.0572 0594	0.0419 4648	65
66	0.1959 8593	0.1421 4879	0.1032 6114	0.0751 2762	0.0547 4253	0.0399 4903	66
67	0.1912 0578	0.1380 0853	0.0997 6922	0.0722 3809	0.0523 8519	0.0380 4670	67
68	0.1865 4223	0.1339 8887	0.0963 9538	0.0694 5970	0.0501 2937	0.0362 3495	68
69	0.1819 9241	0.1300 8628	0.0931 3563	0.0667 8818	0.0479 7069	0.0345 0948	69
70	0.1775 5358	0.1262 9736	0.0899 8612	0.0642 1940	0.0459 0497	0.0328 6617	70
71	0.1732 2300	0.1226 1880	0.0869 4311	0.0617 4942	0.0439 2820	0.0313 0111	71
72	0.1689 9805	0.1190 4737	0.0840 0300	0.0593 7445	0.0420 3655	0.0298 1058	72
73	0.1648 7615	0.1155 7998	0.0811 6232	0.0570 9081	0.0402 2637	0.0283 9103	73
74	0.1608 5478	0.1122 1357	0.0784 1770	0.0548 9501	0.0384 9413	0.0270 3908	74
75	0.1569 3149	0.1089 4521	0.0757 6590	0.0527 8367	0.0368 3649	0.0257 5150	75
76	0.1531 0389	0.1057 7205	0.0732 0376	0.0507 5353	0.0352 5023	0.0245 2524	76
77	0.1493 6965	0.1026 9131	0.0707 2827	0.0488 0147	0.0337 3228	0.0233 5737	77
78	0.1457 2649	0.0997 0030	0.0683 3650	0.0469 2449	0.0322 7969	0.0222 4512	78
79	0.1421 7218	0.0967 9641	0.0660 2560	0.0451 1970	0.0308 8965	0.0211 8582	79
80	0.1387 0457	0.0939 7710	0.0637 9285	0.0433 8433	0.0295 5948	0.0201 7698	80
81	0.1353 2153	0.0912 3990	0.0616 3561	0.0417 1570	0.0282 8658	0.0192 1617	81
82	0.1320 2101	0.0885 8243	0.0595 5131	0.0401 1125	0.0270 6850	0.0183 0111	82
83	0.1288 0098	0.0860 0236	0.0575 3750	0.0385 6851	0.0259 0287	0.0174 2963	83
84	0.1256 5949	0.0834 9743	0.0555 9178	0.0370 8510	0.0247 8744	0.0165 9965	84
85	0.1225 9463	0.0810 6547	0.0537 1187	0.0356 5875	0.0237 2003	0.0158 0919	85
86	0.1196 0452	0.0787 0434	0.0518 9553	0.0342 8726	0.0226 9860	0.0150 5637	86
87	0.1166 8733	0.0764 1198	0.0501 4060	0.0329 6852	0.0217 2115	0.0143 3940	87
88	0.1138 4130	0.0741 8639	0.0484 4503	0.0317 0050	0.0207 8579	0.0136 5657	88
89	0.1110 6468	0.0720 2562	0.0468 0679	0.0304 8125	0.0198 9070	0.0130 0626	89
90	0.1083 5579	0.0699 2779	0.0452 2395	0.0293 0890	0.0190 3417	0.0123 8691	90
91	0.1057 1296	0.0678 9105	0.0436 9464	0.0281 8163	0.0182 1451	0.0117 9706	91
92	0.1031 3460	0.0659 1364	0.0422 1704	0.0270 9772	0.0174 3016	0.0112 3530	92
93	0.1006 1912	0.0639 9383	0.0407 8941	0.0260 5550	0.0166 7958	0.0107 0028	93
94	0.0981 6500	0.0621 2993	0.0394 1006	0.0250 5337	0.0159 6132	0.0101 9074	94
95	0.0957 7073	0.0603 2032	0.0380 7735	0.0240 8978	0.0152 7399	0.0097 0547	95
96	0.0934 3486	0.0585 6342	0.0367 8971	0.0231 6325	0.0146 1626	0.0092 4331	96
97	0.0911 5596	0.0568 5769	0.0355 4562	0.0222 7235	0.0139 8685	0.0088 0315	97
98	0.0889 3264	0.0552 0164	0.0343 4359	0.0214 1572	0.0133 8454	0.0083 8395	98
99	0.0867 6355	0.0535 9383	0.0331 8221	0.0205 9204	0.0128 0817	0.0079 8471	99
100	0.0846 4737	0.0520 3284	0.0320 6011	0.0198 0004	0.0122 5663	0.0076 0449	100

Table A-2 (Cont.)

n	5½%	6%	6½%	7%	7½%	8%	n
1	0.9478 6730	0.9433 9623	0.9389 6714	0.9345 7944	0.9302 3256	0.9259 2593	1
2	0.8984 5242	0.8899 9644	0.8816 5928	0.8734 3873	0.8653 3261	0.8573 3882	2
3	0.8516 1366	0.8396 1928	0.8278 4909	0.8162 9788	0.8049 6057	0.7938 3224	3
4	0.8072 1674	0.7920 9366	0.7773 2309	0.7628 9521	0.7488 0053	0.7350 2985	4
5	0.7651 3435	0.7472 5817	0.7298 8084	0.7129 8618	0.6965 5863	0.6805 8320	5
6	0.7252 4583	0.7049 6054	0.6853 3412	0.6663 4222	0.6479 6152	0.6301 6963	6
7	0.6874 3681	0.6650 5711	0.6435 0621	0.6227 4974	0.6027 5490	0.5834 9040	7
8	0.6515 9887	0.6274 1237	0.6042 3119	0.5820 0910	0.5607 0223	0.5402 6888	8
9	0.6176 2926	0.5918 9846	0.5673 5323	0.5439 3374	0.5215 8347	0.5002 4897	9
10	0.5854 3058	0.5583 9478	0.5327 2604	0.5083 4929	0.4851 9393	0.4631 9349	10
11	0.5549 1050	0.5267 8753	0.5002 1224	0.4750 9280	0.4513 4319	0.4288 8286	11
12	0.5259 8152	0.4969 6936	0.4696 8285	0.4440 1196	0.4198 5413	0.3971 1376	12
13	0.4985 6068	0.4688 3902	0.4410 1676	0.4149 6445	0.3905 6198	0.3676 9792	13
14	0.4725 6937	0.4423 0096	0.4141 0025	0.3878 1724	0.3633 1347	0.3404 6104	14
15	0.4479 3305	0.4172 6506	0.3888 2652	0.3624 4602	0.3379 6602	0.3152 4170	15
16	0.4245 8109	0.3936 4628	0.3650 9533	0.3387 3460	0.3143 8699	0.2918 9047	16
17	0.4024 4653	0.3713 6442	0.3428 1251	0.3165 7439	0.2924 5302	0.2702 6895	17
18	0.3814 6590	0.3503 4379	0.3218 8969	0.2958 6392	0.2720 4932	0.2502 4903	18
19	0.3615 7906	0.3305 1301	0.3022 4384	0.2765 0833	0.2530 6913	0.2317 1206	19
20	0.3427 2896	0.3118 0473	0.2837 9703	0.2584 1900	0.2354 1315	0.2145 4821	20
21	0.3248 6158	0.2941 5540	0.2664 7608	0.2415 1309	0.2189 8897	0.1986 5575	21
22	0.3079 2567	0.2775 0510	0.2502 1228	0.2257 1317	0.2037 1067	0.1839 4051	22
23	0.2918 7267	0.2617 9726	0.2349 4111	0.2109 4688	0.1894 9830	0.1703 1528	23
24	0.2766 5656	0.2469 7855	0.2206 0198	0.1971 4662	0.1762 7749	0.1576 9934	24
25	0.2622 3370	0.2329 9863	0.2071 3801	0.1842 4918	0.1639 7906	0.1460 1790	25
26	0.2485 6275	0.2198 1003	0.1944 9579	0.1721 9549	0.1525 3866	0.1352 0176	26
27	0.2356 0450	0.2073 6795	0.1826 2515	0.1609 3037	0.1418 9643	0.1251 8682	27
28	0.2233 2181	0.1956 3014	0.1714 7902	0.1504 0221	0.1319 9668	0.1159 1372	28
29	0.2116 7944	0.1845 5674	0.1610 1316	0.1405 6282	0.1227 8761	0.1073 2752	29
30	0.2006 4402	0.1741 1013	0.1511 8607	0.1313 6712	0.1142 2103	0.0993 7733	30
31	0.1901 8390	0.1642 5484	0.1419 5875	0.1227 7301	0.1062 5212	0.0920 1605	31
32	0.1802 6910	0.1549 5740	0.1332 9460	0.1147 4113	0.0988 3918	0.0852 0005	32
33	0.1708 7119	0.1461 8622	0.1251 5925	0.1072 3470	0.0919 4343	0.0788 8893	33
34	0.1619 6321	0.1379 1153	0.1175 2042	0.1002 1934	0.0855 2877	0.0730 4531	34
35	0.1535 1963	0.1301 0522	0.1103 4781	0.0936 6294	0.0795 6164	0.0676 3454	35
36	0.1455 1624	0.1227 4077	0.1036 1297	0.0875 3546	0.0740 1083	0.0626 2458	36
37	0.1379 3008	0.1157 9318	0.0972 8917	0.0818 0884	0.0688 4729	0.0579 8572	37
38	0.1307 3941	0.1092 3885	0.0913 5134	0.0764 5686	0.0640 4399	0.0536 9048	38
39	0.1239 2362	0.1030 5552	0.0857 7509	0.0714 5501	0.0595 7580	0.0497 1341	39
40	0.1174 6314	0.0972 2219	0.0805 4075	0.0667 8038	0.0554 1935	0.0460 3093	40
41	0.1113 3947	0.0917 1905	0.0756 2512	0.0624 1157	0.0515 5288	0.0426 2123	41
42	0.1055 3504	0.0865 2740	0.0710 0950	0.0583 2857	0.0479 5617	0.0394 6411	42
43	0.1000 3322	0.0816 2962	0.0666 7559	0.0545 1268	0.0446 1039	0.0365 4084	43
44	0.0948 1822	0.0770 0908	0.0626 0619	0.0509 4643	0.0414 9804	0.0338 3411	44
45	0.0898 7509	0.0726 5007	0.0587 8515	0.0476 1349	0.0386 0283	0.0313 2788	45
46	0.0851 8965	0.0685 3781	0.0551 9733	0.0444 9859	0.0359 0961	0.0290 0730	46
47	0.0807 4849	0.0646 5831	0.0518 2848	0.0415 8747	0.0334 0428	0.0268 5861	47
48	0.0765 3885	0.0609 9840	0.0486 6524	0.0388 6679	0.0310 7375	0.0248 6908	48
49	0.0725 4867	0.0575 4566	0.0456 9506	0.0363 2410	0.0289 0582	0.0230 2693	49
50	0.0687 6652	0.0542 8836	0.0429 0616	0.0339 4776	0.0268 8913	0.0213 2123	50

Table A-3

Amount of a Simple Annuity $s_{\overline{n}|i} = \dfrac{(1+i)^n - 1}{i}$

n	$\frac{1}{4}\%$	$\frac{1}{3}\%$	$\frac{5}{12}\%$	$\frac{1}{2}\%$	$\frac{7}{12}\%$	$\frac{2}{3}\%$	n
1	1.0000 0000	1.0000 0000	1.0000 0000	1.0000 0000	1.0000 0000	1.0000 0000	1
2	2.0025 0000	2.0033 3333	2.0041 6667	2.0050 0000	2.0058 3333	2.0066 6667	2
3	3.0075 0625	3.0100 1111	3.0125 1736	3.0150 2500	3.0175 3403	3.0200 4444	3
4	4.0150 2502	4.0200 4448	4.0250 6952	4.0301 0013	4.0351 3631	4.0401 7807	4
5	5.0250 6258	5.0334 4463	5.0418 4064	5.0502 5063	5.0586 7460	5.0671 1259	5
6	6.0376 2523	6.0502 2278	6.0628 4831	6.0755 0188	6.0881 8354	6.1008 9335	6
7	7.0527 1930	7.0703 9019	7.0881 1018	7.1058 7939	7.1236 9794	7.1415 6597	7
8	8.0703 5110	8.0939 5816	8.1176 4397	8.1414 0879	8.1652 5285	8.1891 7641	8
9	9.0905 2697	9.1209 3802	9.1514 6749	9.1821 1583	9.2128 8349	9.2437 7092	9
10	10.1132 5329	10.1513 4114	10.1895 9860	10.2280 2641	10.2666 2531	10.3053 9606	10
11	11.1385 3642	11.1851 7895	11.2320 5526	11.2791 6654	11.3265 1396	11.3740 9870	11
12	12.1663 8277	12.2224 6288	12.2788 5549	12.3355 6237	12.3925 8529	12.4499 2602	12
13	13.1967 9872	13.2632 0442	13.3300 1739	13.3972 4018	13.4648 7537	13.5329 2553	13
14	14.2297 9072	14.3074 1510	14.3855 5913	14.4642 2639	14.5434 2048	14.6231 4503	14
15	15.2653 6520	15.3551 0648	15.4454 9896	15.5365 4752	15.6282 5710	15.7206 3267	15
16	16.3035 2861	16.4062 9017	16.5098 5520	16.6142 3026	16.7194 2193	16.8254 3688	16
17	17.3442 8743	17.4609 7781	17.5786 4627	17.6973 0141	17.8169 5189	17.9376 0646	17
18	18.3876 4815	18.5191 8107	18.6518 9063	18.7857 8791	18.9208 8411	19.0571 9051	18
19	19.4336 1727	19.5809 1167	19.7296 0684	19.8797 1685	20.0312 5593	20.1842 3844	19
20	20.4822 0131	20.6461 8137	20.8118 1353	20.9791 1544	21.1481 0493	21.3188 0003	20
21	21.5334 0682	21.7150 0198	21.8985 2942	22.0840 1101	22.2714 6887	22.4609 2536	21
22	22.5872 4033	22.7873 8532	22.9897 7330	23.1944 3107	23.4013 8577	23.6106 6487	22
23	23.6437 0843	23.8633 4327	24.0855 6402	24.3104 0322	24.5378 9386	24.7680 6930	23
24	24.7028 1770	24.9428 8775	25.1859 2053	25.4319 5524	25.6810 3157	25.9331 8976	24
25	25.7645 7475	26.0260 3071	26.2908 6187	26.5591 1502	26.8308 3759	27.1060 7769	25
26	26.8289 8619	27.1127 8414	27.4004 0713	27.6919 1059	27.9873 5081	28.2867 8488	26
27	27.8960 5865	28.2031 6009	28.5145 7549	28.8303 7015	29.1506 1035	29.4753 6344	27
28	28.9657 9880	29.2971 7062	29.6333 8622	29.9745 2200	30.3206 5558	30.6718 6587	28
29	30.0382 1330	30.3948 2786	30.7568 5866	31.1243 9461	31.4975 2607	31.8763 4497	29
30	31.1133 0883	31.4961 4395	31.8850 1224	32.2800 1658	32.6812 6164	33.0888 5394	30
31	32.1910 9210	32.6011 3110	33.0178 6646	33.4414 1666	33.8719 0233	34.3094 4630	31
32	33.2715 6983	33.7098 0154	34.1554 4090	34.6086 2375	35.0694 8843	35.5381 7594	32
33	34.3547 4876	34.8221 6754	35.2977 5524	35.7816 6686	36.2740 6045	36.7750 9711	33
34	35.4406 3563	35.9382 4143	36.4448 2922	36.9605 7520	37.4856 5913	38.0202 6443	34
35	36.5292 3722	37.0580 3557	37.5966 8268	38.1453 7807	38.7043 2548	39.2737 3286	35
36	37.6205 6031	38.1815 6236	38.7533 3552	39.3361 0496	39.9301 0071	40.5355 5774	36
37	38.7146 1171	39.3088 3423	39.9148 0775	40.5327 8549	41.1630 2630	41.8057 9479	37
38	39.8113 9824	40.4398 6368	41.0811 1945	41.7354 4942	42.4031 4395	43.0845 0009	38
39	40.9109 2673	41.5746 6322	42.2522 9078	42.9441 2666	43.6504 9562	44.3717 3009	39
40	42.0132 0405	42.7132 4543	43.4283 4199	44.1588 4730	44.9051 2352	45.6675 4163	40
41	43.1182 3706	43.8556 2292	44.6092 9342	45.3796 4153	46.1670 7007	46.9719 9191	41
42	44.2260 3265	45.0018 0833	45.7951 6547	46.6065 3974	47.4363 7798	48.2851 3852	42
43	45.3365 9774	46.1518 1436	46.9859 7866	47.8395 7244	48.7130 9018	49.6070 3944	43
44	46.4499 3923	47.3056 5374	48.1817 5357	49.0787 7030	49.9972 4988	50.9377 5304	44
45	47.5660 6408	48.4633 3925	49.3825 1088	50.3241 6415	51.2889 0050	52.2773 3806	45
46	48.6849 7924	49.6248 8371	50.5882 7134	51.5757 8497	52.5880 8575	53.6258 5365	46
47	49.8066 9169	50.7902 9999	51.7990 5581	52.8336 6390	53.8948 4959	54.9833 5934	47
48	50.9312 0842	51.9596 0099	53.0148 8521	54.0978 3222	55.2092 3621	56.3499 1507	48
49	52.0585 3644	53.1327 9966	54.2357 8056	55.3683 2138	56.5312 9009	57.7255 8117	49
50	53.1886 8278	54.3099 0899	55.4617 6298	56.6451 6299	57.8610 5595	59.1104 1837	50

Table A-3 (Cont.)

n	$\frac{1}{4}\%$	$\frac{3}{8}\%$	$\frac{5}{12}\%$	$\frac{1}{2}\%$	$\frac{7}{12}\%$	$\frac{2}{3}\%$	n
51	54.3216 5449	55.4909 4202	56.6928 5366	57.9283 8880	59.1985 7877	60.5044 8783	51
52	55.4574 5862	56.6759 1183	57.9290 7388	59.2180 3075	60.5439 0381	61.9078 5108	52
53	56.5961 0227	57.8648 3154	59.1704 4502	60.5141 2090	61.8970 7659	63.3205 7009	53
54	57.7375 9252	59.0577 1431	60.4169 8854	61.8166 9150	63.2581 4287	64.7427 0722	54
55	58.8819 3650	60.2545 7336	61.6687 2600	63.1257 7496	64.6271 4870	66.1743 2527	55
56	60.0291 4135	61.4554 2194	62.9256 7902	64.4414 0384	66.0041 4040	67.6154 8744	56
57	61.1792 1420	62.6602 7334	64.1878 6935	65.7636 1086	67.3891 6455	69.0662 5736	57
58	62.3321 6223	63.8691 4092	65.4553 1881	67.0924 2891	68.7822 6801	70.5266 9907	58
59	63.4879 9264	65.0820 3806	66.7280 4930	68.4278 9105	70.1834 9791	71.9968 7706	59
60	64.6467 1262	66.2989 7818	68.0060 8284	69.7700 3051	71.5929 0165	73.4768 5625	60
61	65.8083 2940	67.5199 7478	69.2894 4152	71.1188 8066	73.0105 2691	74.9667 0195	61
62	66.9728 5023	68.7450 4136	70.5781 4753	72.4744 7507	74.4364 2165	76.4664 7997	62
63	68.1402 8235	69.9741 9150	71.8722 2314	73.8368 4744	75.8706 3411	77.9762 5650	63
64	69.3106 3306	71.2074 3880	73.1716 9074	75.2060 3168	77.3132 1281	79.4960 9821	64
65	70.4839 0964	72.4447 9693	74.4765 7278	76.5820 6184	78.7642 0655	81.0260 7220	65
66	71.6601 1942	73.6862 7959	75.7868 9183	77.9649 7215	80.2236 6442	82.5662 4601	66
67	72.8392 6971	74.9319 0052	77.1026 7055	79.3547 9701	81.6916 3580	84.1166 8765	67
68	74.0213 6789	76.1816 7352	78.4239 3168	80.7515 7099	83.1681 7034	85.6774 6557	68
69	75.2064 2131	77.4356 1243	79.7506 9806	82.1553 2885	84.6533 1800	87.2486 4867	69
70	76.3944 3736	78.6937 3114	81.0829 9264	83.5661 0549	86.1471 2902	88.8303 0633	70
71	77.5854 2345	79.9560 4358	82.4208 3844	84.9839 3602	87.6496 5394	90.4225 0837	71
72	78.7793 8701	81.2225 6372	83.7642 5860	86.4088 5570	89.1609 4359	92.0253 2510	72
73	79.9763 3548	82.4933 0560	85.1132 7634	87.8408 9998	90.6810 4909	93.6388 2726	73
74	81.1762 7632	83.7682 8329	86.4679 1499	89.2801 0448	92.2100 2188	95.2630 8611	74
75	82.3792 1701	85.0475 1090	87.8281 9797	90.7265 0500	93.7479 1367	96.8981 7335	75
76	83.5851 6505	86.3310 0260	89.1941 4880	92.1801 3752	95.2947 7650	98.5441 6118	76
77	84.7941 2797	87.6187 7261	90.5657 9108	93.6410 3821	96.8506 6270	100.2011 2225	77
78	86.0061 1329	88.9108 3519	91.9431 4855	95.1092 4340	98.4156 2490	101.8691 2973	78
79	87.2211 2857	90.2072 0464	93.3262 4500	96.5847 8962	99.9897 1604	103.5482 5726	79
80	88.4391 8139	91.5078 9532	94.7151 0435	98.0677 1357	101.5729 8939	105.2385 7898	80
81	89.6602 7934	92.8129 2164	96.1097 5062	99.5580 5214	103.1654 9849	106.9401 6950	81
82	90.8844 3004	94.1222 9804	97.5102 0792	101.0558 4240	104.7672 9723	108.6531 0397	82
83	92.1116 4112	95.4360 3904	98.9165 0045	102.5611 2161	106.3784 3980	110.3774 5799	83
84	93.3419 2022	96.7541 5917	100.3286 5253	104.0739 2722	107.9989 8070	112.1133 0771	84
85	94.5752 7502	98.0766 7303	101.7466 8859	105.5942 9685	109.6289 7475	113.8607 2977	85
86	95.8117 1321	99.4035 9527	103.1706 3312	107.1222 6834	111.2684 7710	115.6198 0130	86
87	97.0512 4249	100.7349 4059	104.6005 1076	108.6578 7968	112.9175 4322	117.3905 9997	87
88	98.2938 7060	102.0707 2373	106.0363 4622	110.2011 6908	114.5762 2889	119.1732 0397	88
89	99.5396 0527	103.4109 5947	107.4781 6433	111.7521 7492	116.2445 9022	120.9676 9200	89
90	100.7884 5429	104.7556 6267	108.9259 9002	113.3109 3580	117.9226 8367	122.7741 4328	90
91	102.0404 2542	106.1048 4821	110.3798 4831	114.8774 9048	119.6105 6599	124.5926 3757	91
92	103.2955 2649	107.4585 3104	111.8397 6434	116.4518 7793	121.3082 9429	126.4232 5515	92
93	104.5537 6530	108.8167 2614	113.3057 6336	118.0341 3732	123.0159 2601	128.2660 7685	93
94	105.8151 4972	110.1794 4856	114.7778 7071	119.6243 0800	124.7335 1891	130.1211 8403	94
95	107.0796 8759	111.5467 1339	116.2561 1184	121.2224 2954	126.4611 3110	131.9886 5859	95
96	108.3473 8681	112.9185 3577	117.7405 1230	122.8285 4169	128.1988 2103	133.8685 8298	96
97	109.6182 5528	114.2949 3089	119.2310 9777	124.4426 8440	129.9466 4749	135.7610 4020	97
98	110.8923 0091	115.6759 1399	120.7278 9401	126.0648 9782	131.7046 6960	137.6661 1380	98
99	112.1695 3167	117.0615 0037	122.2309 2690	127.6952 2231	133.4729 4684	139.5838 8790	99
100	113.4499 5550	118.4517 0537	123.7402 2243	129.3336 9842	135.2515 3903	141.5144 4715	100

n	$\frac{1}{4}\%$	$\frac{1}{3}\%$	$\frac{5}{12}\%$	$\frac{1}{2}\%$	$\frac{7}{12}\%$	$\frac{2}{3}\%$	n
101	114.7335 8038	119.8465 4439	125.2558 0669	130.9803 6692	137.0405 0634	143.4578 7680	101
102	116.0204 1434	121.2460 3287	126.7777 0589	132.6352 6875	138.8399 0929	145.4142 6264	102
103	117.3104 6537	122.6501 8632	128.3059 4633	134.2984 4509	140.6498 0877	147.3836 9106	103
104	118.6037 4153	124.0590 2027	129.8405 5444	135.9699 3732	142.4702 6598	149.3662 4900	104
105	119.9002 5089	125.4725 5034	131.3815 5675	137.6497 8701	144.3013 4253	151.3620 2399	105
106	121.2000 0152	126.8907 9217	132.9289 7990	139.3380 3594	146.1431 0037	153.3711 0415	106
107	122.5030 0152	128.3137 6148	134.4828 5065	141.0347 2612	147.9956 0178	155.3935 7818	107
108	123.8092 5902	129.7414 7402	136.0431 9586	142.7398 9975	149.8589 0946	157.4295 3537	108
109	125.1187 8217	131.1739 4560	137.6100 4251	144.4535 9925	151.7330.8643	159.4790 6560	109
110	126.4315 7913	132.6111 9208	139.1834 1769	146.1758 6725	153.6181 9610	161.5422 5937	110
111	127.7476 5807	134.0532 2939	140.7633 4859	147.9067 4658	155.5143 0225	163.6192 0777	111
112	129.0670 2722	135.5000 7349	142.3498 6255	149.6462 8032	157.4214 6901	165.7100 0249	112
113	130.3896 9479	136.9517 4040	143.9429 8697	151.3945 1172	159.3397 6091	167.8147 3584	113
114	131.7156 6902	138.4082 4620	145.5427 4942	153.1514 8428	161.2692 4285	169.9335 0074	114
115	133.0449 5820	139.8696 0702	147.1491 7754	154.9172 4170	163.2099 8010	172.0663 9075	115
116	134.3775 7059	141.3358 3905	148.7622 9911	156.6918 2791	165.1620 3832	174.2135 0002	116
117	135.7135 1452	142.8069 5851	150.3821 4203	158.4752 8704	167.1254 8354	176.3749 2335	117
118	137.0527 9830	144.2829 8170	152.0087 3429	160.2676 6348	169.1003 8220	178.5507 5618	118
119	138.3954 3030	145.7639 2498	153.6421 0401	162.0690 0180	171.0868 0109	180.7410 9455	119
120	139.7414 1888	147.2498 0473	155.2822 7945	163.8793 4681	173.0848 0743	182.9460 3518	120
121	141.0907 7242	148.7406 3741	156.9292 8894	165.6987 4354	175.0944 6881	185.1656 7542	121
122	142.4434 9935	150.2364 3953	158.5831 6098	167.5272 3726	177.1158 5321	187.4001 1325	122
123	143.7996 0810	151.7372 2766	160.2439 2415	169.3648 7344	179.1490 2902	189.6494 4734	123
124	145.1591 0712	153.2430 1842	161.9116 0717	171.2116 9781	181.1940 6502	191.9137 7699	124
125	146.5220 0489	154.7538 2848	163.5862 3887	173.0677 5630	183.2510 3040	194.1932 0217	125
126	147.8883 0990	156.2696 7458	165.2678 4819	174.9330 9508	185.3199 9475	196.4878 2352	126
127	149.2580 3068	157.7905 7349	166.9564 6423	176.8077 6056	187.4010 2805	198.7977 4234	127
128	150.6311 7575	159.3165 4207	168.6521 1616	178.6917 9936	189.4942 0071	201.1230 6062	128
129	152.0077 5369	160.8475 9721	170.3548 3331	180.5852 5836	191.5995 8355	203.4638 8103	129
130	153.3877 7308	162.3837 5587	172.0646 4512	182.4881 8465	193.7172 4779	205.8203 0690	130
131	154.7712 4251	163.9250 3506	173.7815 8114	184.4006 2557	195.8472 6507	208.1924 4228	131
132	156.1581 7062	165.4714 5184	175.5056 7106	186.3226 2870	197.9897 0745	210.5803 9190	132
133	157.5485 6604	167.0230 2335	177.2369 4469	188.2542 4184	200.1446 4741	212.9842 6117	133
134	158.9424 3746	168.5797 6676	178.9754 3196	190.1955 1305	202.3121 5785	215.4041 5625	134
135	160.3397 9355	170.1416 9931	180.7211 6293	192.1464 9062	204.4923 1210	217.8401 8396	135
136	161.7406 4304	171.7088 3831	182.4741 6777	194.1072 2307	206.6851 8393	220.2924 5185	136
137	163.1449 9464	173.2812 0111	184.2344 7680	196.0777 5919	208.8908 4750	222.7610 6820	137
138	164.5528 5713	174.8588 0511	186.0021 2046	198.0581 4798	211.1093 7744	225.2461 4198	138
139	165.9642 3927	176.4416 6779	187.7771 2929	200.0484 3872	213.3408 4881	227.7477 8293	139
140	167.3791 4987	178.0298 0669	189.5595 3400	202.0486 8092	215.5853 3710	230.2661 0148	140
141	168.7975 9775	179.6232 3937	191.3493 6539	204.0589 2432	217.8429 1823	232.8012 0883	141
142	170.2195 9174	181.2219 8351	193.1466 5441	206.0792 1894	220.1136 6858	235.3532 1688	142
143	171.6451 4072	182.8260 5678	194.9514 3214	208.1096 1504	222.3976 6498	237.9222 3833	143
144	173.0742 5357	184.4354 7697	196.7637 2977	210.1501 6311	224.6949 8470	240.5083 8659	144
145	174.5069 3921	186.0502 6190	198.5835 7865	212.2009 1393	227.0057 0544	243.1117 7583	145
146	175.9432 0655	187.6704 2944	200.4110 1023	214.2619 1850	229.3299 0539	245.7325 2100	146
147	177.3830 6457	189.2959 9753	202.2460 5610	216.3332 2809	231.6676 6317	248.3707 3781	147
148	178.8265 2223	190.9269 8419	204.0887 4800	218.4148 9423	234.0190 5787	251.0265 4273	148
149	180.2735 8854	192.5634 0747	205.9391 1778	220.5069 6870	236.3841 6904	253.7000 5301	149
150	181.7242 7251	194.2052 8550	207.7971 9744	222.6095 0354	238.7630 7670	256.3913 8670	150

Table A-3 (Cont.)

n	$\frac{3}{4}\%$	1%	$1\frac{1}{4}\%$	$1\frac{1}{2}\%$	$1\frac{3}{4}\%$	2%	n
1	1.0000 0000	1.0000 0000	1.0000 0000	1.0000 0000	1.0000 0000	1.0000 0000	1
2	2.0075 0000	2.0100 0000	2.0125 0000	2.0150 0000	2.0175 0000	2.0200 0000	2
3	3.0225 5625	3.0301 0000	3.0376 5625	3.0452 2500	3.0528 0625	3.0604 0000	3
4	4.0452 2542	4.0604 0100	4.0756 2695	4.0909 0338	4.1062 3036	4.1216 0800	4
5	5.0755 6461	5.1010 0501	5.1265 7229	5.1522 6693	5.1780 8939	5.2040 4016	5
6	6.1136 3135	6.1520 1506	6.1906 5444	6.2295 5093	6.2687 0596	6.3081 2096	6
7	7.1594 8358	7.2135 3521	7.2680 3762	7.3229 9419	7.3784 0831	7.4342 8338	7
8	8.2131 7971	8.2856 7056	8.3588 8809	8.4328 3911	8.5075 3045	8.5829 6905	8
9	9.2747 7856	9.3685 2727	9.4633 7420	9.5593 3169	9.6564 1224	9.7546 2843	9
10	10.3443 3940	10.4622 1254	10.5816 6637	10.7027 2167	10.8253 9945	10.9497 2100	10
11	11.4219 2194	11.5668 3467	11.7139 3720	11.8632 6249	12.0148 4394	12.1687 1542	11
12	12.5075 8636	12.6825 0301	12.8603 6142	13.0412 1143	13.2251 0371	13.4120 8973	12
13	13.6013 9325	13.8093 2804	14.0211 1594	14.2368 2960	14.4565 4303	14.6803 3152	13
14	14.7034 0370	14.9474 2132	15.1963 7988	15.4503 8205	15.7095 3253	15.9739 3815	14
15	15.8136 7923	16.0968 9554	16.3863 3463	16.6821 3778	16.9844 4935	17.2934 1692	15
16	16.9322 8183	17.2578 6449	17.5911 6382	17.9323 6984	18.2816 7721	18.6392 8525	16
17	18.0592 7394	18.4304 4314	18.8110 5336	19.2013 5539	19.6016 0656	20.0120 7096	17
18	19.1947 1849	19.6147 4757	20.0461 9153	20.4893 7572	20.9446 3468	21.4123 1238	18
19	20.3386 7888	20.8108 9504	21.2967 6893	21.7967 1636	22.3111 6578	22.8405 5863	19
20	21.4912 1897	22.0190 0399	22.5629 7854	23.1236 6710	23.7016 1119	24.2973 6980	20
21	22.6524 0312	23.2391 9403	23.8450 1577	24.4705 2211	25.1163 8938	25.7833 1719	21
22	23.8222 9614	24.4715 8598	25.1430 7847	25.8375 7994	26.5559 2620	27.2989 8354	22
23	25.0009 6336	25.7163 0183	26.4573 6695	27.2251 4364	28.0206 5490	28.8449 6321	23
24	26.1884 7059	26.9734 6485	27.7880 8403	28.6335 2080	29.5110 1637	30.4218 6247	24
25	27.3848 8412	28.2431 9950	29.1354 3508	30.0630 2361	31.0274 5915	32.0302 9972	25
26	28.5902 7075	29.5256 3150	30.4996 2802	31.5139 6896	32.5704 3969	33.6709 0572	26
27	29.8046 9778	30.8208 8781	31.8808 7337	32.9866 7850	34.1404 2238	35.3443 2383	27
28	31.0282 3301	32.1290 9669	33.2793 8429	34.4814 7867	35.7378 7977	37.0512 1031	28
29	32.2609 4476	33.4503 8766	34.6953 7659	35.9987 0085	37.3632 9267	38.7922 3451	29
30	33.5029 0184	34.7848 9153	36.1290 6880	37.5386 8137	39.0171 5029	40.5680 7921	30
31	34.7541 7361	36.1327 4045	37.5806 8216	39.1017 6159	40.6999 5042	42.3794 4079	31
32	36.0148 2991	37.4940 6785	39.0504 4069	40.6882 8801	42.4121 9955	44.2270 2961	32
33	37.2849 4113	38.8690 0853	40.5385 7120	42.2986 1233	44.1544 1305	46.1115 7020	33
34	38.5645 7819	40.2576 9862	42.0453 0334	43.9330 9152	45.9271 1527	48.0338 0160	34
35	39.8538 1253	41.6602 7560	43.5708 6963	45.5920 8789	47.7308 3979	49.9944 7763	35
36	41.1527 1612	43.0768 7836	45.1155 0550	47.2759 6921	49.5661 2949	51.9943 6719	36
37	42.4613 6149	44.5076 4714	46.6794 4932	48.9851 0874	51.4335 3675	54.0342 5453	37
38	43.7798 2170	45.9527 2361	48.2926 4243	50.7198 8538	53.3336 2365	56.1149 3962	38
39	45.1081 7037	47.4122 5085	49.8982 2921	52.4806 8366	55.2669 6206	58.2372 3841	39
40	46.4464 8164	48.8863 7336	51.4895 5708	54.2678 9391	57.2341 3390	60.4019 8318	40
41	47.7948 3026	50.3752 3709	53.1331 7654	56.0819 1232	59.2357 3124	62.6100 2284	41
42	49.1532 9148	51.8789 8946	54.7973 4125	57.9231 4100	61.2723 5654	64.8622 2330	42
43	50.5219 4117	53.3977 7936	56.4823 0801	59.7919 8812	63.3446 2278	67.1594 6777	43
44	51.9008 5573	54.9317 5715	58.1883 3687	61.6888 6794	65.4531 5367	69.5026 5712	44
45	53.2901 1215	56.4810 7472	59.9156 9108	63.6142 0096	67.5985 8386	71.8927 1027	45
46	54.6897 8799	58.0458 8547	61.6646 3721	65.5684 1398	69.7815 5908	74.3305 6447	46
47	56.0999 6140	59.6263 4432	63.4354 4518	67.5519 4018	72.0027 3637	76.8171 7576	47
48	57.5207 1111	61.2226 0777	65.2283 8824	69.5652 1929	74.2627 8425	79.3535 1927	48
49	58.9521 1644	62.8348 3385	67.0437 4310	71.6086 9758	76.5623 8298	81.9405 8966	49
50	60.3942 5732	64.4631 8218	68.8817 8989	73.6828 2804	78.9022 2468	84.5794 0145	50

Table A-3 (Cont.)

n	$\frac{3}{4}$%	1%	$1\frac{1}{4}$%	$1\frac{1}{2}$%	$1\frac{3}{4}$%	2%	n
51	61.8472 1424	66.1078 1401	70.7428 1226	75.7880 7046	81.2830 1361	87.2709 8948	51
52	63.3110 6835	67.7688 9215	72.6270 9741	77.9248 9152	83.7054 6635	90.0164 0927	52
53	64.7859 0136	69.4465 8107	74.5349 3613	80.0937 6489	86.1703 1201	92.8167 3746	53
54	66.2717 9562	71.1410 4688	76.4666 2283	82.2951 7136	88.6782 9247	95.6730 7221	54
55	67.7688 3409	72.8524 5735	78.4224 5562	84.5295 9893	91.2301 6259	98.5865 3365	55
56	69.2771 0035	74.5809 8192	80.4027 3631	86.7975 4292	93.8266 9043	101.5582 6432	56
57	70.7966 7860	76.3267 9174	82.4077 7052	89.0995 0606	96.4686 5752	104.5894 2961	57
58	72.3276 5369	78.0900 5966	84.4378 6765	91.4359 9865	99.1568 5902	107.6812 1820	58
59	73.8701 1109	79.8709 6025	86.4933 4099	93.8075 3863	101.8921 0405	110.8348 4257	59
60	75.4241 3693	81.6696 6986	88.5745 0776	96.2146 5171	104.6752 1588	114.0515 3942	60
61	76.9898 1795	83.4863 6655	90.6816 8910	98.6578 7149	107.5070 3215	117.3325 7021	61
62	78.5672 4159	85.3212 3022	92.8152 1022	101.1377 3956	110.3884 0522	120.6792 2161	62
63	80.1564 9590	87.1744 4252	94.9754 0034	103.6548 0565	113.3202 0231	124.0928 0604	63
64	81.7576 6962	89.0461 8695	97.1625 9285	106.2096 2774	116.3033 0585	127.5746 6216	64
65	83.3708 5214	90.9366 4882	99.3771 2526	108.8027 7215	119.3386 1370	131.1261 5541	65
66	84.9961 3353	92.8460 1531	101.6193 3933	111.4348 1374	122.4270 3944	134.7486 7852	66
67	86.6336 0453	94.7744 7546	103.8895 8107	114.1063 3594	125.5695 1263	138.4436 5209	67
68	88.2833 5657	96.7222 2021	106.1882 0083	116.8179 3098	128.7669 7910	142.2125 2513	68
69	89.9454 8174	98.6894 4242	108.5155 5334	119.5701 9995	132.0204 0124	146.0567 7563	69
70	91.6200 7285	100.6763 3684	110.8719 9776	122.3637 5295	135.3307 5826	149.9779 1114	70
71	93.3072 2340	102.6831 0021	113.2578 9773	125.1992 0924	138.6990 4653	153.9774 6937	71
72	95.0070 2758	104.7099 3121	115.6736 2145	128.0771 9738	142.1262 7984	158.0570 1875	72
73	96.7195 8028	106.7570 3052	118.1195 4172	130.9983 5534	145.6134 8974	162.2181 5913	73
74	98.4449 7714	108.8246 0083	120.5960 3599	133.9633 3067	149.1617 2581	166.4625 2231	74
75	100.1833 1446	110.9128 4684	123.1034 8644	136.9727 8063	152.7720 5601	170.7917 7276	75
76	101.9346 8932	113.0219 7530	125.6422 8002	140.0273 7234	156.4455 6699	175.2076 0821	76
77	103.6991 9949	115.1521 9506	128.2128 0852	143.1277 8292	160.1833 6441	179.7117 6038	77
78	105.4769 4349	117.3037 1701	130.8154 6863	146.2746 9967	163.9865 7329	184.3059 9558	78
79	107.2680 2056	119.4767 5418	133.4506 6199	149.4688 2016	167.8563 3832	188.9921 1549	79
80	109.0725 3072	121.6715 2172	136.1187 9526	152.7108 5247	171.7938 2424	193.7719 5780	80
81	110.8905 7470	123.8882 3694	138.8202 8020	156.0015 1525	175.8002 1617	198.6473 9696	81
82	112.7222 5401	126.1271 1931	141.5555 3370	159.3415 3798	179.8767 1995	203.6203 4490	82
83	114.5676 7091	128.3883 9050	144.3249 7787	162.7316 6105	184.0245 6255	208.6927 5180	83
84	116.4269 2845	130.6722 7440	147.1290 4010	166.1726 3597	188.2449 9239	213.8666 0683	84
85	118.3001 3041	132.9789 9715	149.9681 5310	169.6652 2551	192.5392 7976	219.1439 3897	85
86	120.1873 8139	135.3087 8712	152.8427 5501	173.2102 0389	196.9087 1716	224.5268 1775	86
87	122.0887 8675	137.6618 7499	155.7532 8945	176.8083 5695	201.3546 1971	230.0173 5411	87
88	124.0044 5265	140.0384 9374	158.7002 0557	180.4604 8230	205.8783 2555	235.6177 0119	88
89	125.9344 8604	142.4388 7868	161.6839 5814	184.1673 8954	210.4811 9625	241.3300 5521	89
90	127.8789 9469	144.8632 6746	164.7050 0762	187.9299 0038	215.1646 1718	247.1566 5632	90
91	129.8380 8715	147.3119 0014	167.7638 2021	191.7488 4889	219.9299 9798	253.0997 8944	91
92	131.8118 7280	149.7850 1914	170.8608 6796	195.6250 8162	224.7787 7295	259.1617 8523	92
93	133.8004 6185	152.2828 6933	173.9966 2881	199.5594 5784	229.7124 0148	265.3450 2094	93
94	135.8039 6531	154.8056 9803	177.1715 8667	203.5528 4971	234.7323 6850	271.6519 2135	94
95	137.8224 9505	157.3537 5501	180.3862 3151	207.6061 4246	239.8401 8495	278.0849 5978	95
96	139.8561 6377	159.9272 9256	183.6410 5940	211.7202 3459	245.0373 8819	284.6466 5898	96
97	141.9050 8499	162.5265 6548	186.9365 7264	215.8960 3811	250.3255 4248	291.3395 9216	97
98	143.9693 7313	165.1518 3114	190.2732 7980	220.1344 7868	255.7062 3947	298.1663 8400	98
99	146.0491 4343	167.8033 4945	193.6516 9580	224.4364 9586	261.1810 9866	305.1297 1168	99
100	148.1445 1201	170.4813 8294	197.0723 4200	228.8030 4330	266.7517 6789	312.2323 0591	100

Table A-3 (Cont.)

n	$2\frac{1}{2}\%$	3%	$3\frac{1}{2}\%$	4%	$4\frac{1}{2}\%$	5%	n
1	1.0000 0000	1.0000 0000	1.0000 0000	1.0000 0000	1.0000 0000	1.0000 0000	1
2	2.0250 0000	2.0300 0000	2.0350 0000	2.0400 0000	2.0450 0000	2.0500 0000	2
3	3.0756 2500	3.0909 0000	3.1062 2500	3.1216 0000	3.1370 2500	3.1525 0000	3
4	4.1525 1563	4.1836 2700	4.2149 4288	4.2464 6400	4.2781 9113	4.3101 2500	4
5	5.2563 2852	5.3091 3581	5.3624 6588	5.4163 2256	5.4707 0973	5.5256 3125	5
6	6.3877 3673	6.4684 0988	6.5501 5218	6.6329 7546	6.7168 9166	6.8019 1281	6
7	7.5474 3015	7.6624 6218	7.7794 0751	7.8982 9448	8.0191 5179	8.1420 0845	7
8	8.7361 1590	8.8923 3605	9.0516 8677	9.2142 2626	9.3800 1362	9.5491 0888	8
9	9.9545 1880	10.1591 0613	10.3684 9581	10.5827 9531	10.8021 1423	11.0265 6432	9
10	11.2033 8177	11.4638 7931	11.7313 9316	12.0061 0712	12.2882 0937	12.5778 9254	10
11	12.4834 6631	12.8077 9569	13.1419 9192	13.4863 5141	13.8411 7879	14.2067 8716	11
12	13.7955 5297	14.1920 2956	14.6019 6164	15.0258 0546	15.4640 3184	15.9171 2652	12
13	15.1404 4179	15.6177 9045	16.1130 3030	16.6268 3768	17.1599 1327	17.7129 8285	13
14	16.5189 5284	17.0863 2416	17.6769 8636	18.2919 1119	18.9321 0937	19.5986 3199	14
15	17.9319 2666	18.5989 1389	19.2956 8088	20.0235 8764	20.7840 5429	21.5785 6359	15
16	19.3802 2483	20.1568 8130	20.9710 2971	21.8245 3114	22.7193 3673	23.6574 9177	16
17	20.8647 3045	21.7615 8774	22.7050 1575	23.6975 1239	24.7417 0689	25.8403 6636	17
18	22.3863 4871	23.4144 3537	24.4996 9130	25.6454 1288	26.8550 8370	28.1323 8467	18
19	23.9460 0743	25.1168 6844	26.3571 8050	27.6712 2940	29.0635 6246	30.5390 0391	19
20	25.5446 5761	26.8703 7449	28.2796 8181	29.7780 7858	31.3714 2277	33.0659 5410	20
21	27.1832 7405	28.6764 8572	30.2694 7068	31.9692 0172	33.7831 3680	35.7192 5181	21
22	28.8628 5590	30.5367 8030	32.3289 0215	34.2479 6979	36.3033 7795	38.5052 1440	22
23	30.5844 2730	32.4528 8370	34.4604 1373	36.6178 8858	38.9370 2996	41.4304 7512	23
24	32.3490 3798	34.4264 7022	36.6665 2821	39.0826 0412	41.6891 9631	44.5019 9887	24
25	34.1577 6393	36.4592 6432	38.9498 5669	41.6459 0829	44.5652 1015	47.7270 9882	25
26	36.0117 0803	38.5530 4225	41.3131 0168	44.3117 4462	47.5706 4460	51.1134 5376	26
27	37.9120 0073	40.7096 3352	43.7590 6024	47.0842 1440	50.7113 2361	54.6691 2645	27
28	39.8598 0075	42.9309 2252	46.2906 2734	49.9675 8298	53.9933 3317	58.4025 8277	28
29	41.8562 9577	45.2188 5020	48.9107 9930	52.9662 8630	57.4230 3316	62.3227 1191	29
30	43.9027 0316	47.5754 1571	51.6226 7728	56.0849 3775	61.0070 6966	66.4388 4750	30
31	46.0002 7074	50.0026 7818	54.4294 7098	59.3283 3526	64.7523 8779	70.7607 8988	31
32	48.1502 7751	52.5027 5852	57.3345 0247	62.7014 6867	68.6662 4524	75.2988 2937	32
33	50.3540 3445	55.0778 4128	60.3412 1005	66.2095 2742	72.7562 2628	80.0637 7084	33
34	52.6128 8531	57.7301 7652	63.4531 5240	69.8579 0851	77.0302 5646	85.0669 5938	34
35	54.9282 0744	60.4620 8181	66.6740 1274	73.6522 2486	81.4966 1800	90.3203 0735	35
36	57.3014 1263	63.2759 4427	70.0076 0318	77.5983 1385	86.1639 6581	95.8363 2272	36
37	59.7339 4794	66.1742 2259	73.4578 6930	81.7022 4640	91.0413 4427	101.6281 3886	37
38	62.2272 9664	69.1594 4927	77.0288 9472	85.9703 3626	96.1382 0476	107.7095 4580	38
39	64.7829 7906	72.2342 3275	80.7249 0604	90.4091 4971	101.4644 2398	114.0950 2309	39
40	67.4025 5354	75.4012 5973	84.5502 7775	95.0255 1570	107.0303 2306	120.7997 7424	40
41	70.0876 1737	78.6632 9753	88.5095 3747	99.8265 3633	112.8466 8760	127.8397 6295	41
42	72.8398 0781	82.0231 9645	92.6073 7128	104.8195 9778	118.9247 8854	135.2317 5110	42
43	75.6608 0300	85.4838 9234	96.8486 2928	110.0123 8169	125.2764 0402	142.9933 3866	43
44	78.5523 2308	89.0484 0911	101.2383 3130	115.4128 7696	131.9138 4220	151.1430 0559	44
45	81.5161 3116	92.7198 6139	105.7816 7290	121.0293 9204	138.8499 6510	159.7001 5587	45
46	84.5540 3443	96.5014 5723	110.4840 3145	126.8705 6772	146.0982 1353	168.6851 6366	46
47	87.6678 8530	100.3965 0095	115.3509 7255	132.9453 9043	153.6726 3314	178.1194 2185	47
48	90.8595 8243	104.4083 9598	120.3882 5659	139.2632 0604	161.5879 0163	188.0253 9294	48
49	94.1310 7199	108.5406 4785	125.6018 4557	145.8337 3429	169.8593 5720	198.4266 6259	49
50	97.4843 4879	112.7968 6729	130.9979 1016	152.6670 8366	178.5030 2828	209.3479 9572	50

Table A-3 (Cont.)

n	$2\frac{1}{2}\%$	3%	$3\frac{1}{2}\%$	4%	$4\frac{1}{2}\%$	5%	n
51	100.9214 5751	117.1807 7331	136.5828 3702	159.7737 6700	187.5356 6455	220.8153 9550	51
52	104.4444 9395	121.6961 9651	142.3632 3631	167.1647 1768	196.9747 6946	232.8561 6528	52
53	108.0556 0629	126.3470 8240	148.3459 4958	174.8513 0639	206.8386 3408	245.4989 7354	53
54	111.7569 9645	131.1374 9488	154.5380 5782	182.8453 5865	217.1463 7262	258.7739 2222	54
55	115.5509 2136	136.0716 1972	160.9468 8984	191.1591 7299	227.9179 5938	272.7126 1833	55
56	119.4396 9440	141.1537 6831	167.5800 3099	199.8055 3991	239.1742 6756	287.3482 4924	56
57	123.4256 8676	146.3883 8136	174.4453 3207	208.7977 6151	250.9371 0960	302.7156 6171	57
58	127.5113 2893	151.7800 3280	181.5509 1869	218.1496 7197	263.2292 7953	318.8514 4479	58
59	131.6991 1215	157.3334 3379	188.9052 0085	227.8756 5885	276.0745 9711	335.7940 1703	59
60	135.9915 8995	163.0534 3680	196.5168 8288	237.9906 8520	289.4979 5398	353.5837 1788	60
61	140.3913 7970	168.9450 3991	204.3949 7378	248.5103 1261	303.5253 6190	372.2629 0378	61
62	144.9011 6419	175.0133 9110	212.5487 9786	259.4507 2511	318.1840 0319	391.8760 4897	62
63	149.5236 9330	181.2637 9284	220.9880 0579	270.8287 5412	333.5022 8333	412.4698 5141	63
64	154.2617 8563	187.7017 0662	229.7225 8599	282.6619 0428	349.5098 8608	434.0933 4398	64
65	159.1183 3027	194.3327 5782	238.7628 7650	294.9683 8045	366.2378 3096	456.7980 1118	65
66	164.0962 8853	201.1627 4055	248.1195 7718	307.7671 1567	383.7185 3335	480.6379 1174	66
67	169.1986 9574	208.1976 2277	257.8037 6238	321.0778 0030	401.9858 6735	505.6698 0733	67
68	174.4286 6314	215.4435 5145	267.8268 9406	334.9209 1231	421.0752 3138	531.9532 9770	68
69	179.7893 7971	222.9068 5800	278.2008 3535	349.3177 4880	441.0236 1679	559.5509 6258	69
70	185.2841 1421	230.5940 6374	288.9378 6459	364.2904 5876	461.8696 7955	588.5285 1071	70
71	190.9162 1706	238.5118 8565	300.0506 8985	379.8620 7711	483.6538 1513	618.9549 3625	71
72	196.6891 2249	246.6672 4222	311.5524 6400	396.0565 6019	506.4182 3681	650.9026 8306	72
73	202.6063 5055	255.0672 5949	323.4568 0024	412.8988 2260	530.2070 5747	684.4478 1721	73
74	208.6715 0931	263.7192 7727	335.7777 8824	430.4147 7550	555.0663 7505	719.6702 0807	74
75	214.8882 9705	272.6308 5559	348.5300 1083	448.6313 6652	581.0443 6193	756.6537 1848	75
76	221.2605 0447	281.8097 8126	361.7285 6121	467.5766 2118	608.1913 5822	795.4864 0440	76
77	227.7920 1709	291.2640 7469	375.3890 6085	487.2796 8603	636.5599 6934	836.2607 2462	77
78	234.4868 1751	301.0019 9693	389.5276 7798	507.7708 7347	666.2051 6796	879.0737 6085	78
79	241.3489 8795	311.0320 5684	404.1611 4671	529.0817 0841	697.1844 0052	924.0274 4889	79
80	248.3827 1265	321.3630 1855	419.3067 8685	551.2449 7675	729.5576 9854	971.2288 2134	80
81	255.5922 8047	332.0039 0910	434.9825 2439	574.2947 7582	763.3877 9497	1020.7902 6240	81
82	262.9820 8748	342.9640 2638	451.2069 1274	598.2665 6685	798.7402 4575	1072.8297 7552	82
83	270.5566 3966	354.2529 4717	467.9991 5469	623.1972 2952	835.6835 5680	1127.4712 6430	83
84	278.3205 5566	365.8805 3558	485.3791 2510	649.1251 1870	874.2893 1686	1184.8448 2752	84
85	286.2785 6955	377.8569 5165	503.3673 9448	676.0901 2345	914.6323 3612	1245.0870 6889	85
86	294.4355 3379	390.1926 6020	521.9852 5329	704.1337 2839	956.7907 9125	1308.3414 2234	86
87	302.7964 2213	402.8984 4001	541.2547 3715	733.2990 7753	1000.8463 7685	1374.7584 9345	87
88	311.3663 3268	415.9853 9321	561.1986 5295	763.6310 4063	1046.8844 6381	1444.4964 1812	88
89	320.1504 9100	429.4649 5500	581.8406 0581	795.1762 8225	1094.9942 6468	1517.7212 3903	89
90	329.1542 5328	443.3489 0365	603.2050 2701	827.9833 3354	1145.2690 0659	1594.6073 0098	90
91	338.3831 0961	457.6493 7076	625.3172 0295	862.1026 6688	1197.8061 1189	1675.3376 6603	91
92	347.8426 8735	472.3788 5189	648.2033 0506	897.5867 7356	1252.7073 8692	1760.1045 4933	92
93	357.5387 5453	487.5502 1744	671.8904 2073	934.4902 4450	1310.0792 1933	1849.1097 7680	93
94	367.4772 2339	503.1767 2397	696.4065 8546	972.8698 5428	1370.0327 8420	1942.5652 6564	94
95	377.6641 5398	519.2720 2568	721.7808 1595	1012.7846 4845	1432.6842 5949	2040.6935 2892	95
96	388.1057 5783	535.8501 8645	748.0431 4451	1054.2960 3439	1498.1550 5117	2143.7282 0537	96
97	398.8084 0177	552.9256 9205	775.2246 5457	1097.4678 7577	1566.5720 2847	2251.9146 1564	97
98	409.7786 1182	570.5134 6281	803.3575 1748	1142.3665 9080	1638.0677 6976	2365.5103 4642	98
99	421.0230 7711	588.6288 6669	832.4750 3059	1189.0612 5443	1712.7808 1939	2484.7858 6374	99
100	432.5486 5404	607.2877 3270	862.6116 5666	1237.6213 0461	1790.8559 5627	2610.0251 5693	100

Table A-3 (Cont.)

n	$5\frac{1}{2}\%$	6%	$6\frac{1}{2}\%$	7%	$7\frac{1}{2}\%$	8%	n
1	1.0000 0000	1.0000 0000	1.0000 0000	1.0000 0000	1.0000 0000	1.0000 0000	1
2	2.0550 0000	2.0600 0000	2.0650 0000	2.0700 0000	2.0750 0000	2.0800 0000	2
3	3.1680 2500	3.1836 0000	3.1992 2500	3.2149 0000	3.2306 2500	3.2464 0000	3
4	4.3422 6638	4.3746 1600	4.4071 7463	4.4399 4300	4.4729 2188	4.5061 1200	4
5	5.5810 9103	5.6370 9296	5.6936 4098	5.7507 3901	5.8083 9102	5.8666 0096	5
6	6.8880 5103	6.9753 1854	7.0637 2764	7.1532 9074	7.2440 2034	7.3359 2904	6
7	8.2668 9384	8.3938 3765	8.5228 6994	8.6540 2109	8.7873 2187	8.9228 0336	7
8	9.7215 7300	9.8974 6791	10.0768 5648	10.2598 0257	10.4463 7101	10.6366 2763	8
9	11.2562 5951	11.4913 1598	11.7318 5215	11.9779 8875	12.2298 4883	12.4875 5784	9
10	12.8753 5379	13.1807 9494	13.4944 2254	13.8164 4796	14.1470 8750	14.4865 6247	10
11	14.5834 9825	14.9716 4264	15.3715 6001	15.7835 9932	16.2081 1906	16.6454 8746	11
12	16.3855 9065	16.8699 4120	17.3707 1141	17.8884 5127	18.4237 2799	18.9771 2646	12
13	18.2867 9814	18.8821 3767	19.4998 0765	20.1406 4286	20.8055 0759	21.4952 9658	13
14	20.2925 7203	21.0150 6593	21.7672 9515	22.5504 8786	23.3659 2066	24.2149 2030	14
15	22.4086 6350	23.2759 6988	24.1821 6933	25.1290 2201	26.1183 6470	27.1521 1393	15
16	24.6411 3999	25.6725 2808	26.7540 1034	27.8880 5355	29.0772 4206	30.3242 8304	16
17	26.9964 0269	28.2128 7976	29.4930 2101	30.8402 1730	32.2580 3521	33.7502 2569	17
18	29.4812 0483	30.9056 5255	32.4100 6738	33.9990 3251	35.6773 8785	37.4502 4374	18
19	32.1026 7110	33.7599 9170	35.5167 2176	37.3789 6479	39.3531 9194	41.4462 6324	19
20	34.8683 1801	36.7855 9120	38.8253 0867	40.9954 9232	43.3046 8134	45.7619 6430	20
21	37.7860 7550	39.9927 2668	42.3489 5373	44.8651 7678	47.5525 3244	50.4229 2144	21
22	40.8643 0965	43.3922 9028	46.1016 3573	49.0057 3916	52.1189 7237	55.4567 5516	22
23	44.1118 4669	46.9958 2769	50.0982 4205	53.4361 4090	57.0278 9530	60.8932 9557	23
24	47.5379 9825	50.8155 7735	54.3546 2778	58.1766 7076	62.3049 8744	66.7647 5922	24
25	51.1525 8816	54.8645 1200	58.8876 7859	63.2490 3772	67.9778 6150	73.1059 3995	25
26	54.9659 8051	59.1563 8272	63.7153 7769	68.6764 7036	74.0762 0112	79.9544 1515	26
27	58.9891 0943	63.7057 6568	68.8568 7725	74.4838 2328	80.6319 1620	87.3507 6836	27
28	62.2335 1045	68.5281 1162	74.3325 7427	80.6976 9091	87.6793 0991	95.3388 2983	28
29	67.7113 5353	73.6397 9832	80.1641 9159	87.3465 2927	95.2552 5816	103.9659 3622	29
30	72.4354 7797	79.0581 8622	86.3748 6405	94.4607 8632	103.3994 0252	113.2832 1111	30
31	77.4194 2926	84.8016 7739	92.9892 3021	102.0730 4137	112.1543 5771	123.3458 6800	31
32	82.6774 9787	90.8897 7803	100.0335 3017	110.2181 5426	121.5659 3454	134.2135 3744	32
33	88.2247 6025	97.3431 6471	107.5357 0963	118.9334 2506	131.6833 7964	145.9506 2044	33
34	94.0771 2207	104.1837 5460	115.5255 3076	128.2587 6481	142.5596 3310	158.6266 7007	34
35	100.2513 6378	111.4347 7987	124.0346 9026	138.2368 7835	154.2516 0558	172.3168 0368	35
36	106.7651 8879	119.1208 6666	133.0969 4513	148.9134 5984	166.8204 7600	187.1021 4797	36
37	113.6372 7417	127.2681 1866	142.7482 4656	160.3374 0202	180.3320 1170	203.0703 1981	37
38	120.8873 2425	135.9042 0578	153.0268 8259	172.5610 2017	194.8569 1258	220.3159 4540	38
39	128.5361 2708	145.0584 5813	163.9736 2996	185.6402 9158	210.4711 8102	238.9412 2103	39
40	136.6056 1407	154.7619 6562	175.6319 1590	199.6351 1199	227.2565 1960	259.0565 1871	40
41	145.1189 2285	165.0476 8356	188.0479 9044	214.6095 6983	245.3007 5857	280.7810.4021	41
42	154.1004 6360	175.9505 4457	201.2711 0981	230.6322 3972	264.6983 1546	304.2435 2342	42
43	163.5759 8910	187.5075 7724	215.3537 3195	247.7764 9650	285.5506 8912	329.5830 0530	43
44	173.5726 6850	199.7580 3188	230.3517 2453	266.1208 5125	307.9669 9080	356.9496 4572	44
45	184.1191 6527	212.7435 1379	246.3245 8662	285.7493 1084	332.0645 1511	386.5056 1738	45
46	195.2457 1936	226.5081 2462	263.3356 8475	306.7517 6260	357.9693 5375	418.4260 6677	46
47	206.9842 3392	241.0986 1210	281.4525 0426	329.2243 8598	385.8170 5528	452.9001 5211	47
48	219.3683 6679	256.5645 2882	300.7469 1704	353.2700 9300	415.7533 3442	490.1321 6428	48
49	232.4336 2696	272.9584 0055	321.2954 6665	378.9989 9951	447.9348 3451	530.3427 3742	49
50	246.2174 7645	290.3359 0458	343.1796 7198	406.5289 2947	482.5299 4709	573.7701 5642	50

Table A-4

Present Value of a Simple Annuity $a_{\overline{n}|i} = \dfrac{1 - (1 + i)^{-n}}{i}$

n	$\frac{1}{4}\%$	$\frac{1}{3}\%$	$\frac{5}{12}\%$	$\frac{1}{2}\%$	$\frac{7}{12}\%$	$\frac{2}{3}\%$	n
1	0.9975 0623	0.9966 7774	0.9958 5062	0.9950 2488	0.9942 0050	0.9933 7748	1
2	1.9925 2492	1.9900 4426	1.9875 6908	1.9850 9938	1.9826 3513	1.9801 7631	2
3	2.9850 6227	2.9801 1056	2.9751 7253	2.9702 4814	2.9653 3732	2.9604 4004	3
4	3.9751 2446	3.9668 8760	3.9586 7804	3.9504 9566	3.9423 4034	3.9342 1196	4
5	4.9627 1766	4.9503 8631	4.9381 0261	4.9258 6633	4.9136 7722	4.9015 3506	5
6	5.9478 4804	5.9306 1759	5.9134 6318	5.8963 8441	5.8793 8083	5.8624 5205	6
7	6.9305 2174	6.9075 9228	6.8847 7661	6.8620 7404	6.8394 8384	6.8170 0535	7
8	7.9107 4487	7.8813 2121	7.8520 5970	7.8229 5924	7.7940 1874	7.7652 3710	8
9	8.8885 2357	8.8518 1516	8.8153 2916	8.7790 6392	8.7430 1780	8.7071 8917	9
10	9.8638 6391	9.8190 8487	9.7746 0165	9.7304 1186	9.6865 1314	9.6429 0315	10
11	10.8367 7198	10.7831 4107	10.7298 9376	10.6770 2673	10.6245 3667	10.5724 2035	11
12	11.8072 5384	11.7439 9442	11.6812 2200	11.6189 3207	11.5571 2014	11.4957 8180	12
13	12.7753 1555	12.7016 5557	12.6286 0283	12.5561 5131	12.4842 9509	12.4130 2828	13
14	13.7409 6314	13.6561 3512	13.5720 5261	13.4887 0777	13.4060 9268	13.3242 0028	14
15	14.7042 0264	14.6074 4364	14.5115 8766	14.4166 2465	14.3225 4470	14.2293 3802	15
16	15.6650 4004	15.5555 9167	15.4472 2422	15.3399 2502	15.2336 8156	15.1284 8148	16
17	16.6234 8133	16.5005 8970	16.3789 7848	16.2586 3186	16.1395 3427	16.0216 7035	17
18	17.5795 3250	17.4424 4821	17.3068 6654	17.1727 6802	17.0401 3350	16.9089 4405	18
19	18.5331 9950	18.3811 7762	18.2309 0443	18.0823 5624	17.9355 0969	17.7903 4177	19
20	19.4844 8828	19.3167 8832	19.1511 0815	18.9874 1915	18.8256 9315	18.6659 0242	20
21	20.4334 0477	20.2492 9069	20.0674 9359	19.8879 7925	19.7107 1398	19.5356 6466	21
22	21.3799 5488	21.1786 9504	20.9800 7661	20.7840 5896	20.5906 0213	20.3996 6688	22
23	22.3241 4452	22.1050 1167	21.8888 7297	21.6756 8055	21.4653 8738	21.2579 4723	23
24	23.2659 7957	23.0282 5083	22.7938 9839	22.5628 6622	22.3350 9930	22.1105 4361	24
25	24.2054 6591	23.9484 2275	23.6951 6853	23.4456 3803	23.1997 6732	22.9574 9365	25
26	25.1426 0939	24.8655 3763	24.5926 9895	24.3240 1794	24.0594 2070	23.7988 3475	26
27	26.0774 1585	25.7796 0561	25.4865 0517	25.1980 2780	24.9140 8852	24.6346 0406	27
28	27.0098 9112	26.6906 3682	26.3766 0266	26.0676 8936	25.7637 9968	25.4648 3847	28
29	27.9400 4102	27.5986 4135	27.2630 0680	26.9330 2423	26.6085 8295	26.2895 7464	29
30	28.8678 7134	28.5036 2925	28.1457 3291	27.7940 5397	27.4484 6689	27.1088 4898	30
31	29.7933 8787	29.4056 1055	29.0247 9626	28.6507 9997	28.2834 7993	27.9226 9766	31
32	30.7165 9638	30.3045 9523	29.9002 1205	29.5032 8355	29.1136 5030	28.7311 5662	32
33	31.6375 0262	31.2005 9325	30.7719 9540	30.3515 2592	29.9390 0610	29.5342 6154	33
34	32.5561 1234	32.0936 1454	31.6401 6139	31.1955 4818	30.7595 7524	30.3320 4789	34
35	33.4724 3126	32.9836 6898	32.5047 2504	32.0353 7132	31.5753 8549	31.1245 5088	35
36	34.3864 6510	33.8707 6642	33.3657 0128	32.8710 1624	32.3864 6445	31.9118 0551	36
37	35.2982 1955	34.7549 1670	34.2231 0501	33.7025 0372	33.1928 3955	32.6938 4653	37
38	36.2077 0030	35.6361 2960	35.0769 5105	34.5298 5445	33.9945 3808	33.4707 0848	38
39	37.1149 1302	36.5144 1488	35.9272 5416	35.3530 8900	34.7915 8716	34.2424 2564	39
40	38.0198 6336	37.3897 8228	36.7740 2904	36.1722 2786	35.5840 1374	35.0090 3209	40
41	38.9225 5697	38.2622 4147	37.6172 9033	36.9872 9141	36.3718 4465	35.7705 6168	41
42	39.8229 9947	39.1318 0213	38.4570 5261	37.7982 9991	37.1551 0653	36.5270 4803	42
43	40.7211 9648	39.9984 7388	39.2933 3040	38.6052 7354	37.9338 2588	37.2785 2453	43
44	41.6171 5359	40.8622 6633	40.1261 3816	39.4082 3238	38.7080 2904	38.0250 2437	44
45	42.5108 7640	41.7231 8903	40.9554 9028	40.2071 9640	39.4777 4221	38.7665 8050	45
46	43.4023 7047	42.5812 5153	41.7814 0111	41.0021 8547	40.2429 9143	39.5032 2566	46
47	44.2916 4137	43.4364 6332	42.6038 8492	41.7932 1937	41.0038 0258	40.2349 9238	47
48	45.1786 9463	44.2888 3387	43.4229 5594	42.5803 1778	41.7602 0141	40.9619 1296	48
49	46.0635 3580	45.1383 7263	44.2386 2832	43.3635 0028	42.5122 1349	41.6840 1949	49
50	46.9461 7037	45.9850 8900	45.0509 1617	44.1427 8635	43.2598 6428	42.4013 4387	50

n	$\frac{1}{4}\%$	$\frac{1}{3}\%$	$\frac{5}{12}\%$	$\frac{1}{2}\%$	$\frac{7}{12}\%$	$\frac{2}{3}\%$	n
51	47.8266 0386	46.8289 9236	45.8598 3353	44.9181 9537	44.0031 7907	43.1139 1775	51
52	48.7048 4176	47.6700 9205	46.6653 9439	45.6897 4664	44.7421 8301	43.8217 7260	52
53	49.5808 8953	48.5083 9739	47.4676 1267	46.4574 5934	45.4769 0108	44.5249 3967	53
54	50.4547 5265	49.3439 1767	48.2665 0224	47.2213 5258	46.2073 5816	45.2234 5000	54
55	51.3264 3656	50.1766 6213	49.0620 7692	47.9814 4535	46.9335 7895	45.9173 3444	55
56	52.1959 4669	51.0066 3999	49.8543 5046	48.7377 5657	47.6555 8802	46.6066 2362	56
57	53.0632 8847	51.8338 6046	50.6433 3656	49.4903 0505	48.3734 0980	47.2913 4796	57
58	53.9284 6730	52.6583 3268	51.4290 4885	50.2391 0950	49.0870 6856	47.9715 3771	58
59	54.7914 8858	53.4800 6580	52.2115 0093	50.9841 8855	49.7965 8846	48.6472 2289	59
60	55.6523 5769	54.2990 6890	52.9907 0632	51.7255 6075	50.5019 9350	49.3184 3334	60
61	56.5110 7999	55.1153 5106	53.7666 7850	52.4632 4453	51.2033 0754	49.9851 9868	61
62	57.3676 6083	55.9289 2133	54.5394 3087	53.1972 5824	51.9005 5431	50.6475 4836	62
63	58.2221 0557	56.7397 8870	55.3089 7680	53.9276 2014	52.5937 5739	51.3055 1161	63
64	59.0744 1952	57.5479 6216	56.0753 2959	54.6543 4839	53.2829 4024	51.9591 1749	64
65	59.9246 0800	58.3534 5065	56.8385 0250	55.3774 6109	53.9681 2617	52.6083 9486	65
66	60.7726 7631	59.1562 6311	57.5985 0871	56.0969 7621	54.6493 3836	53.2533 7238	66
67	61.6186 2974	59.9564 0842	58.3553 6137	56.8129 1165	55.3265 9986	53.8940 7852	67
68	62.4624 7355	60.7538 9543	59.1090 7357	57.5252 8522	55.9999 3358	54.5305 4158	68
69	63.3042 1302	61.5487 3299	59.8596 5832	58.2341 1465	56.6693 6230	55.1627 8965	69
70	64.1438 5339	62.3409 2989	60.6071 2862	58.9394 1756	57.3349 0867	55.7908 5064	70
71	64.9813 9989	63.1304 9490	61.3514 9738	59.6412 1151	57.9965 9520	56.4147 5230	71
72	65.8168 5774	63.9174 3678	62.0927 7748	60.3395 1394	58.6544 4427	57.0345 2215	72
73	66.6502 3216	64.7017 6424	62.8309 8172	61.0343 4222	59.3084 7815	57.6501 8756	73
74	67.4815 2834	65.4834 8595	63.5661 2287	61.7257 1366	59.9587 1896	58.2617 7573	74
75	68.3107 5146	66.2626 1058	64.2982 1365	62.4136 4543	60.6051 8869	58.8693 1363	75
76	69.1379 0670	67.0391 4676	65.0272 6670	63.0981 5466	61.2479 0922	59.4728 2811	76
77	69.9629 9920	67.8131 0308	65.7532 9464	63.7792 5836	61.8869 0229	60.0723 4581	77
78	70.7860 3411	68.5844 8812	66.4763 1002	64.4569 7350	62.5221 8952	60.6678 9319	78
79	71.6070 1657	69.3533 1042	67.1963 2533	65.1313 1691	63.1537 9239	61.2594 9654	79
80	72.4259 5169	70.1195 7849	67.9133 5303	65.8023 0538	63.7817 3229	61.8471 8200	80
81	73.2428 4458	70.8833 0082	68.6274 0550	66.4699 5561	64.4060 3044	62.4309 7549	81
82	74.0577 0033	71.6444 8587	69.3384 9511	67.1342 8419	65.0267 0798	63.0109 0281	82
83	74.8705 2402	72.4031 4206	70.0466 3413	67.7953 0765	65.6437 8590	63.5869 8954	83
84	75.6813 2072	73.1592 7780	70.7518 3482	68.4530 4244	66.2572 8507	64.1592 6114	84
85	76.4900 9548	73.9129 0146	71.4541 0936	69.1075 0491	66.8672 2625	64.7277 4285	85
86	77.2968 5335	74.6640 2139	72.1534 6991	69.7587 1135	67.4736 3007	65.2924 5979	86
87	78.1015 9935	75.4126 4591	72.8499 2854	70.4066 7796	68.0765 1706	65.8534 3687	87
88	78.9043 3850	76.1587 8330	73.5434 9730	71.0514 2086	68.6759 0759	66.4106 9888	88
89	79.7050 7581	76.9024 4182	74.2341 8818	71.6929 5608	69.2718 2197	66.9642 7041	89
90	80.5038 1627	77.6436 2972	74.9220 1313	72.3312 9958	69.8642 8033	67.5141 7591	90
91	81.3005 6486	78.3823 5521	75.6069 8403	72.9664 6725	70.4533 0273	68.0604 3964	91
92	82.0953 2654	79.1186 2645	76.2891 1272	73.5984 7487	71.0389 0910	68.6030 8574	92
93	82.8881 0628	79.8524 5161	76.9684 1101	74.2273 3818	71.6211 1923	69.1421 3815	93
94	83.6789 0900	80.5838 3882	77.6448 9063	74.8530 7282	72.1999 5284	69.6776 2068	94
95	84.4677 3966	81.3127 9616	78.3185 6329	75.4756 9434	72.7754 2950	70.2095 5696	95
96	85.2546 0315	82.0393 3172	78.9894 4062	76.0952 1825	73.3475 6869	70.7379 7049	96
97	86.0395 0439	82.7634 5355	79.6575 3422	76.7116 5995	73.9163 8975	71.2628 8460	97
98	86.8224 4827	83.4851 6965	80.3228 5566	77.3250 3478	74.4819 1193	71.7843 2245	98
99	87.6034 3967	84.2044 8802	80.9854 1642	77.9353 5799	75.0441 5436	72.3023 0707	99
100	88.3824 8846	84.9214 1663	81.6452 2797	78.5426 4477	75.6031 3606	72.8168 6132	100

Table A-4 (Cont.)

n	$\frac{1}{4}\%$	$\frac{1}{3}\%$	$\frac{5}{12}\%$	$\frac{1}{2}\%$	$\frac{7}{12}\%$	$\frac{2}{3}\%$	n
101	89.1595 8450	85.6359 6342	82.3023 0172	79.1469 1021	76.1588 7596	73.3280 0794	101
102	89.9347 4763	86.3481 3630	82.9566 4901	79.7481 6937	76.7113 9283	73.8357 6948	102
103	90.7079 7768	87.0579 4315	83.6082 8117	80.3464 3718	77.2607 0538	74.3401 6835	103
104	91.4792 7948	87.7653 9185	84.2572 0947	80.9417 2854	77.8068 3219	74.8412 2684	104
105	92.2486 5784	88.4704 9021	84.9034 4511	81.5340 5825	78.3497 9174	75.3389 6706	105
106	93.0161 1755	89.1732 4606	85.5469 9928	82.1234 4104	78.8896 0240	75.8334 1099	106
107	93.7816 6339	89.8736 6717	86.1878 8310	82.7098 9158	79.4262 8241	76.3245 8045	107
108	94.5453 0014	90.5717 6130	86.8261 0765	83.2934 2446	79.9598 4996	76.8124 9714	108
109	95.3070 3256	91.2675 3618	87.4616 8397	83.8740 5419	80.4903 2307	77.2971 8259	109
110	96.0668 6539	91.9609 9951	88.0946 2304	84.4517 9522	81.0177 1971	77.7786 5820	110
111	96.8248 0338	92.6521 5898	88.7249 3581	85.0266 6191	81.5420 5770	78.2569 4523	111
112	97.5808 5126	93.3410 2224	89.3526 3317	85.5986 6856	82.0633 5480	78.7320 6480	112
113	98.3350 1372	94.0275 9692	89.9777 2598	86.1678 2942	82.5816 2863	79.2040 3788	113
114	99.0872 9548	94.7118 9062	90.6002 2504	86.7341 5862	83.0968 9674	79.6728 8531	114
115	99.8377 0123	95.3939 1092	91.2201 4112	87.2976 7027	83.6091 7654	80.1386 2779	115
116	100.5862 3564	96.0736 6536	91.8374 8493	87.8583 7838	84.1184 8537	80.6012 8589	116
117	101.3329 0338	96.7511 6149	92.4522 6715	88.4162 9690	84.6248 4047	81.0608 8002	117
118	102.0777 0911	97.4264 0680	93.0644 9841	88.9714 3970	85.1282 5896	81.5174 3048	118
119	102.8206 5747	98.0994 0877	93.6741 8929	89.5238 2059	85.6287 5787	81.9709 5743	119
120	103.5617 5308	98.7701 7486	94.2813 5033	90.0734 5333	86.1263 5414	82.4214 8089	120
121	104.3010 0058	99.4387 1248	94.8859 9203	90.6203 5157	86.6210 6460	82.8690 2076	121
122	105.0384 0457	100.1050 2905	95.4881 2484	91.1645 2892	87.1129 0598	83.3135 9678	122
123	105.7739 6965	100.7691 3195	96.0877 5918	91.7059 9893	87.6018 9493	83.7552 2859	123
124	106.5077 0040	101.4310 2852	96.6849 0541	92.2447 7505	88.0880 4798	84.1939 3568	124
125	107.2396 0139	102.0907 2610	97.2795 7385	92.7808 7070	88.5713 8159	84.6297 3743	125
126	107.9696 7720	102.7482 3199	97.8717 7479	93.3142 9921	89.0519 1210	85.0626 5308	126
127	108.6979 3237	103.4035 5348	98.4615 1846	93.8450 7384	89.5296 5577	85.4927 0173	127
128	109.4243 7144	104.0566 9782	99.0488 1506	94.3732 0780	90.0046 2877	85.9199 0238	128
129	110.1489 9894	104.7076 7225	99.6336 7475	94.8987 1423	90.4768 4716	86.3442 7389	129
130	110.8718 1939	105.3564 8397	100.2161 0764	95.4216 0619	90.9463 2692	86.7658 3499	130
131	111.5928 3730	106.0031 4016	100.7961 2379	95.9418 9671	91.4130 8393	87.1846 0430	131
132	112.3120 5716	106.6476 4800	101.3737 3323	96.4595 9872	91.8771 3399	87.6006 0029	132
133	113.0294 8345	107.2900 1462	101.9489 4596	96.9747 2509	92.3384 9278	88.0138 4135	133
134	113.7451 2065	107.9302 4713	102.5217 7191	97.4872 8865	92.7971 7592	88.4243 4571	134
135	114.4589 7321	108.5683 5262	103.0922 2099	97.9973 0214	93.2531 9893	88.8321 3150	135
136	115.1710 4560	109.2043 3816	103.6603 0306	98.5047 7825	93.7065 7722	89.2372 1673	136
137	115.8813 4224	109.8382 1079	104.2260 2794	99.0097 2960	94.1573 2616	89.6396 1926	137
138	116.5898 6758	110.4699 7754	104.7894 0542	99.5121 6876	94.6054 6097	90.0393 5688	138
139	117.2966 2601	111.0996 4538	105.3504 4523	100.0121 0821	95.0509 9682	90.4364 4724	139
140	118.0016 2196	111.7272 2131	105.9091 5708	100.5095 6041	95.4939 4878	90.8309 0785	140
141	118.7048 5981	112.3527 1227	106.4655 5061	101.0045 3772	95.9343 3185	91.2227 5614	141
142	119.4063 4395	112.9761 2519	107.0196 3547	101.4970 5246	96.3721 6091	91.6120 0941	142
143	120.1060 7875	113.5974 6696	107.5714 2121	101.9871 1688	96.8074 5078	91.9986 8485	143
144	120.8040 6858	114.2167 4448	108.1209 1739	102.4747 4316	97.2402 1619	92.3827 9952	144
145	121.5003 1778	114.8339 6460	108.6681 3350	102.9599 4344	97.6704 7177	92.7643 7038	145
146	122.1948 3071	115.4491 3415	109.2130 7900	103.4427 2979	98.0982 3208	93.1434 1429	146
147	122.8876 1168	116.0622 5995	109.7557 6332	103.9231 1422	98.5235 1160	93.5199 4797	147
148	123.5786 6502	116.6733 4879	110.2961 9584	104.4011 0868	98.9463 2470	93.8939 8805	148
149	124.2679 9503	117.2824 0743	110.8343 8590	104.8767 2506	99.3666 8570	94.2655 5104	149
150	124.9556 0601	117.8894 4262	111.3703 4280	105.3499 7518	99.7846 0882	94.6346 5335	150

478

Table A-4 (Cont.)

n	$\frac{3}{4}\%$	1%	$1\frac{1}{4}\%$	$1\frac{1}{2}\%$	$1\frac{3}{4}\%$	2%	n
1	0.9925 5583	0.9900 9901	0.9876 5432	0.9852 2167	0.9828 0098	0.9803 9216	1
2	1.9777 2291	1.9703 9506	1.9631 1538	1.9558 8342	1.9486 9875	1.9415 6094	2
3	2.9555 5624	2.9409 8521	2.9265 3371	2.9122 0042	2.8979 8403	2.8838 8327	3
4	3.9261 1041	3.9019 6555	3.8780 5798	3.8543 8465	3.8309 4254	3.8077 2870	4
5	4.8894 3961	4.8534 3124	4.8178 3504	4.7826 4497	4.7478 5508	4.7134 5951	5
6	5.8455 9763	5.7954 7647	5.7460 0992	5.6971 8717	5.6489 9762	5.6014 3089	6
7	6.7946 3785	6.7281 9453	6.6627 2585	6.5982 1396	6.5346 4139	6.4719 9107	7
8	7.7366 1325	7.6516 7775	7.5681 2429	7.4859 2508	7.4050 5297	7.3254 8144	8
9	8.6715 7642	8.5660 1758	8.4623 4498	8.3605 1732	8.2604 9432	8.1622 3671	9
10	9.5995 7958	9.4713 0453	9.3455 2591	9.2221 8455	9.1012 2291	8.9825 8501	10
11	10.5206 7452	10.3676 2825	10.2178 0337	10.0711 1779	9.9274 9181	9.7868 4805	11
12	11.4349 1267	11.2550 7747	11.0793 1197	10.9075 0521	10.7395 4969	10.5753 4122	12
13	12.3423 4508	12.1337 4007	11.9301 8466	11.7315 3222	11.5376 4097	11.3483 7375	13
14	13.2430 2242	13.0037 0304	12.7705 5275	12.5433 8150	12.3220 0587	12.1062 4877	14
15	14.1369 9495	13.8650 5252	13.6005 4592	13.3432 3301	13.0928 8046	12.8492 6350	15
16	15.0243 1261	14.7178 7378	14.4202 9227	14.1312 6405	13.8504 9677	13.5777 0931	16
17	15.9050 2492	15.5622 5127	15.2299 1829	14.9076 4931	14.5950 8282	14.2918 7188	17
18	16.7791 8107	16.3982 6858	16.0295 4893	15.6725 6089	15.3268 6272	14.9920 3125	18
19	17.6468 2984	17.2260 0850	16.8193 0759	16.4261 6837	16.0460 5673	15.6784 6201	19
20	18.5080 1969	18.0455 5297	17.5993 1613	17.1686 3879	16.7528 8130	16.3514 3334	20
21	19.3627 9870	18.8569 8313	18.3696 9495	17.9001 3673	17.4475 4919	17.0112 0916	21
22	20.2112 1459	19.6603 7934	19.1305 6291	18.6208 2437	18.1302 6948	17.6580 4820	22
23	21.0533 1473	20.4558 2113	19.8820 3744	19.3308 6145	18.8012 4764	18.2922 0412	23
24	21.8891 4614	21.2433 8726	20.6242 3451	20.0304 0537	19.4606 8565	18.9139 2560	24
25	22.7187 5547	22.0231 5570	21.3572 6865	20.7196 1120	20.1087 8196	19.5234 5647	25
26	23.5421 8905	22.7952 0366	22.0812 5299	21.3986 3172	20.7457 3166	20.1210 3576	26
27	24.3594 9286	23.5596 0759	22.7962 9925	22.0676 1746	21.3717 2644	20.7068 9780	27
28	25.1707 1251	24.3164 4316	23.5025 1778	22.7267 1671	21.9869 5474	21.2812 7236	28
29	25.9758 9331	25.0657 8530	24.2000 1756	23.3760 7558	22.5916 0171	21.8443 8466	29
30	26.7750 8021	25.8077 0822	24.8889 0623	24.0158 3801	23.1858 4934	22.3964 5555	30
31	27.5683 1783	26.5422 8537	25.5692 9010	24.6461 4582	23.7698 7650	22.9377 0152	31
32	28.3556 5045	27.2695 8947	26.2412 7418	25.2671 3874	24.3438 5897	23.4683 3482	32
33	29.1371 2203	27.9896 9255	26.9049 6215	25.8789 5442	24.9079 6951	23.9885 6355	33
34	29.9127 7621	28.7026 6589	27.5604 5644	26.4817 2849	25.4623 7789	24.4985 9172	34
35	30.6826 5629	29.4085 8009	28.2078 5822	27.0755 9458	26.0072 5100	24.9986 1933	35
36	31.4468 0525	30.1075 0504	28.8472 6737	27.6606 8431	26.5427 5283	25.4888 4248	36
37	32.2052 6576	30.7995 0994	29.4787 8259	28.2371 2740	27.0690 4455	25.9694 5341	37
38	32.9580 8016	31.4846 6330	30.1025 0133	28.8050 5163	27.5862 8457	26.4406 4060	38
39	33.7052 9048	32.1630 3298	30.7185 1983	29.3645 8288	28.0946 2867	26.9025 8883	39
40	34.4469 3844	32.8346 8611	31.3269 3316	29.9158 4520	28.5942 2955	27.3554 7924	40
41	35.1830 6545	33.4996 8922	31.9278 3522	30.4589 6079	29.0852 3789	27.7994 8945	41
42	35.9137 1260	34.1581 0814	32.5213 1874	30.9940 5004	29.5678 0136	28.2347 9358	42
43	36.6389 2070	34.8100 0806	33.1074 7530	31.5212 3157	30.0420 6522	28.6615 6233	43
44	37.3587 3022	35.4554 5352	33.6863 9536	32.0406 2223	30.5081 7221	29.0799 6307	44
45	38.0731 8136	36.0945 0844	34.2581 6825	32.5523 3718	30.9662 6261	29.4901 5987	45
46	38.7823 1401	36.7272 3608	34.8228 8222	33.0564 8983	31.4164 7431	29.8923 1360	46
47	39.4861 6775	37.3536 9909	35.3806 2442	33.5531 9195	31.8589 4281	30.2865 8196	47
48	40.1847 8189	37.9739 5949	35.9314 8091	34.0425 5365	32.2938 0129	30.6731 1957	48
49	40.8781 9542	38.5880 7871	36.4755 3670	34.5246 8339	32.7211 8063	31.0520 7801	49
50	41.5664 4707	39.1961 1753	37.0128 7575	34.9996 8807	33.1412 0946	31.4236 0589	50

n	$\frac{3}{4}\%$	1%	$1\frac{1}{4}\%$	$1\frac{1}{2}\%$	$1\frac{3}{4}\%$	2%	n
51	42.2495 7525	39.7981 3617	37.5435 8099	35.4676 7298	33.5540 1421	31.7878 4892	51
52	42.9276 1812	40.3941 9423	38.0677 3431	35.9287 4185	33.9597 1913	32.1449 4992	52
53	43.6006 1351	40.9843 5072	38.5854 1660	36.3829 9690	34.3584 4632	32.4950 4894	53
54	44.2685 9902	41.5686 6408	39.0967 0776	36.8305 3882	34.7503 1579	32.8382 8327	54
55	44.9316 1193	42.1471 9216	39.6016 8667	37.2714 6681	35.1354 4550	33.1747 8752	55
56	45.5896 8926	42.7199 9224	40.1004 3128	37.7058 7863	35.5139 5135	33.5046 9365	56
57	46.2428 6776	43.2871 2102	40.5930 1855	38.1338 7058	35.8859 4727	33.8281 3103	57
58	46.8911 8388	43.8486 3468	41.0795 2449	38.5555 3751	36.2515 4523	34.1452 2650	58
59	47.5346 7382	44.4045 8879	41.5600 2419	38.9709 7292	36.6108 5526	34.4561 0441	59
60	48.1733 7352	44.9550 3841	42.0345 9179	39.3802 6889	36.9639 8552	34.7608 8668	60
61	48.8073 1863	45.5000 3803	42.5033 0054	39.7835 1614	37.3110 4228	35.0596 9282	61
62	49.4365 4455	46.0396 4161	42.9662 2275	40.1808 0408	37.6521 3000	35.3526 4002	62
63	50.0610 8640	46.5739 0258	43.4234 2988	40.5722 2077	37.9873 5135	35.6398 4316	63
64	50.6809 7906	47.1028 7385	43.8749 9247	40.9578 5298	38.3168 0723	35.9214 1486	64
65	51.2962 5713	47.6266 0777	44.3209 8022	41.3377 8618	38.6405 9678	36.1974 6555	65
66	51.9069 5497	48.1451 5621	44.7614 6195	41.7121 0461	38.9588 1748	36.4681 0348	66
67	52.5131 0667	48.6585 7050	45.1965 0563	42.0808 9125	39.2715 6509	36.7334 3478	67
68	53.1147 4607	49.1669 0149	45.6261 7840	42.4442 2783	39.5789 3375	36.9935 6351	68
69	53.7119 0677	49.6701 9949	46.0505 4656	42.8021 9490	39.8810 1597	37.2485 9168	69
70	54.3046 2210	50.1685 1435	46.4696 7562	43.1548 7183	40.1779 0267	37.4986 1929	70
71	54.8929 2516	50.6618 9539	46.8836 3024	43.5023 3678	40.4696 8321	37.7437 4441	71
72	55.4768 4880	51.1503 9148	47.2924 7431	43.8446 6677	40.7564 4542	37.9840 6314	72
73	56.0564 2561	51.6340 5097	47.6962 7093	44.1819 3771	41.0382 7560	38.2196 6975	73
74	56.6316 8795	52.1129 2175	48.0950 8240	44.5142 2434	41.3152 5857	38.4506 5662	74
75	57.2026 6794	52.5870 5124	48.4889 7027	44.8416 0034	41.5874 7771	38.6771 1433	75
76	57.7693 9746	53.0564 8638	48.8779 9533	45.1641 3826	41.8550 1495	38.8991 3170	76
77	58.3319 0815	53.5212 7364	49.2622 1761	45.4819 0962	42.1179 5081	39.1167 9578	77
78	58.8902 3141	53.9814 5905	49.6416 9640	45.7949 8485	42.3763 6443	39.3301 9194	78
79	59.4443 9842	54.4370 8817	50.0164 9027	46.1034 3335	42.6303 3359	39.5394 0386	79
80	59.9944 4012	54.8882 0611	50.3866 5706	46.4073 2349	42.8799 3474	39.7445 1359	80
81	60.5403 8722	55.3348 5753	50.7522 5389	46.7067 2265	43.1252 4298	39.9456 0156	81
82	61.0822 7019	55.7770 8666	51.1133 3717	47.0016 9720	43.3663 3217	40.1427 4663	82
83	61.6201 1930	56.2149 3729	51.4699 6264	47.2923 1251	43.6032 7486	40.3360 2611	83
84	62.1539 6456	56.6484 5276	51.8221 8532	47.5786 3301	43.8361 4237	40.5255 1579	84
85	62.6838 3579	57.0776 7600	52.1700 5958	47.8607 2218	44.0650 0479	40.7112 8999	85
86	63.2097 6257	57.5026 4951	52.5136 3909	48.1386 4254	44.2899 3099	40.8934 2156	86
87	63.7317 7427	57.9234 1535	52.8529 7688	48.4124 5571	44.5109 8869	41.0719 8192	87
88	64.2499 0002	58.3400 1520	53.1881 2531	48.6822 2237	44.7282 4441	41.2470 4110	88
89	64.7641 6875	58.7524 9030	53.5191 3611	48.9480 0234	44.9417 6355	41.4186 6774	89
90	65.2746 0918	59.1608 8148	53.8460 6035	49.2098 5452	45.1516 1037	41.5869 2916	90
91	65.7812 4981	59.5652 2919	54.1689 4850	49.4678 3696	45.3578 4803	41.7518 9133	91
92	66.2841 1892	59.9655 7346	54.4878 5037	49.7220 0686	45.5605 3860	41.9136 1895	92
93	66.7832 4458	60.3619 5392	54.8028 1518	49.9724 2055	45.7597 4310	42.0721 7545	93
94	67.2786 5467	60.7544 0982	55.1138 9154	50.2191 3355	45.9555 2147	42.2276 2299	94
95	67.7703 7685	61.1429 8002	55.4211 2744	50.4622 0054	46.1479 3265	42.3800 2254	95
96	68.2584 3856	61.5277 0299	55.7245 7031	50.7016 7541	46.3370 3455	42.5294 3386	96
97	68.7428 6705	61.9086 1682	56.0242 6698	50.9376 1124	46.5228 8408	42.6759 1555	97
98	69.2236 8938	62.2857 5923	56.3202 6368	51.1700 6034	46.7055 3718	42.8195 2505	98
99	69.7009 3239	62.6591 6755	56.6126 0610	51.3990 7422	46.8850 4882	42.9603 1867	99
100	70.1746 2272	63.0288 7877	56.9013 3936	51.6247 0367	47.0614 7304	43.0983 5164	100

n	2½%	3%	3½%	4%	4½%	5%	n
1	0.9756 0976	0.9708 7379	0.9661 8357	0.9615 3846	0.9569 3780	0.9523 8095	1
2	1.9274 2415	1.9134 6970	1.8996 9428	1.8860 9467	1.8726 6775	1.8594 1043	2
3	2.8560 2356	2.8286 1135	2.8016 3698	2.7750 9103	2.7489 6435	2.7232 4803	3
4	3.7619 7421	3.7170 9840	3.6730 7921	3.6298 9522	3.5875 2570	3.5459 5050	4
5	4.6458 2850	4.5797 0719	4.5150 5238	4.4518 2233	4.3899 7674	4.3294 7667	5
6	5.5081 2536	5.4171 9144	5.3285 5302	5.2421 3686	5.1578 7248	5.0756 9207	6
7	6.3493 9060	6.2302 8296	6.1145 4398	6.0020 5467	5.8927 0094	5.7863 7340	7
8	7.1701 3717	7.0196 9219	6.8739 5554	6.7327 4487	6.5958 8607	6.4632 1276	8
9	7.9708 6553	7.7861 0892	7.6076 8651	7.4353 3161	7.2687 9050	7.1078 2168	9
10	8.7520 6393	8.5302 0284	8.3166 0532	8.1108 9578	7.9127 1818	7.7217 3493	10
11	9.5142 0871	9.2526 2411	9.0015 5104	8.7604 7671	8.5289 1692	8.3064 1422	11
12	10.2577 6460	9.9540 0399	9.6633 3433	9.3850 7376	9.1185 8078	8.8632 5164	12
13	10.9831 8497	10.6349 5533	10.3027 3849	9.9856 4785	9.6828 5242	9.3935 7299	13
14	11.6909 1217	11.2960 7314	10.9205 2028	10.5631 2293	10.2228 2528	9.8986 4094	14
15	12.3813 7773	11.9379 3509	11.5174 1090	11.1183 8743	10.7395 4573	10.3796 5804	15
16	13.0550 0266	12.5611 0203	12.0941 1681	11.6522 9561	11.2340 1505	10.8377 6956	16
17	13.7121 9772	13.1661 1847	12.6513 2059	12.1656 6885	11.7071 9143	11.2740 6625	17
18	14.3533 6363	13.7535 1308	13.1896 8173	12.6592 9697	12.1599 9180	11.6895 8690	18
19	14.9788 9134	14.3237 9911	13.7098 3742	13.1339 3940	12.5932 9359	12.0853 2086	19
20	15.5891 6229	14.8774 7486	14.2124 0330	13.5903 2634	13.0079 3645	12.4622 1034	20
21	16.1845 4857	15.4150 2414	14.6979 7420	14.0291 5995	13.4047 2388	12.8211 5271	21
22	16.7654 1324	15.9369 1664	15.1671 2484	14.4511 1533	13.7844 2476	13.1630 0258	22
23	17.3321 1048	16.4436 0839	15.6204 1047	14.8568 4167	14.1477 7489	13.4885 7388	23
24	17.8849 8583	16.9355 4212	16.0583 6760	15.2469 6314	14.4954 7837	13.7986 4179	24
25	18.4243 7642	17.4131 4769	16.4815 1459	15.6220 7994	14.8282 0896	14.0939 4457	25
26	18.9506 1114	17.8768 4242	16.8903 5226	15.9827 6918	15.1466 1145	14.3751 8530	26
27	19.4640 1087	18.3270 3147	17.2853 6451	16.3295 8575	15.4513 0282	14.6430 3362	27
28	19.9648 8866	18.7641 0823	17.6670 1885	16.6630 6322	15.7428 7351	14.8981 2726	28
29	20.4535 4991	19.1884 5459	18.0357 6700	16.9837 1463	16.0218 8853	15.1410 7358	29
30	20.9302 9259	19.6004 4135	18.3920 4541	17.2920 3330	16.2888 8854	15.3724 5103	30
31	21.3954 0741	20.0004 2849	18.7362 7576	17.5884 9356	16.5443 9095	15.5928 1050	31
32	21.8491 7796	20.3887 6553	19.0688 6547	17.8735 5150	16.7888 9086	15.8026 7667	32
33	22.2918 8094	20.7657 9178	19.3902 0818	18.1476 4567	17.0228 6207	16.0025 4921	33
34	22.7237 8628	21.1318 3668	19.7006 8423	18.4111 9776	17.2467 5796	16.1929 0401	34
35	23.1451 5734	21.4872 2007	20.0006 6110	18.6646 1323	17.4610 1240	16.3741 9429	35
36	23.5562 5107	21.8322 5250	20.2904 9381	18.9082 8195	17.6660 4058	16.5468 5171	36
37	23.9573 1812	22.1672 3544	20.5705 2542	19.1425 7880	17.8622 3979	16.7112 8734	37
38	24.3486 0304	22.4924 6159	20.8410 8736	19.3678 6423	18.0499 9023	16.8678 9271	38
39	24.7303 4443	22.8082 1513	21.1024 9987	19.5844 8484	18.2296 5572	17.0170 4067	39
40	25.1027 7505	23.1147 7197	21.3550 7234	19.7927 7388	18.4015 8442	17.1590 8635	40
41	25.4661 2200	23.4123 9997	21.5991 0371	19.9930 5181	18.5661 0949	17.2943 6796	41
42	25.8206 0683	23.7013 5920	21.8348 8281	20.1856 2674	18.7235 4975	17.4232 0758	42
43	26.1664 4569	23.9819 0213	22.0626 8870	20.3707 9494	18.8742 1029	17.5459 1198	43
44	26.5038 4945	24.2542 7392	22.2827 9102	20.5488 4129	19.0183 8305	17.6627 7331	44
45	26.8330 2386	24.5187 1254	22.4954 5026	20.7200 3970	19.1563 4742	17.7740 6982	45
46	27.1541 6962	24.7754 4907	22.7009 1813	20.8846 5356	19.2883 7074	17.8800 6650	46
47	27.4674 8255	25.0247 0783	22.8994 3780	21.0429 3612	19.4147 0884	17.9810 1571	47
48	27.7731 5371	25.2667 0664	23.0912 4425	21.1951 3088	19.5356 0654	18.0771 5782	48
49	28.0713 6947	25.5016 5693	23.2765 6450	21.3414 7200	19.6512 9813	18.1687 2173	49
50	28.3623 1168	25.7297 6401	23.4556 1787	21.4821 8462	19.7620 0778	18.2559 2546	50

Table A-4 (Cont.)

n	2½%	3%	3½%	4%	4½%	5%	n
51	28.6461 5774	25.9512 2719	23.6286 1630	21.6174 8521	19.8679 5003	18.3389 7663	51
52	28.9230 8072	26.1662 3999	23.7957 6454	21.7475 8193	19.9693 3017	18.4180 7298	52
53	29.1932 4948	26.3749 9028	23.9572 6043	21.8726 7493	20.0663 4466	18.4934 0284	53
54	29.4568 2876	26.5776 6047	24.1132 9510	21.9929 5667	20.1591 8149	18.5651 4556	54
55	29.7139 7928	26.7744 2764	24.2640 5323	22.1086 1218	20.2480 2057	18.6334 7196	55
56	29.9648 5784	26.9654 6373	24.4097 1327	22.2189 1940	20.3330 3404	18.6985 4473	56
57	30.2096 1740	27.1509 3566	24.5504 4760	22.3267 4943	20.4143 8664	18.7605 1879	57
58	30.4484 0722	27.3310 0549	24.6864 2281	22.4295 6676	20.4922 3602	18.8195 4170	58
59	30.6813 7290	27.5058 3058	24.8177 9981	22.5284 2957	20.5667 3303	18.8757 5400	59
60	30.9086 5649	27.6755 6367	24.9447 3412	22.6234 8997	20.6380 2204	18.9292 8953	60
61	31.1303 9657	27.8403 5307	25.0673 7596	22.7148 9421	20.7062 4118	18.9802 7574	61
62	31.3467 2836	28.0003 4279	25.1858 7049	22.8027 8289	20.7715 2266	19.0288 3404	62
63	31.5577 8377	28.1556 7261	25.3003 5796	22.8872 9124	20.8339 9298	19.0750 8003	63
64	31.7636 9148	28.3064 7826	25.4109 7388	22.9685 4927	20.8937 7319	19.1191 2384	64
65	31.9645 7705	28.4528 9152	25.5178 4916	23.0466 8199	20.9509 7913	19.1610 7033	65
66	32.1605 6298	28.5950 4031	25.6211 1030	23.1218 0961	21.0057 2165	19.2010 1936	66
67	32.3517 6876	28.7330 4884	25.7208 7951	23.1940 4770	21.0581 0684	19.2390 6606	67
68	32.5383 1099	28.8670 3771	25.8172 7489	23.2635 0740	21.1082 3621	19.2753 0101	68
69	32.7203 0340	28.9971 2399	25.9104 1052	23.3302 9558	21.1562 0690	19.3098 1048	69
70	32.8978 5698	29.1234 2135	26.0003 9664	23.3945 1498	21.2021 1187	19.3426 7665	70
71	33.0710 7998	29.2460 4015	26.0873 3975	23.4562 6440	21.2460 4007	19.3739 7776	71
72	33.2400 7803	29.3650 8752	26.1713 4275	23.5156 3885	21.2880 7662	19.4037 8834	72
73	33.4049 5417	29.4806 6750	26.2525 0508	23.5727 2966	21.3283 0298	19.4321 7937	73
74	33.5658 0895	29.5928 8107	26.3309 2278	23.6276 2468	21.3667 9711	19.4592 1845	74
75	33.7227 4044	29.7018 2628	26.4066 8868	23.6804 0834	21.4036 3360	19.4849 6995	75
76	33.8758 4433	29.8075 9833	26.4798 9244	23.7311 6187	21.4388 8383	19.5094 9519	76
77	34.0252 1398	29.9102 8964	26.5506 2072	23.7799 6333	21.4726 1611	19.5328 5257	77
78	34.1709 4047	30.0099 8994	26.6189 5721	23.8268 8782	21.5048 9579	19.5550 9768	78
79	34.3131 1265	30.1067 8635	26.6849 8281	23.8720 0752	21.5357 8545	19.5762 8351	79
80	34.4518 1722	30.2007 6345	26.7487 7567	23.9153 9185	21.5653 4493	19.5964 6048	80
81	34.5871 3875	30.2920 0335	26.8104 1127	23.9571 0754	21.5936 3151	19.6156 7665	81
82	34.7191 5976	30.3805 8577	26.8699 6258	23.9972 1879	21.6207 0001	19.6339 7776	82
83	34.8479 6074	30.4665 8813	26.9275 0008	24.0357 8730	21.6466 0288	19.6514 0739	83
84	34.9736 2023	30.5500 8556	26.9830 9186	24.0728 7240	21.6713 9032	19.6680 0704	84
85	35.0962 1486	30.6311 5103	27.0368 0373	24.1085 3116	21.6951 1035	19.6838 1623	85
86	35.2158 1938	30.7098 5537	27.0886 9926	24.1428 1842	21.7178 0895	19.6988 7260	86
87	35.3325 0671	30.7862 6735	27.1388 3986	24.1757 8694	21.7395 3009	19.7132 1200	87
88	35.4463 4801	30.8604 5374	27.1872 8489	24.2074 8745	21.7603 1588	19.7268 6857	88
89	35.5574 1269	30.9324 7936	27.2340 9168	24.2379 6870	21.7802 0658	19.7398 7483	89
90	35.6657 6848	31.0024 0714	27.2793 1564	24.2672 7759	21.7992 4075	19.7522 6174	90
91	35.7714 8144	31.0702 9820	27.3230 1028	24.2954 5923	21.8174 5526	19.7640 5880	91
92	35.8746 1604	31.1362 1184	27.3652 2732	24.3225 5695	21.8348 8542	19.7752 9410	92
93	35.9752 3516	31.2002 0567	27.4060 1673	24.3486 1245	21.8515 6499	19.7859 9438	93
94	36.0734 0016	31.2623 3560	27.4454 2680	24.3736 6582	21.8675 2631	19.7961 8512	94
95	36.1691 7089	31.3226 5592	27.4835 0415	24.3977 5559	21.8828 0030	19.8058 9059	95
96	36.2626 0574	31.3812 1934	27.5202 9387	24.4209 1884	21.8974 1655	19.8151 3390	96
97	36.3537 6170	31.4380 7703	27.5558 3948	24.4431 9119	21.9114 0340	19.8239 3705	97
98	36.4426 9434	31.4932 7867	27.5901 8308	24.4646 0692	21.9247 8794	19.8323 2100	98
99	36.5294 5790	31.5468 7250	27.6233 6529	24.4851 9896	21.9375 9612	19.8403 0571	99
100	36.6141 0526	31.5989 0534	27.6554 2540	24.5049 9900	21.9498 5274	19.8479 1020	100

Table A-4 (Cont.)

n	5½%	6%	6½%	7%	7½%	8%	n
1	0.9478 6730	0.9433 9623	0.9389 6714	0.9345 7944	0.9302 3256	0.9259 2593	1
2	1.8463 1971	1.8333 9267	1.8206 2642	1.8080 1817	1.7955 6517	1.7832 6475	2
3	2.6979 3338	2.6730 1195	2.6484 7551	2.6243 1604	2.6005 2574	2.5770 9699	3
4	3.5051 5012	3.4651 0561	3.4257 9860	3.3872 1126	3.3493 2627	3.3121 2684	4
5	4.2702 8448	4.2123 6379	4.1556 7944	4.1001 9744	4.0458 8490	3.9927 1004	5
6	4.9955 3031	4.9173 2433	4.8410 1356	4.7665 3966	4.6938 4642	4.6228 7966	6
7	5.6829 6712	5.5823 8144	5.4845 1977	5.3892 8940	5.2966 0132	5.2063 7006	7
8	6.3345 6599	6.2097 9381	6.0887 5096	5.9712 9851	5.8573 0355	5.7466 3894	8
9	6.9521 9525	6.8016 9227	6.6561 0419	6.5152 3225	6.3788 8703	6.2468 8791	9
10	7.5376 2583	7.3600 8705	7.1888 3022	7.0235 8154	6.8640 8096	6.7100 8140	10
11	8.0925 3633	7.8868 7458	7.6890 4246	7.4986 7434	7.3154 2415	7.1389 6426	11
12	8.6185 1785	8.3838 4394	8.1587 2532	7.9426 8630	7.7352 7827	7.5360 7802	12
13	9.1170 7853	8.8526 8296	8.5997 4208	8.3576 5074	8.1258 4026	7.9037 7594	13
14	9.5896 4790	9.2949 8393	9.0138 4233	8.7454 6799	8.4891 5373	8.2442 3698	14
15	10.0375 8094	9.7122 4899	9.4026 6885	9.1079 1401	8.8271 1974	8.5594 7869	15
16	10.4621 6203	10.1058 9527	9.7677 6418	9.4466 4860	9.1415 0674	8.8513 6916	16
17	10.8646 0856	10.4772 5969	10.1105 7670	9.7632 2299	9.4339 5976	9.1216 3811	17
18	11.2460 7447	10.8276 0348	10.4324 6638	10.0590 8691	9.7060 0908	9.3718 8714	18
19	11.6076 5352	11.1581 1649	10.7347 1022	10.3355 9524	9.9590 7821	9.6035 9920	19
20	11.9503 8248	11.4699 2122	11.0185 0725	10.5940 1425	10.1944 9136	9.8181 4741	20
21	12.2752 4406	11.7640 7662	11.2849 8333	10.8355 2733	10.4134 8033	10.0168 0316	21
22	12.5831 6973	12.0415 8172	11.5351 9562	11.0612 4050	10.6171 9101	10.2007 4366	22
23	12.8750 4239	12.3033 7898	11.7701 3673	11.2721 8738	10.8066 8931	10.3710 5895	23
24	13.1516 9895	12.5503 5753	11.9907 3871	11.4693 3400	10.9829 6680	10.5287 5828	24
25	13.4139 3266	12.7833 5616	12.1978 7673	11.6535 8318	11.1469 4586	10.6747 7619	25
26	13.6624 9541	13.0031 6619	12.3923 7251	11.8257 7867	11.2994 8452	10.8099 7795	26
27	13.8980 9991	13.2105 3414	12.5749 9766	11.9867 0904	11.4413 8095	10.9351 6477	27
28	14.1214 2172	13.4061 6428	12.7464 7668	12.1371 1125	11.5733 7763	11.0510 7849	28
29	14.3331 0116	13.5907 2102	12.9074 8984	12.2776 7407	11.6961 6524	11.1584 0601	29
30	14.5337 4517	13.7648 3115	13.0586 7591	12.4090 4118	11.8103 8627	11.2577 8334	30
31	14.7239 2907	13.9290 8599	13.2006 3465	12.5318 1419	11.9166 3839	11.3497 9939	31
32	14.9041 9817	14.0840 4339	13.3339 2925	12.6465 5532	12.0154 7757	11.4349 9944	32
33	15.0750 6936	14.2302 2961	13.4590 8850	12.7537 9002	12.1074 2099	11.5138 8837	33
34	15.2370 3257	14.3681 4114	13.5766 0892	12.8540 0936	12.1929 4976	11.5869 3367	34
35	15.3905 5220	14.4982 4636	13.6869 5673	12.9476 7230	12.2725 1141	11.6545 6822	35
36	15.5360 6843	14.6209 8713	13.7905 6970	13.0352 0776	12.3465 2224	11.7171 9279	36
37	15.6739 9851	14.7367 8031	13.8878 5887	13.1170 1660	12.4153 6952	11.7751 7851	37
38	15.8047 3793	14.8460 1916	13.9792 1021	13.1934 7345	12.4794 1351	11.8288 6899	38
39	15.9286 6154	14.9490 7468	14.0649 8611	13.2649 2846	12.5389 8931	11.8785 8240	39
40	16.0461 2469	15.0462 9687	14.1455 2687	13.3317 0884	12.5944 0866	11.9246 1333	40
41	16.1574 6416	15.1380 1592	14.2211 5199	13.3941 2041	12.6459 6155	11.9672 3457	41
42	16.2629 9920	15.2245 4332	14.2921 6149	13.4524 4898	12.6939 1772	12.0066 9867	42
43	16.3630 3242	15.3061 7294	14.3588 3708	13.5069 6167	12.7385 2811	12.0432 3951	43
44	16.4578 5063	15.3831 8202	14.4214 4327	13.5579 0810	12.7800 2615	12.0770 7362	44
45	16.5477 2572	15.4558 3209	14.4802 2842	13.6055 2159	12.8186 2898	12.1084 0150	45
46	16.6329 1537	15.5243 6990	14.5354 2575	13.6500 2018	12.8545 3858	12.1374 0880	46
47	16.7136 6386	15.5890 2821	14.5872 5422	13.6916 0764	12.8879 4287	12.1642 6741	47
48	16.7902 0271	15.6500 2661	14.6359 1946	13.7304 7443	12.9190 1662	12.1891 3649	48
49	16.8627 5139	15.7075 7227	14.6816 1451	13.7667 9853	12.9479 2244	12.2121 6341	49
50	16.9315 1790	15.7618 6064	14.7245 2067	13.8007 4629	12.9748 1157	12.2334 8464	50

Table A-5

$$\text{Values of } 1/s_{\overline{n}|i} \qquad \frac{1}{s_{\overline{n}|i}} = \frac{i}{(1+i)^n - 1} \qquad \left(\frac{1}{a_{\overline{n}|i}} = \frac{1}{s_{\overline{n}|i}} + i \right)$$

n	$\frac{1}{4}\%$	$\frac{1}{3}\%$	$\frac{5}{12}\%$	$\frac{1}{2}\%$	$\frac{7}{12}\%$	$\frac{2}{3}\%$	n
1	1.0000 0000	1.0000 0000	1.0000 0000	1.0000 0000	1.0000 0000	1.0000 0000	1
2	0.4993 7578	0.4991 6805	0.4989 6050	0.4987 5312	0.4985 4591	0.4983 3887	2
3	0.3325 0139	0.3322 2469	0.3319 4829	0.3316 7221	0.3313 9643	0.3311 2095	3
4	0.2490 6445	0.2487 5347	0.2484 4291	0.2481 3279	0.2478 2310	0.2475 1384	4
5	0.1990 0250	0.1986 7110	0.1983 4026	0.1980 0997	0.1976 8024	0.1973 5105	5
6	0.1656 2803	0.1652 8317	0.1649 3898	0.1645 9546	0.1642 5260	0.1639 1042	6
7	0.1417 8928	0.1414 3491	0.1410 8133	0.1407 2854	0.1403 7653	0.1400 2531	7
8	0.1239 1035	0.1235 4895	0.1231 8845	0.1228 2886	0.1224 7018	0.1221 1240	8
9	0.1100 0462	0.1096 3785	0.1092 7209	0.1089 0736	0.1085 4365	0.1081 8096	9
10	0.0988 8015	0.0985 0915	0.0981 3929	0.0977 7057	0.0974 0299	0.0970 3654	10
11	0.0897 7840	0.0894 0402	0.0890 3090	0.0886 5903	0.0882 8842	0.0879 1905	11
12	0.0821 9370	0.0818 1657	0.0814 4082	0.0810 6643	0.0806 9341	0.0803 2176	12
13	0.0757 7595	0.0753 9656	0.0750 1866	0.0746 4224	0.0742 6730	0.0738 9385	13
14	0.0702 7510	0.0698 9383	0.0695 1416	0.0691 3609	0.0687 5962	0.0638 8474	14
15	0.0655 0777	0.0651 2491	0.0647 4378	0.0643 6436	0.0639 8666	0.0636 1067	15
16	0.0613 3642	0.0609 5223	0.0605 6988	0.0601 8937	0.0598 1068	0.0594 3382	16
17	0.0576 5587	0.0572 7056	0.0568 8720	0.0565 0579	0.0561 2632	0.0557 4880	17
18	0.0543 8433	0.0539 9807	0.0536 1387	0.0532 3173	0.0528 5165	0.0524 7363	18
19	0.0514 5722	0.0510 7015	0.0506 8525	0.0503 0253	0.0499 2198	0.0495 4361	19
20	0.0488 2288	0.0484 3511	0.0480 4963	0.0476 6645	0.0472 8556	0.0469 0696	20
21	0.0464 3947	0.0460 5111	0.0456 6517	0.0452 8163	0.0449 0050	0.0445 2176	21
22	0.0442 7278	0.0438 8393	0.0434 9760	0.0431 1380	0.0427 3251	0.0423 5374	22
23	0.0422 9455	0.0419 0528	0.0415 1865	0.0411 3465	0.0407 5329	0.0403 7456	23
24	0.0404 8121	0.0400 9159	0.0397 0472	0.0393 2061	0.0389 3925	0.0385 6062	24
25	0.0388 1298	0.0384 2307	0.0380 3603	0.0376 5186	0.0372 7055	0.0368 9210	25
26	0.0372 7312	0.0368 8297	0.0364 9581	0.0361 1163	0.0357 3043	0.0353 5220	26
27	0.0358 4736	0.0354 5702	0.0350 6978	0.0346 8565	0.0343 0460	0.0339 2664	27
28	0.0345 2347	0.0341 3299	0.0337 4572	0.0333 6167	0.0329 8082	0.0326 0317	28
29	0.0332 9093	0.0329 0033	0.0325 1307	0.0321 2914	0.0317 4853	0.0313 7123	29
30	0.0321 4059	0.0317 4992	0.0313 6270	0.0309 7892	0.0305 9857	0.0302 2166	30
31	0.0310 6449	0.0306 7378	0.0302 8663	0.0299 0304	0.0295 2299	0.0291 4649	31
32	0.0300 5569	0.0296 6496	0.0292 7791	0.0288 9453	0.0285 1482	0.0281 3875	32
33	0.0291 0806	0.0287 1734	0.0283 3041	0.0279 4727	0.0275 6791	0.0271 9231	33
34	0.0282 1620	0.0278 2551	0.0274 3873	0.0270 5586	0.0266 7687	0.0263 0176	34
35	0.0273 7533	0.0269 8470	0.0265 9809	0.0262 1550	0.0258 3691	0.0254 6231	35
36	0.0265 8121	0.0261 9065	0.0258 0423	0.0254 2194	0.0250 4376	0.0246 6970	36
37	0.0258 3004	0.0254 3957	0.0250 5336	0.0246 7139	0.0242 9365	0.0239 2013	37
38	0.0251 1843	0.0247 2808	0.0243 4208	0.0239 6045	0.0235 8316	0.0232 1020	38
39	0.0244 4335	0.0240 5311	0.0236 6736	0.0232 8607	0.0229 0925	0.0225 3687	39
40	0.0238 0204	0.0234 1194	0.0230 2644	0.0226 4552	0.0222 6917	0.0218 9739	40
41	0.0231 9204	0.0228 0209	0.0224 1685	0.0220 3631	0.0216 6046	0.0212 8928	41
42	0.0226 1112	0.0222 2133	0.0218 3637	0.0214 5622	0.0210 8087	0.0207 1031	42
43	0.0220 5724	0.0216 6762	0.0212 8295	0.0209 0320	0.0205 2836	0.0201 5843	43
44	0.0215 2855	0.0211 3912	0.0207 5474	0.0203 7541	0.0200 0110	0.0196 3180	44
45	0.0210 2339	0.0206 3415	0.0202 5008	0.0198 7117	0.0194 9740	0.0191 2875	45
46	0.0205 4022	0.0201 5118	0.0197 6743	0.0193 8894	0.0190 1571	0.0186 4772	46
47	0.0200 7762	0.0196 8880	0.0193 0537	0.0189 2733	0.0185 5465	0.0181 8732	47
48	0.0196 3433	0.0192 4572	0.0188 6263	0.0184 8503	0.0181 1291	0.0177 4626	48
49	0.0192 0915	0.0188 2077	0.0184 3801	0.0180 6087	0.0176 8932	0.0173 2334	49
50	0.0188 0099	0.0184 1285	0.0180 3044	0.0176 5376	0.0172 8278	0.0169 1749	50

Table A-5 (Cont.)

n	$\frac{1}{4}\%$	$\frac{1}{3}\%$	$\frac{5}{12}\%$	$\frac{1}{2}\%$	$\frac{7}{12}\%$	$\frac{2}{3}\%$	n
51	0.0184 0886	0.0180 2096	0.0176 3891	0.0172 6269	0.0168 9230	0.0165 2770	51
52	0.0180 3184	0.0176 4418	0.0172 6249	0.0168 8675	0.0165 1694	0.0161 5304	52
53	0.0176 6906	0.0172 8165	0.0169 0033	0.0165 2507	0.0161 5585	0.0157 9266	53
54	0.0173 1974	0.0169 3259	0.0165 5164	0.0161 7686	0.0158 0824	0.0154 4576	54
55	0.0169 8314	0.0165 9625	0.0162 1567	0.0158 4139	0.0154 7337	0.0151 1160	55
56	0.0166 5858	0.0162 7196	0.0158 9176	0.0155 1797	0.0151 5056	0.0147 8951	56
57	0.0163 4542	0.0159 5907	0.0155 7927	0.0152 0598	0.0148 3918	0.0144 7885	57
58	0.0160 4308	0.0156 5701	0.0152 7760	0.0149 0481	0.0145 3863	0.0141 7903	58
59	0.0157 5101	0.0153 6522	0.0149 8620	0.0146 1392	0.0142 4836	0.0138 8949	59
60	0.0154 6869	0.0150 8319	0.0147 0457	0.0143 3280	0.0139 6787	0.0136 0973	60
61	0.0151 9564	0.0148 1043	0.0144 3221	0.0140 6096	0.0136 9666	0.0133 3926	61
62	0.0149 3142	0.0145 4650	0.0141 6869	0.0137 9796	0.0134 3428	0.0130 7763	62
63	0.0146 7561	0.0142 9098	0.0139 1358	0.0135 4337	0.0131 8033	0.0128 2442	63
64	0.0144 2780	0.0140 4348	0.0136 6649	0.0132 9681	0.0129 3440	0.0125 7923	64
65	0.0141 8764	0.0138 0361	0.0134 2704	0.0130 5789	0.0126 9612	0.0123 4171	65
66	0.0139 5476	0.0135 7105	0.0131 9489	0.0128 2627	0.0124 6515	0.0121 1149	66
67	0.0137 2886	0.0133 4545	0.0129 6972	0.0126 0163	0.0122 4116	0.0118 8825	67
68	0.0135 0961	0.0131 2652	0.0127 5121	0.0123 8366	0.0120 2383	0.0116 7168	68
69	0.0132 9674	0.0129 1395	0.0125 3908	0.0121 7206	0.0118 1289	0.0114 6150	69
70	0.0130 8996	0.0127 0749	0.0123 3304	0.0119 6657	0.0116 0805	0.0112 5742	70
71	0.0128 8902	0.0125 0687	0.0121 3285	0.0117 6693	0.0114 0906	0.0110 5919	71
72	0.0126 9368	0.0123 1185	0.0119 3827	0.0115 7289	0.0112 1567	0.0108 6657	72
73	0.0125 0370	0.0121 2220	0.0117 4905	0.0113 8422	0.0110 2766	0.0106 7933	73
74	0.0123 1887	0.0119 3769	0.0115 6498	0.0112 0070	0.0108 4481	0.0104 9725	74
75	0.0121 3898	0.0117 5813	0.0113 8586	0.0110 2214	0.0106 6690	0.0103 2011	75
76	0.0119 6385	0.0115 8332	0.0112 1150	0.0108 4832	0.0104 9375	0.0101 4773	76
77	0.0117 9327	0.0114 1308	0.0110 4170	0.0106 7908	0.0103 2517	0.0099 7993	77
78	0.0116 2708	0.0112 4722	0.0108 7629	0.0105 1423	0.0101 6099	0.0098 1652	78
79	0.0114 6511	0.0110 8559	0.0107 1510	0.0103 5360	0.0100 0103	0.0096 5733	79
80	0.0113 0721	0.0109 2802	0.0105 5798	0.0101 9704	0.0098 4514	0.0095 0222	80
81	0.0111 5321	0.0107 7436	0.0104 0477	0.0100 4439	0.0096 9316	0.0093 5102	81
82	0.0110 0298	0.0106 2447	0.0102 5534	0.0098 9552	0.0095 4496	0.0092 0360	82
83	0.0108 5639	0.0104 7822	0.0101 0954	0.0097 5028	0.0094 0040	0.0090 5982	83
84	0.0107 1330	0.0103 3547	0.0099 6724	0.0096 0855	0.0092 5935	0.0089 1955	84
85	0.0105 7359	0.0101 9610	0.0098 2833	0.0094 7021	0.0091 2168	0.0087 8266	85
86	0.0104 3714	0.0100 6000	0.0096 9268	0.0093 3513	0.0089 8727	0.0086 4904	86
87	0.0103 0384	0.0099 2704	0.0095 6018	0.0092 0320	0.0088 5602	0.0085 1857	87
88	0.0101 7357	0.0097 9713	0.0094 3073	0.0090 7431	0.0087 2781	0.0083 9115	88
89	0.0100 4625	0.0096 7015	0.0093 0422	0.0089 4837	0.0086 0255	0.0082 6667	89
90	0.0099 2177	0.0095 4602	0.0091 8055	0.0088 2527	0.0084 8013	0.0081 4504	90
91	0.0098 0004	0.0094 2464	0.0090 5962	0.0087 0493	0.0083 6047	0.0080 2616	91
92	0.0096 8096	0.0093 0592	0.0089 4136	0.0085 8724	0.0082 4346	0.0079 0994	92
93	0.0095 6446	0.0091 8976	0.0088 2568	0.0084 7213	0.0081 2903	0.0077 9629	93
94	0.0094 5044	0.0090 7610	0.0087 1248	0.0083 5950	0.0080 1709	0.0076 8514	94
95	0.0093 3884	0.0089 6485	0.0086 0170	0.0082 4930	0.0079 0757	0.0075 7641	95
96	0.0092 2957	0.0088 5594	0.0084 9325	0.0081 4143	0.0078 0038	0.0074 7001	96
97	0.0091 2257	0.0087 4929	0.0083 8707	0.0080 3583	0.0076 9547	0.0073 6588	97
98	0.0090 1776	0.0086 4484	0.0082 8309	0.0079 3242	0.0075 9275	0.0072 6394	98
99	0.0089 1508	0.0085 4252	0.0081 8124	0.0078 3115	0.0074 9216	0.0071 6415	99
100	0.0088 1446	0.0084 4226	0.0080 8145	0.0077 3194	0.0073 9363	0.0070 6642	100

Table A-5 (Cont.)

n	$\frac{1}{4}\%$	$\frac{1}{3}\%$	$\frac{5}{12}\%$	$\frac{1}{2}\%$	$\frac{7}{12}\%$	$\frac{2}{3}\%$	n
101	0.0087 1584	0.0083 4400	0.0079 8366	0.0076 3473	0.0072 9711	0.0069 7069	101
102	0.0086 1917	0.0082 4769	0.0078 8782	0.0075 3947	0.0072 0254	0.0068 7690	102
103	0.0085 2439	0.0081 5327	0.0077 9387	0.0074 4610	0.0071 0986	0.0067 8501	103
104	0.0084 3144	0.0080 6068	0.0077 0175	0.0073 5457	0.0070 1901	0.0066 9495	104
105	0.0083 4027	0.0079 6987	0.0076 1142	0.0072 6481	0.0069 2994	0.0066 0668	105
106	0.0082 5082	0.0078 8079	0.0075 2281	0.0071 7679	0.0068 4261	0.0065 2013	106
107	0.0081 6307	0.0077 9340	0.0074 3589	0.0070 9045	0.0067 5696	0.0064 3527	107
108	0.0080 7694	0.0077 0764	0.0073 5061	0.0070 0575	0.0066 7294	0.0063 5205	108
109	0.0079 9241	0.0076 2347	0.0072 6691	0.0069 2264	0.0065 9052	0.0062 7042	109
110	0.0079 0942	0.0075 4084	0.0071 8476	0.0068 4107	0.0065 0965	0.0061 9033	110
111	0.0078 2793	0.0074 5972	0.0071 0412	0.0067 6102	0.0064 3028	0.0061 1175	111
112	0.0077 4791	0.0073 8007	0.0070 2495	0.0066 8242	0.0063 5237	0.0060 3464	112
113	0.0076 6932	0.0073 0184	0.0069 4720	0.0066 0526	0.0062 7590	0.0059 5895	113
114	0.0075 9211	0.0072 2500	0.0068 7083	0.0065 2948	0.0062 0081	0.0058 8465	114
115	0.0075 1626	0.0071 4952	0.0067 9582	0.0064 5506	0.0061 2708	0.0058 1171	115
116	0.0074 4172	0.0070 7535	0.0067 2213	0.0063 8195	0.0060 5466	0.0057 4008	116
117	0.0073 6846	0.0070 0246	0.0066 4973	0.0063 1013	0.0059 8353	0.0056 6974	117
118	0.0072 9646	0.0069 3082	0.0065 7857	0.0062 3956	0.0059 1365	0.0056 0065	118
119	0.0072 2567	0.0068 6041	0.0065 0863	0.0061 7021	0.0058 4499	0.0055 3278	119
120	0.0071 5607	0.0067 9118	0.0064 3988	0.0061 0205	0.0057 7751	0.0054 6609	120
121	0.0070 8764	0.0067 2311	0.0063 7230	0.0060 3505	0.0057 1120	0.0054 0057	121
122	0.0070 2033	0.0066 5617	0.0063 0584	0.0059 6918	0.0056 4602	0.0053 3618	122
123	0.0069 5412	0.0065 9034	0.0062 4049	0.0059 0441	0.0055 8194	0.0052 7289	123
124	0.0068 8899	0.0065 2558	0.0061 7621	0.0058 4072	0.0055 1894	0.0052 1067	124
125	0.0068 2491	0.0064 6188	0.0061 1298	0.0057 7808	0.0054 5700	0.0051 4951	125
126	0.0067 6186	0.0063 9919	0.0060 5078	0.0057 1647	0.0053 9607	0.0050 8937	126
127	0.0066 9981	0.0063 3751	0.0059 8959	0.0056 5586	0.0053 3615	0.0050 3024	127
128	0.0066 3873	0.0062 7681	0.0059 2937	0.0055 9623	0.0052 7721	0.0049 7208	128
129	0.0065 7861	0.0062 1707	0.0058 7010	0.0055 3755	0.0052 1922	0.0049 1488	129
130	0.0065 1942	0.0061 5825	0.0058 1177	0.0054 7981	0.0051 6216	0.0048 5861	130
131	0.0064 6115	0.0061 0035	0.0057 5435	0.0054 2298	0.0051 0602	0.0048 0325	131
132	0.0064 0376	0.0060 4334	0.0056 9782	0.0053 6703	0.0050 5077	0.0047 4878	132
133	0.0063 4725	0.0059 8720	0.0056 4216	0.0053 1197	0.0049 9639	0.0046 9518	133
134	0.0062 9159	0.0059 3191	0.0055 8736	0.0052 5775	0.0049 4286	0.0046 4244	134
135	0.0062 3675	0.0058 7745	0.0055 3339	0.0052 0436	0.0048 9016	0.0045 9052	135
136	0.0061 8274	0.0058 2381	0.0054 8023	0.0051 5179	0.0048 3828	0.0045 3942	136
137	0.0061 2952	0.0057 7097	0.0054 2787	0.0051 0002	0.0047 8719	0.0044 8911	137
138	0.0060 7707	0.0057 1890	0.0053 7628	0.0050 4902	0.0047 3688	0.0044 3959	138
139	0.0060 2539	0.0056 6760	0.0053 2546	0.0049 9879	0.0046 8733	0.0043 9082	139
140	0.0059 7446	0.0056 1704	0.0052 7539	0.0049 4930	0.0046 3853	0.0043 4280	140
141	0.0059 2425	0.0055 6721	0.0052 2604	0.0049 0055	0.0045 9046	0.0042 9551	141
142	0.0058 7476	0.0055 1809	0.0051 7741	0.0048 5250	0.0045 4311	0.0042 4893	142
143	0.0058 2597	0.0054 6968	0.0051 2948	0.0048 0516	0.0044 9645	0.0042 0305	143
144	0.0057 7787	0.0054 2195	0.0050 8224	0.0047 5850	0.0044 5048	0.0041 5786	144
145	0.0057 3043	0.0053 7489	0.0050 3566	0.0047 1252	0.0044 0518	0.0041 1333	145
146	0.0056 8365	0.0053 2849	0.0049 8975	0.0046 6718	0.0043 6053	0.0040 6947	146
147	0.0056 3752	0.0052 8273	0.0049 4447	0.0046 2250	0.0043 1653	0.0040 2624	147
148	0.0055 9201	0.0052 3760	0.0048 9983	0.0045 7844	0.0042 7316	0.0039 8364	148
149	0.0055 4712	0.0051 9309	0.0048 5580	0.0045 3500	0.0042 3040	0.0039 4166	149
150	0.0055 0284	0.0051 4919	0.0048 1238	0.0044 9217	0.0041 8825	0.0039 0029	150

Table A-5 (Cont.)

n	$\frac{3}{4}\%$	1%	$1\frac{1}{4}\%$	$1\frac{1}{2}\%$	$1\frac{3}{4}\%$	2%	n
1	1.0000 0000	1.0000 0000	1.0000 0000	1.0000 0000	1.0000 0000	1.0000 0000	1
2	0.4981 3200	0.4975 1244	0.4968 9441	0.4962 7792	0.4956 6295	0.4950 4950	2
3	0.3308 4579	0.3300 2211	0.3292 0117	0.3283 8296	0.3275 6746	0.3267 5467	3
4	0.2472 0501	0.2462 8109	0.2453 6102	0.2444 4479	0.2435 3237	0.2426 2375	4
5	0.1970 2242	0.1960 3980	0.1950 6211	0.1940 8932	0.1931 2142	0.1921 5839	5
6	0.1635 6891	0.1625 4837	0.1615 3381	0.1605 2521	0.1595 2256	0.1585 2581	6
7	0.1396 7488	0.1386 2828	0.1375 8872	0.1365 5616	0.1355 3059	0.1345 1196	7
8	0.1217 5552	0.1206 9029	0.1196 3314	0.1185 8402	0.1175 4292	0.1165 0980	8
9	0.1078 1929	0.1067 4036	0.1056 7055	0.1046 0982	0.1035 5813	0.1025 1544	9
10	0.0966 7123	0.0955 8208	0.0945 0307	0.0934 3418	0.0923 7534	0.0913 2653	10
11	0.0875 5094	0.0864 5408	0.0853 6839	0.0842 9384	0.0832 3038	0.0821 7794	11
12	0.0799 5148	0.0788 4879	0.0777 5831	0.0766 7999	0.0756 1377	0.0745 5960	12
13	0.0735 2188	0.0724 1482	0.0713 2100	0.0702 4036	0.0691 7283	0.0681 1835	13
14	0.0680 1146	0.0669 0117	0.0658 0515	0.0647 2332	0.0636 5562	0.0626 0197	14
15	0.0632 3639	0.0621 2378	0.0610 2646	0.0599 4436	0.0588 7739	0.0578 2547	15
16	0.0590 5879	0.0579 4460	0.0568 4672	0.0557 6508	0.0546 9958	0.0536 5013	16
17	0.0553 7321	0.0542 5806	0.0531 6023	0.0520 7966	0.0510 1623	0.0499 6984	17
18	0.0520 9766	0.0509 8205	0.0498 8479	0.0488 0578	0.0477 4492	0.0467 0210	18
19	0.0491 6740	0.0480 5175	0.0469 5548	0.0458 7847	0.0448 2061	0.0437 8177	19
20	0.0465 3063	0.0454 1531	0.0443 2039	0.0432 4574	0.0421 9122	0.0411 5672	20
21	0.0441 4543	0.0430 3075	0.0419 3749	0.0408 6550	0.0398 1464	0.0387 8477	21
22	0.0419 7748	0.0408 6372	0.0397 7238	0.0387 0332	0.0376 5638	0.0366 3140	22
23	0.0399 9846	0.0388 8584	0.0377 9666	0.0367 3075	0.0356 8796	0.0346 6810	23
24	0.0381 8474	0.0370 7347	0.0359 8665	0.0349 2410	0.0338 8565	0.0328 7110	24
25	0.0365 1650	0.0354 0675	0.0343 2247	0.0332 6345	0.0322 2952	0.0312 2044	25
26	0.0349 7693	0.0338 6888	0.0327 8729	0.0317 3196	0.0307 0269	0.0296 9923	26
27	0.0335 5176	0.0324 4553	0.0313 6677	0.0303 1527	0.0292 9079	0.0282 9309	27
28	0.0322 2871	0.0311 2444	0.0300 4863	0.0290 0108	0.0279 8151	0.0269 8967	28
29	0.0309 9723	0.0298 9502	0.0288 2228	0.0277 7878	0.0267 6424	0.0257 7836	29
30	0.0298 4816	0.0287 4811	0.0276 7854	0.0266 3919	0.0256 2975	0.0246 4992	30
31	0.0287 7352	0.0276 7573	0.0266 0942	0.0255 7430	0.0245 7005	0.0235 9635	31
32	0.0277 6634	0.0266 7089	0.0256 0791	0.0245 7710	0.0235 7812	0.0226 1061	32
33	0.0268 2048	0.0257 2744	0.0246 6786	0.0236 4144	0.0226 4779	0.0216 8653	33
34	0.0259 3053	0.0248 3997	0.0237 8387	0.0227 6189	0.0217 7363	0.0208 1867	34
35	0.0250 9170	0.0240 0368	0.0229 5111	0.0219 3363	0.0209 5082	0.0200 0221	35
36	0.0242 9973	0.0232 1431	0.0221 6533	0.0211 5240	0.0201 7507	0.0192 3285	36
37	0.0235 5082	0.0224 6805	0.0214 2270	0.0204 1437	0.0194 4257	0.0185 0678	37
38	0.0228 4157	0.0217 6150	0.0207 1983	0.0197 1613	0.0187 4990	0.0178 2057	38
39	0.0221 6893	0.0210 9160	0.0200 5365	0.0190 5463	0.0180 9399	0.0171 7114	39
40	0.0215 3016	0.0204 5560	0.0194 2141	0.0184 2710	0.0174 7209	0.0165 5575	40
41	0.0209 2276	0.0198 5102	0.0188 2063	0.0178 3106	0.0168 8170	0.0159 7188	41
42	0.0203 4452	0.0192 7563	0.0182 4906	0.0172 6426	0.0163 2057	0.0154 1729	42
43	0.0197 9338	0.0187 2737	0.0177 0466	0.0167 2465	0.0157 8666	0.0148 8993	43
44	0.0192 6751	0.0182 0441	0.0171 8557	0.0162 1038	0.0152 7810	0.0143 8794	44
45	0.0187 6521	0.0177 0505	0.0166 9012	0.0157 1976	0.0147 9321	0.0139 0962	45
46	0.0182 8495	0.0172 2775	0.0162 1675	0.0152 5125	0.0143 3043	0.0134 5342	46
47	0.0178 2532	0.0167 7111	0.0157 6406	0.0148 0342	0.0138 8836	0.0130 1792	47
48	0.0173 8504	0.0163 3384	0.0153 3075	0.0143 7500	0.0134 6569	0.0126 0184	48
49	0.0169 6292	0.0159 1474	0.0149 1563	0.0139 6478	0.0130 6124	0.0122 0396	49
50	0.0165 5787	0.0155 1273	0.0145 1763	0.0135 7168	0.0126 7391	0.0118 2321	50

n	¾%	1%	1¼%	1½%	1¾%	2%	n
51	0.0161 6888	0.0151 2680	0.0141 3571	0.0131 9469	0.0123 0269	0.0114 5856	51
52	0.0157 9503	0.0147 5603	0.0137 6897	0.0128 3287	0.0119 4665	0.0111 0909	52
53	0.0154 3546	0.0143 9956	0.0134 1653	0.0124 8537	0.0116 0492	0.0107 7392	53
54	0.0150 8938	0.0140 5658	0.0130 7760	0.0121 5138	0.0112 7672	0.0104 5226	54
55	0.0147 5605	0.0137 2637	0.0127 5145	0.0118 3018	0.0109 6129	0.0101 4337	55
56	0.0144 3478	0.0134 0824	0.0124 3739	0.0115 2106	0.0106 5795	0.0098 4656	56
57	0.0141 2496	0.0131 0156	0.0121 3478	0.0112 2341	0.0103 6606	0.0095 6120	57
58	0.0138 2597	0.0128 0573	0.0118 4303	0.0109 3661	0.0100 8503	0.0092 8667	58
59	0.0135 3727	0.0125 2020	0.0115 6158	0.0106 6012	0.0098 1430	0.0090 2243	59
60	0.0132 5836	0.0122 4445	0.0112 8993	0.0103 9343	0.0095 5336	0.0087 6797	60
61	0.0129 8873	0.0119 7800	0.0110 2758	0.0101 3604	0.0093 0172	0.0085 2278	61
62	0.0127 2795	0.0117 2041	0.0107 7410	0.0098 8751	0.0090 5892	0.0082 8643	62
63	0.0124 7560	0.0114 7125	0.0105 2904	0.0096 4741	0.0088 2455	0.0080 5848	63
64	0.0122 3127	0.0112 3013	0.0102 9203	0.0094 1534	0.0085 9821	0.0078 3855	64
65	0.0119 9460	0.0109 9667	0.0100 6268	0.0091 9094	0.0083 7952	0.0076 2624	65
66	0.0117 6524	0.0107 7052	0.0098 4065	0.0089 7386	0.0081 6813	0.0074 2122	66
67	0.0115 4286	0.0105 5136	0.0096 2560	0.0087 6376	0.0079 6372	0.0072 2316	67
68	0.0113 2716	0.0103 3889	0.0094 1724	0.0085 6033	0.0077 6597	0.0070 3173	68
69	0.0111 1785	0.0101 3280	0.0092 1527	0.0083 6329	0.0075 7459	0.0068 4665	69
70	0.0109 1464	0.0099 3282	0.0090 1941	0.0081 7235	0.0073 8930	0.0066 6765	70
71	0.0107 1728	0.0097 3870	0.0088 2941	0.0079 8727	0.0072 0985	0.0064 9446	71
72	0.0105 2554	0.0095 5019	0.0086 4501	0.0078 0779	0.0070 3600	0.0063 2683	72
73	0.0103 3917	0.0093 6706	0.0084 6600	0.0076 3368	0.0068 6750	0.0061 6454	73
74	0.0101 5796	0.0091 8910	0.0082 9215	0.0074 6473	0.0067 0413	0.0060 0736	74
75	0.0099 8170	0.0090 1609	0.0081 2325	0.0073 0072	0.0065 4570	0.0058 5508	75
76	0.0098 1020	0.0088 4784	0.0079 5910	0.0071 4146	0.0063 9200	0.0057 0751	76
77	0.0096 4328	0.0086 8416	0.0077 9953	0.0069 8676	0.0062 4285	0.0055 6447	77
78	0.0094 8074	0.0085 2488	0.0076 4436	0.0068 3645	0.0060 9806	0.0054 2576	78
79	0.0093 2244	0.0083 6983	0.0074 9341	0.0066 9036	0.0059 5748	0.0052 9123	79
80	0.0091 6821	0.0082 1885	0.0073 4652	0.0065 4832	0.0058 2093	0.0051 6071	80
81	0.0090 1790	0.0080 7179	0.0072 0356	0.0064 1019	0.0056 8828	0.0050 3405	81
82	0.0088 7136	0.0079 2851	0.0070 6437	0.0062 7583	0.0055 5936	0.0049 1110	82
83	0.0087 2847	0.0077 8887	0.0069 2881	0.0061 4509	0.0054 3406	0.0047 9173	83
84	0.0085 8908	0.0076 5273	0.0067 9675	0.0060 1784	0.0053 1223	0.0046 7581	84
85	0.0084 5308	0.0075 1998	0.0066 6808	0.0058 9396	0.0051 9375	0.0045 6321	85
86	0.0083 2034	0.0073 9050	0.0065 4267	0.0057 7333	0.0050 7850	0.0044 5381	86
87	0.0081 9076	0.0072 6418	0.0064 2041	0.0056 5584	0.0049 6636	0.0043 4750	87
88	0.0080 6423	0.0071 4089	0.0063 0119	0.0055 4138	0.0048 5724	0.0042 4416	88
89	0.0079 4064	0.0070 2056	0.0061 8491	0.0054 2984	0.0047 5102	0.0041 4370	89
90	0.0078 1989	0.0069 0306	0.0060 7146	0.0053 2113	0.0046 4760	0.0040 4602	90
91	0.0077 0190	0.0067 8832	0.0059 6076	0.0052 1516	0.0045 4690	0.0039 5101	91
92	0.0075 8657	0.0066 7624	0.0058 5272	0.0051 1182	0.0044 4882	0.0038 5859	92
93	0.0074 7382	0.0065 6673	0.0057 4724	0.0050 1104	0.0043 5327	0.0037 6868	93
94	0.0073 6356	0.0064 5971	0.0056 4425	0.0049 1273	0.0042 6017	0.0036 8118	94
95	0.0072 5571	0.0063 5511	0.0055 4366	0.0048 1681	0.0041 6944	0.0035 9602	95
96	0.0071 5020	0.0062 5284	0.0054 4541	0.0047 2321	0.0040 8101	0.0035 1313	96
97	0.0070 4696	0.0061 5284	0.0053 4941	0.0046 3186	0.0039 9480	0.0034 3242	97
98	0.0069 4592	0.0060 5503	0.0052 5560	0.0045 4268	0.0039 1074	0.0033 5383	98
99	0.0068 4701	0.0059 5936	0.0051 6391	0.0044 5560	0.0038 2876	0.0032 7729	99
100	0.0067 5017	0.0058 6574	0.0050 7428	0.0043 7057	0.0037 4880	0.0032 0274	100

Table A-5 (Cont.)

n	$2\frac{1}{2}\%$	3%	$3\frac{1}{2}\%$	4%	$4\frac{1}{2}\%$	5%	n
1	1.0000 0000	1.0000 0000	1.0000 0000	1.0000 0000	1.0000 0000	1.0000 0000	1
2	0.4938 2716	0.4926 1084	0.4914 0049	0.4901 9608	0.4889 9756	0.4878 0488	2
3	0.3251 3717	0.3235 3036	0.3219 3418	0.3203 4854	0.3187 7336	0.3172 0856	3
4	0.2408 1788	0.2390 2705	0.2372 5114	0.2354 9005	0.2337 4365	0.2320 1183	4
5	0.1902 4686	0.1883 5457	0.1864 8137	0.1846 2711	0.1827 9164	0.1809 7480	5
6	0.1565 4997	0.1545 9750	0.1526 6821	0.1507 6190	0.1488 7839	0.1470 1747	6
7	0.1324 9543	0.1305 0635	0.1285 4449	0.1266 0961	0.1247 0147	0.1228 1982	7
8	0.1144 6735	0.1124 5639	0.1104 7665	0.1085 2783	0.1066 0965	0.1047 2181	8
9	0.1004 5689	0.0984 3386	0.0964 4601	0.0944 9299	0.0925 7447	0.0906 9008	9
10	0.0892 5876	0.0872 3051	0.0852 4137	0.0832 9094	0.0813 7882	0.0795 0457	10
11	0.0801 0596	0.0780 7745	0.0760 9197	0.0741 4904	0.0722 4818	0.0703 8889	11
12	0.0724 8713	0.0704 6209	0.0684 8395	0.0665 5217	0.0646 6619	0.0628 2541	12
13	0.0660 4827	0.0640 2954	0.0620 6157	0.0601 4373	0.0582 7535	0.0564 5577	13
14	0.0605 3652	0.0585 2634	0.0565 7073	0.0546 6897	0.0528 2032	0.0510 2397	14
15	0.0557 6646	0.0537 6658	0.0518 2507	0.0499 4110	0.0481 1381	0.0463 4229	15
16	0.0515 9899	0.0496 1085	0.0476 8483	0.0458 2000	0.0440 1537	0.0422 6991	16
17	0.0479 2777	0.0459 5253	0.0440 4313	0.0421 9852	0.0404 1758	0.0386 9914	17
18	0.0446 7008	0.0427 0870	0.0408 1684	0.0389 9333	0.0372 3690	0.0355 4622	18
19	0.0417 6062	0.0398 1388	0.0379 4033	0.0361 3862	0.0344 0734	0.0327 4501	19
20	0.0391 4713	0.0372 1571	0.0353 6108	0.0335 8175	0.0318 7614	0.0302 4259	20
21	0.0367 8733	0.0348 7178	0.0330 3659	0.0312 8011	0.0296 0057	0.0279 9611	21
22	0.0346 4661	0.0327 4739	0.0309 3207	0.0291 9881	0.0275 4565	0.0259 7051	22
23	0.0326 9638	0.0308 1390	0.0290 1880	0.0273 0906	0.0256 8249	0.0241 3682	23
24	0.0309 1282	0.0290 4742	0.0272 7283	0.0255 8683	0.0239 8703	0.0224 7090	24
25	0.0292 7592	0.0274 2787	0.0256 7404	0.0240 1196	0.0224 3903	0.0209 5246	25
26	0.0277 6875	0.0259 3829	0.0242 0540	0.0225 6738	0.0210 2137	0.0195 6432	26
27	0.0263 7687	0.0245 6421	0.0228 5241	0.0212 3854	0.0197 1946	0.0182 9186	27
28	0.0250 8793	0.0232 9323	0.0216 0265	0.0200 1298	0.0185 2081	0.0171 2253	28
29	0.0238 9127	0.0221 1467	0.0204 4538	0.0188 7993	0.0174 1461	0.0160 4551	29
30	0.0227 7764	0.0210 1926	0.0193 7133	0.0178 3010	0.0163 9154	0.0150 5144	30
31	0.0217 3900	0.0199 9893	0.0183 7240	0.0168 5535	0.0154 4345	0.0141 3212	31
32	0.0207 6831	0.0190 4662	0.0174 4150	0.0159 4859	0.0145 6320	0.0132 8042	32
33	0.0198 5938	0.0181 5612	0.0165 7242	0.0151 0357	0.0137 4453	0.0124 9004	33
34	0.0190 0675	0.0173 2196	0.0157 5966	0.0143 1477	0.0129 8191	0.0117 5545	34
35	0.0182 0558	0.0165 3929	0.0149 9835	0.0135 7732	0.0122 7045	0.0110 7171	35
36	0.0174 5158	0.0158 0379	0.0142 8416	0.0128 8688	0.0116 0578	0.0104 3446	36
37	0.0167 4090	0.0151 1162	0.0136 1325	0.0122 3957	0.0109 8402	0.0098 3979	37
38	0.0160 7012	0.0144 5934	0.0129 8214	0.0116 3192	0.0104 0169	0.0092 8423	38
39	0.0154 3615	0.0138 4385	0.0123 8775	0.0110 6083	0.0098 5567	0.0087 6462	39
40	0.0148 3623	0.0132 6238	0.0118 2728	0.0105 2349	0.0093 4315	0.0082 7816	40
41	0.0142 6786	0.0127 1241	0.0112 9822	0.0100 1738	0.0088 6158	0.0078 2229	41
42	0.0137 2876	0.0121 9167	0.0107 9828	0.0095 4020	0.0084 0868	0.0073 9471	42
43	0.0132 1688	0.0116 9811	0.0103 2539	0.0090 8989	0.0079 8235	0.0069 9333	43
44	0.0127 3037	0.0112 2985	0.0098 7768	0.0086 6454	0.0075 8071	0.0066 1625	44
45	0.0122 6751	0.0107 8518	0.0094 5343	0.0082 6246	0.0072 0202	0.0062 6173	45
46	0.0118 2676	0.0103 6254	0.0090 5108	0.0078 8205	0.0068 4471	0.0059 2820	46
47	0.0114 0669	0.0099 6051	0.0086 6919	0.0075 2189	0.0065 0734	0.0056 1421	47
48	0.0110 0599	0.0095 7777	0.0083 0646	0.0071 8065	0.0061 8858	0.0053 1843	48
49	0.0106 2348	0.0092 1314	0.0079 6167	0.0068 5712	0.0058 8722	0.0050 3965	49
50	0.0102 5806	0.0088 6549	0.0076 3371	0.0065 5020	0.0056 0215	0.0047 7674	50

Table A-5 (Cont.)

n	$2\frac{1}{2}\%$	3%	$3\frac{1}{2}\%$	4%	$4\frac{1}{2}\%$	5%	n
51	0.0099 0870	0.0085 3382	0.0073 2156,	0.0062 5885	0.0053 3232	0.0045 2867	51
52	0.0095 7446	0.0082 1718	0.0070 2429	0.0059 8212	0.0050 7679	0.0042 9450	52
53	0.0092 5449	0.0079 1471	0.0067 4100	0.0057 1915	0.0048 3469	0.0040 7334	53
54	0.0089 4799	0.0076 2558	0.0064 7090	0.0054 6910	0.0046 0519	0.0038 6438	54
55	0.0086 5419	0.0073 4907	0.0062 1323	0.0052 3124	0.0043 8754	0.0036 6686	55
56	0.0083 7243	0.0070 8447	0.0059 6730	0.0050 0487	0.0041 8105	0.0034 8010	56
57	0.0081 0204	0.0068 3114	0.0057 3245	0.0047 8932	0.0039 8506	0.0033 0343	57
58	0.0078 4244	0.0065 8848	0.0055 0810	0.0045 8401	0.0037 9897	0.0031 3626	58
59	0.0075 9307	0.0063 5593	0.0052 9366	0.0043 8836	0.0036 2221	0.0029 7802	59
60	0.0073 5340	0.0061 3296	0.0050 8862	0.0042 0185	0.0034 5426	0.0028 2818	60
61	0.0071 2294	0.0059 1908	0.0048 9249	0.0040 2398	0.0032 9462	0.0026 8627	61
62	0.0069 0126	0.0057 1385	0.0047 0480	0.0038 5430	0.0031 4284	0.0025 5183	62
63	0.0066 8790	0.0055 1682	0.0045 2513	0.0036 9237	0.0029 9848	0.0024 2442	63
64	0.0064 8249	0.0053 2760	0.0043 5308	0.0035 3780	0.0028 6115	0.0023 0365	64
65	0.0062 8463	0.0051 4581	0.0041 8826	0.0033 9019	0.0027 3047	0.0021 8915	65
66	0.0060 9398	0.0049 7110	0.0040 3031	0.0032 4921	0.0026 0608	0.0020 8057	66
67	0.0059 1021	0.0048 0313	0.0038 7892	0.0031 1451	0.0024 8765	0.0019 7758	67
68	0.0057 3300	0.0046 4159	0.0037 3375	0.0029 8578	0.0023 7487	0.0018 7986	68
69	0.0055 6206	0.0044 8618	0.0035 9453	0.0028 6272	0.0022 6745	0.0017 8715	69
70	0.0053 9712	0.0043 3663	0.0034 6095	0.0027 4506	0.0021 6511	0.0016 9915	70
71	0.0052 3790	0.0041 9266	0.0033 3277	0.0026 3253	0.0020 6759	0.0016 1563	71
72	0.0050 8417	0.0040 5404	0.0032 0973	0.0025 2489	0.0019 7465	0.0015 3633	72
73	0.0049 3568	0.0039 2053	0.0030 9160	0.0024 2190	0.0018 8606	0.0014 6103	73
74	0.0047 9222	0.0037 9191	0.0029 7816	0.0023 2334	0.0018 0159	0.0013 8953	74
75	0.0046 5358	0.0036 6796	0.0028 6919	0.0022 2900	0.0017 2104	0.0013 2161	75
76	0.0045 1956	0.0035 4849	0.0027 6450	0.0021 3869	0.0016 4422	0.0012 5709	76
77	0.0043 8997	0.0034 3331	0.0026 6390	0.0020 5221	0.0015 7094	0.0011 9580	77
78	0.0042 6463	0.0033 2224	0.0025 6721	0.0019 6939	0.0015 0104	0.0011 3756	78
79	0.0041 4338	0.0032 1510	0.0024 7426	0.0018 9007	0.0014 3434	0.0010 8222	79
80	0.0040 2605	0.0031 1175	0.0023 8489	0.0018 1408	0.0013 7069	0.0010 2962	80
81	0.0039 1248	0.0030 1201	0.0022 9894	0.0017 4127	0.0013 0995	0.0009 7963	81
82	0.0038 0254	0.0029 1576	0.0022 1628	0.0016 7150	0.0012 5197	0.0009 3211	82
83	0.0036 9608	0.0028 2284	0.0021 3676	0.0016 0463	0.0011 9663	0.0008 8694	83
84	0.0035 9298	0.0027 3313	0.0020 6025	0.0015 4054	0.0011 4379	0.0008 4399	84
85	0.0034 9310	0.0026 4650	0.0019 8662	0.0014 7909	0.0010 9334	0.0008 0316	85
86	0.0033 9633	0.0025 6284	0.0019 1576	0.0014 2018	0.0010 4516	0.0007 6433	86
87	0.0033 0255	0.0024 8202	0.0018 4756	0.0013 6370	0.0009 9915	0.0007 2740	87
88	0.0032 1165	0.0024 0393	0.0017 8190	0.0013 0953	0.0009 5522	0.0006 9228	88
89	0.0031 2353	0.0023 2848	0.0017 1868	0.0012 5758	0.0009 1325	0.0006 5888	89
90	0.0030 3809	0.0022 5556	0.0016 5781	0.0012 0775	0.0008 7316	0.0006 2711	90
91	0.0029 5523	0.0021 8508	0.0015 9919	0.0011 5995	0.0008 3486	0.0005 9689	91
92	0.0028 7486	0.0021 1694	0.0015 4273	0.0011 1410	0.0007 9827	0.0005 6815	92
93	0.0027 9690	0.0020 5107	0.0014 8834	0.0010 7010	0.0007 6331	0.0005 4080	93
94	0.0027 2126	0.0019 8737	0.0014 3594	0.0010 2789	0.0007 2991	0.0005 1478	94
95	0.0026 4786	0.0019 2577	0.0013 8546	0.0009 8738	0.0006 9799	0.0004 9003	95
96	0.0025 7662	0.0018 6619	0.0013 3682	0.0009 4850	0.0006 6749	0.0004 6648	96
97	0.0025 0747	0.0018 0856	0.0012 8995	0.0009 1119	0.0006 3834	0.0004 4407	97
98	0.0024 4034	0.0017 5281	0.0012 4478	0.0008 7538	0.0006 1048	0.0004 2274	98
99	0.0023 7517	0.0016 9886	0.0012 0124	0.0008 4100	0.0005 8385	0.0004 0245	99
100	0.0023 1188	0.0016 4667	0.0011 5927	0.0008 0800	0.0005 5839	0.0003 8314	100

Table A-5 (Cont.)

n	$5\frac{1}{2}\%$	6%	$6\frac{1}{2}\%$	7%	$7\frac{1}{2}\%$	8%	n
1	1.0000 0000	1.0000 0000	1.0000 0000	1.0000 0000	1.0000 0000	1.0000 0000	1
2	0.4866 1800	0.4854 3689	0.4842 6150	0.4830 9179	0.4819 2771	0.4807 6923	2
3	0.3156 5407	0.3141 0981	0.3125 7570	0.3110 5167	0.3095 3763	0.3080 3351	3
4	0.2302 9449	0.2285 9149	0.2269 0274	0.2252 2812	0.2235 6751	0.2219 2080	4
5	0.1791 7644	0.1773 9640	0.1756 3454	0.1738 9069	0.1721 6472	0.1704 5645	5
6	0.1451 7895	0.1433 6263	0.1415 6831	0.1397 9580	0.1380 4489	0.1363 1539	6
7	0.1209 6442	0.1191 3502	0.1173 3137	0.1155 5322	0.1138 0032	0.1120 7240	7
8	0.1028 6401	0.1010 3594	0.0992 3730	0.0974 6776	0.0957 2702	0.0940 1476	8
9	0.0888 3946	0.0870 2224	0.0852 3803	0.0834 8647	0.0817 6716	0.0800 7971	9
10	0.0776 6777	0.0758 6796	0.0741 0469	0.0723 7750	0.0706 8593	0.0690 2949	10
11	0.0685 7065	0.0667 9294	0.0650 5521	0.0633 5690	0.0616 9747	0.0600 7634	11
12	0.0610 2923	0.0592 7703	0.0575 6817	0.0559 0199	0.0542 7783	0.0526 9502	12
13	0.0546 8426	0.0529 6011	0.0512 8256	0.0496 5085	0.0480 6420	0.0465 2181	13
14	0.0492 7912	0.0475 8491	0.0459 4048	0.0443 4494	0.0427 9737	0.0412 9685	14
15	0.0446 2560	0.0429 6276	0.0413 5278	0.0397 9462	0.0382 8724	0.0368 2954	15
16	0.0405 8254	0.0389 5214	0.0373 7757	0.0358 5765	0.0343 9116	0.0329 7687	16
17	0.0370 4197	0.0354 4480	0.0339 0633	0.0324 2519	0.0310 0003	0.0296 2943	17
18	0.0339 1992	0.0323 5654	0.0308 5461	0.0294 1260	0.0280 2896	0.0267 0210	18
19	0.0311 5006	0.0296 2086	0.0281 5575	0.0267 5301	0.0254 1090	0.0241 2763	19
20	0.0286 7933	0.0271 8456	0.0257 5640	0.0243 9293	0.0230 9219	0.0218 5221	20
21	0.0264 6478	0.0250 0455	0.0236 1333	0.0222 8900	0.0210 2937	0.0198 3225	21
22	0.0244 7123	0.0230 4557	0.0216 9120	0.0204 0577	0.0191 8687	0.0180 3207	22
23	0.0226 6965	0.0212 7848	0.0199 6078	0.0187 1393	0.0175 3528	0.0164 2217	23
24	0.0210 3580	0.0196 7900	0.0183 9770	0.0171 8902	0.0160 5008	0.0149 7796	24
25	0.0195 4935	0.0182 2672	0.0169 8148	0.0158 1052	0.0147 1067	0.0136 7878	25
26	0.0181 9307	0.0169 0435	0.0156 9480	0.0145 6103	0.0134 9961	0.0125 0713	26
27	0.0169 5228	0.0156 9717	0.0145 2288	0.0134 2573	0.0124 0204	0.0114 4810	27
28	0.0158 1440	0.0145 9255	0.0134 5305	0.0123 9193	0.0114 0520	0.0104 8891	28
29	0.0147 6857	0.0135 7961	0.0124 7440	0.0114 4865	0.0104 9811	0.0096 1654	29
30	0.0138 0539	0.0126 4891	0.0115 7744	0.0105 8640	0.0096 7124	0.0088 2743	30
31	0.0129 1665	0.0117 9222	0.0107 5393	0.0097 9691	0.0089 1628	0.0081 0728	31
32	0.0120 9519	0.0110 0234	0.0099 9665	0.0090 7292	0.0082 2599	0.0074 5081	32
33	0.0113 3469	0.0102 7293	0.0092 9924	0.0084 0807	0.0075 9397	0.0068 5163	33
34	0.0106 2958	0.0095 9843	0.0086 5610	0.0077 9674	0.0070 1461	0.0063 0411	34
35	0.0099 7493	0.0089 7386	0.0080 6226	0.0072 3396	0.0064 8291	0.0058 0326	35
36	0.0093 6635	0.0083 9483	0.0075 1332	0.0067 1531	0.0059 9447	0.0053 4467	36
37	0.0087 9993	0.0078 5743	0.0070 0534	0.0062 3685	0.0055 4533	0.0049 2440	37
38	0.0082 7217	0.0073 5812	0.0065 3480	0.0057 9505	0.0051 3197	0.0045 3894	38
39	0.0077 7991	0.0068 9377	0.0060 9854	0.0053 8676	0.0047 5124	0.0041 8513	39
40	0.0073 2034	0.0064 6154	0.0056 9373	0.0050 0914	0.0044 0031	0.0038 6016	40
41	0.0068 9090	0.0060 5886	0.0053 1779	0.0046 5962	0.0040 7663	0.0035 6149	41
42	0.0064 8927	0.0056 8342	0.0049 6842	0.0043 3591	0.0037 7789	0.0032 8684	42
43	0.0061 1337	0.0053 3312	0.0046 4352	0.0040 3590	0.0035 0201	0.0030 3414	43
44	0.0057 6128	0.0050 0606	0.0043 4119	0.0037 5769	0.0032 4710	0.0028 0152	44
45	0.0054 3127	0.0047 0050	0.0040 5968	0.0034 9957	0.0030 1146	0.0025 8728	45
46	0.0051 2175	0.0044 1485	0.0037 9743	0.0032 5996	0.0027 9354	0.0023 8991	46
47	0.0048 3129	0.0041 4768	0.0035 5300	0.0030 3744	0.0025 9190	0.0022 0799	47
48	0.0045 5854	0.0038 9765	0.0033 2505	0.0028 3070	0.0024 0527	0.0020 4027	48
49	0.0043 0230	0.0036 6356	0.0031 1240	0.0026 3853	0.0022 3247	0.0018 8557	49
50	0.0040 6145	0.0034 4429	0.0029 1393	0.0024 5985	0.0020 7241	0.0017 4286	50

Table A-6
$(1 + i)^n$, n fractional

n	$1/4\%$	$1/3\%$	$5/12\%$	$1/2\%$	$7/12\%$	$2/3\%$
$1/12$ $1/12$	1.0002 0809	1.0002 7735	1.0003 4656	1.0004 1571	1.0004 8482	1.0005 5387
$1/6$ $2/12$	1.0004 1623	1.0005 5479	1.0006 9324	1.0008 3160	1.0009 6987	1.0011 0804
$1/4$ $3/12$	1.0006 2441	1.0008 3229	1.0010 4004	1.0012 4766	1.0014 5515	1.0016 6252
$1/3$ $4/12$	1.0008 3264	1.0011 0988	1.0013 8696	1.0016 6390	1.0019 4068	1.0022 1730
$5/12$ $5/12$	1.0010 4091	1.0013 8754	1.0017 3401	1.0020 8030	1.0024 2643	1.0027 7240
$1/2$ $6/12$	1.0012 4922	1.0016 6528	1.0020 8117	1.0024 9688	1.0029 1243	1.0033 2780

n	$3/4\%$	1%	$1 1/4\%$	$1 1/2\%$	$1 3/4\%$	2%
$1/12$ $1/12$	1.0006 2286	1.0008 2954	1.0010 3575	1.0012 4149	1.0014 4677	1.0016 5158
$1/6$ $2/12$	1.0012 4611	1.0016 5976	1.0020 7256	1.0024 8452	1.0028 9562	1.0033 0589
$1/4$ $3/12$	1.0018 6975	1.0024 9068	1.0031 1046	1.0037 2909	1.0043 4658	1.0049 6293
$1/3$ $4/12$	1.0024 9378	1.0033 2228	1.0041 4943	1.0049 7521	1.0057 9963	1.0066 2271
$5/12$ $5/12$	1.0031 1819	1.0041 5458	1.0051 8947	1.0062 2287	1.0072 5479	1.0082 8523
$1/2$ $6/12$	1.0037 4299	1.0049 8756	1.0062 3059	1.0074 7208	1.0087 1205	1.0099 5049

n	$2 1/2\%$	3%	$3 1/2\%$	4%	$4 1/2\%$	5%
$1/12$ $1/12$	1.0020 5984	1.0024 6627	1.0028 7090	1.0032 7374	1.0036 7481	1.0040 7412
$1/6$ $2/12$	1.0041 2392	1.0049 3862	1.0057 5004	1.0065 5820	1.0073 6312	1.0081 6485
$1/4$ $3/12$	1.0061 9225	1.0074 1707	1.0086 3745	1.0098 5341	1.0110 6499	1.0122 7223
$1/3$ $4/12$	1.0082 6484	1.0099 0163	1.0115 3314	1.0131 5940	1.0147 8046	1.0163 9636
$5/12$ $5/12$	1.0103 4170	1.0123 9232	1.0144 3715	1.0164 7622	1.0185 0959	1.0205 3728
$1/2$ $6/12$	1.0124 2284	1.0148 8916	1.0173 4950	1.0198 0390	1.0222 5242	1.0246 9508

n	$5 1/2\%$	6%	$6 1/2\%$	7%	$7 1/2\%$	8%
$1/12$ $1/12$	1.0044 7170	1.0048 6755	1.0052 6169	1.0056 5415	1.0060 4492	1.0064 3403
$1/6$ $2/12$	1.0089 6339	1.0097 5879	1.0105 5107	1.0113 4026	1.0121 2638	1.0129 0946
$1/4$ $3/12$	1.0134 7517	1.0146 7385	1.0158 6828	1.0170 5853	1.0182 4460	1.0194 2655
$1/3$ $4/12$	1.0180 0713	1.0196 1282	1.0212 1347	1.0228 0912	1.0243 9981	1.0259 8557
$5/12$ $5/12$	1.0225 5935	1.0245 7584	1.0265 8679	1.0285 9223	1.0305 9222	1.0325 8679
$1/2$ $6/12$	1.0271 3193	1.0295 6301	1.0319 8837	1.0344 0804	1.0368 2207	1.0392 3048

Table A-7
$(1 + i)^{-n}$, n fractional

n	$\frac{1}{4}\%$	$\frac{1}{3}\%$	$\frac{5}{12}\%$	$\frac{1}{2}\%$	$\frac{7}{12}\%$	$\frac{2}{3}\%$
$\frac{1}{12}$ $\frac{1}{12}$	0.9997 9195	0.9997 2272	0.9996 5356	0.9995 8446	0.9995 1542	0.9994 4644
$\frac{1}{6}$ $\frac{2}{12}$	0.9995 8394	0.9994 4552	0.9993 0724	0.9991 6909	0.9990 3107	0.9988 9319
$\frac{1}{4}$ $\frac{3}{12}$	0.9993 7597	0.9991 6840	0.9989 6104	0.9987 5389	0.9985 4696	0.9983 4024
$\frac{1}{3}$ $\frac{4}{12}$	0.9991 6805	0.9988 9135	0.9986 1496	0.9983 3887	0.9980 6308	0.9977 8760
$\frac{5}{12}$ $\frac{5}{12}$	0.9989 6017	0.9986 1438	0.9982 6900	0.9979 2402	0.9975 7944	0.9972 3527
$\frac{1}{2}$ $\frac{6}{12}$	0.9987 5234	0.9983 3749	0.9979 2315	0.9975 0934	0.9970 9603	0.9966 8324

n	$\frac{3}{4}\%$	1%	$1\frac{1}{4}\%$	$1\frac{1}{2}\%$	$1\frac{3}{4}\%$	2%
$\frac{1}{12}$ $\frac{1}{12}$	0.9993 7753	0.9991 7115	0.9989 6533	0.9987 6005	0.9985 5532	0.9983 5114
$\frac{1}{6}$ $\frac{2}{12}$	0.9987 5544	0.9983 4299	0.9979 3172	0.9975 2164	0.9971 1274	0.9967 0500
$\frac{1}{4}$ $\frac{3}{12}$	0.9981 3374	0.9975 1551	0.9968 9919	0.9962 8477	0.9956 7223	0.9950 6158
$\frac{1}{3}$ $\frac{4}{12}$	0.9975 1243	0.9966 8872	0.9958 6772	0.9950 4942	0.9942 3381	0.9934 2086
$\frac{5}{12}$ $\frac{5}{12}$	0.9968 9150	0.9958 6261	0.9948 3732	0.9938 1561	0.9927 9746	0.9917 8285
$\frac{1}{2}$ $\frac{6}{12}$	0.9962 7096	0.9950 3719	0.9938 0799	0.9925 8333	0.9913 6319	0.9901 4754

n	$2\frac{1}{2}\%$	3%	$3\frac{1}{2}\%$	4%	$4\frac{1}{2}\%$	5%
$\frac{1}{12}$ $\frac{1}{12}$	0.9979 4440	0.9975 3980	0.9971 3732	0.9967 3694	0.9963 3865	0.9959 4241
$\frac{1}{6}$ $\frac{2}{12}$	0.9958 9302	0.9950 8565	0.9942 8283	0.9934 8453	0.9926 9070	0.9919 0128
$\frac{1}{4}$ $\frac{3}{12}$	0.9938 4586	0.9926 3754	0.9914 3652	0.9902 4274	0.9890 5610	0.9878 7655
$\frac{1}{3}$ $\frac{4}{12}$	0.9918 0291	0.9901 9545	0.9885 9835	0.9870 1152	0.9854 3482	0.9838 6815
$\frac{5}{12}$ $\frac{5}{12}$	0.9897 6416	0.9877 5937	0.9857 6831	0.9837 9084	0.9818 2679	0.9798 7601
$\frac{1}{2}$ $\frac{6}{12}$	0.9877 2960	0.9853 2928	0.9829 4637	0.9805 8068	0.9782 3198	0.9759 0007

n	$5\frac{1}{2}\%$	6%	$6\frac{1}{2}\%$	7%	$7\frac{1}{2}\%$	8%
$\frac{1}{12}$ $\frac{1}{12}$	0.9955 4821	0.9951 5603	0.9947 6585	0.9943 7764	0.9939 9140	0.9936 0710
$\frac{1}{6}$ $\frac{2}{12}$	0.9911 1623	0.9903 3552	0.9895 5909	0.9887 8690	0.9880 1891	0.9872 5507
$\frac{1}{4}$ $\frac{3}{12}$	0.9867 0399	0.9855 3836	0.9843 7958	0.9832 2759	0.9820 8230	0.9809 4365
$\frac{1}{3}$ $\frac{4}{12}$	0.9823 1139	0.9807 6444	0.9792 2719	0.9776 9953	0.9761 8136	0.9746 7258
$\frac{5}{12}$ $\frac{5}{12}$	0.9779 3834	0.9760 1365	0.9741 0176	0.9722 0256	0.9703 1588	0.9684 4160
$\frac{1}{2}$ $\frac{6}{12}$	0.9735 8477	0.9712 8586	0.9690 0317	0.9667 3649	0.9644 8564	0.9622 5045

n	k					p					
		.05	.10	.15	.20	.25	.30	.35	.40	.45	.50
1	0	.9500	.9000	.8500	.8000	.7500	.7000	.6500	.6000	.5500	.5000
	1	.0500	.1000	.1500	.2000	.2500	.3000	.3500	.4000	.4500	.5000
2	0	.9025	.8100	.7225	.6400	.5625	.4900	.4225	.3600	.3025	.2500
	1	.0950	.1800	.2550	.3200	.3750	.4200	.4550	.4800	.4950	.5000
	2	.0025	.0100	.0225	.0400	.0625	.0900	.1225	.1600	.2025	.2500
3	0	.8574	.7290	.6141	.5120	.4219	.3430	.2746	.2160	.1664	.1250
	1	.1354	.2430	.3251	.3840	.4219	.4410	.4436	.4320	.4084	.3750
	2	.0071	.0270	.0574	.0960	.1406	.1890	.2389	.2880	.3341	.3750
	3	.0001	.0010	.0034	.0080	.0156	.0270	.0429	.0640	.0911	.1250
4	0	.8145	.6561	.5220	.4096	.3164	.2401	.1785	.1296	.0915	.0625
	1	.1715	.2916	.3685	.4096	.4219	.4116	.3845	.3456	.2995	.2500
	2	.0135	.0486	.0975	.1536	.2109	.2646	.3105	.3456	.3675	.3750
	3	.0005	.0036	.0115	.0256	.0469	.0756	.1115	.1536	.2005	.2500
	4	.0000	.0001	.0005	.0016	.0039	.0081	.0150	.0256	.0410	.0625
5	0	.7738	.5905	.4437	.3277	.2373	.1681	.1160	.0778	.0503	.0312
	1	.2036	.3280	.3915	.4096	.3955	.3602	.3124	.2592	.2059	.1562
	2	.0214	.0729	.1382	.2048	.2637	.3087	.3364	.3456	.3369	.3125
	3	.0011	.0081	.0244	.0512	.0879	.1323	.1811	.2304	.2757	.3125
	4	.0000	.0004	.0022	.0064	.0146	.0284	.0488	.0768	.1128	.1562
	5	.0000	.0000	.0001	.0003	.0010	.0024	.0053	.0102	.0185	.0312
6	0	.7351	.5314	.3771	.2621	.1780	.1176	.0754	.0467	.0277	.0156
	1	.2321	.3543	.3993	.3932	.3560	.3025	.2437	.1866	.1359	.0938
	2	.0305	.0984	.1762	.2458	.2966	.3241	.3280	.3110	.2780	.2344
	3	.0021	.0146	.0415	.0819	.1318	.1852	.2355	.2765	.3032	.3125
	4	.0001	.0012	.0055	.0154	.0330	.0595	.0951	.1382	.1861	.2344
	5	.0000	.0001	.0004	.0015	.0044	.0102	.0205	.0369	.0609	.0938
	6	.0000	.0000	.0000	.0001	.0002	.0007	.0018	.0041	.0083	.0156

*Entries in this table are values of $\binom{n}{k}p^k(1-p)^{n-k}$ for the indicated values of n, k, and p.

n	k	.05	.10	.15	.20	.25	p .30	.35	.40	.45	.50
7	0	.6983	.4783	.3206	.2097	.1335	.0824	.0490	.0280	.0152	.0078
	1	.2573	.3720	.3960	.3670	.3115	.2471	.1848	.1306	.0872	.0547
	2	.0406	.1240	.2097	.2753	.3115	.3177	.2985	.2613	.2140	.1641
	3	.0036	.0230	.0617	.1147	.1730	.2269	.2679	.2903	.2918	.2734
	4	.0002	.0026	.0109	.0287	.0577	.0972	.1442	.1935	.2388	.2734
	5	.0000	.0002	.0012	.0043	.0115	.0250	.0466	.0774	.1172	.1641
	6	.0000	.0000	.0001	.0004	.0013	.0036	.0084	.0172	.0320	.0547
	7	.0000	.0000	.0000	.0000	.0001	.0002	.0006	.0016	.0037	.0078
8	0	.6634	.4305	.2725	.1678	.1001	.0576	.0319	.0168	.0084	.0039
	1	.2793	.3826	.3847	.3355	.2670	.1977	.1373	.0896	.0548	.0312
	2	.0515	.1488	.2376	.2936	.3115	.2965	.2587	.2090	.1569	.1094
	3	.0054	.0331	.0839	.1468	.2076	.2541	.2786	.2787	.2568	.2188
	4	.0004	.0046	.0185	.0459	.0865	.1361	.1875	.2322	.2627	.2734
8	5	.0000	.0004	.0026	.0092	.0231	.0467	.0808	.1239	.1719	.2188
	6	.0000	.0000	.0002	.0011	.0038	.0100	.0217	.0413	.0703	.1094
	7	.0000	.0000	.0000	.0001	.0004	.0012	.0033	.0079	.0164	.0312
	8	.0000	.0000	.0000	.0000	.0000	.0001	.0002	.0007	.0017	.0039
9	0	.6302	.3874	.2316	.1342	.0751	.0404	.0207	.0101	.0046	.0020
	1	.2985	.3874	.3679	.3020	.2253	.1556	.1004	.0605	.0339	.0176
	2	.0629	.1722	.2597	.3020	.3003	.2668	.2162	.1612	.1110	.0703
	3	.0077	.0446	.1069	.1762	.2336	.2668	.2716	.2508	.2119	.1641
	4	.0006	.0074	.0283	.0661	.1168	.1715	.2194	.2508	.2600	.2461
	5	.0000	.0008	.0050	.0165	.0389	.0735	.1181	.1672	.2128	.2461
	6	.0000	.0001	.0006	.0028	.0087	.0210	.0424	.0743	.1160	.1641
	7	.0000	.0000	.0000	.0003	.0012	.0039	.0098	.0212	.0407	.0703
	8	.0000	.0000	.0000	.0000	.0001	.0004	.0013	.0035	.0083	.0176
	9	.0000	.0000	.0000	.0000	.0000	.0000	.0001	.0003	.0008	.0020
10	0	.5987	.3487	.1969	.1074	.0563	.0282	.0135	.0060	.0025	.0010
	1	.3151	.3874	.3474	.2684	.1877	.1211	.0725	.0403	.0207	.0098
	2	.0746	.1937	.2759	.3020	.2816	.2335	.1757	.1209	.0763	.0439
	3	.0105	.0574	.1298	.2013	.2503	.2668	.2522	.2150	.1665	.1172
	4	.0010	.0112	.0401	.0881	.1460	.2001	.2377	.2508	.2384	.2051

Table A-8 (Cont.)

n	k	.05	.10	.15	.20	.25	.30	.35	.40	.45	.50
10	5	.0001	.0015	.0085	.0264	.0584	.1029	.1536	.2007	.2340	.2461
	6	.0000	.0001	.0012	.0055	.0162	.0368	.0689	.1115	.1596	.2051
	7	.0000	.0000	.0001	.0008	.0031	.0090	.0212	.0425	.0746	.1172
	8	.0000	.0000	.0000	.0001	.0004	.0014	.0043	.0106	.0229	.0439
	9	.0000	.0000	.0000	.0000	.0000	.0001	.0005	.0016	.0042	.0098
	10	.0000	.0000	.0000	.0000	.0000	.0000	.0000	.0001	.0003	.0010
11	0	.5688	.3138	.1673	.0859	.0422	.0198	.0088	.0036	.0014	.0005
	1	.3293	.3835	.3248	.2362	.1549	.0932	.0518	.0266	.0125	.0054
	2	.0867	.2131	.2866	.2953	.2581	.1998	.1395	.0887	.0513	.0269
	3	.0137	.0710	.1517	.2215	.2581	.2568	.2254	.1774	.1259	.0806
	4	.0014	.0158	.0536	.1107	.1721	.2201	.2428	.2365	.2060	.1611
	5	.0001	.0025	.0132	.0388	.0803	.1321	.1830	.2207	.2360	.2256
	6	.0000	.0003	.0023	.0097	.0268	.0566	.0985	.1471	.1931	.2256
	7	.0000	.0000	.0003	.0017	.0064	.0173	.0379	.0701	.1128	.1611
	8	.0000	.0000	.0000	.0002	.0011	.0037	.0102	.0234	.0462	.0806
	9	.0000	.0000	.0000	.0000	.0001	.0005	.0018	.0052	.0126	.0269
	10	.0000	.0000	.0000	.0000	.0000	.0000	.0002	.0007	.0021	.0054
	11	.0000	.0000	.0000	.0000	.0000	.0000	.0000	.0000	.0002	.0005
12	0	.5404	.2824	.1422	.0687	.0317	.0138	.0057	.0022	.0008	.0002
	1	.3413	.3766	.3012	.2062	.1267	.0712	.0368	.0174	.0075	.0029
	2	.0988	.2301	.2924	.2835	.2323	.1678	.1088	.0639	.0339	.0161
	3	.0173	.0852	.1720	.2362	.2581	.2397	.1954	.1419	.0923	.0537
	4	.0021	.0213	.0683	.1329	.1936	.2311	.2367	.2128	.1700	.1208
	5	.0002	.0038	.0193	.0532	.1032	.1585	.2039	.2270	.2225	.1934
	6	.0000	.0005	.0040	.0155	.0401	.0792	.1281	.1766	.2124	.2256
	7	.0000	.0000	.0006	.0033	.0115	.0291	.0591	.1009	.1489	.1934
	8	.0000	.0000	.0001	.0005	.0024	.0078	.0199	.0420	.0762	.1208
	9	.0000	.0000	.0000	.0001	.0004	.0015	.0048	.0125	.0277	.0537
	10	.0000	.0000	.0000	.0000	.0000	.0002	.0008	.0025	.0068	.0161
	11	.0000	.0000	.0000	.0000	.0000	.0000	.0001	.0003	.0010	.0029
	12	.0000	.0000	.0000	.0000	.0000	.0000	.0000	.0000	.0001	.0002
13	0	.5133	.2542	.1209	.0550	.0238	.0097	.0037	.0013	.0004	.0001
	1	.3512	.3672	.2774	.1787	.1029	.0540	.0259	.0113	.0045	.0016
	2	.1109	.2448	.2937	.2680	.2059	.1388	.0836	.0453	.0220	.0095
	3	.0214	.0997	.1900	.2457	.2517	.2181	.1651	.1107	.0660	.0349
	4	.0028	.0277	.0838	.1535	.2097	.2337	.2222	.1845	.1350	.0873

Table A-8 (Cont.)

n	k	.05	.10	.15	.20	.25	*p* .30	.35	.40	.45	.50
13	5	.0003	.0055	.0266	.0691	.1258	.1803	.2154	.2214	.1989	.1571
	6	.0000	.0008	.0063	.0230	.0559	.1030	.1546	.1968	.2169	.2095
	7	.0000	.0001	.0011	.0058	.0186	.0442	.0833	.1312	.1775	.2095
	8	.0000	.0000	.0001	.0011	.0047	.0142	.0336	.0656	.1089	.1571
	9	.0000	.0000	.0000	.0001	.0009	.0034	.0101	.0243	.0495	.0873
	10	.0000	.0000	.0000	.0000	.0001	.0006	.0022	.0065	.0162	.0349
	11	.0000	.0000	.0000	.0000	.0000	.0001	.0003	.0012	.0036	.0095
	12	.0000	.0000	.0000	.0000	.0000	.0000	.0000	.0001	.0005	.0016
	13	.0000	.0000	.0000	.0000	.0000	.0000	.0000	.0000	.0000	.0001
14	0	.4877	.2288	.1028	.0440	.0178	.0068	.0024	.0008	.0002	.0001
	1	.3593	.3559	.2539	.1539	.0832	.0407	.0181	.0073	.0027	.0009
	2	.1229	.2570	.2912	.2501	.1802	.1134	.0634	.0317	.0141	.0056
	3	.0259	.1142	.2056	.2501	.2402	.1943	.1366	.0845	.0462	.0222
	4	.0037	.0349	.0998	.1720	.2202	.2290	.2022	.1549	.1040	.0611
	5	.0004	.0078	.0352	.0860	.1468	.1963	.2178	.2066	.1701	.1222
	6	.0000	.0013	.0093	.0322	.0734	.1262	.1759	.2066	.2088	.1833
	7	.0000	.0002	.0019	.0092	.0280	.0618	.1082	.1574	.1952	.2095
	8	.0000	.0000	.0003	.0020	.0082	.0232	.0510	.0918	.1398	.1833
	9	.0000	.0000	.0000	.0003	.0018	.0066	.0183	.0408	.0762	.1222
	10	.0000	.0000	.0000	.0000	.0003	.0014	.0049	.0136	.0312	.0611
	11	.0000	.0000	.0000	.0000	.0000	.0002	.0010	.0033	.0093	.0222
	12	.0000	.0000	.0000	.0000	.0000	.0000	.0001	.0005	.0019	.0056
	13	.0000	.0000	.0000	.0000	.0000	.0000	.0000	.0001	.0002	.0009
	14	.0000	.0000	.0000	.0000	.0000	.0000	.0000	.0000	.0000	.0001
15	0	.4633	.2059	.0874	.0352	.0134	.0047	.0016	.0005	.0001	.0000
	1	.3658	.3432	.2312	.1319	.0668	.0305	.0126	.0047	.0016	.0005
	2	.1348	.2669	.2856	.2309	.1559	.0916	.0476	.0219	.0090	.0032
	3	.0307	.1285	.2184	.2501	.2252	.1700	.1110	.0634	.0318	.0139
	4	.0049	.0428	.1156	.1876	.2252	.2186	.1792	.1268	.0780	.0417
	5	.0006	.0105	.0449	.1032	.1651	.2061	.2123	.1859	.1404	.0916
	6	.0000	.0019	.0132	.0430	.0917	.1472	.1906	.2066	.1914	.1527
	7	.0000	.0003	.0030	.0138	.0393	.0811	.1319	.1771	.2013	.1964
	8	.0000	.0000	.0005	.0035	.0131	.0348	.0710	.1181	.1647	.1964
	9	.0000	.0000	.0001	.0007	.0034	.0116	.0298	.0612	.1048	.1527

Table A-8 (Cont.)

n	k					p					
		.05	.10	.15	.20	.25	.30	.35	.40	.45	.50
15	10	.0000	.0000	.0000	.0001	.0007	.0030	.0096	.0245	.0515	.0916
	11	.0000	.0000	.0000	.0000	.0001	.0006	.0024	.0074	.0191	.0417
	12	.0000	.0000	.0000	.0000	.0000	.0001	.0004	.0016	.0052	.0139
	13	.0000	.0000	.0000	.0000	.0000	.0000	.0001	.0003	.0010	.0032
	14	.0000	.0000	.0000	.0000	.0000	.0000	.0000	.0000	.0001	.0005
	15	.0000	.0000	.0000	.0000	.0000	.0000	.0000	.0000	.0000	.0000
16	0	.4401	.1853	.0743	.0281	.0100	.0033	.0010	.0003	.0001	.0000
	1	.3706	.3294	.2097	.1126	.0535	.0228	.0087	.0030	.0009	.0002
	2	.1463	.2745	.2775	.2111	.1336	.0732	.0353	.0150	.0056	.0018
	3	.0359	.1423	.2285	.2463	.2079	.1465	.0888	.0468	.0215	.0085
	4	.0061	.0514	.1311	.2001	.2252	.2040	.1553	.1014	.0572	.0278
	5	.0008	.0137	.0555	.1201	.1802	.2099	.2008	.1623	.1123	.0667
	6	.0001	.0028	.0180	.0550	.1101	.1649	.1982	.1983	.1684	.1222
	7	.0000	.0004	.0045	.0197	.0524	.1010	.1524	.1889	.1969	.1746
	8	.0000	.0001	.0009	.0055	.0197	.0487	.0923	.1417	.1812	.1964
	9	.0000	.0000	.0001	.0012	.0058	.0185	.0442	.0840	.1318	.1746
	10	.0000	.0000	.0000	.0002	.0014	.0056	.0167	.0392	.0755	.1222
	11	.0000	.0000	.0000	.0000	.0002	.0013	.0049	.0142	.0337	.0667
	12	.0000	.0000	.0000	.0000	.0000	.0002	.0011	.0040	.0115	.0278
	13	.0000	.0000	.0000	.0000	.0000	.0000	.0002	.0008	.0029	.0085
	14	.0000	.0000	.0000	.0000	.0000	.0000	.0000	.0001	.0005	.0018
	15	.0000	.0000	.0000	.0000	.0000	.0000	.0000	.0000	.0001	.0002
	16	.0000	.0000	.0000	.0000	.0000	.0000	.0000	.0000	.0000	.0000
17	0	.4181	.1668	.0631	.0225	.0075	.0023	.0007	.0002	.0000	.0000
	1	.3741	.3150	.1893	.0957	.0426	.0169	.0060	.0019	.0005	.0001
	2	.1575	.2800	.2673	.1914	.1136	.0581	.0260	.0102	.0035	.0010
	3	.0415	.1556	.2359	.2393	.1893	.1245	.0701	.0341	.0144	.0052
	4	.0076	.0605	.1457	.2093	.2209	.1868	.1320	.0796	.0411	.0182
	5	.0010	.0175	.0668	.1361	.1914	.2081	.1849	.1379	.0875	.0472
	6	.0001	.0039	.0236	.0680	.1276	.1784	.1991	.1839	.1432	.0944
	7	.0000	.0007	.0065	.0267	.0668	.1201	.1685	.1927	.1841	.1484
	8	.0000	.0001	.0014	.0084	.0279	.0644	.1134	.1606	.1883	.1855
	9	.0000	.0000	.0003	.0021	.0093	.0276	.0611	.1070	.1540	.1855

Table A-8 (Cont.)

						p					
n	k	.05	.10	.15	.20	.25	.30	.35	.40	.45	.50
17	10	.0000	.0000	.0000	.0004	.0025	.0095	.0263	.0571	.1008	.1484
	11	.0000	.0000	.0000	.0001	.0005	.0026	.0090	.0242	.0525	.0944
	12	.0000	.0000	.0000	.0000	.0001	.0006	.0024	.0081	.0215	.0472
	13	.0000	.0000	.0000	.0000	.0000	.0001	.0005	.0021	.0068	.0182
	14	.0000	.0000	.0000	.0000	.0000	.0000	.0001	.0004	.0016	.0052
	15	.0000	.0000	.0000	.0000	.0000	.0000	.0000	.0001	.0003	.0010
	16	.0000	.0000	.0000	.0000	.0000	.0000	.0000	.0000	.0000	.0001
	17	.0000	.0000	.0000	.0000	.0000	.0000	.0000	.0000	.0000	.0000
18	0	.3972	.1501	.0536	.0180	.0056	.0016	.0004	.0001	.0000	.0000
	1	.3763	.3002	.1704	.0811	.0338	.0126	.0042	.0012	.0003	.0001
	2	.1683	.2835	.2556	.1723	.0958	.0458	.0190	.0069	.0022	.0006
	3	.0473	.1680	.2406	.2297	.1704	.1046	.0547	.0246	.0095	.0031
	4	.0093	.0700	.1592	.2153	.2130	.1681	.1104	.0614	.0291	.0117
	5	.0014	.0218	.0787	.1507	.1988	.2017	.1664	.1146	.0666	.0327
	6	.0002	.0052	.0301	.0816	.1436	.1873	.1941	.1655	.1181	.0708
	7	.0000	.0010	.0091	.0350	.0820	.1376	.1792	.1892	.1657	.1214
	8	.0000	.0002	.0022	.0120	.0376	.0811	.1327	.1734	.1864	.1669
	9	.0000	.0000	.0004	.0033	.0139	.0386	.0794	.1284	.1694	.1855
	10	.0000	.0000	.0001	.0008	.0042	.0149	.0385	.0771	.1248	.1669
	11	.0000	.0000	.0000	.0001	.0010	.0046	.0151	.0374	.0742	.1214
	12	.0000	.0000	.0000	.0000	.0002	.0012	.0047	.0145	.0354	.0708
	13	.0000	.0000	.0000	.0000	.0000	.0002	.0012	.0045	.0134	.0327
	14	.0000	.0000	.0000	.0000	.0000	.0000	.0002	.0011	.0039	.0117
	15	.0000	.0000	.0000	.0000	.0000	.0000	.0000	.0002	.0009	.0031
	16	.0000	.0000	.0000	.0000	.0000	.0000	.0000	.0000	.0001	.0006
	17	.0000	.0000	.0000	.0000	.0000	.0000	.0000	.0000	.0000	.0001
	18	.0000	.0000	.0000	.0000	.0000	.0000	.0000	.0000	.0000	.0000
19	0	.3774	.1351	.0456	.0144	.0042	.0011	.0003	.0001	.0000	.0000
	1	.3774	.2852	.1529	.0685	.0268	.0093	.0029	.0008	.0002	.0000
	2	.1787	.2852	.2428	.1540	.0803	.0358	.0138	.0046	.0013	.0003
	3	.0533	.1796	.2428	.2182	.1517	.0869	.0422	.0175	.0062	.0018
	4	.0112	.0798	.1714	.2182	.2023	.1491	.0909	.0467	.0203	.0074

499

Table A-8 (Cont.)

n	k	.05	.10	.15	.20	.25	.30	.35	.40	.45	.50
19	5	.0018	.0266	.0907	.1636	.2023	.1916	.1468	.0933	.0497	.0222
	6	.0002	.0069	.0374	.0955	.1574	.1916	.1844	.1451	.0949	.0518
	7	.0000	.0014	.0122	.0443	.0974	.1525	.1844	.1797	.1443	.0961
	8	.0000	.0002	.0032	.0166	.0487	.0981	.1489	.1797	.1771	.1442
	9	.0000	.0000	.0007	.0051	.0198	.0514	.0980	.1464	.1771	.1762
	10	.0000	.0000	.0001	.0013	.0066	.0220	.0528	.0976	.1449	.1762
	11	.0000	.0000	.0000	.0003	.0018	.0077	.0233	.0532	.0970	.1442
	12	.0000	.0000	.0000	.0000	.0004	.0022	.0083	.0237	.0529	.0961
	13	.0000	.0000	.0000	.0000	.0001	.0005	.0024	.0085	.0233	.0518
	14	.0000	.0000	.0000	.0000	.0000	.0001	.0006	.0024	.0082	.0222
	15	.0000	.0000	.0000	.0000	.0000	.0000	.0001	.0005	.0022	.0074
	16	.0000	.0000	.0000	.0000	.0000	.0000	.0000	.0001	.0005	.0018
	17	.0000	.0000	.0000	.0000	.0000	.0000	.0000	.0000	.0001	.0003
	18	.0000	.0000	.0000	.0000	.0000	.0000	.0000	.0000	.0000	.0000
	19	.0000	.0000	.0000	.0000	.0000	.0000	.0000	.0000	.0000	.0000
20	0	.3585	.1216	.0388	.0115	.0032	.0008	.0002	.0000	.0000	.0000
	1	.3774	.2702	.1368	.0576	.0211	.0068	.0020	.0005	.0001	.0000
	2	.1887	.2852	.2293	.1369	.0669	.0278	.0100	.0031	.0008	.0002
	3	.0596	.1901	.2428	.2054	.1339	.0716	.0323	.0123	.0040	.0011
	4	.0133	.0898	.1821	.2182	.1897	.1304	.0738	.0350	.0139	.0046
	5	.0022	.0319	.1028	.1746	.2023	.1789	.1272	.0746	.0365	.0148
	6	.0003	.0089	.0454	.1091	.1686	.1916	.1712	.1244	.0746	.0370
	7	.0000	.0020	.0160	.0545	.1124	.1643	.1844	.1659	.1221	.0739
	8	.0000	.0004	.0046	.0222	.0609	.1144	.1614	.1797	.1623	.1201
	9	.0000	.0001	.0011	.0074	.0271	.0654	.1158	.1597	.1771	.1602
	10	.0000	.0000	.0002	.0020	.0099	.0308	.0686	.1171	.1593	.1762
	11	.0000	.0000	.0000	.0005	.0030	.0120	.0336	.0710	.1185	.1602
	12	.0000	.0000	.0000	.0001	.0008	.0039	.0136	.0355	.0727	.1201
	13	.0000	.0000	.0000	.0000	.0002	.0010	.0045	.0146	.0366	.0739
	14	.0000	.0000	.0000	.0000	.0000	.0002	.0012	.0049	.0150	.0370
	15	.0000	.0000	.0000	.0000	.0000	.0000	.0003	.0013	.0049	.0148
	16	.0000	.0000	.0000	.0000	.0000	.0000	.0000	.0003	.0013	.0046
	17	.0000	.0000	.0000	.0000	.0000	.0000	.0000	.0000	.0002	.0011
	18	.0000	.0000	.0000	.0000	.0000	.0000	.0000	.0000	.0000	.0002
	19	.0000	.0000	.0000	.0000	.0000	.0000	.0000	.0000	.0000	.0000
	20	.0000	.0000	.0000	.0000	.0000	.0000	.0000	.0000	.0000	.0000

Column header p spans the probability columns (.05 through .50).

Table A-9
Areas Under the Normal Distribution

$b*$	.00	.01	.02	.03	.04	.05	.06	.07	.08	.09
0.0	.0000	.0040	.0080	.0120	.0160	.0199	.0239	.0279	.0319	.0359
0.1	.0398	.0438	.0478	.0517	.0557	.0596	.0636	.0675	.0714	.0753
0.2	.0793	.0832	.0871	.0910	.0948	.0987	.1026	.1064	.1103	.1141
0.3	.1179	.1217	.1255	.1293	.1331	.1368	.1406	.1443	.1480	.1517
0.4	.1554	.1591	.1628	.1664	.1700	.1736	.1772	.1808	.1844	.1879
0.5	.1915	.1950	.1985	.2019	.2054	.2088	.2123	.2157	.2190	.2224
0.6	.2257	.2291	.2324	.2357	.2389	.2422	.2454	.2486	.2517	.2549
0.7	.2580	.2611	.2642	.2673	.2704	.2734	.2764	.2794	.2823	.2852
0.8	.2881	.2910	.2939	.2967	.2995	.3023	.3051	.3078	.3106	.3133
0.9	.3159	.3186	.3212	.3238	.3264	.3289	.3315	.3340	.3365	.3389
1.0	.3413	.3438	.3461	.3485	.3508	.3531	.3554	.3577	.3599	.3621
1.1	.3643	.3665	.3686	.3708	.3729	.3749	.3770	.3790	.3810	.3830
1.2	.3849	.3869	.3888	.3907	.3925	.3944	.3962	.3980	.3997	.4015
1.3	.4032	.4049	.4066	.4082	.4099	.4115	.4131	.4147	.4162	.4177
1.4	.4192	.4207	.4222	.4236	.4251	.4265	.4279	.4292	.4306	.4319
1.5	.4332	.4345	.4357	.4370	.4382	.4394	.4406	.4418	.4429	.4441
1.6	.4452	.4463	.4474	.4484	.4495	.4505	.4515	.4525	.4535	.4545
1.7	.4554	.4564	.4573	.4582	.4591	.4599	.4608	.4616	.4625	.4633
1.8	.4641	.4649	.4656	.4664	.4671	.4678	.4686	.4693	.4699	.4706
1.9	.4713	.4719	.4726	.4732	.4738	.4744	.4750	.4756	.4761	.4767
2.0	.4772	.4778	.4783	.4788	.4793	.4798	.4803	.4808	.4812	.4817
2.1	.4821	.4826	.4830	.4834	.4838	.4842	.4846	.4850	.4854	.4857
2.2	.4861	.4864	.4868	.4871	.4875	.4878	.4881	.4884	.4887	.4890
2.3	.4893	.4896	.4898	.4901	.4904	.4906	.4909	.4911	.4913	.4916
2.4	.4918	.4920	.4922	.4925	.4927	.4929	.4931	.4932	.4934	.4936
2.5	.4938	.4940	.4941	.4943	.4945	.4946	.4948	.4949	.4951	.4952
2.6	.4953	.4955	.4956	.4957	.4959	.4960	.4961	.4962	.4963	.4964
2.7	.4965	.4966	.4967	.4968	.4969	.4970	.4971	.4972	.4973	.4974
2.8	.4974	.4975	.4976	.4977	.4977	.4978	.4979	.4979	.4980	.4981
2.9	.4981	.4982	.4982	.4983	.4984	.4984	.4985	.4985	.4986	.4986
3.0	.4987	.4987	.4987	.4988	.4988	.4989	.4989	.4989	.4990	.4990

* For $b > 3$, the area under the curve is essentially 0.5.

Table A-10
Exponentials

x	e^x	e^{-x}	x	e^x	e^{-x}	x	e^x	e^{-x}
0.00	1.0 000	1.00 000	0.50	1.6 487	0.60 653	1.00	2.7 183	0.36 788
0.01	1.0 101	0.99 005	0.51	1.6 653	0.60 050	1.50	4.4 817	0.22 313
0.02	1.0 202	0.98 020	0.52	1.6 820	0.59 452	2.00	7.3 891	0.13 534
0.03	1.0 305	0.97 045	0.53	1.6 989	0.58 860	2.50	12 .182	0.08 208
0.04	1.0 408	0.96 079	0.54	1.7 160	0.58 275	3.00	20 .086	0.04 979
0.05	1.0 513	0.95 123	0.55	1.7 333	0.57 695	3.50	33 .115	0.03 020
0.06	1.0 618	0.94 176	0.56	1.7 507	0.57 121	4.00	54 .598	0.01 832
0.07	1.0 725	0.93 239	0.57	1.7 683	0.56 553	4.50	90 .017	0.01 111
0.08	1.0 833	0.92 312	0.58	1.7 860	0.55 990	5.00	148 .41	0.00 674
0.09	1.0 942	0.91 393	0.59	1.8 040	0.55 433	5.50	244 .69	0.00 409
0.10	1.1 052	0.90 484	0.60	1.8 221	0.54 881	6.00	403 .43	0.00 248
0.11	1.1 163	0.89 583	0.61	1.8 404	0.54 335	6.50	665 .13	0.00 150
0.12	1.1 275	0.88 692	0.62	1.8 589	0.53 794	7.00	1096 .6	0.00 091
0.13	1.1 388	0.87 810	0.63	1.8 776	0.53 259	7.50	1717 .7	0.00 055
0.14	1.1 503	0.86 936	0.64	1.8 965	0.52 729	8.00	2981 .0	0.00 034
0.15	1.1 618	0.86 071	0.65	1.9 155	0.52 205	8.50	5914 .6	0.00 021
0.16	1.1 735	0.85 214	0.66	1.9 348	0.51 685	9.00	8103 .1	0.00 012
0.17	1.1 853	0.84 366	0.67	1.9 542	0.51 171	9.50	13360	0.00 009
0.18	1.1 972	0.83 527	0.68	1.9 739	0.50 662	10	22026	0.00 005
0.19	1.2 092	0.82 696	0.69	1.9 937	0.50 158			
0.20	1.2 214	0.81 873	0.70	2.0 138	0.49 659			
0.21	1.2 337	0.81 058	0.71	2.0 340	0.49 164			
0.22	1.2 461	0.80 252	0.72	2.0 544	0.48 675			
0.23	1.2 586	0.79 453	0.73	2.0 751	0.48 191			
0.24	1.2 712	0.78 663	0.74	2.0 959	0.47 711			
0.25	1.2 840	0.77 880	0.75	2.1 170	0.47 237			
0.26	1.2 969	0.77 105	0.76	2.1 383	0.46 767			
0.27	1.3 100	0.76 338	0.77	2.1 598	0.46 301			
0.28	1.3 231	0.75 578	0.78	2.1 815	0.45 841			
0.29	1.3 364	0.74 826	0.79	2.2 034	0.45 384			
0.30	1.3 499	0.74 082	0.80	2.2 255	0.44 933			
0.31	1.3 634	0.73 345	0.81	2.2 479	0.44 486			
0.32	1.3 771	0.72 615	0.82	2.2 705	0.44 043			
0.33	1.3 910	0.71 892	0.83	2.2 933	0.43 605			
0.34	1.4 049	0.71 177	0.84	2.3 164	0.43 171			
0.35	1.4 191	0.70 469	0.85	2.3 396	0.42 741			
0.36	1.4 333	0.69 768	0.86	2.3 632	0.42 316			
0.37	1.4 477	0.69 073	0.87	2.3 869	0.41 895			
0.38	1.4 623	0.68 386	0.88	2.4 109	0.41 478			
0.39	1.4 770	0.67 706	0.89	2.4 351	0.41 066			
0.40	1.4 918	0.67 032	0.90	2.4 596	0.40 657			
0.41	1.5 068	0.66 365	0.91	2.4 843	0.40 252			
0.42	1.5 220	0.65 705	0.92	2.5 093	0.39 852			
0.43	1.5 373	0.65 051	0.93	2.5 345	0.39 455			
0.44	1.5 527	0.64 404	0.94	2.5 600	0.39 063			
0.45	1.5 683	0.63 763	0.95	2.5 857	0.38 674			
0.46	1.5 841	0.63 128	0.96	2.6 117	0.38 289			
0.47	1.6 000	0.62 500	0.97	2.6 379	0.37 908			
0.48	1.6 161	0.61 878	0.98	2.6 645	0.37 531			
0.49	1.6 323	0.61 263	0.99	2.6 912	0.37 158			

Table A-11
Natural Logarithms

x	$\ln x$	x	$\ln x$	x	$\ln x$	x	$\ln x$
.01	−4.60517	0.50	−0.69315	1.00	0.00000	1.5	0.4 0547
.02	−3.91202	.51	−0.67334	1.01	0.00995	1.6	0.4 7000
.03	−3.50656	.52	−0.65393	1.02	0.01980	1.7	0.5 3063
.04	−3.21888	.53	−0.63488	1.03	0.02956	1.8	0.5 8779
		.54	−0.61619	1.04	0.03922	1.9	0.6 4185
.05	−2.99573	.55	−0.59784	1.05	0.04879	2.0	0.6 9315
.06	−2.81341	.56	−0.57982	1.06	0.05827	2.1	0.7 4194
.07	−2.65926	.57	−0.56212	1.07	0.06766	2.2	0.7 8846
.08	−2.52573	.58	−0.54473	1.08	0.07696	2.3	0.8 3291
.09	−2.40795	.59	−0.52763	1.09	0.08618	2.4	0.8 7547
0.10	−2.30259	0.60	−0.51083	1.10	0.09531	2.5	0.9 1629
.11	−2.20727	.61	−0.49430	1.11	0.10436	2.6	0.9 5551
.12	−2.12026	.62	−0.47804	1.12	0.11333	2.7	0.9 9325
.13	−2.04022	.63	−0.46204	1.13	0.12222	2.8	1.0 2962
.14	−1.96611	.64	−0.44629	1.14	0.13103	2.9	1.0 6471
.15	−1.89712	.65	−0.43078	1.15	0.13976	3.0	1.0 9861
.16	−1.83258	.66	−0.41552	1.16	0.14842		
.17	−1.77196	.67	−0.40048	1.17	0.15700		
.18	−1.71480	.68	−0.38566	1.18	0.16551		
.19	−1.66073	.69	−0.37106	1.19	0.17395		
0.20	−1.60944	0.70	−0.35667	1.20	0.18232		
.21	−1.56065	.71	−0.34249	1.21	0.19062		
.22	−1.51413	.72	−0.32850	1.22	0.19885		
.23	−1.46968	.73	−0.31471	1.23	0.20701		
.24	−1.42712	.74	−0.30111	1.24	0.21511		
.25	−1.38629	.75	−0.28768	1.25	0.22314		
.26	−1.34707	.76	−0.27444	1.26	0.23111		
.27	−1.30933	.77	−0.26136	1.27	0.23902		
.28	−1.27297	.78	−0.24846	1.28	0.24686		
.29	−1.23787	.79	−0.23572	1.29	0.25464		
0.30	−1.20397	0.80	−0.22314	1.30	0.26236		
.31	−1.17118	.81	−0.21072	1.31	0.27003		
.32	−1.13943	.82	−0.19845	1.32	0.27763		
.33	−1.10866	.83	−0.18633	1.33	0.28518		
.34	−1.07881	.84	−0.17435	1.34	0.29267		
.35	−1.04982	.85	−0.16252	1.35	0.30010		
.36	−1.02165	.86	−0.15032	1.36	0.30748		
.37	−0.99425	.87	−0.13926	1.37	0.31481		
.38	−0.96758	.88	−0.12783	1.38	0.32208		
.39	−0.94161	.89	−0.11653	1.39	0.32930		
0.40	−0.91629	0.90	−0.10536	1.40	0.33647		
.41	−0.89160	.91	−0.09431	1.41	0.34359		
.42	−0.86750	.92	−0.08338	1.42	0.35066		
.43	−0.84397	.93	−0.07257	1.43	0.35767		
.44	−0.82098	.94	−0.06188	1.44	0.36464		
.45	−0.79851	.95	−0.05129	1.45	0.37156		
.46	−0.77653	.96	−0.04082	1.46	0.37844		
.47	−0.75502	.97	−0.03046	1.47	0.38526		
.48	−0.73397	.98	−0.02020	1.48	0.39204		
.49	−0.71335	.99	−0.01005	1.49	0.39878		

Answers to Odd-Numbered Exercises

Introduction

Section A

1. 8
5. 136
9. −8
13. 19
17. 23

3. 57
7. 13
11. −2
15. −79

Section B

1. −20
5. 0
9. 0

3. −24
7. 96

Section C

1. (a) 0.2; (b) 20%
3. (a) 0.375; (b) 37.5%
5. (a) 1.571428 . . . ; (b) 157.1428 . . . %
7. (a) −1.5; (b) −150%
9. (a) −0.7058823 . . . ; (b) −70.58823 . . . %
11. $105
13. $19.80
15. 83⅓%

Section D

1. 13/12
3. 1/4
5. 3/8
7. 1/13
9. $-360/77$
11. $-189/88$
13. $13\frac{1}{3}\%$
15. 4%
17. -1.2%
19. -107.5%
21. The 3 qt container is cheaper by 8¢ for each 12 qt.
23. The 1 lb 4 oz box is cheaper by 42¢ for each 60 oz.

Section E

1. 576
3. -216
5. $-1/2a$
7. x^{-1}
9. $x^{1/2}$
11. x^{-6}

Section F

1. $3a(x + 2y)$
3. $3a(x - y)(x + y)$
5. $(x + 13)(x - 1)$
7. $(x - 2y)(x + 2y)(x^2 + 4y^2)$
9. $(2x + y)^2$
11. $x(2x - 5)$
13. $x(x + 1)(x - 2)$
15. $x^2(4x - 5)$
17. $x^2(z - 2t^2)^2$
19. $2x(x + y)$

Section G

1. 3
3. 21
5. 19.7
7. -3
9. -1
11. 28/9
13. 79
15. $-21/4$
17. 31 doz
19. 8 books
21. 40 yr

Section H

1. $-1, 9$
3. $-4, -5$
5. 1, 4
7. 1/2, 5
9. $-1, 4/3$
11. $1 + \sqrt{6}, 1 - \sqrt{6}$
13. $-1/2 + (1/2)\sqrt{2}, -1/2 - (1/2)\sqrt{2}$
15. $(1 + \sqrt{73})/6, (1 - \sqrt{73})/6$
17. 4, -3
19. $2 + \sqrt{11}, 2 - \sqrt{11}$
21. No real roots

Section I

1. $x = 1, y = 3$
3. $s = 11, t = 7$
5. $x = -1, t = 6$
7. $1.05 for the bottle, 5¢ for the cork
9. $2.00 shipping, $3.00 per book

Section J

1. $x \leq 2$
3. $x > 8$
5. $x > 0$
7. Lisa is under 12.

Section K

1. 5, 3/5, 4/5, 3/4
3. Sides are 10 and $5\sqrt{3}$, cos $30° = \sqrt{3}/2$, tan $30° = 1/\sqrt{3}$
5. Legs are each $\sqrt{2}$, sin $45° = $ cos $45° = \sqrt{2}/2$, tan $45° = 1$

7. (a) -4 $\quad$ 0 $\qquad\qquad\qquad$ x

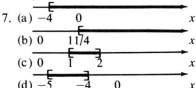

    (b) 0 $\quad$ 1 1/4 $\qquad\qquad$ x

    (c) 0 $\quad$ 1 $\quad$ 2 $\qquad\qquad$ x

    (d) -5 $\quad$ -4 $\quad$ 0 $\qquad$ x

Chapter 1

Section 1.1

1. (a) $y = 2x + 4$; (b) $y = -3x$; (c) $y = -2$; (d) $y = (1/2)x - 1/2$;
   (e) $y = -(1/4)x + 3$
3. 2/5, 3, $-6/5$
5. 121/24
7. $y = -7, y = 1$
11. $2x + 5y = 20, 2x - 5y + 20 = 0$
13. $\sqrt{193}$
15. Breakeven at $x = 166\frac{2}{3}$, $C = R = \$7,500$
17. x is increased to 500.
19. \$33
21. \$30, \$1,400

Section 1.2

3. (a) $3x + y \geq 11$; (b) $5x + 3y \geq 4$; (c) $y \leq 7$ and $x \geq -3$;
   (d) $-1/4 \leq x \leq 3$ and $y \leq 6$.

Section 1.3

3. $x \geq 0, y \geq 0, x + 5y \leq 50, 3x + y \leq 24, 6x + y \leq 42$
5. 9 boxes of the first kind, 4 boxes of the second kind. Profit is \$4.80.
7. 12 of the first type, 6 of the second type. Receipts are \$24. Price should be between \$0.60 and \$1.50.

Section 1.4

1. 36
3. 20
5. $80/3 \leq M \leq 80$
7. 40 suits, no dresses, income is \$3,200.
9. 20/3 grams of A and 20/3 grams of B produce 1,000 calories. Since the conditions say "more of B than of A," strictly speaking, there is no perfect solution. Roughly 6.6 grams of A, 6.7 grams of B is the best possible.

Chapter 2

Section 2.1
1. $(9, -1)$
5. $(-2, 1, 3, 5/2)$
9. $(-2, 1, -3)$
13. $(3, 5, 7)$

3. $(-2, 7, 4)$
7. $(1, -1, 2)$
11. $(-1, 2, 7, 3, -4)$
15. 20 type A, 2 type B, and 8 type C

Section 2.2
1. Inconsistent
3. $(1/2, 3/2)$
5. $x = (13 + n)/4$, $y = (1 + 5n)/4$, $z = n$, for any n.
7. $x = 21/10$, $y = 13/10$
9. $x = (17 + n)/3$, $y = (4n - 1)/3$, $z = n$, $w = -2$, for any n.

Section 2.3
23. $x = 23/3 - k$, $y = 5/3$, $z = k$,
    for any k
27. 385

25. Inconsistent

29. There may be n \$4 ties,
    $5,000 - 3n$ \$2 ties, and
    $2,000 + 2n$ \$1 ties, where n is
    any integer less than 1,667. If
    there are 2,000 \$2 ties, then
    there are 4,000 \$1 ties and 1,000
    \$4 ties.

Section 2.4
31. $(2, 1, -1)$
35. $(-2, 3, 5, 2)$
39. Inconsistent

33. $(1, 1, -1)$
37. $x = 55/13 - k$, $y = k$, $z = 73/26$,
    $w = 233/26$, where k is any
    number.

Section 2.5
1. $P = 6$
5. $P = 14$

3. $P = 18$
7. 25/7 jars of Econo-nut, 1,250/7
   jars of All-nutz, 425/14 jars of
   Lux-O-nuts, profit about \$45.36

Section 2.6
3. Minimum $P = 12$
7. No solution exists
11. $P = 28$

5. Minimum $P = -1/7$
9. 2.81 packages of I, 7.025
   packages of II, 12.752 packages
   of III

Chapter 3

Section 3.1

1. (a) $\begin{pmatrix} 0 & 0 & 0 \\ 3 & 1 & 4 \end{pmatrix}$ (b) Undefined

   (c) $(-4 \quad 8 \quad -10 \quad -4)$

   (d) $\begin{pmatrix} 1 & 0 & 1 \\ -5 & -2 & -1 \end{pmatrix}$ (e) $\begin{pmatrix} 9 \\ 6 \\ -15 \end{pmatrix}$

   (f) $\begin{pmatrix} 5 & -10 & -15 \\ 10 & 10 & 0 \end{pmatrix}$

   (g) $\begin{pmatrix} -4 & -2 & -8 \\ 21 & 10 & -3 \end{pmatrix}$

   (h) Undefined; (i) $\begin{pmatrix} -3/2 \\ -1 \\ 5/2 \end{pmatrix}$

3. $a = b = c = 0$

5. $\begin{pmatrix} 0 & 0 & 0 \\ 1 & 0 & 0 \\ 1 & 1 & 0 \end{pmatrix}$

7. The first row is the cost of the cigars and the tax on the cigars. The second row is the cost of of the cigarettes and the tax on the cigarettes.

Section 3.2

1. (a) Undefined; (b) $\begin{pmatrix} -2 & 7 \\ -15 & 25 \\ -3 & 5 \\ -20 & 37 \end{pmatrix}$

   (c) $\begin{pmatrix} -2 & 9 \\ -9 & 15 \\ 0 & -5 \\ -23 & 49 \end{pmatrix}$

   (d) $\begin{pmatrix} 1 & -1 \\ -6 & 15 \\ -3 & 11 \\ 4 & -5 \end{pmatrix}$

   (e) $\begin{pmatrix} 1 & -31 \\ 20 & -15 \\ 9 & 40 \\ 55 & -176 \end{pmatrix}$ (f) Undefined

5. $x = 3$ or 9

7. $\mathbf{GH} = 25$, $\mathbf{HG} = \begin{pmatrix} -1 & 2 & 4 \\ -3 & 6 & 12 \\ -5 & 10 & 20 \end{pmatrix}$

9. $\begin{pmatrix} 7 & 4 \\ 37 & 29 \\ 32 & 25 \\ 5 & 15 \end{pmatrix}$

Section 3.3

1. $\mathbf{AB} = \begin{pmatrix} 5 & -11 \\ 5 & -9 \end{pmatrix}$, $(\mathbf{AB})^{-1} = (1/10) \begin{pmatrix} -9 & 11 \\ -5 & 5 \end{pmatrix}$ $\mathbf{A}^{-1} = (1/5) \begin{pmatrix} -3 & 2 \\ 1 & 1 \end{pmatrix}$;

$\mathbf{B}^{-1} = (1/2) \begin{pmatrix} 4 & 3 \\ 2 & 1 \end{pmatrix}$

5. (a) $(1/26) \begin{pmatrix} 7 & -16 & 17 \\ 2 & 14 & -10 \\ -5 & 4 & -1 \end{pmatrix}$ (b) $x = 1, y = 1, z = -1$

7. $(1/16) \begin{pmatrix} -92 & 30 \\ -98 & -131 \\ -138 & -23 \end{pmatrix}$

9. (a) $(1/10) \begin{pmatrix} 16 & -20 & 22 & -8 \\ -21 & 25 & -27 & 13 \\ -25 & 35 & -35 & 15 \\ 24 & -30 & 28 & -12 \end{pmatrix}$

(b) $(1/66) \begin{pmatrix} -47 & -12 & -14 & 43 \\ 51 & 6 & 18 & -27 \\ 14 & 12 & 14 & -10 \\ 25 & 12 & -8 & 1 \end{pmatrix}$

Section 3.4

1. (a) $\begin{pmatrix} 125 \\ 125 \end{pmatrix}$

(b) the second component has a surplus of 175

(c) $\begin{pmatrix} 5100/19 \\ 7200/19 \end{pmatrix}$

5. There is no output vector with positive components. Hence the problem is unsolvable in a practical sense.

3. $\mathbf{X} = \begin{pmatrix} k \\ k \end{pmatrix}$, where k is any number

7. (a) $\begin{pmatrix} 0.2 & 0.1 \\ 0.3 & 0.4 \end{pmatrix}$ (b) $\begin{pmatrix} 49 \\ 136 \end{pmatrix}, \begin{pmatrix} 71 \\ 114 \end{pmatrix}$

(c) Payroll increase 70/3 hours, Accounting increase 110/3 hours.

Chapter 4

Section 4.1

1. 44, 3,060

5. -10, 1,005

9. 615/154, 520/154, 425/154, 330/154, . . .

3. $(a + b)/2$

7. 9,990

Section 4.2

1.
End of Year Numbered	Amount Depreciated	Value of Asset
0	0	$10,000
1	$950	9,050
2	950	8,100
3	950	7,150
4	950	6,200
5	950	5,250
6	950	4,300
7	950	3,350
8	950	2,400
9	950	1,450
10	950	500

End of Year Numbered	Amount Depreciated	Value of Asset
0	0	$10,000.00
1	$1,727.27	8,272.73
2	1,554.55	6,718.18
3	1,381.82	5,336.36
4	1,209.09	4,127.27
5	1,036.36	3,090.91
6	863.64	2,227.27
7	690.91	1,536.36
8	518.18	1,018.18
9	345.45	672.73
10	172.73	500.00

3. Ten-year life gives more depreciation under both methods.
5. $8,128.21
7. $17,500

Section 4.3

1. $8(5^{10} - 2^{10})/3(2^{10}) \approx 25,428.6$

3. $-1/3, -6/3^{11}, 9[1 + (1/3)^{21}]/2, 4.5$

5. 4

7. $r = 1/7$; 6, 6/7, 6/49, 6/343

9. $x = \pm 12, y = 36, z = \pm 108$

11. $-103 - 7/3^{19}, -936 - 7[1 - (1/3)^{18}]/6$

Section 4.4

1.

End of Year Numbered	Amount Depreciated	Value of Asset
0	0	$10,000.00
1	$2,000.00	8,000.00
2	1,600.00	6,400.00
3	1,280.00	5,120.00
4	1,024.00	4,096.00
5	819.20	3,276.80
6	655.36	2,621.44
7	524.29	2,097.15
8	419.43	1,677.72
9	335.54	1,342.18
10	268.44	1,073.74

3. 50% per year

End of Year Numbered	Amount Depreciated	Value of Asset
0	0	$32,000
1	$16,000	16,000
2	8,000	8,000
3	4,000	4,000
4	2,000	2,000
5	1,000	1,000

Annual depreciation under straight-line is $6,200. For the sum-of-integers method, the annual depreciations are $10,333.33, 8,266.67, 6,200, 4133.33, and 2,066.67 for years 1 through 5 respectively.

5. Depreciation rate is 20%; after 10 years the scrap value is $2,254.86.

End of Year Numbered	Amount Depreciated	Value of Asset
0	0	$21,000.00
1	$4,200.00	16,800.00
2	3,360.00	13,440.00
3	2,688.00	10,752.00
4	2,150.40	8,601.60
5	1,266.93	7,334.67
6	1,266.93	6,067.74
7	1,266.93	4,800.81
8	1,266.93	3,533.88
9	1,266.93	2,266.95
10	1,266.95*	1,000.00

*2¢ over in order to account for round-off error

7. Depreciation rate is 15%. The asset values at the end of years 0 through 10 respectively are $10,000; 8,500; 7,225; 6,141.25; 5,220.06; 4,437.05; 3,771.50; 3,205.77; 2,724.91; 2,316.17; 1,968.74.

9. Depreciation rate is $66\frac{2}{3}\%$.

End of Year Numbered	Amount Depreciated	Value of Asset
0	0	$81,000
1	$27,000	54,000
2	18,000	36,000
3	12,000	24,000
4	8,000	16,000

For straight-line, the annual depreciation is $16,250. For sum-of-integers, the annual depreciations are $26,000; 19,500; 13,000; 6,500.

Chapter 5

Section 5.1
1. (a) \$424; (b) \$520;
   (c) \$667.50; (d) \$1,026.67
5. 6.09%

3. (a) 20%; (b) $13\frac{1}{3}\%$;
   (c) 17.14%
7. 240%

Section 5.2
1. \$2,859.01

5. \$569.25
9. \$1,096.26

3. (a) \$334.79; (b) \$467.59;
   (c) \$608.33
7. \$579.20

Section 5.3
1. \$2,855.61
5. $50(1 + i)^8 + X + X(1 + i)^{-7} =$
   $100(1 + i)^3 + 100(1 + i)^{-2} +$
   $500(1 + i)^{-17}$. For $i = 3\%$,
   $X = \$244.17$; for $i = 1\frac{1}{2}\%$,
   $X = \$280.64$

3. \$543.23
7. \$622.77
9. \$2,135.68

Section 5.4
1. \$14,316.76
5. \$6,421.34
9. \$2,951.10
13. \$17,297.12
17. \$772.24

3. \$4,006.08
7. \$87.68
11. \$44.32
15. \$1,270.36

Section 5.5
1. \$505.85; \$29.92

3.

Payment Number	Amount of Payment	Interest	Principal Repaid	Principal Outstanding
0	—	—	—	\$200,000.00
1	\$46,194.96	\$10,000.00	\$36,194.96	163,805.04
2	46,194.96	8,190.25	38,004.71	125,800.33
3	46,194.96	6,290.02	39,904.94	85,895.39
4	46,194.96	4,294.77	41,900.19	43,995.20
5	46,194.96	2,199.76	43,995.20	0
Totals	230,974.80	30,974.80	200,000.00	

5. \$137.41

9. 83

7. 21 full payments and a final
   payment of \$7.50.
11. 18

13. $9,799.32; $10,289.28. No final payment is needed; the interest accumulated carries the total over $10,000.

15. 53 full payments and a final payment of $174.91.

Section 5.6

1.
Payment Number	Amount Deposited	Interest Accumulated	Total Accumulation
1	$113.78	—	$113.78
2	113.78	$1.14	228.70
3	113.78	2.29	344.77
4	113.78	3.45	462.00
5	113.78	4.62	580.40
6	113.80	5.80	700.00
Totals	682.70	17.30	

3.
Payment Number	Amount Deposited	Interest Accumulated	Total Accumulation
1	$1,763.14	—	$ 1,763.14
2	1,763.14	$ 30.85	3,557.13
3	1,763.14	62.25	5,382.52
4	1,763.14	94.19	7,239.85
5	1,763.14	126.70	9,129.69
6	1,763.14	159.77	11,052.60
7	1,763.14	193.42	13,009.16
8	1,763.18	227.66	15,000.00
Totals	14,105.16	894.84	

5. The second source is cheaper by $3,241.03 per year.

7. Increase by $388.34 per payment

Section 5.7

1. $9,109.32

3. $16,349.66

5. $4,236.20

7. $9,071.08

9. $286.70

11. $7.16, 6.44, 6.00

Chapter 6

Section 6.1

1. 12.30%

3. 4.91%

5. 4.97%

7. $j_1 = 8.24\%$, $j_{12} = 7.95\%$

Section 6.2
1. $64.47
5. $5,569.95
9. $4,243.76
13. $94,815.45

3. $136.57
7. $1,229.20
11. $82.54, $83.81

Section 6.3
1. $10,000.00
5. The second one is a better investment.
9. $4,678.87
13. $38,670.89

3. $600, $609
7. $5,302.34, $268.43
11. $3,700, $296

Section 6.4
1. $1,396.66
5. $574.12, $577.10
9. $6,144.64, $48,124.26

3. $3,451
7. $2,077.87
11. 3 yr, 8 mo, 8 days; 3 yr, 22 days; 2 yr, 7 mo, 16 days

Section 6.5
1. 5.28%
5. 7.51%
9. 11.70%

3. 3.34%
7. 16.38%
11. 4.78%

Section 6.6
1. $784.18
5. 5.26%
9. 5.79%
13. $928.30; $918.30 or $91\frac{7}{8}$
15. $1,091.42; $1,061.42 or 106

3. $1,074.40
7. 5.71%
11. (a) $1,273.55;   (b) $1,274.82;
   (c) $1,273.32 or $127\frac{3}{8}$

Chapter 7

Section 7.1
1. (a) True;   (b) False;   (c) True;
   (d) False;   (e) True;   (f) True;
   (g) False;   (h) True
5. {2, 4, 6, 8, 10, 11, 12, 13, . . . , 25}
9. {4, 1, 0, 9, 16}
13. $\emptyset$, {#}; $\emptyset$, {@}, {$}, {@, $};
   $\emptyset$, {%}, {¢}, {&}, {%, ¢}, {%, &}, {¢, &}, {%, ¢, &}; 2^n
17. 1,300; 700

3. {10, 11, 12, . . . , 25}, {2, 4, 6, . . . , 24}, {37, 39, 41, . . . , 49}
7. {36, 37, . . . , 50}, {1, 2, 3, . . . , 9, 26, 27, 28, . . . , 50}
11. {8, 6, 4, 2, 0, −2, −4}
15. 19

Section 7.2

1. (a) 3; (b) 1; (c) 3; (d) 1;
   (e) 4
5. $D = \{z: 5 \leq z \leq 21\}$
11. $-3, 1, 5, 15, 37$

3. $R = \{y: 2 \leq y \leq 10\}$

9. For example, $y = f(x) = 2x + 1$
13. (a) 9; (b) 8; (c) 1/4; (d) 1;
    (e) 1; (f) $t^2(x + 3)$; (g) 9; (h) 4

Section 7.3

1. 25/6; 0
5. $V = \{a, e, i, o, u\}$, $E = \{e, n, t,$
   $v\}$, $\{e\} = V \cap E$; $E \cup V$;
   $E \cap V'$
9. {first try, second try}', {first try,
   second try, third try}, {first try,
   never}, {second try, third try,
   fourth try}

3. $\{1, 2, 3, 4, 5, 6, 7, 8, 9, 10\}$
7. $\{(1, 1), (1, 2), (1, 3), (1, 4),$
   $(1, 5), (1, 6), (2, 1), (2, 2), (2, 3),$
   $(2, 4), (2, 5), (2, 6), (3, 1), (3, 2),$
   $(3, 3), (3, 4), (3, 5), (3, 6), (4, 1),$
   $(4, 2), (4, 3), (4, 4), (4, 5), (4, 6),$
   $(5, 1), (5, 2), (5, 3), (5, 4), (5, 5),$
   $(5, 6), (6, 1), (6, 2), (6, 3), (6, 4),$
   $(6, 5), (6, 6)\}$

Section 7.4

3. 5/26, 2/13, 4/13, 3/26
7. 0.3, 0.4, 0.4, 0.1
11. 70%, 20%, 50%, $7.60, $2.60

5. 4/9, 7/9, 7/18, 5/9
9. 1/36, 0, 11/36

Section 7.5

1. See answer to Section 7.3,
   Exercise 7. The probabilities are
   1/36, 2/36, 3/36, 4/36, 5/36,
   6/36, 5/36, 4/36, 3/36, 2/36,
   1/36.

5. 9/47
7. 4/47, 8/47, 15/47

Section 7.6

1. $p(x) = 1/2$ for $x = 0, 1$
5. $p(0) = 0.12$, $p(1) = 0.24$,
   $p(2) = 0.49$, $p(3) = 0.15$

9. $p(0) = 3/15$, $p(1) = 8/15$,
   $p(2) = 4/15$
13. $p(-1{,}500) = 0.4$, $p(-700) = 0.3$,
    $p(100) = 0.2$, $p(1{,}700) = 0.05$,
    $p(2{,}500) = 0.05$; 0.30

3. 5/16, 7/8
7. $p_X(1) = 1/15$, $p_X(2) = 1/3$,
   $p_X(3) = 3/5$, $p_Y(0) = 1/5$,
   $p_Y(1) = 1/5$, $p_Y(2) = 4/15$,
   $p_Y(3) = 1/3$
11. $p(k) = 1/13$ for $k = 1, 2, \ldots, 9$
    and $p(10) = 4/13$

Section 7.7

1. 1/2, 1, 3/2, 2, . . . ; $n/2$ for n flips

3. $-1/19$; i.e., you average a little
   more than a $5¢$ loss on each
   $1.00 bet.

5. 1.67

9. 16/15

13. −$530

17. $p > 4/15$

21. $13.25

7. $E(X) = 38/15$, $E(Y) = 26/15$

11. 85/13

15. 35/6

19. 16

23. $3.75; 6.37\frac{1}{2}$

Section 7.8

1. 35/12

5. 0.7611

9. 104/225

13. 1,225,100

17. 95/13, 1,440/169

3. (a) 15; (b) 2/9

7. $Var(X) = 86/225$, $Var(Y) = 284/225$

11. 1,680/169

15. 17/3, 35/9

Section 7.9

3. Both salesmen should go to street 1 with probability 5/13

7. $v = 100q + 550$

5. $\begin{pmatrix} 3 & -1 \\ -18 & 6 \end{pmatrix}$, (6/7, 1/7), $\begin{pmatrix} 1/4 \\ 3/4 \end{pmatrix}$, $v = 0$

Section 7.10

3. (a) Player I plays Row 4, Player II plays Column 4, $v = 5$

(b) $(1/2, 1/2, 0)$, $\begin{pmatrix} 1/2 \\ 1/2 \\ 0 \end{pmatrix}$, $v = 3/2$

7. Always sell; $q > 1/3$

5. Player I plays the black 3, Player II plays the black 1, $v = 3$.

Section 7.11

1. (a) $(1/2, 1/2)$, $\begin{pmatrix} 0 \\ 1/3 \\ 0 \\ 2/3 \end{pmatrix}$, $v = 1$

(b) $(5/18, 1/2, 0, 2/9)$, $\begin{pmatrix} 10/27 \\ 11/27 \\ 2/9 \end{pmatrix}$, $v = 4/9$

5. (a) $(7/9, 0, 0, 0, 2/9)$, $\begin{pmatrix} 4/9 \\ 5/9 \end{pmatrix}$, $v = 53/9$ (b) $(0, 1, 0, 0)$, $\begin{pmatrix} 0 \\ 1 \end{pmatrix}$,

3. Player I plays black 3 and red 3 each with probability 1/2. Player II plays red 1 and black 2 with probabilities 2/3 and 1/3 respectively, or red 1 and black 3 with probabilities 3/4 and 1/4 respectively (or any weighted average of these two strategies). The value of the game is 3.

7. $(0, 1/2, 1/2)$, $\begin{pmatrix} 0 \\ 1/2 \\ 1/2 \end{pmatrix}$

$v = 5$ (c) $(2/3, 1/3)$, $\begin{pmatrix} 0 \\ 1/2 \\ 1/2 \\ 0 \end{pmatrix}$,

$v = 2$ (d) $(1, 0, 0)$, $\begin{pmatrix} 0 \\ 1 \\ 0 \end{pmatrix}$, $v = 5$

(e) $(1/5, 0, 4/5)$, $\begin{pmatrix} 4/5 \\ 1/5 \\ 0 \end{pmatrix}$, $v = 37/5$

(f) $(0, 1/5, 4/5)$, $\begin{pmatrix} 0 \\ 1/5 \\ 4/5 \\ 0 \end{pmatrix}$, $v = 16/5$

(g) $(0, 0, 1/2, 1/2)$,

$\begin{pmatrix} 0 \\ 0 \\ 1/8 \\ 7/8 \end{pmatrix}$, $v = 11/2$

9. Player I plays red 1 and black 1 each with probability 1/2. Player II plays red 1 and black 2 with probabilities 3/5 and 2/5 respectively. The value of the game is $v = 0$.

Chapter 8

Section 8.1
1. (a) 1/3; (b) 2/7; (c) 2/7
5. 33/80, 49/99, 4/49
9. (a) 1/8; (b) 5/24; (c) 11/24; (d) 3/8
13. 45.5%

3. 11/850, 33/66,640, 33/16,660
7. (a) 2/5; (b) 1/3; (c) 2/15
11. 5/6, 5/7

Section 8.2
1. $P(U_1|W) = 3/4$, $P(U_2|W) = 1/4$
5. $P(\text{small}|\text{rotten}) = 1/8$, $P(\text{medium}|\text{rotten}) = 3/8$, $P(\text{large}|\text{rotten}) = 1/2$
9. 12/25

3. 171/179
7. 8/17, 8/17, 1/17

11. 38%, 0.76

Section 8.3
1. 0.56
5. 0.7, 0.2

9. 65/81
13. Play the strong player first.

3. 0.5
7. Without replacement, 1/84; with replacement, 1/27
11. 2/3; no

Section 8.4

1. (b) 1;   (c) 1/2;   (d) 4, 0
5. For the first model: 1/4, 1/4, 1/4, 1/4; 1.5; 2/3; For the second model: 1/8, 7/32, 21/64, 21/64, 119/64; 27/47
9. (a) 19/48;   (b) 57/157; (c) 43/48
13. 2.44, 4.8448

3. (b) 1/2;   (c) 1/2;   (d) 4.25, 1/3
7. 147/512, 315/512

11. 0.7;   1.12

Section 8.5

1. (a) No;   (b) Yes;   (c) No; (d) Yes
5. (5/13, 8/13)
9. (b) 0.44, 0.576

3. 0.195; (0.4280, 0.2805, 0.2915)

7. 53/80

Section 8.6

1. (b) (1/2, 1/2) Not regular; (d) (0, 1, 0) Not regular
5. $3/7 = 42.86\%$
9. 2/3 smoke Brand C, 1/3 do not

3. $50/201 = 24.88\%$

7. 1/3 laborers, 2/3 professionals
11. Regular, (1/3, 1/4, 1/4, 1/6)

Section 8.7

1. Fall semesters: 1,000; 1,250; 1,312.5; long run, $1333\frac{1}{3}$. Spring semesters: 500, 625, 656.25; long run, $666\frac{2}{3}$.

3. Fall semesters: 1,000, $1,111\frac{1}{9}$, $1,123\frac{37}{81}$; long run, 1,125. Spring semesters: $333\frac{1}{3}$, $370\frac{10}{27}$, $374\frac{118}{243}$; long run, 375.

5. (a) (36/49, 13/49);   (b) (39/49, 10/49);   (c) (186/245, 59/245); (d) (127/147, 20/147)

7. (c) Two-thirds of the time the process is absorbed in the absorbing state nearest the starting point. The expected time until absorption is 2 trials.

9. Expected time until escape: from 1, 37/13 sec; from 2, 53/13 sec; from 3, 43/13 sec. Probabilities of exits: from 1, (5/13, 5/13, 3/13); from 2, (4/13, 4/13, 5/13); from 3, (3/13, 3/13, 7/13).
13. 80/13; 5/13; 77/130

11. (a) The process is absorbed in state 2 with probability 1. Starting from state 1, the expected time absorption is 4/3 steps.   (b) $N = \begin{pmatrix} 2.4 & 0.8 \\ 0.8 & 1.6 \end{pmatrix}$ $B = \begin{pmatrix} 1 \\ 1 \end{pmatrix}$ (c) $N = \begin{pmatrix} 1.6 & 0.8 \\ 0.8 & 2.4 \end{pmatrix}$ $B = \begin{pmatrix} .4 & .6 \\ .2 & .8 \end{pmatrix}$

Chapter 9

Section 9.1

1. 132

3. 160, 70

5. $14! \approx 8.7178 \cdot 10^{10}$

7. $2 \cdot 6! \cdot 8! = 58,060,800$

9. 260,000

11. 1

13. (a) 48;   (b) 16;   (c) 240;   (d) 96

15. 16

17. $2(10!)^2 \approx 2.6336 \cdot 10^{13}$

Section 9.2

1. $\binom{52}{7} \approx 1.3378 \cdot 10^8$

3. 200

5. 30

7. (a) 5,040;   (b) 3,780;
   (c) 50,400

9. 240

11. 720

13. 1,260

15. (a) 20;   (b) 128, if you count
    the possibility that he takes
    none.

17. (a) 5,880;   (b) 19,404

Section 9.3

1.
```
                              1
                          1       1
                      1       2       1
                  1       3       3       1
              1       4       6       4       1
          1       5      10      10       5       1
      1       6      15      20      15       6       1
  1       7      21      35      35      21       7       1
1       8      28      56      70      56      28       8       1
  1   9      36      84     126     126      84      36       9       1
    1    10      45     120     210     252     210     120      45      10      1
  1    11      55     165     330     462     462     330     165      55      11      1
1    12      66     220     495     792     924     792     495     220      66      12      1
```

3. $64x^6 - 96x^5y + 64x^4y^2 -$
   $20x^3y^3 + (15/4)x^2y^4 - (3/8)xy^5 +$
   $(1/64)y^6$

5. $-7/9$

7. $-1,792$

9. $(15/4)x^2y^8$

11. $x^8y^{-8} - 4x^5y^{-6} + 7x^2y^{-4} - 7x^{-1}y^{-2}$

13. $70x^4$

Section 9.4

1. 1/6

3. $4\dfrac{\binom{13}{4}\binom{13}{3}^3}{\binom{52}{13}} \approx 0.105$

5. (a) 579/2,156;   (b) 89/193

7. 2/5

9. $5/4$ 11. $1/462$
13. $95/97 \approx 97.9\%$

Section 9.5
1. $0.2501, 0.4480, 0, 0.0003$ 3. $2.8, 2.24$
5. $10.5, 0.2061, 0.2186, 11$ 7. $0.1296, 0.2074, 0.1659$
9. 0.5520 11. 0.4480
13. 2.67%

Section 9.6
1. $0.5793, 0.9049, 0.0139, 0.0869$ 3. (a) 0.1525;   (b) 0.8351;
5. (a) 0.9733;   (b) at least 0.75;   (c) 0.9770;   (d) 0.9974
   (c) 0.9699 7. $0.0796, 0.9534, 1.0$
9. 0.0516 11. 0.3557
13. The probability that the machine
    is working properly is virtually
    zero.

Chapter 10

Section 10.1
1. (a) Demand, maximum demand   3. (a) Demand, maximum demand
   $= 16$, maximum price $= 4$; $= 4$, maximum price $= 160$;
   (b) Supply, minimum price $= 8$;   (b) Supply, minimum price $= 10$;
   (c) Demand, maximum demand   (c) Demand, maximum demand
   $= 12$, maximum price $= 6$; $= 100$, maximum price 10;
   (d) Demand, maximum demand   (d) Demand, maximum demand
   $= 110/7$, maximum price $= 22$; $= 144$, maximum price $= 144$
   (e) Supply, minimum price $= 40$
5. $x = 3p - 9$ 7. $x + 500p = 20,000$, $P(x) = 40 -$
                                             $x/500$
9. (a) First is supply, $(13/4, 107/8)$; 11. (a) $R(x) = 4x - x^2/4$, $(8, 16)$;
   (b) First is demand, $(140/9,$ (c) $R(x) = 6x - x^2/2$, $(6, 18)$;
   $760/9)$ (d) $R(x) = 22x - 7x^2/5$, $(55/7,$
13. 9(a) $R(x) = 15x - x^2/2$, $(15,$ $605/7)$
    $112.5)$;   9(b) $R(x) = 100x - x^2$,
    $(50, 2,500)$;   10(a) $R(x) = 2x -$
    $x^2/100$ $(100, 100)$;   10(b) $R(x) =$
    $40x - 5x^2$ $(4, 80)$

Section 10.2
1. 5 3. $2x - 3$, positive for $x > 3/2$,
                                             negative for $x < 3/2$
5. $2x - 7$ 9. $y = 2x + 3$
11. 12 13. $3x^2$

Section 10.3

1. (a) $f'(x) = 14x - 6$; (b) $g'(x) = 45x^2 - 24x^3 - 11$; (c) $F'(x) = 12x^{11} + 3x^5$; (d) $H'(x) = 33x^{10} - 32x$

5. (a) $6x$; $y = 6x - 2$; (b) $y = 5x - 3$; (c) $(-1, -8)$

9. $x > -6$; all x

3. $y = 8x + 4$

7. 450

Section 10.4

1. (a) $x = 0$, minimum; (b) $x = -1$, maximum; (c) $x = 1$, minimum; $x = -1$, maximum; (d) $x = 2$, maximum; $x = -2$, minimum; (e) $x = 0$, maximum; $x = 4$, minimum.

5. (a) $2 \le x \le 4$; (b) $x = 8/3$, $p = 32/9$, $R = 256/27$

9. (a) $P(x) = 10,000 - 1,000x$; $R(x) = 10,000x - 1,000x^2$; (b) $C(x) = 2,500 + 1,500x$; $S(x) = -1,000x^2 + 8,500x - 2,500$; (c) $x = 85/20$; (d) Reduce profits by $840; (e) $4,250/coat

13. 17.5 and 7

3. (a) $0 \le x \le 10$; $0 \le p \le 120/11$; (b) $3 \le x \le 13/2$; $0 \le p \le 7$; (c) $0 \le x \le 8$, $0 \le p \le 6$; (d) $0 \le x \le 14$, $0 \le p \le 224$

7. (a) 87/4; (b) $48.50/thousand units.

11. $40' \times 80'$

Section 10.5

1. Minimum at $(-3, -12)$

5. Relative maximum at $(2, 3)$, relative minimum at $(4, -1)$, inflection point at $(3, 1)$

9. No maximum or minimum, inflection point at $(0, 1)$ where the slope is 1, increasing function for all x

13. Minimum at $(0, 0)$, no inflection point

3. Maximum at $(-2/3, 13/3)$

7. No maximum or minimum, horizontal tangent and inflection point at $(0, 0)$, increasing function for all x

11. No maximum or minimum, horizontal tangent and inflection point at $(0, -4)$, decreasing function for all x

15. Minima at $(0, 0)$ and $(2, 0)$, relative maximum at $(1, 1)$, inflection points at $(1 + (1/3)\sqrt{3}, 4/9)$ and $(1 - (1/3)\sqrt{3}, 4/9)$

Section 10.6

1. (a) $(1 - x^2)^5 - 10x^2(1 - x^2)^4$; (b) $50x^4 - 1/x^2 + x^{-1/2} + 2$; (c) $(4/3)x(2x^2 + 7)^{-2/3} + 3/x^2$; (d) $\dfrac{2(x + 1)(x^3 + 3x) - (x + 1)^2(3x^2 + 3)}{(x^3 + 3x)^2}$;

(e) $3\sqrt{x^2 + 1} + 6x^2(x^2 + 1)^{-1/2}$;   (f) $21x^2(x^3 - 2)^6$;   (g) $-11/(3x - 1)^2$;
(h) $x^{-2/3} + 2/x^3$;   (i) $10(x^2 - 5x)^4(2x - 5)$;   (j) $2(x + 1)(x^2 + 2)^3 +$
$6x(x + 1)^2(x^2 + 2)^2$
3. (a) $x = 0$;   (b) $x = -1, x = 1$;   (c) $x = -1 - \sqrt{2}, x = -1 + \sqrt{2}$;
(d) $x = 0, x = -3/2$
5. (a) $y = 20x - 12$;   (b) $4y = 3x + 9$;   (c) $9y = 4x - 2$

Section 10.7

1. At $x = 3$, $Q(3) = 11$

3. At $x = 2$, $Q(2) = 212$

7. 80

9. It would make the optimal point
$x = 0$, $S = -1$; that is, it would
end the business.

11. $10'' \times 10'' \times 5'' \approx 14'' \times$
$14'' \times 5''$

13. $\sqrt[3]{80/3}' \times \sqrt[3]{80/3}' \times$
$(3/4)\sqrt[3]{80/3}' \approx 3' \times 3' \times 2'3''$

Section 10.8

1. (a) $f_x = (1 - y^2)^5$; $f_y = -10xy (1 - y^2)^4$;   (b) $f_x = -2x^{-3} + (1/2)\sqrt{y/x}$;
$f_y = 50y^4 + (1/2)\sqrt{x/y}$;   (c) $f_x = 4xy^2/(x^2 + y^2)^2$; $f_y = -4x^2y/(x^2 + y^2)^2$;
(d) $f_x = x/\sqrt{x^2 + y^2}$, $f_y = y/\sqrt{x^2 + y^2}$
3. (a) $f_{xx} = 0$, $f_{yy} = -10x(1 - y^2)^3(1 - 9y^2)$, $f_{xy} = -10y(1 - y^2)^4$;
(b) $f_{xx} = 6x^{-4} - (1/4)y^{1/2} x^{-3/2}$, $f_{yy} = 200y^3 - (1/4)x^{1/2}y^{-3/2}$, $f_{xy} =$
$(1/4)y^{-1/2}x^{-1/2}$;   (c) $f_{xx} = 4y^2(y^2 - 3x^2)/(x^2 + y^2)^3$; $f_{yy} = -4x^2(x^2 - 3y^2)/$
$(x^2 + y^2)^3$; $f_{xy} = 8xy(x^2 - y^2)/(x^2 + y^2)^3$;   (d) $f_{xx} = y^2/(x^2 + y^2)^{3/2}$, $f_{yy} =$
$x^2/(x^2 + y^2)^{3/2}$, $f_{xy} = -xy/(x^2 + y^2)^{3/2}$
5. 7
7. No solution exists
9. A $12'' \times 12'' \times 12''$ cube

Chapter 11

Section 11.1

1. $a_2 = 2.25$, $a_{10} = 2.5937$, $a_{20} =$
2.6533, $a_{100} = 2.7048$

3. $1,077.88

5. $3,098.98

7. $81.05

9. (a) $9e^{-3x}$;   (b) $(x + 2)e^x$;
(c) $2e^x(e^x + 1)/(e^x - 1)^3$;
(d) $2e^{x^2}(1 + 2x^2)$;   (e) $(9x^6 +$
$18x^3 + 2)e^{x^3}$;   (f) $(9x^6 - 18x^3 +$
$2)e^{x^3}$;   (g) $[2e^x(e^x + 7)^{-1/2} -$
$\bullet e^{2x}(e^x + 7)^{-3/2}]/4$;
(h) $4e^{x^2}[e^{x^2}(1 + 2x + 3x^2) +$
$2(1 + x + x^2)] + 12x^2$

11. (a) $y = x + 1$;   (b) $ey = x$;
(c) $y = 2$

13. $f_x = 2xe^{x^2 + y^2}$, $f_y = 2ye^{x^2 + y^2}$

Section 11.2

1. 2.96%, 3.92%, 4.88%, 5.83%, 6.77%, 7.70%

3. (a) $1/(x + 3)$;   (b) $1 + \ln x$;
(c) $[x \ln x - (x + 1) \ln (x + 1)]/$
$x(x + 1)(\ln x)^2$;   (d) $[3(x^2 + 1) -$
$2x(3x + 5) \ln (3x + 5)]/$
$(3x + 5)(x^2 + 1)^2$;   (e) $2x \ln$
$(e^x + 2) + x^2 e^x/(e^x + 2)$;
(f) $10(1/x + 2x)(\ln x + x^2)^9$;
(g) $6(\ln x)^2/x$;
(h) $2(\ln x)e^{(\ln x)^2}/x$

5. (a) 1;   (b) 2;   (c) 0

7. (a) $x = 1/e$;   (b) $x = 1/2$;
(c) $x = e^{-3/2}$

9. (a) $f_{xx} = 2(y^2 - x^2)/(x^2 + y^2)^2$;
$f_{yy} = 2(x^2 - y^2)/(x^2 + y^2)^2$;
$f_{xy} = -4xy/(x^2 + y^2)^2$;
(b) $f_{xx} = e^{x + y}/(e^x + e^y)^2$; $f_{yy} =$
$e^{x + y}/(e^x + e^y)^2$; $f_{xy} =$
$-e^{x + y}/(e^x + e^y)^2$;   (c) $f_{xx} =$
$(2 + 4x + x^2 + y^2)e^x$; $f_{yy} = 2e^x$;
$f_{xy} = 2ye^x$;   (d) $f_{xx} = -2/x^2$;
$f_{yy} = -3/y^2$; $f_{xy} = 0$

Section 11.3

1. 78

3. 784,111

5. 418,505,500 years

7. $140,296,110

Section 11.4

1. (a) $-4p/(200 - 4p)$;
(b) $-p/2(100 - p)$;   (c) $-5p$;
(d) $-2p/(p + 1)$

3. (a) -1;   (b) -1;   (c) -1;
(d) -1

5. $-14/11 = -1.27$, demand is
reduced by $70/11\% = 6.4\%$

7. $15 \le p \le 31, 0 \le x \le 256$;
at $p = 15$, elasticity is zero; at
$p = 31$, elasticity is undefined.

Section 11.5

1. 1

3. $250/e$

5. Maximum at $x = 0$, $y = 1/$
$\sqrt{2\pi}$; inflections at $x = \pm 1$, $y =$
$1/e\sqrt{2\pi}$

7. $x = 10$, $y = 25$

9. e

Chapter 12

Section 12.1

1. (a) $(1/8)x^8 + c$; (b) $3x^{1/3} + c$;
   (c) $(3/2)x^2 + c$; (d) $7e^x + c$;
   (e) $7x + (5/2)x^2 - e^x + c$;
   (f) $\ln x + c$

5. $f(x) = -(1/3)x^3 + 8x - 22/3$

9. $D(p) = p^{-1}100e^{(1-p^2)/2}$

3. $y = (1/3)x^3 - 2x^2 + 5x + 43/3$

7. $Q(x) = 1 + (1/10)x + 10/x$;
   $Q(10) = 3$

11. (a) $2(x^2 + 1)^{1/2} + c$; (b) $(1/4)(x^3 - 3)^{4/3} + c$; (c) $(2/3)e^{x^{3/2}} + c$; (d) $2 \ln(x^{1/2} + 1) + c$;
    (e) $(1/10)(3x - 4)^{10/3} + c$

13. You cannot factor a function of x through the integral sign. The antiderivative can be found by using binomial theorem to expand the function into a polynomial.

Section 12.2

1. 4
5. 4
9. 32/3
13. (a) 45/2; (b) $(e^{49} - 1)/2$;
    (c) $(26^{5/2} - 5^{5/2})/5$; (d) $(1/2)\ln 5$; (e) 4; (f) 75,937.5;
    (g) $(1/2)(\ln x)^2 - 9/2 + e$

3. 36
7. 2
11. 125/6

Section 12.3

1. 1/3
5. 58/3
9. 12.5

3. 9/2
7. $CS = 50, PS = 150$

Section 12.4

1. $1/8; 7/64; 0; 27/64; 0.488$
9. $m + 1; 1 - 1/2^{m+1}$; approaches 1; $(m + 1)/(m + 2)$; $(m + 1)/(m + 3)(m + 2)^2$; $E(X)$ approaches 1, $\text{Var}(X)$ approaches 0.

3. (a) 3/4; 3/80; (b) $2/\ln 2$; $2(3 \ln 2 - 2)/(\ln 2)^2$
11. $3/32; 205/256; 1; 847/864$; 2, 4/5

Section 12.5

1. 32
5. 404/3

3. 6.6994, error is 0.0046

INDEX